UTAH PLACE NAMES

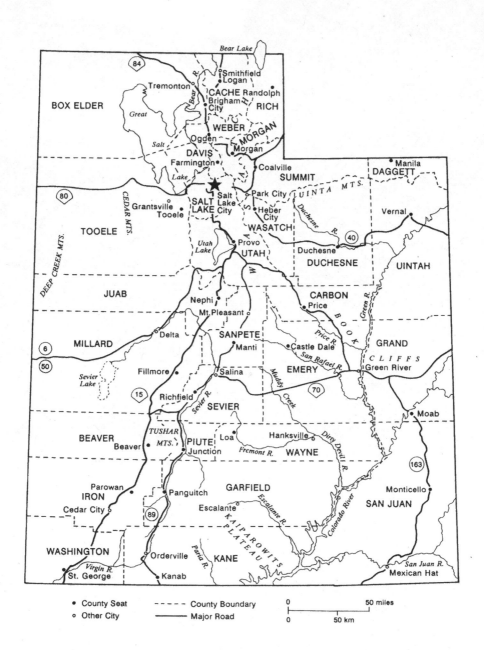

Bear Lake

84

Tremonton

Smithfield
Logan

CACHE Randolph

Brigham
City

BOX ELDER

Great

RICH

WEBER

MORGAN

Salt

Ogden

DAVIS

Morgan

Farmington

Coalville

Manila

Lake

SUMMIT

DAGGETT

80

CEDAR MTS.

Grantsville
Tooele

Salt
Lake
City

Park City

UINTA MTS.

Duchesne R.

Vernal

DEEP CREEK MTS.

SALT
LAKE

Heber
City

40

TOOELE

WASATCH

Utah
Lake

Provo

Duchesne

UINTAH

JUAB

UTAH

DUCHESNE

Nephi

CARBON

Green R.

Mt. Pleasant

Price

6

Delta

SANPETE

BOOK

Price R.

GRAND

50

MILLARD

Manti

Castle Dale

San Rafael R.

CLIFFS

Sevier
Lake

Fillmore

Salina

EMERY

Green River

15

Sevier R.

Richfield

SEVIER

Muddy Creek

70

Moab

TUSHAR
MTS.

Loa

Hanksville

Dirty Devil R.

BEAVER

Beaver

PIUTE
Junction

Fremont R.

WAYNE

163

Parowan

GARFIELD

Monticello

IRON

Panguitch

Cedar City

89

Escalante

Escalante R.

SAN JUAN

Colorado River

WASHINGTON

Orderville

Paria R.

KANE

KAIPAROWITS
PLATEAU

St. George

Virgin R.

Kanab

San Juan R.

Mexican Hat

• County Seat
○ Other City

----- County Boundary
——— Major Road

0   50 miles
0   50 km

UTAH PLACE NAMES

A Comprehensive Guide
To the Origins of Geographic Names

A COMPILATION

John W. Van Cott

The University of Utah Press
Salt Lake City, Utah

4 3 2   1992 1993 1994 1995 1996 1997

The paper in this book meets the standards for
permanence and durability established by the
Committee on Production Guidelines for Book
Longevity of the Council on Library Resources

Library of Congress Cataloging-in-Publication Data

Van Cott, John W., 1911-
    Utah place names / John W. Van Cott.
        p.   cm.
    Includes bibliographical references and index.
    ISBN 0-87480-345-4 (pbk. : alk. paper)
        1. Names, Geographical–Utah. 2. Utah–Geography.   I. Title
    F824.V36 1990
    917.92'003–dc20   90-52741
                                                          CIP

Dedicated to

My wife

Emily

and

Our four children

John F.
Ann C.
Robert J.
and
Linda L.

All of whose help and support has been unlimited

CONTENTS

FOREWORD

If you are among the many who have experienced the frustration of trying to determine the exact location of an event recorded so far in the past that place names and routes have changed, the value of this exhaustive compilation by John W. Van Cott will be readily appreciated. For others, the worth of this book will become apparent as one's knowledge of the land called home is enriched by the bits and pieces of history associated with individual entries.

Archaeologists, biologists, geologists, geographers, historians, outdoor enthusiasts, and workers in a variety of industries and businesses will find value in the following work. As a biologist, I know that the work of colleagues involved in relocating early collection sites will be much simplified by this compilation. As one inescapably captivated by local history, I find each page a fascination. We are fortunate that this report covers the entire state of Utah.

The author is well prepared for the task he has undertaken. For almost two decades he has pored over maps and manuscripts and made innumerable trips to the remote corners of Utah to observe and interview. From that wealth of experience has come a compendium of historical geography that is thorough, authoritative, and highly readable.

Kimball T. Harper
Department of Botany and Range Science
Brigham Young University
Provo, Utah

PREFACE

Utah is a wonderfully endowed state that is enjoyed by the tourist, business person, and permanent resident. The state's secular and religious history, geography, geology, natural history, and people are fascinating and varied enough to satisfy the most adventurous explorer or average citizen. But, this is not a book extolling the varieties and beauties of Utah, it is a compilation of the origins of the geographic names of the state. I have visited most of these places and each has a unique story. Donald Jackson's words are true: "Yet, I wrote my notes with immensely greater confidence, having been there" (250).

A brief comparison of early maps with current maps shows that the names of lakes, mountain ranges, and rivers change with interesting frequency. What was the Grand River of yesteryear is the Colorado River today. Newhouse, Frisco, and Elephant City were once prominent towns in Beaver County; today they are ghost towns simmering in the summer sun and freezing in the snows of winter. The S.O.B. Rapids of the Green River are gone, only to be renamed the emasculated Sob Rapids by order of the U.S. Board on Geographic Names. By similar edict, Nigger Bill Canyon was replaced by Negro Bill Canyon. Recently a suggestion was made that it be renamed Black Bill Canyon because negro is no longer a preferred word.

Questions should be asked such as why did the mining town of Bingham disappear? What happened to that vast elusive Buenaventura River, recorded on maps as having been located in various areas of the West? Why does the town of Ticaboo suddenly appear in the middle of the desert?

Sadly, the origin of many of these stories are not compiled in a single reference. They are scattered in hundreds of isolated books and journals, in the dim memories of third and fourth generations, and in the legends and stories told by sheepherders and cattlemen who roam Utah's vast regions. This book is a tardy attempt to rectify some of these problems by putting this neglected historical information into a single reference.

My own initiation into the geographic name process came in 1940 while working for the old U.S. Grazing Service under the Taylor Grazing Act. I was assigned to vegetation and grazing surveys in the Price, Moab, and Blanding areas. Near Moab the wild beauty of the canyon then known as Nigger Bill Canyon was exposed. At that time, the process of changing the name to Negro Bill Canyon was taking place. As I looked down into those sheer-walled depths while working in the nearby Wilson Mesa, Castle Valley, and Pack Canyon areas, I couldn't help wondering just who or what the areas were named for and why.

Who was Mary Jane, whose name is attached to a nearby canyon? Who was honored by Professor Valley and Creek and the ghost town site of Richardson? What was the story behind Amasa Back and Arths Pasture? Of the possible origins of the name Moab, which was correct? Who named Mount Delano and Mount Belnap over in the Tushar Mountains east of Beaver? What are the Charley Holes and who are they named for? How did Hobble Creek Canyon east of Spanish Fork receive its name? Of the thousands of names throughout Utah (there are 22,500 listed in the official Geographic Names Information System or GNIS of the U.S. Geological Survey), why is there no adequate reference to place name origins? Many people consider this an important part of the state's history.

The U.S. Work Projects Administration, in cooperation with the State of Utah, was in the process of producing an introductory publication on the origin of names, but on towns and counties only. What was really needed was a comprehensive work on all the place names in Utah. The realization dawned on me that the only solution to the problem was to compile the information myself. Although I was both hesitant and tentative, I began the process of locating, researching, and compiling the information. I didn't want a book listing only the vital statistics of latitude, longitude, and altitude, suitable only for the scientist or the statistician. What was needed was an all-encompassing book that the scientist, field worker, or vacationer could refer to and enjoy.

I decided to use the section, township, and range format instead of longitude and latitude for exact location. It can be a frustrating experience to discover an interesting place name but not be provided with historical information or a location, so I also added an exact location in relation to a known point, such as three miles south of Puffer Lake or one mile northwest of The Confluence. Altitude in feet and meters is also included for additional information.

I had another problem: If the complete history of each name were to be included, the work would develop into a four-volume publication, a project that someone should pursue in the future, but not for this initial effort.

The majority of books written about Utah geographic names specialize in ghost towns, cities, and counties—none were all-inclusive. Towns, counties, and ghost towns are important but so are all the physical features with an identifiable name. Many places have obvious stories behind their naming, but the earlier names, variants, and nicknames are also important. These have been listed and cross-referenced, although each place name may not have an individual entry.

In the preliminary stages I researched county and state histories, but in the place-naming process, except in one or two cases, these proved inadequate. My personal opinion is that the county and local historians are capable of doing a better job of compiling information concerning the origins of geographic names that relate to their local area. Inevitably I compiled all the names that were listed on various maps and thus began my project.

Even though Utah is not completely mapped, the most reliable name maps are the U.S. Geological Survey (USGS) 7.5' topographic maps, each covering approximately sixty square miles. If these were unavailable, the USGS 15' maps were used. The 15' maps cover approximately two hundred and forty square miles. On a supplementary basis I reviewed numerous additional maps, such as Bureau of Land Management maps that often included more local legend. The total number of maps reviewed eventually rose to over 1,100. Although the Geographic Names Information System (GNIS) for Utah was published in 1981, it has been a helpful reference work, but not for name sources.

And so, over the years, features in Utah have been named and renamed as the Indian was displaced by later intruders. It was the Indians who provided the earliest names in our state. From their most insignificant basket, shattered bone, or discarded chip to their beautiful pottery and awe-inspiring ruins, their history has given names to Utah places, some of them anglicized and others reminding us of their ancestry and legends. Pahrump, Peteetneet, Skutumpah, Seedskeedee, Wah Wah, and Parunuweap are some names that have endured throughout Utah's history. Shoshone, Ute, Piute, Goshute, Navajo, and Hopi Indian names are represented in Utah, although with no written language most of the ancient Indian names were preempted, anglicized, or bastardized.

The Spanish influence on place names in Utah was initiated when Domínguez and Escalante plodded through these wild lands with their weary party. It was at this time that the Spanish Trail developed, which has a vast name history in itself. The Spanish explorers also added names such as Salina, Castilla, and multiple Escalantes.

All the early adventurers—Indians, Spaniards, mountain men, Mormons, and military—filed their accumulated reports, carved their initials on rocks and trees, or left their remains forgotten on old battlegrounds or near the logs of an overturned raft. The stories of their deeds and place names were researched from journals, musty government records and reports, or obtained in later years from people who were once wide-eyed grandchildren.

Utah is unique in its religious history. Names such as Nephi, Brigham City, Lehi, Widtsoe, St. George, and Snowville would not have been used without the advent of the Mormons—those intrepid, often woefully inept, but thoroughly adaptable religionists whose beliefs demanded that living be more or less isolated and filled with hard work—at least in the early stages.

Many settlers expected to be sorely tested and from these trials came the rich heritage of today's names. Experiences with corrupt politicians, the military, hostile enemies, and new and different weather patterns resulted in names such as Cohab Canyon, U M and Cricket Mountains, Mormon Flat, Hurricane, and Lightning Ridge.

Trials with slave traders of Indian, Spanish, Mexican, black and white descent resulted in interesting names. Hideout Canyon, Horsethief Canyon, Flat Nose George Canyon, and McCarthy Spring are place names that resulted from raids by horse and cattle rustlers—those omnipresent spectrals who would swoop in during the night then disappear in a dusty haze, leaving dead horses and stinking cattle piled up at river crossings or fallen in the desert wastes. Calves too young or weak to keep up would be left as bait for wolf, bear, cougar, or coyote; thus Spanish Bottoms, Cougar Springs, and Coyote Bench were born. Even the bones of man added to the historic name lore. Flat Nose George was killed by a posse in Flat Nose George Canyon.

Language could not exist, history could not be written, and stories could not be told without names. Names are automatically given to things by human beings. This is our only source of communication, for there is no other way to leave a story for posterity than by and with names. Once a name is given, character and identity develop. Indira Gandhi once noted, "When you know a thing by name, you feel much closer to it; even with a bird, if you know it is a robin, there is a different relationship" (Putman, 387).

In 1954 Stegner (449) commented on a lack of an adequate study of Utah place names. Where can a person go to check one source to find Corn Creek or the early town of Peteetneet? Where are Hans Flat, Horseshoe Bend, or Three Step Hill, and how did they come into being?

Name problems are gradually being solved. But competition still grows raucous when politicians compete with the military, dam builders, or other politicians to have their own names implanted on the land, or the dams, or the lakes.

In the past, maps made by different companies were unreliable because conflicting names were used for the same feature. As maps were updated in subsequent years, the names changed with alarming frequency. What should a map maker, a cartographer, call a feature, and by what authority?

Several controversies have arisen over pejorative place names. In earlier days the names did not cause problems because most geographic names were concocted by men in the field, on the range, in the forest, on the trail, or fighting the rivers. If women had been creating names, there would undoubtedly be fewer embarrassing situations today. Men used names that served a purpose at the time, even though the names were sometimes crude. Today, if a name cannot be used in polite society, cannot be said out loud, or causes embarrassment, then a change may be required.

In the final analysis, a name should identify, be useful, and carry its own weight in today's oral or written language. As the maturing frontier society adapted to modern times, new rules changed Jap Flats to Japanese Flats. Paul Bunyans Potty, a natural window in Canyonlands Park, went through the same controversy but managed to hold firm and to emerge unscathed. Mild disputes still continue over names such as Yankee Flats and Squaw Peaks.

Much work has been accomplished in the realm of pejorative place names, but much more remains to be done and eventually each name will have to be dealt with on its own merits. Will the multiple "nipple" names such as Marys or Mollys or Peters Nipple eventually be modified? Heaven forbid! Let us not become too squeamish. Names are history and should be enjoyed because they serve a purpose.

In conclusion, I would like to make one brief plea to each person who has lived in the wild places of Utah, who has been intimately acquainted with the state's name history, and who is someday going "to write a book" on place names and their sources. Make your information available! You have invaluable, irreplaceable knowledge that is useless if kept hidden. Share those bits of information with the public, even if in small pamphlet form or in handwritten manuscript. Write it down. Time is running out for recording pertinent personal history that will be useful to later descendants. There is an obligation here that should not be ignored.

I accept full responsibility for all errors of commission or omission. Inasmuch as this is an ongoing project (and there are, at a rough estimate, at least 40 percent more place names in Utah that still have an unaccounted history), I would appreciate receiving any corrections or additions. They will be enthusiastically received, seriously considered, gratefully acknowledged, and hopefully a supplemental publication will eventually be added as one more contribution to the name history of Utah. Through its geographic names and its history, long live a very noble state.

ACKNOWLEDGMENTS

A research-compilation project such as this is the contribution of many written and oral sources. Of these, the major references are listed in the bibliography. Unfortunately many sources for individual place names must remain unmentioned because so much information was obtained through conversations with people I met while conducting field research. There is no reliable way to verify the accuracy of the information I acquired in these chance encounters. I accepted the stories as they were related to me; this is better than no record at all. And there is more than a fifty-fifty chance that the name sources are valid. To these many contributing partners, I give heartfelt thanks.

Certain individuals and institutions must be specially mentioned. I express my appreciation for the prompt response filled with excellent advice when I wrote Wallace Stegner for his thoughts on the book while contemplating its inception. He is a noted authority on place names in Utah. I also wish to thank Kimball T. Harper for his kind remarks and contributions.

I appreciate the help of Blaine Furniss of Brigham Young University's Botany and Range Science Department for reviewing, suggesting, and taking untold hours out of his busy schedule to help iron out and clarify problems.

The Botany and Range Science Department of BYU and its parent, the College of Biological and Agricultural Science, have both been most supportive. The department chairpersons, from the late Dr. Dayna Stocks to Dr. Wilford Hess, have been encouraging and cooperative in providing office space, equipment, and maps—over eleven hundred of them. Maps are the lifeblood and soul of a project such as this.

Donald Orth, executive secretary of the U.S. Board on Geographic Names in Washington, D.C., has been most helpful. On two occasions he gave me access to the Board's geographic names files.

Special note must be made of the cooperation and help of Dr. David E. Miller's widow, Helen L., and their son David, Jr. Dr. Miller and I were working on a joint authorship of a geographic names of Utah book when he unexpectedly died. He was a noted historian and former chairman of the history department of the University of Utah. The family most graciously let me use Dr. Miller's place name files.

Dr. Jay Haymond, coordinator of Historical Collections and Research at the Utah Historical Society and also chairman of the Utah State Committee on Geographic Names, has always been helpful and supportive of this project. I express my appreciation both to Dr. Haymond and to the committee members for their support.

Thanks also go to the director of the Bean Museum and curator of its herbarium, Dr. Stan Welsh, who helped guide me through the mysteries of the professional logger's names for trees. For therein lies the reasons why White Pine Creek and Lake is where blue spruce and Englemann spruce are harvested and Red Pine Creek is where Douglas fir are harvested.

Thanks are extended to Rhea Toyn, postmistress in the extreme northwest part of Utah. She provided valuable help with the Grouse Creek and Raft River region names.

Edson Alvey of Escalante helped me several times. His typescript glossary, now in the Utah Historical Society Library in Salt Lake City, has provided valuable information on the Kaiparowits Plateau, the Hole-in-the-Rock, and Escalante country. Orrin Miller was helpful with Tooele County names. For one very puzzling place name: Goshen's early name of Sodom (Sodum), I thank Nancy M. Bradford, town clerk of

Goshen. Dr. Dick Murdock (retired) of BYU and John Clegg guided me through many lakes, canyons, and the Clegg names for the western Uinta Mountains. Elden Wilckens of the U.S. Forest Service assisted with central and western Uinta Mountain names.

On two occasions, I spoke with Pearl Baker in her Green River home about the books she has written and the names centering around the old Biddlecome Ranch (Ekker Ranch) out of Hanksville and the Robbers Roost, which is Butch Cassidy, the Sundance Kid, and the Wild Bunch country. Also, I was fortunate in being able to chat about early place names with Lulu Betenson of Circleville just one month before she passed away. She was not only over ninety years old, but was Butch Cassidy's younger sister.

To Ned Chaffin of San Bernardino, California, thanks for all the assistance on many river bottoms and canyon place names in Canyonlands National Park.

Thanks to the staff of the University of Utah Press and to Hope Hendricks for editing and formatting the manuscript.

To my daughter Linda, your talents used in producing this, your father's dream-child, are very much appreciated.

To Emily, my wife of fifty-three years, I am forever grateful for your patience through numerous moves while we established ourselves and for being my partner on many field trips in those early days—in the high country, but *never* in the desert. I appreciate your help in reviewing the manuscript. Your forte has been an optimism that this project would be completed.

A BRIEF HISTORY
OF THE GEOGRAPHIC
NAMES OF UTAH

Just as your personal name is important to you, geographic names are important to the community, the state, and the historian. Communication is virtually impossible without names. Legal papers, maps, geographic or geologic descriptions and locations must have names, and on names rest history.

The history of the regulation and control of geographic names is an important concern because everyone is directly or indirectly affected by these regulations and controls. The stories behind the names in this book illustrate how our environment, culture, and heritage were shaped by history. Major John Wesley Powell named the Dirty Devil River, but how far up the river did he intend the name to apply? After considerable litigation, it was decided the name applied only as far as the junction of the Fremont and Muddy rivers. Upon such decisions rest water rights, grazing rights, and, in the early days, even land rights.

On a national scale this name problem became evident and was finally acted upon in 1890. Prior to that time too many features had duplicate names, making the naming process confusing and unreliable. Applications for new names or decisions between competing names had no legal base or established rules to follow. Since cartographers require precise information, they were having difficulty compiling accurate, reliable maps. To make matters worse, private map makers were competing with one another, which also resulted in less-than-accurate maps.

Some states attempted to compile state name books, but these projects were tedious because neighboring states failed to cooperate and no federal laws existed to use as a guideline. One example was the fiasco resulting over the naming of Nevada's Boulder Dam—or was it Hoover Dam? A more recent example is the controversy over renaming Florida's Cape Canaveral to Cape Kennedy. As a result of public pressure, the name was changed back to Cape Canaveral. Such incidents illustrate the problems of confused, misinterpreted, or misguided place-naming.

On September 4, 1890, the U.S. Board on Geographic Names was established by presidential executive order. Unfortunately, the board was not authorized to make decisions because it was given an evaluating, organizing, and listing function only. Even though the organization was ineffective, it was an important beginning.

The lack of a board had been a problem for many years. For example, in the Utah Territory of 1847 problems occurred when new immigrants named features that were previously named by the native Indians. Prominent among those native tribes were the Shoshones, Goshutes, Piutes (Pahutes), Navajoes, and Utes. From them we have names such as Washakie (Shoshone), Ibapa (Goshute), Kanosh (Piute), Oljieto (Navajo), and Ouray (Ute). Because the tribes had no written language, preserving the original phonetics and names became difficult. The people attempting to record Indian names added to this confusion because they were often illiterate and spelled words as they thought they were pronounced. The Indian word for water, for instance, was spelled "Pa," "Pa'a," "Pah," "Paw," or "Pai." It was a hopeless situation for those dedicated to protecting early native languages.

The first known outside influence on the early Indian cultures in Utah Territory were recorded by Domínguez and Escalante in their 1776 expedition. The Spanish place names listed in the written records were strongly influenced by the Catholic Church they represented. One example is present-day Mount Timpanogos—the explorers called the mountain "El Sierra Blanca de los Timpanois."

Very few name changes transpired in the area over the next forty years. Then in 1818 a major but subtle invasion occurred which forever changed the name history of the region. From the east William Henry Ashley and his "enterprising young men" brought names that would be permanently implanted on western name history. The group represented English, Scottish, French, Dutch, Scandinavian, and German ancestry. Some of the dozens of place names of the early trappers and adventurers were Ashley National Forest, Jedediah Smith Mountain, Bridger Lake, and former Carson County, named for Kit Carson.

During the same period, a group including the French Canadian Peter Skene Ogden came from the northwest. The city of Ogden is named after him. From the Southwest, out of Taos, New Mexico, came another French Canadian, Etienne Provost whose name honors Provo River, Canyon, and City.

The mountain men trapped and explored in the area until the early 1840s when resources dwindled, demands changed, and the wagon trains began making the tortuous route into the West. It was at this time that the remainder of these earlier individualists were forced to turn to other pursuits such as professional scouting, acting as guides, and farming and/or ranching.

The Bartelson-Bidwell wagon train was the first to leave wagon tracks across what is presently Utah; they also left many imprints with their names. Pilot Mountain and Donner-Reed Pass reflect the activities of that period. Though tragic in their poorly developed and executed plans, the Donner-Reed party helped break the trail for the great drama of the following year of 1847 when the first and second Mormon migrations arrived in the Great Salt Lake Valley.

The Mormons, with their close-knit families and strong religious convictions, immediately began naming their new surroundings. Within hours, Ensign Peak was named. And soon Great Salt Lake City, Great Salt Lake, and Emigration Canyon entered the records.

The Mormons named more places in Utah than any other individual or group. From the Bible they bestowed Hebron, Salem, and Canaan. Today Utah ranks high on the list of states with Bible-connected names. From their alternate scripture, the Book of Mormon, came Nephi, Lehi, Moroni, Manti, and Bountiful.

Prospectors, lumbermen, railroadmen, cattlemen, and sheepmen also contributed to Utah's place names. Most of the names were given by males since they were out in the field, the forest, the desert, or on the range. Their hard-working and long-suffering wives kept the home fires, raised and cared for the children and developed gardens among many other activities. Utah honors many wonderful women with Lydia's Canyon, Kiz, Mount Ellen, and the town of Annabella, named for Isabella Dalton and Ann Roberts, two early pioneer women who settled in that community.

The developing farms, ranches, towns, and cities attracted outlaws who took advantage of the weak and the unwary and left their names during the wild period between 1870 and the early 1900s. Flat Nose George and Blue John both died violently, leaving their names on canyons north of the town of Green River. Silver Tip, killed by an Arizona sheriff, gave his name to a spring near the north end of the Robbers Roost country. Even though an alert citizen killed bank robbers Billy McCarthy and his son Fred, they left their names for McCarthy Springs and Canyon.

In 1860-61 the Pony Express and the Overland Stage passed through, leaving names on many features, among them Overland Canyon and Pass.

Wallace Stegner wrote that Major Powell and his river runners contributed more place names to Utah than any other group or individual except the Mormons. From Powell's expeditions we have Browns Park, Desolation Canyon, Cataract Canyon, Glen Canyon, and Lake Powell.

One of Utah's Mormon converts was Andrew Jenson, a man whose enthusiasm for history helped him eventually become an assistant Mormon church historian. In 1919 he published the "Origin of Western Geographic Names," then in March 1940, as part of the program of the Work Projects Administration and Utah Writers Projects, he produced a small publication called the *Origins of Utah Place Names*. The emphasis of this book was on the name of towns, cities, and counties.

The National Board on Geographic Names had to be reorganized if it was to be of any benefit to the program. So in 1947 that goal was accomplished when the board received the authority to standardize names on federal lands and maps, and to establish uniform rules and regulations for all domestic geographic names. The board could now deal with name proposals and problems in all states.

Several other important events occurred in the past. In 1900, Henry Gannett published *A Gazetteer of Utah* and in 1944 Kate Carter wrote "Origins of State Names" in the fifth volume of *Heart Throbs of the West*.

The Work Projects Administration and Zoology Department of the University of Utah produced the *Gazetteer of Utah Localities and Altitudes* in 1952, in 1961 Rufus Wood Leigh published *Five Hundred Utah Place Names*, then in 1972 the National Place Name Survey Committee was formed.

The following summarizes events up to 1984 that led to the formation of committees and organizations affecting the governance of place names in Utah.

Several problems occurred because a state or central organization had never been established to protect place names. Concerns were also expressed that Utahns were not given enough input on the federal name decisions for their state. Historians and geographic names buffs could not find comprehensive reference material on Utah place names. Therefore, steps were taken to form a committee to work on the geographic names of Utah. At the request of Dr. Byrd Granger, director of the National Place Names Survey, Dr. David Miller, former chairman of the University of Utah History Department, started a program to remedy the situation. James Jacobs, a retired U.S. National Forest supervisor and member of the American Name Society, was contacted by Donald Orth, executive secretary of the National Board on Geographic Names. Orth proposed that James Jacobs and Dr. Miller be co-chairmen of the National Place Names Survey in Utah. Jacobs voluntarily withdrew in favor of Miller, who was then appointed director of the project.

I had been conducting research for a place names book on Utah and was invited to join the project. Wendy Hassibe was chief public service officer in the Salt Lake City offices of the map division of the United States Geological Survey when she was invited to join. She was working to encourage place names studies in the region. Kent Malan, a cartographer in the Regional Offices of the U.S. Forest Service in Ogden, was also asked to join since he was heavily involved in name research in his daily activities. He was also the backbone of the formation of the *Utah Geographic Names Handbook*, an assignment Malan and I undertook. The first edition appeared in October 1975 and a revised edition was published in July 1976.

Supervising, guiding, advising, and encouraging was Dr. Jay Haymond, librarian of the Utah State Historical Society and executive secretary of our committee. It was the concerted effort of these people, with the full cooperation of the National Board in Washington, D.C., and the National Place Name Survey, that culminated in a committee for the control of geographic names in Utah.

On October 24, 1973, the first planning meeting was held and Dr. Miller was moved to chair the committee. He appointed Dr. Haymond as associate director. A tentative name for the committee was "The Committee on Place Names of Utah." By January of 1975 the committee name had been modified to "The Utah State Committee on Geographic Names," which was approved and accepted by the Utah State History Board. At this point all new names or name changes, all adjudications involving place names, would be submitted to the Utah Committee on Geographic Names and through them to the United States Board on Geographic Names for review and acceptance or rejection by both the state and national organizations. A tentative first edition of the *Utah Geographic Names Handbook*, a guide and instructional manual, was published in October 1975.

In January 1976, Governor Calvin Rampton formally established the Utah State Committee on Geographic Names by executive order.

The First Conference on Intermountain Geographic Names, initiated by the Utah Committee, was held in November 1977 to advance interstate relations and study interstate problems on geographic names. Representatives from Montana, Oregon, Washington, and California attended. A vote was made to continue the meeting on an annual basis.

The tragic news of Dr. David Miller's death was announced on August 21, 1978. He was replaced by Kent Malan, with Dr. Haymond continuing as executive secretary.

At the Fifth Annual Western States Geographic Names Conference in 1981, Kent Malan made a resolution that Jay Haymond be made permanent secretary for the conference. The resolution passed. Wendy Hassibe volunteered to keep the Geographic Names Information System records current. Donald Orth suggested that the Canadian Provinces and northern states of Mexico be included on the invitation list to study the problems of naming features on the international border.

On August 20, 1982, twelve individuals met to form a new Utah Place Names Society and I was appointed as first president. I also agreed to formulate a tentative constitution. The goals of the new society are as follows:

1. To search out the folklore and origins of Utah's place names.
2. To hold at least two meetings a year to encourage local interest in place names and their cultural origins.
3. To encourage and sponsor the preparation of papers on the history of place names through original research.
4. To help locate the remaining original sources of information on Utah's place names.
5. To provide a central location for information on place names at the Utah State Historical Society Library where storage, protection, and study will be properly carried out.
6. To provide a central location for assisting county committees working on local place names.
7. To encourage general interest in Utah place names by promoting articles in local newspapers.
8. To develop a newsletter for the purpose of communicating more efficiently with our membership.

During the 1983 seventh annual meeting of the Western States Geographic Names Conference held in Boise, Idaho, it was announced that the conference was now fully incorporated and officially recognized by the laws of Utah, with Articles of Incorporation filed February 8, 1984.

The first issue of the Utah Place Names Society newsletter was distributed in 1984 and Keith Rosevear, cartographer/supervisor, Utah State Department of Transportation, assumed office as president of the Utah Place Names Society, replacing me, whose term had expired.

INSTRUCTIONS

In order to clarify the system used to present the information in this book, the following instructions should be used. An asterisk (*) following a place name indicates past or present inhabitation. North Creek is the creek. North Creek* is the settlement. Shauntie* was a previously inhabited ghost town site. Antelope Peak or Circle Cliffs would not have an asterisk. Repeated use of the inhabited place name in a single entry will not continue to carry the asterisk.

The county where the place name is located follows in bold print and parentheses.

A series of letters and numbers end each entry. The first group is the section, township, and range as closely as can be pinpointed (i.e., S12,T3S,R4W,SLM, or USM). A section equals approximately one square mile, reflecting U.S. Geological Survey topographic map sections. Because Utah is not completely mapped, some entries are incomplete. In this case, whatever information is available will be provided.

The second group of numbers, when present, is altitude in feet followed by meters in parentheses. Altitude is not included with canyons or deserts with varying altitudes.

The third set of numbers refers to sources listed in the bibliography at the end of the book. There are periodic references to a main source where more specific information is presented in parentheses. Volume numbers are preceded with a "v". If a slash follows the volume number, this refers to the number of the publication. For example, 555(v32/5) is reference number 555, volume 32, number 5.

The "D.L." number occasionally appearing after the reference numbers refers to the U.S. Board on Geographic Names "Decision List." See 531 and 532 in the Bibliography.

Where indicated, "MRN" means more research is needed to provide more complete information.

Several place name entries do not provide information on section/township/range, elevation, references, and/or decision list numbers. Although most of the entries list at least one of the four, all the sources were not always available. In any case, the information will be presented in the following order: (1) section/township/range, (2) elevation, (3) references, and (4) decision list number. If any of the four are missing, the available information will begin at the left margin.

". . . there is no part of the world where nomenclature is so rich, poetical, humorous, and picturesque as the United States of America."
Dingman quoting Robert Louis Stevenson.

"A name is a mark or a term put upon a place or a person to enable those people or things to be the subject of discourse."
Most any dictionary.

You can neither talk to nor about without a name.
Anonymous.

Humpty Dumpty, "Tell me your name?"
Alice, "My name is Alice, but—"
"It's a stupid name enough!" Humpty Dumpty interrupted impatiently. "What does it mean?"
"Must a name mean something?" Alice asked doubtfully.
"Of course it must," Humpty Dumpty said with a short laugh. "My name means the shape I am—and a good handsome shape it is too. With a name like yours you might be any shape almost."
Lewis Carroll, *Alice's Adventures in Wonderland* and *Through the Looking Glass.*

". . . is a word or a combination of words by which a person, place, idea, etc., is known or designated."
Most any dictionary.

"A name is a first element in any identification."
Anonymous.

"I'd sooner be in Escalante" was the remark that gave Sooner Bench its name.
See SOONER BENCH in text.

- A -

A-1 PEAK (**Summit**) is located on the west end of the Uinta Mountains, one and one-half mile northeast of Kletting Peak and three miles northeast of Hayden Peak. The name is an arbitrary code number which will be used until a permanent name is assigned. Since code-named peaks are only listed on special maps, no further reference will be made to them in this publication.
T1S,R10E,SLM; 12,377' (3,773m). 594.

AARON* (**San Juan**) is named after Aaron Asay. See Hatch*.

ABAJO MOUNTAINS (**San Juan**) are six miles west of Monticello*. The name originated during the Old Spanish Trail days of the 1700s and is Spanish for "low" or "down." The mountains are also known locally as the "Blue Mountains" or the "Blues" because of their dark somber blue color as seen from a distance. They are laccolithic in origin and isolated. The highest point is Abajo Peak at 11,360' (3,463m).
T33,34S,R21,22,23E,SLM. 314, 406, 492, 602.

ABAJO PEAK (**San Juan**) is on the east side of the Abajo Mountains and is the highest peak in the range. The peak was named by Ferdinand V. Hayden of the U.S. Topographical Engineers who surveyed in this area in 1873. A local name used during the early 1900s was Shay Mountain.
T34S,R22E,SLM; 11,360' (3,463m). 530.

ABERCROMBIE PEAK (**Tooele**) is located in the Deep Creek Mountains about one mile southeast of Dry Canyon and one mile southwest of Willow Spring. It was named for an early prospector from nearby Gold Hill*.

S34,T9S,R18W,SLM; 8,182' (2,494m). 152, 494.

ABERDEEN* (**Iron**) was a small settlement established by Rufus Novil and George Wood a short distance east of Cedar City*. The townsite was never very desirable, so it was soon abandoned.
S13,14,T36S,R11W,SLM; 5,920' (1,804m). 567.

ABES LAKE (**Summit**) is at the west end of the Uinta Mountains, one and one-half miles north of the west end of Notch Mountain. The lake was named after Abraham Marchant of Peoa* who headed the group which converted it into a reservoir.
S13,T1S,R8E,SLM; 9,840' (2,999m). 298.

ABRAHAM* (**Millard**) is five miles west of Sutherland* and eight miles northwest of Delta*. The site was settled in 1890 and named for Abraham H. Cannon, a Mormon elder and settler in the area.
S26,T16S,R8W,SLM; 4,591' (1,399m). 542.

ACORD FORK (**Sanpete**) originates eight miles southeast of Spring City* and drains west into Temple Fork. It was named for the man who helped acquire some of the necessary timbers and lumber to build the historic Mormon Temple in nearby Manti*.
S29,30,T16S,R5E,SLM. 602.

ACORD LAKES (**Sevier**) are near the head of Convulsion Canyon west of Old Woman Plateau. See Acord Fork for name source.
S9,16,T22S,R4E,SLM; 7,975' (2,431m). 602.

ADAIRVILLE* (**Garfield**). See Widtsoe*.

1

ADAIRVILLE* (**Kane**) was located forty-five miles east of Kanab*, one-half mile north of US-89, near the Paria River. The area was settled in 1873 and named for the Thomas Adair family. After severe flooding in 1883 and 1884 most of the residents moved upstream to Paria* (Pahrea[h]). The settlement was finally abandoned in 1885 because of flash floods and drought. The site is now a ghost town.
S33,T42S,R1W,SLM; 4,400' (1,341m). 89, 288, 455, 516.

ADAMS CANYON (**Davis**) originates six miles east of Layton* where it drains westward into Holmes Reservoir. The canyon was named for Elias Adams, a pioneer of the late 1850s who settled at the mouth of the canyon and established a small whip-saw lumber operation.
S16,T4N,R1E,SLM. 88.

ADAMS HEAD PEAK (**Garfield**) is fifteen miles northeast of Panguitch* on the Sevier Plateau. The peak was named by the U.S. Geological Survey and has a Powell survey cairn on top. The peak was used as a lookout for fires, hostile Indians, and other emergencies. Two possible origins are cited for the name. Either a Mr. Adams was one of the early lookouts or the peak has the outline of a human head when looked at from a certain angle.
T33S,R4W,SLM; 10,426' (3,178m). 100(v17), 494, 567.

ADAMS RIVER (**Washington**). See Virgin River.

ADAMSVILLE* (**Beaver**) is small agricultural community on U-21 eight miles west of Beaver*. It was first settled in the spring of 1862 by David B. Adams and three other families; the settlement was named Adamsville in 1867 after its founder. An earlier name for the community was Beaver Iron Works*. Wales* was also a temporary name honoring the many Welsh people who

lived there during the early period.
S30,T29S,R8W,SLM; 5,521' (1,683m). 100 (v17), 355.

ADAX LAKE (**Summit**) is in the west Uinta Mountains one and one-half miles north northwest of Notch Mountain. Seven miles east southeast is Mirror Lake. The word is a corruption of the name "Adix" which was used by Cardie Clegg, an early developer and freighter in the area. Clegg was referring to his son-in-law, Vern Adix.
S14,T1S,R8E,SLM; 9,700' (2,957m). 379.

ADELAIDE PARK* (**Millard**) is six miles up Corn Creek southeast of Kanosh*. James Mills Paxton and his second wife Adelaide lived there and homesteaded the land under the Squatters Rights Act. At a public gathering on May 24, 1935, the spot was dedicated as a park.
S4,T24S,R4½E,SLM; 5,575' (1,699m). 508.

ADOBE MESA (**Grand**) is on the northwest slopes of the La Sal Mountains, east of and near Castle Valley. The name is a corruption of Doby Brown, a man who homesteaded in this area.
S11,T25S,R23E,SLM to S20,T25S,R24E, SLM; 7,000' (2,134m). 146.

ADVENTURE* (**Washington**) was between Grafton* and Rockville* near the Virgin River. It was founded in 1860 by Phillip Klingensmith and others from Iron County. Adventure was abandoned when flooding and other problems sent the settlers up-river to a new townsite called Rockville. Adventure was named because the residents felt it was truly an adventure to move into and attempt to tame this primitive, desert region. Today Adventure is a ghost town site. See Rockville.
S2,T42S,R11W,SLM; 3,750' (1,143m). 100 (v13), 89.

AGATE* (**Grand**) is located on US-6/50, thirty-eight miles east of Green

River*. This small, temporary settlement on the Cisco Desert south of Cisco* was named for local agate deposits.

AJAX* (Tooele) was in the heart of Rush Valley on U-36, midway between St. John Station* and Vernon*. The site was originally settled in 1863 by Welsh farmers as a hay and livestock area. At this time it was known as Center* for its location in the center of the valley between Stockton* and Vernon. In 1869 William Ajax transferred his store operation from Salt Lake City* to the area and began selling supplies to local miners and ranchers. He excavated an underground business area where the extreme winter and summer temperatures were greatly subdued. He developed a complete underground department store, cafe, and hotel. When the railroad came through, travel to and from more distant destinations became easier, mines declined, families moved out, and business diminished. William Ajax died in 1899. By 1914 the site was abandoned and became a ghost town.
S27,T6S,R5W,SLM; 5,064' (1,544m). 89, 100(v13), 567.

AKIN* (Millard). See Delta*.

ALBION BASIN (Salt Lake) is at the head of Little Cottonwood Canyon between Secret Lake and Mt. Wolverine. The basin was named by English developers who arrived in the 1870s to invest in the mining boom that developed in the basin. Albion is an old poetic Celtic name for England or Great Britain.
NW¼,T3S,R3E,SLM; 9,300' (2,835m). 444.

ALDRIDGE* (Wayne) was at the mouth of Pleasant Creek on U-24, eleven miles east of the Capitol Reef National Park headquarters. It was settled in 1882 by Mosiah Behunin and by 1890 developed into a small community. The settlers produced fruits, alfalfa, melons, and a variety of vegetables. It was abandoned by 1900 partly because of insufficient arable land.
S19,T29S,R8E,SLM; 4,800' (1,463m). 485.

ALEXANDER* (Duchesne). See Altonah*.

ALEXANDER LAKE (Summit) is in the southwest section of the Uinta Mountains, between Iron Mine Mountain and Haystack Mountain. The lake was named for an early explorer and settler.
S36,T2S,R8E,SLM; 9,350' (2,850m). 298.

ALFALFA* (Millard). See Sugarville*.

ALHAMBRA ROCK (San Juan) is an intrusive dike three miles southwest of Mexican Hat* and four miles south of the Goosenecks of the San Juan River. The feature was named by early Spaniards when they passed through the area. The contour of the rock suggested the Alhambra, the medieval Moorish castle of Granada, Spain.
5,000' (1,524m). 314.

ALKALI CANYON (San Juan) originates five miles northeast of Blanding*. The alkaline waters of this canyon drain southeast into Montezuma Creek.
S28,T35S,R23E,SLM to S24,T39S,R24E, SLM.

ALLEN CANYON (San Juan) originates seven miles north of Aneth* and drains south into the San Juan River. John and Peter Allen were early settlers who raised their families here and gave their name to this canyon and the canyon in the following entry.
S18,T40S,R25E,SLM to S2,T41S,R20E,SLM. 406, 567.

ALLEN CANYON (San Juan) originates on the northern slopes of Mt. Linnaeus in the Abajo Mountains and drains south into Cottonwood Creek. Ten miles to the southeast is Blanding*. See the preceding Allen Canyon.
S6,T36S,R21E,SLM (at mouth). 406, 567.

ALLEN CREEK (Daggett) originates in the northeast section of the Uinta

Mountains, seven miles northwest of Mount Lena and west of the junction of U-44 and U-260. The creek drains north into Flaming Gorge Reservoir four miles west of the dam, named for Lewis Allen who herded his cattle in this area. S31,T2N,R22E,SLM to S18,T2N,R22E,SLM. 172.

ALLEN CREEK (**Garfield**) originates on Escalante Mountain eleven miles southwest of Escalante* and drains southeast into Upper Valley. The creek was named after Philo Allen, Sr., who ranched nearby. S19,T35S,R1E,SLM to S34,T35S,R1E,SLM. 12. D.L. 6504.

ALLEN DUMP (**Garfield**) is an extensive sandy bench or upland five miles northeast of Sunset Flat and the Hole-in-the-Rock. Escalante* is twenty miles west. The Allen brothers ran their stock on this bench. S16,T37S,R6E,SLM; 5,817' (1,773m). 12.

ALLEN LAKE (**Duchesne**) is in the southwest section of the Uinta Mountains, two miles east of Governor Dern Lake. District Ranger Floyd L. Allen was killed by lightning while on duty there in August 1938. S14,T3N,R8W,USM; 10,400' (3,170m). 100 (v2), 309.

ALLEN LAKE (**Duchesne**) is in the south central section of the Uinta Mountains midway between Carrot Lake and Lake Atwood. Jess Allen was the first person to stock the lake with fish. 10,990' (3,350m). 309.

ALLIGATOR LAKE (**Summit**) is in the north central section of the Uinta Mountains eight miles north of Kings Peak, near the head of Henrys Fork. The general outline of the lake resembles an alligator. 10,033' (3,058m).

ALLRED HOLLOW (**Beaver**) is northeast of Beaver* on the South Fork of North Creek. It drains northwest into the South Fork. In the 1880s Indians stole William Allred's horse in the hollow. Allred was able to recover his horse but one Indian was killed in the ensuing fight. S35,T29S,R6W,SLM. 355.

ALLRED LAKE (**Duchesne**) is in the south central section of the Uinta Mountains between Lake Atwood and Mount Emmons where it drains into Atwood Creek. Ken Allred, a fireguard, was the first to stock this lake with fish. 11,000' (3,353m). 309.

ALLRED SPRING (**Beaver**) is at the head of the East Fork of Baker Canyon. The spring was named after Orson Allred, an Indian fighter who camped at the spring in the early 1870s. S35,T29S,R6W,SLM; 9,725' (2,964m). 355.

ALMA* (**Sevier**). See Monroe*.

ALMA* (**Weber**). See West Weber*.

ALMA TAYLOR HOLLOW (**Uintah**) originates at Alma Taylor Lake in the eastern Uinta Mountains. Taylor Mountain is six miles north. See Alma Taylor Lake. 567.

ALMA TAYLOR LAKE (**Uintah**) is in the northeast section of the Uinta Mountains at the head of Alma Taylor Hollow. Taylor Mountain was also named for Alma Taylor and is located six miles northeast. Taylor was a 1877 pioneer who, with his brother Teancum, ran cattle near the lake and on Taylor Mountain. 9,000' (2,743m). 567.

ALPINE* (**Utah**) is on U-74 five miles north of American Fork* near the mouth of American Fork Canyon. It was first settled in the fall of 1850 by W. H. Hooper, Quincy Knowlton, and George M. Burgess who developed a cattle ranch in the area. Several early names for the

settlement include Fort Wordsworth* for William S. Wordsworth, Dry Creek Settlement*, and later, Mountainville*, because of the adjacent high mountains. Brigham Young is reported to have liked the name Mountainville, but considered Alpine more expedient and appropriate. Following legislative action, the settlement of Mountainville was incorporated as the City of Alpine on January 10, 1855.
S24,T4S,R1E,SLM; 4,957' (1,511m). 270, 288, 314, 360, 542.

ALTA* (Salt Lake) is at the head of Little Cottonwood Canyon east of Sandy*. In 1864, General Connor's soldiers from Fort Douglas* discovered silver ore when they were surveying in the canyon. By 1866 a small mining community was established which the miners named Central City* because of its central location around surrounding mines. In 1871 another community developed down the canyon. The citizens named it Alta, a Spanish word for "high" or "upper." Central City was gradually absorbed into Alta because of increasing population and development. At one time Alta was a lively mining town with over 9,500 inhabitants. The ore was so rich it was profitable to haul it by oxen down the canyon then fifty miles north to Ogden*. From there it was shipped by train to San Francisco where the ore was loaded onto ships and transported around Cape Horn to Swansea*, Wales for refining. Eventually the mines at Alta were depleted and the canyon community diminished as avalanches and fires continued to plague the area. Today Alta is a thriving summer and winter recreation center; skiing and summer festivals now assume international importance. Avalanche danger has been reduced thanks to a very active U.S. Forest Service program.
T3S,R3E,SLM; 8,600' (2,621m). 89, 314, 360, 444, 454, 466(3 Oct. 1965), 542.

ALTAMONT* (Duchesne) is on the upper benchlands of the south central slopes of the Uinta Mountains. Three miles to the north is Altonah* and four miles to the east is Bluebell*. Altamont received its name in 1936 through a contest sponsored by the high school student body. The composite name submitted by Clarence Snyder refers to Altonah and Mt. Emmons, a nearby peak.
S25,T1S,R4W,USM; 6,380' (1,945m). 165, 567.

ALTON* (Kane) is a livestock and ranching community near the head of Long Valley, twenty miles northeast of Glendale* at the base of the beautiful Sunset Cliffs. These cliffs are part of the west boundary of the Paunsaugunt Plateau. Alton's earliest name was Roundys Station* after Lorenzo Wesley Roundy and his family. Roundy built two log cabins there but was forced to abandon his ranch site because he was having trouble with the Indians. He drowned in 1876 while ferrying supplies across the Colorado River. The site was later named Graham* for Graham Duncan MacDonald, a pioneer of nearby Ranch*. MacDonald was a bookkeeper for an adjacent sawmill; he also helped haul lumber for the construction of the St. George* Mormon temple. Alton was an outgrowth of nearby Upper Kanab* and was considered part of that settlement at one time. As time passed, various names were discussed for Alton-to-be, but none were accepted until a drawing was held at a community social in 1912. Among the names put into a hat for the drawing was one suggested by Charles R. Pugh who had been reading a book about the Alton Fjord in Norway, known for the height of its surrounding mountains. A two-year-old child drew the name from the hat.
S12,T39S,R6W,SLM; 7,036' (2,145m). 100 (v17), 288, 360, 455, 515, 542.

ALTON AMPHITHEATER (Kane) is a semi-enclosed area two miles in diameter, surrounded by mountains and cliffs on the headwaters of Kanab Creek. The

name comes from the community located within its confines. See Alton*.
T39S,R5,6W,SLM; ca. 6,900' (2,103m).

ALTONAH* (Dúchesne) is in the upper benchland country adjacent to the south central Uinta Mountains. Altamont* is three miles south and Mountain Home* is five miles west southwest. The site was originally settled in 1906, but was named Alexander* after Robert and Milton Alexander who were early settlers. After the townsite was finalized in January 1912, its name was changed to Altonah which refers to its comparative altitude. There was also an early temporary name variant—Queen City* meaning queen of all it surveyed.
S13,14,T1S,R4W,USM; 6,680' (2,036m). 89, 165, 360, 542, 567.

ALTUS* (Summit) was located at what is presently Parleys Summit, the highest point along the highway between Salt Lake City* and Park City*. Altus was settled in 1900 as a temporary way station, but was soon abandoned. It completely disappeared after the I-80 freeway was built.
S9,T1S,R3E,SLM; 7,025' (2,141m). 542.

ALUMBED HOLLOW (Sevier) originates south of Steves Mountains, draining southwest into Salina Creek. It is named for the small spring of alum water in the hollow.
S35,T21S,R2E,SLM to S9,T22S,R2E,SLM. 567.

ALUNITE* (Piute) was formerly a small mining community fifteen miles south of Marysvale* on the eastern slope of Deer Trail Mountain. The area was settled in 1914 after Tom Gillan, a local prospector, discovered the mineral alunite. The mines were shut down after World War I when a need for the alunite subsided. Today the mines are a center for the production of alunite and its by-products, for which the community was originally named. The old settlement of Alunite was never reestablished and is a ghost town site.
89, 242.

ALVEY WASH (Garfield) originates on the southeast slopes of Death Ridge at the north end of the Kaiparowits Plateau. It drains to the north northeast to Escalante* then southeast into Harris Wash. Today the middle section of Alvey Wash is called Tenmile Wash and the lower section is called Harris Wash. Alvey Wash was named after William Alvey, an initial settler who grazed horses along the upper reaches of the wash. Alvey Wash was one of the first places to be named by members of the Powell Survey.
S20,28,T37S,R2E,SLM to S15,T36S,R4E, SLM. 12, 602.

AMALGA* (Cache) is a small agricultural community on U-218 three miles west of Smithfield*. It was first settled in 1860 by Hans Jorgensen. When the Amalgamated Sugar Company built a sugar beet processing plant there, the name was changed to Amalga.
S13,T13N,R1W,SLM; 4,448' (1,356m). 449, 567, 542.

AMASA BACK (Grand) is a three-mile-long ridge or hogsback in a large U-shaped bend of the Colorado River located approximately five miles southwest of Moab*. The feature was named for Amasa Larson, a tall, lanky cattleman who entered the area in the early 1880s.
S6,7,18,19,T26S,R21E,SLM; 5,000' (1,524m). 578.

AMERICAN FORK* (Utah) is at the north end of Utah Lake on US-91 and the American Fork River. It was first settled by Mormons in 1850. The town took its name from the river which was named much earlier. Previous town names were McArthursville* (Arthursville*) for Duncan McArthur who was an early settler, and Lake City* for its proximity to Utah Lake. Fort Wall* was built here in 1852 and

6

completed in 1855. See American Fork River.
S13,14,23,24,T5S,R1E,SLM;   4,617'
(1,407m). 27, 100(v17), 288, 314, 542, 555(v53/1).

AMERICAN FORK CANYON (Utah). See American Fork River.

AMERICAN FORK CREEK (Utah). See American Fork River.

AMERICAN FORK RIVER (Utah) originates on the south slopes of Mount Baldy (Bald Mountain) south of Little Cottonwood Canyon and one mile northeast of Twin Peaks. It drains through American Fork Canyon to enter Utah Valley and Utah Lake. Three possible reasons for having this name are listed; it is very likely that all are involved: (1) It was named to avoid confusion with the Spanish Fork River to the south where the Domínguez and Escalante party entered the Utah Valley. They originally named this river the El Rio de Santa Ana. (2) Before the Mormons entered the valley, it was named by American goldseekers who camped there while passing through on their way to California. (3) It was named by early trappers and mountain men who worked the creek for beaver as early as 1822.
S35,T5S,R1E,SLM (mouth of creek). 27, 129, 270, 288, 314, 384, 542.

AMETHYST LAKE (Summit) is the dominant lake of a small cluster of lakes in the Amethyst Lake Basin. The name comes from the dramatic blue color of the water. See Amethyst Lake Basin.

AMETHYST LAKE BASIN (Summit) is a ruggedly beautiful basin on the northern slopes of the western Uinta Mountains at the head of Ostler Fork of the Stillwater. It rests between two magnificent peaks—Ostler on the southwest and Lamotte on the northeast—and takes its name from the dominant lake in the basin.

NE¼,T1S,R10E,SLM; ca. 10,800' (3,292m).

AMY LAKE (Duchesne) is in the southwest section of the Uinta Mountains in the Four Lakes Basin. MRN
S2,T3N,R8W,USM; 10,800' (3,292m).

ANASAZI CANYON (San Juan) originates on the northern slopes of Navajo Mountain five miles northeast of Rainbow Bridge National Monument. It drains into the Colorado River (Lake Powell). See Anasazi Indian Village State Historical Site for name source.
530. D.L. 6001.

ANASAZI INDIAN VILLAGE STATE HISTORICAL SITE (Garfield) is the site of an ancient Anasazi Indian village in what is now Boulder*. In 1959, initial excavations were started and it is believed that the people of the village lived there from 1075 A.D. to 1275 A.D. Anasazi means "Ancient Ones" in Navajo. The site is now a state park which has a beautiful visitor center and a walk-through trail allowing sightseers to visit the ruins.
S25,T33S,R4E,SLM; 6,575' (2,004m).

ANCHOR LAKE (Summit) is at the western end of the Uinta Mountains two miles west of Notch Mountain and two and one-half miles northwest of Mount Watson. The lake was named by the U.S. Forest Service for its anchor-like shape.
S22,T1S,R8E,SLM; 10,390' (3,167m). 298.

ANCHORAGE* (Davis) is a community developed between Syracuse* on the west and Laytona* on the east, one mile south of Clearfield*. It was built during World War II for employees of the Clearfield Naval Depot. One might surmise a naval origin in this community name.
S13,T4N,R2W,SLM; 4,306' (1,337m).

ANDERSON JUNCTION* (Washington) is an exit at the junction of I-15 and U-17, five miles south of Pintura*. In 1853 this area was referred to as

McPhersons Flat*. In 1863, a miner by the name of Peter Anderson was called by the Mormon Church to help settle along the Muddy River in what is now Nevada. While traveling south, he arrived at McPherson's Flat when his wife became ill, so they decided to stay and homestead. The area became known as Anderson's Ranch. Today the I-15 freeway passes over the old ranch property where there is a numbered exit called Anderson Junction on I-15 south. S27,T40S,R13W,SLM; 3,750' (1,143m). 154, 542, 546.

ANDERSON MEADOW (**Beaver**) surrounds the Anderson Meadow Reservoir near the head of the south fork of the Beaver River in the Tushar Mountains. It was named for William R. Anderson who fenced the area, raised livestock, and bred horses there prior to 1880. S9,T30S,R5W,SLM; 9,355' (2,851m). 125.

ANDERSON MEADOW RESERVOIR (**Beaver**). See Anderson Meadow.

ANDERSON RANCH (**Washington**). See Anderson Junction.

ANDY MILLER FLATS (**Garfield**) is adjacent to and north of the Mille Crag Bend of the Colorado River, five miles east of the mouth of the Dirty Devil River. Andy Miller was an early sheepherder who ran his sheep in the area. S16,T33S,R15E,SLM (in part); 4,800'-5,388' (1,463m-1,642m). 102.

ANETH* (**San Juan**) is a small community on a point north of the junction of McElmo Creek and the San Juan River. It was the site of a Navajo trading post during the early 1880s. In 1886 it was named Holyoak* after an early settler. In the 1900s the name was changed to Anseth*, then Aneth for an operator of the local trading post. The discovery of oil and gas in the area accelerated settlement and population growth. S16,21,T41S,R25E,SLM; 4,531' (1,381m).

314, 406, 578.

ANGEL ARCH (**San Juan**) is on Salt Creek in Canyonlands National Park about eleven miles south southeast of Squaw Creek Campground. It was named in the 1950s by Chaffee C. Young who visualized it as a reverential figure with the head bowed as if in prayer. One could imagine wings on this figure. A less popular name for this feature is Pegasus Arch, for the winged horse of Greek mythology. T31S,R20E,SLM. 311, 466(1 Nov. 1978).

ANGEL COVE (**Wayne**). See Angels Point.

ANGEL COVE SPRING (**Wayne**). See Angels Point.

ANGELS LANDING (**Washington**) is a dramatic sandstone monolith deep in Zion Canyon National Park across the river and north of Cable Mountain. This is a water-carved formation with a partially flattened dome that was eroded out of the Mukuntuweap Plateau. Wind blowing sand has aided in the erosion, leaving unusual formations, undercuttings, caves, and coves. Angels Landing was named by the Reverend Frederick Vining Fisher of Ogden*, Utah. The nearby Great White Throne was visualized as the throne of Deity, which Fisher felt Angels would never land on but would reverently pause at the foot of to pay their obeisance from nearby Angels Landing. T42S,R9E,SLM; 5,785' (1,763m). 438, 546, 600.

ANGELS POINT (**Wayne**) is an elevated projection of land pointing to the southwest between Robbers Roost Canyon, and South Fork on the north and No Mans Canyon on the south. Seven miles to the east is the Ekker Ranch house, known earlier as the Biddlecome Ranch. To the west, Angels Point looks down onto the Dirty Devil River and the mouth of Beaver Canyon.

8

The name is taken from Angels Trail which passes through this area. There is also an Angel Cove and Angel Cove Spring adjacent on the Dirty Devil River down below. See Angels Trail.
S2,T29S,R13E,SLM; 5,000' (1,524m). 25.

ANGELS TRAIL (Wayne). Livestock were once herded along this trail, some of which were rustled from the regions to the west around the Henry Mountains. The livestock trail headed east down Beaver Canyon (Beaver Box) and crossed the Dirty Devil River at Angel Cove. From there the trail went up the precipitous slopes to the head of Angels Point, then east past Deadmans Hill and onto Roost Flats. It is recorded that the outlaw Cap Brown was one of the earliest users of the trail. Brown named the trail in the early 1870s because only an angel with wings could make it out of the Dirty Devil River area and up onto the point.
T29S,R14E,SLM to T29S,R13E,SLM. 25.

ANGLE* (Sevier) is a small agricultural and ranching community in Grass Valley. It is adjacent to U-62, fifteen miles north of Antimony* and twenty miles south of Koosharem*. Early names were Lower Grass Valley* because it was situated in the valley, and Spring Creek* because of its early location by Spring Creek. The name comes from the sharp right angle the road takes from the main highway into the community.
S35,T29S,R2W,SLM; 6,410' (1,954m). 242, 360, 567.

ANNABELLA* (Sevier) is on U-258 east of Central* and south of Richfield*. The Harry Dalton and Joseph Powell families settled there in the spring of 1871. Their first homes were dugouts. There are two versions of the origin of the community's name: (1) The name is derived from Ann S. Roberts and Isabella Dalton who were two of the first women to settle in the area. (2) The name was taken from a story whose heroine was named Annabella. The first version is preferred.

The town was previously named Omni Point* because it was on the point of the mountain two miles from Omni* (Richfield). Omni was a prominent individual in the Book of Mormon.
S18,T24S,R2W,SLM; 5,301' (1,616m). 288, 360, 542, 567, 584, 585.

ANNABELLA RESERVOIR (Sevier) is on Glenwood Mountain east of Monroe* on the Sevier Plateau. Drainage is northwest into Cottonwood Creek. It is named after the town the reservoir serves.
S10,T25S,R2W,SLM; 9,835' (2,998m).

ANNIE MAE CREEK (Wasatch) originates in the southwest section of the Uinta Mountains and drains south into Wolf Creek. On the east is Rhoades Canyon and to the west is Twin Creek. Annie Mae Creek is a clear, cold water creek on the old freighter road between Tabiona*/Hanna* and Kamas* or Heber*. A long-time freighter operator from this area had to obtain culinary water from that particular creek for his wife Annie Mae. She preferred the water from this creek because she claimed it was of superior quality. Over the years, her insistence for the creek water eventually gave her name to the creek.
S16,21,T1N,R9W,USM. 595.

ANT VALLEY (Cache) is south of Hardware Ranch in the Bear River Range. Sheep Creek and Blacksmith Fork both drain through this valley. The valley name comes from the numerous ant hills observed in the valley by the first pioneers.
NW½,T9N,R3E,SLM; 6,000' (1,829m). 567.

ANTELOPE* (Duchesne) was an early "Stringtown" on Antelope Creek, one and one-half miles southeast of present-day Bridgeland*. It was first settled during the 1905 land rush. A man named Saunders built a store and service station there and named it Antelope after the creek. Later, Antelope and Arcadia* (six miles north) were combined and

Bridgeland developed. Some of the first settlers were J. P. Christensen and Webb Lumpkin. Today, hay and cattle ranches predominate in the area where antelope were once plentiful.
S10,15,16,T4S,R3W,USM; 5,350' (1,631m). 165.

ANTELOPE FLAT (**Daggett**) is north of Flaming Gorge Reservoir and west of Goslin Mountain. Antelope Hollow and other "Antelope" geographic names are found in the vicinity.
T3N,R21,22,23E; 6,200'-6,800' (1,890m-2,073m).

ANTELOPE ISLAND (**Davis**) is located in the southeast sector of the Great Salt Lake, west of Farmington Bay. Osborne Russell, a trapper, made an 1841 entry in his journal referring to the presence of antelope and buffalo on the island. The island had various early names which were used interchangeably, such as Antelope, Church, and Buffalo Island. The name Church Island originated from the Mormon Church's early use of the island as a herd ground around 1849.
T2,3N,R3W,SLM; 6,596' (2,010m). 88, 100 (v2), 360, 546.

ANTELOPE MOUNTAIN (**Millard**) is thirteen miles west southwest of Cove Fort*. The mountain and the surrounding desert area provided habitat for early herds of antelope that roamed there. The animals watered at nearby Antelope Spring.
S22,23,26,T17S,R13W,SLM;7,230'(2,204m).

ANTELOPE PEAK (**Beaver**) is south of the south end of the San Francisco Mountains and two miles south southeast of Antelope Springs.
S29,T23S,R13W,SLM; 6,829' (2,081m).

ANTELOPE PEAK (**Iron**) is at the north end of the Antelope Range, twenty-three miles west of Cedar City* and ten miles northeast of Newcastle*. The peak was a landmark on this particular part of the Old Spanish Trail.

S16,T35S,R14W,SLM; 6,557' (1,999m).

ANTELOPE RANGE (**Iron**) has a north-south orientation and is northwest of Iron Mountain and twenty miles west of Cedar City*. Newcastle* is five miles southwest. In earlier times the area was known as Crows Nest, because the down timber was so tangled it was difficult to harvest in addition to impeding travel. Silver Peak is the highest point in the range.
S35,T36S,R14W,SLM; 7,272' (2,217m).

ANTELOPE SPRING (**Iron**) is at the north end of the Antelope Range and the south end of the Escalante Desert. Eleven miles to the southwest is Newcastle*. The spring lies on the Old Spanish Trail.
S4,T35S,R14W,SLM; 5,500' (1,676m).

ANTELOPE SPRING* (**Millard**) is two and one-half miles northwest of Antelope Mountain on the old Mormon Trail and the old stage route from Salt Lake City* to Kanosh*. The spring is six miles east of Black Rock* and twenty-eight miles southwest of Kanosh. At one time there was a hotel, barn, dance hall, and saloon there. Current reports indicate that antelope are again being established in this area.
S9,T25S,R9W,SLM; 5,063' (1,543m). 355.

ANTELOPE SPRINGS (**Beaver**) is on the southeast slopes of the Wah Wah Valley and west of the south end of the San Francisco Mountains. Nineteen miles to the east is Milford*. The early Piute Indians called the springs Sembits (Rose Bush) for the wild roses found at the spring.
S13,T28S,R13W,SLM; 5,575' (1,699m). 125.

ANTELOPE VALLEY (**Garfield**) is in Robbers Roost country at the head of Robbers Roost Canyon. Fifteen miles to the south southwest is the Ekker Ranch (the old Biddlecome Ranch on earlier maps). Blue John Canyon and Horseshoe Canyon are located to the east. Large

numbers of antelope were in the area when the cattlemen and sheepmen first arrived.
T27S,R15E,SLM; 5,400'-5,600' (1,646m-1,707m).

ANTELOPE WASH (Beaver) originates in the Indian Peak area of the Needle Range and is fed by Upper and Lower Indian Springs. It drains to the northeast between Sawtooth Peak and Indian Peak and into Pine Valley Wash. The name comes from the antelope found in the valley.

ANTIMONY* (Garfield) is four miles south of the Otter Creek Reservoir on U-22. In early 1873 about twenty-two men, including A. K. Thurber and George Bean, arrived here while on a peace-keeping mission with the Fish Lake Indians. They had agreed to meet the Indians at Cedar Grove near Koosharem*. While near the present site of Antimony they caught and earmarked several coyote pups. This incident led to the area's first name—Coyote*. The meadowlands were used as early as 1873 for grazing but several families moved in to establish a permanent settlement in 1878. In 1880 antimony (stibnite), a metal used in alloys, was discovered in nearby Coyote Canyon, so Coyote became a mining town as well as a ranching community. In 1921 the town of Coyote was renamed Antimony after the metal mined in the area.
S10,15,T31S,R2W,SLM; 6,444' (1,964m). 100(v17), 145, 314, 360, 602.

ANTIMONY CREEK (Garfield) originates on the Aquarius Plateau. It drains to the northwest, entering the east fork of the Sevier River one and one-half miles south of Antimony*. See Antimony*.
S10,15,T31S,R2W,SLM; 6,444' (1,964m).

ANTONE FLAT (Garfield) is a section of rangeland four miles northeast of Escalante* between Mamie Creek on the east and Pine Creek on the west. To the north is the Aquarius Plateau and to the south is the Escalante River. The area was named for Antone Woerner, an early Escalante settler.
S2,T35S,R3E,SLM. 12.

APPLEDALE* (Box Elder) is a rural area three miles west of Corinne*. It was first settled in 1895 and became known for its abundant apple orchards.
S33,34,T10N,R3W,SLM; 4,238' (1,292m). 139, 542, 567.

AQUARIUS PLATEAU (Garfield, Wayne) is south of Bicknell*, Torrey*, Grover*, and Teasdale*. Northwest is Antimony* and south are Escalante*, Boulder*, and the Escalante River. The plateau is approximately thirty-five miles long, fifteen miles wide, and was named in the mid-1870s by A. H. Thompson of the Powell Surveys. According to many this is the grandest of all the high plateaus.

It is best described by some of the explorers, geologists, and surveyors who worked their way over the plateau. Dellenbaugh reported that "The slopes we were crossing were full of leaping torrents and clear lakes. They were so covered with these that the plateau afterwards was given the name Aquarius." Captain Dutton best puts into words the sublime and awesome grandeur of this vast primitive wilderness, "Its broad summit is clad with dense forests of spruces opening in grassy parks, and sprinkled with scores of lakes filled by the melting snows. We have seen it afar off, its long straight crest-line stretched across the sky like the threshold of another world. On three sides, south, west, and east, it is walled by dark battlements of volcanic rock, and its long slopes beneath descend into the dismal desert. The explorer who sits upon the brink of its parapet looking off into the southern and eastern haze, who skirts its lava-cap or clambers up and down its vast ravines, who builds his campfire by the borders of its snow-fed lakes or stretches himself beneath its giant pines and spruces, forgets that he is a geologist

11

and feels himself a poet . . . [I have] seen its dull, expressionless ramparts grow upward into walls of majestic proportions and sublime import."

Thompson is claimed to be the first white man to cross the back of the Aquarius. Today local usage breaks the Aquarius into three main sections: Boulder Mountain is east, Escalante Mountain is west, and the Aquarius Plateau is in the center but includes all three. The highest point is Bluebell Knoll at 11,253' (3,430m).
T30-33S,R1W-R6E,SLM. 159, 160, 175, 314, 496, 602.

ARAGO CITY* (**Beaver**) is a ghost town site in the Star Range about ten miles southwest of Milford*. Nearby is the ghost town site of Shauntie* which seems to have been a center for these early mining towns on the west side of Picacho Peak near the head of Shauntie and Moscow washes. MRN
S26,T28S,R12W,SLM; 6,200' (1,890m). 89, 288.

ARAPIEN VALLEY (**Sanpete**), has a north-south orientation and is south of Sterling* and Ninemile Reservoir. It extends south of Mayfield* between Axtell* and Order Mountain. The valley was named for Chief Arapien (Arapene, Arrapene), a Piute chieftain and younger half-brother of the well-known Chief Walker. Arapien took over the entire chieftainship after Chief Walker died. The valley was a favorite camping ground for the tribe.
S19,T20S,R1,2E,SLM; 5,500' (1,676m).

ARCADIA* (**Duchesne**) is west of U-86, four and one-half miles north of Bridgeland*. Arcadia was settled in 1908. The name was suggested by William H. Smart who was president of the Duchesne Mormon Stake at that time. The word refers to an ancient Greece region of quiet pastoral beauty and simple pleasures. It was previously named Red Cap* for a chief of the Ute Tribe. See also Antelope* and Bridgeland*.

S16,17,T3S,R3W,USM; 5,380' (1,640m). 100(v17), 165, 508, 542.

ARCH CANYON (**Iron**) originates in Cedar Breaks National Monument at Point Supreme and drains northwest into Ashdown Creek and Cedar Canyon. It received its name from the two fine arches within the canyon.
S34,35,T36S,R9W,SLM. 530.

ARCH CANYON (**San Juan**) originates on the southwest slopes of the Abajo Mountains, two miles south of the Kigalia Ranger Station and Kigalia Point. The canyon drains southeast into upper Comb Wash and received its name from the many natural arches in the surrounding region.
S25,T38S,R20E,SLM (mouth of canyon).

ARCHES NATIONAL PARK (**Grand**) is two miles northwest of Moab*, near U-191. The southern border of the park lies along the Colorado River. A miner named Alexander Ringhoffer has been given tentative credit for discovery and mention of the numerous natural windows, arches, and bridges in this area. On April 12, 1929, President Herbert Hoover proclaimed it a national monument. In the fall of 1936, the first car was driven into the park by Harry Goulding of Monument Valley. Frank Pinkley, superintendent of the Southwestern National Monuments and first superintendent of Arches National Monument is given credit for recommending the name for the park. On November 16, 1971, President Richard Nixon signed a congressional bill establishing the area as Arches National Park. The park contains a remarkable concentration of natural geological features, arches, windows, and bridges and is now an international tourist attraction.
T24,25S,R21,22E,SLM. 325, 546.

ARGENTA* (**Salt Lake**) is eight miles up Big Cottonwood Canyon close to the mouth of Mill D South Fork. This early

silver mining camp of the 1870s was given the Latin name for silver (*Argentum*). The camp lasted for ten years before burning down. It was not rebuilt.
S18,T2S,R3E,SLM; 7,300' (2,225m). 89, 494.

ARGO POINT (**Weber**) is on the southeast sector of Fremont Island in the Great Salt Lake. The Argo was a small boat used by the Wenner family who lived in a stone house they had built and occupied on the island from 1886 to 1891. In classical mythology, the Argo was the ship in which Jason sailed in his quest for the Golden Fleece. See Fremont Island.
S21,T5N,R4W,SLM. 133.

ARGYLE* (**Rich**) was once three miles southwest of Randolph*. It was initially settled around 1875 by John Kennedy and his family who gave the settlement its first name, Kennedyville*. The name was changed to Argyle during an 1895 Sunday church service because the new arrivals were of Scottish descent and Argyle was the name of a Scottish shire or county. As transportation improved, more community activities were centered around nearby Randolph so people gradually moved away from Argyle. This withdrawal continued until the area became completely rural and by 1915 Argyle ceased to exist.
S1,T10N,R6E,SLM; 6,340' (1,932m). 89, 100(v13,17), 288, 567.

ARGYLE CANYON (**Carbon, Duchesne**) originates at Argyle Ridge on the West Tavaputs Plateau. It drains east-southeast into Nine Mile Canyon. Argyle Ridge roughly parallels Argyle Canyon. MRN
S17,T11S,R11E,SLM to S4,T12S,R14E,SLM.

ARINOSA* (**Tooele**) is nineteen miles east of Wendover* in the heart of the Salt Flats. Today it is a seldom-used siding with no permanent residents on the Western Pacific Railroad near I-80. In the 1880s it was a railroad main-

tenance camp, but it was abandoned in 1955 partly because it lacked culinary water and because of improved transportation. The exact source of the name is unknown but it is probably a corruption of the Spanish "arido" meaning "dry" or "arid."
S21,T1S,R16W,SLM; 4,215' (1,285m). 498.

ARRAPENE* (**Sanpete**). See Mayfield* and Arapien Valley.

ARSENAL HILL (**Salt Lake**) was once a name for the hill where the state capitol now stands. Long before the capitol was built it was known as Prospect Hill. Later, explosives magazines for the territory were stored there and it became known as Arsenal Hill. In April 1876 the powder magazines accidentally detonated, causing extensive damage. Today the state capitol building is located there and it is known as Capitol Hill.
S31,T1N,R1E,SLM; 4,550' (1,387m). 555 (v52/3), 567.

ARTHS PASTURE (**Grand**) is an area of rangeland eight miles west of Moab* and US-160. It was named for Arth Taylor, an early settler who ran his cattle there.
T25S,R20E,SLM; 5,100' (1,554m). 530. D.L. 6901.

ARTHUR* (**Salt Lake**) was one and one-half miles east of Garfield* near the southern tip of the Great Salt Lake. It was a mining town built in 1910 by the Utah Copper Company and Boston Consolidated Milling. The last house was moved in 1958 and the site was demolished to make way for further expansion of the local mining industry. The town was named for U.S. President Chester A. Arthur.
S23,24,T1S,R3W,SLM; 4,400' (1,341m). 89, 360, 542.

ASAY* (**Garfield**) was five and one-half miles south of present-day Hatch* where Asay Creek crosses US-89. It was first settled in 1872 by Joseph Asay and his

wife, Sarah Ann, and family. Joseph was the first postmaster in Asay and he also ran a small store. In 1880 the communities of Asay, Johnson*, and Castle* were absorbed and moved closer to Hatch (known earlier as Hatchtown*). The town of Asay perished in the late 1890s when a nearby sawmill burned down.
S24,T37S,R6W,SLM; 7,000' (2,134m). 100 (v13), 145, 567.

ASAY BENCH (Garfield, Kane) is north of the headwaters of Asay Creek and the confluence of Strawberry Creek with Swains Creek. Asay Bench was Joseph Asay's grazing lands. See Asay*.
T36S,R6W,SLM.

ASAY CREEK (Garfield) originates at the confluence of Strawberry Creek and Swains Creek. It drains northeast into the Sevier River five miles south of Hatch. See Asay*.
S5,T38S,R6W,SLM to S24,T37S,R6W,SLM. 289, 600.

ASH CREEK (Washington) originates at the confluence of North Ash Creek and Kanarra Creek and drains south past Pintura* into the Virgin River. It was named by early Mormon leader John D. Lee for the small single-leaf ash tree (Fraxinus anomala) that grows along the banks.
S1,T39S,R13W,SLM to S23,T41S,R13W, SLM. 314, 600. D.L. 6102.

ASHDOWN CREEK (Iron) originates on the western slopes of Cedar Breaks National Monument and drains west into the head of Coal Creek. The creek was named for George Ashdown who developed the region and owned a ranch and two sawmills on the creek. There are several natural bridges in the area.
S27,T36S,R9W,SLM to S36,T36S,R10W, SLM. 530, 567.

ASHLEY* (Uintah). See Vernal*.

ASHLEY CENTER* (Uintah). See Vernal*.

ASHLEY CREEK (Uintah). The South Fork originates at Lake Wilde two miles west southwest of Leidy Peak, and drains southeast. The North Fork originates one mile northeast of Leidy Peak at Hacking Lake. They join several miles southeast, near Taylor Mountain. The main stream drains through Ashley Valley and empties into the Green River. The creek was named for General William H. Ashley who led mountain men and trappers into this area. There is an Ashley Spring and an Ashley Gorge nearby.
S31,T5S,R23E,SLM (mouth of creek). 129, 172, 371, 372.

ASHLEY SPRING (Uintah) is found in Ashley Gorge along Ashley Creek which is what the spring was named after. The spring provides water for the town of Vernal*.
567.

ASHLEY TWIN LAKES (Uintah) are two alpine lakes separated by a narrow neck. The lakes are located in the southeast section of the Uinta Mountains on the headwaters of Ashley Creek, South Fork. See Ashley Creek for name source.
10,332' (3,149m).

ASHLEY VALLEY (Uintah) is a large valley with a northwest-southeast orientation with the main drainage going into Ashley Creek. The valley is twenty miles long and six to eight miles wide. Within the valley's boundaries are Maeser* and Vernal* to the northwest and Jensen* and Naples* to the east. See Ashley Creek for name source.
T4,5S,R21,22E,SLM; ca. 5,200' (1,585m).

ASHTON* (Washington). See Pintura* (Washington).

ASPEN GROVE* (Utah) is a beautiful sub-alpine recreation area at the head of the North Fork of the Provo River on the east slopes of Mount Timpanogos.

The principal trail head for Timpanogos Peak departs here. The grove receives its name from the predominant plant species, the quaking aspen (*Populus tremuloides*).
S1,T5S,R4E,SLM; 6,851' (2,088m).

ASPEN HOLLOW (**Beaver**) is on the southern slopes of Little Shelly Baldy Peak and drains into Indian Creek. It was named for the abundance of quaking aspen in the hollow.
S24,T27S,R6W,SLM.

ASPEN HOLLOW SPRING (**Beaver**) is in Aspen Hollow.
S24,T27S,R6W,SLM; 9,000' (2,743m).

ASPEN LAKE (**Duchesne**) is in the south central section of the Uinta Mountains on the headwaters of Atwine Creek. The lake drains east into Lake Fork River and Moon Lake. Aspen Lake received its name because of the numerous aspen trees. It is also known as Colorow Lake, named for Chief Colorow, a war chief of the Whiteriver Utes who camped near the lake during a dispute with the Whiterocks Indian Agency.
S32,T23N,R6W,USM; 10,260' (3,127m). 100 (v17), 595.

ASPHALT RIDGE (**Uintah**) is a prominent ridge, twelve miles long, several miles west southwest of Vernal*. It has a northwest-southeast orientation and contains natural deposits of asphalt which were used in constructing nearby US-40.
S19,T4S,R21E,SLM to S1,T6S,R21E,SLM; 6,687' (2,038m). 546, 567.

ASPHALT WASH (**Uintah**) originates at the confluence of the West and Center Forks, fourteen miles northeast of Rainbow* and four and one-half miles south of the White River. It flows north into the White River. A vein of asphalt is exposed along the wash.
S13,T10,R23E,SLM (at mouth).

ATCHISON CREEK (**Beaver**) originates on the west slope of Twin Peaks of the Indian Peak Range. It drains west into Hamlin Valley Wash in the southwest corner of the county. MRN
S27,T30S,R18W,SLM.

ATHERLY RESERVOIR (**Tooele**) is in Rush Valley one and one-half miles west of Faust* on Faust Creek. MRN
S28,T7S,R5W,SLM; 5,210' (1,588m).

ATKIN* (**Millard**). See Delta*.

ATKINVILLE* (**Washington**) was a small pioneer settlement on the east side of the Virgin River, ten miles south southwest of St. George*. It was first settled by the William Atkin family and was one of several settlements in this area including Price City* and Bloomington* which did not survive floods, sickness, and drought. Bloomington has recently been revitalized and today is a flourishing community.
S2,T43S,R16W,SLM; 2,475' (754m). 89, 154.

ATWOOD CREEK (**Duchesne**) originates at Atwood Lake, five miles southeast of Kings Peak and two and one-half miles north of Mount Emmons. It drains east into the upper Uinta River. The creek was named for Wallace W. Atwood, a well-known geologist who studied Uinta Mountain glaciation.
100(v2), 172, 309.

ATWOOD LAKE (**Duchesne**) is in the south central section of the Uinta Mountains, three miles north of Mount Emmons. Drainage is east southeast into the Uinta River. See Atwood Creek for name source.
11,030' (3,362m).

AUGER HOLE LAKE (**Garfield**) is on the Aquarius Plateau, three miles south southeast of Roundy Reservoir near the head of Pine Creek. It received its name from the boggy condition of the lake.
9,200' (2,804m). 12.

15

AUGUSI CANYON (**Uintah**) originates forty-five miles northwest of Grand Junction*, Colorado, and five miles west of the Colorado border. It drains southwest between Dry Burn Canyon and Rat Hole Canyon and empties into Bitter Creek. It is named after an Indian named Augusi who lived and farmed along Bitter Creek near the mouth of Augusi Canyon.
S27,35,T13S,R25E,SLM to S18,T14S,R25E, SLM. 530.

AUGUSTA NATURAL BRIDGE (**San Juan**). See Natural Bridges National Monument.

AURORA* (**Sevier**) is west of the Sevier River on U-256, four miles southwest of Salina*. It was first settled in 1875 by people from Provo*. An earlier name was Willow Bend* because it was on a bend of the Sevier River which was heavily overgrown with willows. The post office rejected the name because they felt the name "willow" was being overused. Numan Van Louvan suggested the name Aurora because of the colorful tints of the surrounding hills—it reminded him of the Roman goddess of the dawn. The name change was made on August 2, 1897, and Van Louvan was subsequently made postmaster.
S5,T22S,R1W,SLM; 5,187' (1,581m). 100 (v17), 567, 569, 585.

AUSTIN* (**Sevier**) is on U-118 near the Sevier River, three miles north of Monroe*. In 1910-11, the Elsinore Sugar Factory was built nearby and the town developed to house the factory workers. It was locally known as Frog Town* for the large number of frogs living along the Sevier River. The town was formally named Austin for George Austin, agricultural superintendent of the sugar factory. When the sugar factory closed in 1928, the community remained.
S34,T24S,R2W,SLM; 5,300' (1,615m). 360, 542.

AVERETT CANYON (**Kane**) is a tributary of the upper Paria River and originates southeast of Bryce Canyon National Park near Indian Hollow. The canyon drains southeast into Willis Creek and then into the Paria River. On August 21, 1866, Elijah Averett, Jr., was killed, George Ishum was wounded, and Hyrum Pollock died from incidental exposure when six men isolated from a larger group were attacked by Indians.
S8,T38S,R3W,SLM to S23,T38S,R3W,SLM. 100(v17), 159, 224, 455, 515.

AVINTAQUIN CREEK (**Duchesne**) originates on the West Tavaputs Plateau, fifteen miles east northeast of Soldier Summit at the confluence of the West and South Forks. The creek drains through Avintaquin Canyon to enter Strawberry River at the Pinnacles. MRN S5,T6S,R8W,USM to S24,T4S,R8W,USM.

AVON* (**Cache**) is a small agricultural community on U-165 eleven miles south of Logan* and three miles southeast of present-day Paradise*. It was settled in 1860 and originally known as Paradise, but was abandoned in 1868 because the settlers were having trouble with the Indians. Mrs. Orson Smith named the community in honor of Avon*, England, the birthplace of William Shakespeare.
S10,T9N,R1E,SLM; 5,012' (1,528m). 100 (v17), 288, 449, 494, 542, 546.

AWAPA PLATEAU (**Piute**) is a high, wind-swept, semi-barren, eastward-sloping plateau, northeast of the Aquarius Plateau and directly south of the Fishlake Plateau. It is thirty miles long, twenty miles wide, more or less treeless and is a cheerless and repulsive plateau composed of lava, sloping toward Rabbit Valley. The plateau is bordered on the north by U-24, on the west by Parker Mountain, and Thousand Lake Mountain is located east. The name is Piute and means "a water hole among the cedars."
T27-30S,R1,2W,SLM; 9,995' (3,046m) (highest point). 175, 314, 420.

AXHANDLE CANYON (**Sanpete**) originates in the San Pitch Mountains
southwest of Wales*. It drains southeast
into the Sanpete River. MRN
S17,T16S,R2E,SLM to ca. S30,T16S,R3E,
SLM.

AXTELL* (**Sanpete**) is on US-89 between Gunnison* and Salina*. The town
was settled in 1870 and received the
name Willow Creek* for the small,
willow-lined creek where the settlement
was located. It received the name Axtell
on March 15, 1876, after Axel Einerson,
an early settler.
S20,T20S,R1E,SLM; 5,135' (1,565m). 288,
360, 368, 494, 542.

AZTEC BUTTE (**San Juan**) is a large
conical butte in Canyonlands National
Park at the north end of the Grand View
Point. There are Indian ruins on the
butte and in the surrounding area, hence
the colorful name—even though it is
inaccurate.
T28S,R19E,SLM; 6,298' (1,920m).

AZTEC CREEK (**San Juan**) drains
through the lower reaches of Forbidden
Canyon. The creek originates in Arizona,
drains north, and empties into Lake
Powell. It was named for the Indian ruins
along the creek.
567.

AZURE CLIFFS (**Emery, Grand**). See
Book Cliffs.

AZURE LAKE (**Summit**) is at the base
of Haystack Mountain at the west end of
the Uinta Mountains. The name is
descriptive of the lake color.
S12,T2S,R8E,SLM; 10,000' (3,048m).

- B -

BAC-BONE* (**Kane**) is off US-89, fifteen miles west of Big Water* (formerly Glen Canyon City*). Alex Joseph, a polygamous cult leader, and his followers named and temporarily occupied Bac-Bone in late 1975 and early 1976 before moving to Glen Canyon City, which they renamed Big Water*.
S31,T42S,R1E,SLM; 4,800' (1,463m). 466 (6 Dec. 1975, 4 July 1976), 578.

BACCHUS* (**Salt Lake**) is a small community on U-111, on the eastern slopes of the Oquirrh Mountains. Bacchus was the former site of the small pioneer village of Coonville*. The name was changed from Coonville to Bacchus in 1915 when the Hercules Powder Company established an explosives manufacturing plant there. They named the community in honor of T. E. Bacchus, vice president of the company and superintendent of the Bacchus plant. With improved transportation, the workers moved to more favorable locations. Between 1930 and 1960 the town deteriorated into a ghost town.
S8,T2S,R2W,SLM; 4,910' (1,497m). 89, 100 (v17), 272, 360, 542, 567.

BACHELOR BASIN (**Grand**) is a small alpine basin on the northwest slopes of the La Sal Mountains, four miles southeast of Castleton*. It was named for about three hundred isolated prospectors from Leadville, Colorado, who mined and prospected in the area.
S34,T25S,R24E,SLM; 7,500' (2,286m). 146.

BACHELOR CANYON (**Summit**) originates four miles west of Echo* and five miles northeast of East Canyon Reservoir and drains northeast into the Weber River. In the spring of 1860, William Bachelor and Charles S. Appleby moved from Salt Lake City* to settle on the land at the mouth of the canyon.
S28-S15,T3N,R4E,SLM. 508.

BADGER ISLAND (**Tooele**) is a small island—sometimes no more than a sandbar—between Stansbury and Carrington Islands in the southwest quadrant of the Great Salt Lake. It was named after the common badger, an abundant animal during low lake levels. 4,210' (1,283m).

BADLAND CLIFFS (**Duchesne**) lie along the northern ridge of upper Argyle Canyon on the West Tavaputs Plateau. The Argyle drains into Minnie Maud Creek. The term *badlands* describes this area which is extremely rugged, highly eroded, and more or less uninhabitable.
T11S,R11,12E,SLM.

BAER CANYON (**Davis**) originates in the Wasatch Mountains three miles east of Kaysville*. It drains west into the Great Salt Lake. John Baer (also listed as Bair) was an early settler who built a sawmill in the canyon.
S33,T4N,R1E,SLM (to the lake mud flats). 567.

BAGPIPE BUTTES (**Wayne**) is at the southern end of the Elaterite Basin on the west side of the Colorado River in Canyonlands National Park. The extending pinnacles of the buttes resemble a bagpipe and are prominent landmarks in this area.
S36,T30S,R16E,SLM; 6,679' (2,036m).

BAILEY MOUNTAIN (**Beaver**) is at the north end of the Mineral Mountains near the head of Negro Mag Wash. Minersville* and Adamsville* are located south and Milford* is west. The

mountain is named after the spring. See also Negro Mag Wash.
S13,T27S,R9W,SLM; 8,307' (2,532m). 355.

BAILEY RIDGE (**Beaver**) is at the north end of the Mineral Mountains along the northeast slopes of Bailey Mountain. See Bailey Spring for name source.
S12,T27S,R9W,SLM; 7,600' (2,316m). 355.

BAILEY SPRING (**Beaver**) is at the north end of Bailey Mountain at the head of Negro Mag Wash. The spring is claimed to have medicinal value. It was named after its discoverer, Dr. Ralph Bailey, who established squatter's rights there in the 1870s. Bailey also tried to introduce a sanitarium in the area, which he wanted to name Roosevelt Radium Warm Springs.
S12,T27S,R9W,SLM; 7,000' (2,134m). 125, 355.

BAIR CANYON (**Davis**). See Baer Canyon.

BAKER BENCH (**Garfield**) is a benchland south of Choprock Bench and southwest of the Circle Cliffs. It extends south to the Escalante River. The bench was named for the Baker family of Boulder.
T36,37S,R7E,SLM. 12.

BAKER CANYON (**Beaver**) originates on the western slopes of the Tushar Mountains at the junction of the north and east forks, northeast of Beaver*. The canyon was named by early pioneers in honor of Phillip Baker, one of Beaver's initial settlers.
S20,T29S,R6W,SLM. 125.

BAKING SKILLET KNOLL (**Wayne**) is in the Burr Desert, twenty miles southeast of Hanksville* and ten miles east of the Henry Mountains. The knoll has the general shape of a baking skillet.
S16,T30S,R13E,SLM; 5,485' (1,672).

BALD EAGLE MOUNTAIN (**Box Elder**) is at the northern end of the Pilot Range, east of the Utah-Nevada line and nine miles southwest of Lucin*. Bald eagles are common in the area, especially during wintertime.
S3,T6N,R19W,SLM; 8,028' (2,447m).

BALD HILLS (**Iron**) is five miles northwest of Enoch* and ten miles northwest of Cedar City*. The name comes from the barren or bald appearance of the hills.
S4,9,T34S,R12W,SLM; ca. 5,857' (1,785m).

BALD KNOLL CANYON (**Sevier**) originates in the Valley Mountains north of Aurora* and drains into the Sevier River Valley northwest of Redmond*. The canyon received its name from nearby Bald Knoll.
S2,T21S,R2W,SLM to S15,T21S,R1W,SLM.

BALD MOUNTAIN (**Duchesne, Summit**) is at the west end of the Uinta Mountains, one mile west southwest of Mirror Lake. Since the upper part of the mountain is above the timberline, it is lacking in heavy vegetation. Variants include Mount Baldy and Old Baldy.
S27,T1S,R9E,SLM; 11,943' (3,640m). 309.

BALD MOUNTAIN (**Tooele**) is part of the crest of the Deep Creek Range and is named because of the lack of trees along this segment of the crest. The small ranching community of Ibapah* is located eight miles northwest.
NW¼,S16,T10S,R18E,SLM; 9,645' (2,940m).

BALD MOUNTAIN PASS (**Duchesne**) is between Bald Mountain and Murdock Mountain. The area is a center for the origin of several of Utah's principal river systems. The pass separates the Weber River drainage to the northwest from the Provo River drainage to the southwest. The Duchesne River drains to the south and the Bear River drains to the north. It is named after Bald Mountain.
S34,35,T1S,R9E,SLM; 10,620' (3,237).

BALD RIDGES (**Beaver**) is east of the Mineral Mountains and west of the north end of Beaver Valley. The ridges are devoid of vegetation.
S23,25,26,36,T27S,R8E,SLM; ca. 7,858' (2,395m).

BALDWIN RIDGE (**Beaver**) is on the western slopes of the Tushar Mountains between North Creek, South Fork, and Pine Creek. It was named after Jesse Baldwin, an early sheriff of Beaver County who used the ridge as a pasture for his horses.
S24,T28S,R6W,SLM; 9,234' (2,815m). 567.

BALFOUR* (**Box Elder**) is a ghost town several miles west of Corinne*. It was a temporary Union Pacific Railroad camp near what was known as the Wanda Hot Springs, but it perished when the railroad was completed. Although the site was originally known as Balfour, Rasmus Hansen changed it to Hansen*. It was later changed to Connor*, in honor of the military commander at Fort Douglas in Salt Lake City*. MRN
567.

BALLARD* (**Uintah**) was a small temporary community west of Bottle Hollow. It was originally named Wilson* for President Woodrow Wilson, then the name was changed to Ballard, for a Mormon church apostle.

BALDY HILL (**Beaver**) is a small but prominent hill across the Beaver River, north of Minersville*. There is very little vegetation in the area.
S1,12,T30S,R10W,SLM; 5,469' (1,667m).

BANNER* (**Duchesne**). See Mount Emmons*.

BAPTIST DRAW (**Emery**) is a small draw originating at the south end of the San Rafael Swell in Sinbad Country. It drains east into the head of Chute Canyon. Joe Swasey, an early settler, cattleman and prospector, is reported to have "baptized" his dog here by tossing it into one of the waterpockets.
193.

BARBERRA HOLLOW (**Duchesne**) originates in the southwest section of the Uinta Mountains on the slopes of Tabby Mountain. It drains east to the Duchesne River, one mile southeast of Tabiona*. A man named Barberra had a homestead at the mouth of the canyon.
S33,T1S,R8W,SLM to S5,T2S,R7W,SLM. 595.

BARKER RESERVOIR (**Garfield**) is at the head of North Creek on Escalante Mountain at the west end of the Aquarius Plateau. There is also a lower Barker Reservoir in this area. The Barker family was prominent in the early history of the area.
9,564' (2,915m).

BARN HILLS (**Millard**) is a high lone valley in the center of the hill country between Blind Valley and Tule Valley. Jack Watson used the hills for his cattle around 1910. He called this valley his barn because when his cattle were in the area, they were semi-protected and less inclined to roam, hence were "in the barn." An earlier name for this area was "The Ibex Hills." Variant: Barn.
T21,22S,R14W,SLM; 5,790' (1,765m). D.L. 6103.

BARNEY LAKE (**Garfield**) is on the southern slopes of the Aquarius Plateau, two miles southeast of Jacobs Reservoir and three miles east of Roundy Reservoir. The Barney family was prominent in the settlement of nearby Escalante* and the surrounding country. The lake was named for Joseph S. Barney, an early sheepman.
9,950' (3,033m). 12.

BARNEY RESERVOIR (**Garfield**) is in the center of Seep Flat, fifteen miles from Escalante*, on the road to the Hole-in-the-Rock. See Barney Lake for name source.
S12,T37S,R43,SLM; 5,405' (1,647m). 12.

BARNEY TOP (**Garfield**) is an alpine area in the Escalante Mountains west of Escalante*. South Creek, Dry Creek, Spencer Canyon, and Cherry Creek head here. Almon Thompson of the Powell Survey called it Table Top Mountain. The name was changed to Barney Top because this was Joseph Barney's early sheep range.
T35S,R1W,SLM; 10,400' (3,170m). 12, 602.

BARREL SPRING CANYON (**Beaver**) is at the southern end of the San Francisco Mountains, draining into Morehouse Canyon. The canyon was named Barrel Spring because a barrel was sunk into the ground to save the slow-surfacing spring water.
S25,T26S,R13W,SLM. 125.

BARRIER CANYON (**Wayne**). See Horseshoe Canyon.

BARRIER CREEK (**Wayne**) drains Horseshoe Canyon. See Horseshoe Canyon.

BARTHOLOMEW BENCH (**Utah**). See Bartholomew Canyon.

BARTHOLOMEW CANYON (**Utah**) originates on the southeast slopes of Provo Peak and drains southeast into the left fork of Hobble Creek. It was named for Joseph Bartholomew who made the first road into the canyon to cut and gather wood. A sawmill was built and used there for several years. Bartholomew Bench is close by and is named after the same man.
S6,T7S,R4E,SLM to S21,T7S,R4E,SLM. 270.

BARTONS CANYON (**Beaver**). See Bartons Hollow.

BARTONS HOLLOW (**Beaver**) originates on the slopes of the Mineral Mountains. It drains southeast via Cherry Creek into Indian Creek northwest of Adamsville*. It was named for John H. Barton of Beaver* who prospected in the area.
S1,T29S,R9W,SLM. 125.

BARTONS HOLLOW SPRING (**Beaver**) is at the head of Bartons Hollow. See Bartons Hollow for name source.

BASIN* (**Duchesne**). The name is taken from the natural landform where widely dispersed settlements such as Cedarview* and Monarch* were established in late 1905 and 1906. See The Crescent*.
S28,33,T1S,R1W,USM.

BASIN* (**Grand**) is on the western slopes of Mount Waas in the La Sal Mountains. Moab* is eighteen miles west. Basin was a miner's settlement which developed in 1898 and received its name from the Miners Basin Mining District. After 1908, the settlement declined rapidly as mining activity decreased.
9,900' (3,018m). 89.

BATEMAN SPRING (**Beaver**) is on the eastern slopes of the Wah Wah Mountains, draining east into the Wah Wah Valley at Revenue Basin. The spring was named after J. A. Bateman who ran stock there during the 1930s.
S22,T28S,R15W,SLM; 6,400' (1,951m). 567.

BATES CANYON (**Tooele**). See Ophir Canyon.

BATESVILLE* (**Tooele**). Bates Creek originates at Lowe Peak on the southwest slopes of the Oquirrh Mountains and drains southwest into Rush Valley. In 1850 Ormus E. Bates and his family settled at the mouth of what is presently Ophir Canyon. The settlement was known for a time as Knowllen* or Nowlenville* but eventually assumed the family name and became Batesville. In 1852-53 the people built a fort to protect themselves from the Indians. The settlers named it Rose Springs Fort*, but the railroad later changed the name to Fort Erda*. The settlement, Batesville, lasted until 1873.
S23,T5S,R4W,SLM; 5,800' (1,768). 100(v17), 153, 494, 567.

BATTLE CREEK* (Utah). See Pleasant Grove*.

BATTLE CREEK CANYON (Utah) originates east of Pleasant Grove* on the western slopes of Mount Timpanogos and drains into Utah Lake. On February 28, 1849, a compliment of thirty to forty men under the command of Captain John Scott pursued a band of Ute Indians into this area. This was the first tragic conflict between the Indians and the whites following the arrival of the Mormons into the Great Salt Lake Valley. Four Indians were listed as dead, although reports vary.
S22,23,27,T5S,R2E,SLM. 270.

BATTLESHIP BUTTE (Emery) is six miles north northwest of Green River*, at the east end of Little Elliot Mesa. The butte has the general shape of a battleship.
S23,24,T20S,R15E,SLM.

BAUER* (Tooele) is a small mining community five miles southwest of Tooele*, west of and adjacent to U-36. It was first settled in 1855 and named for B. F. Bauer, a local mine operator. It had the earlier name of Buhl*.
S13,T4S,R5W,SLM; 5,000' (1,524m). 542.

BEACON HILL (Box Elder) is the high point on Fremont Island in the Great Salt Lake. The hill was used for signaling in times of trouble.
S12,T6N,R5W,SLM; 4,785' (1,458m). 371.

BEAR BASIN (Wasatch) is at the headwaters of the Bear, Buck, and Dip Vat hollows on the west end of the Uinta Mountains. Over a period of years, a homesteader named Elloc Evans shot several bears in the basin for his winter meat.
S17,18,20,T4S,R7E,SLM. 298.

BEAR CANYON (Beaver) originates on the western slopes of the Tushar Mountains and drains northwest into Pole Creek. The name originated when James E. Hoops killed a large grizzly bear in the canyon around 1898.
S21,22,T28S,R6W,SLM. 125.

BEAR CANYON* (Carbon). See Royal*.

BEAR CREEK (Garfield) originates on Boulder Mountain of the Aquarius Plateau, east of Jacobs Reservoir and northwest of Bear Lake. It drains southeast into Boulder Creek. In the early days of settlement, the pioneers had frequent problems with bears.
S4,T33S,R4E,SLM (at mouth). 12.

BEAR CREEK (Garfield, Iron) originates nine miles northeast of Paragonah* at the southern end of Upper Bear Valley. It drains northeast through Middle and Lower Bear Valley to eventually enter the Sevier River. It received its name from several bear-related incidents in the area during settlement.
S27,T33S,R7W,SLM to S10,T33S,R5W,SLM. 12.

BEAR HOLLOW (Weber) originates on Lightning Ridge five miles northeast of Causey Reservoir and north of the head of the Ogden River, South Fork. It drains southwest into Wheat Grass Canyon and the Causey Reservoir. Mr. and Mrs. Thomas Causey had their camp destroyed there by a grizzly bear. See Causey Reservoir.
S4,9,T7N,R4E,SLM. 567.

BEAR LAKE (Garfield) is on Boulder Mountain of the Aquarius Plateau near the head of Bear Creek. See Bear Creek (Garfield) for name source.
9,677' (2,950m).

BEAR LAKE (Rich) is a deep, cold-water lake astride the Idaho-Utah border. It is about twenty-two miles long and two to six miles wide. In the early 1800s the lake was a popular area for trappers and yearly rendezvous were held there for trappers of white, black, and Indian

descent. Today it is an important water source, a recreation site for fishing, boating, and water-skiing, in addition to being an attractive site for condominiums and luxurious summer homes. It was once called Little Lake to distinguish it from the much larger Great Salt Lake. Donald McKenzie of Hudson Bay Fur Company, probably influenced by the large number of bears in the area and by the recent naming of the adjacent Bear River, has the honor of naming the lake. He sent out a dispatch to the northwest from "Black Bear's Lake," on September 10, 1819. The word "Black" was soon dropped.
T13,14,15N,R5,6E,SLM (in Utah); 5,924' (1,806m). 100(v17), 163(20 May 1973), 240, 372, 496, 542, 546.

BEAR LAKE STATE RECREATION AREA (Rich). Is centered around Bear Lake. The headquarters are on Bear Lake and US-89, one mile north of Garden City*. See Bear Lake.

BEAR RIVER (Utah, Idaho, Wyoming) originates on the northwest slopes of the Uinta Mountains at the confluence of the Hayden and Stillwater forks. It drains into Wyoming and Idaho as far north as Soda Springs where it makes an abrupt U-turn back into Utah and the Great Salt Lake at the Bear River Bay National Bird Refuge. It flows over five hundred miles yet ends up less than sixty miles from its source. Michel Bourdon, a twenty-one-year-old French Canadian trapper of the Hudson Bay Fur Company, is given credit for naming the river. He named it the Bear River in 1818 while trapping in the area, then was killed by Indians there the following year. The river had several other names such as Mud River, White Mud River, and Miller River. The Indians also had names for the river such as the Quee-yah-pah for Tobacco Root Water or Gull-yay-pah for Tobacco Water. These names refer to the color of the river water in its lower reaches. The name Michel Bourdon gave refers to the numerous black, brown, and grizzly bears found in the region at that time. The Bear River is the largest river located entirely inside the Great Basin. Nearby Bear Lake was named the following year by McKenzie. See Bear Lake.
S32,T2N,R10E,SLM to S1,T9R,R4W,SLM. 100(v17), 314, 542, 546.

BEAR RIVER CITY* (Box Elder) is on U-84 along the Bear River about eight miles south of Tremonton*. It was initially settled in 1866 by Scandinavian Mormon converts who were assigned to live in this area by their church. Their first homes were dugouts. The settlers drew their community name from the nearby river.
S12,T3W,R10N,SLM; 4,255' (1,297m). 139, 288, 360, 542.

BEAR RIVER BAY (Box Elder) is at the mouth of the Bear River in the northeast section of the Great Salt Lake, fifteen miles west of Brigham City*. This area is designated as a national wildlife and migratory bird refuge. The bay was named for the river.
S8,T9N,R3,4W,SLM; 4,205' (1,282m).

BEAR RIVER RANGE (Cache) is a mountain range with a north-south orientation east of Logan*. Logan Canyon, Logan River, and Blacksmith Fork cut through the range from east to west into Cache Valley. The mountains were named after the nearby Bear River which flows in a giant bow or bend around the northern end of the mountains. The Bear River Range is about seventy miles long. Naomi Peak is the highest point.
T11-14N,R2,3E,SLM; 9,980' (3,042m). D.L. 8401.

BEAR RIVER VALLEY (Box Elder) is at the northern end of Willard Bay and the Bear River Bay section of the Great Salt Lake, between the West Hills and the Wellsville Hills. Both the Malad River and the Bear River drain through the valley.
T10,11N,R3W,SLM; 4,270' (1,301m).

BEAR TRAP CREEK (**Summit**) originates at the western end of the Uinta
Mountains. It drains northeast into the
Smith and Morehouse Creek and was a
prime location for trapping bears in the
1870s and 1880s.
S1,11,12,T1S,R7E,SLM. 298.

BEAR VALLEY (**Iron**) is in the mountains northeast of Paragonah* where it
has a northeast-southwest orientation. It
is divided into the Lower, Middle, and
Upper Bear valleys. U-20 passes through
the northern end of the valley and Bear
Valley Creek originates at the southern
end of the valley. The old wagon road
from Paragonah to Panguitch* passed
through this area. The name refers to the
many bear encounters of the early days.
T32,33S,R6,7W,SLM; 7,000'-7,500' (2,134m-
2,286m). 40, 175, 567.

BEAR VALLEY (**Sevier**) has a north-
south orientation eight miles north
northwest of Koosharem* and thirteen
miles east of Monroe*. The valley was
named by a party led by Albert K.
Thurber while they were on their way to
Cedar Grove to negotiate a peace treaty
with the Fishlake Indians. In the valley
they passed the freshly killed and skinned
corpse of a large bear. Its fat, milky-
white, and bloated body shone in the
sunlight and created an impressive sight.
T25S,R1W,SLM; 6,600' (2,012m). 40, 585.

BEARS EARS (**San Juan**) are two
prominent land features resembling bear
ears. The small mesas are located near
the southern end of Elk Ridge, west of
the Abajo Mountains. Nearby to the west
is Natural Bridges National Monument.
The Spanish called the mesas Orejas del
Oso (Ears of the Bear).

BEARSKIN FLAT (**Beaver**) is in the
Mineral Mountains north of Bearskin
Mountain and south of the head of
Cunningham Wash. It received its name
from nearby Bearskin Mountain.
S18,T27S,R8W,SLM; 7,400' (2,257m).

BEARSKIN MOUNTAIN (**Beaver**) is in
the Mineral Mountains north of
Wildhorse Mountain and east of Little
Bearskin Mountain. The name resulted
from an incident involving a Piute Indian
named Pant, who killed a large bear in
the vicinity and draped the bearskin out
on some shrubs to dry.
S17,T17S,R8W,SLM; 9,095' (2,772m). 355,
567.

BEAVER* (**Beaver**) is in the eastern
part of Beaver County near I-15 and the
Beaver River. It was settled from
Parowan* in February 1856 by Captain
Simeon F. Howd and others. This settlement broke up the ninety miles of lonely
road through wild, uninhabited territory
between Fillmore* and Parowan. The
town received its name from the river
and later became the county seat.
S21,22,T29S,R7W,SLM; 5,891' (1,796m).
384, 395, 567.

BEAVER BOTTOMS (**Beaver, Millard**)
are flat bottomlands and pasturelands
south of Millard County's Red Rock
Knoll and Black Rock. The area extends
south into Beaver County along the
Beaver River where the river drains
north then loses its identity as a river.
T27S,R10W,SLM. 355.

BEAVER BOTTOMS* (**Beaver**) was an
early small settlement that developed
along the Beaver River, seven miles
north of Milford*.
567.

BEAVER CANYON (**Beaver**) originates
east of Beaver* at Merchant Valley and
drains west, ending east of Beaver. The
canyon name comes from the river
draining through it.
S17,T29S,R5W,SLM to S13,T29S,R7W,SLM.

BEAVER COUNTY is in southwestern
Utah, bounded on the east by Piute
County, on the north by Millard County,
and on the south by Iron County. It was
created from a section of Iron County on

January 5, 1856, and was named for the once plentiful beaver.
6, 360.

BEAVER DAM* (Box Elder) is a small rural community on U-69 near the mouth of Willow Creek. It is near the Bear River, between Deweyville* and Mendon*, and was first settled in 1867 by people from Providence* and Deweyville. It was named for the numerous beaver dams found along the creek. The first co-op dairy in Utah was established here in 1868.
S3,T12N,R2W,SLM; 4,595' (1,401m). 139, 163(25 July 1973), 270, 542.

BEAVER DAM MOUNTAINS (Washington) have a north-south orientation and are located in southwestern Utah. The mountains are bounded on the west by Beaver Dam Wash and the Nevada state line, and on the east by the White Hills and St. George. The old highway that went through Santa Clara and followed the Old Spanish Trail cuts through the southern part of the mountains. The mountains were named after nearby Beaver Dam Wash.
T41,42,43S,R18W,SLM; 7,746' (2,361m). 316.

BEAVER DAM WASH (Washington) originates at Beaver Dam State Park in Nevada. It drains south-southeast, crossing the state line into Utah, paralleling the Beaver Dam Mountains and continuing south into Arizona to flow into the Virgin River northeast of Littlefield*. It leaves the state at Utah's lowest point—ca. 2,100' (640m). Jedediah Smith called it Pautch Creek because of the plentiful beaver and beaver dams in the upper reaches.
T38-43S,R19-20W,SLM. 314, 372, 438, 462. D.L. 7403.

BEAVER IRON WORKS* (Beaver) was an early name for Adamsville*.

BEAVER LAKE (Summit) is in the central section of the Uinta Mountains, two and one-half miles west of Haystack Mountain. In this same vicinity are Duck, Weir, Hidden, and Fire lakes. The lake is inhabited by beaver.
S10,T2S,R8E,SLM; 9,920' (3,023m). 298.

BEAVER LAKE (Beaver) does not exist today. It was a natural lake six miles north of Beaver* on the Beaver River and was the source for the name of the nearby Beaver Lake Mountains. The lake gradually disappeared with increased use of Beaver River water. It is shown on maps of the 1870s (see George M. Wheeler's Atlas, Sheet Map No. 59).
S7,T27S,R10W,SLM; 4,970' (1,515m). 578.

BEAVER LAKE (Beaver) was a small natural lake on the Beaver River drainage system located ten miles north of Milford*. It disappeared as sediment filled in the lake bed and the river water dissipated.
S7,18,T26S,R10W,SLM.

BEAVER LAKE MOUNTAINS (Beaver) are ten miles north of Milford*. The mountains are named for the small, shallow Beaver Lake, located in earlier times southeast on the Beaver River. The lake no longer exists. See Beaver Lake (Beaver).
T26S,R11,12W,SLM; 6,895' (2,102m). 360, 383.

BEAVER MOUNTAINS (Beaver) is a popular or common name for the Tushar Mountains, east of Beaver*. These should not be confused with the Beaver Mountains to the northwest in Millard County. See Tushar Mountains.

BEAVER RESERVOIR (Beaver) was on the Beaver River, eight miles north of Milford*. It no longer exists, since it served its purpose in early settlement days. The reservoir filled in with sediment and was not reclaimed.
S31,32,T26S,R10W,SLM; 4,920' (1,500m).

BEAVER RIDGE (**Beaver**) is in the foothills nine miles southeast of Beaver*, at the summit of Nevershine Hollow. I-15 passes through the hollow and over the ridge which is also the summit at that point. It receives its name from its proximity to Beaver.
S35,T30S,R7W,SLM; 6,673' (2,034m).

BEAVER RIVER (**Beaver**) originates in the Tushar Mountains east of Beaver* at the confluence of the South Fork and several other creeks and springs. It drains west past Beaver, Milford*, and the southern end of the Mineral Range then turns north and disappears into the ground at the Beaver Bottoms near Red Rock Knoll and Black Rock in Millard County. In earlier days it was known for its large number of beaver colonies. Jedediah Smith called it "The Lost River" and Domínguez and Escalante called it "El Rio de Tejedor" (The Beaver River). T29S,R6W,SLM to S14,T19S,R9W,SLM. 129, 360, 372, 583.

BEAVER RIVER VALLEY (**Beaver**) applies to that generalized area through which the Beaver River flows after it reaches the valley west of the Tushar Mountains. Eastern Beaver Valley is the area near Beaver* and Adamsville*. Western Beaver Valley is commonly called the Milford Valley and is also part of the Escalante Desert.

BEAVER SINKS (**Millard**) is an indefinite area southwest of Black Rock where the Beaver River gradually disappears into the sandy ground.

BECKS (**Salt Lake**) was a siding on the Union Pacific Railroad in North Salt Lake near the hot springs of the same name.
S14,T1N,R1W,SLM; 4,221' (1,287m).

BECKS HOT SPRINGS (**Salt Lake**) was in the northwest section of Salt Lake City* in the hot springs area. In 1885 John Beck bought the property, built a cement swimming pool and accompanying buildings, and opened it to the public. There was a shallow lake nearby where the runoff collected. The buildings and pool have since been dismantled.
S14,T1N,R1W,SLM; 4,221' (1,287m). 252, 494, 546.

BECKWITH PLATEAU (**Emery**) is west of the Green and south of the Price rivers. In 1853 Captain John W. Gunnison of the U.S. Reconnaissance Survey was assigned to survey along the 39th Parallel with Lieutenant E. G. Beckwith, the second in command. They crossed the Green River where the town of Green River* is now located. Shortly after, in western Utah Territory, Gunnison and several of his men were massacred by Indians. Beckwith assumed command of the survey party and completed the assignment. The river crossing eventually assumed Gunnison's name and Beckwith was honored with his name being given to the plateau.
T18,19S,R15,16E,SLM; 6,802' (2,073m). 27, 371.

BEDGROUND LAKE (**Duchesne**) is in the southwest section of the Uinta Mountains on the upper Fish Creek drainage. One and one-half miles west is Governor Dern Lake. The Bedground Lake area was once a favored bedding ground for sheep and a campground for the herders.
S15,T3N,R8W,USM; 10,500' (3,200m). 578.

BEEF BASIN (**San Juan**) is thirteen miles south of The Confluence (of the Green and Colorado rivers) and ten miles north of Dark Canyon and Woodenshoe Canyon. At one time the Scorup Cattle Company held their beef cattle here until the roundup was over.
T32S,R18,19E,SLM; 6,300'-6,400' (1,920m-1,951m). 567.

BEEF BASIN WASH (**San Juan**) originates on the western slopes of the Abajo Mountains, draining northwest into

Gypsum Canyon. It received its name from the basin into which it drains.
T32,33S,R18,19E,SLM.

BEEF HOLLOW (Cache) originates one mile north of Green Canyon and three miles southeast of Hyde Park*. It drains west into the valley between North Logan* and Hyde Park. In pioneer times the Indians stole two beef cows in Hyde Park, took them up this canyon, then slaughtered them for food. A variant is Beef Canyon.
S17,18,T12N,R1E,SLM. 567.

BEEHIVE ARCH (Garfield) is three miles south of The Confluence on the Colorado River. It lies west of and near the Spanish Bottoms. In profile it has the shape of a beehive. The name was submitted by Kent Frost and approved prior to 1962.
T30S,R18E,SLM.

BEEHIVE MOUNTAIN (Sevier). See Beehive Peak.

BEEHIVE PEAK (Sevier) is in the Pavant Range west of Aurora* and north of Richfield*. Erosion has caused its shape to resemble the Utah State beehive symbol. From the east it looks like a beehive and from the west it appears as a red pyramid. Variant: Beehive Mountain.
S36,T21S,R2½W,SLM; 9,018' (2,749m). 530, 584.

BEEHIVE POINT (Daggett) is at the end of Kingfisher Canyon in what is now Flaming Gorge Reservoir. This stretch was a rampaging river when it was first explored by Major Powell and his party in the late 1860s. Here the river reversed its direction around a large protruding point that was prominently exposed and inhabited by numerous hovering and fluttering kingfishers. These wheeling, noisy birds reminded Powell of an active beehive so he named the canyon and point accordingly. Below Beehive Point is the beginning of Hideout Canyon. See also Kingfisher Canyon.
S11,T2N,R20E,SLM; 6,125' (1,867m). 159, 160, 420, 496.

BEERS PASS (Beaver) is at the extreme north side of the Needles Range, on an unimproved road leading from Pine Valley to Antelope Valley. See Beers Tunnel Spring (Beaver) for name source.
S9,T26S,R18W,SLM; 6,350' (1,935m). 125.

BEERS TUNNEL SPRING (Beaver) is at the extreme north end of the Needles Range, south of Beers Pass. The spring was named after James Beers who had a stage station nearby. Halfway Summit is further north on U-21.
S16,T26S,R18W,SLM; 6,400' (1,951m).

BEETLE CREEK (Beaver) originates in the Tushar Mountains on Big Flat and drains north into Hy Hunt Creek. In 1922 the U.S. Forest Service treated a beetle infestation here. Variant: Beetle Canyon.
S13,24,T29S,R5W,SLM. 125.

BEHUNIN CANYON (Washington) originates in Zion National Park, one and one-half miles west of Angels Landing. It drains south into Heaps Canyon at Emerald Pools and was named for Isaac Behunin, an early pioneer whose family joined him in building a cabin and developing a farm in the area.
S33,T40S,R10W,SLM (draining south). 530, 532, 600.

BEIRDNEAU PEAK (Cache) is in the Bear River Range east northeast of North Logan*. Mount Jardine is four miles north and Beirdneau Campground in Logan Canyon is three miles south. The peak and campground were named for Nehemiah W. Beirdneau, an early Logan* settler.
8,914' (2,717m).

BELL SPRING (Beaver) is near the head of Bell Spring Hollow. A bell was

found by the spring; thus the origin of the name.
S6,T27S,R6W,SLM; 7,400' (2,256m). 567.

BELL SPRING HOLLOW (Beaver) originates in the west foothills of the north Tushar Mountains at Bell Spring. It drains northwest towards Pine Creek and Cove Fort* and takes its name from the spring.
S6,T27S,R6W,SLM (at head).

BELLS CANYON (Salt Lake) originates in the mountains south of Lambs Canyon, one and one-half miles northeast of Lone Peak. It drains northwest into the southern end of the Great Salt Lake Valley. The mouth of the canyon is one-half mile south of Granite*.
S11,T3S,R1E,SLM (at mouth).

BELLVIEW* (Washington). See Pintura*.

BELMONT* (Box Elder) was three and one-half miles north of Garland* and west of Fielding*. The community was formerly named Riverside* around 1893. Belmont served as a station on the Malad branch of the Union Pacific Railroad. In 1902, the Malad Valley Central Railroad built a line between Brigham City* and Malad*, Idaho. On October 10, 1910, the station was named Riverside, so the Utah community and railroad station changed their name to Chevers*. The public felt this was an unacceptable name, so they voted to change the name to Belmont.
S35,T13N,R3,SLM; 4,360' (1,329m). 567.

BELNAP* (Sevier) was a station and a siding on the Denver and Rio Grande Railroad (now abandoned) in Marysvale Canyon north of Marysvale*. In 1894 the rails reached this point three miles south of Sevier*. Rail service through the canyon was discontinued in 1971, which led to the abandonment of the station. It was named for the mountain peak in the Tushar Mountains to the west.
S20,T26S,R4W,SLM. 360, 496, 584.

BEN LOMOND PEAK (Weber) is three and one-half miles north of North Ogden*. All agree that the name honors a mountain of the same name in Scotland, but it is uncertain if it was first applied by a Scotsman named Robert Montgomery or was named by a Scottish woman who settled in North Ogden during the pioneer period.
S9,T7N,R1W,SLM; 9,712' (2,960m). 100 (v17), 274, 314, 360.

BENCH* (Uintah). See Vernal*.

BENDER MOUNTAIN (Daggett) is east of Clay Basin and south of the Wyoming line. It was named for Bill Bender, leader of the Powder Springs Gang, a group of rustlers, horse thieves, and part-time ranchers. Bender died of pneumonia in 1897.
S2,T3N,R25E,SLM; 8,297' (2,529m). 80, 172, 303.

BENJAMIN* (Utah) is an agricultural community along U-147 and U-228, three miles north of Payson* and four miles west of Spanish Fork*. It was established in 1860 and named after Benjamin Franklin Stewart, one of its founders. The community was established in 1862-63 by Benjamin's brother, Andrew Jackson, and other settlers from Payson. MRN
S20,21,29,T8S,R2E,SLM; 4,528' (1,380m). 270, 288, 494, 567.

BENMORE* (Tooele) is in Rush Valley, one-half mile southeast of Vernon*, near U-36. The town was established in 1905 as an outgrowth of Vernon. One version of the name source states that it was named "Ben" for Israel Bennion and "More" for Charles H. Skidmore, who surveyed the settlement site. Another version suggests the "More" represents the Moore family, one of the prominent early families.
S28,T8S,R5W,SLM; 5,578' (1,700m). 270, 288, 494, 542, 567.

BENNETT* (Uintah) is six and one-half miles south of Whiterocks* and five

miles northeast of Roosevelt*. It was one of the many townsites laid out shortly after the Uintah Basin was opened to homesteading in 1905. The site was officially laid out in 1914 but had been settled earlier by John B. Bennett. Before that, James Jones filed for a townsite which he wanted to name Cuneal*. He was not successful.
NE¼,S25,T1S,R1W,USM; 5,448' (1,661m). 97, 100(v17), 542, 567.

BENNETT SPRING (Beaver) is in Sheeprock Canyon on the western slopes of the Tushar Mountains, four miles north of North Creek*. The spring was named for J. F. Bennett who prospected in the area around 1874.
S8,T28S,R6W,SLM. 125.

BENNINGTON* (Washington). See Leeds*.

BENNION* (Salt Lake) is on U-68, two miles south of Taylorsville* and three miles southwest of Murray*. The name honors the William Bennion family, who were prominent early residents. Their community was an outgrowth of Taylorsville, from which Bennion separated in 1905.
S15,22,T2S,R1W,SLM; 4,377' (1,334m). 144, 288, 360, 494, 567.

BENNION CREEK (Tooele) originates in the Sheeprock Mountains on the southeast slopes of Dutch Peak, ten miles south southeast of Vernon*. It drains north into Vernon Creek. Samuel and Mary Bennion were early settlers in this area.
NW¼,T10S,R6W,SLM to S16,T9S,R5W,SLM. 508.

BENSON* (Cache) is eight miles northwest of Logan*. In 1870 the Charles Reese and Israel J. Clark families settled there from Logan. On May 3, 1871, the settlement was organized by Moses Thatcher, an apostle of the Mormon Church, and Bishop William B. Preston of Logan, a Mormon elder. Bishop Preston suggested a name honoring Ezra T. Benson, a presiding elder of the Mormon Church in that area.
S11,T12N,R1W,SLM; 4,426' (1,349m). 100 (v17), 360, 449, 567.

BERNARD CREEK (Davis) originates northeast of Centerville* and drains west into the valley. The creek was named for James Bernard in the spring of 1848.
S35,T3N,R1E,SLM to S6,T2N,R1E,SLM. 88.

BERRY CANYON (Kane). Variant: Berry Valley. See Long Valley.

BERRYPORT CANYON (Utah) originates at Bald Knoll on the Wallsburg Ridge, seven miles southwest of Wallsburg*, and drains south into the Left Fork of Hobble Creek. There, an abundant growth of service berries in the area were harvested each summer by the early settlers.
S14,T6S,R4E,SLM to S2,T7S,R4E,SLM. 270.

BERRYVILLE* (Kane). See Glendale*.

BERYL* (Iron) is a Union Pacific Railroad siding nine miles northwest of Newcastle* and thirteen miles north of Beryl Junction*. This area was once referred to as the Escalante Desert but today is known as the Escalante Valley. Improved irrigation and deep well pumping has allowed most of it to become agriculturally productive. In 1901 it was named Beryl, a word of French origin which identifies the semi-precious stone found in the vicinity.
S32,T33S,R16W,SLM; 5,147' (1,569m). 314, 360, 542.

BERYL JUNCTION (Iron) is at the southern end of the Escalante Valley, northwest of Newcastle* and fifteen miles south of Beryl*. It is the uninhabited junction of U-18, U-56, U-98.
S33,T35S,R16W,SLM; 5,182' (1,579m).

BETENSON FLAT (Beaver) is in the Tushar Mountains at the head of the East Fork of the Beaver River. An earlier name was Dry Flat. It was named in the early 1900s after Blaine Betenson. S1,T30S,R5W; 9,680' (2,950m). 125.

BETH LAKE (Summit) is in the southwest section of the Uinta Mountains between Trident and Haystack Lakes. Two miles northwest is Haystack Mountain. MRN
S18,T2S,R9E,SLM; 9,730' (2,966m).

BETSY LAKE (Duchesne) is in the southwest section of the Uinta Mountains near Grandaddy Lake. One-half mile west is Mohawk Lake. MRN
S32,T3N,R8W,USM; 10,350' (3,155m).

BICKNELL* (Wayne) is five miles south of Lyman* on U-24. The town was originally settled in 1879 and named Thurber* for Albert King Thurber, an Indian interpreter, local Mormon church official, and early explorer of Rabbit Valley. A. K. Thurber led the group who went to Cedar Grove near Koosharem* to sign a peace treaty with the Fish Lake Indians. In 1914, Thomas W. Bicknell, a historian and educator from Providence, Rhode Island, offered a library of one thousand volumes to any town in Utah that would name their town after him. At the time, George C. Brinkerhoff was filling a mission for the Mormon Church in Rhode Island and approached Bicknell about his offer. The towns of Thurber in Wayne County and Grayson* in San Juan County vied for the prize. A compromise was proposed in which Thurber would receive half of the library if the town changed its name to Bicknell. Grayson received the other half of the library after changing the town name to Blanding*, the maiden name of Bicknell's wife. A record of this action was made in the courthouse in April 1916.
S26,T28S,R3E,SLM; 7,125' (2,172m). 90, 288, 485, 516, 542, 546.

BICKNELL BOTTOMS (Wayne) are the bottomlands along the Fremont River south of Bicknell*.

BIDDLECOME RANCH (Wayne). See Ekker Ranch*.

BIDDLECOME RIDGE (Emery) has a north-south orientation and is eight miles northwest of Ferron*. It was named for the Biddlecome family, who ran cattle there in the early 1900s. Joe Biddlecome grew up there but eventually established the Biddlecome Ranch out in the heart of the Robbers Roost country. Today the Biddlecome Ranch is known as the Ekker Ranch.
S16,21,28,34,T19S,R6E,SLM; 8,147' (2,483m). 24.

BIG BOWN BENCH (Garfield) is northeast of and near the Escalante River between Death Hollow and Silver Falls Creek. This is the larger of the two Bown benches. There is also Bowns Lake, Bowns Point, and Bowns Reservoir. Will Bown was an early sheep and cattleman who ran his stock in these areas. See Little Bown Bench.
S6,T35S,R6E,SLM (center of bench); 5,800' (1,768m). 12, 534, 602.

BIG CANYON (Salt Lake). See Parleys Canyon (Salt Lake).

BIG CANYON CREEK (Salt Lake). See Parleys Creek (Salt Lake).

BIG CAVE HOLLOW (Beaver). See Cave Hollow (Beaver).

BIG CEDAR COVE (Beaver) is in the Mineral Mountains west of Bailey Mountain. There is a heavy concentration of juniper trees in the area.
S14,T27S,R9W,SLM; 6,500' (1,981m).

BIG CHIEF (San Juan) is a gigantic sandstone monolith rising over nine hundred feet in Monument Valley, approximately two miles south of Monument Pass. Variant: Big Indian.
S25,T43S,R16E,SLM; 6,370' (1,942m).

BIG COTTONWOOD CANYON (Salt Lake) originates in the Wasatch

Mountains at Brighton*, sixteen miles from Butlerville*. It drains west, entering the Great Salt Lake Valley at Wasatch Boulevard and Seventy-fifth South and continues west to eventually empty into the Jordan River. Cottonwoods are plentiful in Utah, and every community and region seems to have its share of cottonwood trees and names. This particular cottonwood-named canyon yielded abundant water, water power, timber, and both winter and summer recreation. Cottonwood Canyon was named by Brigham Young and was a favorite recreational area among the early settlers of the Salt Lake region.
S35,T2S,R3E,SLM to S25,T2S,R1E,SLM. 360, 567, 578.

BIG COTTONWOOD CANYON (**Washington**). See Cottonwood Canyon (Washington).

BIG COVE (**Beaver**) is on the western slopes of the Tushar Mountains between Baker Canyon, East Fork, and the Beaver River. It is a natural open amphitheater.
S24,T29S,R6W,SLM; 5,900' (1,798m).

BIG CREEK (**Rich**) originates on the eastern slopes of the Monte Cristo Range at the Little Crawford Spring west of Woodruff Park. It drains northeast into Crawford Canyon, emerges from the mountains, and empties into the Bear River two miles southwest of Randolph*. It was larger than nearby Little Creek and is also the largest creek in Rich County.
S12,T9N,R4E,SLM to S34,T11N,R7E,SLM. 567.

BIG CREEK (**Rich**) originates at the Big Spring in the foothills five miles southwest of the south end of Bear Lake. It meanders for about five miles as a large slow-moving stream through marshy meadowland, then empties into the south end of Bear Lake.
S4,T12N,R5E,SLM to S24,T13N,R5E,SLM.

BIG ELK LAKE (**Summit**) is in the southwest section of the Uinta Mountains three and one-half miles west of Haystack Mountain. The lake is known for the elk that inhabit the area. Little Elk Lake is further south.
S5,T2S,R8E,SLM; 10,025' (3,056m). 298.

BIG FLAT (**Beaver**) is a large semi-flat alpine meadow on the summit south of ·Puffer Lake in the Tushar Mountains. Iant and Beetle creeks originate there and U-135 passes through the flat. It was named Big Flat because of its open terrain surrounded by forest.
S18,T29S,R4W,SLM; 10,205' (3,110m). 125.

BIG FLAT SPRING (**Beaver**) is a small seep-spring, three-eighths of a mile south of the Big Flat Ranger Station on the Big Flat up Beaver Canyon. It was developed in 1929 by the U.S. Forest Service for watering stock.
S18,T29S,R4W,SLM; 10,100' (3,078m). 125.

BIG HOLLOW (**Beaver**) is a large open drainage system of good pastureland in the upper valley north of Beaver*. It drains southwest past Manderfield* into Indian Creek.
S13,14,22,T28S,R7W,SLM.

BIG HOLLOW (**Garfield**) originates in rugged rimrock canyon country, five miles northwest of Boulder* and drains south to enter Sweetwater Creek, five miles southwest of Boulder. It was crossed at its widest point during the early days of wagon travel.
S8,T33S,R4E,SLM to S6,T34S,R4E,SLM.

BIG HOLLOW (**Utah**) is in northwest Mapleton*, southeast of Springville*. There was once a large grove of juniper trees in what is now the Evergreen Cemetery. This grove extended southeast to surround and define the Big Hollow area.
S9,T8S,R3E,SLM; 4,650' (1,417m). 134(29 Feb. 1976).

BIG HORSESHOE (**Sanpete**) is a spectacular cirque on the summit of the Wasatch Plateau at the head of Canal Canyon, three miles southwest of Haystack Mountain. It is considerably larger than the Little Horseshoe to the west.
S36,T16S,R4E,SLM; 10,800' (3,292m).

BIG INDIAN (**San Juan**). See Big Chief (San Juan).

BIG JOHN FLAT (**Beaver**) is in the Tushar Mountains southwest of Delano Peak on the Sawmill Fork of Merchant Creek. It was named for Big John Murdock, an early Beaver* resident.
S27,T28S,R5W,SLM; 10,000' (3,048m). 355.

BIG LAKE (**Duchesne**) is on Tabby Mountain in the southwest section of the Uinta Mountains. One and one-half miles southeast is the smaller Little Lake.
S29,T1S,R8W,USM; 9,890' (3,014m).

BIG LAKE (**Garfield**) is on the Aquarius Plateau, four miles northwest of Roundy Reservoir, near the head of Spring Draw. It is the largest lake in the area.
SW¼,T31S,R2E,SLM; 9,877' (3,011m).

BIG LAKE (**Garfield**) is on Boulder Mountain in the eastern part of the Aquarius Plateau, north of Boulder*.
T31S,R4E,SLM.

BIG LAKE (**Kane**) is west of and near Kanab Creek, seven and one-half miles north of Kanab*. It is the largest body of water in the area.
S17,T42S,R6W,SLM; 5,350' (1,631m).

BIG LAKE (**Sevier**) is on Cove Mountain eight miles east of Monroe* and two miles east of the Annabella Reservoir. It is a large, shallow, irrigation reservoir which was previously named Mecham Reservoir after the original developer.
T25S,R2W,SLM; 9,421' (2,841m). 585.

BIG MOUNTAIN (**Morgan, Salt Lake**) is on the county line east of the head of City Creek Canyon and Mountain Dell Canyon. This was the largest, most difficult mountain the Mormon pioneers confronted on their western migration to the Great Salt Lake Valley.
S6,7,17,T1N,R3E,SLM; 8,472' (2,582m). 100 (v17), 567.

BIG PASS (**Box Elder**) is a prominent pass, east of Tangent Peak, which goes through the Hogup Mountains.
T9N,R11W,SLM; 5,450' (1,661m).

BIG PINTO SPRING (**Beaver**) is at the head of Pinto Creek in the Indian Peak Range. The multi-colored background inspired the name.
S35,T30S,R18W,SLM; 3,178' (969m). 125.

BIG ROCK CANDY MOUNTAIN (**Sevier**) is five miles north of Marysvale* on US-89. It is a cluster of irregular, multi-colored hills. This unusual site was named by Ken Olsen and others during the summer of 1929 when they jokingly placed a sign with this name onto a post at the base of the mountain. Haywire Mac (Harry McClintock), a brakeman on the nearby Denver and Rio Grande Railroad, had just written the song "Big Rock Candy Mountain." Olsen also put up a sign calling the nearby spring "Lemonade Springs." The names held. Today the area has been commercialized with food, lodging, and neon lights.
S29,T26S,R4W,SLM; 5,800' (1,768m). 206, 360, 567. D.L. 7902.

BIG SAGE (**Kane**) is a large sagebrush flat on the Kaiparowits Plateau between Left Hand and Right Hand Collett forks.
S16,21,22,T38S,R3E,SLM; 6,700' (2,042m). 12.

BIG SAND LAKE STATE BEACH (**Duchesne**) is three miles south of Bluebell* at the junction of U-87 and U-199. It received its name from the

nearby Big Sand Wash that was used in constructing the reservoir.
S16,21,T2S,R3W,USM; 5,885' (1,794m).

BIG SAND WASH (Duchesne) originates in the south central section of the Uinta Mountains, four miles north of Bluebell*. It drains south through the Big Sand Wash Reservoir into Dry Gulch Creek.
S8,T1S,R3W,USM to S35,T2S,R2W,USM.

BIG SAND WASH RESERVOIR (Duchesne) is on the Big Sand Wash, three miles south of Bluebell*. The reservoir is surrounded by the state park.
S16,21,T2S,R3W,USM; 5,885' (1,794m).

BIG SLOUGH (Beaver) originates in the lowlands of the Beaver River, south of Beaver*. It drains southwest, paralleling the Beaver River which it rejoins after two miles.
S21,29,30,T29S,R7W,SLM.

BIG SPENCER FLATS (Garfield). See Spencer Flats.

BIG SPRING (Daggett) is in the north central section of the Uinta Mountains, three miles northeast of Sheep Creek Lake and two and one-half miles south of Jessen Butte. The water disappears underground at Lost Creek, approximately eighteen miles west of where it re-emerges at Big Spring.
S16,T2N,R19E,SLM; 6,975' (2,126m). 172.

BIG SPRING (Tooele) is a small body of water at Timpie* near the Western Pacific Railroad siding and I-80, where a small dam has caused natural ponds to develop. Fifteen miles southeast is Grantsville*. The Piute word "timp" means "rock." See Timpie Lake. Variant: Timp Lake.
S8,9,T1S,R7W,SLM; 4,220' (1,286m).

BIG TRIANGLE (Grand) is a large section of land shaped like a triangle which is formed by Coates Creek and Triangle Canyon. To the north are Westwater and Marble canyons.

S3,9,10,T22S,R25E,SLM; 5,000' (1,524m).

BIG TWIST CREEK (Beaver) originates on the western slope of Birch Creek Mountain in the Tushar Range, draining southwest into South Creek. The course of the creek is very irregular with many unexpected twists and turns. Little Twist Creek is located north.
S13,T30S,R5W,SLM. 125.

BIG WASH (Beaver) originates on the northern slopes of the Shauntie Hills, draining past Milford* into the Beaver River. It is a long, wide wash.
T27,28S,R10-12W,SLM.

BIG WASH (Beaver) originates south of Minersville* in the Black Mountains. It drains northwest into the Escalante Desert southwest of Minersville.
S3,T31S,R9W,SLM to SW¼,T30S,R10W, SLM.

BIG WASH RESERVOIR (Beaver) is near the head of Big Wash on the northern slopes of the Shauntie Hills in the Star Range. Milford* is ten miles east.
S4,T28S,R12W,SLM; 5,825' (1,775m).

BIG WATER* (Kane) is on US-89, nineteen miles northwest of Page*, Arizona. It was known as Glen Canyon City* during the construction of nearby Glen Canyon Dam. In 1983, the town was incorporated as Big Water at the instigation of Alex Joseph, the town's first mayor. See Bac-Bone*.
S11,T43S,R2E,SLM; 4,100' (1,250m). 466(29 Dec. 1983).

BILL ALLRED CANYON (Sanpete) is a small canyon originating west of the Big and Little Horseshoe, draining north into Pigeon Hollow. It is not part of the creek. See Bill Allred Creek for name source.
S20,29,T16S,R4E,SLM.

BILL ALLRED CREEK (Sanpete) originates in the mountains south of Spring

City* and west of the Little Horseshoe. It drains west through Little Pigeon Hollow into the San Pitch River. The Allred family were original settlers in nearby Spring City.
S20,T16S,R4E,SLM to S27,T16S,R3E,SLM. 508.

BILLIES MOUNTAIN (Utah) is ten miles up Spanish Fork Canyon, across and to the northwest from Thistle* Junction. Billie, known as Uncle Billie, was the son of Aaron Johnson, an early settler in the area. Local history records that Billie's team and wagon got stuck in the mud up on the mountain and considerable effort was required to get Billie, his horses, and wagon out. Recently, a massive earth slide caused tremendous damage to Thistle, the Spanish Fork River, and the nearby railroad.
S22,23,T9S,R5E,SLM; 6,676' (2,035m). 509.

BILLY WEST CANYON (Iron) originates four miles south southwest of Parowan* and drains southeast into Parowan Canyon. MRN
S10,11,T35S,R9W,SLM.

BINGHAM* (Salt Lake) was a community in Bingham Canyon, fifteen miles southwest of Salt Lake City*. It was disincorporated on November 2, 1971, with the expansion of the Bingham open-pit copper mine. Today the town has disappeared. Bingham was named after Sanford and Thomas Bingham, early Mormon stockmen who ran their cattle in the canyon from 1848 to 1850. A sawmill built at the mouth of the canyon supplied much of the timber used to build the Mormon Tabernacle in Salt Lake City. It was General Connor's men from Fort Douglas who staked the first mining claim in the canyon. Gold, silver, lead, and then copper were mined there. At its peak, Bingham was nearly seven miles long but less than a city block wide. Early name variants were Binghams Herd House*, Binghams Gulch* and later, after the town was established,

Jinxtown*. Fires and floods often swept through the canyon and avalanches were common during the winter. Despite all this danger, the population reached fifteen thousand at one time.
S13,23,T3S,R3W,SLM. 89, 314, 494, 542, 546. D.L. 6803.

BINGHAM CANYON (Salt Lake) has been severely altered over the years with the intrusion of the nearby open-pit copper mine. See Bingham*.

BINGHAM FORT* (Weber). See Lynne* (Weber).

BINGHAM JUNCTION* (Salt Lake). See Midvale*.

BIRCH CREEK (Beaver) originates on the western slope of Birch Creek Mountain at the junction of the North and Middle forks, southeast of Beaver*. Birch Lake is two miles northeast of the creek source. The creek has a heavy growth of birch trees (Betula) along its banks.
S12,T30S,R6W,SLM to S1,T30S,R7W,SLM. 100(v17).

BIRCH CREEK (Piute) originates on the eastern slopes of the Circleville Mountains of the Tushar Range. It drains southeast into the Sevier River. Birch trees are plentiful along the creek.
S24,T30S,R5W,SLM to S34,T30S,R4W,SLM.

BIRCH CREEK CLOVER BEDS (Beaver) are in the more open and less rugged area south of Birch Lake. Clover (Trifolium) grows abundantly there.
S1,T30S,R6W,SLM; 9,000' (2,743m).

BIRCH CREEK MOUNTAIN (Beaver) is included in the Tushar Mountain Range east southeast of Beaver*, on the headwaters of Birch Creek. Variant: Birch Mountain.
S7,8,17,T30S,R5W,SLM; 10,733' (3,271m).

BIRCH LAKE (Beaver) is in the Tushar Range on the headwaters of Birch Creek,

from which it receives its name.
S36,T29S,R6W,SLM; 8,815' (2,687m). 125.

BIRCH SPRING CREEK (Beaver)
originates on the south slope of Pole
Mountain in the Tushar Range. It drains
south into Tanner Hollow.
S10,T28S,R6W,SLM.

BIRD ISLAND (Box Elder) is in the
southwest section of Great Salt Lake
about four miles north of Carrington
Island. The island is about seventy feet
high and one-half mile in circumference.
In earlier times many birds such as
pelicans, cormorants, and gulls nested on
the island. When the lake level dropped,
the island became connected to land and
the bird population was depleted by
predators. A variant name for the island
is Hat Island, which came from
Stansbury's men in the early 1850s
because it has a cone shape, resembling
a hat.
133, 314, 604.

BIRDSEYE* (Utah) is at the junction of
Thistle Creek and Bennie Creek, seven
miles south southwest of Thistle Junction.
It was settled in 1885 and named Summit
Basin*, then in 1897 the name was
changed to Clinton*. Later, the town was
named Birdseye for the nearby birdseye
marble quarries in the Indianola* area to
the southeast.
S26,T10S,R3E,SLM; 5,400' (1,646m). 542,
567, 578.

BITTER CREEK (Grand) originates on
the East Tavaputs Plateau north of the
Book Cliffs, at the junction of the East,
Middle, and West forks. It drains south
into the Colorado River at Westwater*.
The water is alkaline and unpalatable.
S23,T16S,R25E,SLM (to the Colorado
River).

BITTER CREEK (Uintah) originates at
Baxter Pass in Colorado and crosses into
Utah three miles north of the
Uintah-Grand County line. It joins the

White River about twenty miles southeast
of Ouray*, Utah. The water near the
source is sweet and fresh but it gradually
increases in alkalinity as it approaches
the mouth. Sweet Water Creek joins it
along its course.
S18,T15S,R26E,SLM to S11,T10S,R22E,SLM
(in Utah). 602.

BLACK BOX CANYON (Emery) lies six
miles in a straight line northwest of
where I-70 crosses the San Rafael River,
sixteen miles west of Green River*. It is
a slot-like canyon with dark-colored walls
through which the San Rafael River
drains. It was in this canyon that Sid
Swasey made a monumental leap with his
horse (see Swazys Leap).
T21S,R13E,SLM. 193.

BLACK CANYON (Beaver) originates
on the northern slope of the Black
Mountains in Iron County and drains
north to cross the county line into the
Escalante Desert near Mound Pond. See
Black Mountain for name source.
T30,31S,R11W,SLM.

BLACK CANYON (Garfield). The head
is thirteen miles south of Antimony* at
the north end of Johns Valley. It drains
north toward the mouth of Antimony
Creek and is named for the black lava
rock surroundings.
S2,T33S,R2W,SLM to S35,T31S,R2W,SLM.

BLACK CANYON (Sanpete) originates
at the summit of the mountains east of
Spring City*. It drains southeast into
Lowry Water which in turn enters Joes
Valley Reservoir. The name comes from
the black lava rock surroundings and the
heavy stands of dark-colored vegetation.
S16,T16S,R5E,SLM to S5,T17S,R6E,SLM.
152.

BLACK CAP MOUNTAIN (Sevier) is a
conical butte one and one-half miles east
of Salina* and one mile north of Salina
Canyon. The mountain top is a two-
hundred-and-fifty-foot-thick cap of lava

which has protected it from the erosion that has leveled the surrounding area. S29,T21S,R1E,SLM; 6,362' (1,939m). 175.

BLACK DRAGON CANYON (Emery) originates on the Jackass and Rattlesnake benches of the Sinbad country of San Rafael Swell. It drains east, cutting through the San Rafael Reef, to empty into the San Rafael River at the Tidwell Bottoms. An Indian pictograph resembling a dragon-like figure on the canyon wall led to the canyon name. S6,7,T22S,R13E,SLM to S32,T21S,R14E, SLM. 193.

BLACK HILL (Box Elder) is ten miles west of Park Valley*. It is a lava rock hill with dark-colored vegetation, consisting of mostly cedars. S22,27,T13N,R15W,SLM. 567.

BLACK HILL SPRING (Box Elder) is on Black Hill, ten miles west of Park Valley*. S15,T13N,R15W,SLM. 567.

BLACK HOLLOW (Beaver) is on the benchland west of the Tushar Mountains, eight miles north of Manderfield*. The local vegetation creates a dark, shaded background. S13,T27S,R7W,SLM.

BLACK LAKE (Garfield) is between McGath and Dry lakes on the southern slopes of Boulder Mountain of the Aquarius Plateau. The reflection of the heavy background vegetation on the water of the lake is quite dark. T32S,R3E,SLM; 9,640' (2,938m).

BLACK MOUNTAIN (Beaver) is on the western slopes of the Tushar Mountains east of Beaver* and south of the Beaver River. The dark pinyon pine, juniper, and exposed dark lava rock inspired the mountain name. S30,T29S,R6W,SLM; 7,340' (2,237m).

BLACK MOUNTAIN (Beaver) is southeast of Minersville*.

S29,T30S,R9W,SLM; 6,897' (2,102m).

BLACK MOUNTAIN (Iron) is nine miles southeast of Cedar City* and five miles southwest of Cedar Breaks. The mountain got its name because of the lava rock and dark vegetation in the area. S24,T37S,R10W,SLM; 10,375' (3,162m).

BLACK MOUNTAIN RANGE (Beaver) is a range of mountains with an east-west orientation, lying south of the Beaver-Iron County line. Parowan Canyon cuts through the west end. The mountains have a lava rock base and dark green vegetation. T31S,R9W,SLM. 583.

BLACK RIDGE (Beaver) is on the western slopes of the Tushar Mountains northeast of Beaver*. Johnson Draw is at its northwest extension. S4,5,8,T29S,R6W,SLM; 7,600' (2,316m). 125.

BLACK RIDGE (Washington) is an imposing lava ridge with a northeast-southwest orientation which parallels Ash Creek. It is the southern boundary of the Great Basin in this area. Ash Creek drains south into the Virgin and Colorado River systems instead of into the Great Basin. The Black Ridge was a formidable obstacle to travel and was often bypassed by immigrants going to California. They preferred a route through Pinto* and around the Pine Valley Mountains to the west. T38-40S,R12,13W,SLM. 154, 423, 438.

BLACK ROCK (Millard) is a large black butte in the desert twelve miles southwest of Delta*. It rises three thousand feet above the desert floor and has a three- to four-mile diameter. It was an important landmark for early travelers. T18,19S,R8W,SLM. 89, 516.

BLACK ROCK* (Millard) was an early settlement several miles east of Black

Rock. It was settled in 1874 and named after the nearby rock formation. The town was soon abandoned and today it is a seldom-used railroad siding.
S22,T24S,R10W,SLM; 4,853' (1,479m). 89, 516, 542.

BLACK ROCK (Salt Lake) is at the south end of the Great Salt Lake, twenty miles west of Salt Lake City*. It has always served as a landmark for travelers and natives alike. At one time it functioned as a dock for boats when the experimentation on water freighting between the north and south shores of the lake was being conducted. At the north end of the lake is Corinne* which served as the loading and unloading points for northward freighting. Black Rock was named July 27, 1847, when Brigham Young and others visited the site. There is also a report (530, p. 323) that the rock was given a similar name by the Donner-Reed party. The site was developed into a full-scale resort in 1878. Its popularity rose and fell with fluctuations in the lake level. Its doom was thought to be sealed in 1963 when the water receded to its lowest recorded level. Then in the 1980s the lake rose far above previously recorded levels, covering picnic tables, beaches, restrooms, and other facilities.
S18,T1S,R3W,SLM; 4,205' (1,282m). 100 (v2), 275, 360, 567, 591.

BLACK ROCK DESERT (Millard) is west of Meadow*, Kanosh*, and Flowell*, and south of Clear Lake. It received its name from nearby Black Rock.
T21S,R7W,SLM.

BLACK ROCK PASS (Millard) is at the northern end of the San Francisco Mountains, seven miles west of Black Rock.
S28,T24S,R11W,SLM; 5,215' (1,590m).

BLACK ROCK VALLEY (Garfield) is five miles south of Panguitch Lake. The name comes from the black volcanic rock

in the area.
S28,34,T36S,R7W,SLM; 8,200' (2,499m).

BLACK ROCK VOLCANO (Millard) is an extinct volcano in the Pavant Valley west of Kanosh*. There are several volcanic cones in this area.
S13,T23S,R6W,SLM.

BLACKS CANYON (Washington) origi- nates on the southwest slopes of the West Temple monolith, one and one-half miles northwest of Springdale*. It drains southeast through Springdale into the Virgin River, North Fork. The name honors Joseph Black, an early explorer and pioneer in Zion Canyon.
S29,T41S,R10W,SLM. 532, 602.

BLACKS FORK* (Summit) is one and one-half miles south of the Wyoming border, near the Meeks Cabin Reservoir. It is near Blacks Fork of the Green River from which it receives its name. Blacks Fork was a lumber town which existed from 1870 to 1930. At its peak, the town supported fifty to one hundred lumbermen, but is now a ghost town. It was also an early government commissary post.
S28,T3N,R12E,SLM; 8,840' (2,694m).

BLACKS FORK (Summit) originates on the north central slopes of the Uinta Mountains, on Tokawana Peak and Mount Lovenia, draining northeast into the Green River. It was named in the 1820s for Arthur Black of the Ashley Fur Company.
S34,T3N,R12E,SLM. 89, 172, 215, 342, 371, 372.

BLACKSMITH FORK CREEK (Cache) originates in the Monte Cristo Mountains east of Ant Valley, three and one-half miles southeast of the Hardware Ranch. The creek drains northwest through Blacksmith Fork Canyon into the Logan River. There are two versions of the name source. One comes from an inci- dent where Jedediah Smith and his party had to return to a set of cached black-

smith tools in the canyon in order to re-shoe their horses. The other version is that the fork was named after Andrew Anderson, a blacksmith.
S3,T9N,R4E,SLM to S9,T11N,R1E,SLM. 372, 567.

BLACKSMITH FORK CANYON (Cache) is the part of the Blacksmith Fork that passes through the Bear River Range east of Hyrum*.

BLAIR BASIN (Daggett) is eight miles north of Blair Spring and twenty-eight miles northeast of Vernal*. See Blair Spring for name source.
S19,T1S,R24E,SLM; 7,700' (2,347m).

BLAIR DRAW (Daggett) originates at Blair Spring on the southern slopes of Diamond Mountain. It drains southeast into Stone Bridge Draw and the Green River. See Blair Spring.
S1,T3S,R23E,SLM to S3,T4S,R24E,SLM. 567.

BLAIR SPRING (Daggett) is at the head of Blair Draw. Duncan Blair, a squaw man, ran his cattle there in the 1880s and 1890s.
S1,T3S,R23E,SLM; 7,100' (2,164m). 567.

BLAKE* (Emery). See Green River*, Utah (Emery).

BLANCHARD* (Weber) was a small community south of what is today West Weber*. It was named after the Blanchard brothers, who owned the largest farm in the area. Blanchard has been absorbed into the West Weber, Garland*, and Taylor* complex west of Ogden. See West Weber for further details.
S16,T6N,R2W,SLM; 4,240' (1,292m).

BLANDING* (San Juan) is on US-163 and the White Mesa, midway between Monticello* and Bluff*. It was first settled in 1887 as White Mesa*. About 1908 the name was changed to Grayson* in honor of Nellie Lyman Grayson, a pioneer settler. In 1914 Thomas W. Bicknell, a wealthy easterner, offered a one-thousand-volume library to any town in Utah that would take his name. Thurber* (now Bicknell*) and Grayson (now Blanding) vied for the prize. A compromise was made in which Thurber received half of the library in exchange for taking the name of Bicknell. Grayson received the other half in exchange for taking the maiden name of Bicknell's wife, Blanding.
S26,27,34,35,T36S,R22E,SLM; 6,088' (1,856m). 100(v17), 288, 314, 406.

BLAWN MOUNTAIN (Beaver) is in the Wah Wah Mountains at the head of Blawn Wash. Around 1900 it was named after Billy Blawn who had built a cabin there, probably near the Blawn Spring. See Blawn Wash Spring for additional information.
S30,32,33,T29S,R15W,SLM; 8,250'(2,515m).

BLAWN WASH (Beaver) originates on the eastern slopes of the Wah Wah Mountains at Lamerdorf Peak, then drains into the Escalante Desert. The old Jockey Freight Road (see Jockey Road) follows the wash for a distance. See Blawn Wash Spring.
S19,T29S,R15W,SLM to S9,T31S,R14W, SLM. D.L. 7404.

BLAWN WASH SPRING (Beaver) is near the head of Blawn Wash, southeast of Lamerdorf Peak, in the Wah Wah Mountains. It was named for Billy Blawn who built a cabin there around 1900. Blonde Wash has been used on some maps. Another researcher mentions a William Bellond, a prospector and cattleman who lived and worked in this vicinity around 1872. Therefore, the exact source for the name is unclear and needs further research. MRN
S28,T29S,R15W,SLM; 6,840' (2,085m). 125, 532(No. 7404, Oct.-Dec. 1974).

BLIND SPRING (Garfield) is a spring that is difficult to find. It is on the northern slopes of Blind Spring Moun-

tain, ten miles northeast of Panguitch*. It drains north into Sanford Creek, Right Fork.
8,225' (2,507m).

BLIND SPRING MOUNTAIN (Garfield) is at the southern end of the Sevier Plateau, twelve miles northeast of Panguitch*. It received its name from Blind Spring, which is on the mountain.
9,534' (2,906m).

BLIND SPRING (Box Elder) is nine miles northwest of Tremonton*, west of and near US-30S. The spring is in a draw and can only be seen from a certain angle. The first person to settle the Blind Spring area was the father of Adolph Harris, who sold water to the teamsters that passed the spring.
S10,T12N,R4W,SLM; 4,800' (1,463m). 567.

BLIND VALLEY (Millard) is in the heart of the Confusion Range. Fifteen miles north is US-6,50. Blind Valley is isolated and completely enclosed by mountains and hills.
T21,22S,R14,15W,SLM; 5,600' (1,707m).

BLIZZARD LAKE (Wasatch) is in the southwest section of the Uinta Mountains, three miles south southwest of Mirror Lake. An early surveying party was caught in a blizzard in this area.
S9,T3N,R9W,USM; 10,300' (3,139m). 530.

BLOCK MESAS (Kane) are midway between Zion National Park and the Coral Pink Sand Dunes. Here they rise as a group of isolated, flat-topped mesas with steep rising flanks. Several canyons originate on the mesas: Cottonwood, Bay Bill, Merwin, Joseph, and Setheys canyons are among them.
S2,T3S,R8,9W,SLM; 6,625' (2,019m).

BLOOMINGTON* (Millard). See Hinckley*.

BLOOMINGTON* (Washington) is three and one-half miles southwest of St. George*. In 1870 a small group of settlers led by William Carpenter and Harrison Pearce separated from Price*, an early settlement two miles south of St. George. They moved one mile further south, near the Virgin River, to establish their own community. Lars James Larsen built the first house, which was made of rock, and for a period of time the community was known as St. James* in honor of Larsen. Shortly after, noticing and appreciating the beautiful spring flowers appearing on the hillsides two to three weeks earlier than elsewhere, the settlers named their community Bloomington. A series of alternating flash floods and drought began in 1880 and people began moving to other areas. For all practical purposes the community was abandoned by 1930. Today as people realize the advantages and opportunities of Bloomington's milder climate it has re-developed as a vital new residential area with a community center, golf course, and beautiful homes.
S14,T43S,R16W,SLM; 2,480' (756m). 100 (v17), 154, 360, 578.

BLOOMINGTON HILLS* (Washington) is southwest of St. George*, near Bloomington*.

BLUBBER CREEK (Garfield) originates at the Sunset Cliffs west of Bryce Canyon National Park and eight miles southwest of Tropic Reservoir. It drains east into the Sevier River, East Fork. It is a quiet creek, and on warm days swamp gasses bubble off from decaying vegetation.
S35,36,T37S,R4½W,SLM. 567.

BLUE BENCH (Duchesne) is a benchland northeast of Duchesne*. The small community of Blumesa* is located in this area and was named after the bench. Beautiful blue lupines color the bench in the springtime.
T2,3S,R3-5W,USM; 5,800'-6,000' (1,768m-1,829m).

BLUE CASTLE BUTTE (Emery) is six miles north northwest of Green River* in Blue Castle Canyon. It is a comparatively

small butte with a castle shape and a bluish tinge to its base.
S12,T20S,R15E,SLM; 5,250' (1,600m).

BLUE CASTLE CANYON (Emery) originates on the Beckwith Plateau northwest of Green River*. It drains southeast into the Green River, passing Blue Castle Butte from which it receives its name.
S32,T19W,R15E,SLM to S17,T20S,R15E, SLM.

BLUE CHIEF MESA (Grand) is five miles east of the mouth of the Dolores River. It was named in the 1890s for the nearby mine of the same name.
S19,25,36,T15S,R24E,SLM; 5,000' (1,524m). 578.

BLUE CREEK (Box Elder) originates in upper Blue Creek Valley, twelve miles north of Blue Creek Spring. The creek drains through the Blue Creek Reservoir, then flows south into the north bay of Great Salt Lake. The waters of the spring and creek are very blue.
S1,T14N,R6W,SLM to T9N,R5W,SLM. 567, 578.

BLUE CREEK* (Box Elder) was a settlement fifteen miles southeast of Snowville* on I-80 and US-30S. Two and one-half miles south is Blue Creek Spring from which the site received its name. The settlement was established in the 1890s and was abandoned in the 1900s.
S17,18,T13N,R5W,SLM; 4,691' (1,430m). 516, 567.

BLUE CREEK RESERVOIR (Box Elder) was built on Blue Creek in 1904. It is one mile northwest of Howell*.
S31,T13N,R5W,SLM; 4,589' (1,399m).

BLUE CREEK SPRING (Box Elder) is one mile north of the Blue Creek Reservoir and twenty miles west northwest of Tremonton*. The spring was named for the bluish cast of the water. Variant: Blue Springs.
S29,T13N,R5W,SLM; 4,610' (1,405m).

BLUE CREEK VALLEY (Box Elder) is traversed by Blue Creek. Howell* is in the center of the valley.

BLUE FLY CREEK (Garfield) originates on the Paunsaugunt Plateau eight miles west of central Bryce Canyon National Park. The creek drains into the Sevier River, East Fork. The blue fly (blue bottle fly) is quite common in the area.
S27,T36S,R4½W,SLM. 100(v17).

BLUE JAY SPRING (Beaver) is on the northwest slopes of Indian Peak near the head of Miners Cabin Wash. Large numbers of blue jays inhabit the area, especially in the spring and fall.
S7,T29S,R18W,SLM; 7,700' (2,347m). 125, 577.

BLUE JOHN CANYON (Wayne) originates in the high Roost country south of the Roost Flats, draining northeast into Horseshoe Canyon. This entire area is now part of Canyonlands National Park. The canyon was named after John Griffith, or "Blue John," an outlaw and cattle rustler who arrived in the area around 1889-1900. He reportedly had one blue eye and one brown eye which had a cast in it. Griffith's nickname was originated by Ink Harris, another outlaw.
S16,T29S,R15E,SLM to S36,T27S,R15E, SLM. 25, 303.

BLUE JOHN SPRING (Wayne) is on the eastern ridge of Blue John Canyon. Horseshoe Canyon is midway between the head and mouth of the spring. Blue John built a cabin next to the spring. The spring was named by Joe Biddlecome. See Blue John Canyon.
5,800' (1,768m). 24, 25, 303.

BLUE LAKE (Beaver) is on Blue Lake Creek at the head of North Creek, South Fork. The name refers to the blue lake water.
S4,T28S,R5W,SLM; 9,700' (2,957m). 125, 355.

41

BLUE LAKE (**Duchesne**) is in the southwest section of the Uinta Mountains in the Naturalist Basin. One mile northwest is Mount Agassiz. The lake has a deep blue color.
S32,T4N,R8W,USM; 10,925' (3,330m). 298.

BLUE LAKE (**Garfield**) is in the Escalante Mountains twenty miles northwest of Escalante* in the cluster of lakes at the head of North Creek. The lake is a deep blue color.
9,700' (2,957m). 12.

BLUE LAKE (**Summit**) is in the southwest section of the Uinta Mountains on the upper Provo River drainage, one-half mile south of Haystack Mountain. The lake is quite blue.
S13,T2S,R8E,USM; 9,990' (3,045m). 602.

BLUE LAKE (**Summit**) is at the west end of the Uinta Mountains, one mile east of Boyer Lake. The lake is named for the blue water.
S35,T2N,R8E,SLM; 9,850' (3,002m).

BLUE LAKE (**Tooele**) is fifteen miles south of Wendover*. It is a body of comparatively clear, tepid, spring water. Scuba enthusiasts have requested that this small lake become Utah's first underwater or scuba park. It has been used for scuba diving for some time. The waters are blue.
S5,T4S,R19W,SLM; 4,241' (1,296m).

BLUE LAKE (**Uintah**) is in the eastern section of the Uinta Mountains on the headwaters of Dry Fork. The lake is blue.
T4N,R1E,USM; 11,250' (3,429m).

BLUE LAKE CREEK (**Beaver**) is a small creek originating near the summit of the Tushar Mountains on the southern slopes of Mount Belnap. It drains through Blue Lake into the head of North Creek, South Fork and receives its name from Blue Lake.
S31,T28S,R5W,SLM.

BLUE LAKES (**Tooele**) is a cluster of shallow, intensely blue lakes located three miles northeast of Grantsville*. The lakes form a collector system for creek overflow in the area.
S20,29,T2S,R5W,SLM; 4,239' (1,319m). 100 (v2).

BLUE MESA (**Wayne**) is eight miles southwest of Hanksville* and three miles south of Blue Valley and the Fremont River. The mesa received its name from the bluish-colored Mancos shale that is so prominent in the region.
T29S,R10E,SLM; 5,031' (1,533m).

BLUE MOUNTAIN PLATEAU (**Uintah**) is west of and near the Colorado State line between Cluff Creek and the Green River. Early mountain men described the mountains to the east in Colorado as having a bluish color. The plateau takes its name from the mountain.
100(v17).

BLUE MOUNTAINS (**Beaver**) are southeast of the Wah Wah Mountains. The deep blue-black color of the mountains are caused by volcanic rocks and cedars.
S14,23,26,35,T30S,R14W,SLM; 7,595' (2,315m).

BLUE MOUNTAINS (**San Juan**) is a local name for the Abajo Mountains. Variant: The Blues.

BLUE NOTCH (**San Juan**) is a distinctive precipice at the head of Blue Notch Canyon west of and near Lower White Canyon. The predominant soil in the area is a blue clay.
5,350' (1,631m).

BLUE NOTCH CANYON (**San Juan**) originates at the Blue Notch, west of lower White Canyon. It drains southwest, entering the Colorado River at Good Hope Bay in the Glen Canyon National Recreation Area.
S36,T35S,R13E,SLM (at mouth).

BLUE PEAK (**Beaver**) is the highest point in the Blue Mountains.
S26,T30S,R14W,SLM; 7,594' (2,315m).

BLUE PEAK (**Sevier**) is on the Sevier Plateau southwest of Cove Mountain and three and one-half miles northwest of Koosharem*. From a distance the peak has a bluish-black appearance.
S16,T26S,R1W,SLM; 8,544' (2,604m).

BLUE RIBBON SUMMIT (**Beaver**) is on the northern slopes of Black Mountain south of the Minersville Reservoir. The name was taken from the nearby Blue Ribbon mine.
S27,T30S,R9W,SLM; 6,600' (2,012m). 578.

BLUE SPRING (**Garfield**) is at the head of Blue Spring Creek four miles southwest of Panguitch Lake into which it drains. It was named for the deep blue waters of the spring.
S18,T36S,R7W,SLM; 8,675' (2,644m). 12.

BLUE SPRING CREEK (**Garfield**) originates at the Blue Spring three miles southwest of Panguitch Lake into which it drains.
S5,7,8,15,T36S,R7W,SLM. 12.

BLUE SPRING MOUNTAIN (**Iron**) is five miles southwest of Panguitch Lake. Blue Spring originates at the head of Blue Creek on the northeast slope of the mountain.
S23,24,T36S,R8W,SLM; 9,894' (3,016m). 567.

BLUE SPRING VALLEY (**Garfield**) is three miles southwest of Panguitch Lake with Blue Spring Creek draining through it.
S7,18,T36S,SLM; 8,650' (2,637m).

BLUE VALLEY (**Beaver**) is a small valley near I-15 in the foothills southeast of Beaver*. The lava rock and sagebrush in the valley have a bluish tint.
S24,26,T30S,R7W,SLM; 6,450' (1,966m). 125, 355.

BLUE VALLEY (**Wayne**) follows the Fremont River six miles west of Hanksville*. The valley was named for the bluish tint of the Mancos shale formation.
S20,21,22,T28S,R10E,SLM; 4,440' (1,353m).

BLUE VALLEY* (**Wayne**). See Giles*.

BLUEACRE* (**Beaver**) is a mining ghost town site northwest of Milford*, at the south end of the Beaver Lake Mountains. The settlement received its name from the blue lupine flowers that grew prolifically in the springtime. As the mine resources were depleted around 1906, Blueacre was abandoned.
S7,T27S,R11W,SLM; 5,900' (1,798m). 125.

BLUEBELL* (**Duchesne**) is a small agricultural community on U-199 and the benchland, four miles north of Big Sand Wash Reservoir. Heber Powell suggested that the town be named after the bluebells that grew on the bench land each spring. A post office was assigned to Bluebell on November 4, 1911.
S27,T1S,R3W,USM; 6,203' (1,891m). 165, 542.

BLUEBELL CREEK (**Grand**) originates on the East Tavaputs Plateau on the northeast slopes of Moonwater Point. The creek drains west into the Green River and was named for the numerous bluebells growing along the creek.
T16S,R17E,SLM.

BLUEBELL LAKE (**Duchesne**) is in the south central section of the Uinta Mountains, on the headwaters of the Yellowstone and Garfield creeks. It was named for the abundant bluebells growing near the lake.
S31,32,T4N,R5W,USM; 10,894' (3,320m).

BLUES, THE (**Garfield**) are bluish-colored clay foothills located northeast of Henrieville* on U-54 to Escalante*. Before the road was improved, traveling through this area and over the pass was

a treacherous experience—especially in wet weather when the clay became slippery.
S36,T36S,R1W,SLM; 7,800' (2,377m). 602.

BLUFF* (San Juan) is on US-163 midway between Mexican Hat* and Blanding*. The town was established on April 6, 1880, by the Hole-in-the-Rock expedition of the Mormon Church's San Juan Mission. William Hutchings of Beaver* originally named the town Bluff City* in reference to the prominent bluffs along the San Juan River. The word "City" was dropped to avoid confusion with Iowa's Council Bluffs*, which was occasionally referred to as Bluff City*. Bluff City was the first Anglo-Saxon settlement in San Juan County. Life was difficult during the early years, when it was half-humorously suggested that the town itself was one big bluff.
S20,21,22,T28S,R10E,SLM; 4,440' (1,353m). 288, 314, 360, 406, 542.

BLUFFDALE* (Salt Lake) is on U-68, two miles south of Riverton*. The town was originally part of West Jordan*. It was named on August 8, 1886, for the bluffs along the nearby Jordan River.
S10,T4S,R1W,SLM; 4,435' (1,352m). 163 (2 Oct. 1978, 1B), 288, 542, 546.

BLUMESA* (Duchesne) was a small community seven miles northeast of Duchesne* on the Blue Bench. It was laid out in 1914 by Hugh M. Woodward and was named for the blue lupines and sage growing on the bench. The community was unsuccessful and was soon abandoned.
S13,T3S,R4W,USM; 5,918' (1,804m). 542, 595.

BOLLIE LAKE (Duchesne) is on the Uinta River, four miles east northeast of the U-Bar Ranch. Mount Emmons is four miles northwest. "Bollie" means "bald" or "baldy." The lake was named after the sparsely vegetated mountain in the vicinity.

BOLLIE MOUNTAIN (Duchesne). See Bollie Lake.
S17,T3N,R3W,USM; 10,650' (3,246m). 567.

BONANZA* (Uintah) was forty miles southeast of Jensen* on U-45. Byron Colton believed his claim on the gilsonite vein there would develop into a very rich strike. Gilsonite is a natural asphalt found only in this area. "Bonanza" is the Spanish word for prosperity, a rich strike, or boom. Bonanza was established in 1888.
S23,T9S,R24E,SLM; 5,456' (1,663m). 100 (v17), 314, 360, 542, 567.

BONETA* (Duchesne) is three miles southeast of Altamont*, near U-87, on the south central slopes of the Uinta Mountains. It was first established by Moroni Fisher and others on September 19, 1909. The town was named by one of its co-founders, Peter B. Madsen, for its favorable location. "Boneta" means pretty or beautiful in Spanish.
S23,T1S,R4W,USM; 6,455' (1,967m). 165, 314, 542, 567.

BONETA BEND (Wayne) is on the lower Green River, two miles south of the mouth of Millard Canyon. One and one-half miles west are the Buttes of the Cross. See Boneta* for name source.
S24,25,T40S,R21E,SLM; 4,320' (1,317m). 159, 422.

BONNEVILLE SPEEDWAY (Tooele) is on the Bonneville Salt Flats several miles northeast of Wendover*. World-class speed contests by motorcycles, automobiles, and bicycles are held here. The area is a remnant of prehistoric Lake Bonneville, which left a large deposit of rock-hard salt that makes an ideal high-speed track.
T1N,R17W,SLM; 4,245' (1,294m).

BOOK CLIFFS (Grand) are a massive escarpment several miles in length, laced by highly eroded indentations which give the impression of the leaves of a partly

opened book. The cliffs extend from Helper* on the west to Grand Junction* and the Colorado River on the east. Book Cliffs is the central feature of three vast escarpments that Powell named in 1868. The northernmost is the Brown Cliffs, known today as the Roan Cliffs, and the southernmost is the Sunset Cliffs located near Alton*. The cliffs had previously been named the Book Mountains by Lieutenant Gunnison, whose name took precedence.
100(v17), 160, 175, 314, 360, 422.

BOOKER LAKE (Summit) is in the southwest section of the Uinta Mountains between the southern slopes of Notch Mountain and Wall Lake. It was named after an early trapper.
S30,T1S,R9E,SLM; 10,500' (3,200m). 602.

BOREN MESA (Grand) is on the western slopes of the La Sal Mountains southwest of the head of Mill Creek. Carlos Boren settled in the area and became a cattleman in 1878, while Emil Boren prospected nearby.
S32,33,T26S,R24E,SLM; 9,000' (2,743m). 146.

BOSMAN CREEK (Beaver) originates on the western slopes of the Tushar Mountains between Bosman Ridge and Driggs Ridge. The creek drains northwest into North Creek, South Fork. Some records indicate that the creek and the ridge were named for a Captain Bosman (Boosman) of nearby Fort Cameron. It was reported that he hunted there during the 1880s. Personal correspondence by a compiler with the United States Board on Geographic Names in Washington, D.C., gave this response: "We called the old military post section of the National Archives to see if it had any record of a Captain Bosman, Boosman, or Bausman who had been stationed at Fort Cameron. No record of an officer with any of these names could be found." MRN
S29,T28S,R5W,SLM. 125, 577.

BOSMAN RIDGE (Beaver) is on the western slopes of the Tushar Mountains between Bosman Creek and Lion Creek. Puffer Lake is southeast. See Bosman Creek for name source.
S20,T28S,R5W,SLM. 125.

BOTHWELL* (Box Elder) is on U-102, four and one-half miles west of Tremonton*. It was named in 1894 to honor the builders of the Bothwell Canal; John R. Bothwell was president of the waterworks at that time. The canal was used to divert water from the Bear River in order to enhance the agricultural potential of this region. Before 1894 it was called Rowville* in honor of William Rowe and his family, who were early pioneers in the area.
S1,2,T11N,R4W,SLM; 4,330' (1,320m). 100 (v17), 139, 360.

BOTTLE HOLLOW (Uintah) is a one-mile-long draw with an east-west orientation, west of Fort Duchesne* and one mile south of US-40. During the 1880s while U.S. soldiers were stationed at Fort Duchesne, the gully was used as a dump for empty liquor bottles. The soldiers were not allowed to return to the fort from neighboring settlements (i.e. Roosevelt*) until they had discarded their bottles. The name Bottle Hollow became accepted.
S22,T2S,R1E,USM; 5,000' (1,524m). 360, 573.

BOULDER* (Garfield) is on U-12, on the eastern part of the Aquarius Plateau. Almon Thompson of the Powell survey named the town Boulder after the nearby mountain. It was settled between 1889 and 1894, even though cattle had been brought into the area as early as 1879. At that time, Nichole Johnson and August Anderson of Richfield* brought in five hundred head to graze on Boulder Mountain. Except for pack train or horseback, Boulder was isolated until 1935 when the U.S. Civilian Conservation Corps completed a road that could be

used by wagons and automobiles.
S25,26,T33S,R4E,SLM; 6,675' (2,035m).
143, 145, 315, 542, 546.

BOULDER* (**San Juan**) was twelve miles southeast of Monticello* and east of Boulder Creek. It was a small settlement established in 1910 by John Butt, who filed the first claim in 1909. This unsuccessful community was soon abandoned.
S18,19,30,T34S,R25E,SLM; 6,785' (2,068m). 406.

BOULDER CANYON (**Beaver**) is in the foothills south of Beaver* and drains north into South Creek. It is named for the large number of lava boulders in the canyon.
S12,13,T30S,R7W,SLM.

BOULDER CREEK (**Garfield**) originates on Boulder Mountain on the east side of the Aquarius Plateau. It drains south into the Escalante River, passing through Boulder City*. It was named by Pardon Dodds of the Powell survey for the large lava and sandstone boulders in the area.
S22,T35S,R5E,SLM (at mouth). 159, 315, 602.

BOULDER CREEK (**Wayne**) originates on Boulder Mountain in the northeast section of the Aquarius Plateau. It drains northeast to enter the Fremont River between Torrey* and Teasdale*. There are numerous lava boulders located in this region.
T30S,R4E,SLM to S14,T29S,R4E,SLM.

BOULDER MEADOW (**Garfield**) is an alpine meadow at the east end of the Aquarius Plateau, on the south side of Boulder Mountain.
10,960' (3,341m).

BOULDER MOUNTAIN (**Garfield**) is north of Boulder City* and south of Grover* and Teasdale*. The mountain makes up the eastern section of the Aquarius Plateau. It was named by Almon Thompson of the Powell survey.

"Boulder Mountain" is the term local inhabitants use most frequently rather than the name Aquarius Plateau. Through a combination of common usage and early name assignment, the present-day Aquarius Plateau has been unofficially divided into three sections. The eastern area is Boulder Mountain, the western section is Escalante Mountain, and the central area—as well as the entire plateau—is the Aquarius Plateau. The name "Boulder" refers to the numerous large lava and sandstone boulders in the area.
T31S,R4,5E,SLM; 10,800'-11,200' (3,292m-3,414m). 143, 145, 315, 542, 546.

BOULDER SPRING (**Beaver**) is on the east side of South Twin Flat Mountain in the Mineral Mountains. It is surrounded by massive granite boulders.
S6,T28S,R8W,SLM; 7,620' (2,323m).

BOULDERVILLE* (**Summit**). See Marion*.

BOUNDARY BUTTE MESA (**San Juan**) is seventeen miles south of the San Juan River and southwest of White Mesa Village*. It is close to the Navajo and Apache Indian reservations, boundary, near the Utah-Arizona border.
T43S,R22E,SLM; 5,595' (1,705m). 567.

BOUNTIFUL* (**Davis**) is eight miles north of Salt Lake City* on I-15 and U-106. It was initially settled in 1847 by Perrigrine Sessions, Jezreel Shoemaker, and John Perry and their families. It has the distinction of being the second city settled by the Mormon pioneers in the Utah Territory. The name has been changed on several occasions. It was originally known as Calls Settlement* for Anson Call, who stopped to visit the area. The name was then changed to Sessions Settlement* for Perrigrine Sessions. For a time it was called North Mill Creek Canyon Ward* to distinguish it from Mill Creek Canyon Ward, east of Salt Lake City. This name was soon shortened to North Canyon Ward*. In

1854 the first post office identified the town as North Canyon Settlement*. The town was also known as Stoker* in honor of John Stoker, the first Mormon bishop in the area. He finally suggested the name "Bountiful" after an ancient city mentioned in the Book of Mormon. Bountiful was unanimously accepted and the name has remained unchanged since February 27, 1855.
S19,20,T2N,R1E,SLM; 4,408' (1,344m). 27, 88, 201, 275, 360, 546, 567, 586(v1).

BOUNTIFUL FORT* (Davis). The settlers of Bountiful* decided they needed a fort for protection against Indians. Construction began in 1854 and continued for two years, but the fort was never completed. See Bountiful*.

BOUNTIFUL PEAK (Davis) is at the heads of Ricks, Davis, and Farmington creeks, northeast of Centerville*. Five miles southwest is Bountiful*, from which it receives its name.
S27,T3N,R1E,SLM; 9,259' (2,822m).

BOURBON LAKE (Summit) is at the west end of the Uinta Mountains, seven miles north of Mirror Lake and one-half mile west of U-150. MRN
S35,T1N,R9E,SLM; 9,790' (2,984m).

BOVINE TOWN* (Box Elder) is near Kelton*, on the former Central Pacific Railroad. The railroad company named the town after nearby Bovine Mountain. "Bovine" referred to the region's cattle industry, which used Bovine Town as its center of operation.

BOWDEN LAKE (Duchesne) is in the south central section of the Uinta Mountains on the headwaters of the Uinta River, one-half mile south of the Kidney Lakes. Joe Bowden was the first individual to stock this lake with fish.
10,693' (3,259m). 309.

BOWDIE CANYON (San Juan) originates on the Dark Canyon Plateau, ten miles east of the end of Cataract Canyon. It drains northwest into lower Cataract Canyon of the Colorado River. There is also a Bowdie Point nearby to the north. MRN

BOWKNOT BEND (Emery) is in Labyrinth Canyon of the Colorado River, between Keg Spring Canyon and Horseshoe Canyon. It was named by Major Powell because the river takes a gigantic, almost completely circular bend. Powell's men called it a "bowknot of a river."
S36,T25S,R17E,SLM. 160, 420, 422, 609. D.L. 6402.

BOWNS BENCH (Garfield). See Big Bowns Bench and Little Bowns Bench.

BOWNS LAKE (Garfield) is a small lake on the southeast slopes of Boulder Mountain of the Aquarius Plateau, northeast of Boulder*. Bowns Point and Bowns Reservoir are in the vicinity. It was named for Will Bown, an early sheep and cattleman in the area.
10,100' (3,078m). 12, 530.

BOWNS POINT (Garfield) is an upland point on the southeast section of Boulder Mountain of the Aquarius Plateau. Bowns Lake is one mile south. See Bowns Lake for name source.

BOWNS RESERVOIR (Garfield) is on the eastern slope of the Aquarius Plateau, four miles east of the Boulder*-Grover* Road. The reservoir drains south into Oak Creek. See Bowns Lake for name source.
T31S,R6E,SLM. 12, 602.

BOX, THE (Garfield) is a section of canyon on upper Pine Creek, four miles east southeast of Posy Lake. At this point the creek cuts through the escarpment of the Aquarius Plateau to form a canyon with vertical walls.
12.

BOX CANYON (Summit) originates in the southwest section of the Uinta

47

Mountains, one and one-half miles west of Erickson Basin. It drains north into Red Pine Creek. "Box" is applied to many of these rugged, dead-end canyons with precipitous walls.
S35,T1S,R7E,SLM to S13,T1S,R7E,SLM.

BOX CREEK (Piute) originates on the eastern slopes of Marysvale Peak and drains east into Grass Valley. The Tom Box family settled on the creek and gave it their name.
S8,T29S,R2W,SLM to S4,T28S,R1W,SLM. 100(v17), 360, 585.

BOX ELDER CITY* (Box Elder). See Brigham City*.

BOX ELDER CANYON (Box Elder) originates east of Brigham City* and drains west into the north end of the Great Salt Lake. It was named by William Davis in 1851 when he noted the large number of box elder trees growing along the canyon floor.
S20,21,T9N,R1W,SLM. 100(v17), 435, 546, 567.

BOX ELDER COUNTY was created in March 1856 when the county was separated from Weber County. It was named for the box elder trees around the mouth of Box Elder Canyon.

BOX ELDER CREEK (Box Elder) originates five miles northeast of Willard* on the northern slopes of Black Mountain. It drains north into the head of Box Elder Canyon.
S9,T8N,R1W,SLM to S19,T9N,R1W,SLM.

BOX ELDER LAKE (Box Elder) is two miles northwest of Brigham City*. It was named after Brigham City's earlier name.
567.

BOX ELDER PEAK (Box Elder) is between Honeyville* and Wellsville*. The peak was named after Brigham City*'s former name.
S1,T10N,R2W,SLM; 9,372' (2,857m).

BOX ELDER VALLEY (Box Elder). Mantua* is in the center of the valley, east of Brigham City*. Variant: Little Valley.
139.

BOYER LAKE (Summit) is at the west end of the Uinta Mountains, nine miles northeast of Smith and Morehouse Reservoir.
S34,T2N,R8E,SLM; 9,429' (2,874m).

BP SPRING (Grand) is on the East Tavaputs Plateau at the head of Chandler Canyon. It was there that cattleman Preston Nutter tolerated a whipping by an Indian to prevent possible or further hostilities. The Indian used—in the crude cowboy language of that day—a "bull prick" whip. Such a whip was made of braided rawhide with the dried genitalia of a bull serving as the core.
S8,T16S,R19E,SLM; 8,000' (2,438m). 555 (v32/3), 578.

BRADBURY CANYON (Summit) originates four miles west southwest of Hoytsville*. It drains southeast into the Weber River and was named for Thomas Bradbury, an early settler in Hoytsville.
S36,T2N,R4E,SLM to S5,T1N,R5E,SLM. 508.

BRADFORD* (Box Elder) was established as a railroad siding northwest of Brigham City*. It was a sugarbeet-loading facility for the Utah-Idaho Sugar Company and named for William Bradford, the company's master mechanic. The station was later moved to Brigham City.
567.

BRADSHAW CITY* (Beaver) was a mining camp built near the Cave Mine north of Minersville*. John Bradshaw apparently discovered the Cave Mine, literally by following his dream. Variant: Cave Mine Camp*.
S12,T29S,R10W,SLM; 6,400' (1,951m). 456, 516.

BRADSHAW MOUNTAIN (Beaver) is six miles north of Minersville* between Cave and Guyo canyons. See Bradshaw City* for name source.
S7,T29S R9E,SLM; 8,011' (2,442m). 456.

BRIAN HEAD* (Iron) is a dominant headland of the Markagunt Plateau east of Cedar City*. There are two name origins: (1) It was named for a geologist named Brian who used it as a survey point. (2) It was named for William Jennings Bryan, a popular man at that time. Today Brian Head is a year-round recreation and residential site.
S12,T36S,R9W,SLM; 11,307' (3,446m). 226, 314, 360, 508, 567.

BRIDAL VEIL FALLS (Utah) is on US-189 in Provo Canyon, east of Orem*, between Springdell* and Vivian Park*. Captain J. H. Simpson of the U.S. Topographical Engineers observed the falls in 1859. He originally named the falls the Beautiful Cascade but later changed it to Bridal Veil Falls.
S34,T5S,R3E,SLM. 360, 477.

BRIDGE CANYON (Kane) originates in Bryce Canyon National Park and drains east into Willis Creek. It is named for the natural bridge at the head of the canyon.
NW¼,T38S,R4W,SLM. 314, 546, D.L. 1 July 1934 to 30 June 1935.

BRIDGE CREEK (San Juan) originates on the western slopes of Navajo Mountain. It drains northwest under the Rainbow Bridge (from which it receives its name) into Aztec Creek of Forbidden Canyon.

BRIDGELAND* (Duchesne) is a scattered agricultural community nine miles east of Duchesne* on the old highway (now U-86). The community center is located where the highway crosses the river on an important bridge built in the early 1900s. Mileage was measured from this point during the early days of the town. William Smart

recommended the name Bridgeland. The bridge drew neighboring communities Antelope* and Arcadia* closer together.
S41,T4S,R3W,USM; 5,297' (1,615m). 89, 165, 542.

BRIDGER CREEK (Rich) originates in Wyoming and drains into Utah at the Bear River, north of the Crawford Mountains. It was named for Jim Bridger, the famous mountain man and scout.
S17,20,T12N,R8E,SLM (in Utah).

BRIDGER JACK MESA (San Juan) is six miles north of La Sal Junction* near US-160. Bridger Jack is remembered as a Piute Indian medicine man who attempted to cure Posey's sick child. Unfortunately, the boy died and Bridger Jack was killed shortly thereafter.
S27,T28S,R22E,SLM; 5,810' (1,771m). 146, 475.

BRIDGER LAKE (Summit) is in the north central section of the Uinta Mountains near China and Marsh lakes. The lake was named for Jim Bridger, the well-known trapper and scout.
S29,T3N,R14E,SLM; 9,350' (2,850m).

BRIGGS CAMP CREEK (Beaver) originates east of LaBaron Lake in the Tushar Mountains and drains north into Iant Creek. See Briggs Creek for name source.
S2,T30S,R5W,SLM.

BRIGGS CANYON (Beaver) is a synonym for Briggs Hollow.

BRIGGS CREEK (Beaver) originates on the western slopes of the Tushar Mountains and drains northwest into North Creek, South Fork. John Briggs, a sheepherder of the middle 1800s, herded sheep in this area.
S31,T28S,R5W,SLM to S26,T28S,R6W,SLM. 100(v17). 125.

BRIGGS HOLLOW (Beaver) originates on the western slopes of the Tushar

Mountains, one mile south of Indian Creek. It drains west southwest into North Beaver Valley. See Briggs Creek for name source.
S31,T27S,R6W,SLM.

BRIGGS RIDGE (Beaver) has a northwest-southeast orientation and is on the western slopes of the Tushar Mountains near Briggs Creek. John Briggs ran his sheep on this ridge.
S31,T28S,R5W,SLM to S25,T28S,R6W,SLM; 9,100' (2,774m). 100(v17), 125.

BRIGHAM CITY* (Box Elder) is on I-15 and US-89,91,30 at the mouth of Box Elder Canyon. The town was originally called Box Elder* from 1850 to 1851, a name taken from the creek upon which it was founded. For the next two years the town was known as Youngsville*. Finally on January 12, 1867, the city was named Brigham City to honor Brigham Young, the second leader of the Mormon Church.
S23,24,25,T9N,R2W,SLM; 4,439' (1,353m). 27, 100(v17), 139, 288, 314, 360, 542, 567.

BRIGHAM PEAK (Piute). See Mount Brigham.

BRIGHAM PLAINS (Kane) are in south central Utah, north of US-89 and east of the Cockscomb. The name is derived from the dominant stand of ephedra (Mormon tea, Brigham tea, or joint fir) that grows in the area. Brigham tea was a concoction the impoverished early Mormon pioneers made from the steepings of tender ephedra (Mormon tea) tips. The drink was mixed with milk, when available, and sugar or a substitute sweetener. This tea is still occasionally used.
T41,42S,R1W,SLM; 6,500' (1,981m). 578.

BRIGHAM TEA BENCH (Garfield) is east of the Escalante River, ten miles east northeast of Tenmile Flat. See Brigham Plains for name source.
S24,25,T35S,SLM; 5,400' (1,646m).

BRIGHTON* (Salt Lake) was a small community on what is now central Twenty-first South in Salt Lake City*. It was settled in the fall of 1849, then absorbed by an expanding Salt Lake City. It was named for the Brighton family who made their home there.

BRIGHTON* (Salt Lake) is a recreational community at the end of U-152 in upper Big Cottonwood Canyon. The town was originally named Silver Lake* after the small lake nearby. There are various claims for the name source. It could have been named after a city in England, or for Thomas W. Brighton or William Stuart Brighton, both of whom built homes in the area.
S35,T2S,R3E,SLM; 8,730' (2,661m). 100 (v17), 288, 314, 360, 542.

BRIGHTON LAKE (Salt Lake). See Silver Lake.

BRISTLECONE CANYON (Iron) originates in the east central part of Cedar Breaks National Monument and drains southwest into Arch Creek. Bristlecone Ridge is north of the canyon. Both receive their names from the bristlecone pine (Pinus aristata), the dominant pine species in the area.

BRITTS MEADOW (Beaver) is in the Beaver River Canyon of the Tushar Mountains at the junction of Lake Stream and Hy Hunt Creek. It was named for Newell K. Britt, a surveyor for the U.S. Geological Survey who worked in the area in 1885.
S15,T29S,R11W,SLM; 8,800' (2,682m). 355.

BROADHEAD LAKE (Wasatch) is in the southwest section of the Uinta Mountains, five miles northeast of Iron Mine Mountain and three and one-half miles east of Alexander Lake. See Broadhead Meadows.
S33,T3N,R9W,USM; 9,950' (3,033m).

BROADHEAD MEADOWS (Wasatch) are at the west end of the Uinta

Mountains, west of and near Murdock Basin. An early settler named Broadhead logged and grazed this area in the late 1800s.
S3,4,10,16,T2S,R9E,SLM;   9,500'-10,000' (2,896m-3,048m). 298.

BROKEN BOW ARCH (Kane) is on upper Willow Gulch, east of the Kaiparowits Plateau and south of Fortymile Gulch. It was named by Alvey Edson when he found a broken Indian bow under the arch.
T40S,R8E,SLM; 4,000' (1,219m). 12, 602. D.L. 7902.

BROMIDE BASIN (Garfield) is in the Henry Mountains above the old mining town of Eagle City*, at the head of Crescent Creek. This was the center of early local mining activities. There was also a temporary mining camp named Bromide* in the basin.
S34,T31S,R10E,SLM; 10,400' (3,170).

BROMIDE* (Garfield). See Bromide Basin.

BROMLEYS CANYON (Summit) originates four miles west of Coalville* and drains north northeast into the Weber River. See Bromleys Station* for name source.
S2,T2N,R4E,SLM to S25,T3N,R4E,SLM. D.L. 6901.

BROMLEYS STATION* (Summit) is in Echo Canyon northeast of present-day Echo*. It is on the Overland Stage Road between Echo Station* and Weber Station*. It was also known as Hanging Rock Station* for its unique location near a large outcrop of conglomerate rock. James Bromley was an early settler who ran the station.
516.

BROOKLYN* (Sevier). In 1873 a few Mormon colonists moved south from Elsinore* to the south bank of the Sevier River. The settlement received its name from the earliest prominent settler, John Brooks Wasden. In June 1909, the community was absorbed into Elsinore.
S32,T24S,R2W,SLM; 5,328' (1,624m). 288, 360, 368, 585.

BROWN CITY* (Utah). On November 19, 1858, an application was made for the establishment of an early non-Mormon city in the Utah Territory. The proposed town location was the Provo Bench area and was to be named Brown City. The plan fell through when the Utah territorial legislature refused to endorse the application.
575.

BROWN CLIFFS (Grand). See Roan Cliffs.

BROWN DUCK LAKE (Duchesne) is in the Brown Duck Lake Basin of the Lake Fork River drainage.
S5,6,T2N,R6W,USM; 10,186' (3,105m).

BROWNS FORT* (Weber) was erected in 1850 by Captain James Brown in what is now west central Ogden*. Today's location would be on Twenty-ninth Street, east of the Union Pacific Railroad station. Browns Fort replaced the Miles Goodyear Fort on the nearby Weber River, which inundated the fort with its rising waters.
S32,T6N,R1W,SLM; 4,310' (1,314m). 274, 275, 546.

BROWNS HOLE (Daggett). See Browns Park.

BROWNS HOLE (San Juan) is four miles northeast of La Sal Junction at the head of Muleshoe Canyon where Cottonwood Canyon and Buck Hollow meet. In 1882 a prospector named Doby Brown settled there.
S23,26,T28S,R23E,SLM; 6,000' (1,829m). 475, 514.

BROWNS HOLE (Weber) is eight miles northeast of Huntsville* on Elk Creek near the Middle Fork of the Ogden River. Harvey Brown cut logs there in

anticipation of transporting them to a sawmill. The area was so rugged he failed to get the logs out and was forced to abandon them.
S23,24,T7N,R2E,SLM; 6,600' (2,012m). 567.

BROWNS PARK (Daggett) is in extreme northeast Utah, northwest Colorado, and south central Wyoming. It is an isolated basin, thirty-five miles long and five to six miles wide, surrounded by mountains. It is presently a grazing area for cattle and sheep, but has an increasing tendency toward recreational activities such as river running, fishing, and hunting. It was once a rendezvous area for trappers, mountain men, outlaws, rustlers, and bank robbers. Fort Davy Crockett was built in the basin in 1837 by Philip Thompson and William Craig. There are several stories as to how Browns Hole received its name. In 1827, French-Canadian trapper Baptiste Brown (several names and several spellings are listed for him) settled there. He is given most of the credit for being the original name source. However, names such as Bibleback Brown, Henry Bosun Brown, Charles Brown, and Ephraim Brown are also entered in the published names list coinciding with this area. Major Powell, who passed through this area with his survey crew in the late 1860s and early 1870s, changed the name from Browns Hole to Browns Park because he felt it was a more appropriate, attractive, euphonious, and aesthetic name.
T1,2N,R24E,SLM; 5,500'-6,000' (1,676m-1,829m). 159, 172, 204, 271, 303, 314, 360, 546.

BROWNSVILLE* (Weber). See Ogden* (Weber).

BRUMLEY CREEK (Grand) originates between Mount Mellenthin and Mount Peale in the La Sal Mountains and drains west into Pack Creek. A man named Brumley ran the Gold Basin sawmill on the upper reaches of the creek.
S14,T27S,R24E,SLM to S22,T27S,R23E, SLM. 567.

BRUMLEY RIDGE (Grand) is ten miles southeast of Moab*, between Brumley and Mill creeks. See Brumley Creek for name source.
S10,T27S,R23E,SLM.

BRUSH CREEK (Uintah) originates ten miles northeast of Vernal* at the junction of Big Brush and Little Brush creeks. It drains south southeast into the Green River. Major Powell's party named the creek for the heavy growth of shrubs and underbrush along the banks. Domínguez and Escalante crossed the Green River near the mouth of this creek.
S13,T3S,R22E,SLM to S9,T5S,R23E,SLM. 160, 271, 583.

BRUSH HOLLOW (Beaver) originates on the west side of the Tushar Mountains, north of Wildcat and Indian creeks. It drains northwest toward Cove Creek and was named for the heavy growth of scrub oak along the hollow.
S17,T27S,R6W,SLM (at source). 125.

BRUSHY BASIN (San Juan) is on the southern slopes of the Abajo Mountains, six miles south of Mount Linnaeus. It drains south into the Brushy Basin Wash and is named for its heavy growth of upland desert shrubs.
S7,18,T35S,R22E,SLM; ca. 7,500' (2,286m). 555(v32), 609, 610.

BRUSHY BASIN WASH (San Juan) originates at Brushy Basin and drains south into Cottonwood Creek.
S6,T35S,R22E,SLM to S10,T37S,R21E,SLM.

BRYCE CANYON (Garfield) originates in the center of Bryce Canyon National Park and continues east to the Paria River. It was named for Ebenezer Bryce, a pioneer cattleman who homesteaded there in the fall of 1875.
100(v17), 229, 314, 546, 600. D.L. 1 July 1934 to 30 June 1935.

BRYCE CANYON AMPHITHEATER (Garfield) is the large semicircular area in the part of the park circumscribed by the Pink Cliffs at the head of Bryce Creek.

BRYCE CANYON NATIONAL PARK (Garfield) has a north-northeast by south-southwest orientation and runs parallel to the Sevier River, East Fork. The canyon drainage goes into the Paria River. The spectacularly colorful Pink Cliffs, named by Major Powell's survey party at the center of the National Park, are the east escarpment of the Paunsaugunt Plateau. The Pink Cliffs have been sculptured by water, wind, and gravity into pinnacles, columns, cliffs, castles, and shapes of indescribable form and beauty. The park is not a canyon per se, but the edge of a plateau which can be enjoyed from above or from the depths below. The park was established in 1928 by President Hoover. See Bryce Canyon for name source.

BRYCE CREEK (Garfield) is the principal creek that drains Bryce Canyon National Park.

BUCK PASTURE (Beaver) is in the Circleville Mountains at the south end of the Tushar Mountains, between Anderson Meadow Reservoir and LaBaron Lake. Deer are plentiful in this area.
S9,T30S,R5W,SLM; 9,750' (2,972m). 125.

BUCK PASTURE (Uintah) is now only a part of the large Oaks Park Reservoir. Early sheep men fenced this area and corralled their buck sheep there during certain periods of the year.
S1,12,T1S,R10E,SLM; 9,278' (2,828m). 567.

BUCK RIDGE (Beaver) is in the Tushar Mountains between Three Creek, South Fork, and Hy Hunt Creek. Large numbers of deer gathered on the ridge.
S22,23,T29S,R5W,SLM; 9,750' (2,972m). 125.

BUCKEYE LAKE (Summit) is in the southwest section of the Uinta Moun-

tains, two and one-half miles south of Washington Lake and Haystack Mountain.
S19,T2S,R9E,SLM; 9,675' (2,961m).

BUCKHORN FLAT (Iron) is in the Parowan Valley twenty miles southwest of Beaver* and thirty-three miles northeast of Cedar City*. The area was named after Buckhorn Springs.
T32S,R8W,SLM; 5,764' (1,757m). 360, 546.

BUCKHORN SPRING (Beaver) is on the northeast slopes of Indian Peak in the Indian Peak Mountains. It drains into the head of Turkey Wash. The name originated when mountain sheep horns were found there.
S27,T28S,R18W,SLM; 6,650' (2,027m). 125.

BUCKHORN SPRINGS (Iron) is on the flats midway between Beaver* and Parowan*, three miles north of a present-day I-15 rest stop. These were well-known springs in early Utah territorial history. Fremont passed there in the 1840s. Wagon trains and freighters on the old California road stopped there. It was also a favorite water hole for desert big horn sheep, antelope, mule deer, and other wildlife. Molted horns were fastened to a post planted near the springs so they could be spotted from afar. John Ayre and his family settled there around 1879. Later, a small community grew up with the name Buckhorn Springs* but overuse of the available water resulted in abandonment. Modern deep-well pumping and improved irrigation have recently permitted the construction of several comfortable homes, and people have settled in the region once more.
S23,T32S,R8W,SLM; 5,764' (1,757m). 89, 100(v13), 136, 288, 314, 516.

BUCKHORN SPRINGS* (Iron). See Buckhorn Springs.

BUCKHORN WASH (Emery) originates seven miles south southeast of Cleveland*, where the Buckhorn Reservoir is now located. It drains southeast into the San Rafael River. The wash is vital as a primary access road into the San Rafael Swell country from the north. It was also part of the escape route for Butch Cassidy and Elza Lay after the Castle Gate payroll robbery, as they escaped with Joe Walker toward the Roost country. Variant: Buckhorn Draw. 25, 193, 303.

BUENAVENTURA RIVER. The word is Spanish for good luck or good fortune. Over the years several rivers—imaginary or otherwise—have held the name. These included the present-day Green River and an imaginary river that was supposed to have drained directly from the Great Salt Lake west to the Pacific Ocean. Jedediah Smith explored the region and discovered that no westward-flowing river existed from the Great Salt Lake. See Green River.
314, 371, 372, 496, 546.

BUENO* (Grand). See Moab*.

BUFFALO ISLAND (Davis). See Antelope Island.

BUHL* (Tooele). See Bauer*.

BULL FLAT (Box Elder) is in the central Raft River Mountains at the head of Bull Canyon, east of the head of Clear Creek Canyon. Buffalo grazed there in the early days. The name was applied by early stockmen.
S20,T14N,R13W,SLM. 567.

BULL MOUNTAIN (Washington) is the central section of the Bull Valley Mountains. See the Bull Valley Mountains for name origin.
S22,32,T38S,R17W,SLM; 6,463' (1,970m).

BULL RUN CANYON (Garfield) originates near the head of Carcass Canyon between Alvey Wash and the Straight Cliffs of the Kaiparowits. It drains northwest into Alvey Wash at Little

Valley. Wild cattle used to run in the area.
S4,T37S,R3E,SLM to S25,T36S,R2E,SLM. 12.

BULL RUSH CREEK (Piute) originates at the west base of Bull Rush Peak, twelve miles south of Circleville*. It drains west into the Sevier River and receives its name from the bulrush plant (*Scirpus*) which is quite common along the lower reaches of the creek.
S24,T32S,R5W,SLM (at mouth).

BULL RUSH PEAK (Piute) is twelve miles south of Circleville* and five miles east of US-89. The peak was named after the creek.
T32S,R4½W,SLM; 9,377' (2,858m).

BULL VALLEY (Kane) originates in the southeast section of Bryce Canyon at Lonely Spring. It drains east southeast into the Bull Valley Gorge and the Paria River. The name refers to the cattle herds that grazed in the valley.

BULL VALLEY (San Juan) is midway between The Confluence and Dark and Woodenshoe canyons. It is a small valley where bulls were temporarily held during roundup. In the late 1800s and early 1900s, the Scorup Cattle Company, owned by Al and Jim Scorup, ran their cattle there.
NW¼,T32S,R18E,SLM; 6,500' (1,981m).

BULL VALLEY GORGE (Kane) originates south of Cannonville* in Bull Valley. It is a massive, rugged gorge that drains southeast into the Paria River. The gorge was named for the valley it drains.
S28,T38S,R3W,SLM (to Sheep Creek and the Paria River).

BULL VALLEY MOUNTAINS (Washington) are bounded on the north by the Escalante Desert and Enterprise* and on the south by Veyo* and Gunlock*. Nearby Mountain Meadows

was a favorite camping site for emigrants on their way to California. It was also the site of the Mountain Meadows Massacre of 1857. The name for the mountains resulted from an incident when some cattle escaped from the Mountain Meadows camps. The cattle were eventually captured and used to build up local herds or butchered for food by the local settlers.
T38,39S,R17W,SLM. 154, 311, 530, 546.

BULLBERRY* (Wayne). See Teasdale*.

BULLBERRY CREEK (Piute) is three miles west of Circleville*. The creek is named for the bullberry shrub which is synonymous with the more commonly used name of buffalo berry (*Shepherdia argentea*). The buffalo berry was a favorite food of early Indians and an ingredient of pemmican. Pemmican was a mixture of fat, buffalo jerky or other dried meat, and the berries. Pressed and wrapped in skin, the resultant paste preserved well, was nutritious, and kept its flavor.
S24,25,T30S,R5W,SLM to S26,T30S,R4W, SLM. 578.

BULLBERRY SLOUGH (Beaver) originates in the lowlands west of Beaver* and drains southwest where it links with the Big Slough to drain into the Beaver River. See Bullberry Creek for name source.
S20,29,T29S,R7W,SLM.

BULLET CANYON (San Juan) originates on the eastern slopes of Cedar Mesa, south of the Bears Ears and drains west into Grand Gulch. The original name prior to 1894 was Graham Canyon for C. C. Graham, an early digger (prior to 1894) of the ancient ruins found in the canyon. MRN
S4,T39S,R18E,SLM to S1,T38S,R17E,SLM. 610.

BULLFROG CREEK (Garfield, Kane) originates on the northwest slopes of Mount Pennell in the Henry Mountains. It drains northwest, turns abruptly at Turn of Bullfrog and continues south into what is now Bullfrog Bay and Bullfrog Marina on Lake Powell. Large numbers of frogs lived in the seeps and shallows along the creek.
S3,T33S,R10E,SLM (to Bullfrog Bay). 496.

BULLFROG CREEK (Piute) originates on the eastern slopes of Circleville Mountain, five miles west of Circleville*. It drains east into Circle Valley and is known for its bullfrogs.
S24,25,T30S,SLM to S26,T30S,R4W,SLM. 496, 578.

BULLION* (Piute). See Bullion City* (Piute).

BULLION CANYON (Iron) originates in the Crows Nest section of the Antelope Range at Silver Peak. It drains northwest into the Escalante Desert. Silver and some gold were mined there from the 1890s from 1910.
S26,27,T35S,R15W,SLM (at mouth). 100 (v17), 567.

BULLION CANYON (Piute) originates on the eastern slopes of the Tushar Mountains between Mount Belnap and Delano Peak. It drains east northeast with Marysvale* at its mouth. The creek draining through the canyon is Pine Creek. An early synonym for Bullion Canyon was Pine Canyon. The name came from the gold, silver, lead, and copper which was extracted from the canyon mines.
S25,T27S,R4W,SLM (at mouth). 175, 242.

BULLION CITY* (Piute) is five miles up Bullion Canyon west southwest of Marysvale*. It was established in 1868 and for a time was the county seat. In the spring of 1869 some two hundred miners came to Marysvale and settled near the mine in Pine Canyon (Bullion Canyon). The place then became known as Bullion City. When the ore dropped

in value the community was abandoned and became a ghost town.
S5,T28S,R4W,SLM; 7,945' (2,422m). 27, 89, 242, 360, 516, 586(v1).

BULLIONVILLE* (Tooele) was once a small silver mining camp established in 1870 at the north end of the Dugway Range. It was soon abandoned because of a lack of water and is now a ghost town. The name reflects dreams of vast fortunes that never materialized.
ca. S34,T9S,R12W,SLM; 5,000' (1,524m). 516.

BULLIONVILLE* (Uintah) was in the eastern Uinta Mountains at the head of Big Brush Creek and the mouth of Government Creek. In 1882 prospectors found what they believed to be a rich strike. Cabins were built and the place was named Bullionville in anticipation of great riches. Very little ore was found and today it is a ghost town.
S28,T1S,R21E,SLM; 8,525' (2,598m). 89, 100(v17), 516, 542.

BULLOCK DRAW (Emery) originates on the San Rafael Swell west of the Head of Sinbad. It drains northwest into Coal Wash, South Fork. The draw was fenced and used at certain times to separate the bulls from the rest of the herds.
S16,T22S,R10E,SLM. 193.

BUMBLEBEE CANYON (Iron) originates on the northeast slopes of the Harmony Mountains near the Bumblebee Spring. It drains south into Mare Hollow. See Bumblebee Spring for name source.
S26,35,T37S,R13W,SLM. 360. D.L. 6102.

BUMBLEBEE LAKE (Iron) is near Bumblebee Spring.

BUMBLEBEE MOUNTAIN (Iron) is west of Antelope Peak, the south end of Wah Wah Valley, and northwest of the Blue Mountains.
S32,T29S,R14W,SLM; 6,625' (2,019m). 360.

BUMBLEBEE SPRING (Iron) is on the northeast slopes of Bumblebee Mountain. It is common in arid country when various types of wildlife congregate near water; this could be magpies, jays, or even a hornet nest. At this spring bees and wasps were especially prevalent; hence the name, which was first used casually but eventually took hold.
S32,T29S,R14W,SLM; 6,270' (1,911m). 360.

BUNCETOWN* (Sanpete). See Sterling*.

BUNCEVILLE* (Sanpete). See Sterling*.

BUNCHGRASS CREEK (Cache) originates on the Bear River Range west of the Logan River on the eastern slopes of Mount Magog. The creek drains into the Logan River. Bunchgrass and wheatgrass is plentiful along the creek, probably from reseeding practices.

BUNKER CREEK (Iron, Garfield) originates six miles northeast of Cedar Breaks National Monument and drains east into Spring Creek and Panguitch Lake. It was named for John Bunker, who ran his livestock in the area.
S5,T36S,R8W,SLM to S7,T36S,R7W,SLM. 567.

BUNTING CANYON (Kane) originates in the Vermillion Cliffs, three miles west southwest of Kanab*. It drains east northeast into Kanab Creek and is named after James L. Bunting.
S28,29,30,T43S,R6W,SLM. 100(v17).

BURBANK* (Millard) was an early Mormon farming community established in the 1870s in Snake River Valley south of Pruess Lake. An early post office was nearby at the Dearden Ranch. The community was named for Margie Burbank Clay, wife of Judge E. W. Clay. A combination of outlaws, cattle and horse rustlers, in addition to uncertain water, caused the abandonment of the community in the 1880s.
S36,T23S,R20W,SLM; 5,420' (1,652m). 100 (v17), 516.

BURBANK HILLS (**Millard**) are east of Garrison*, Lake Pruess, and Lake Creek. See Burbank* for name source.
T22,23S,R18W,SLM; 7,815' (2,382m).

BURCH CREEK (**Weber**) originates on the southern slopes of Mount Ogden and drains into the Weber River. Two brothers, Robert and James Burch, first settled on the creek and for a while the settlement was called Burch Creek*. Today it is part of South Ogden*.
S6,T5N,R1E,SLM to S6,T5N,R1W,SLM. 274, 567.

BURCH CREEK* (**Weber**). See South Ogden* (Weber).

BURG ON THE BEAR* (**Box Elder**). See Corinne* (Box Elder).

BURKHOLDER DRAW (**Grand**) originates nine miles east of Moab* on the Porcupine Rim of Castle Valley. It drains west into Mill Creek, North Fork. Joseph Burkholder was a prospector there in 1879.
S1,T26S,R23E,SLM to S6,T26S,R23E,SLM. 146.

BURMEISTER* (**Tooele**). See Burmester* (Tooele).

BURMESTER* (**Tooele**) was a station on the Western Pacific Railroad on the south shore of Great Salt Lake. It was first known as Grants Station*, but in 1906 it was renamed after Frank T. Burmester, a landowner. He later sold his land to the Morton Salt Company. Variant: Burmeister*.
S31,T1S,R5W,SLM; 4,217' (1,285m). 567.

BURNING HILLS (**Kane**) have a northwest-southeast orientation on the southwest slopes of the Kaiparowits Plateau between Last Chance Creek and Navajo Canyon. The Smokey Mountains are close by. This region has had problems with smoldering coal deposits and occasional underground rumblings are reported. Also, possibly due to the

above, the landscape is hot and dry, which is accentuated by a burning sun on the reddish soil.
T40-41S,R5E,SLM; 5,200'-5,600' (1,585m-1,707m). 578.

BURNT FLAT (**Beaver**) is on Circleville Mountain at the south end of the Tushar Mountains. Burnt Flat was named after a range fire damaged the area.
S3,T30S,R5W,SLM; 9,850' (3,002m).

BURNT FORK CREEK (**Summit**) originates in the north central Uinta Mountains at Burnt Fork Lake, and drains north into Wyoming. It is recorded that "Burns" was misinterpreted as "Burnt." A Burns family owned and operated a ranch in this area.
S16,T3N,R17E,SLM (in Utah). 172.

BURNT FORK LAKE (**Summit**) is at the head of Burnt Fork Creek. See Burnt Fork Creek for name source.
10,640' (3,243m).

BURNT HOLLOW (**Garfield**) originates at Burnt Spring and drains northwest into Circle Valley. See Burnt Spring.
S26,T31S,R3W,SLM to S5,T31S,R3W,SLM.

BURNT SPRING (**Garfield**) is at the head of Burnt Hollow, eight miles southeast of Circleville*. This was once a thickly timbered area of blue spruce and quaking aspen, which was destroyed by fire.
S26,T31S,R3W,SLM. 567.

BURR CANYON (**Garfield**) is that part of the Burr Trail which cuts through the Waterpocket Fold east of Wagon Box Mesa. See Burr Trail for further details and name origin.
S16,T34S,R8E,SLM.

BURR CREEK (**Sevier**) originates at the Burr Springs on the eastern slopes of Cove Mountain. The creek drains southeast, passing north of Burrville* into Otter Creek. It was named for the Charles C. Burr family, who were the

original settlers of Burrville. See Burr Top and Burr Trail.
S27,T25S,R1W,SLM to S12,T26S,R1W,SLM.

BURR DESERT (Wayne) is a vast grazing area northeast of the Henry Mountains between the Dirty Devil River and Bull Mountain of the Henry Mountains. See Burr Top and Burr Trail.
T30S,R13E,SLM.

BURR POINT (Wayne) is a narrow section of land in the southwest corner of the Burr Desert. See Burr Top and Burr Trail.
SW¼,T30S,R13E,SLM.

BURR SPRING (Sevier) is three miles northeast of Burrville* at the head of Burr Creek. See Burrville for name source.
S27,T25S,R1W,SLM; 7,520' (2,292m).

BURR TOP (Garfield) is a grazing area on the Aquarius Plateau between Jacobs Reservoir and McGath Lake. This area was named after John Atlantic Burr, one of four sons of the Charles Clark Burr family who initially settled Burrville*. John's parents emigrated from Scotland to Utah via an ocean route around Cape Horn, then travelled overland from California. John was born during the voyage—hence the middle name. There are several geographic names honoring John A. Burr, but the best known is probably the Burr Trail. John's death was as tragic as his life was dramatic. He died on the open range while trying to relieve a severe prostate and bladder problem with a piece of bailing wire.
10,000'-10,400' (3,048m-3,170m). 360, 578, 602.

BURR TRAIL (Garfield) was developed by John Atlantic Burr to move his livestock between winter and summer grazing and to market. The two general terminals of the trail were Boulder* and Grass Valley near Koosharem*, and Angle*, Hall's Crossing*, and the Bullfrog Marina at the southeast end.

The trail passes through what is some of the wildest and least traveled country in Utah. See Burr Top and The Muley Twist.

BURRVILLE* (Sevier) is on Burr Creek west of the junction of U-24 and U-62. As far back as 1872 attempts were made to establish homesteads and ranches in this Grass Valley region. These endeavors failed because of Indian problems, isolation, and severe winters. In 1875 the Charles C. Burr family settled there and the site was named after them. See Burr Trail.
S12,T26W,R1W,SLM; 7,000' (2,134m).

BURTNER* (Millard). See Delta*.

BUSBY CANYON (Tooele) originates on the northeast slopes of Dutch Mountain, five miles north of Gold Hill. It drains northeast onto the mud flats of the Great Salt Lake Desert. MRN
T7S,R17,18W,SLM.

BUTCH CASSIDY DRAW (Garfield) originates on Horse Bench and drains south southwest into Red Creek, six miles east of US-89 and the Bryce Canyon Junction. It was named for Robert LeRoy Parker (Butch Cassidy), outlaw and leader of the Wild Bunch outlaws.
S7,T35S,R4W,SLM to S26,T35S,R4½W,SLM. 25.

BUTCHERVILLE* (Salt Lake). See Federal Heights* (Salt Lake).

BUTLER CANYON (Garfield) originates south of the Burr Desert, Poison Spring Canyon, and west of the Dirty Devil River. It drains south into North Wash. Monte Butler utilized this area for several years. Butler has been given credit for several canyon and wash names in the region. He was an outlaw who occasionally led the Wild Bunch during the 1890s.
SW¼,T32S,R13E,SLM (at mouth). 25, 475.

BUTLER CANYON (**Garfield**) originates east of Beef Basin, ten miles south of The Needles in Canyonlands National Park. It drains north northwest into Chesler Canyon. See Butler Canyon above for name origin.
T32S,R19E,SLM to S36,T30½S,R18E,SLM.

BUTLER FLAT (**San Juan**) is near the mouth of Butler Wash in Canyonlands National Park. One mile east is Chesler Park. See Butler Canyon for name source.

BUTLER WASH (**Garfield**) originates on the eastern slopes of the Henry Mountains south of Bull Mountain and drains east into Poison Spring Canyon. See Butler Canyon for name source.
S19,T31S,R11E,SLM to S3,T31S,R12E,SLM.

BUTLER WASH (**San Juan**) originates southwest of the Abajo Mountains, east of Comb Ridge and drains south into the San Juan River. This area was named for John Butler of the Hole-in-the-Rock expedition who was one of the first white scouts to enter the San Juan country.
S7,T37S,R21E,SLM to S12,T41S,R20E,SLM. 100(v17), 359.

BUTLER WASH (**San Juan**) originates near the southeast side of Beef Basin in Canyonlands National Park. It drains north northeast into Chesler Canyon at the north end of Butler Flats. See Butler Canyon for name source.
S36,T30½S,R18E,SLM (at mouth).

BUTLERVILLE* (**Garfield**) was a short-lived settlement located south of Henrieville*. The predominant settlers were Butlers.

BUTLERVILLE* (**Salt Lake**) was located around Twenty-seventh East and Seventieth South, southeast of Salt Lake City*. It was settled in 1877 by the five Butler brothers and their families. In 1901, the town was named after Alva Butler. He was the first bishop of the new Butlerville Ward of the Mormon Church. The community grew up around a paper mill, built in 1861, which supplied paper for the Deseret News. The settlers also harvested lumber from nearby Big Cottonwood Canyon. It was humorously suggested that with five Butlers and only four McGies as the first settlers, the voting favored the name Butlerville. Today the expanded area is called Cottonwood Heights*.
S22,27,T2S,R1E,SLM; 4,800' (1,463m). 82, 252, 288, 360.

BUTTE OF THE CROSS (**Wayne**) is two miles west of the Anderson and Unknown bottoms of the Green River. The formation was named by the men of the Powell river expedition because when they first saw the feature from a distance, they thought it was a single butte appearing in the form of a cross. Closer examination proved it to be two buttes aligned to form the cross.
ca. S16,T28S,R17E,SLM; 5,638' (1,718m). 420, 422, 496.

BUTTERFIELD* (**Salt Lake**). See Herriman* (Salt Lake).

BUTTERFIELD CANYON (**Salt Lake**) originates at the south end of the Oquirrh Mountains northeast of the Butterfield Peaks. It drains northeast. Thomas Butterfield, one of the first settlers of nearby Herriman*, built the road up Butterfield Canyon.
S11,T4S,R3W,SLM to S32,T2S,R3W,SLM. 100(v17), 252, 360.

BUTTERFIELD PEAKS (**Salt Lake, Tooele, Utah**) is on the county line at the head of Butterfield Canyon, left-hand fork. See Butterfield Canyon.
S15,16,T4S,R3W,SLM; 9,370' (2,856m).

BUTTERFLY LAKE (**Duchesne**) is at the west end of the Uinta Mountains on Hayden Pass. Hayden Peak is two miles northeast. The lake has the general shape of a butterfly.
S24,T4N,R9E,SLM; 10,340' (3,152m). 298.

BUYSVILLE* (**Wasatch**) was a small settlement between Daniels* and Charleston*. It was named for Edward Buys, an early settler. The settlement was later absorbed into both Daniels and Charleston.
S13,T4S,R4E,SLM; 5,540' (1,689m). 377, 567.

- C -

C CANYON (Carbon) originates on the summit east of Indianola*. It is a gigantic C-shaped canyon that drains northwest into Fish Creek, west of the Scofield Reservoir.
S10,T12S,R5E,SLM.

CABLE MOUNTAIN (Washington) is in Zion National Park, six miles up the canyon from park headquarters. In 1900 David Flanigan devised and built a cable system for dropping lumber from the top of the mountain to the canyon bottom. Flanigan got the idea from a similar system developed at Shunesburg*. This system used cables and wheels to transport mail from the top of the cliffs to the valley bottom, thus avoiding the arduous trek by mule or on foot up and down the old Wiggle Trail.
6,496' (1,980m). 78, 154, 311, 600.

CABBAGE VALLEY (Iron) is eight miles southeast of Cedar City* near the head of Shurtz Canyon. It was named for the small wild cabbage plants that grow in the valley. The plant blooms in the spring and livestock seem to favor it over other plants.
S14,T37S,R11W,SLM; 7,600' (2,316m). 567.

CACHE COUNTY was created in 1856 in the north central part of the state. Early trappers "cached" furs and supplies in Cache Valley, which was the name given to the county. It is bordered by Rich, Morgan, and Box Elder counties. See Cache Valley.

CACHE JUNCTION* (Cache) is ten miles northwest of Mendon*, near a spring. The site was initially settled by Sylvanus Collett in 1867. The town was established in 1890 as an outgrowth of Benson* and it became an important railroad junction on the Union Pacific Railroad. Originally this area was divided into Petersboro No. 1* and No. 2*. No. 2 became Cache Junction. The railroad no longer uses the stop but a cafe and a few local residents still remain.
S30,T13N,R1W,SLM; 4,448' (1,356m). 360, 449, 542, 567.

CACHE VALLEY (Cache) is a large, beautiful, graben valley in the north central part of the state. The well-known communities of Logan*, Hyrum*, Wellsville*, and Smithfield* are located there. Maughns Fort* was the first settlement in the valley. The valley was also a popular rendezvous site for mountain men and Indians. Willow Valley was its first name for the valley; the name was used until the summer of 1826 when a trapper was killed in a cave-in. A reliable account records that this trapper was employed by Smith, Jackson, and Sublette of the Rocky Mountain Fur Company. He was accidentally buried alive while excavating a cave intended for the safe storage (cache) of furs. The body was left where it was buried. The valley was also referred to as Logan's Hole in memory of Ephraim Logan who was killed by Indians near Jackson*, Wyoming, around 1826. Ephraim's grave is located up nearby Logan Canyon.
T10-14N,R1E,R1W,SLM. 449, 546, 578.

CACTUS POND (Beaver) is north of the mouth of Black Canyon that drains out of the Black Mountains toward Minersville*. Cacti are common around the pond.
S36,T29S,R11W,SLM; 5,070' (1,545m).

CAINEVILLE* (Wayne) was on the left bank of the Fremont River, sixty-five miles southeast of Loa*. In 1882, the

Mormon Church sent Elijah Cutler Behunin to open this area for settlement. He was the first man to take a wagon through Capitol Wash (now known as Capitol Reef Gorge) in the Capitol Reef National Park. The town he established was named to honor John T. Caine, Utah Territory's representative to Congress. Periodic flooding caused the people to abandon their homes in Caineville and much arable land was lost. Erosion and abandonment eventually reverted this area to open range and ranch land. Today, much of this area is again under cultivation because of improved irrigation techniques. Presently there are no substantial settlements along this stretch of the river, and Caineville could best be called a ghost town. S35,T29S,R8E,SLM; 4,750' (1,448m). 89, 97, 100(v13), 288, 485, 546, 567.

CAJON MESA (San Juan) is west of the Colorado border where the Hovenweep National Monument of the Square Tower Group Ruins is also located. "Cajon" is Spanish for box or a ravine—a canyon. T39S,R25E,SLM.

CALDER LAKE (Salt Lake). See Nibley Lake (Salt Lake).

CALDER POND (Uintah). See Matt Warner Reservoir (Uintah).

CALF CANYON (Garfield) originates in the northwest section of the Kaiparowits Plateau and drains northwest into Alvey Wash. Early stockmen kept their weaner calves separate from the cows in the canyon. S17,T36S,R3E,SLM to S1,T36S,R2E,SLM. 12.

CALF CANYON (San Juan) originates west of the Abajo Mountains between Ruin Canyon and Beef Basin Wash. It drains northwest into Beef Basin Wash near the mouth of Ruin Canyon. During roundup, when the cattle were being sorted, branded, or trailed out to market, the calves were held in this canyon. The

bulls were held in Bull Valley northwest of Beef Basin. T33S,R18,19E,SLM.

CALF CREEK (Garfield) originates west of Boulder* and one mile west of New Home Bench on the southern slopes of the Aquarius Plateau. It drains south through the Calf Creek Falls into the Escalante River. Weaner calves were held in the canyon. The canyon has one of the more beautiful waterfalls in the state. S4,T34S,R4E,SLM to S12,T35S,R4E,SLM. 12, 602.

CALICO PEAK (Kane) is one and one-quarter miles west of the old ghost town of Paria*. The nearby multiple-colored formations suggested the name. S12,T41S,R2W,SLM; 5,881' (1,793m).

CALLAO* (Juab) is west of Fish Springs* and north of Trout Creek*, on the old Overland and Pony Express route south of the Gold Hill Mining area. In 1860, the Pony Express established a station known as Willow Springs* at a time when gold was discovered in nearby Gold Hill*. In 1870, E. W. Tripp, his wife, and small son established a ranch there. In 1895 the name was changed to Callao because there were several places named Willow Springs that were previously established in the territory. An old prospector who had been to Peru imagined a resemblance to Callao, Peru, and suggested the name. For a while the old Lincoln Highway passed through Callao. Today about twenty-seven residents live in Callao and it is the last town in Utah to use a one-room schoolhouse. T11S,R17W,SLM. 89, 314, 347, 360, 498, 516, 542.

CALLS FORT* (Box Elder) was seven miles north of Brigham City* on U-89 at the base of the Wellsville Mountains. It was settled in 1854 and named after Anson V. Call, who built the local fort. Calls Fort was on the northern frontier

of the territory for many years during this early period. In 1855 Thomas Harper and his family arrived. Call hired Harper as manager of his farm and in 1906 Harper's name was given to the settlement. He also became the Mormon bishop in that area. In 1871 the precinct was divided: the south side became Lake Side* and the north side was Calls Fort. Today the entire vicinity is listed as Calls Fort.
S15,T10N,R2W,SLM; 4,282' (1,305m). 27, 100(v17), 139, 275, 360, 567.

CALLS FORT CANYON (Box Elder) originates on the southern slopes of Box Elder Peak, three and one-half miles east of Honeyville*. It drains southwest into Bear Valley at Calls Fort*.
S1,T10N,R2W,SLM to S11,T10N,R2W,SLM.

CALLS SETTLEMENT* (Davis). See Bountiful*.

CAMELBACK RIDGE (Tooele) is in the Dugway Proving Grounds military area and named for its distinctive profile.
S15,22,26,T8S,R10W,SLM; 5,501' (1,677m).

CAMERON* (Carbon). See Royal* (Carbon).

CAMERON WASH (Garfield) originates at Dry Lake five miles southeast of Panguitch Lake. It drains north into Rock Canyon and was named for John Cameron, an early stockman there.
S18,19,30,T36S,R6W,SLM.

CAMP CREEK (Iron) originates on the northern slopes of Horse Ranch Mountain, four miles southeast of Kanarraville*. It drains northwest into Kanarra Creek and was a favorite camping spot.
S18,T38S,R12W,SLM to S30,T38S,R12W, SLM. 567.

CAMP FLAT (Garfield) is near the head of Carcass Canyon midway between Alvey Wash and Right Hand Collett Canyon. It was a popular camping area

for early stockmen.
S8,17,T37S,R3E,SLM; 7,081' (2,158m). 12.

CAMP FLOYD* (Utah) was established on July 4, 1858, by Brigadier General Albert Sidney Johnston. He was in command of the Utah Expeditionary Forces composed of approximately three thousand men, freighters, camp workers, and numerous camp followers. Colonel Phillip St. George Cooke succeeded Johnston, and on February 6, 1861, changed the name to Fort Crittenden*, in honor of Senator J. J. Crittenden of Kentucky. He made the change because of the strong anti-union tendencies that were then openly manifested by John B. Floyd, the U.S. Secretary of War. The camp was abandoned in July 1861 as a result of the Civil War. Today it is a military cemetery and a state historical site located one-half mile south southwest of Fairfield* on U-73. See Fairfield*.
S32,T6S,R1W,SLM; 4,900' (1,494m). 27, 89, 270, 360, 384, 516, 546.

CAMP RAWLINS* (Utah). See Fort Rawlins* (Utah).

CAMP RELIEF* (Tooele). See Stockton* (Tooele).

CAMP SPRING* (Garfield) is a spring in the upper area of Right Hand Collett Canyon. It was a favorite camping spot for stockmen.
S36,T37S,R2E,SLM; 6,190' (1,887m). 12.

CAMP WILLIAMS* (Salt Lake) is headquarters of the Utah National Guard near the Jordan Narrows, one mile southwest of the Point of the Mountain. The camp was established by President Woodrow Wilson in 1914-15 as a military reservation. It was named in 1928 for Brigadier General W. G. Williams.
S26,T4S,R1W,SLM; 4,800' (1,463m). 360.

CAMPBELL CANYON (Garfield) originates in Bryce Canyon National Park and drains east through Tropic* into the Paria River. The canyon was named after

Ralph Allen Campbell, who arrived in Tropic in the summer of 1897. He held squatters rights from Tropic to the mouth of the canyon.
S1,T37S,R3W,SLM (at mouth). 530.

CANAAN CREEK (Garfield) originates on the eastern slopes of Canaan Peak at the north end of the Kaiparowits Plateau. It drains northeast to form the headwaters of Coal Bed Canyon. See Canaan Mountain for name source.
S9,T37S,R1E,SLM to S3,T36S,R2E,SLM. D.L. 6504.

CANAAN MOUNTAIN (Garfield) is a cattle range southwest of Escalante* at the north end of the Kaiparowits Plateau. It was named by A. H. Thompson of the Powell surveys for the biblical name Canaan because it seemed so fruitful and desirable. The word means "low mountain" in Hebrew. In 1870 the Mormon Church owned and operated a large co-op cattle ranch there, known as the Canaan Ranch.
S9,T37S,R1E,SLM; 9,293' (2,833m). 12, 100 (v17), 602.

CANAAN PEAK (Garfield) is the high point of Canaan Mountain.
D.L. 6504.

CANAL CANYON (Sanpete) originates southeast of Spring City* at the Big Horseshoe and drains northwest into Sanpete Valley. See Canal Creek.
S36,T16S,R4E,SLM to S15,T16S,R4E,SLM.

CANAL CREEK (Sanpete) drains through Canal Canyon. The water is used extensively for irrigation.
508.

CANAL CREEK* (Sanpete). See Chester*.

CANE SPRING (Garfield) is on Hansen Creek in the Cane Spring Desert, seven miles north of Bullfrog Basin and one mile east of U-276. Cattails (Typha) growing around the spring suggested the name.
4,043' (1,232m).

CANE SPRING DESERT (Garfield) is south southwest of Mount Ellsworth in the Henry Mountains. It received its name from nearby Cane Spring.
T36,37S,R11E,SLM; 4,000'-5,000' (1,219m-1,327m).

CANNON* (Cache). See Cornish*.

CANNON* (Salt Lake) was an early settlement on the west bank of the Jordan River between Fifth and Twelfth South. It was eventually absorbed into Salt Lake City*. George Q. Cannon was an early settler and Mormon church official there.
S2,11,T1S,R1W,SLM; 4,225' (1,288m). 567.

CANNONVILLE* (Garfield) is on U-54 five miles south southeast of Tropic* and one-half mile west of Henrieville*. It was established in 1874 by James L. Thompson and others with their families. An early name was Clifton* in recognition of the surrounding cliffs and rugged terrain. The name was changed to Cannonville for George Q. Cannon, a Mormon church official. It was humorously called Gunshot* because it was not large enough to be a cannon. See also Clifton* and Georgetown*.
S19,30,T37S,R2W,SLM; 6,000' (1,829m). 89, 145, 288, 360, 542, 567.

CANYON CREEK (Salt Lake). See Parleys Canyon.

CANYON CREEK (Salt Lake). See Emigration Creek (Canyon).

CANYONLANDS NATIONAL PARK is an extensive park that has the confluence of the Green and the Colorado rivers at its center. It was established in 1964. The numerous deep canyons in this wilderness region suggest the name.

CAPITOL GORGE (Wayne) is the branch of the Fremont River Gorge that

drains Capitol Reef. The gorge drains into Pleasant Creek near Notom*. In pioneer (pre-bridge) days, travellers taking the Fremont River Gorge were forced to cross and recross the river even though it periodically flooded. Capitol Gorge was an alternate route taken to avoid the Fremont River Gorge. Butch Cassidy and the Wild Bunch used the Capitol Gorge many times in their travels. Today a modern highway and several bridges have tamed the Fremont River and the unpredictable Capitol Gorge is now just a hikers' paradise. See Capitol Reef National Park for name source.
T30S,R7E,SLM. 25, 303, 546.

CAPITOL HILL* (Salt Lake) is a section of Salt Lake City* at the north end of State Street where the state capitol was built. It was first named Prospect Hill then Arsenal Hill because military explosive magazines were located there. In 1876 a massive explosion destroyed the military complex and today the capitol building beautifies the spot.
S31,T1N,R1E,SLM; 4,500' (1,372m). 567.

CAPITOL REEF NATIONAL MONUMENT (Wayne). See Capitol Reef National Park.

CAPITOL REEF NATIONAL PARK (Wayne) extends along the Waterpocket Fold from near Lake Powell's Bullfrog Marina to Cathedral Valley. U-24 bisects the park. The pioneer town of Fruita* is near the center of the park. Today a small one-room schoolhouse is all that remains of that town. The events leading to the area's national park status began when a small parcel of the land was set aside as a state park in 1925-26 and was included in what was known as The Wayne Wonderland. In 1937 it became a national monument. Then, in 1971 the area was greatly expanded and designated a national park. Two factors influenced the name. The word "capitol" was inspired by the massive, heavily eroded, rounded rock formations that resemble the domes of federal buildings. The geologic upthrust, which creates the scenic attraction of the area, has been called a reef. The word "reef" was coined by sailors in the Australian gold rush to describe the gold bearing ridges near Bendigo, Australia, which resembled rock or coral barriers in the seas. The Indian ruins and the picturesque scenery of this area inspired novelist Zane Grey, who wrote several books about the area. In addition, the Wild Bunch, Butch Cassidy, and other well-known outlaws frequently hid out in or passed through the region in earlier days.
T29S,R6E,SLM. 25, 314, 360, 496, 546.

CAPITOL WASH (Wayne) originates on the southeast slopes of Miners Mountain. It drains east through the Capitol Gorge.
T30S,R7E,SLM.

CARBON* (Carbon). See Heiner* (Carbon).

CARBON COUNTY was established in 1892 and named for the large deposits of coal in the area. Price City* is the county seat and US-6 and U-10 are the principle highways passing through the county. The Green River serves as the county border on the east side.
6, 314, 360.

CARBONATE GULCH (Beaver) originates in the southeast part of the San Francisco Mountains and drains southeast into Big Wash. It was named for the carbonate mine that was located in the gulch around 1872.
S7,17,T27S,R12W,SLM. 125.

CARBONVILLE* (Carbon) is a small, recently developed community on US-6,50, two and one-half miles northwest of Price*. It received its name from the coal-mining industry.
S6,7,T14S,R10E,SLM; 5,650' (1,722m). 578.

CARCASS* (Wayne). See Grover* (Wayne).

CARCASS CANYON (**Garfield**) originates at the north end of the Kaiparowits Plateau, twelve miles south of Escalante*. It drains southeast into the Right Hand Collett Canyon at the Straight Cliffs. Livestock sometimes get trapped and die in the wash while trying to get to the water.
S4,T37S,R3E,SLM (head of wash). 12.

CARCASS CREEK (**Wayne**) originates on the northeast slopes of Boulder Mountain. It drains north northeast to join Rock Creek and the Fremont River southeast of Torrey*. Livestock are frequently lost along this creek because the creek bed is narrow and rocky and has steep sides. Animals that go down to drink sometimes slip and fall and are unable to get out.
S30,T30S,R5E,SLM to S26,T29S,R5E,SLM. 485.

CARCASS WASH (**Kane**) originates three miles south of Dance Hall Rock at the junction of the right and left forks of Carcass Wash, and two miles east of Sooner Bench. It drains northeast into Fortymile Gulch.
T40S,R8E,SLM. 12, 359, 546, 602.

CARD CANYON (**Cache**) originates in the Bear River Mountains, twelve miles east of Logan*. It drains northeast into the Logan River at Card Campground and was named for Charles Card, an early pioneer in the area.
567.

CARL LAKE (**Duchesne**) is on the southern slopes of East Grandaddy Mountain at the west end of the Uinta Mountains. Two miles northwest is Grandaddy Lake. Carl Wilcken placed his name on a board while working trails in the area, then left the board at the unnamed lake. His name was accepted.
S10,T2N,R8W,USM; 10,080' (3,072m). 594.

CARLISLE* (**San Juan**) is six miles north of Monticello*. It was first settled in the 1880s by George Washington Johnson. In 1898 the name was changed from Indian Creek* to Carlisle when Harold and Edmund S. Carlisle gained control of the property. The brothers invested $720,000 in British capital for the development of a ranch in Utah Territory. They established their headquarters at the old Double Cabin Springs where a post office was granted. The Carlisle brothers also had sizable holdings in New Mexico and Kansas.
S36,T32S,R23E,SLM; 6,950' (2,118m). 406, 409, 475.

CARMEL JUNCTION* (**Washington**). See Mount Carmel Junction* (Washington).

CAROLINE BRIDGE (**San Juan**). See Natural Bridges National Monument (San Juan).

CAROLYN LAKE (**Duchesne**) is in the southwest section of the Uinta Mountains between Four Lakes and Naturalist Basin. It was named for the daughter of Ralph Giles, a U.S. Forest Service employee.
S33,T3N,R8W,USM; 10,500' (3,200). 578, 594.

CARPENTER BASIN (**Grand**) is on the southwest slopes of the La Sal Mountains at the head of Cottonwood Creek. The basin drains into Muleshoe Canyon. A Mr. Carpenter homesteaded there.
S9,T28S,R24E,SLM. 578.

CARRINGTON ISLAND (**Tooele**) is an oval-shaped island in the Great Salt Lake with a varying size and shape because of changing water levels. The island is approximately two miles long and is north of Stansbury Island and west of Antelope Island. The island was named by Captain Howard Stansbury for Albert Carrington, a Mormon, who acted as an assistant on the survey.
T3N,R7W,SLM; 4,727' (1,441m). 100(v2), 314, 360, 492, 546.

CARROT LAKE (Duchesne) is in the south central Uinta Mountains, one and one-half miles north northeast of Mount Emmons. There is a heavy growth of wild carrot around the lake.
10,830' (3,301m).

CARSON* (Emery). See Elmo* (Emery).

CARSON COUNTY no longer exists. When Nevada Territory was created by Congress in 1861, this county, formerly a part of Utah Territory, was eliminated. It was named for Kit Carson, famous scout, trapper, and frontiersman.
6, 542.

CART CREEK (Daggett) originates in the eastern Uinta Mountains, three and one-half miles northeast of East Park Reservoir. It drains southeast then north, entering Flaming Gorge Reservoir near the dam. In earlier days, large two-wheeled carts were used for logging this area. Major Powell named the creek Francis Creek for Francis Bishop, a cartographer for his second expedition. Francis's name is still applied to a fork of Cart Creek. See Francis Creek.
T1N,R21E,SLM to S21,T2N,R22E,SLM. 172, 360, 555(v35).

CARTER CREEK (Daggett) originates at Browne Lake, seven miles north northeast of Leidy Peak on the northeast slopes of the Uinta Mountains. It drains east, entering the Flaming Gorge Reservoir at Red Canyon. Judge Carter built a cabin and fireplace for freighters at a campsite where Beaver Creek enters Carter Creek. Major Powell named this creek Kettle Creek but the name did not catch on. See also Carter Road.
S32,T2N,R19E,SLM (to Red Canyon). 172, 578.

CARTER ROAD (Daggett, Summit, Uintah) was a road running from Carter Station* in Wyoming, through Lone Tree* to Fort Bridger*, Wyoming. It crossed Henrys Fork seven times, passing through Clay Basin, the upper end of Browns Park, Linwood*, and Manila*. From there the road passed over the Uinta Mountains to Fort Thornburg* at the mouth of Ashley Creek, six and one-half miles northwest of Vernal*. The road was an early Indian trail that the whites began using in 1865 when it was developed by Major Noyes Baldwin, the commissary officer of Fort Bridger. The road was first developed because of Indian troubles in Colorado where the Indian agent, Meeker, and Major Thornburg(h) had recently been killed in a series of conflicts. The road was built by, and named for, Judge William Alexander Carter, Sr., who was heavily involved in business dealings at Fort Bridger where he was a postmaster, trader, and settler. His son, William A. Carter, Jr., who was born at the fort, took over the responsibilities of the road after his father died of pneumonia while working on the road. Fort Thornburg, the southern terminal, was abandoned in 1884.
172, 555(35/3).

CARTERVILLE* (Utah) at Eighth to Twelfth South along Tenth East has been incorporated into Orem City*. It was first settled in May 1875 by John and Jane Carter. They were soon followed by additional Carters and other settlers.
S24,T6S,R2E,SLM; 4,750' (1,448m). 270, 394.

CASA DEL ECO MESA (San Juan) is two miles south of the San Juan River and five miles southwest of Montezuma Creek*. The name is Spanish and means Home of Echo Mesa.
T41S,R22E,SLM; 5,000' (1,524m). D.L. 6103.

CASCADE MOUNTAIN (Utah) is part of the Wasatch Range. It is a rugged, precipitous mountain with numerous small cascades and waterfalls on its flanks. The mountain faces the Provo Valley between Provo Canyon and Rock Canyons. Bridal Veil Falls is on the

northern slope and is thought to be the most scenic waterfall.
T6S,R3E,SLM; 10,908' (3,338m).

CASCADE SPRING (Wasatch) is at the mouth of Bear Canyon on Deer Creek, three and one-half miles northwest of lower Deer Creek Reservoir. Today it is a state park, remarkable for the cascading waters from fast-flowing springs that splash down over fern- and flower-covered rocks. Walks, resting places, bridges, and nature trails enhance the park.
S24,T4S,R3E,SLM; 6,263' (1,909m).

CASS CREEK (Garfield) originates on the southern slopes of Cass Creek Peak north of Mount Hillers, in the Henry Mountains. It drains into Pennell Creek and is named for Cass Hite, who prospected in the area. He established the small community of Hite*, which is now covered by the waters of Lake Powell. Cass Hite is given credit for being the first white man to discover the natural bridges of Natural Bridges National Monument. See Hite* and Ticaboo Creek.
S31,32,T33S,R11E,SLM.

CASS CREEK PEAK (Garfield) is at the head of Cass Creek in the Henry Mountains, two miles northwest of Mount Hillers. See Cass Creek.
S28,T33S,R11E,SLM; 9,428' (2,874m).

CASSIDY ARCH (Wayne) is in Capitol Reef National Park north of the mouth of the Grand Wash. It was named for Butch Cassidy (Robert L. Parker) of the Wild Bunch, who often passed this way in the late 1800s and early 1900s.
S26,T29S,R6E,SLM.

CASTILLA SPRINGS* (Utah) is three miles up from the mouth of Spanish Fork Canyon. Today the warm water sulphur springs form a swampy area alongside US-6,50. In the 1890s the springs were the site of a popular resort including hotel, cabins, bathing, and other recreational facilities. The resort was built in 1891 but was destroyed by fire in 1942 and never rebuilt. The springs were named by early travellers along this part of the Old Spanish Trail after the province of Castile in Spain.
S18,T9S,R4E,SLM; 4,920' (1,500m). 270, 314, 360.

CASTLE. There are many castle names in Utah because much of the terrain, especially in southern Utah, simulates castles, cathedrals with columns, and turrets. All of these features have, in various ways, a general castellated appearance. No attempt has been made to list them all.

CASTLE* (Garfield) was in Castle Valley between Cedar Breaks and Panguitch Lake. It was an early settlement established along the tributaries of the upper Sevier River, near the divide where the headwaters of the south-draining Virgin River originates. The area was pioneered in 1872 by Meltiar Hatch and his two wives, Parmelia Snyder Hatch and Mary Ann Ellis Hatch. The family operated a cattle ranch. The town was named for the spectacular castle-like topography of the surrounding cliffs. See also Hatch*.
S21,22,27,T36S,R8W,SLM; 9,600' (2,926m). 145, 292.

CASTLE CLIFF WASH (Washington) originates at Jarvis Peak west of St. George*. It drains southwest out of the Beaver Dam Mountains. Old US-91 followed this wash down through the Joshua Tree Forest, as it leaves the southwest corner of Utah to enter Arizona. The Old Spanish Trail also followed this route. At the base of the wash is Castle Cliff from which the name is taken.
T42,43S,R18W,SLM.

CASTLE CREEK (Grand) originates on Manns Peak at the junction of Dry Fork and the west fork of Mill Creek. It drains northwest through Castle Valley (from

68

which it receives its name) into the Colorado River.
S26,T26S,R24E,SLM to S35,T24S,R22E, SLM.

CASTLE CREEK (**San Juan**) originates near the Clay Hill Divide, the mouth of Steer Pasture Canyon, and the Irish Green Spring. It drains southwest into the San Juan River. The creek received its name from the castle-like Indian ruins one mile northeast, up the creek from the Green Water Spring. The Hole-in-the-Rock expedition passed through this canyon in February 1880 on their way to Bluff* and Montezuma*.
SE¼,T39S,R14E,SLM to S25,T40S,R12E, SLM (at mouth). 359.

CASTLE DALE* (**Emery**) is on U-10 and Cottonwood Creek in Castle Valley, ten miles northeast of Ferron*. The initial desire of the community was to named their town Castle Vale*, but the post office listed it as Castle Dale and it was never changed. There are many castle-like geologic formations in the region.
S33,34,T18S,R8E,SLM; 5,771' (1,759m). 100 (v17), 314, 360, 542.

CASTLE GATE* (**Carbon**) was a century-old coal mining town in lower Price Canyon. The town was first settled in 1888. Because of expanding coal operations, the houses were moved or dismantled and the people relocated in late 1974. Castle Gate received its name from the twin rock towers in the canyon where the highway entered the town. One tower was destroyed when the highway was widened and modernized. Butch Cassidy robbed the Pleasant Valley Coal Company payroll here on April 21, 1897, and escaped into Roost country.
S36,T12S,R9E,SLM; 6,147' (1,874m). 25, 542, 546.

CASTLE ISLAND (**Weber**). See Fremont Island (Weber).

CASTLE LAKE (**Duchesne**) is near Hayden Pass, one and one-half miles east of Mirror Lake at the west end of the Uinta Mountains. The lake is near a mountainous rock formation resembling a castle with multiple turrets and spires.
S2,T4N,R9W,USM; 10,340' (3,152m). 530.

CASTLE LAKE (**Summit**) is in the north central section of the Uinta Mountains at the head of Henrys Fork. It is two miles north of Mount Powell. Castle-like features adjacent to the lake suggested the name.
11,363' (3,463m).

CASTLE LAKE (**Summit**) is in the southwest section of the Uinta Mountains, two miles west of the head of Shingle Creek. See above for name source.
S2,T2S,R7E,SLM; 9,875' (3,010m).

CASTLE PEAK (**Duchesne**) is between the upper part of Pariette Draw and Pariette Bench. The peak has the profile of a castle.
S4,T9S,R17E,SLM; 5,345' (1,629m).

CASTLE PEAK (**Summit**) is at the west end of the Uinta Mountains near Castle Lake. Kamas* is eight and one-half miles east southeast.
S2,T2S,R7E,SLM; 10,234' (3,119m).

CASTLE ROCK (**Summit**) is in Echo Canyon, six miles southwest of Wasatch*. It has the rough outline of an ancient castle. The Castle Rock Pony Express Station was located here until it closed in 1867. In 1872 it became a stop for the Union Pacific Railroad. The David Moore and David Rees families moved in temporarily, but today it is a ghost town site located on private land.
S6,T4N,R7E,SLM; 6,500' (1,981m). 89, 100 (v17), 567, 516.

CASTLE ROCK (**Weber**) is the highest point on Fremont Island in the Great

Salt Lake. This name was an early synonym for the entire island, Castle Rock Island. Early Mormon settlers named it for its distinctive profile. See Fremont Island.
S7,T5N,R4W,SLM; 4,995' (1,522m). 360, 371, 546.

CASTLE VALLEY (Grand) has a northwest-southeast orientation and is ten miles east of Moab*, bordering the Colorado River. Castle Creek drains through the valley. Unusual features such as towers and buttes around the margin of the valley suggested the name.
T25S,R23E,SLM; 4,400'-5,500' (1,341m-1,676m). 422, 514, 546.

CASTLE VALLEY (Emery) is between the Wasatch Plateau and the San Rafael Swell. I-70 forms the southern boundary. Ferron*, Castle Dale*, and Cleveland* are all located in this area. U-10 passes through the valley and the San Rafael River has its headwaters there. It is a region of precipitate escarpments and unusual rock formations and was named by the early travelers passing through on the Old Spanish Trail.
T19-21S,R7-8E,SLM. 420, 546.

CASTLE VALLEY (Garfield) opens at the mouth of Castle Creek. Early settlers included Meltiar Hatch and his two wives. See Castle* (Garfield).
S21,22,27,T36S,R8W,SLM; 9,600' (2,926m). 145, 360, 567.

CASTLETON* (Grand) is a small community in Castle Valley east of Moab*. In earlier days it was occupied by miners and sheepherders who mined and grazed their flocks on the nearby La Sal Mountains. It was also a focal point and supply center for the entire region. By 1879 there were cabins along Castle Creek and the population eventually peaked in 1895. As the nearby mines were depleted, the community was abandoned. Today small ranches, homesites, and recreational facilities are growing in the area.

S25,T25S,R23E,SLM; 5,900' (1,798m). 146, 360, 494, 567.

CASTO CANYON (Garfield) originates on the southern slopes of Casto Bluff, north of Bryce Canyon National Park and east of Panguitch*. It drains west into Casto Wash and the Sevier River. A Mr. Casto was an early Panguitch farmer. 494. D.L. 7402.

CAT PASTURE (Kane) is near the head of Coyote Gulch, Dry Fork, between the Escalante River and the Kaiparowits Plateau. Bobcats were once abundant in this area.
5,000' (1,524m). 12.

CAT PEAK (Utah) is on Reservation Ridge at the head of Kyune Creek, six and one-half miles southeast of Soldier Summit. Cougars roamed this region in previous times, giving the name.
S6,T11S,R9E,SLM; 9,758' (2,974m).

CATARACT CANYON (Garfield, San Juan, Wayne) is one of several Colorado River canyons. It starts three miles below The Confluence at Spanish Bottoms and extends down to Millecrag Bend in Straight Canyon east of the mouth of the Dirty Devil River. It was named by Major Powell for its numerous cataracts.
159, 160, 314, 360, 422, 496.

CATHEDRAL, THE (Summit) is in the north central section of the Uinta Mountains between the right- and left-hand forks of the Bear River, East Fork. It is a secluded area surrounded by cliffs.
S33,T1N,R11E,SLM; 12,224' (3,726m).

CATHEDRAL IN THE DESERT (Kane) is a large natural alcove at the head of Clear Creek, two miles northwest of Hole-in-the-Rock. It was named by Bob Fullmer, a photographer from Los Angeles.
T40½S,R9E,SLM.

CATHEDRAL VALLEY (Emery, Sevier, Wayne) is at the north end of Capitol

Reef National Park. Unusual spires, cliffs, and castle-like formations in the region suggested the name. Lower Cathedral Valley is located to the southeast.
T27S,R6E,SLM.

CATSTAIR CANYON (Kane) is a steep, rocky, transverse canyon cutting directly through the lower Cockscomb. It is the main pass through the Cockscomb on US-89 between Kanab*, Utah, and Page*, Arizona. The canyon was named because only a cat could work its way through this section (before the canyon was blasted out to make way for the highway).
S25,36,T42S,R2W,SLM.

CAUSEY RESERVOIR (Weber) is east northeast of Ogden* at the junction of Wheat Grass Canyon and the south fork of Ogden River. Thomas Causey and his wife built and ran a sawmill there. Nearby Bear Hollow, which drains into Wheat Grass Canyon, is where a grizzly bear invaded their camp.
S26,34,35,T7N,R3E,SLM; 5,692' (1,735m). 567.

CAUSEY SPRING (Weber) is one mile north of Causey Reservoir in Dry Bread Hollow. See Causey Reservoir.
S23,T7N,R3E,SLM.

CAVE CANYON (Beaver) originates on the western slopes of the Mineral Range east of Milford* and north of Minersville*. It drains west into the Beaver River and was named for the cave discovered by John Bradshaw near the mouth of the canyon in 1859. The cave became the entrance to Bradshaw's mine in March 1871. See Cave Mine Camp.
S4,T29S,R9W,SLM to S12,T29S,R10W,SLM. 355, 456.

CAVE HOLLOW (Beaver) originates on the western slopes of the Tushar Mountains south of Baker Canyon and drains west into the Beaver River. The area was named for the large but shallow cave near its mouth. Variant: Big Cave Hollow.
S21,T29S,R6W,SLM.

CAVE LAKES CANYON (Kane) originates two miles northeast of Coral Pink Sand Dunes State Park and drains east into Three Lakes Canyon. As water drains into the sandstone pockets along the canyon bottom it forms small bodies of water called waterpockets or potholes. The canyon is a site of primitive ruins and was named for the caves the ancient peoples inhabited.
S34,T42S,R7W,SLM to S30,T42S,R6W,SLM. 455, 546.

CAVE MINE CAMP* (Beaver) was a temporary mining settlement in a draw on the south side of Cave Canyon near the mine of the same name. The mine was discovered through a dream John Bradshaw had in the 1870s. See Bradshaw City* and Cave Canyon.
S12,T29S,R10W,SLM; 6,400' (1,951m). 355, 456.

CCC RESERVOIR (Beaver) is in the center of Pine Valley near the mouth of Turkey Wash. It was built by the Civilian Conservation Corps (CCC) in the 1940s.
S31,T27S,R16W,SLM; 5,514' (1,681m).

CECRET LAKE (Salt Lake) is at the head of Little Cottonwood Canyon, one-half mile southwest of the end of the canyon. The lake is located in an isolated area.
T3S,R3E,SLM; 9,850' (3,002m).

CEDAR BREAKS (Iron) is a massive multi-colored amphitheater on the southwest escarpment of the Markagunt Plateau, eighteen miles east of Cedar City* at the headwaters of Ashdown Creek. "Breaks" was a term used by the early settlers, meaning a badlands area. Cedar trees are quite common in the area.
314, 360.

CEDAR BREAKS NATIONAL MONU-
MENT (Iron) was established on August
22, 1933, and centers around the Cedar
Breaks area.

CEDAR CITY* (Iron) is on I-15 between Parowan* and St. George* and
was named for the large number of
cedar trees (Juniperus osteosperma) in the
valley when the settlers first arrived. It
was first called Little Muddy*, then Coal
Creek*, receiving its name from the
creek where the community was first
established. It was marked for settlement
by Parley P. Pratt and company on
December 1, 1849, and settled November
11, 1851, by Henry Lunt and a party of
fifty people out of Parowan. The early
intentions for the city were to produce
iron from the recently discovered iron
ore deposits to the west.
S10,11,14,T36S,R11W,SLM;5,834'(1,778m).
288, 360, 567.

CEDAR COUNTY was established on
January 5, 1856. The county was named
after the numerous cedar trees in the
region. It was absorbed into Utah County
in 1862.
6, 516.

CEDAR CREEK* (Box Elder) was a
small settlement four miles southeast of
Strevell*, Idaho, and one half mile south
of US-30. The community was named for
the creek. John Jenson settled there and
ran a store and stage line station.
Ranching and dry farming was about all
the area could support.
S1,T14N,R12W,SLM; 5,155' (1,571m). 360,
567.

CEDAR FORT* (Utah) is on U-73 west
of the north end of Utah Lake and four
and one-half miles north of Fairfield*.
The abundance of cedar trees suggested
the name. On January 5, 1856, by legislative act, the settlements of Cedar
Valley were organized into a county with
Cedar Fort as the county seat. The entire

area was later absorbed into Utah
County.
S6,T6S,R2W,SLM; 5,069' (1,545m). 100
(v17), 270.

CEDAR GROVE (Sevier) was near
Koosharem*. In 1873 it was the site of
the signing of a peace treaty between the
Mormons and the Fishlake Indians. The
Mormons were represented by A. K.
Thurber, George Bean, and their party.
The trees that were once in the grove no
longer exist.
100(v5,17), 360.

CEDAR HILLS* (Utah) is between
Alpine* and Pleasant Grove* on U-146.
Cedar Hills was established as a
community in the fall of 1977. The local
cedar-covered hills suggested the name.
S8,17,T5S,R2E,SLM; 4,800' (1,463m). 163
(2 Nov. 1977), 399, 466(11 April 1978).

CEDAR MESA (San Juan) parallels
U-261 north northwest of the Valley of
the Gods, east of Grand Gulch. Cedars
are plentiful on the mesa.
T38-40S,R18E,SLM; 6,400'-6,700' (1,951m-
2,042m). 443.

CEDAR MOUNTAINS (Tooele) are a
low range of mountains with a north-
south orientation, south of Low* and
Low Pass, and west of Skull Valley. The
historic Hastings Pass winds its way
through the Cedar Mountains.
T4S,R9,10W,SLM; 7,712' (2,351m).

CEDAR SPRING (Box Elder) is on the
southwest slopes of the northern
Promontory Mountains, five miles
southwest of Sunset Pass. It was named
for nearby Cedar Grove. A Mr. Heders
discovered and named the spring in 1860.
S34,T11N,R7W,SLM; 4,875' (1,486m). 567.

CEDAR SPRINGS* (Millard). See
Holden*.

CEDAR VALLEY (Iron) has
Kanarraville* at the south end, Cedar

City* in the east central region, and Rush Lake to the north. Cedar trees are plentiful in this area.
T34-37S,R11,12W,SLM; 5,500' (1,676m). 360, 423.

CEDAR VALLEY (Utah) is west of Utah Lake and the Lake Mountains. West of the valley are the Oquirrh Mountains and the Thorpe Hills. The valley was originally settled in 1852 by Alfred Bell.
T5,6S,R1,2W,SLM; 4,890' (1,490m). 567.

CEDAR VIEW RESERVOIR (Duchesne) is in the south central section of the Uinta Mountains, eleven miles northwest of Neola*. Cedar and pinyon pine trees are plentiful.
S20,T2W,R2N,USM; 8,024' (2,446m).

CEDARVIEW* (Uintah) is a small agricultural community surrounded by rolling cedar-covered hills. The town was first developed in 1912 and is on U-121, five miles south of Neola*. The area supports ranching and gas and oil production.
S30,T1S,R1W,USM; 5,450' (1,661m). 89, 288, 542.

CENTER* (Tooele) was midway between St. John* and Vernon* on U-36. It was first settled in 1863 by Welsh pioneers and became a hay, livestock, and general supply source for nearby ranches, the miners of Ophir*, and other nearby settlements and mines. It was here that Mr. William Ajax and his wife started what became their famous underground store, restaurant, and supply center. See Ajax*. It was abandoned in 1914 and today Center is a ghost town site.
S27,T6S,R5W,SLM; 5,044' (1,544m). 100 (v17), 542.

CENTER CANYON (Wasatch) originates at Mare Spring, four miles southwest of Heber Mountain. It drains west southwest into Daniels Canyon. Since the mouth of this canyon was centrally located in Daniels Canyon, it became an important mileage and resting point for early freighters.
S11,T5S,R6E,SLM to S20,T5S,R6E,SLM.

CENTER CREEK (Beaver) originates at the south end of the Wah Wah Mountains north of Lamerdorf Peak. It drains northeast into Quartz Creek and the Wah Wah Valley.
S5,6,T29S,R15W,SLM.

CENTER CREEK (Iron) originates in the mountains six miles northeast of Cedar Breaks National Monument. The creek drains north into Parowan Canyon. The creek was named by Parley P. Pratt and his party in 1849 when it became the central point of the initial colonization of Iron County. See Parowan*.
S31,32,T35S,R8W,SLM to S36,T34S,R9W, SLM. 423.

CENTER CREEK* (Iron). See Parowan*.

CENTER CREEK (Wasatch) originates three miles southwest of Heber Mountain and ten miles southeast of Heber City*. The creek is midway between Daniels Creek and Lake Creek.
S2,T5S,R6E,SLM to S9,T4S,R5E,SLM. 567.

CENTER CREEK* (Wasatch) is five miles south southeast of Heber City* and two miles north of the mouth of Daniels Canyon. In 1860 the town received its name from the creek on which the community first settled.
S10,15,T4S,R5E,SLM; 5,927' (1,807m). 567.

CENTERFIELD* (Sanpete) is on US-89 two miles south of Gunnison* and eight miles north of Redmond*. In 1869 a group of squatters from Gunnison moved into the area then known as The Field. On August 29, 1896, The Field* became Centerfield because it was in the center of Gunnison Valley.
S28,29,T19S,R1E,SLM; 5,095' (1,553m). 152, 288, 360, 542.

CENTERVILLE* (Davis) is two miles north of Bountiful*, just east of I-15. The original name was Deuel Creek* because the settlement was established on the Creek named for Osmyn M. Deuel. Later it became Cherry Settlement* for the Benjamin Cherry family, then the town was named Centerville. Other early settlers included Thomas Grover and family and the Charles C. Rich group.
S7,8,18,T1E,R2N,SLM; 4,350' (1,326m). 27, 88, 100(v17), 275, 288, 360, 516, 542.

CENTRAL* (Sevier) is four and one-half miles south of Richfield* on US-89. In 1877 the settlers accepted the name Inverury*, which comes from a Scottish town meaning "between two waters." In 1940 the name was changed to Central because the town was in the central part of the valley and the county. Some of the early settlers were the William A. Stewart and Joseph Evans families.
S14,23,T24S,R3W,SLM; 5,297' (1,615m). 100(v17), 360, 542, 567, 584, 585.

CENTRAL* (Washington) is six miles west of Pine Valley*, near the Santa Clara River. The town was aptly named because it occupies a central position among Enterprise*, Gunlock*, Veyo*, and Pine Valley.
S21,11,T39S,R16W,SLM; 5,200' (1,585m). 154, 542.

CENTRAL* (Weber). See Roy*.

CENTRAL CITY* (Salt Lake) was a temporary mining camp in Little Cottonwood Canyon that was soon absorbed into Alta*.

CENTRAL PARK* (Salt Lake). See South Salt Lake*.

CEPHALOPOD GULCH (Salt Lake) is at the base of the foothills just northeast of the University of Utah campus. It heads on the southwest slopes of Mount Van Cott and is known for its fossils. In 1921 Asa Mathews described the Lower Triassic Cephalopod fauna found in this area.
S34,T1N,R1E,SLM. 508.

CHA CANYON (San Juan) originates on the northern slopes of the Navajo Mountains and drains north into the San Juan River. Cha means "beaver" in the Navajo language.

CHAIN LAKES (Duchesne) is a series of alpine lakes arranged like the links in a chain near the central section of the Uinta Mountains, three miles east of Mount Emmons. The four principal lakes of the chain are Lower, Middle, Upper, and Fourth Chain lakes.
T4N,R3W,USM; 10,500'-11,000' (3,200m-3,353m). 165.

CHALK CREEK (Beaver) originates at the south end of the Wah Wah Mountains. It drains northeast into Quartz Creek and the Wah Wah Valley through chalkish-colored soil.
S5,6,T29S,R15W,SLM. 100(v17).

CHALK CREEK (Millard) originates three miles east southeast of Fillmore* at the junction of the north and south forks. It drains northwest into the Pavant Valley at The Sink. See above for name source.
S35,T21S,R4W,SLM to S31,32,T20S,R5W, SLM. 135, 567.

CHALK CREEK (Summit) originates on the northwest slopes of the Uinta Mountains, south of Seven Tree Flat. The creek drains through chalky soil past Coalville* into the Echo Reservoir.
S8,T2N,R9E,SLM to S8,T2N,R5E,SLM.

CHALK CREEK CANYON (Millard). See Chalk Creek (Millard).

CHAMBERS* (Daggett). See Manila*.

CHAMPLIN MOUNTAINS (Tooele). See Simpson Mountains.

CHAMPLIN PEAK (Juab) is the high point of the Gilson Mountains north of

Leamington*. See Simpson Mountains.
S7,T14S,R3W,SLM; 7,504' (2,287m).

CHANDLER CANYON (Uintah) origi-
nates on the East Tavaputs Plateau at
BP Springs and drains northwest into the
Green River. The canyon was given the
maiden name of the wife of U. F.
Steward, the assistant geologist of Major
Powell's expedition.
S8,T16S,R19E,SLM (to Green River). 159,
515(v7).

CHANDLER PASTURE (Uintah) is on
the East Tavaputs Plateau north of and
near Chandler Canyon.
S22,27,T15S,R18E,SLM; 7,700' (2,347m).

CHANDLER POINT (Uintah) is a large
elevated landform southwest of the elbow
of Chandler Canyon.
S6,7,T16S,R19E,SLM.

CHARLESTON* (Wasatch) is at the
northeast section of Deer Creek
Reservoir, at the junction of U-113 and
US-89. The town was settled in 1852.
There are two versions of the name
source. The first and more accepted is
that it was named for Charles Shelton,
who surveyed the town. The other
suggests that James Herbert stopped
there on his mail route and told the men
at the herders' cabin that if they would
put up a mailbox, he would deliver mail
to them. A Mr. Winterton, one of the
herders, remembered hearing of
Charleston*, South Carolina, so he made
a mailbox, put it in a crotch of a tree
and used that name.
S14,T4S,R4E,SLM; 5,440' (1,658m). 100
(v17), 288, 360, 542, 567.

CHARLESTON CREEK (Box Elder)
originates three and one-half miles south
southeast of Yost* and drains northwest
into Johnson Creek. The creek was
named for Charley Yost, who rode the
range there in 1860-70.
S15,23,25,T14N,R15W,SLM. 139.

CHARLEY FLAT (Emery). See Charley
Holes.

CHARLEY HOLES (Emery) is on
Crawford Draw in the Sinbad country of
the San Rafael Swell. It drains into
upper Straight Wash. The holes are a
series of natural depressions or water
holes in the draw five miles southeast of
The Wickiup, a giant rock formation.
The holes were named for Charley
Swasey, who ran cattle there. Nearby is
Charley Flat.
S1,T23S,R11E,SLM; 6,400' (1,951m). 193.

CHEATUM* (Salt Lake) was a small
temporary mining settlement up Little
Cottonwood Canyon. The settlement was
established during the late 1800s, but did
not last long after the local mines closed
down. Most settlements of this type
consisted of a boardinghouse, one or two
saloons, and the tents or frame shacks
where the miners lived.
454.

CHECKERBOARD MESA
(Washington) is part of the White Cliffs
near the east entrance to Zion National
Park. The name reflects the many eroded
check lines in the crossbedded white
sandstone that makes up the mesa.
S29,T41S,R9W,SLM. 530, 532.

CHEESEBOX, THE (San Juan) is five
miles northwest of Natural Bridges
National Monument. It is a small,
circular butte with perpendicular sides
and a flat top that looks like an old-
fashioned cheesebox.
S18,T36S,R17E,SLM; 6,325' (1,928m).

CHEESEBOX CANYON (San Juan)
originates five miles north northeast of
The Cheesebox from which it receives its
name. The canyon drains southwest into
White Canyon.
S22,T35S,R17E,SLM to T36S,R16E,SLM.

CHENEY CREEK (**Rich**) originates at Cheney Springs, four miles west southwest of Pickleville* near the south end of Bear Lake. It drains southeast into Meadowville Creek and was named for Joseph Cheney, an early settler.
S2,11,T4E,R13N,SLM to S20,T13N,R5E,SLM. 567.

CHENEY SPRINGS (**Rich**) are at the head of Cheney Creek four miles west southwest of Pickleville*. Nearby are North Cheney Springs. See Cheney Creek for name source.
S11,T13S,R4E,SLM.

CHEPETA CANYON (**Duchesne**) originates on the East Tavaputs Plateau about six miles west of the Colorado line and north of the Book Cliffs. It drains north into Bitter Creek. Variant: Chipeta. See Chepeta Lake for name source.
S4,T16S,R25E,SLM to S5,T15S,R25E,SLM.

CHEPETA LAKE (**Duchesne**) is in the central section of the Uinta Mountains at the head of Whiterocks River. The lake was named for the wife of Ouray, a Uinta Ute Indian chief. Chepeta was a very important person herself, as she worked with and helped her people. The name means "rippling water."
S29,32,T5N,R1W,USM; 10,560' (3,219m). 100(v17), 309.

CHERRY CREEK (**Beaver**) originates on the southeast slopes of the Mineral Mountains and drains east into Indian Creek, north of Adamsville*. Chokecherry (*Prunus virginiana*) is plentiful along the creek.
S10,T29S,R9W,SLM to S17,T29S,R8W,SLM.

CHERRY CREEK (**Cache**) originates on the western slopes of Cherry Peak in the Bear River Range. It drains west past Richmond*, into the Cub River. Chokecherry is common along the creek.
S21,T14N,R1E,SLM (at mouth).

CHERRY CREEK (**Garfield**) originates on the eastern slopes of Barney Top of the Escalante Mountains. It drains east into Main Canyon west of Escalante*. Wild chokecherry is abundant along the creek area.
S10,T38S,R1E,SLM (at mouth).

CHERRY CREEK (**Juab**) originates in the West Tintic Mountains and drains south southwest into Cherry Creek Wash, then sinks into the desert. Wild chokecherry is common along the creek.
S7,T11S,R4W,SLM to S2,T14S,R8W,SLM.

CHERRY CREEK* (**Juab**) was one and one-half miles southwest of Maple Peak on Cherry Creek. It was a temporary tent town operating around 1883 while the construction of a reservoir and a pipeline to Eureka* took place. The camp took the name of the creek, but was dismantled when the pipeline was completed.
S24,T11S,R5W,SLM; 6,416' (1,956m). 516.

CHERRY CREEK SETTLEMENT* (**Davis**). See Centerville* (Davis).

CHERRY CREEK SPRING (**Beaver**) is in the southeastern Mineral Mountains near the head of Cherry Creek.
S11,T29S,R9W,SLM; 6,800' (2,073m).

CHERRY PEAK (**Cache**) is in the mountains east of Richmond* at the head of Cherry Creek.

CHESLER PARK (**San Juan**) is in the heart of The Needles country of Canyonlands National Park, east of and near the Grabens and seven miles south southeast of The Confluence. It is a park-like area, completely surrounded by high, eroded, sandstone formations. The area was named for an early horse rancher who ran his operation in the vicinity.
T31S,R19E,SLM; 5,500' (1,676m). 578.

CHESSMAN CANYON (**Iron**) originates in the east central sector of Cedar Breaks National Monument at Chessman Overlook. It drains southwest into

Ashdown Creek. The eroded landforms resemble chessmen.
S33,T36S,R9W,SLM. 567.

CHESTER* (Sanpete) is four miles west of Spring City* at the junction of U-11 and U-117. The town was settled by David Candland in the middle 1800s. In the beginning the town was named Canal Creek* after the waterway from which the community received its water. Candland then changed the name to Chesterfield* after his hometown in England; it was later reduced to Chester. This community is considered the closest to the geographic center of Utah.
S35,T15S,R3E,SLM; 5,510' (1,679m). 288, 542, 546, 569.

CHESTER PONDS (Sanpete) are a series of small spring-fed ponds near Chester* from which the ponds receive their name.
S25,26,T15S,R3E,SLM; 5,600' (1,707m).

CHICKEN CREEK (Juab) originates in the San Pitch Mountains, nine miles southeast of Levan*. The creek drains northeast into the Juab Valley and the Sevier River. Wild sage hens were plentiful in the area when it was originally settled.
S20,T15S,R2E,SLM to S31,T1S,R1E,SLM. 578.

CHICKEN CREEK* (Juab). See Juab* (Juab).

CHICKEN CREEK RESERVOIR (Juab) is on Chicken Creek on the west side of Juab Valley.
S17,20,T15S,R1W,SLM; 5,050' (1,539m).

CHIMNEY TOWN* (Rich) was at the south end of Bear Lake. This town was one of several communities that was abandoned as the inhabitants moved into or were absorbed by Laketown*. See Round Valley* and Laketown*.

CHINA LAKE (Summit) is on the north central slopes of the Uinta Mountains on the east fork of Smiths Fork. Bridge Lake and Marsh Lake are in the vicinity. A Chinese man and his mule reportedly drowned here in the late 1800s. Another story suggests the lake is so deep in places that one could sink to China before touching bottom.
S6,T2N,R14E,SLM; 9,408' (2,868m). 567. D.L. 6901.

CHINA LAKE MEADOWS (Summit) is one-half mile south of China Lake.

CHINA WALL* (Uintah) was a short-lived mining camp associated with the gilsonite mining between Harrison* and Watson*.

CHINATOWN (Morgan) was fifteen miles up Lost Creek, northeast of Devils Slide. About eighteen acres of unusually eroded and colored rock formations that resemble Chinese pagodas suggested the name.
378.

CHINATOWN* (Washington) was close to the Robbers Roost near Hurricane* (the location of this area is unclear). When the Hurricane canal was under construction, a work camp was set up where the men lived in dugouts along the bank. Someone remarked that the place looked like a Chinatown and the name held.

CHINLE CREEK (San Juan) originates in the Navajo Indian country of northeastern Arizona. It drains north, cutting through the Comb Ridge from east to west and into the San Juan River. "Chinle" is a Navajo word meaning "where water comes out of."
S28,T41S,R20E,SLM (at mouth). 314, 360, 567. D.L. 6302, 7102.

CHLORIDE CANYON (Iron) originates at the junction of the north and south forks in the Antelope Range, twenty-three miles west of Cedar City*. The canyon drains westward. In 1890, silver chloride was discovered in the canyon and a mining camp was established. The mining operation continued until 1910. S19,T35S,R14W,SLM to S11,14,T35S,R15W, SLM. 360, 567.

CHOCOLATE PEAK (Box Elder) is two miles north northeast of Deweyville* in the Wellsville Range. The shape of the peak reminds some of a chocolate drop. S33,T2W,R12N,SLM; 6,535' (1,992m). 578.

CHOKECHERRY HOLLOW (Beaver) originates in the mountains west of the north end of Beaver Valley. It drains southeast to enter Fortuna Canyon and Wildcat Creek. Chokecherry (*Prunus virginiana*) trees are plentiful in this area. S24,T27S,R8W,SLM.

CHOKECHERRY PEAK (Beaver) is at the south end of the Tushar Mountains at the head of the South Fork of South Creek. The peak received its name from the creek. S33,T30S,R5W,SLM; 9,987' (3,044m).

CHOKECHERRY SPRING (Beaver) is three miles north of Indian Peak in the Indian Peak range. There is an abundance of chokecherry trees in this area. S5,T29S,R1S,SLM; 7,320' (2,331m).

CHOKECHERRY SPRING (Kane) is on the upper Left Fork of Lydias Canyon, seven miles northwest of Glendale*. Chokecherry is plentiful. S25,T39S,R8W,SLM.

CHOPROCK BENCH (Garfield) is east of Escalante*, between Silver Falls Creek and Bench on the west, and Baker Bench and the Circle Cliffs on the east. It is an extremely rugged benchland cut by numerous deep canyons, washes, and impassable eroded areas of rimrock. T36S,R7E,SLM; 5,700' (1,737m). 12.

CHRISTIANBURG* (Sanpete) is three miles east of Gunnison* near US-89, along the San Pitch River. The town was originally settled in 1873 and named for

the Christiansen brothers: Julius, Theodore, and Titus, who were the first to settle there with their families. S23,T19S,R1E,SLM; 5,203' (1,586m). 360, 466(28 Sept. 1985).

CHRISTIANSEN CANYON (Tooele) originates in the Deep Creek Range, four miles east northeast of Ibapah* on the northern slopes of North Peak. It drains west into Deep Creek Valley. Pete Christiansen ran cattle along nearby Deep Creek. S8,T9S,R18W,SLM to S3,T9S,R19W,SLM. 100(v17).

CHRISS LAKE (Garfield) is on the southern slopes of Boulder Mountain of the Aquarius Plateau. It drains into West Deer Creek. T32S,R5E,SLM.

CHRISTMAS CITY* (Utah) was up Provo Canyon, one mile from Olmstead* on the south side of the road. The settlement consisted of a service station and small grocery store. The people who ran these establishments selected the name and for a while it gained a small reputation. When the highway was widened, Christmas City was demolished. S6,T6S,R3E,SLM; 4,851' (1,479m).

CHRISTMAS MEADOWS (Summit) is on the Stillwater Fork of Bear River on the northern slopes of the Uinta Mountains. Disney's beautiful film *Perry* was produced in this lush meadow where the stream lazily meanders after rushing down from Amethyst Lake. Mr. Christmas, a prospector from California, lived there for seven years. S15,22,T1N,R10E,SLM; 8,775' (2,675m). 360, 466(24 Dec. 1984).

CHURCH ISLAND (Davis). See Antelope Island.

CHURCH ROCK (San Juan) is a landmark in Dry Valley at the junction of US-163 and U-211, which leads into the

east side of Canyonlands National Park. The rock is a chapel-shaped sandstone formation.
S24,T31S,R23,SLM; 6,254' (1,906m).

CIGAR CREEK CANYON (Kane) is at the head of Reese Canyon on the Kaiparowits Plateau and drains southwest. MRN
S9,T26S,R7W,SLM; 7,048' (2,148m).

CIRCLE CLIFFS (Garfield). The eastern boundary of this raised basin is the Waterpocket Fold. To the west is Boulder* and the drainage into the Escalante River. The eastern section of the Aquarius Plateau (Boulder Mountain) is north and East Moody Canyon and the head of Stevens Canyon is south. The cliffs are a five-hundred-square-mile area surrounding a vast open range of rugged hinterland forming striking shapes and colors. The cliffs were named by Grove Karl Gilbert, a noted U.S. Geological Survey geologist. Other references suggest that the cliffs were named by the Powell Survey.
12, 57, 602.

CIRCLE LAKE (Garfield) is an oval lake at the southern edge of the Aquarius Plateau near the head of Boulder Creek, West Fork. Crescent Lake and Half Moon Lake are also in the area.
T41S,R4E,SLM; 10,800' (3,292m).

CIRCLE SPRING (Kane) surfaces from an alcove on the east side of Collett Top of the Kaiparowits.
S35,T38S,R4E,SLM; 6,240' (1,902m). 12.

CIRCLE VALLEY (Piute). The town of Circleville* is in the center of this valley. The Circleville Mountains are west and Kingston* and Junction* are north. Valleys surrounded by mountains are often called circle valleys and are quite common in Utah.

CIRCLEVILLE* (Piute) is in the heart of Circle Valley, twenty-six miles north of Panguitch*. It is a productive agricultural and livestock community on the Sevier River. Circleville was an early county seat before being moved to Bullion City*, which is now a ghost town. In 1864 Brigham Young called fifty families from Sanpete County to settle the region under the general supervision of LDS Apostle Orson Hyde, with William Allred as presiding elder. William Anderson was one of the settlers; he suggested the name Circleville.
S25,26,T30S,R4W,SLM; 6,063' (1,848m). 27, 242, 314, 360, 542, 586.

CIRCLEVILLE CANYON (Garfield) originates along the Sevier River, fourteen miles north of Panguitch* where the river cuts through the mountains. It ends three miles southwest of Circleville* and received its name from the valley.
S13,T32S,R5W,SLM to S4,T31S,R4W,SLM.

CIRCLEVILLE MOUNTAINS (Beaver) are at the south end of the Tushar Mountains. The name is taken from Circleville* and the Circle Valley, located six miles to the east.
S15,22,T30S,R5W,SLM; 11,331' (3,454m). 567.

CISCO* (Grand) was at the mouth of Cisco Wash on US-6 (I-70) in the early days. It was an ore and coal shipping, outfitting, and supply center that was initially settled around 1887 by John Martin, a surveyor. Large ranches developed in the surrounding countryside and numerous holding corrals were built for loading livestock onto trains. Today it is much smaller in size and importance. Although the name origin is unclear, one reference said cisco means broken pieces of coal or coal dust. Another suggests it is an Indian name for a type of fish. In Spanish, cisco means disturbance or row. A frontier cattle and mining town usually

has a wild reputation, so this seems the most likely name origin. Since I-70 now bypasses Cisco, the town will probably shrink even further.
S24,T21S,R23E,SLM; 4,352' (1,326m). 100 (v17), 146, 314, 360, 542, 578.

CITY CREEK (Cache) originates in the Bear River Range on the western slopes of Mount Naomi. It drains west through Richmond* into Cub Creek and is the town's water source.
S28,T14N,R1E,SLM (at mouth). 435.

CITY CREEK (Salt Lake) originates northeast of Salt Lake City* on the northern slopes of Lookout Peak. It drains southwest through City Creek Canyon near the capitol building. When the pioneers entered the valley, this creek was the first one diverted for irrigation before plowing was started. It was also the source of the original Salt Lake City water supply. On Sunday, August 22, 1847, Brigham Young named the creek during the first general conference of the Mormon Church.
27, 100(v17), 252, 314.

CITY CREEK PEAK (Beaver) is in the Tushar Mountains on the county line, one and one-half miles east of Puffer Lake. The peak was named after nearby City Creek.
S5,T29S,R4W,SLM; 11,165' (3,403m).

CITY OF THE PLAINS* (Weber). See Plain City* (Weber).

CLARENCE CREEK (Garfield) originates twelve miles north of the north end of Bryce Canyon National Park and drains southeast past Clarence Creek Spring into Hunt Creek. It was named for Clarence Showalter, who used the area as a range for his sheep during the 1890s. See also Showalter Creek and Bench.
S22,T34S,R4W,SLM. 567.

CLARENCE CREEK SPRING (Garfield) is near the head of Clarence Creek.

CLARION* (Sanpete) was four miles west of Centerfield* and five miles southwest of Gunnison* on the west side of the Sevier River. In August 1911, the Jewish Agricultural and Colonial Association of Philadelphia* purchased six thousand acres of land from the Utah State Land Board. The Jewish association dispatched an engineer and an advance party of twelve men (some with families) to survey the area and prepare the ground for homes and crops. Homes, a church, and a school were built, followed by a canal, then a post office in 1915. After six years of crop failures, the colony was declared bankrupt in 1917. The soil was alkaline and inappropriate for intensive cultivation, so the settlers gradually dispersed. Japanese families then moved into the area in 1921, but World War II disrupted their settlement and the land reverted to the local citizens. Most of the foreign residents of Clarion were gone by 1934.
S35,T19S,R1W,SLM; 5,100' (1,554m). 89, 152, 360, 466(17 June 1982), 555(v36/2).

CLARK LAKE (Grand) is a small reservoir near Oowah Lake on Upper Mill Creek southeast of Moab*. The lake was named for Robert Clark of Moab.
S23,T26S,R22E,SLM; 8,800' (2,682m). 578.

CLARK VALLEY (Carbon) is a large valley, four-tenths of a mile northwest of East Carbon City* and south of the Book and Roan cliffs. MRN
T14S,R12E,SLM; 5,700'-5,900' (1,737m-1,798m).

CLARKDALE* (Kane) was an early pioneer settlement of ranches that the Clark and Lee families established at the head of Skutumpah Canyon in 1870. The settlement is located where Skutumpah

Creek, Red Wash, and Thompson Creek join, all of which drain into Johnson Canyon. Clarkdale was a way station on the old road to Kanab* that passed through Upper Kanab* (Alton*). Dellenbaugh of the Powell surveys camped at the settlement one night in 1871 and called it Clarkdale because three of the few families there were Clarks. The town was also called Skutumpah* for the creek. "Skutumpah" is a Piute word that refers to a creek where squirrels and rabbitbrush are plentiful. Today Clarkdale is private ranch property. Variants: Clarkston*, Skutumpah*, Skumpah*, Skoots-Pah*, and Skoompa*.
S5,6,7,T41S,R4½W,SLM; 6,000' (1,829m). 159, 422, 455, 515.

CLARKSTON* (Cache) is on Clarkston Creek at the junction of U-142 and U-170. It was settled in 1864-65 by a group including Israel Justus Clark, an Indian interpreter. The town was named by E. T. Benson in honor of its founder. Clarkston was one of the early Utah towns that assumed an earlier name of Stringtown* because the first homes were built along the only existing road.
S26,27,T14N,R2W,SLM; 4,884' (1,489m). 249(15 Oct. 1979), 288, 360, 435, 449, 542.

CLARKSTON* (Kane). See Clarkdale*.

CLAWSON* (Emery) is on U-10 seven miles southwest of Castle Dale* and three and one-half miles northeast of Ferron*. It was settled in the spring of 1897 by the families of Edward Jorgenson, Elias Blackburn, Guy King, and others. The original name was Kingsville* for the King family. The early location was two miles east of present-day Clawson. Mormon church leaders advised the move to the present site in 1902. On October 25, 1904, Mormon Apostle Rudger Clawson came to organize a ward and the town name was changed from Kingsville to Clawson in his honor.

S26,T29S,R7E,SLM; 5,944' (1,812m). 100 (v17), 360, 542.

CLAY BASIN (Daggett) is north of Browns Park. The Mountain Home Range and the Green River are located south. Jesse Ewing Canyon leads from the west end of Browns Park into the east end of Clay Basin. Clay Basin Creek and Clay Basin Meadows are also in the vicinity. In the 1870s a Mr. Clay from New England established the Middlesex Land and Cattle Company with the aid of eastern investors. He moved into the area north of Browns Park (Browns Hole) and purchased several ranches with the intention of monopolizing the livestock industry in that area. He was eased out by the local competition, cattle rustlers, cold winters, and sheep. The basin was named after him.
T3N,R24E,SLM; 6,200'-6,600' (1,890m-2,012m). 80, 172.

CLAY CANYON (Garfield) originates east of the Waterpocket Fold and Halls Creek on Big Thompson Mesa. It drains southeast into Upper Bullfrog Creek and receives its name from the clay-alkaline soil of the badlands through which it drains.
S36,T35S,R9E,SLM (part of canyon). 567.

CLAY HILLS (San Juan) are north of the San Juan River and the Red House Cliffs. They have a northeast-southwest orientation. This blue clay formation was a formidable obstacle to the Hole-in-the-Rock expedition of 1879 because the hills were extremely slippery when wet. Today the Clay Hills are controlled and passed over by highway U-263.
T38S,R39S,R14,15E,SLM; 6,580' (2,006m). 359, 567.

CLAY HILLS DIVIDE (San Juan) is the point where U-263 leaves Castle Creek, passes over the Clay Hills and drops down through the Red House Cliffs.
359.

CLAYTON SPRING (**Garfield**) is at the head of Antimony Creek on the Aquarius Plateau, eight miles west northwest of Posy Lake. The cluster of Clayton Lakes at the head of North Creek are located three miles south. Both the spring and the lakes are named for Albert Clayton, an early pioneer. He kept a dairy at the spring.
10,025' (3,056m). 602.

CLEAR CREEK* (**Box Elder**) is a small ranch community on Clear Creek three miles southwest of Strevell* on the north central side of the Raft River Mountains. It received its name from the creek. An earlier name was Nafton* for a Mr. Naft, who established a cattle and horse ranch there around 1900-11. 1953 maps list the area as Nafton while later maps show it as Clear Creek.
S36,T15N,R13W,SLM; 5,600' (1,707m). 508.

CLEAR CREEK (**Box Elder**) originates in the meadows four miles northeast of George Peak in the Raft River Mountains. It drains northeast, crossing into Idaho near Strevell*. It has clear, sweet-tasting water.
S23,T14N,R14W,SLM to S25,T15N,R13W, SLM (Utah-Idaho border).

CLEAR CREEK* (**Carbon**) is five and one-half miles south of Scofield* on Mud Creek at the south end of Pleasant Valley. A camp was established there in the early 1870s to harvest mine props for the local coal mines. Then in 1898 an exceptionally good vein of coal was uncovered and the camp expanded into a town which flourished and peaked from 1910 to 1920. By the mid-1950s the town began to decline. Recently some of the old homes have been bought and rejuvenated as summer homes. During deer season the population of Clear Creek doubles.
S33,T13S,R7E,SLM; 8,303' (2,531m). 89, 607.

CLEAR CREEK CANYON (**Sevier**) originates at the summit between the Pavant Mountains and the Tushar Mountains. It drains east into the Sevier River at Sevier*. The canyon is ruggedly beautiful and the creek water is exceptionally clear.
S34,T25S,R5W,SLM to S31,T26S,R4W,SLM.

CLEAR LAKE (**Millard**) is ten miles west of Deseret* and is part of the storage system of the lower Sevier River. See Clear Lake* (Millard).
T19,20S,R7W,SLM; 4,590' (1,399m). 89, 100 (v13), 148, 567.

CLEAR LAKE* (**Millard**) is several miles west of Clear Lake. In 1897, C. W. Aldrich, a representative of a New York firm, developed a siding, shipping point, and an agricultural and stock-grazing center. Aldrich used the nearby lake for naming the operation. The area was a natural wild hay and winter grazing center and several families eventually settled there. Water fluctuations, increasing soil alkalinity, and other problems prevented further development and the project slowly deteriorated. Today it is the Clear Lake Waterfowl Management Area, which is owned and operated by the Utah Division of Wildlife Resources.
T19S,R8W,SLM; 4,590' (1,399m). 89, 516, 542.

CLEARFIELD* (**Davis**) is northwest of Layton* and south of Roy* on US-91 (I-15). Clearfield is an outgrowth of Syracuse* and was settled in 1877 by Richard and Emily Hamblin who started with a small dugout with a thatched roof. The settlement received its name from the attractive, open surroundings. Sand Ridge* was an earlier name that was changed when Miss Minnie Christensen, a school teacher, suggested the present name. Today it has become an important city surrounding the Hill Air Force Base and the Freeport Center.
S1,T4N,R2W,SLM; 4,487' (1,368m). 88, 100 (v17), 360, 542, 567.

CLEGG CANYON (Wasatch) originates in the mountains northeast of Daniels Canyon and drains southwest into Daniels Canyon. It was named for Henry Clegg, an early settler who developed a road into the canyon to obtain bark for tanning leather.
S10,T5S,R6E,SLM. 113, 270, 379.

CLEGG LAKE (Summit) is at the west end of the Uinta Mountains, one mile west of Bald Mountain. It was named for John H. Clegg, who was instrumental in developing some of the reservoirs in the region.
S23,33,T1S,R9E,SLM; 10,500' (3,200m). 113, 298, 379.

CLEOPATRAS CHAIR (Wayne) is a geologic formation resembling a gigantic throne in present-day Canyonlands National Park, east of the north end of The Spur. The name was suggested by various surveyors during a period of exotic place naming. Similar names from that period are Little Egypt, Sinbad, and Vishnu.
NW¼,T29S,R17E,SLM; 6,520' (1,987m). 497, 546.

CLEVELAND* (Emery) is a small agricultural settlement on U-155, fourteen miles north northeast of Castle Dale*. The original settlers came from Huntington* and Scofield* in 1885 to established this community. The name honors President Grover Cleveland.
S13,T17S,R9E,SLM; 5,735' (1,748m). 349, 542.

CLEVELAND* (Garfield). See Spry*.

CLEVELAND LAKE (Duchesne) is at the head of the west fork of Whiterocks River, one-half mile west of Queant Lake.
T4N,R2W,USM.

CLEVELAND LAKE (Duchesne) is near Cleveland Peak and south of Ottoson Basin. It received its name from the peak.

S1,T3N,R7W,USM; 11,172' (3,405m).

CLEVELAND PEAK (Duchesne) is in the southwest section of the Uinta Mountains at the head of the east fork of Rock Creek. The peak divides Squaw Basin from Ottoson Basin. George H. Wilcken named the peak in 1925 for President Cleveland, who was a loud, rumbling speaker. The peak occasionally roars and rumbles when falling rocks, small avalanches, and rock slides are triggered by violent weather. When this occurs, the noise echoes back and forth among the cliffs.
S1,T3N,R7W,USM; 12,584' (3,836m). 595.

CLEVELAND RESERVOIR (Emery) is near Lake Canyon on the Wasatch Plateau and drains into the left fork of Huntington Creek. The reservoir was named after the adjacent community.
S22,27,T14S,R6E,SLM; 8,750' (2,667m).

CLEVELAND-LLOYD DINOSAUR QUARRY (Emery) is eighteen miles east of Cleveland*. The "Cleveland" half of the name comes from the nearby town. "Lloyd" refers to Malcolm Lloyd, Jr., a Princeton Law School graduate who partially financed research and excavation at the quarry. It was established primarily as an archaeological and research center for students, and the first excavations were made by the University of Utah in 1931. A research center is located at the site.
S21,28,T17S,R11E,SLM; 5,750' (1,753m). 79.

CLIFF ARCH (Kane) is in Coyote Gulch of the Escalante River drainage system. It is the smallest of the eight Escalante arches that have been measured. The name developed because the flying buttress-like arch clings to the side of the canyon wall.
NE¼,T39S,R8E,SLM. 369.

CLIFF CREEK (Duchesne) can be found in the central section of the Uinta Mountains where it originates at Cliff

Lake and drains down a short rugged drop into the Whiterocks River. It receives its name from the lake it drains. S16,21,23,T4N,R1W,USM.

CLIFF LAKE (Duchesne) is at the head of Cliff Creek in the central section of the Uinta Mountains. Four miles southeast is Paradise Park Reservoir. Cliff Lake receives its name from the nearby cliffs.
S22,T4N,R1W,USM; 10,348' (3,154m).

CLIFF LAKE (Summit) is at the west end of the Uinta Mountains, south of and between Mount Watson and Wall Lake. Rugged cliffs rise above it.
S31,T1S,R9E,SLM; 10,230' (3,118m). 530.

CLIFF LAKE (Summit) is in the north central section of the Uinta Mountains on the headwaters of Henrys Fork near Mount Powell. The nearby cliffs suggested the name.
11,443' (3,488m).

CLIFF RIDGE (Uintah) has a east northeast-west southwest orientation. The ridge is on the Colorado border, but a large section parallels US-40 in Utah. Dinosaur National Monument and Split Mountain Canyon are located eight miles north. In some areas the cliffs rise 1,800 feet (549m) from the base. The name is suggestive of the ridge profile.
T5S,R24,25E,SLM; 8,228' (2,508m).

CLIFTON* (Tooele) is a ghost town site in the Clifton Hills, four and one-half miles south of Gold Hill* and fifty miles south of Wendover*. Valuable ore was discovered there in 1858 and in 1872 a smelter was built. The production at the smelter did not meet expectations and was soon closed down. The town received its name from the surrounding broken, rugged country.
S25,T8W,R18W,SLM; 6,200' (1,890m). 89, 367.

CLIFTON* (Garfield) is a ghost town site one mile south of Cannonville*.

Several villages were settled in this area during the mid-1870s, but an erratic water supply and flooding forced the settlers to abandon the villages. The communities were absorbed into nearby Cannonville. Clifton was named by Willis E. Robinson for the surrounding cliffs. See Cannonville*.
S30,T37S,R2W,SLM; 5,800' (1,768m). 89, 145, 567, 600.

CLIFTON HILLS (Tooele) is located five miles south of Gold Hill*. It is a small cluster of hills that includes Montezuma Peak, the highest point. The hills received their name from the early mining camp of Clifton*. See Clifton* (Tooele).
SW¼,T8S,R17W,SLM; 7,370' (2,246m). 89.

CLINTON* (Utah). See Birdseye* (Utah).

CLINTON* (Davis) is one mile west of Sunset and two miles southwest of Roy on U-37. During the 1870s, James Hill and his family settled this small village that was named by Joseph D. Burnett. Today the residences are dispersed and there is no central business area. Earlier names were The Range*, Sand Ridge*, The Basin*, and The Summit*.
S27,T5N,R2W,SLM; 4,423' (1,348m). 88, 100 (v17), 360.

CLIVE SIDING* (Tooele) was ten miles east of Knolls* on the Western Pacific Railroad where I-80 and the railroad pass over the Cedar Mountains. This temporary maintenance camp and siding was abandoned in 1955. MRN
T1S,R11W,SLM; 4,285' (1,306m). 498.

CLOVER* (Tooele) is a small agricultural community on the east side of Johnsons Pass on Clover Creek and U-215. The settlement was originally named Johnsons Settlement* for Luke S. Johnson, an early settler. The name was then changed to Shambip*, a Goshute Indian word for rush or bulrush plants. Shambip was then called Johnson* up

until 1856 when G. S. Craig renamed the town Clover after a nearby flat covered with native clover. At this time, John Bennion built a small cabin and wintered a few cattle in the area. Clover and St. John* have since merged to become Rush Valley City*.
S31,T5S,R5W,SLM; 5,165' (1,574m). 153, 288, 360, 367, 542.

CLOVER CREEK* (Juab). See Mona* (Juab).

CLUFF* (Summit) was an early settlement that was absorbed into Coalville*. It was named for William W. Cluff, a Mormon stake president and early mayor of Coalville. The settlement was previously called Spring Hollow* for the many springs located in the area.
288, 567.

CLYDE LAKE (Summit) is in the southwest section of the Uinta Mountains, one-fourth mile northwest of Wall Lake. The lake was named for Clyde Maycock, who had moved into the area and built cabins near Trial Lake.
S30,T1S,R9E,SLM; 10,425' (3,178m). 379.

CLYDES SPRING (Emery) is at the head of Clydes Spring Canyon, which drains northeast off The Spur into the head of Horsethief Canyon. The spring was named for Clyde Tidwell who ran cattle in the region with his father, Tom, and his brothers Frank, Keep, and Rowland. The old Tidwell Ranch is four miles northwest of Clydes Spring, toward Horseshoe Canyon. This entire area is now part of Canyonlands National Park.
S1,T28S,R16E,SLM; 5,575' (1,699m). 578.

CLYDES SPRING CANYON (Emery) originates on the east side of The Spur, west of Millard Canyon. It drains northeast into the head of Horsethief Canyon. See Clydes Spring.
SW¼,T27S,R17E,SLM.

COAL BED CANYON (Garfield) originates at the north end of the Kaiparowits Plateau at the junction of Willow Creek and Canaan Creek. It drains northeast into Alvey Wash. Don Shurtz opened a vein of coal in this canyon which was mined for many years.
S3,T36S,R2E,SLM to S36,T35S,R2E,SLM. 12. D.L. 6504.

COAL BED CANYON (San Juan) originates near the small agricultural community of Northdale* in Dolores County, Colorado. It drains southeast into Montezuma Canyon. Coal beds are exposed in the canyon.
S35,T36S,R24E,SLM (at mouth).

COAL CANYON (Emery, Grand). See Gray Canyon.

COAL CITY* (Carbon) was up Consumers Wash, nine miles west of Spring Glen* and eight miles north of the coal-mining town of Wattis*. The area was grazing land until 1885 when the town was laid out and settled by George Storrs. Oak Springs Bench* was the first town name; the name was later changed to Cedar Mesa Ranch*. In 1921 it was called Great Western* after the mining company operating in the vicinity, then the name was changed to Coal City. The town began to slow down in 1935 and was completely abandoned by 1940. At one time, the famous boxer Jack Dempsey lived and trained in Coal City and the town temporarily adopted the name Dempseyville*. It was hoped that Dempsey would invest in local coal properties and consideration was given to permanently changing the town name to Dempsey City*. Dempsey decided not to invest, however, and the name Coal City was retained.
S3,T14S,R8E,SLM; 7,050' (2,149m). 89, 100 (v17), 542, 607.

COAL CREEK (Iron) originates in Cedar Canyon east of Cedar City* at the

junction of Ashdown and Crow creeks and drains west into the valley. Parley P. Pratt first named the creek Little Muddy. When coal was discovered in the fall of 1851, the name was changed to Coal Creek.
S36,T36S,R10W,SLM (at head). 27, 136, 423.

COAL CREEK* (Iron). See Cedar City*.

COAL WASH (Emery) originates on the San Rafael Swell north of the head of Sinbad country, at the junction of the North and South forks. It drains into North Salt Wash. There are three different reports on the origin of the name. One suggests the name comes from evidence of coal in the wash. Another suggests it was a tar seep mistaken for coal. A third records that the canyon was quite cold, hence the name Cold Wash.
S28,T20S,R9E,SLM. 193, 567.

COALVILLE* (Sanpete). See Wales* (Sanpete).

COALVILLE* (Summit) is at the mouth of Chalk Creek on the Weber River, near Echo Reservoir. Coalville is the county seat of Summit County. The community was originally settled by H. B. Wild, A. B. Williams, their families, and others. In 1858, Thomas Rhodes discovered and developed coal deposits in this area; the operation was called the Church Mines by the Mormon Church. An earlier name was Chalk Creek*, after the local creek. After the coal discovery, the community changed the name to Coalville because many of the miners came from Coalville*, England. The coal mines are no longer active.
S8,9,T2N,R5E,SLM; 5,586' (1,703m). 27, 151, 288, 314, 542, 567.

COBB SPRING (Beaver) is in the Mountain Home Range, draining west into Hamlin Valley. The spring was named after Ernest Cobb, a stockman of the 1870s.

S17,T26S,R19W,SLM; 7,500' (2,286m). 125.

COCKSCOMB (Garfield, Kane) parallels Cottonwood Creek and Wash with Cads Crotch on the east. The Cockscomb extends south into Arizona and US-89 passes through it at Catstair Canyon. This jagged geologic feature has a north-south orientation and at the north end becomes prominent above the horizon just south of Canaan Peak. The sharp, incised, heavily eroded sawtooth profile of this feature resembles the comb of a rooster.
T37-44S,R1,2W,R1E (in Utah).

COFFIN LAKE (Summit) is in the central section of the Uinta Mountains on the headwaters of the middle fork of Beaver Creek. The lake has the general shape of a coffin.
10,853' (3,308m).

COHAB CANYON (Wayne) is a small canyon originating in Capitol Reef National Park. It is one-half mile south of the ghost town of Fruita* and drains northeast into the Fremont River. The canyon received its name from the early Mormon settlers who occasionally fled to the canyon to avoid federal officers who pursued them over their polygamist beliefs.
S2,14,T29S,R6E,SLM. 100(v17).

COLD SPRING (Beaver) is on the northern slopes of Wittwer Hill on the northwest side of the Tushar Mountains. The water is quite cold as it flows from the quartzite rock.
S8,T27S,R6W,SLM; 8,350' (2,545m). 125.

COLLEGE* (Cache). See College Ward*.

COLLEGE WARD* (Cache) is midway between Logan* and Wellsville* on US-89. In 1877, just one month before his death, Brigham Young deeded this farmland he held under his name to the local Mormon church authorities to help maintain the Utah State Agricultural

College (Utah State University) at Logan. In 1879 the first settlers were permitted to move onto the land and start constructing their homes. This was the beginning of a new community, College Ward.
S19W,T11N,R1W,SLM; 4,490' (1,369m). 288, 360, 449, 546.

COLLETT CANYON (**Garfield**) is divided into the Right Hand Collett and the Left Hand Collett. Both originate at the north end of the Kaiparowits Plateau about twelve miles from Escalante* on the Hole-in-the-Rock road. The two Collett Canyons unite to form Twenty-mile Wash. It was named for Reuben Collett, whose cattle ranged there.
T37,38S,R4E,SLM. 12, 602.

COLLETT TOP (**Kane**) was the rangeland on the Kaiparowits Plateau at the head of the Collett Canyons. See Collett Canyon.
S33,34,T38S,R4E,SLM; 6,450' (1,966m).

COLLINS GULCH (**Salt Lake**) originates two miles south of Alta* on the northern slopes of Mount Baldy, and drains north into Little Cottonwood Creek at Alta*. It was named for Charles Collins, an early prospector who worked in and around Alta. Collins died of a heart attack while removing his tools from a tunnel in a mine he had just sold. Today the gulch is part of the large recreational center surrounding Alta.
NW¼,T3S,R3E,SLM. 454, 546.

COLLINSTON* (**Box Elder**) is a small agricultural community on U-69, three miles south southeast of Fielding*. The town had an earlier name of Hampton* or Hampton Ford* for Ben Hampton, who operated a toll ferry across the Bear River in 1867-68. Hampton was changed to Collinston to honor Collins Fulmer, a favorite conductor on the Utah Northern Railroad. At that time James Standing bought the ferry and bridge rights from Hampton and William Godbe and moved the town site one mile east to higher ground.
S17,T12N,R2W,SLM;   4,417'   (1,346m). 100(v17), 360, 542, 546, 567.

COLOB (**Washington**). See Kolob.

COLORADO RIVER originates high on the western slopes of the Rocky Mountains north of Grand Lake in Colorado. The river drains southwest into eastern Utah and the Canyonlands National Park, gathering in the Green River at The Confluence, then the Dirty Devil, the Escalante, and the San Juan Rivers (among others) as it leaves Utah through Lake Powell.

Various sections of the river have had different names during its history. The giant Cocopa Indians who lived near the mouth of the river kept warm in the cool autumn nights by using firebrands. For this reason, Diaz called that section of the river the Rio del Tizon (Firebrand River). It was also called the Buena Guia of Alarcon. At various times it has also been known as the Rio Grande de Buena Esperanze (River of Good Hope); River of Mystery; San Clemente (Merciful); Red River, and some local Indians near the Grand Canyon called it the Pahaweep (Water Down Deep in the Earth).

The name "Colorado" originated in 1604 when Onate gave the Spanish name "Rio Colorado" (reddish-tinted river) to what is today the Little Colorado River. "Rio Colorado" was gradually transferred to the largest river in the area, the Grande River, from the mouth to The Confluence. In the early 1800s' writings, the name evolved into Colorado del Occidente and its many variations. American explorers and trappers gradually anglicized the Spanish versions into the name Colorado River of the West, which then became the present-day Colorado River. It is now one of the oldest geographic names originated by white men in the United States.

In order to solve the problem of having names that were still being used for different sections of the river, in 1921 the U.S. Congress changed the river's name to "Colorado." However, the earlier name, "Grand(e)," was still in effect for the section from the Colorado border to The Confluence in Utah. So the Utah legislature followed the national program and changed this last section to "Colorado." The entire river is now officially known as the Colorado River. 129, 159, 160, 314, 420, 422, 429, 501, 546, 583.

COLTON* (Utah) is on US-6,50 at the junction of the Price and White rivers. The community was a junction and a railroad siding that served Scofield*. It was established in 1883 as Pleasant Valley Junction* and later, in the mid-1890s, the name was changed to Colton for William F. Colton, a railroad official. The community was abandoned in the 1950s as improved equipment made longer railroad hauls more efficient. As a result, the demand for coal shipments from Scofield and Pleasant Valley was reduced. S22,T11S,R8E,SLM; 7,180' (2,188m). 89, 100(v17), 494, 542, 546.

COLUMBIA* (Carbon) is part of East Carbon City*, one and one-half miles south southwest of Dragerton*. On July 23, 1973, Dragerton and Columbia were incorporated into East Carbon City. Columbia was built in 1922 to house miners who mined coal for the Columbia Steel Plant at Ironton* between Provo* and Springville*. Columbia received its name from the mine. S17,18,T15S,R4E,SLM; 6,200' (1,890m). 100 (v17), 288, 360, 546.

COLUMBINE CANYON (Iron) originates in the northeast section of Cedar Breaks National Monument and drains southwest into Rattle Creek. The canyon received its name from the beautiful Columbine wildflower (Aquilega). S25,26,T36S,R9W,SLM.

COLUMBINE RIDGE (Iron) has a northeast-southwest orientation north of Columbine Canyon in the Cedar Breaks National Monument. See Columbine Canyon.

COMB RIDGE (San Juan) extends from the southwest slopes of the Blue Mountains (Abajo) south into Monument Valley. It is a sharp-toothed ridge resembling the comb of a rooster. The ridge obstructed the passage of the Hole-in-the-Rock expedition, but they were finally able to overcome it by moving south along the base to the San Juan River. There they were again able to travel east. T36-43S,R20,21E,SLM. 58, 359, 360, 406, 546, 567.

COMB WASH (San Juan) is parallel to Comb Ridge. The Hole-in-the-Rock expedition followed this wash to the San Juan River before moving east. The wash was an ancient Indian trail. See Comb Ridge.

COMO SPRINGS* (Morgan) is one mile east of Morgan*. Dr. T. S. Wadsworth named this well-known recreational center after the birthplace of Mrs. Samuel Francis. She was born near Lake Como in northern Italy. S31,T4N,R3E,SLM; 5,082' (1,549m). 378.

CONFLUENCE, THE (San Juan) is the junction of the Colorado and the Green rivers. T30S,R19E,SLM. 160, 422, 496.

CONFUSION RANGE (Juab, Millard) has a north-south orientation between the Snake and Tule valleys. The range is named for its rugged isolation and confusing topography. The high point is King Top. T14-20S,R15,17W,SLM; 8,350' (2,545'). 477, 546.

CONGER MOUNTAINS (Millard) has a north-south orientation west of the Confusion Range. It is named for an early cattleman who ran his livestock in

this area.
T18-20S,R17-18W,SLM; 7,973' (2,430m).
567.

CONGRESSMAN NATURAL BRIDGE
(San Juan). See Natural Bridges National
Monument.

CONNELLSVILLE* (Emery) was three
miles up Coal Canyon, which drains into
Huntington Canyon. It was settled in
1875 and named after the coking center
in Connellsville*, Pennsylvania. After
three years of frustration and failure,
Connellsville was abandoned.
S11,T14S,R6E,SLM; 8,700' (2,652m). 89,
516.

CONNER BASIN (Daggett) is in the
northeast section of the Uinta Mountains.
Jessen Butte is one and one-half miles
east. The basin was named for Sam and
Al Conner, outlaws and horse thieves,
killed in the basin by a local posse.
S35,36,T3N,R18E,SLM; 7,500' (2,286m).
172.

CONNOR* (Box Elder) was a railroad
siding and workers' camp several miles
west of Corinne* and south of Connor
Springs. The camp was first named
Balfour* until section foreman Rasmus
Hansen put in a side track: the town
then became known as Hansen*. Later it
was named Connor for nearby Connor
Springs. Today it is a ghost town site.
See Connor Springs.

CONNOR SPRINGS (Box Elder) is fourteen miles northwest of Corinne* and
three miles southwest of Penrose*. The
springs were named for Colonel Patrick
E. Connor, the commander of Fort
Douglas in the mid-1800s. Connor
encouraged his men to explore and
prospect for valuable minerals while they
were in the area.
S6,T10N,R4W,SLM; 4,260' (1,298m). 516,
567.

CONSUMERS* (Carbon) was eleven
miles west of Spring Glen*, where the

road leads up Consumers Wash into the
North Fork of Gordon Creek at the end
of U-139. Sweet* and National* are in
the vicinity. In 1920 A. E. Gibson,
superintendent of the Spring Canyon
mine, developed a mine known as the
Gibson. The settlement also took the
name Gibson*. In 1924 the Consumers
Mutual Coal Company took over both
the town and the mine and changed the
community name to Consumers. The
town peaked and then closed down by
1950.
S17,T13S,R8E,SLM; 7,500' (2,286m). 89,
100(v17), 607.

CONSUMERS WASH (Carbon) originates four and one-half miles east
northeast of Spring Glen*, between
Wildcat and Spring canyons. It drains
west southwest into the Price River.
S27,35,36,T13S,R9E,SLM.

COOK CORNER* (Beaver) is little more
than a point on the map southwest of
Milford* and east of Hay Spring. The
name is that of a family who settled
there. It is no longer applied locally.
S11,T29S,R11W,SLM; 5,019' (1,530m). 578.

COOKSVILLE* (Box Elder). See Grouse
Creek*.

COON CANYON (Salt Lake) originates
on the eastern slopes of the Oquirrh
Range at the junction of the Left and
Right forks, and drains east through
Bacchus*, into Salt Lake Valley. The
canyon was named for Abraham Coon,
who settled at the mouth of the canyon
in 1854. See Bacchus*.
S14,T2S,R3W,SLM to S5,T2S,R2W,SLM.

COON PEAK (Salt Lake). See
Farnsworth Peak and Bacchus*.

COONVILLE* (Salt Lake) is a ghost
town site where Bacchus* is now located.
See Bacchus* and Coon Canyon.

CO-OP CREEK (Summit) originates at
the west end of the Uinta Mountains,

one mile southeast of Castle Lake. The creek drains south into Beaver Creek in the Provo River drainage. The name comes from a cooperative work agreement in the early logging days of the region.
S11,14,27,T2W,R7E,SLM. 298.

CO-OP CREEK (Wasatch) originates in the southwest section of the Uinta Mountains, six miles southeast of the head of the Strawberry River. The creek drains into the Strawberry Reservoir in an area where community livestock grazed under the control of common herders.
S5,T2S,R11W,USM to S12,T3S,R12W,USM.

CO-OP FLAT (Iron) is between Pryor Knoll and Urie Creek, east of the headwaters of Shurtz Creek. The early Cedar Co-op sheep herd was held there during the summer months.
S18,19,T37S,R10W,SLM; 9,200' (2,804m). 567.

CO-OP KNOLL (Iron) is a prominent knoll on Kanarra Mountain on Kanarraville* Co-operative rangeland. Co-op Spring is one-half mile south.
S3,T38S,R11W,SLM; 9,775' (2,979m). 567.

CO-OP SPRING (Iron) is on Kanarra Mountain, east of Kanarraville* and one-half mile southeast of Co-op Knoll. See Co-op Knoll.
S2,T38S,R11W,SLM; 9,375' (2,857m). 567.

CO-OP VALLEY SINKS (Iron) is a mountain valley depression southeast of Parowan* where drainage water collects and is used by stockmen.
S25,26,T34S,R8W,SLM; 8,426' (2,568m). 567.

COPE CANYON (Garfield) originates at the Pink Cliffs in northeast Bryce Canyon National Park. The canyon drains southeast into the headwaters of the Paria River. Thomas H. Cope was born in Leeds*, England, then came to Tropic* in May 1896 where he purchased a farm at the mouth of the canyon which was then named for him.
S23,T36S,R3W,SLM (at mouth). 100(v17), 530.

COPENHAGEN* (Sanpete) was an early name for Manti*. Many early settlers were people of Danish descent.

COPES BASIN (Beaver) is near the mouth of Beaver River, South Fork, and the power house, and was named for William Copeland, who operated a sawmill in the basin during in the 1880s.
S25,T29S,R6W,SLM; 7,500' (2,286m). 567.

COPPER CANYON (San Juan) originates between Hoskinnini Mesa and Nokai Mesa at the junction of the east and west forks of Copper Creek. Sixteen miles southeast is Goulding*. The canyon drains northwest into the San Juan River. Prospecting for copper, gold, and silver was carried on in the canyon during the late 1800s.
S22,T43S,R13E,SLM to S13,T41S,R12E, SLM.

COPPER GLOBE (Emery) is an area of the San Rafael Swell south of Devils Canyon, at the head of Cat Canyon. Copper ore has been mined there.
T23S,R9E,SLM; 7,500' (2,286m). 193.

COPPER GULCH (Beaver) originates on the western slopes of the San Francisco Mountains north of Indian Grave Peak. It drains west into Wah Wah Valley. The name is related to the early mining of copper ore.
S3,4,T27S,R13W,SLM. 125.

COPPERFIELD* (Salt Lake) was in the south fork of Bingham Canyon, southwest of Salt Lake City*. Copperfield was an alpine mining town established in 1929 and named for the rich copper ore mined in Bingham Canyon. The town was once known as Upper Bingham*, but was eventually overrun by the ever-expanding open-pit copper mine. Copperfield was completely evacuated by

the 1950-55 period.
6,700' (2,042m). 578.

COPPERTON* (Salt Lake) is a model mining town built at the mouth of Bingham Canyon on Rattlesnake Flat. It was built in 1926 by the Utah Copper Company to provide housing for its employees when nearby Bingham* became overcrowded.
S17,18,T3S,R2W,SLM; 5,500' (1,676). 100 (v17), 360, 542.

CORAL PINK SAND DUNES (Kane) are at the northwest base of the Moquith Mountains, nine miles west of Kanab*. The dunes are a beautiful coral pink color and are approximately nine to ten miles long. The dunes are formed when south-blowing winds lose strength when passing over the Moquith Mountains. This change in wind velocity creates sand deposits in the valley. The area is now a state park.
S4,T43S,R7W,SLM to S3,T44S,R8W,SLM; 6,000' (1,829m). 578.

CORINNE* (Box Elder) is on U-83 four miles west of Brigham City*. It was one of the rare towns in Utah Territory established by anti-Mormons determined to compete with and overcome all Mormon influence. In March 1869, plans for the town were initiated and financed by Mark A. Gilmore and five companions, all men of means. The settlement was then incorporated on February 8, 1870, with the intention that it evolve into a large, thriving city. In the early competitive days, the developing community had many names: Connor* for General Patrick E. Connor, an anti-Mormon and commanding officer at Fort Douglas; Bear River* and Burg on the Bear* after the adjacent river. The name Corinne was claimed by several sources. General J. A. Williamson's daughter was the first white child born there—she was named Corinne. (This version is deemed most authentic.) Corinne of Italy was the heroine of a novel published in 1807 and has been claimed as the inspiration for

the name. Others suggested the town was named for a well-known dance hall girl named Corinne. Still others suggest that the town was named for Corinne LaVaunt (Lavont), a well-known actress who visited the town. The name could have been the result of any one of these claims. Despite plans for a thriving lake port, freighting center, railroad center, smelting center, cultural center, university, opera house, and other optimistic dreams, anticipated growth never occurred.
S6,T9N,R2W,SLM; 4,229' (1,289m). 89, 139, 288, 360, 542, 546.

CORK RIDGE (Beaver) is on the western slopes of the Tushar Mountains between Pole Creek and Pine Creek. "Cork Ridge" was a corruption of "Cart Ridge," the original name. Carts with large wheels were used to haul the lumber from the ridge.
S22,28,T28S,R6W,SLM. 125.

CORN CREEK (Garfield) originates on the eastern slopes of Barney Top, twelve miles up Main Canyon west of Escalante*, and drains east into Main Canyon. In 1875 Philo Allen and his son Edmund wintered their cattle in Main Canyon, built a house near the mouth of present-day Corn Creek, and planted a successful crop of corn.
S4,5,7,T35S,R1E,SLM. 602.

CORN CREEK (Millard) originates at the junction of the East and West forks, nine miles southeast of Kanosh*. It drains west into the desert. Pioneers noted that the Indians had planted corn near the creek.
S32,T23S,R4W,SLM to S5,T23S,R6W,SLM. D.L. 8503.

CORNER CANYON (Salt Lake) originates four miles southeast of Draper* in the extreme southeast corner of the Salt Lake Valley. It drains west into the valley.
S1,T4S,R1E,SLM to S4,R1E,SLM. 508.

CORNISH* (Cache) is on U-23 and U-61, four miles north of Trenton* and three and one-half miles west of Lewiston*. Early names were Ransom*, Trenton*, and Cannon*. In 1907, the railroad changed the name from Cannon to Cornish in honor of William D. Cornish, vice president of the Union Pacific Railroad at that time.
S3,4,9,10,T14N,R1W,SLM; 4,480' (1,366m). 249(15 Oct. 1979), 360, 542.

CORRAL CANYON (Beaver) originates on the western slopes of the Mineral Mountains at Rock Corral Springs. It links with Ranch Canyon to drain northwest into the Beaver River at Yellow Banks. There is a natural rock corral at the head of the canyon.
S14,T28S,R9W,SLM to S32,T27S,R10W, SLM. 125.

CORRAL CANYON (Beaver) originates in the Wah Wah Mountains southeast of Sewing Machine Pass and drains northwest into the open canyon at Lime Point.
S8,T27S,R15W,SLM to S36,T26S,R16W, SLM. 125.

CORRY POINT (Iron) is a point of land seven miles south of Cedar Breaks Lodge. It extends down into the junction between Deep Creek and O'Neil Gulch and was named for Andrew Corry, a sheep and dairyman who operated in the area.
S11,T38S,R10W,SLM to S25,T38S,R10W, SLM; 8,000' (2,438m). 567.

CORSON PEAK (Daggett) is the highest point of Phil Pico Mountain. It is located in the northeastern Uinta Mountains, two miles south of the Wyoming border. The King survey named it in 1871 for Lieutenant Joseph Kirby Corson, assistant surgeon on the expedition.
S29,T3N,R28E,SLM; 9,576' (2,919m). 494. D.L. 6601.

COSMOPOLITAN* (Summit) was three miles north of Park City*. It was a temporary community made up of forty

families who worked in the quarry. They processed paving blocks and dressed stone to ship to Salt Lake City*. The operation collapsed when the cement plant at Devils Slide opened.
S28,33,T1S,R4E,SLM; 6,700' (2,042m). 567.

COTTON CREEK (Box Elder) originates in the Grouse Creek Mountains near the south side of Cotton Thomas Basin. It drains south southeast into the head of Grouse Creek and was named for William C. (Cotton) Thomas. See Cotton Thomas Basin.
S15,16,T13N,R17W,SLMtoS13,T12N,R18W, SLM. 567.

COTTON THOMAS BASIN (Box Elder) is at the head of Basin Creek, which drains east into the South Fork of Junction Creek. William C. (Cotton) Thomas was a pioneer who moved to this area with his family from Brigham City* in 1869.
T13,14N,R17W,SLM; 6,550' (1,996m). 100 (v13), 139, 567, 578.

COTTONWOOD* (Salt Lake) is the area in the eastern Salt Lake Valley between Thirty-ninth and Sixty-second South and from Thirteenth East to the east foothills. It was an early settlement that expanded southeast in 1848 and was named for the luxuriant growth of cottonwood trees growing along the creek. It was the first active farming district outside of Salt Lake City* proper to be farmed by the pioneers. Variant: Big Cottonwood*.
T2S,R1E,SLM; 4,400' (1,341m). 567, 578.

COTTONWOOD* (Washington). See Harrisburg*.

COTTONWOOD CANYON (Kane) originates in the upland basin country, eight miles northwest of Kanab*, and drains south through the Vermillion Cliffs into Arizona. Cottonwoods are plentiful along the banks.
S10,T43S,R7W,SLM to S10,T44S,R7W,SLM (in Utah).

COTTONWOOD CANYON (**Washington**) originates on the southern slopes of Pine Valley Mountain at the junction of the West and Middle forks. It drains south into Quail Creek where I-15 presently is and where early Harrisburg* once was located.
S27,T40S,R15W,SLM to S23,T41S,R14W, SLM.

COTTONWOOD CREEK (**Beaver**) originates in the Indian Peak Mountains of the Needle Range. It drains into Sheep Creek at the Sheep Creek Reservoir. Cottonwoods are plentiful in this area.
T29S,R30S,R17W,SLM.

COTTONWOOD SPRING (**Beaver**) is near the head of Cottonwood Wash on the eastern slopes of the Mountain Home Range.
S25,T26S,R19W; 6,850' (2,088m).

COTTONWOOD WASH (**Beaver**) originates on the eastern slopes of the Mountain Home Range and drains northwest toward the Pine Valley Hardpan.
T26S,R19W,SLM.

COTTONWOODS*, THE (**Beaver**). See Minersville*.

COUGAR CANYON (**Kane**) originates ten miles northwest of Glendale* and drains south into Muddy Creek. Jacob H. Crasley killed a record-sized cougar there in 1910.
S1,12,T40S,R8W,SLM. 567.

COUGAR CANYON (**Piute**) is on the eastern slopes of the Tushar Mountains and drains southeast into Order Canyon. This was once cougar country.
S15,16,T29S,R4W,SLM. 567.

COUGAR CREEK (**Beaver**) originates on the western slopes of the Tushar Mountains, southwest of Puffer Lake and drains north into Lake Stream. This was once cougar country.
S15,T29S,R5W,SLM.

COUGAR MOUNTAIN (**Washington**) is in the northwest section of Zion Canyon National Park between North Creek and Coalpits Wash. Many cougars were found here during the earlier days.
S3,10,T41S,R11W,SLM; 6,479' (1,975m).

COUGAR SPRING (**Beaver**) is in the north central section of the Needle Mountains of the Mountain Home Range. It drains west into Hamblin Valley Wash on the Utah-Nevada border.
S9,T27S,R19W,SLM; 7,300' (2,225m).

COURTHOUSE WASH (**Grand**) originates at Courthouse Pasture, twelve miles northwest of Moab* near US-160. It drains southeast into the Colorado River and receives its name from the numerous monolithic sandstone features that are found along its course.
S20,29,T24S,R20E,SLM to S27,T25S,R21E, SLM. 514, 546.

COVE* (**Cache**) is seven miles north of Richmond*. In 1863 Goudy Hogan relocated his house from Richmond to the area near the mill that was built on High Creek in 1862. Hogan became one of the first settlers of Cove. The settlement was in a geographically protected area and was first called Coveville*.
S28,T25S,R3W,SLM; 5,548' (1,691m). 360, 449, 542, 567.

COVE* (**Sevier**) is a small community in a semi-protected area on US-89 between Joseph* and Sevier*.
S28,T25S,R3W,SLM; 5,548' (1,691m).

COVE CREEK (**Millard**) originates at the summit east of Cove Fort* between the south end of the Pavant Range and the Tushar Mountains. It drains west past Cove Fort, from which it receives its name, then disappears into the desert at Beaver Bottoms.
S19,30,T25S,R5W,SLM to T25S,R10W,SLM (at Beaver Bottoms). 314, 355.

COVE FORT* (**Millard**) was built in a geographically protected area at the crossing of Cove Creek (near junction of I-70 and I-15) and the old California road. Ira Hinckley built this outpost fort under the direction of Brigham Young during the Indian wars of the 1860s. In pioneer times, Cove Creek was the southern boundary of the Pah Vant Indian lands. Today Cove Fort is acknowledged as the best preserved of the old forts of Utah.
S25,T25S,R7W,SLM; 5,998' (1,828m). 89, 314, 360, 542, 546.

COVE RIVER (**Sevier**) is a small river originating against the foothills, two miles north of Glenwood* (Glen Cove*). The river drains southwest into the Sevier River and received its name from the community.
S23,34,T23S,R2W,SLM.

COVEVILLE* (**Cache**). See Cove* (Cache).

COW CAMP WELL* (**Beaver**) is a watering tank for cattle in the Pine Valley, north of U-21 and south of the Pine Valley Hardpan.
S19,T26S,R16W,SLM; 5,214' (1,589m).

COW CANYON (**Kane**) originates at the Waterpocket Fold and drains southwest into the Escalante River. Wild cattle, which had escaped from domestic herds, roamed this area in earlier days.
T39S,R9E,SLM. 12.

COW HOLLOW (**Beaver**) originates on the western slopes of the Mineral Mountains at McEwen Springs. It drains west into the Beaver River east of Milford* and was named for an incident involving a cow carcass in the hollow.
S22,T28S,R9W,SLM. 125.

COW TRACK RESERVOIR (**Beaver**) is in Pine Valley south of the Pine Valley Hardpan and west of Lime Point. Cow trails converging towards the reservoir can be seen from a distance.

S25,T26S,R17W,SLM; 5,220' (1,591m). 578.

COWBOY PASS (**Millard**) is in the Confusion Range south of Plympton Ridge. It is a well-known pass on the cattle trail through the Confusion Range between Snake and Tule valleys.
SW¼,T17S,R17W,SLM; 5,718' (1,743m). 578.

COWBOY PASTURE SPRING (**Emery**) is on Coal Wash, North Fork of the San Rafael Swell and was a favorite camping spot of early stockmen.
193.

COWBOY SPRING (**Beaver**) is in the foothills west of the north end of Beaver Valley. Archie Brooks, a cowpuncher, developed and named the spring in 1916.
S12,T28S,R8W,SLM; 7,100' (2,164m). 567.

COWPUNCHER PASTURE (**Garfield**) is on the southern slopes of the Aquarius Plateau at the junction of the two main forks of Pine Creek. Early cowboys used this area as a pasture for their horses. It later served as a forest ranger's pasture.
7,940' (2,420m). 12.

COYOTE* (**Garfield**). See Antimony*.

COYOTE* (**Grand**). See La Sal*.

COYOTE BENCH (**Beaver**) is on the western slopes of the south Tushar Mountains, between South Creek and Coyote Creek. Coyotes roam the area.
S28,33,T30S,R6W,SLM; 7,050' (2,149m).

COYOTE GULCH (**San Juan**) originates at Fiftymile Mountain of the Kaiparowits Plateau and drains east into the Escalante River at Stevens Arch. The gulch is one of the larger drainage systems leading into the Escalante River. It is also known for its large number of natural arches. Coyotes are prevalent throughout the area.
S29,30,T39S,R7E,SLM (to Escalante River). 12.

COYOTE NATURAL BRIDGE (**Kane**) is a large natural bridge in Coyote Gulch of the Escalante drainage system. The bridge was named after the gulch. T39S,R8E,SLM.

COYOTE SPRING (**Beaver**) is on the southwest slopes of the San Francisco Mountains, north of Carbonate Gulch. According to legend, a coyote dug a hole in the ground here and water seeped out. S6,T27S,R12W; 6,775' (2,065m). 125.

CRAFTON* (**Millard**). In 1874 the David Crafts family and others established this small settlement in the salt marshes twelve miles west of Deseret*. After they built a small reservoir, the community was also called Laketown*. Crafton was abandoned in 1906-7 because of drought, excess alkalinity, and crop failures. 89, 100(v17), 508.

CRAFTS LAKE (**Millard**) is in the Sevier River channel along the salt marsh desert, two miles southwest of the Gunnison Massacre monument and eight miles southwest of Hinckley*. See Crafton*. S7,T18S,R8W,SLM; 4,555' (1,388m).

CRAGGY CANYON (**Uintah**). See Split Mountain.

CRANDALL CITY* (**Summit**). See Rockport* (Summit).

CRANER PEAK (**Tooele**) is in the center of the Lakeside Mountains bordering the west side of the Great Salt Lake. S26,T2N,R9W,SLM; 6,625' (2,019m).

CRATER KNOLL (**Beaver**) is an extinct volcanic crater in the foothills west of the north end of Beaver Valley. S11,T27S,R8W,SLM; 7,702' (2,348m).

CRATER LAKES (**Sevier**) are on the Mytoge Mountains east of Fish Lake. The entire area is of volcanic origin and two of the shallow craters are filled with water. S2,11,T26S,R2E,SLM; 9,503' (2,897m) and 9,510' (2,899m).

CRAWFORD DRAW (**Emery**) originates south of The Wickiup in the Sinbad country of the San Rafael Swell. It drains southeast into the head of Straight Wash. Both Nathaniel "Tan" Crawford and George Crawford ran cattle here in earlier days. S27,35,T22S,R11E,SLM (upper section of draw). 193.

CRAWFORD MOUNTAINS (**Rich**) have a northeast-southwest orientation along the Utah-Wyoming line and are bordered on the south and west by the Bear River. The high point is Rex Peak. The mountains were named for the Crawfords, who ran their cattle there in 1875. T9-11N,R7,8E,SLM; 7,996' (2,437m). 100 (v17), 360, 466(15 June 1978), 567.

CRAWFORD WASH (**Washington**) is four miles northeast of the ghost town of Shunesburg* and three miles southeast of the Zion Canyon-Mount Carmel highway tunnel. It was named for William Robinson Crawford, an early Mormon bishop and pioneer who lived in the vicinity. T42S,R10W,SLM. 530.

CRAZY CREEK (**Beaver**) originates in the Tushar Mountains and drains southeast into Merchant Creek. One report on the name origin states that the creek was named for the unexpected sharp changes in its course. Another says that the name of the creek had to do with Lousy Jim, an early eccentric prospector and sheepherder who lived nearby on Lousy Jim Creek. S8,T29S,R5W,SLM. 100(v17), 355, 567.

CRESCENT, THE (**Duchesne**) is a landform several square miles in size, located four miles north of Roosevelt* and east

of U-121. Several temporary communities including Crescent*, Cedarview*, Basin*, Monarch*, and others were established in this area. All failed and today it is an agricultural region with a few scattered homes and farms that may or may not have again picked up some of the old community names.
S28,33,T1S,R1W,USM; 5,200' (1,585m). 89, 165.

CRESCENT* (Duchesne). In 1905-6 several people attempted to settle this and several other sites in The Crescent, a land area two to four miles north of Roosevelt*. See The Crescent.
S2,3,T2S,R1W,USM; 5,150' (1,570m).

CRESCENT* (Salt Lake) is a small settlement on US-91, three miles south of Sandy City*. It was an early outgrowth of nearby Draper* and was named by Nils August Nilson. Nilson's selection of the name was influenced by the crescent curve in the Wasatch Mountains.
S18,19,T3S,R1E,SLM; 4,425' (1,349m). 288, 360, 542, 567.

CRESCENT JUNCTION* (Grand) is at the junction of US-163, I-70, and US-6,50, eighteen miles east of Green River*. Originally it was a wayside stop and service station but it has recently expanded to include permanent residents. The name comes from the crescent-shaped configuration of the Book Cliffs near the junction.
S33,T21S,R19E,SLM; 4,900' (1,494m).

CRESCENT LAKE (Cache) is in the Bear River Range, five miles north northeast of Naomi Peak and Mount Gog. It has a general crescent shape.
R2E,T14N,SLM; 8,450' (2,576m).

CRESCENT LAKE (Garfield) is near Trail Point at the south end of the Boulder Mountain section of the Aquarius Plateau. Nearby are Circle, Half Moon, and Horseshoe lakes. Crescent Lake is between the headwaters of Boulder Creek, East and West forks.

The shape of the lake has the gentle curve of a crescent.
T31S,R4E,SLM; 10,800' (3,292m).

CRICKET HILLS (Millard) have a north-south orientation and run along the eastern border of Sevier Lake. The hills were named by John R. Murdock, who ran stock there in the early 1880s. In season he found great hoards of "Mormon" crickets moving out of the hills into the lower valleys.
T20-23S,R9E,10E,SLM; 7,040' (2,146m). 567.

CROCODILE LAKE (Kane) lies six miles north of Kanab* along US-89 at the mouth of a cave. The opening of the cave was thought to resemble the mouth of a huge crocodile.
S30,T42S,R6W,SLM; 5,478' (1,670m). 567.

CROOKED CREEK (Summit) originates at the west end of the Uinta Mountains on the western slopes of Hoyt Peak and drains into Beaver Creek. It cuts a crooked course through the valley.
S36,T1S,R6E,SLM to S36,T1S,R5E,SLM.

CROSS CANYON (San Juan) originates near the Colorado-Utah line. The canyon crosses into Utah north of the Holly Group Ruins of the Hovenweep National Monument and drains west into Nancy Patterson Canyon northeast of the Hatch Trading Post. The canyon runs east west instead of north south, which is the common orientation of the other canyons in this vicinity.
S22,T38S,R26E,SLM to S33,T38S,R25E,SLM (in Utah).

CROSSING OF THE FATHERS (Kane, San Juan). This famous crossing is now buried under several hundred feet of Lake Powell waters. It was here in November 1776 that the Domínguez and Escalante party finally found a way to cross the Colorado River on their return to New Mexico. The Indians called it Ute Ford and the Spaniards called it El Vado de los Padres. Padre Bay of Lake Powell,

which now covers the crossing, was named to honor what used to be the mouth of Padre Creek.
T43S,R5E,SLM. 420, 583.

CROTON CANYON (Kane) originates on the Kaiparowits Plateau at the junction of Sunday Canyon and Rogers Canyon and drains south into Last Chance Creek. The word "Croton" has several meanings including that of a type of insect or plant (i.e., *Croton tiglium*) having medicinal properties.
S1,T41S,R5E,SLM to S30,T41S,R6E,SLM.

CROUSE CANYON (Daggett). See Crouse Creek.

CROUSE CREEK (Daggett) originates in the eastern Uinta Mountains at Crouse Reservoir. It drains north northeast to enter the Green River at the mouth of Swallow Canyon. It was named for Charles Crouse, a bullwhacker who became a rancher here in 1880. An earlier name was Jimmie Reed Creek after Jimmie and his wife, Margaret: they built a cabin in 1876 at the mouth of the creek.
S23,T1S,R24E,SLM to S2,T1N,R25E,SLM. 172, 609.

CROUSE RESERVOIR (Uintah) is in the eastern Uinta Mountains on Pot Creek, eight miles north of Diamond Mountain. See Crouse Creek.
S23,T1S,R24E,SLM; 7,165' (2,184m). 172, 609.

CROW SEEP (Garfield) is in Robbers Roost country near the Ekker (Joe Biddlecome) Ranch. Joe caught a jet black wild mustang at the spring and named it Crow. The spring is named for the horse.
S14,T29S R14E,SLM; 5,825' (1,775m). 24.

CROWLEYVILLE* (Sanpete) is a part of Centerfield* midway between Axtell* and Centerfield on US-89. It is still known as Crowleyville. John (Crowley) Nielsen and his family arrived in the area

around 1890. John's nickname, Crowley, was a place where he lived in Denmark before he emigrated.
S5,T20S,R1E,SLM; 5,100' (1,554m). 360.

CROWS NEST (Iron). See Antelope Range.

CROYDON* (Morgan) is a small community at the junction of Lost Creek and the Weber River. A group, including the families of George Knight and James Walker, settled there in 1862. The community's first name was Lost Creek* after the nearby creek on which the families settled. The name was changed to Croydon because the majority of settlers were from Croydon, England.
S20,T4N,R4E,SLM; 5,350' (1,631m). 378, 542.

CRYSTAL* (Millard). See Flowell*.

CRYSTAL CANYON (Juab) originates one mile southeast of the ghost town site of Diamond*. It drains southeast into Diamond Gulch. Early prospectors thought they were finding diamonds when the crystals were actually valueless quartz. See also Diamond*.
S8,16,17,T11S,R2W,SLM. 89.

CRYSTAL CARBON* (Grand) is approximately seventeen miles northwest of Cisco* near the mouth of Diamond and Flume canyons. In 1926 a plant was built that utilized the plentiful natural gas to manufacture carbon black. The company town consisted of two rows of houses built out of tin sheeting. The town was named after the West Virginia company that owned the operation. The plant closed and went out of business after Texas companies produced the product at a more competitive price.
S7,T18S,R23E,SLM; 5,350' (1,631m). 146.

CRYSTAL PEAK (Box Elder) is at the east end of the Raft River Mountains at the head of Crystal Hollow. Crystal Spring is on the eastern slopes at the head of Crystal Hollow. The springwater

formed minute crystals on the surrounding rocks. The peak received its name from the spring.
S28,T14N,R12W,SLM; 7,770' (2,368m). 578.

CRYSTAL PEAK (**Millard**) is at the northern end of the Wah Wah Mountains near the southern end of the Confusion Mountains. The peak is composed of white pumice-like volcanic material that makes it visible from a great distance.
S24,T23S,R16W,SLM; 7,106' (2,166m). 567.

CRYSTAL SPRING (**Beaver**) is on the western slopes of the San Francisco Mountains, across the summit from the head of Sawmill Canyon. The water is unusually clear.
S22,T26S,R13W,SLM; 7,000' (2,134m).

CRYSTAL SPRING (**Box Elder**) was discovered in 1884. See Crystal Peak (Box Elder).
567.

CUB ISLAND (**Box Elder**) is in Great Salt Lake at the north end of Gunnison Island. It becomes part of Gunnison Island in low water, which is how the name originated. In other words, the cub belongs to the lioness—Gunnison Island.
4,300' (1,311m). 133, 360.

CUB RIVER (**Cache**) originates in Idaho and drains into Utah northeast of Lewiston*, to enter the Bear River. Legend suggests that when Brigham Young was crossing the Bear River near this section, he named the smaller river the Cub River.
S34,T15N,R1E,SLM to S6,T13,R1E,SLM. 100 (v17), 567.

CUBERANT LAKE (**Summit**) is at the western end of the Uinta Mountains, two and one-half miles north of Reids Peak. This long, slender lake has a Ute Indian name meaning long.
S15,T1S,R9E,SLM; 10,420' (3,176m). 298, 530.

CUDDYBACK LAKE (**Garfield**) is on the Aquarius Plateau two miles east of McGath Lake. Cuddyback was a local stockman and early peace officer.
T32S,R3E,SLM; 9,560' (2,914m). 602.

CULLEN CREEK (**Beaver**) originates in the Tushar Mountains on the western slopes of City Creek Peak and drains into Puffer Lake. It was named for Mat Cullen, a mining man who spent his vacations in the vicinity between 1878 and 1882.
S6,T29S,R4W,SLM. 100(v17), 125.

CULVERT CANYON (**Iron**) originates on the southern slopes of Stoddard Mountain of the Harmony Mountains, west of Cedar City*. The canyon drains south into Pace Draw. The forest road crosses the canyon near its mouth where a large culvert was installed.
S19,29,32,T37S,R13E,SLM. 567.

CUMMINGS MESA (**San Juan**) is south of and near the Colorado River, six miles west of Navajo Mountain. Byron H. Cummings, an archaeologist and geologist who worked and studied in the region, contributed to the overall knowledge of the pre-history of southeast Utah.
R8E,T43S,SLM; 6,000' (1,829m). 567.

CUNEAL* (**Uintah**). See Bennett*.

CUNNINGHAM HILL (**Beaver**) is in the benchlands east of the Mineral Mountains near Cunningham Wash. It was named for Cunningham Matthews, an early settler.
S3,T28S,R8W,SLM; 6,200' (1,890m). 125.

CUNNINGHAM WASH (**Beaver**) originates in the northeast Mineral Mountains, north of Bearskin Mountain and northwest of Beaver*. It drains south into Wildcat Creek. See Cunningham Hill.
S8,T27S,R8W,SLM to S35,T28S,R8W,SLM.

CURLEW VALLEY (**Box Elder**) is in north central Utah, north of Great Salt Lake. Northeast and east are Snowville* and the Hansel Mountains. The valley was named after the long-billed curlew, a long-legged bird with a long, down-curved bill. Nearby to the south is the Locomotive Springs Waterfowl Management Area. Variant: Curley Valley.
T13,14N,R8,9,10W,SLM; 4,400' (1,341m). 89, 578. D.L. 7702.

CURRANT CANYON (**Duchesne**) originates in the Badland Cliffs north of Nine Mile Canyon. The canyon drains south into Nine Mile Creek between Trail and Petes canyons. The wild currant is common in the area.
S36,T11S,R14E,SLM (at mouth).

CURRANT CREEK (**Wasatch**) originates south of the west end of the Uinta Mountains at the junction of the Left and South forks of Pass Creek. The creek drains southeast into Red Creek. Wild currants grow around the creek area.
S35,T1S,R11W,USM to S34,T3S,R8W,USM.

CURRANT CREEK PEAK (**Wasatch**) is near the head of Currant Creek, Left Fork, southeast of Heber*.
S19,T1S,R11W,USM; 10,554' (3,217m).

CURRY CANYON (**Emery**) originates on the Big Horn benches and drains into the Green River. It was named for the Curry brothers, who were local outlaws along with their Uncle, Flat Nose George. Eventually, all the Currys were killed by gunfire.
S12,14,T18S,R16E,SLM. 24, 303, 415.

CURTIS CREEK (**Cache**) originates eight miles east northeast of Hardware Ranch and drains west into Blacksmith Fork. It was named for Lehi Curtis, who was the original owner of Hardware Ranch*. See Hardware Ranch.
S14,T10N,R4E,SLM (at mouth).

CURTIS RIDGE (**Cache**) is east of the Hardware Ranch* and has an east northeast-west southwest orientation. See Curtis Creek.
T10N,R4E,SLM; 8,884' (2,708m).

CUTTHROAT LAKE (**Summit**) is at the west end of the Uinta Mountains, three miles west of Hayden Peak. Cutthroat trout were planted in the lake.
S14,T1S,R9E,SLM; 9,990' (3,045m). 578.

CUTLER RESERVOIR (**Cache**) was constructed at the junction of the Little Bear River and the Bear River, near Newton*.
T1,2W,R12,13N,SLM; 4,407' (1,343m).

CYCLONE LAKE (**Garfield**) is five miles north northwest of Lake Posy on the Aquarius Plateau. It is a beautiful alpine lake one-half mile in length. A wide swath of trees near the lake have been blown down, seemingly by a cyclone or tornado.
9,865' (3,007m). 12, 567.

CYS CACHE LAKE (**Beaver**) is in the Tushar Mountains on the Beaver River, South Fork, east of Hi Low Lake. The lake was first stocked with fish in 1914 by the game warden, Cyrus Davis. It was named Cys Cache Lake after fishing in the lake was legalized.
S30,T29S,R5W,SLM; 7,700' (2,347m). 125.

- D -

DAGGETT COUNTY is in the extreme northeast corner of the state. The county was created in January 1918 and is the most recently established Utah county. It was named for Ellsworth Daggett, first surveyor general of Utah. He surveyed an important irrigation canal that brought water to the county. Manila* is the county seat.
6, 172, 360.

DAGGETT LAKE (Daggett) is in the northeast section of the Uinta Mountains on the headwaters of Sheep Creek, South Fork. Two miles northwest is Spirit Lake. See Daggett County for name source.
10,462' (3,189m).

DAIRY CANYON (Kane) originates in the high country between Johnson and Kanab canyons and drains into Johnson Canyon. A pioneer dairy was once located in the canyon.
S9,T43S,R1W,SLM to S35,T42S,R1W,SLM. 100(v17), 567.

DAIRY RIDGE (Rich) is four miles east of Monte Cristo Peak. A local man and his family used to move onto the ridge every summer. They brought their milk cows for producing milk, butter, and cheese to sell to employees of the sawmill located in the area.
S13,14,T4E,R8N,SLM to S8,18,T8N,R5E, SLM; 8,100' (2,469m). 567.

DAIRY VALLEY CREEK (Box Elder) originates near Dairy Valley in the mountains of northeastern Nevada. The creek crosses the state line into Utah and drains east into Etna Creek. Specific "dairy" names recall local farmers who moved their families and milk cows to the lush summer pastures to live in seasonal tents or cabins. They produced dairy products which they sold to miners, loggers, passing immigrants, or the military. Their cheese and butter could be barreled for export, via freight wagons, to neighboring markets.
S33,T11S,R18W,SLM (at mouth).

DAKOTA HILL (Kane) is an exposed hill in heavily eroded country, five miles northeast of The Narrows in Zion National Park. It is capped with conglomerate gravel, which lends the geologic name to this hill.
S7,T40S,R9W,SLM; 6,661' (2,030m). 530.

DALLES* (Millard). See Delle*.

DALTON* (Washington) was an 1864 settlement at the mouth of what became known as Daltons Wash. John Dalton, his four wives, and several others settled this area, one and one-half miles up the Virgin River from Virgin*. Dalton was abandoned in 1866 because of Indian problems and was never resettled.
89, 154, 311, 600.

DALTON CREEK (Morgan) originates two miles north of Francis Peak on the Davis County line. Ted Dalton gave his name to the creek after he settled at the mouth.
S21,T4N,R1E,SLM to S8,T4N,R2E,SLM. 100 (v17), 378.

DAN LEIGH HOLLOW (Iron) originates on Cedar Mountain northwest of Black Mountain and drains south into O'Neil Gulch. Daniel T. Leigh homesteaded in the hollow.
S15,22,T37S,R10W,SLM. 567.

DANCE HALL ROCK (Kane) is on the old Hole-in-the-Rock road, forty-five miles east of Escalante*. The members

of the expedition camped by this feature while waiting for a passage (the Hole) to be blasted out of the rock. This passage would provide a passageway down through the cliffs to the river crossing below. Dance Hall Rock is a large, natural sandstone amphitheater with a comparatively flat base located seventeen miles from the Hole. The amphitheater was large enough to hold meetings or socials. Members of the expedition camped at Dance Hall Rock for approximately four months before they conquered the Hole, crossed the river, and moved on.
S1,T40S,R7E,SLM; 4,725' (1,440m). 359, 546, 602.

DANDY CROSSING (Garfield) is an early name for the Hite Crossing near the mouth of the Dirty Devil River. It was considered a good, comparatively easy or "dandy" crossing. See Hite Crossing.

DANGER CAVE* (Tooele) is at the Danger Cave State Historical Monument, one mile northeast of Wendover*. The name comes from an incident that occurred during archaeological excavations when a large slab of rock fell from the ceiling and narrowly missed the workers. Apparently the cave was inhabited around 10,000 B.C.
S8,T1S,R19W,SLM; 4,285' (1,306m). 360, 569.

DANIELS* (Wasatch) is a community near the mouth of Daniels Canyon on Daniels Creek. Daniels was first settled by Aaron Daniels. Nearby, Edward Buys settled Buysville*, which was soon absorbed into Daniels. Earlier names were Lake Creek* and Center Creek*, each a small settlement located next to their respective creeks. Center Creek still exists, but Lake Creek was absorbed into Heber City*.
S17,18,T4S,R5E,SLM; 5,711' (1,741m). 100(v17), 288, 360, 377, 567.

DANIELS CANYON (Wasatch). See Daniels Creek.

DANIELS CREEK (Wasatch) originates at the head of Daniels Canyon and Daniels Pass, seventeen miles southeast of Heber City*. The creek drains northwest through Daniels Canyon into Deer Creek Reservoir. See Daniels* for name source.
S21,T6W,R12W,USM to S23,T4S,R4E,SLM.

DANISH FLATS (Grand) is eight miles north of Cisco* and was named for the early Danish settlers who attempted to homestead in the area.
T20S,R24-25E,SLM; 4,500' (1,372m). 578.

DANISH KNOLL (Sanpete) is on the summit of the Wasatch Plateau near the skyline drive, southeast of Ephraim*. One and one-half miles south is Swedish Knoll. These two names reflect the influence of the early Scandinavians who settled the area during pioneer times.
S2,T18S,R4E,SLM; 10,356' (3,157m).

DARK CANYON (San Juan) originates at Elk Ridge, eighteen miles northwest of Blanding* and drains northwest into the Colorado River. It is a deep, wild, rugged, isolated canyon.
S18,T35S,R20E,SLM (to the Colorado River).

DARK CANYON PLATEAU (San Juan) is near Middle Dark Canyon. Fable Valley, Youngs Canyon, and Bowdie Canyon all head on the plateau. The plateau received its name from the nearby canyon.

DAVE CANYON (Garfield) originates on the northern end of the Kaiparowits Plateau and drains northwest into Alvey Wash. Dave Moosman homesteaded at the mouth of the canyon.
S20,T36S,R3E,SLM to S13,T36S,R2E,SLM. 12. D.L. 6504.

DAVENPORT CANYON (Cache). See Davenport Creek.

DAVENPORT CREEK (Cache) originates fourteen miles southeast of Avon* and three miles south of Sharp Mountain. The creek drains northwest into the Little Bear River, South Fork. James Davenport cut timber here for the railroad. Nearby James Peak was named for the same man.
S27,T8N,R2E,SLM to S22,T9N,R1E,SLM. 567, 578.

DAVES HOLLOW (Garfield) originates on the Paunsaugunt Plateau near the Bryce Canyon National Park visitor center. It drains northwest into the Sevier River, East Fork. Daves Hollow was named for David O. Littlefield, who settled in Cannonville* in 1876 and began grazing sheep in the area in 1880.
S25,T36S,R4W,SLM to S10,11,T36S,R4W, SLM. 530, 531(1 July 1934 to 30 June 1935).

DAVID E. MILLER HILL (Weber) is the high point at the south end of Fremont Island. It was named for David E. Miller, a noted Utah historian. Miller was a charter member and first chairman of the Utah Committee on Geographic Names. This book is dedicated to Dr. Miller, a personal friend. The name for the hill was initiated and formalized by the Utah State Committee on Geographic Names on November 13, 1980.
S17,T5N,R4W,SLM. 578. D.L. 8103.

DAVIS* (Uintah). See Naples*.

DAVIS CANYON (San Juan) originates nine miles south southeast of Cave Spring Line Camp near the head of Horse Canyon. It drains north northeast into Indian Creek.
T32S,R20E,SLM to S33,T30S,R21E,SLM.

DAVIS COUNTY was one of the original eight counties created on October 5, 1850, at the legislative assembly of the Territory of Deseret. The area north of Salt Lake City* was organized into a county and named in honor of Daniel C. Davis, a captain in the Mormon Battalion and commanding officer of the Mormon Volunteers. Davis had died four months earlier on June 1, 1850, forty miles west of Fort Kearney, Nebraska, where he was buried on the prairie.
6, 88, 314, 360.

DAVIS CREEK (Davis) originates on the western slopes of Bountiful Peak, four miles east of Farmington*. The creek drains west into Farmington Bay in the Great Salt Lake. See Davis County for name source.
S27,T3N,R1E,SLM to S36,T3N,R1W,SLM.

DAVIS FLATS (Garfield) are on the Aquarius Plateau near Cyclone Lake, three miles northwest of Posy Lake. Johnny Davis and his brother George ran their sheep on the flats. See also Davis Gulch.
9,900' (3,018m). 12, 602.

DAVIS FORT (Box Elder) was built in 1853 on the present site of Brigham City* to help protect against the Indians. It was also known as Old Fort. It was named for William Davis who, with his family, settled there on March 11, 1851. Davis was also the first Mormon bishop at the fort.
163(8 Sept. 1934), 275, 360.

DAVIS GULCH (Kane) originates at Fiftymile Point near the southwest ridge of the Kaiparowits Plateau and drains northwest into the Escalante River. Several well-known natural arches are in this gulch. See Davis Flat for name source.
T41S,R8½E,SLM to T40S,R9E,SLM.

DAVIS HOLLOW (Uintah) originates in the eastern Uinta Mountains on the slopes of Taylor Mountain. It drains southeast into Big Brush Creek. Bill

Davis, an early sheep permittee, was blinded by dynamite caps in nearby Davis Park.
S31,32,34,T1S,R21E,SLM. 309, 567.

DAVIS LAKES (**Duchesne**) are in the central section of the Uinta Mountains on the headwaters of the Uinta River. Bob Davis was an early guide in the area and the first to stock this cluster of lakes with fish.
11,050' (3,368m). 309.

DAVIS PARK (**Uintah**). See Davis Hollow.

DAVIS SPRING (**Uintah**) is at the head of Davis Hollow.

DAY SPRING (**Iron**) is between Kanarra Mountain and Cedar Mountain west of Crystal Creek. Thomas Day herded sheep in this area.
S1,T38S,R11W,SLM; 9,200' (2,804m). 567.

DAYS CANYON (**Utah**) originates two and one-half miles south southeast of Hobble Creek, Right and Left forks. The canyon drains north into the Right Fork at the Guard Station and the Cherry Picnic area which was first opened and utilized by Abraham Day.
S3,T8W,R4E,SLM. 100(v17), 270.

DE MILLE PEAK (**Washington**) is near the southern boundary of Zion Canyon National Park, three miles south of the ghost town of Shunesburg*. The peak was named for Bishop Oliver De Mille of the Mormon Church, one of the founders of nearby Shunesburg.
6,697' (2,041m). 530, 600. D.L. 1 July 1934 to 30 June 1935.

DE MOISY PEAK (**Morgan, Weber**) is on the county line, two miles south southwest of Snow Basin. MRN
S8,T5N,R1E,SLM; 9,369' (2,856m).

DEAD HORSE POINT (**Grand**) is between Shafer Canyon and Shafer Basin in the Dead Horse Point State Park, twelve airline miles southwest of Moab*. The point is a prominent abutment on a steep-walled mesa. It is about 400 yards wide and has vertical cliff walls that drop over two thousand feet. The narrow neck leading into the mesa is approximately thirty yards wide. There are several versions to the name origin. One story has rustlers either shooting or abandoning their stolen herd in order to escape a posse. Another more accepted version records that in 1894, Arthur Taylor, a Moab stockman, was herding cattle between the La Sal Mountains summer range and the winter range along the river when he came upon a large waterpocket, typical of this arid slickrock and desert region. The water level was visible but inaccessible. Several dead horses were nearby. Unable to reach water, the horses had apparently died of thirst. The proximity of the dead horses to the point on the mesa gave rise to the name.
S5,T27S,R20E,SLM; 5,906' (1,800m). 314, 514, 546, 555(v26).

DEAD LAKE (**Uintah**) is on the Whiterocks River drainage, in the Paradise Park area of the southeastern section of the Uinta Mountains. There is no obvious plant or animal life in the lake.
S8,T3N,R1E,USM; 10,050' (3,063m). 309.

DEAD MARE WASH (**Garfield**) originates midway between Henrieville* and Escalante* near the summit. A mare died there.
S18,T36S,R1E,SLM (at mouth). 12.

DEAD OX CANYON (**Morgan**) originates seven miles south southwest of Porterville* and drains east into East Canyon Creek. There are several variations of the name source. They all suggest that several oxen were lost by early immigrants, either during a big storm or by starvation.
S26,27,28,29,T2N,R3E,SLM. 100(v17), 378, 567.

DEADMAN HILL (Wayne) is midway between the Biddlecome (Ekker) Ranch and the head of the South Fork of Robbers Roost Canyon. It was here that a young cowhand, who had recently joined an outlaw gang, was shot by a pursuing posse. The outlaws were moving east along the Old Angel Trail. The youngster died and was buried near the west end of what then became Deadman Hill.
S35,T28S,R14E,SLM; 6,047' (1,843m). 25.

DEADMAN LAKE (Uintah) is at the head of Dry Fork, five miles west of Leidy Peak. Deadman Lake received its name when an old prospector decided to stay in the mountains and work through the winter in the early 1900s. He was last seen in October by Dick Murdock and John Murray. When they returned in late spring he was found dead. Apparently he had frozen to death in his tent.
S32,T1N,R18E,SLM; 10,800' (3,292m). 442.

DEADMAN RIDGE (Garfield) is southeast of Escalante* on the road to Hole-in-the-Rock between Seep Flat and Tenmile Flat. Myron Shurts was killed by lightning here on May 10, 1912.
S33,34,T36S,R4E,SLM; 5,450' (1,661m). 12.

DEAN LAKE (Duchesne) is in the southwest section of the Uinta Mountains and is one of the four lakes in the Four Lakes Basin. It was named for Dean Clyde.
S2,11,T3N,R8W,USM. 113.

DEATH CREEK (Box Elder) originates in Death Valley in northeastern Nevada and drains east into Utah. The body of an aged Indian was found by the creek. The valley in Nevada and the Reservoir in Utah are both named from the creek.
S4,T10N,R19W,SLM to S18,T11N,R18W,SLM (in Utah). 525.

DEATH CREEK RESERVOIR (Box Elder) is near the Nevada border on Death Creek, from which it received its name.

S21,T11N,R19W,SLM; 5,845' (1,782m).

DEATH HOLLOW (Garfield) originates near Hells Backbone north of Escalante* and drains south into the Escalante River. The trail across the hollow is rugged and precipitous. When livestock lost their footing, they would plunge to their death on the underlying rocks.
NW¼,T35S,R4E,SLM (at mouth). 12.

DEATH RIDGE (Garfield) is at the head of Alvey Wash and Trap Canyon Wash on the Kaiparowits Plateau south southeast of Canaan Peak. A herd of cattle were trapped on the ridge in a snowstorm and most of them perished.
S19,20,T37S,R2E,SLM; 7,956' (2,425m). 12.

DEATH RIDGE RESERVOIR (Garfield) is on Death Ridge.
S19,T37S,R2E,SLM; 7,100' (2,164m).

DEEP CANYON (Cache) originates in the north Wellsville Mountains. It drains west, serving Mendon* with culinary water. The upper canyon is steep and rugged.
S14,T11N,R2W,SLM.

DEEP CANYON (San Juan) originates on the Rainbow Plateau several miles east of the junction of the San Juan River and the Colorado River (Lake Powell). It is a deep and narrow canyon that drains north into the San Juan River.

DEEP CREEK (Box Elder) originates in Idaho and drains south, passing through the Rose Ranch Reservoir. The creek has a deep, heavily eroded streambed. The water eventually disappears into the ground west of Locomotive Springs.
S25,T15N,R8W,SLM to T11N,R10W,SLM (in Utah).

DEEP CREEK (Garfield) originates on the Aquarius Plateau near Cyclone Lake. It drains southeast into Pine Creek at The Box. It has steep, heavily eroded sides.

12.

DEEP CREEK* (Tooele). See Ibapah*.

DEEP CREEK (Tooele) originates at the junction of East, Middle, and West creeks, in the Deep Creek Valley, one-half mile southwest of Ibapah*. The creek drains north through the valley and evaporates into the Great Salt Lake Desert. See Ibapah* for name source.
S21,T9S,R19W,SLM to T15S,R17W,SLM. D.L. 8202.

DEEP CREEK (Wasatch) originates four miles east of Strawberry Reservoir and drains southeast through Deep Creek Canyon into Currant Creek. The canyon through which the creek drains is quite deep.
S20,T3S,R10W,USM to S21,T3S,R9W,USM.

DEEP CREEK CANYON (Wasatch). See Deep Creek (Wasatch).

DEEP CREEK MOUNTAINS (Tooele) have a north-south orientation near the headwaters of Deep Creek, from which they receive their name. The high point is Ibapah Peak.
T9-12S,SLM to R18-19W,SLM; 12,087' (3,684m).

DEEP CREEK VALLEY (Tooele) is on both sides of the headwaters of Deep Creek, with Ibapah* located within the valley west of the Deep Creek Range.
T8-13S,R18-19W,SLM; ca. 5,500' (1,676m).

DEEP LAKE (Sevier) is on the western slopes of Cove Mountain, one-half mile southeast of Annabella Reservoir and three miles southwest of Big Lake. William Marble and a Mr. Mecham claimed the waters of Deep and Long lakes for irrigation.
T25S,R2W,SLM; 9,900' (3,018m). 361.

DEER CANYON (Garfield) originates on the eastern slopes of Barney Top of the Escalante Mountains. It drains east into Main Canyon west of Escalante*.

The canyon is known for its good deer hunting during season.
S18,T35S,R1E,SLM to S13,T35S,R1E,SLM.

DEER CREEK (Beaver) originates on the western slopes of the Tushar Mountains and drains southeast into Merchant Creek, West Fork. Mule deer inhabit the area.
S5,9,T29S,R5W,SLM.

DEER CREEK (Utah) originates five miles south southwest of Alta*. The creek drains into the reservoir at Tibble Fork and American Fork Canyon. Mule deer are plentiful in the canyon.
S2,T4S,R2E,SLM to S7,T4S,R3E,SLM.

DEER CREEK* (Utah) was in upper American Fork Canyon where the Tibble Fork reservoir is presently located. Four and one-half miles further up, at Dutchman Flat, was the ghost town of Forest City*. Deer Creek was an early mining and railroad community where the American Fork Railroad built an upper terminal in 1872. The settlement began to deteriorate as early the late 1870s and was a ghost town by 1880.
S7,T4S,R3E,SLM; 6,380' (1,945m). 89.

DEER CREEK CANYON (Sevier) origi-nates in the Pavant Range, nine miles west northwest of Richfield*. It drains southeast into Cottonwood Creek and into the Sevier River. Early prospectors and miners hunted deer in the canyon.
S3,T23S,R3W,SLM to S16,T23S,R3W,SLM. 100(v17), 567.

DEER CREEK LAKE STATE RECREATION AREA (Wasatch) is in Heber Valley, at the junction of the Provo River and Deer Creek, fifteen miles east of Provo*. The area was designated as a state recreation area in January 1971.
S5,T5S,R4E,SLM; 5,417' (1,651m).

DEER CREEK RESERVOIR (Wasatch) was built at the junction of Deer Creek and the Provo River.

DEER LAKE (**Beaver**) is one-half mile east of Otter Lake and south of Puffer Lake in the Tushar Mountains. Deer are numerous in this area.
S11,T29S,R5W,SLM; 9,250' (2,819m).

DEER LAKE (**Beaver**) is in the Tushar Mountains, one-half mile north of Kents Lake. Deer are numerous here.
S31,T29S,R5W,SLM; 9,575' (2,918m).

DEER TRAIL MOUNTAIN (**Piute**) is on the eastern slopes of the Tushar Mountains, four miles southwest of Marysvale*. The mountain receives its name from an incident in September 1878 when one Joseph Smith was deer hunting along this trail and discovered a lead-bearing vein of ore.
S10,14,15,T28S,R4W,SLM;10,826'(3,300m). 216.

DEFIANCE HOUSE (**San Juan**) is a prehistoric ruin found in Forgotten Canyon. Jesse Jennings, an archaeologist, discovered the ruins in 1959 and named them for the three apparently defiant warriors bearing shields and weapons shown in pictographs on the wall just above the ruins. See Forgotten Canyon.
SW¼,T37S,R12E,SLM. D.L. 8202.

DELANO PEAK (**Beaver**). See Mount Delano.

DELICATE ARCH (**Grand**) is in the Salt Wash area of Arches National Park and lies one and one-half miles east of the Wolfe Cabin near Winter Camp Wash. This feature is one of the grandest and most photogenic of Utah's natural arches. The early cowboys called the arch The Schoolmarms Bloomers. The present name demonstrates a more artistic, aesthetic approach.
S4,T24S,R22E,SLM.

DELL LOT HOLLOW (**Sevier**) originates on the eastern slopes of the Pavant Range. It drains southeast into the Sevier River Valley. In 1880 while Dell Lott was hauling timbers out of the hollow, his team ran away and wrecked his outfit.
S13,T25S,R4½W,SLM to S22,T25S,R3W, SLM. 100(v17).

DELLE* (**Tooele**) is ten miles east of Low* and sixty-five miles west of Salt Lake City* near I-80. It was established in 1880 as a maintenance camp and dispatch center for the Western Pacific Railroad where it crossed the Great Salt Lake Desert. Today it is a gas station, cafe, and siding only. An early name was Dalles Spring* but this was shortened to Delle by railroad personnel for telegraphic efficiency. "Dalles" is French and refers to water.
S5,T1S,R8W,SLM; 4,200' (1,280m). 314, 498.

DELLENBAUGH BUTTE (**Emery**) is near the mouth of the San Rafael River. Frederick Dellenbaugh was not quite eighteen when he was hired for the second trip of Major Powell's Green and Colorado River expedition. He was the expedition artist and assistant photographer. As the team worked their way down the river, Dellenbaugh remarked that this particular butte looked like an art gallery. Major Powell suggested it be named for the artist. There are Indian ruins on the top of the butte.
159, 160, 204, 217, 314, 360, 420, 515, 609.

DELTA* (**Millard**) is sixty-six miles southwest of Nephi* on US-6,50 near the Sevier River. The name describes the flatland (delta) along the Sevier River before the river drains into the Sevier Lake Sink. The town was first settled in 1906 and named Akin* for a railroad employee. The name was changed to Burtner* after a railroad official, then Melville* for an early settler involved in the Melville Irrigation Company. The name Melville confused the Postal Service because it was too similar to Millville* in Cache County, so the name Delta was finally accepted.
S12,T16S,R7W,SLM; 4,629' (1,411m). 89, 288, 314, 360, 567.

DEMPSEYVILLE* (**Carbon**). See Coal City*.

DENMARK WASH (**Sevier**) originates in the hill country, four and one-half miles northwest of Aurora*. The wash drains east southeast into the Sevier River. The name reflects the influence of the Scandinavian immigrants among the early settlers. U-63 passes through the wash.
S14,T21S,R2W,SLM to S26,T21S,R1W,SLM. 289.

DERN LAKE (**Duchesne**). See Governor Dern Lake.

DESERET* (**Millard**) is an agricultural community on U-257, nine miles southwest of Delta*. The settlement was established in 1860 and received its name from nearby Fort Deseret*. "Deseret" is a term from Mormon scripture meaning "honeybee." In March 1891, Deseret was divided into three communities: Oasis*, Deseret (in the center), and Bloomington* (later known as Hinckley*) on the northwest.
S4,5,T18S,R7W,SLM; 4,580' (1,396m). 61 (Ether 2:3), 312, 360, 507, 542.

DESERET PEAK (**Tooele**) is the high point of the Stansbury Range. See Deseret* (Millard) for name source.
T4N,R7W,SLM; 11,031' (3,362m).

DESERET RAILROAD STATION* (**Weber**). See Uintah* (Weber).

DESERET STATE was that portion of northern California lying east of the Sierra Nevada Mountains and west of the Rocky Mountains, from Latitude 33° to the border of Oregon and including a seaport at San Diego. This large region was initiated as the provisional state of Deseret (see Deseret* for name origin). The name lasted only as long as it took the U.S. Congress to eliminate it by creating the Territory of Utah in September 1850. The name Utah is derived from the Ute Indian Tribe. The

beehive, honoring the term "deseret" survives as part of the state seal.
6, 27, 374, 546.

DESERT COUNTY was one of original four counties created in the Territory of Utah in March 1852. It extended from the Great Salt Lake to California and was discontinued January 1862.
6, 374.

DESERT LAKE (**Emery**) is six miles east of Cleveland*. In 1885 it was recognized as a favorable place to build a dam to save the wastewater draining from Cleveland farmlands. It received its name from the surrounding desert. See Desert Lake*.
S3,10,11,T17S,R10E,SLM; 5,574' (1,699m). 89, 100(v2,13), 360, 516.

DESERT LAKE* (**Emery**) was north of Desert Lake. In the spring of 1888 the Thomas and Samuel Wells families and others settled in this area. In 1906 they surveyed a townsite and built log cabins to live in while they constructed a canal. The agricultural value of the soil deteriorated with an excessive alkali buildup, so the settlers moved over to nearby Victor*. Desert Lake became a ghost town. See Desert Lake.
S34,T16S,R10E,SLM; 5,617' (1,712m). 89, 100(v13).

DESERT LAKE WASH (**Emery**) originates in the desert south of the Huntington Airport and east of the Huntington Reservoir. The wash drains east into Desert Lake, from which it received its name.
S8,T17S,R9E,SLM to S3,T17S,R10E,SLM.

DESERT RANCH RESERVOIR (**Beaver**) is a small reservoir in the desert rangelands of Pine Valley between U-21 and the Pine Valley Hardpan, west of the Wah Wah Mountains.
S12,T26S,R17W,SLM; 5,155' (1,571m).

DESERT SEEP WASH (**Emery**) originates at the Desert Lake marshes, four

miles east of Cleveland*, and drains northeast into the Price River.
S11,T17S,R10E,SLM to S24,T16S,R11E, SLM.

DESERT SPRING (Iron) is three miles northwest of Modena* on the west side of the Escalante Desert. In early freighting days this was one of the camp stops on the road from Milford* to the mines of Nevada. Ben Tasker, an outlaw and cattle rustler, often used Desert Spring as his headquarters.
S23,T34S,R19W,SLM; 5,600' (1,707m). 516, 567.

DESOLATION CANYON (Carbon) is a ninety-seven-mile-long section of the Green River. It is south of Ouray* and extends downstream from the mouth of Nine Mile Creek to the mouth of Florence Canyon. The canyon was named by members of Major Powell's expedition because it was wildly desolate, had tortuous rapids, and was a wilderness of gray and brown cliffs.
S35,T11S,R18E,SLM to S3,T17S,R17E,SLM. 160, 204, 360, 420, 422, 496.

DETROIT MOUNTAINS (Juab, Millard). See Drum Mountains and Joy*.

DEVIL CANYON (San Juan) originates on the southeast slopes of the Abajo Mountains, seven miles southwest of Monticello*, and drains southeast into Montezuma Creek. US-163 crosses the canyon. Devil Canyon is dry most of the year except when a heavy storm hits the upper reaches, it quickly fills with flood waters that dash against the walls in a wild rush down the canyon. Flash floods were dreaded by the early freighters traveling through these canyons. Many cattle and wagons have been washed away by flash floods.
S31,T34S,R23E,SLM to S2,T37S,R24E,SLM. 567.

DEVIL CREEK (Beaver) originates south of Beaver* at South Creek and drains through the lowlands to enter the Beaver River near Minersville Reservoir. The creek meanders, swamps, and treacherous bogs are a known danger point for livestock.
T29S,R7,8W,SLM; 5,700' (1,737m). 125.

DEVILS CHAIR (Weber) is an alternate name given to a part of the Devils Gate in lower Weber Canyon. See Devils Gate.

DEVILS GARDEN (Garfield) is southeast of Escalante* about eighteen miles out on the Hole-in-the-Rock road. It is an area of sandstone sculptured into strange, distorted dwarf and mushroom-like figures. Devils Garden was named by Edson Alvey, a local naturalist.
S13,24,T37S,R4E,SLM; 5,290' (1,612m). 12, 602.

DEVILS GARDEN (Grand) is an area in Arches National Park where unusually shaped sandstone features are found.
S17,21,T23S,R21E,SLM; 5,100' (1,554m).

DEVILS GATE (Box Elder) is in the Grouse Creek Mountains at the head of Joe Dahar Creek where the walls of the canyon close in on the creek.
S14,T13N,R18W,SLM; 6,200' (1,890m).

DEVILS GATE (Weber) is on the lower Weber River. In pioneer times this was a formidable obstacle where the walls closed in at this point and the river was forced through a narrow "gateway," making it a very dangerous passageway. At one time windlasses and ropes were used to transport cargo through Devils Gate and a toll station was built just below it. The railroad finally blasted through the gate and the canyon was widened and straightened. Today both I-80 and the railroad pass through with ease.
S32,T5N,R1E,SLM; 4,750' (1,448m). 100 (v17), 546.

DEVILS GATE VALLEY (Box Elder) is an upland valley near the Box Elder, Cache, and Weber County line. Mantua*

is four miles northwest. The valley is at the head of Devils Hole Canyon from which it receives its name.
S11,12,13,14,T8N,R1W,SLM; 6,500' (1,981m).

DEVILS HOLE CANYON (Box Elder) originates at Devils Gate Valley, four miles southeast of Mantua*. It drains northwest into Box Elder Creek and receives its name from its rugged, steep terrain.
S3,11,T8N,R1W,SLM.

DEVILS PLAYGROUND (Box Elder) is in the Bovine Mountains at the south end of the Grouse Creek Mountains.
S10,15,T9N,R16W, SLM.

DEVILS SLIDE (Morgan) is on the south side of Weber Canyon. The slide is a geologic formation consisting of two vertical, parallel limestone reefs twenty feet apart. The feature rises approximately forty feet above the canyon slope to form a giant chute that extends several hundred feet up and down the mountainside.
S19,T4N,R4E,SLM. 494, 544.

DEVILS SLIDE* (Morgan) is a small industrial community in Weber Canyon at the Devils Slide, from which it receives its name (see Devils Slide).
S19,T4N,R4E,SLM; 5,229' (1,594m).

DEWEY* (Grand) is a small ranching community at the junction of the Dolores and Colorado rivers. There are two versions of the name source. The first and most preferred states that Dewey Smith, a prospector, camped by the river ford around 1880. Today a bridge named for Dewey crosses the river at this point. Another version suggests that the name was taken from a raft used to ferry supplies and equipment down river to the mouth of Professor Creek. The raft was named for Admiral Dewey.
S18,T23S,R24E,SLM; 4,110' (1,253m). 100 (v17), 146, 360.

DEWEY BRIDGE (Grand). See Dewey*.

DEWEY CANYON (Box Elder) originates in the Wellsville Mountains, three miles southeast of Deweyville*. It drains west into the Bear River. See Dewey Spring for name source.
S15,16,T11N,R2W,SLM.

DEWEY SPRING (Box Elder) is by Deweyville*. The spring was named for John C. Dewey, who settled the area after William Empey left in 1864. See Deweyville* (Box Elder).
S8,T11N,R2W,SLM; 4,325' (1,318m).

DEWEY SPRING (Grand) is one-half mile northeast of Dewey* and the Dewey Bridge. It was named for Dewey Smith, a prospector who operated here in the 1880s. See Dewey* (Grand).
S8,T23S,R24E,SLM; 4,175' (1,273m).

DEWEYVILLE* (Box Elder) was originally settled by William Empey in 1864 in the Dewey Spring area. The spring was first known as Empeys Spring. After Empey moved out, John C. Dewey and his family settled in the community and changed the name to Dewey Spring*. When a post office was established on September 29, 1873, the town name was changed to Deweyville.
S8,T11N,R2W,SLM; 4,323' (1,318m). 100 (v17), 139, 289, 360, 567.

DIAMOND* (Juab) is a mining ghost town site among the old defunct mines, five miles south of Eureka*. Diamond was first settled in 1870 when a Jewish lapidary discovered crystals in the area that he cut and sold as valuable gems. Other prospectors were finding brilliant crystals and claiming diamond mines. An adjoining canyon was named Crystal Canyon. The last house in Diamond was moved in 1923.
S8,T11S,R2W,SLM; 6,240' (1,902m). 89, 546, 567.

DIAMOND FORK (**Utah**) originates in the Wasatch Mountains, nine miles east of the junction of Hobble Creek, Right and Left forks. It drains south to Three Forks and into the Spanish Fork River. Diamond Fork was named for a rancher who ran his sheep in the canyon.
S25,T7S,R5E,SLM to S17,T9W,R4E,SLM. D.L. 6803.

DIAMOND GULCH (**Uintah**) originates six miles southwest of Crouse Reservoir northeast of Vernal*. It drains southeast into Jones Hole Creek. See Diamond Mountain (Uintah) for name source.
S17,T2S,R24E,SLM to S1,T3S,R25E,SLM.

DIAMOND LAKE (**Summit**) is in the southwest section of the Uinta Mountains in the center of the Trial, Star, and Lost lakes area. It is a small lake that sparkles in the sunshine.
S32,T1S,R9E,SLM; 9,800' (2,987m).

DIAMOND MOUNTAIN (**Uintah**) has a northeast-southwest orientation in the eastern Uinta Mountains. Its northwest exposure is at Diamond Mountain Plateau and its southeast exposure is at Jones Hole Creek. Diamond Mountain in Utah has consistently, but erroneously, been tied to the great 1872 diamond hoax that was instigated by Phillip Arnold and John Slack and exposed by Clarence King, director of the United States Geologic Survey. The diamond hoax actually occurred at Diamond Mountain in northwestern Colorado. Diamond Mountain (Utah) was named for Jim Diamond who ran cattle on the mountain (no relation to the legendary New York Diamond Jim). Diamond Gulch to the north is also mistakenly tied into the diamond hoax incident.
T2,3S,R24,25E,SLM. 39, 80, 160, 172, 303, 309, 360, 496, 516, 546.

DIAMOND MOUNTAIN PLATEAU (**Uintah**) is in the southeast Uinta Mountains and runs parallel to Diamond Gulch. The name comes from adjacent Diamond Mountain.

T2S,R23E,SLM; 7,987' (2,434m).

DIANAS THRONE (**Kane**) is a prominent saddle on a sandstone ridge near US-89, four miles southeast of Carmel Junction*. In 1920, the feature was named by William W. Seegmiller for the Roman goddess Diana, maiden huntress, goddess of the moon and hunting, and the protectress of women.
S3,4,T42S,R7W,SLM; 7,054' (2,150m). 567.

DIKE LAKE (**Uintah**) is in the group of lakes about one and one-half miles west southwest of Leidy Peak. An igneous dike, rare in the Uinta Mountains, forms a prominent cliff along the north shore of the lake.
10,792' (3,289m). 578.

DILLY CANYON (**Emery**) originates on Valley Mountain and drains south into Range Creek northwest of Green River*. Tom Dilly was an early cowman and part-time outlaw who operated in the late 1800s in the Price*, Woodside*, Florence Creek, and Rattlesnake Canyon areas.
S4,T17S,R16E,SLM (at mouth). 25, 303.

DIME LAKE (**Duchesne**) is a small circular lake on the southern slopes of the Uinta Mountains at the head of Shale Creek, near Fox Lake.
10,704' (3,263m).

DINOSAUR NATIONAL MONUMENT (**Uintah**) is a remote area of northeastern Utah and northwestern Colorado that centers around the Dinosaur Quarry and the scenic geologic upheavals and erosions of Split Mountain and Canyon, Gates of Lodore, and the Yampa and Green rivers. It was set aside as a national monument in 1915 and received its name from the adjacent Dinosaur Quarry. See Dinosaur Quarry.

DINOSAUR QUARRY (**Uintah**) is on U-149 north of Jensen*, Utah. In 1909 Earl Douglass of the Carnegie Museum first discovered dinosaur fossils in an

unusual concentration of fossil bones that is unsurpassed anywhere in the world. The excavation of fossils still continues. See Dinosaur National Monument.
167, 542.

DIPPING VAT SPRINGS (Box Elder) is in the southeast part of Grouse Creek Valley. This was where early sheep men installed vats for dipping their sheep.
567.

DIRTY DEVIL RIVER (Garfield, Wayne) originates at the junction of the Fremont and Muddy rivers that join northeast of Hanksville* to form the Dirty Devil. This river then drains southeast into the Colorado River. During one of Powell's expeditions, the party drew near the mouth of the then unnamed river and someone shouted, "How is she, Jack?" and Jack replied, "Oh, she's a dirty devil!" This is the origin of the name. When the river was first named by the Powell group, they made no distinction as to how far upriver the name would apply or which branch the name continued on. This problem was finally solved by the courts. Powell later changed the name to Fremont River to honor John Charles Fremont, cartographer and pathfinder, but the name Dirty Devil continued its popularity, so the name Fremont now applies only to the principal upper fork. Powell's party subsequently named Bright Angel Creek further down the Colorado River in Grand Canyon National Park to counteract the naming of the Dirty Devil. Inasmuch as they had honored the devil they felt obligated to honor the good spirits as well.
S2,T28S,R11E,SLM to S21,T33S,R14E,SLM.
159, 160, 422, 496, 542.

DISAPPOINTMENT HILLS (Millard) are in the Confusion Mountains northeast of Plympton Ridge and west of White (Tule) Valley. The name is associated with the frustrations and disappointments endured by Captain Simpson and his party during the 1850s while surveying and exploring the region.
S31,32,T15½S,R16W,SLM; 6,000' (1,829m). 477.

DIVIDE CANYON (San Juan) originates on Tarantula Mesa about ten miles south of Notom*. The canyon drains north as part of the headwaters of Sandy Creek east of the Waterpocket Fold. Divide Canyon is between the headwaters of Sandy Creek, draining north into the Fremont River. Halls Creek drains south into the Colorado River (Lake Powell).
S31,T32S,R8E,SLM (at mouth). MRN

DIVIDE LAKE (Duchesne) is in the central Uinta Mountains on the headwaters of Shale Creek, one and one-half miles north of Fox Lake. Divide Lake is near the crest at the division of two drainage systems.
11,217' (3,419m).

DIVIDE LAKE (Garfield) is on the southern slopes of the Aquarius Plateau, between and dividing the east and west forks of Boulder Creek.
R4E,T31S,SLM; 9,575' (2,918m). 508.

DIVIDEND* (Utah) was a small mining community two and one-half miles east of Eureka*. It paid off for those miners who kept their mining shares. One of the miners, E. J. Raddatz, named this town that began to deteriorate after the mine closed in 1949.
S15,T10S,R2W,SLM; 5,900' (1,798m). 89, 100(v17), 516.

DIXIE SPRINGS* (Washington) is a recently established community on I-15 between Harrisburg Junction* and Hurricane*. The town was named for the adjacent springs. Since pioneer days the term "Dixie" has been applied to Utah's southwestern section that has much warmer year-round temperatures in comparison to the rest of the state.

DOBIETOWN* (Utah) was a temporary settlement on the outskirts of Fairfield* (Camp Floyd*) that was soon absorbed into Fairfield. The lack of local timber for building homes suggested the name. Adobe bricks were very accessible and easy to use. See Fairfield* and Camp Floyd* references.

DOCTOR CANYON (Sevier) originates on Fishlake Plateau, three miles west of Fish Lake and drains southeast into Fish Lake. Doctor H. H. St. John and his brother built a small cabin in the canyon in 1885. Later they built a large luxurious home at the mouth of the creek that was used as both a residence and hospital. S12,T26S,R1E,SLM to S19,T26S,R2E,SLM. 285, 584.

DODDS HOLLOW (Daggett) originates sixteen miles northwest of Vernal* and drains southeast into Big Brush Creek. It was named for Captain Pardon Dodds, who helped build a road through the area that included Dodds Hollow. Dodds was the first Ute Indian agent in the Uintah Basin after the Indians were relocated into the basin. S5,8,9,T2S,R21E,SLM.

DOG VALLEY (Garfield) is four miles south of the Circleville Mountains near Fremont Pass. Prairie dogs were common in the valley. S29,32,T31S,R5W,SLM; 7,470' (2,277m).

DOG VALLEY (Juab) is eight miles west of Nephi* and north of U-132. It was named for the prairie dogs that were common in the valley. T12-14S,R2W,SLM; 5,500' (1,676m).

DOLL HOUSE (Kane) is west of the Spanish Bottoms on the Colorado River. This highly eroded area of sandstone pinnacles, spires, domes, and other unusual shapes is part of Canyonlands National Park. T30S,R18E,SLM. D.L. 6901.

DOLLAR LAKE (Summit) is in the north central section of the Uinta Mountains on the headwaters of Henrys Fork, two miles west of Gilbert Peak. Ed

Oaks caught a five-pound rainbow trout there in the 1920s and named the lake because of its circular shape. 10,785' (3,287m). 309.

DOLLAR LAKE (Uintah) is in the eastern section of the Uinta Mountains on the headwaters of the Whiterocks River, East Fork. Whiterocks Lake is one-fourth mile north. The lake has a circular shape. S2,T4N,R1W,USM; 10,500' (3,200m).

DOLORES RIVER (Grand) drains from Colorado into the Colorado River in Utah, midway between Cisco* and Moab*. The mouth of the river is at Dewey*. The Old Spanish Trail followed part of the river. The Spaniards named it Rio Nuestra Senora de los Dolores or River of Our Lady of Sorrows. The Domínguez-Escalante expedition named it El Rio de San Bernardo. S8,T23S,R24E,SLM (at mouth). 157, 314, 583.

DOLPHIN ISLAND (Box Elder) is in the Great Salt Lake but becomes part of the mainland when the lake is low. The island is shaped like a dolphin. 4,275' (1,202m). 567.

DOME CANYON (Millard) is in the center of the House Range, originating at the summit and draining west into Tule (White) Valley. The canyon was named by Captain J. H. Simpson during his road survey of 1859. He thought the high bluffs at the canyon entrance had a dome-like appearance. T17S,R13W,SLM. 477.

DOME ISLAND (Salt Lake). See Stansbury Island.

DONKEY CREEK (Wayne) originates at Donkey Reservoir on the northern slopes of Boulder Mountain, the eastern section of the Aquarius Plateau, and drains north northeast into the Fremont River. Early settlers in the area would travel by burro to Teasdale* for supplies. There are

several "Donkey" names in the region such as Donkey Point, Donkey Meadows, and Donkey Reservoir.
S19,T29S,R5E,SLM (at mouth). 100(v17).

DONNER CANYON (Tooele) originates in the northwest section of the county on the northern slopes of Graham Peak in the Silver Island Mountains. The canyon drains northeast into the salt desert. Nearby is Donner-Reed Pass. Both the canyon and the pass names originated from the passing of the Donner-Reed party of 1846-47.
T3N,R17W,SLM. 506, 542.

DONNER-REED PASS (Tooele) is in the center of the Silver Island Mountains in the northwest part of the county. See Donner Canyon.
T3N,R17W,SLM; 4,420' (1,347m).

DORA* (Duchesne). See Duchesne*.

DORITY CANYON (Garfield). See Dougherty Canyon (Garfield).

DORRY CANYON (San Juan) originates on the northwest slopes of Mount Tukuhnikivatz of the La Sal Mountains. It drains northwest into Brumley Canyon. Dorry Crouse ran his sheep in the canyon.
S7,8,16,T27S,R24E,SLM. 146.

DOUBLE CABINS* (San Juan). See Carlisle*.

DOUBLEUP HOLLOW (Beaver) originates on Black Mountain south of Greenville* and drains north onto the Greenville Bench. The name is a reminder of the pre-automobile days when teams of horses or oxen had to be doubled up to pull heavy loads over difficult terrain.
S31,T30S,R8W,SLM. 578.

DOUGHERTY CANYON (Garfield) is on Escalante Mountain at the head of Twitchell Creek. (Dougherty is sometimes spelled Dority).

S24,T33S,R1W,SLM; 9,800' (2,987m). 12.

DOUGLAS CANYON (San Juan). See Johns Canyon (San Juan).

DOUGLAS MESA (San Juan) is west of the Goosenecks of the San Juan River and northwest of Mexican Hat*. Jim (James) Douglas was a prospector in the area during the early 1900s. In 1909, he discovered gold on a sand bar of the San Juan River. Before he could work his find, the river rose and flooded the bar. Jim waited around until 1929 to recover his gold bonanza, but became discouraged and frustrated. He committed suicide by jumping off the San Juan River bridge at Mexican Hat.
T40,41S,R16,17E,SLM; 6,000' (1,829m). 546, 567.

DOUGLAS WASH (San Juan) originates at the south end of Douglas Mesa, south of the San Juan River. It drains east into Halgaitoh Wash and receives its name from the mesa.
S30,T42S,R17E,SLM to S36,T42S,R17E, SLM.

DOVE CREEK (Box Elder) originates at the junction of its various forks in the Raft River Mountains, ten miles south southwest of Yost*. The creek drains southeast into the Great Salt Lake Desert at the Sinks of Dove Creek. Early settlers found numerous mourning doves there.
S32,T15N,R13W,SLM to S8,T10N,R12W, SLM. 100(v17), 567.

DOVER* (Sanpete) was on the west side of the Sevier River opposite Fayette*. The town was named after Dover*, England, the hometown of several of Dover's settlers. The area was originally settled by John E. Fosgren, who made a few improvements then moved on. In 1877 William Robinson and others established homesteads in the area. By the 1890s the land became alkaline as a result of improper irrigation methods, so the village declined. During the 1930s a

drought struck simultaneously with the development of an epidemic. This forced the abandonment of Dover, which then became a ghost town.
S26,T18S,R1W,SLM; 5,060' (1,542). 89, 360, 567.

DOWD CREEK (**Daggett**) originates in the eastern Uinta Mountains at Dowd Spring on the west side of Dowd Mountain. Dowd Creek drains south into Carter Creek. See the mountain for name source.
S29,30,T2N,R20E,SLM.

DOWD HOLE (**Daggett**) is a small natural basin in the northeastern Uinta Mountains west of Dowd Mountain, at the head of Dowd Creek. The area was named for Cleophas J. Dowd, murdered April 11, 1897, by his partner, Charles Reasor. See Dowd Mountain.
S29,30,T2N,R20E,SLM; 7,640' (2,329m).

DOWD MOUNTAIN (**Daggett**) is in the northeastern section of the Uinta Mountains at the head of Hideout Draw. Dowd Hole is in the vicinity. The mountain was named for Cleophas J. Dowd, who homesteaded in this area from 1857-97. He ran his horses on the mountain. Dowd's dealings were often suspect and after ill feelings festered for some time, he was killed by his partner, Charles Reasor. A U.S. Forest Service sign is posted by Dowd's gravesite.
S21,22,T2N,R20E,SLM; 8,100' (2,469m). 172.

DRAGERTON* (**Carbon**). See East Carbon City*.

DRAGON* (**Uintah**) was on Evacuation Creek at the mouth of Dragon Canyon. Twenty miles north is Bonanza*. The town received its name from the nearby Black Dragon Mine where gilsonite was originally discovered. The mine was named for the imagined shape of the gilsonite deposit as it appeared on the surface of the ground. This particular type of asphaltum is not known to exist

in any other area in the world. The mine was discovered in the 1860s and when the Uintah Railroad first went through, it was known as Dragon Junction*. A fire, change in transportation facilities, and other factors caused the entire area to decline, although the mining continues to this day.
S12,T12S,R25E,SLM; 5,772' (1,759m). 50, 89, 100(v17), 360, 494.

DRAGON CANYON (**Juab**) originates three miles south of Eureka* on the southern slopes of Mammoth Peak. It drains southwest into the Tintic Valley and receives its name from the Dragon Mines at the head of the canyon.
S29,T10S,R2W,SLM to S36,T11S,R3W,SLM. 578.

DRAGON CANYON (**Uintah**) originates at the elbow of the Atchee Ridge of the East Tavaputs Plateau. The canyon drains north northeast into Evacuation Creek at the ghost town site of Dragon*. See Dragon* for name source.
S22,T13S,R25E,SLM to S12,T12S,R25E, SLM.

DRAPER* (**Salt Lake**) is in the southeast corner of the Great Salt Lake Valley, four miles southwest of the mouth of Little Cottonwood Canyon. The town was first known as Willow Creek* for the creek the settlers used. They also used the region as a grazing area for their cattle. The town name was then changed to Brownsville* for Ebenezer Brown and family who arrived in 1849. Later, the name was again changed to honor William Draper, the town's first Mormon bishop. The Draper family settled in the area in 1850.
S28,29,T3S,R1E,SLM; 4,550' (1,387m). 252, 288, 360, 542, 567, 604.

DRAPER* (**Sanpete**). See Freedom*.

DRIPPING SPRING (**Beaver**) is at the south end of the Mineral Mountains west of Adamsville*. The spring drains west

into Lincoln Gulch.
S21,T29S,R9W,SLM; 6,780' (2,067m).

DROMEDARY PEAK (Salt Lake) is in the front range of the Wasatch Mountains, one mile east of Twin Peaks. When viewing the peak from a particular angle, it resembles a dromedary camel.
T3S,R2E,SLM; 11,107' (3,385m). 578.

DRUID ARCH (San Juan) is in the Needles section of Canyonlands National Park, near the head of Elephant Canyon. The arch has an imagined similarity to the Stonehenge of England, an area where the ancient Druids worshipped.
S16,T31S,R19E,SLM.

DRUM MOUNTAIN (Juab, Millard) has a northwest-southeast orientation in the north central section of Millard County and the south central section of Juab County. Lady Laird Peak is the high point. An early name was Detroit Mountains. There are two versions for the name source. The mountain is claimed to be shaped like a drum when viewed from a certain angle. It is also claimed that, at certain times, rumbling and echoing are often heard in the mountains. To the south are the Little Drum Mountains. See Detroit Mountains and Joy*.
T14,15S,R11W,SLM; 6,982' (2,128m). 100 (v17), 567.

DRUNKARD HOLLOW (Utah). See Drunker Hollow.

DRUNKER HOLLOW (Utah) is a small hollow eight miles northwest of Soldier Summit where it drains into Tie Fork. It was a place where miners congregated for their drinking sprees.
S1,2,T10S,R6E,SLM. 283.

DRY BREAD HOLLOW (Weber) originates four miles north of the Causey Reservoir between Huntsville* and Woodruff* and drains south into the Causey Reservoir. At one time, workers constructing a road in the area ran out

of supplies but voted to stay to complete the road despite a lack of food. The last several days the workers lived on old dry bread and water.
S12,14,23,26,T7N,R3E,SLM. 100(v17), 567.

DRY CANYON (Beaver) originates northeast of Blawn Mountain at the south end of the Wah Wah Mountains. The canyon drains northeast into Willow Creek and into the Wah Wah Valley. The canyon is dry throughout most of the year.
S14,15,T29S,R15W,SLM.

DRY CANYON (Utah) originates at Lightning Peak, five miles southeast of Bridal Veil Falls and drains southeast into Hobble Creek, Left Fork. It was named for the large number of dead quaking aspen trees found in the canyon.
S19,T6S,R4E,SLM to S2,T7S,R4E,SLM. 270.

DRY CREEK (Beaver) originates in Beaver Valley three miles north of Beaver*. It drains south through Greenville* into the Beaver River and remains dry part of the year.
T29S,R8W,SLM.

DRY CREEK* (Utah). See Lehi*.

DRY CREEK SETTLEMENT* (Utah). See Alpine*.

DRY FLAT (Beaver). See Betenson Flat.

DRY FORK* (Uintah) is a small ranching community on Dry Fork, eleven miles northwest of Vernal*. The fork is dry part of the year. Variant: Mountain Dell*.
S15,T3S,R20E,SLM; 6,475' (1,974m). 100 (v17), 542.

DRY FORK (Uintah) originates at the junction of North Fork and Split Creek, four miles south of Marsh Peak. The fork drains southeast.
S30,T3S,R21E,SLM (at mouth).

116

DRY LAKE (Cache) is a large sink at the summit of the Wellsville Mountains near the head of Wellsville Canyon. During the spring run-off period, water collects here to form a sizable shallow lake. As the lake waters recede, the expanding dry areas are then utilized for planting and pasturage. US-189 and US-91 pass through the sink.
S28,29,32,33,T10N,R1W,SLM. 5,638' (1,718m).

DRY LAKE (Piute) is five miles northeast of Junction*. The lake is dry during several months of the year.
S21,28,T29S,R2½W,SLM; 7,600' (2,316m). 567.

DRY POLE HOLLOW (Cache) is the first large hollow east of Providence* and north of Providence Canyon. It originates at Little Baldy and drains to the west into the north end of Providence. Even though a forest fire killed the trees, they were all left standing.
S12,T11N,R1E,SLM. 567.

DRY TOWN* (Cache). See River Heights*.

DRY WASH (Kane) originates at Petes Cove on the west side of the Kaiparowits. It drains south southeast into Last Chance Creek and is intermittently dry.
S6,T39S,R4E,SLM to S34,T40S,R4E,SLM.

DUBINKY SPRING (Grand). See Dubinky Wash.

DUBINKY WASH (Grand) originates fifteen miles northwest of Moab* and drains southwest into Hell Roaring Canyon. Red and Dubinky Anderson, brothers, were camping at Valley City* to the northeast when they suddenly became frightened at a supposed apparition in an abandoned house. One of the brothers fled barefoot and was finally located at the spring. Both spring and wash gradually assumed the Dubinky name. The head of the wash is at the spring.

S24,25,T24S,R18E,SLM. 146.

DUBLIN WASH (Sanpete) originates in the Cedar Hills, four and one-half miles north northwest of Mount Pleasant*. The wash drains southeast into the San Pitch River. MRN
S8,16,21,T14S,R4E,SLM.

DUCHESNE* (Duchesne) is on US-40 at the junction of the Strawberry and Duchesne rivers. It was initially settled in 1904 when the Uinta Basin was opened to white settlers. The name Duchesne was the first name requested for the community. The postal service refused because the name would conflict with nearby Fort Duchesne*. In 1905, the town was named Dora* for the daughter of A. M. Murdock, who owned the first store there. Subsequently the name changed to Theodore* in honor of President Theodore Roosevelt. When a nearby town took the name of Roosevelt* in 1915, the original request for Duchesne was finally accepted. See Duchesne River for name source.
S1,T4S,R5W,USM; 5,510' (1,679m). 100(v17), 165, 309, 314, 360, 530, 542.

DUCHESNE COUNTY was created in 1914 by petition of the citizens of the eastern portion of what was then Wasatch County. See Duchesne River for name source.
6, 360, 542.

DUCHESNE RIVER (Duchesne, Uintah) originates at the southwestern section of the Uinta Mountains at the foot of Mount Agassiz. The river drains south southeast through Duchesne* into the Green River. Prior to 1875 the present Duchesne River was known as the Uinta River. As one of the more historic and prominent rivers of Utah, there has been much confusion in past writings as to the river's name history and relative relationships with the mouths of the nearby White and Uinta rivers. The river was supposedly named in the 1830s after the early French trapper in the area,

Du Chasne. Others suggest that the name was derived from an early Indian chief. Name sources relating to Indian chiefs often crop up whether based on fact or fiction. Another version suggests that Father DeSmet may have influenced the name in honor of Rose Du Chesne, founder of the Society of the Sacred Heart in America. Another record claims the river was named for Fort Duquesne, built by the French in 1754 where Pittsburgh, Pennsylvania, is located. Another reference records an Ute Indian word "doo-shane," which means "dark canyon." Parts of the river, especially in the Uinta Mountain areas, drain through dark canyons. Still another source suggests the river was named for Andre Duchesne, the French geographer and historian. There is also a chance that the actual name source will never be found. Unless there is a reference the author has not briefed, this would be an intriguing research project for an enthusiastic toponymist.
T3N,R8,9W,USM to S32,T5S,R3E,USM. 159, 160, 298, 314, 496, 530, 542, 555(v9).

DUCK CREEK (**Kane**) originates at the junction of Sage Valley Creek and Deer Hollow Creek in the lava fields north of Navajo Lake. The creek drains east into the Duck Creek Sinks of the Markagunt Plateau. Ducks are attracted to the quiet areas of the creek.
S5,T38S,R8W,SLM to S5,8,T38S,R7W,SLM. 578.

DUCK CREEK (**Rich**) originates in the hill country southwest of the south end of Bear Lake and drains east into the Bear River. Several small ponds and sloughs along the drainage system attract wild ducks.

DUCK LAKE (**Summit**) is at the west end of the Uinta Mountains in the Provo River drainage, one and one-half miles west of Haystack Mountain. Nearby are Fire Island and Weir lakes. It was named by Morgan Park because wild ducks prefer this lake over neighboring lakes.

S3,T2S,R8E,SLM; 9,780' (2,981m). 113, 298.

DUCKETT RIDGE (**San Juan**) has a north-south orientation southeast of the Abajo Mountains. John Duckett worked a mine at the north end of the ridge.
SW¼,T34S,R22E,SLM; 10,139' (3,090m). 530.

DUGOUT CREEK (**Garfield**) originates on the western slopes of Mount Ellen of the Henry Mountains. It drains west northwest into Sweetwater Creek, on the eastern slopes of Wildcat Mesa. Early stockmen and settlers lived in dugouts along the creek.
S34,T31S,R10E,SLM to S12,T31S,R8E,SLM. 578.

DUGOUT SPRING (**Emery**) is on Dugout Wash in the San Rafael Desert, eight miles northeast of the Flat Tops. Drainage flows north into the San Rafael River. The early cowboys lived in dugouts in this vicinity. There is a Lower Dugout Spring nearby.
S22,28,T25S,R14E,SLM; 4,800' (1,463m).

DUGOUT STATION* (**Utah**) was a stop on the Pony Express route between Salt Lake City* and Fairfield*. It was ten miles northeast of Camp Floyd* and was also known as Joes Dugout Station. It was named for Joe "Shropshire" Dorton.
T5S,R1W,SLM. 516.

DUGOUT WASH (**Emery**) originates on the Sweetwater Reef, four to five miles east of the Flat Tops in the San Rafael Desert. It drains north northeast into the San Rafael River. See Dugout Spring for name source.
S33,T26S,R14E,SLM to S17,T24S,R15E, SLM.

DUGWAY* (**Tooele**) was initiated in 1942 as a military installation with restricted entry. Approximately one thousand people live in this area. In pioneer days, the name developed from a novel procedure where one long, winding horizontal trench was dug along a steep slope where travel was essential. The trench held the two wheels on the upper side of a wagon, preventing it from slipping downhill or tipping over. 4,840' (1,475m). 360, 498.

DUGWAY PASS (Juab) is between the north end of the Thomas Range and the south end of the Dugway Range. This was Simpson's Short Cut Pass, named in May 1858.
T11S,R11W,SLM; 5,410' (1,649m). 477.

DUNCAN CREEK (Beaver) originates on the Bosman Ridge of the west Tushar Mountains, five miles west northwest of Puffer Lake. The creek drains southwest into Merchant Creek. MRN
S29,33,T28S,R5W,SLM. 125.

DUNCAN CREEK (Iron) originates on Duncan Mountain on the northern slopes of the Harmony Mountains. The creek drains northeast through Duncan Canyon into Cedar Valley where it disappears into the ground. It was named for Chapman Duncan, an early cattleman and rancher who was prominent in the development of Old Iron Town*. Chapman was also involved in the settlement of Duncans Retreat*.
S17,T37S,R13W,SLM to S2,T36S,R12W, SLM. 567.

DUNCAN MOUNTAIN (Iron) is at the head of Duncan Creek, which is south of U-56 and sixteen miles west of Cedar City*. See Duncan Creek for name source.
S8,T37S,R13W,SLM; 7,743' (2,360m).

DUNCANS RETREAT* (Washington) was on the upper Virgin River, halfway between present-day Virgin* and Grafton*. It was first settled by Chapman Duncan, Alma Minerly, and others during the winter of 1861-62. The area was washed out by the floods of January 1862 and the settlers were forced to move. Duncan "retreated" to Duncans Retreat after making a surveying error on an irrigation ditch project at Virgin.

S31,T41S,R11W,SLM. 89, 100(v13), 154, 311.

DURKEE CREEK (Piute) originates on the northwest slopes of Marysvale Peak near Durkee Springs and drains into the Sevier River. A Mr. Durkee lived at the springs and ran his cattle and sheep in the nearby mountains and canyons during the summer months.
S3,T27S,R2½W,SLM to S20,T27S,R3W,SLM. 89.

DURKEE SPRING (Piute) is on the southwest slopes of Marysvale Peak at the head of Durkee Creek. See Durkee Creek for name source.
S13,T27S,R3W,SLM; 7,325' (2,233m).

DUTCH JOHN* (Daggett) is two miles north of Flaming Gorge Dam. The settlement was built to house Flaming Gorge Dam construction workers. Today it houses the employees of the Flaming Gorge National Recreation Area centered around the dam and the lake. In the early 1860s, "Dutch" John Hanselena, a horse trader and miner from Schleswig, Prussia, settled in the Red Canyon Bottoms and prospected in the area. He held a copper claim on the north side of Red Canyon and left his name on several nearby sites. The nickname, "Dutch John," came from his strong accent. Nearby are Dutch John Mountains, Flat, Canyon, Spring, Bench, etc.
S1,2,11,12,T2N,R22E,SLM; 6,325' (1,928m). 172, 309, 314.

DUTCH HOLLOW (Summit) originates four and one-half miles west of Park City* where it drains northeast into Kimball Creek. Dutch Pete was a prospector who lived in nearby Park City. He killed himself at the hollow while on a drunken binge, thinking his money had been stolen. After his suicide, the wallet was found where he had misplaced it.
S1,11,T2S,R3E,SLM. 567.

DUTCH MOUNTAIN (Tooele) is three miles north northeast of the Ochre

Mountains and two miles north northwest of the old ghost town of Gold Hill*. Some of the early prospectors in the area were Dutch.
T7S,R18W,SLM; 7,260' (2,213m). 567.

DUTCHMANS ARCH (**Emery**) is north of I-70 on the San Rafael Swell, one mile east of Ghost Rock. The arch was named for a Dutchman who worked for John Seely, an early cowman.
S34,T22S,R10E,SLM. 193.

DYER* (**Uintah**) is a ghost town site on the eastern slopes of Dyer Mountain, north northeast of Vernal*. The settlement was established in 1887 by Lewis B. Dyer, a cowboy who discovered copper in the area and operated a mine nearby. The mine was abandoned in 1900.
S16,T1S,R21E,SLM; 9,875' (3,010m). 89, 172.

DYER MOUNTAIN (**Uintah**) is in the eastern Uinta Mountains at the head of Big Brush Creek. Steinaker Reservoir is fifteen miles south. See Dyer*.
S8,16,T1S,R21E,SLM; 10,248' (3,124m).

- E -

E. T. CITY* (Tooele) was at the south end of Great Salt Lake where Lake Point* is presently located. It was named for Ezra Taft Benson, an early miller and Mormon Church official. E. T. Benson brought cattle here to be pastured. It was first settled by Peter Maughan and Geo. W. Bryan and others in early summer of 1854. In 1923 the name was changed to Lake Point*.
S2,T2S,R4W,SLM; 4,243' (1,298m). 89, 100(v17), 153.

EAGLE CANYON (Emery) originates on the San Rafael Swell near the Head of Sinbad and the San Rafael Knob. It drains northwest into North Salt Wash. Green River* is thirty miles east. Present-day I-70 crosses near the canyon head. The canyon is a rugged, isolated area which is a common nesting area for eagles. A tongue-in-cheek comment has been made that if an eagle ever did get to the bottom of the canyon, it wouldn't be able to fly out.
S4,9,T23S,R10E,SLM to S25,T21S,R8E,SLM. 100(v70), 193.

EAGLE CITY* (Wayne) is a ghost town site on the southeast slopes of Mount Ellen of the Henry Mountains, near the head of Crescent Creek. Bromide Basin is two miles west. It was a small mining camp established in the 1880s for the mines in the Bromide Basin area. By 1900 it was abandoned. The name comes from the area's isolation, altitude, and the prevalence of eagles.
S36,T31S,R10E,SLM; 7,800' (2,377m). 25, 89, 273, 567.

EAGLE GATE (Salt Lake) is in Salt Lake City* on State and South Temple streets, extending over the north-south traffic. The gate, first erected in 1889, had an eagle with outspread wings over the main entrance of Brigham Young's private grounds. The eagle was part of the perimeter wall. Brigham Young had the wall built for protection against Indian raids, in addition to furnishing gainful employment for early pioneers. Truman O. Angell designed the gate and Ralph Ramsey carved the wooden eagle using a specimen killed in nearby City Creek Canyon as a model. The eagle was carved from five blocks of wood, one each for the body, head, and neck, and two more for the wings. It was removed in 1890 to widen the street and permit passage of the new electric streetcars— public transportation. In 1891 it was sent east, electroplated, and returned to its original site.
100(v3), 546.

EARLS DRAW (Emery) originates at the Swazy Cabin on the San Rafael Swell, two miles south of Ghost Rock, where it drains east. MRN
S9,T23S,R10E,SLM to S1,T23S,R10E,SLM. 193.

EARLY WEED BENCH (Kane) is twenty-two miles from Escalante* on the Hole-in-the-Rock road east of Sunset Flat. The desert sands in this area warm up in the spring just a bit early. This encourages the local desert plants to mature before those in the surrounding areas.
NW¼,T38S,R6E,SLM; 5,550' (1,692m). 12.

EAST BAKER BENCH (Garfield) is near Baker Bench. See Baker Bench.

EAST BOULDER LAKES (Garfield) are a small cluster of lakes on the Aquarius Plateau at the head of East Boulder Draw. The lakes receive their

name from the mountain and the creek into which they drain.
T31S,R4E,SLM; 11,040' (3,365m).

EAST CANYON (Cache) originates at Porcupine Reservoir, east and southeast of Avon*.
S12,13,T9N,R1E,SLM (at mouth).

EAST CANYON (Morgan) originates near Kimballs Junction* over the summit east from the head of Parleys Canyon. The canyon drains in a northerly direction to enter the Weber River. The Mormon pioneers named the canyon in 1847. It had an earlier name of Bauchmins Creek after a local trapper.
S8,T1S,R4E,SLM to S27,T4N,R2E,SLM. 100 (v17), 542, 567.

EAST CANYON LAKE STATE REC-REATION AREA (Morgan) is thirty miles northeast of Salt Lake City* near U-65. It is a six-hundred-and-eighty-acre mountain lake that received its name from the canyon.
S10,15,23,T2N,R3E,SLM; 5,662' (1,726m). 569.

EAST CANYON RESERVOIR (Morgan). See above. D.L. 6002.

EAST CARBON CITY* (Carbon) is on U-123, one mile west of Sunnyside and south of the Book and Roan cliffs. It is primarily a coal mining community and the name is related to that industry. On July 23, 1973, Dragerton* and Columbia* incorporated into East Carbon City.
S1,2,17,18,T15S,R13E,SLM; 6,300'(1,920m). 360.

EAST CLARK BENCH (Garfield) is between the lower reaches of Wahweap and the Paria River. The temporary settlement of Bac-bone* was on the west side of the bench. The bench was named for Owen Washington Clark, an early cattleman.
T43S,R1,2E,SLM. 578.

EAST FISH LAKE (Uintah) is on the east side of Bollie Mountain as opposed to West Fish Lake which is on the west side of Bollie. The lake empties into Burnt Fork.
567.

EAST GARLAND* (Box Elder) is on U-154 and the west side of the Bear River, three miles northeast of Garland*. The settlement was started in 1884 when John A. Larson moved from Bear River City* and built a home on the site of a former stage station. In 1889 the early name for the entire area, which included what became Garland*, East Garland, and North Garland*, was Sunset*. On November 20, 1904, the East Garland Mormon ward was created, thus establishing the community. Today it is prime agricultural land with encroaching residential sites. See Garland* for name source.
S19,T12N,R2W,SLM; 4,300' (1,311m). 251.

EAST GRANDADDY MOUNTAIN (Duchesne) is in the southwest Uinta Mountains near Grandaddy Lake and two miles east of West Grandaddy Mountain. The mountain received its name from the lake.
S2,3,4,9,10,11,T2N,R8W,USM; 11,659' (3,554m).

EAST JORDAN* (Salt Lake). See Midvale*.

EAST KAYSVILLE* (Davis). See Fruit Heights*.

EAST LAYTON* (Davis) is one and one-half miles east of Layton*. The town was formerly a part of Layton from which it received its name. It has since become an important residential community for nearby Hill Field Air Base. On Tuesday, January 13, 1981, East Layton was signed out of existence and absorbed into Layton.
S14,T4N,R1W,SLM; 4,700' (1,433m). 360, 466(15 Jan. 1981, 4C).

EAST MILL CREEK* (**Salt Lake**) is on the southeast perimeter of Greater Salt Lake City* at about Thirty-third South and Wasatch Boulevard (3300 East). It became a subdivision of Salt Lake City on Mill Creek as the creek emerged from the Wasatch Range.
T1S,R1E,SLM.

EAST MOODY CANYON (**Garfield**) originates at the Waterpocket Fold southeast of the southern tip of the Circle Cliffs. It drains southwest into the Escalante River. See Moody Creek.
T36S,R9E,SLM to T37S,R7E,SLM.

EAST OF THE NAVAJO (**San Juan**) is a vast wilderness on the western slopes of the Kaiparowits Plateau. It lies between Navajo and Rogers canyons and receives its name from Navajo Canyon.
S39,T40S,R5E,SLM.

EAST PARK RESERVOIR (**Uintah**) is in the southeast section of the Uinta Mountains, four miles east northeast of Oaks Park, at the head of Little Brush Creek. The reservoir is in an alpine meadow.
9,017' (2,748m).

EAST PLYMOUTH* (**Box Elder**) is three miles east of Plymouth* and four miles north northeast of Fielding*. In 1876 John W. Hess of Davis County settled there with his family, intending to experiment with dry-farm agriculture. He planted, harvested, and thus became one of the pioneers of dry farming in this region. Other people moved in and the community became known as Hessville*. In 1891 Hessville assumed the name of East Plymouth because of its geographic location relative to Plymouth. In 1892 members of the community became dissatisfied and chose a new community to the south that was eventually known as Fielding.
S18,T13N,R12W,SLM; 4,465' (1,361m). 251, 360.

EAST SHINGLE CREEK LAKE (**Summit**) is at the west end of the Uinta Mountains on the headwaters of Shingle Creek. The lake received its name from the creek.
S6,T2S,R8E,SLM; 9,700' (2,957m).

EAST TAVAPUTS PLATEAU (**Uintah, Grand**) is a high tableland north of the Roan or Brown Cliffs, south of the Uinta Basin. The Tavaputs Plateau is divided by Desolation and Gray canyons of the Green River. Powell named both canyons in addition to the Tavaputs Plateau, after a Ute Indian headman.
160, 422, 542.

EAST WEBER* (**Weber**). See Uintah*.

EASTERN BEAVER VALLEY (**Beaver**) is synonymous with the Beaver Valley or Upper Valley between Beaver* and Adamsville* as opposed to the Western Beaver Valley or Lower Valley which is synonymous with the Milford Valley area.
125.

EASTLAND* (**San Juan**) is a small ranching community fourteen miles southeast of Monticello* near the head of Horsehead Canyon and three miles south of US-666. The town was established in 1949 and named as being east of Monticello.
S24,T34S,R25E,SLM; 6,880' (2,097m). 406.

EASTON* (**Weber**). See Uintah*.

ECHO* (**Summit**) is near the north end of Echo Reservoir. In 1854 James Bromley settled there as station manager for the Overland Stage Company and in 1860 the Pony Express established a station there. In 1861 the Overland telegraph office was set up in the express station, and the town of Echo was established as an important communication and travel stop. It became more important when the Union Pacific Railroad came through and pushed the

community into a modern-day railroad boomtown. In 1929 the depression hit and, with improved technology helping the railroad, the old town died. Today it is a small placid community that received its name from the canyon where the resonance of the surrounding cliffs bounces echoes back and forth across the canyon. See Echo Canyon.
S24,T31N,R4E,SLM; 5,459' (1,664m). 163(27 Dec. 1935), 314, 288, 466(8 March 1978), 542.

ECHO CANYON (Summit) originates at Wasatch*, close to the southwestern corner of Wyoming. The canyon drains southwest and ends near the mouth of Echo Creek at the Weber River. Throughout the history of the West, the canyon has been a principal Indian and trapper's trail and later a pioneer road. I-80 passes through the canyon today. In 1846 the Harlan-Young party made the first wagon tracks down Echo Canyon. They were followed a week or ten days later by the Donner-Reed party. The following year the Mormons made the same route. Numerous reports and journals comment on the strange reverberations that bounce back and forth in the canyon. Some reported the sound of carpenter hammers on boards. Other reports suggest the sound of lowing cattle and braying donkeys or mules. See Echo*.
S2,T5N,R7E,SLM to S25,T3N,R4E,SLM.

ECHO CANYON CREEK (Summit) drains through Echo Canyon. In earlier days it was known as Red Fork Creek and later as Egans Creek.
516.

ECHO LAKE (Duchesne) is in the Murdock Basin in the southwest section of the Uinta Mountains. The lake is in an area where the surrounding cliffs reverberate echoes.
S10,15,T3N,R9W,USM; 9,750' (2,972m).

ECHO RESERVOIR (Summit) is on the Weber River between the mouth of Echo Canyon and Coalville*. The reservoir received its name from the canyon.
S30,T3N,R5E,SLM to S17,T2N,R5E,SLM; 5,560' (1,695m).

EDEN* (Weber) is on the North Fork of the Ogden River, north of Pineview Reservoir. The first home was a log cabin built in 1857 for summer herdsmen Erastus Bingham and Joseph Hardy. A community was established in 1859 when fifteen families moved in via North Ogden Canyon and Pass. The settlers hired a government surveyor, Washington Jenkins, to plat the town. Jenkins said he thought the area was one of the most beautiful sites he had every surveyed and suggested the biblical name Eden. An earlier temporary name was North Fork Town*.
S35,T7N,R1E,SLM; 4,947' (1,508m). 274, 288, 360, 542, 546, 567.

EDGEMONT* (Utah) is a subdivision in northeast Provo*. The town is on U-78, US-189, and the mouth of Little Rock Canyon, at the base of the Wasatch Mountains.
S19,T6S,R3E,SLM; 4,783' (1,458m).

EDWIN BRIDGE (San Juan). See Natural Bridges National Monument.

EGANS CREEK (Summit). See Echo Canyon. Howard Egan was one of the first 1847 pioneers to arrive in the Salt Lake Valley. He was a noted scout, Pony Express rider, and was involved in the development of the Overland Stage.
371.

EGG ISLAND (Davis) is off the west coast of Antelope Island in Great Salt Lake. Captain Stansbury and his men named it after they obtained seventy-six heron eggs from the nesting birds on the island. It is a small island that becomes

part of Antelope Island when the lake level is low. The island is a nesting site for gulls, herons, pelicans, cormorants, and other birds.
4,300' (1,311m). 100(v2), 133, 360, 371, 492, 542.

EGYPT (Garfield) is west of and near the Escalante River between Harris Wash and Twentyfive Mile Wash. It is a desert area of sand dunes and unusual geologic features of obelisks and pillars that remind one of ancient Egypt.
T37S,R6E,SLM; 5,400' (1,646m). 12, 497.

EIGHTMILE CREEK (Millard) is eight miles southwest of Scipio* where it drains southwest into the desert.
S27,34,T18S,R4W,SLM to S22,T19S,R5W, SLM. 567.

EKKER RANCH (Wayne) is on the Roost Flats, south of the head of Robbers Roost Canyon, South Fork. Early maps list it as Biddlecome Ranch, which was founded by Joe and Millie Biddlecome. The ranch was established in what was then the heart of the Robbers Roost country during a period when bank robbing and cattle rustling gangs were active. Butch Cassidy and his gang played a substantial role in these activities. Descendants of the Biddlecomes and the Ekkers now own the property and the cattle ranch continues to operate.
S14,T29S,R14E,SLM (headquarters); 5,799' (1,768m). 24, 25, 303.

ELATERITE BASIN (Wayne) is a vast tract of land seven miles west of The Confluence of the Green and Colorado rivers. The word "elaterite" is the soft, flexible, mineral resin that oozes out of the rocks in the basin.
T30S,R17E,SLM; 5,200' (1,585m).

ELATERITE BUTTE (Wayne) is a large butte on the east side of Elaterite Basin.
T30S,R17E,SLM; 6,552' (1,997m).

ELBERTA* (Utah) is a small rural community near the southwest tip of Utah Lake, three miles west of Goshen*. It was established in 1895 and was first called Mount Nebo* for the nearby peak. The next name came from the Early Elberta peach orchards planted there by Ernest Rognan. Records indicate that the name was given intentionally to attract settlers. It reminds one of how Fruitland*, Duchesne County, received its name. Today Elberta is still a fruit-producing town.
S8,9,16,17,T10S,R1W,SLM; 4,660' (1,420m). 100(v17), 542.

ELBOW LAKE (Duchesne) is in the central section of the Uinta Mountains on the headwaters of the Whiterocks River, one mile west of Chepeta Lake. The lake has a right-angled shape like the crook of an elbow.
S30,31,T6N,R1W,USM; 10,900' (3,322m).

ELBOW, THE (Piute) is five miles northeast of Junction* and three miles northeast of Piute Reservoir. It is an open benchland shaped like an elbow that rests against the hills near the mouth of Tibadore Canyon. Supposedly the climate is a bit milder there than the surrounding area and the crops grow better because the surrounding hills protect the crops from frost.
S28,32,T28S,R2½W,SLM; 6,450' (1,966m). 567. D.L. 8503.

ELECTRIC FENCE RESERVOIR (Beaver) is in the Pine Valley south of the Pine Valley Hardpan.
S8,T26S,R16W,SLM; 5,170' (1,576m).

ELEPHANT BACK (Beaver) is in the Indian Peak Mountains of the Needle Range near Sawtooth Peak. The name is a descriptive term for a land feature with a rounded top.
S15,T28S,R18W,SLM; 7,071' (2,155m).

ELEPHANT CANYON (**Beaver**) is in the Star Range southwest of Milford* and drains southeast toward the Escalante Desert. The canyon is named for the Elephant Mine that operated in 1871.
S30,T28S,R11W,SLM. 100(v17), 125.

ELEPHANT CANYON (**San Juan**) originates at Druid Arch in the Needles section of Canyonlands National Park. The canyon drains north past Elephant Hill into the Colorado River and receives its name from the numerous dome-like, elephant-back sandstone formations near the canyon.
S16,T31S,R19E,SLM (to the Colorado River).

ELEPHANT CITY* (**Beaver**) is a ghost town site in the Star Range southwest of Milford*. The city received its name from the adjacent Elephant Mine. Both the city and the mine were in or near Elephant Canyon. The city thrived from 1871 to 1875, along with other famous ghost towns such as Star City*, Shenandoah City*, South Camp*, Shauntie*, and others.
T28S,R12W,SLM. 355.

ELEPHANT HILL (**San Juan**) is in Canyonlands National Park at the north end of the Needles section between Big Spring and Elephant canyons. The base of the hill is the end of a two-wheel-drive road and the beginning of the four-wheel-drive road leading to The Confluence, The Grabens, and Chesler Park. Before the national park era, when this area was known as the Scorup-Somerville grazing range, the cattle company paid a cat operator two hundred dollars to cut a road from one side of the hill to the other. The road could have been built over an easier route, but the operator decided to take the quickest route his equipment could handle. Today the road has become a challenge—a rite of passage—into the hinterland on the east side. One feels a sense of "arriving" after surviving a return trip over Elephant Hill. The hill, and the other similar features in the region, take their names from the heavily eroded elephant-back sandstone domes that are quite common in the area.
S27,T30S,R19E,SLM; 5,300' (1,615m). 126.

ELGIN* (**Grand**) is on the east side of the Green River across from Green River*. In 1905, Elgin was established as a siding on the Denver and Rio Grande Western Railroad, and a post office was granted on March 5, 1898. The town quickly became a fruit-growing center, but over the years unexpected freezing periods and the cost of pumping water from the river caused the community to decline. Today the town has been revitalized by the addition of motels and tourist activities. Elgin has now been absorbed into Green River.
S15,T21S,R16E,SLM; 4,075' (1,242m). 89, 146.

ELIZABETH CAVE (**Uintah**) is ten miles northwest of Vernal* in Dry Fork Canyon. L. C. Thorne and his daughter, Mary Lew Thorne, were searching for archaeological specimens when they entered a cave and discovered a well-preserved female mummy. Mary Lew named the mummy Elizabeth.
ca. S23,T3S,R20E,SLM. 567.

ELK CREEK (**Daggett**) originates in the northeastern section of the Uinta Mountains, two miles north of Trout Creek Park. It drains north into Carter Creek. Elk are numerous in the region.

ELK HORN SPRINGS* (**Iron**). See Enoch*.

ELK MOUNTAIN CREEK (**Grand**). See Mill Creek.

ELK MOUNTAIN MISSION* (**Grand**). See Moab*.

ELK MOUNTAINS (**San Juan**). See La Sal Mountains.

ELK RIDGE (San Juan) is a prominent ridge west of the Abajo Mountains with a north-south orientation. The ridge threads its way between the heads of many of the isolated canyons that originate in this area. Some of these canyons are Texas, Dark, Deadman, and Poison canyons. The ridge was a strategic trail of the early Ute Indians. Elk were plentiful in the region.
T33-36S,R19E,SLM. 406, 567.

ELKHORN* (Wasatch). See Hailstone*.

ELKHORN CANYON (Summit) originates at the Elkhorn Divide, six miles northeast of Rockport Reservoir. The canyon drains northwest into Chalk Creek, South Fork. See Elkhorn Divide.
S22,T1N,R6E,SLM to S9,T2N,R6E,SLM.

ELKHORN DIVIDE (Summit) is a four-mile-long ridge with a north-south orientation located six miles northeast of Rockport Reservoir. Elk congregate in the region near the Sargent Lakes.
S5,8,17,T1N,R6E,SLM; 8,524' (2,598m).

ELLIOT MESA (Emery) is on Beckwith Plateau, twelve miles north of Green River*. It was named for Scott Elliott, an Englishman who had settled on the Big Spring Ranch near present-day Sunnyside.
T19S,R15E,SLM; 6,991' (2,131m). 25.

ELMO* (Emery) is a small, dispersed agricultural community east of U-10 and eight miles north of Huntington*. Elmo was settled in 1908 by people from Cleveland*, although it was filed upon as early as 1904. The origin of the name is uncertain, but folklore suggests a reference to a popular novel of the day, St. Elmo.
S32,33,T16S,R10E,SLM; 5,694' (1,736m). 100(v5), 360, 542, 567.

ELSINORE* (Sevier) is on US-89 and the Sevier River, six miles south of Richfield*. The community was first settled in the spring of 1874 by James C.

Jensen, Jens Iver Jensen, and others. The town was given its official name at the suggestion of Mormon Stake President Joseph A. Young because the site reminded him of Elsinore, Denmark, where he had visited. The town had an earlier name of Little Denmark* because many of the early settlers were immigrants of that country.
S28,29,T24S,R3W,SLM; 5,342' (1,628m). 100(v17), 360, 546, 585.

ELWOOD* (Box Elder) is on US-30S, two miles southeast of Tremonton*. It was established in 1879 with an early name of Manila Ward* in honor of Commodore George Dewey's victory in the Spanish American War. The name was changed to Elwood by the postal authorities to avoid confusion with the Manila Voting Precinct. Mr. Davidson, a cattle and sheepman, was the first white settler in Elwood.
S23,24,T11N,R3W,SLM; 4,295' (1,309m). 251, 360.

EMERALD LAKE (Sanpete) is on the western slopes of Block Mountain, two and one-half miles southwest of Heliotrope Mountain. The name reflects the beautiful emerald color of the lake.
S17,T20S,R4E,SLM; 10,135' (3,089m).

EMERALD LAKE (Utah) is a small snow-melt lake on the eastern slope of Mount Timpanogos at the bottom of the cirque.
S7,8,T5S,R3E,SLM; 10,375' (3,162m).

EMERALD LAKES (Sevier) are two small, beautiful, high-alpine lakes between U M Plateau and Sheep Valley. The lakes have a distinctive emerald color.
S16,T24S,R3E,SLM; 10,260' (3,127m).

EMERY* (Emery) is on U-10 fifteen miles southwest of Ferron*. The town was first called Muddy Creek* after the nearby creek. It was later named Emery in honor of George W. Emery, of Tennessee, who was appointed governor

of Utah Territory in 1875. See Emery County.
S4,9,T22S,R6E,SLM; 6,262' (1,909m). 6, 27, 288, 360, 542, 567.

EMERY COUNTY was established in 1880 and named to honor George W. Emery, territorial governor of Utah, 1875-80. Originally, the proposed name was Castle County, but it was decided that honoring the governor was more important. Emery County is the only county in Utah named in honor of a Utah state governor.
6, 374.

EMIGRANT PASS (Box Elder) is at the south end of the Grouse Creek Mountains, passing over an extension known today as the Bovine Mountains. The westward traveling immigrants of the Bartelson-Bidwell party of 1841 had to work their way over this extension on the pass.
T9N,R16W,SLM; 6,097' (1,858m). 251, 371.

EMIGRANT PASS (Sevier) is on I-70 at the summit, six miles west of Fremont Junction. This important pass in this Fish Lake Plateau area south of Musinia Peak, is an important landmark and guide point.
S29,T23S,R4E,SLM; 7,880' (2,402m).

EMIGRANT SPRING* (Box Elder) is two and one-half miles south of Cedar Creek*, an early stage station. The Emigrant Spring was named by early immigrants who passed this area on their journey west and northwest.
S24,T14N,R12W,SLM; 5,575' (1,699m). 567.

EMIGRATION CANYON (Salt Lake) originates in the Wasatch Mountains east of Salt Lake City* and drains southwest into the Jordan River. For a short time the early name was Canyon Creek. Shortly after, it was renamed Emigration Canyon because of the historic importance to the pioneers of 1847 who

traveled through it to enter the Great Salt Lake Valley in 1847.
S27,T1N,R2E,SLM to S11,T1S,R1E,SLM. 27, 100(v17), 252, 360.

EMMAVILLE* (Salt Lake) is a ghost town site, one and one-fourth miles north of the mouth of Little Cottonwood Canyon near Deaf Smith Canyon. The settlers were predominantly miners, rock quarry freighters, and various day laborers. It is believed to have been named after the Emma Mine up Little Cottonwood Canyon, which in turn was named for the daughter of the co-discoverer of the Emma Mine, Robert B. Chisholm. The town was first settled in 1868-69, but began to decline in 1871 when improved railroad facilities in the canyon, an epidemic, and a disastrous fire in Emmaville changed the course of local history.
S1,T3S,R1E,SLM; 5,200' (1,585m). 89, 163(22 May 1972), 360, 356, 516, 567.

EMPEYS SPRINGS* (Box Elder). See Deweyville*.

EMPIRE CANYON (Summit) originates three and one-half miles south of Park City*. The canyon drains north to become the main street of Park City*. It was named for the Empire Mining Company, the developer of a large mine in the vicinity in 1887.
S28,T2S,R4E,SLM to S16,T2S,R4E,SLM. 508.

ENGLISH FORT* (Salt Lake). See Granger*.

ENOCH* (Iron) is six miles north of Cedar City* and west of old US-91. The community had an early name of Elkhorn Springs* because elk horns were found by the springs. Joel, Seth, Nephi, and Sextus Johnson were the first settlers in 1851, resulting in the name Fort Johnson* and later Johnsons Settlement*. The name Enoch was given to the

settlement in 1884 when some of the settlers were living under the Order of Enoch, or the United Order. Enoch was an ancient biblical prophet who "walked with God."
S7,T35S,R10W,SLM; 5,548' (1,691m). 136, 266(Genesis 5:34), 288, 314, 516, 542, 567.

ENOCH CITY* (Summit). See Rockport* (Summit).

ENSIGN PEAK (Salt Lake) is in the foothills north of Salt Lake City*, one and one-fourth miles north of the state capitol building. Wilford Woodruff wrote in 1847, "We went north of the camp about five miles and we all went on to the top of a high peak in the edge of the mountain, which we considered a good place to raise an ensign. So we named it 'Ensign Peak.' I was the first person that ascended this hill which we had thus named. Brother Young was very weary in climbing to the peak—he being feeble. Had not yet recovered from effects of Mt. Fever" (604, p. 168).
S30,T1N,R1E,SLM; 5,414' (1,650m). 27, 129, 163(15 Sept. 1934), 252, 604.

ENTERPRISE* (Morgan) is at the northwest end of Morgan Valley, five miles northwest of Morgan*. This small community was settled in 1862. The name represents a compliment to the settlers for their enterprise, hard work, and steadfastness in developing the settlement.
S9,T4N,R2E,SLM; 4,967' (1,514m). 360, 378, 567.

ENTERPRISE* (Washington) is a small agricultural community located on U-18 at the south end of the Escalante Desert near the mouth of Shoal Creek. Many Enterprise settlers came from Hebron*, a settlement located further up Shoal Creek. These people gradually started to abandon Hebron because the local mines were shutting down, an earthquake struck in 1902, and there was a lack of water. The 1906 San Francisco earthquake demolished the last of old Hebron, and

the new, undamaged Enterprise now had a population of approximately one hundred families. Enterprise was originally named Shoal Creek*. The name change reflected their ability to adjust to unexpected problems. The settlers considered their new home an enterprising community. See Hebron*.
S13,14,T37S,R17W,SLM; 5,329' (1,624m). 154, 288, 314, 542, 546.

ENTERPRISE RESERVOIR (Washington) is eight miles west of Enterprise* on Little Pine Creek. The site includes an upper and lower Enterprise Reservoir, both named after the community they serve.
S33,34,T37S,R18W,SLM.

EPHRAIM* (Sanpete) is in the Sanpete Valley on US-89 between Mount Pleasant* and Manti*. The town was originally called Pine Creek+, then for a short period of time, Cottonwood*. When the settlers established themselves and were able to fortify, Cottonwood was renamed Fort Ephraim*, honoring one of the tribes of Israel. When Ephraim was founded, it was the intention to locate another town on the west side of the San Pitch River and name it Manassa*, in order to honor both sons of Joseph who were sold into Egypt. Manassa was never built.
S3,4,9,10,T17S,R3E,SLM; 5,515' (1,681m). 288, 360, 542, 567.

EPHRAIM CANYON (Sanpete) originates on the Wasatch Plateau east of Ephraim*. Ephraim Creek drains through the canyon into the San Pitch River and received its name from the town it serves.
S13,T17S,R13E,SLM (at head).

EPHRAIM HANKS STATION* (Salt Lake). See Hanks Station*.

EPHRAIMS GRAVE (Cache). Ephraim Logan's grave is in Logan Canyon, Right Fork, four and one-half miles south southwest of Temple Peak. Logan City*,

down the canyon to the west, and the canyon were both named for this early trapper.
7,200' (2,195m). 578.

EPHS HOLE (Beaver) is on the north side of the Beaver River, east of Big Cove and west of Lousy Jim Creek. Ephraim Puffer, one of Beaver's early sheriffs, often hunted deer in the hollow. S18,19,T29S,R5W,SLM; 8,500' (2,591m). 125.

ERICKSON BASIN (Summit). See Erickson Creek (Summit).
S31,32,T1S,R8E,SLM; 9,600' (2,926m).

ERICKSON CREEK (Summit) originates at the southwest section of the Uinta Mountains in Erickson Basin, one-half mile southwest of Big Elk Lake. The creek drains north into the headwaters of Smith and Morehouse Creek. This area, including Erickson Basin and North and South Erickson lakes, was logged off during the early 1900s by one Mr. Erickson, a lumberman.
S29,30,31,T1S,R8E,SLM. 298.

ERICKSON WASH (Juab, Tooele) originates at Erickson Pass on the southwest slopes of the Sheeprock Mountains, six miles north of Delta*. The wash drains south, disappearing into the desert at the Old River Bed east of Keg Mountain.
S11,T10S,R7W,SLM to S4,T12S,R8W,SLM.

ERNIE CANYON (Emery) originates on the San Rafael Swell, six miles south of present-day I-70 and drains through the San Rafael Reef into Iron Wash. MRN
S24,T23S,R11E,SLM to S4,T24S,R13E,SLM.

ERNIES COUNTRY (Garfield) is five miles southwest of The Confluence and west of Cataract Canyon in Canyonlands National Park. Ernie Larson was an early sheepman.
T30½,31S,R17,18E,SLM; ca. 5,100' (1,554m). 326.

ESCALANTE* (Garfield) is in Potato Valley on U-12 and the upper reaches of the Escalante River. The town was first named Potato* or Spud Valley* for the edible wild potatoes that grew in the area. The name was changed to Escalante by Almon Thompson of the Powell surveys. The name honors the famous Spanish explorer who passed this area far to the west in 1776 with the leader of the expedition, Domínguez. The members of the expedition never came near the valley. The valley was discovered by whites in 1866 during the Black Hawk War when a group of Mormon cavalry ventured into the valley while pursuing Indians. In 1876 Philo Allen, Sr., built the first log cabin at the mouth of Corn Creek in Main Canyon.
S8,17,18,T35S,R33E,SLM; 5,812' (1,771m). 12, 100(v1,5), 288, 314, 360, 385, 496, 515, 546, 602.

ESCALANTE BASIN (Garfield) is the region drained by the tributaries of the upper Escalante River. The basin was named by the Almon Thompson party of the Powell surveys.
422.

ESCALANTE CANYON (Garfield) originates south of the northwest end of the Kaiparowits Plateau and drains south into Last Chance Creek. See Escalante*.
T38S,R2E,SLM at S34,T39S,R3E,SLM (headwaters of Last Chance Creek). 12.

ESCALANTE DESERT (Beaver, Iron) is a vast flatland located twenty-five miles west of Cedar City* and north of Enterprise* and Newcastle*. In ancient times this area was part of Lake Bonneville. The desert is sometimes referred to as the Escalante Valley and was named for Escalante of the 1776 Domínguez and Escalante expedition. Domínguez and Escalante are believed to be the first white men to enter this region. Due to recent deep-well drilling and above-ground sprinkling with high-

pressure pumps, the area is rapidly being converted to pasture land, alfalfa, and other field crops. The word "desert" may soon become passe.
T31-36S,R12-18W,SLM; 5,150' (1,570m). 578.

ESCALANTE MOUNTAIN (Garfield) is the western part of the Aquarius Plateau. The eastern section of the Aquarius is Boulder Mountain. See Escalante River for name source.
T32,33,34S,R1E,R1W,SLM; 10,400' (3,170m).

ESCALANTE NATURAL BRIDGE (Garfield) is on the Escalante River between the mouths of Sand and California creeks. This feature was named after the river.
T35S,R4E,SLM; 5,400' (1,646m). 602.

ESCALANTE RIVER (Garfield) originates five miles southwest of Escalante* at the junction of Upper Valley, Birch, and North creeks. The river drains southeast into the Colorado River. This was the last river in the United States to be discovered and added to maps. It is considered one of the most crooked rivers in the United States. Geologist Herbert E. Gregory measured a fourteen-mile straight line sector of the river and found it to be thirty-five miles long. The river was named by Almon Thompson of the Powell surveys to honor the first white man to have crossed this wilderness area, even though Escalante never entered this locality. Thompson also provided an earlier name of Potato Creek or Potato Valley Creek after the valley the river drained. Today, sections of the river have been set apart as a wilderness area.
T35-40S,R2-9E,SLM. 100(v1), 159, 360, 422, 496, 515, 602.

ESKDALE* (Millard) is a small agricultural community in the Snake Valley west of the Conger Range. It was founded as a religious community, The Order of Aaron, by the spiritual head,

Dr. M. L. Glendenning, who was of royal background and very fond of his history. The family lands were located on the River Esk in Scotland.
S35,T19S,R19W,SLM; 4,972' (1,515m). 578.

ETHER PEAK (Utah) is in the Wasatch Mountains, four miles east southeast of Springville*, south of Hobble Creek. Ether was an honored name in Mormon Church scripture.
S6,T8S,R4E,SLM; 7,533' (2,296m). 61.

ETNA* (Box Elder) is five miles southwest of Grouse Creek* on Etna and Warm creeks, east of the Nevada border. There is no longer an established community today. It was first settled in 1875 by Valison and Alma C. Tanner and its early name was West Fork* (of Grouse Creek). A permanent name was required before mail could be delivered, so Charlie Morris, the mail carrier, chose Etna.
S18,T11N,R18W,SLM; 5,203' (1,586m). 251, 525, 567.

EUREKA* (Juab) is a mining community on US-6,50 in the Tintic Mountains, twelve miles west of Goshen*. It was settled when gold was discovered in the area in 1869. More than six communities sprang up to provide housing for the incoming miners. "Eureka" is Greek for "I have found it."
S18,T10S,R2W,SLM; 6,442' (1,964m). 134 (29 Feb. 1976), 288, 314, 360, 542.

EUREKA PEAK (Juab) is one mile south of Eureka*, from which the name is derived.
S19,T10S,R2W,SLM; 7,916' (2,413m).

EVACUATION CREEK (Utah) originates in Colorado, enters Utah south of the White River, and drains northwest. The waters are highly diarrheic.
S7,T10S,R25E,SLM (at mouth). 578.

EVANS* (Box Elder) was a small community and siding on the old Oregon Short Line Railroad, two miles west of

Bear River City*. The Utah-Idaho Sugar Company named the siding to honor Mase Evans, manager of the company. S31,T10N,R3W,SLM; 4,259' (1,298m). 567.

EVANSVILLE* (**Utah**). See Lehi* (Utah).

EVERMAN LAKE (**Duchesne**) is at the west end of the Uinta Mountains in Naturalist Basin. Two miles northwest is Mount Agassiz. The lake was named after Barton Warren Everman, a naturalist and one of Agassiz's students. Many places in this area were named for students of Agassiz, the great naturalist. S33,T4N,R8W,USM; 10,500' (3,200m). 309.

EXPLORER CANYON (**Kane**) is in the lower Escalante River basin. The canyon originates between the heads of Bowns and Fence canyons and drains into the Escalante River. It was named for a group of Scouts from Salt Lake City* who explored the canyon. T39S,R9E,SLM.

EYE OF THE NEEDLE (**Beaver**) is a small natural window high up on Lime Point on the western slopes of the Wah Wah Mountains near U-21. The feature is visible from the highway. S36,T26S,R16W,SLM; 6,641' (2,024m).

EZRA M C BENCH (**Kane**) is a grazing area between Fools Canyon and the Escalante River. It was named for Ezra McInelly, an Escalante cattleman. T38S,R8E,SLM. 12.

- F -

FABLE VALLEY (**San Juan**) is on the Dark Canyon Plateau near Dark Canyon.

FACTORY BENCH (**Wayne**) has a north-south orientation near Factory Butte where it receives its name. The Fremont River and the ghost town site of Giles* is located at the southern end of the bench.
T27,28S,R10E,SLM; 4,800' (1,463m).

FACTORY BUTTE (**Wayne**) is five miles north of the Fremont River, between North Cainville Mesa and Factory Bench. The butte has the appearance of a gigantic factory building.
S22,23,26,27,T27S,R9E,SLM; 6,385' (1,946m).

FACTORY FARM* (**Kane**). See Hidden Lake and Orderville*.

FAILURE CANYON (**Summit**) originates in the southwest section of the Uinta Mountains and drains north into Beaver Creek. A Ute Indian, Beaver Creek Charlie, went broke mining in the canyon.
S28,33,T2S,R7E,SLM. 567.

FAIRFIELD* (**Utah**) is five miles south of Cedar Fort* on U-73 on the west side of Utah Lake. The town was established in 1855 when John Carson, his four brothers, and others settled in the valley. The developing community was rudely challenged when it found itself hopelessly involved with the fortunes of the incoming Johnston's Army of 1858-59. The army established a nearby camp called Camp Floyd*. The ensuing population explosion quickly rose to over seven thousand soldiers, teamsters, gamblers, and camp followers of various persuasions. The settlement was soon known as

Frogtown*. Frogtown became Fairfield in 1861 in honor of Amos Fielding, who participated in establishing the community. The pleasant views from the community out over the surrounding fields is also connected to the town name. Today, except for historical memories, a magnificent overland stagecoach inn, and a nearby military cemetery, it is again a quiet, small, relaxed community. See also Camp Floyd*.
S29,32,T6S,R2W,SLM; 4,877' (1,487m). 27, 81, 89, 100(v17), 268, 313, 360, 384, 542, 546, 569.

FAIRMONT* (**Weber**) was first settled in 1852. In 1923 it was organized as a separate entity from parts of Kanesville*, Riverdale*, Roy*, and Wilson*. The town was named for the beautiful nearby mountains and surrounding pleasant view.
SE¼,T6N,R2W,NE¼,T5N,R2W,SLM; 4,200'-4,400' (1,280m-1,341m). 542, 567.

FAIRVIEW* (**Garfield**). See Panguitch*.

FAIRVIEW* (**Garfield**) is eleven miles south of Hanksville* on the Sawmill Basin Road. It is a large ranch located on the eastern slopes of the Henry Mountains and named for its attractive views.
S8,T30S,R11E,SLM; 5,150' (1,570m). 25, 273.

FAIRVIEW* (**Sanpete**) was settled six miles north of Mount Pleasant* on US-89. Its early name was North Bend* because it was on a bend in the San Pitch River. In 1864, following a suggestion by Archibald Anderson, it was renamed Fairview for its attractive surroundings.
S1,2,6,T14S,R4E,SLM; 6,000' (1,829m). 288, 322, 542, 567.

FAIRVIEW LAKES (Sanpete) is a small cluster of alpine lakes six and one-half miles east of Fairview*. The water flows to Fairview from the lakes in Cottonwood Canyon Creek.
S36,T13S,R5E,SLM; 8,975' (2,736m).

FAIRY POOL (Salt Lake). See Lake Phoebe.

FAIRYLAND CANYON (Garfield) originates in Bryce Canyon National Park at Fairyland Point, one and one-half miles northeast of the visitor center, and drains southeast into Campbell Canyon west of Tropic*. The name reflects the fragile beauty of the canyon, heavily eroded out of the Pink Cliffs.
T36S,R3W,SLM.

FAIRYLAND POINT (Garfield) is in Bryce Canyon National Park at the head of Fairyland Canyon, one and one-half miles northeast of the visitor center. This is an extension of the Pink Cliffs. See Fairyland Canyon.
7,758' (2,365m).

FALSE CREEK (Garfield). See Alvey Wash.

FARMINGTON* (Davis) is on U-106 twelve miles north of Salt Lake City*. Hector Caleb Haight arrived here with his cattle in the fall of 1847; he lived through the winter in a tent. In 1848 he built a cabin and the area was known as Haights Bench* as well as North Cottonwood Creek*, for the creek near the settlement. The name was later changed to Miller's Settlement* for Daniel A. Miller, who is credited with plowing the first field. The town finally became Farmington on February 18, 1852, as a reminder of the rich soil that encouraged a life-style of farming.
S19,T3N,R1E,SLM; 4,302' (1,311m). 88, 275, 288, 360, 542, 567.

FARMINGTON BAY (Davis) is the bay of the Great Salt Lake that rests midway between Farmington* and Bountiful*. The bay was named for the adjacent community.
4,207' (1,282m).

FARMINGTON CANYON (Davis) originates in the mountains east of Farmington*, from which it receives its name.
S17,18,T3N,R1E,SLM.

FARMINGTON CREEK (Davis) drains through Farmington Canyon.
S26,T3N,R1E,SLM to S35,T3N,R1W,SLM.

FARMINGTON FLATS (Davis) is an open, flat area near the summit of the mountains east of Farmington*. Farmington Creek drains the flats.
S23,25,T3N,R1E,SLM; 7,600' (2,316m).

FARMINGTON LAKE (Davis) is in the mountains east of Farmington* and north of Bountiful Peak.
S22,T3N,R1E,SLM; 8,100' (2,469m).

FARNSWORTH PEAK (Salt Lake, Tooele) is in the Oquirrh Mountains, four miles south of the Great Salt Lake. The peak was originally named Coon Peak honoring Abraham Coon, a pioneer. After television stations placed broadcasting equipment on the peak, the name was changed to honor Philo T. Farnsworth, a Utah native who invented television units.
S8,T2S,R3W,SLM; 9,054' (2,760m). 546. D.L. 6803.

FARR WEST* (Weber) is three miles east of Plain City* on U-84 and I-15. The name developed because it was west of Farrs Fort* and named for Lorin Farr, first president of the Weber Stake of the Mormon Church. It had an earlier name of West Harrisville* because early settlers Chauncey W. West, J. S. Taylor, and others came from nearby Harrisville*. See Farrs Fort*.
S35,36,T7N,R2W,SLM; 4,260' (1,298m). 274, 288, 360, 542, 567.

FARRS FORT* (Weber) is in North Ogden*, one block north of the Ogden River and one and one-half miles west of the mouth of the Ogden Canyon. In 1850 Lorin Farr, Ezra Chase, and others built the fort. A spring was inside the fort and the houses formed the basic outside wall. In 1853 the people moved out of the fort and onto the surrounding land. The fort was named for Lorin Farr. See Farr West*.
S21,T6N,R1W,SLM; 4,380' (1,335m).

FAUST* (Tooele) is at the south end of Rush Valley where the old Pony Express Trail crosses the Union Pacific Railroad. Atherly Reservoir is one and one-half miles west. Faust was named for H. J. "Doc" Faust who rode the Pony Express out of this station, operated a mail station on a local section of the Overland Trail, and later purchased the station and area for his ranch. H. J. Faust was also important in Utah agricultural history for helping upgrade the quality of beef cattle on his ranch. Today the site is an unimportant siding on the railroad.
S27,T7S,R5W,SLM; 5,253' (1,601m). 134(29 Feb. 1976), 360, 406, 542, 555(v32).

FAUST CREEK (Tooele) originates in the general area between the Vernon Hills and Vernon* at the southern end of Rush Valley. The creek drains north through the Atherly Reservoir to the lowlands near Rush Lake. See Faust*.
S4,11,T9S,R5W,SLM to S3,T5S,R5W,SLM. D.L. 7402.

FAXON LAKE (Duchesne) is in the Naturalist Basin at the southwest section of the Uinta Mountains. One and one-half miles west is Mount Agassiz. The lake is named after naturalist Charles Edward Faxon, one of Agassiz's students.
S28,T4N,R8W,USM; 10,980' (3,347m). 298, 309.

FAYETTE* (Sanpete) is on U-28 five miles northwest of Gunnison*. It was settled in 1861 by James Bartholomew, soon abandoned, then re-established in 1866. The original name was Warm Creek* for the name of the creek upon which the people settled. Fayette was the name finally chosen because the Mormon Church was first organized in Fayette*, Seneca County, New York.
S19,30,T18S,R1E,SLM; 4,040' (1,231m). 152, 288, 314, 360, 542, 567.

FEDERAL HEIGHTS* (Salt Lake) is today a small but prosperous subdivision of Salt Lake City at the east end of South Temple Street. In 1850, Charles Popper, a Jewish butcher, immigrated to the United States from Germany. By 1854 he had worked his way to the Great Salt Lake Valley where he obtained a contract to provide beef to Fort Douglas*. He purchased land at the mouth of Dry Canyon, what is known today as Federal Heights. Here he operated his slaughtering yards, a candle and soap factory, and a butcher shop downtown on Main Street. Popperton*, the place name at the head of South Temple Street, was established. Later it became known as Butcherville*, in reference to Popper's principal business. About the time of the Spanish-American war, Charles Popper faded from the scene and his property was appropriated by the federal government for Fort Douglas. In 1907 the land was annexed to Salt Lake City* from Fort Douglas and the name Federal Heights was commonly used.
S33,T1N,R1E,S4,T1S,R1E,SLM.466(14 Sept. 1986), 508.

FEHR LAKE (Duchesne) is in the southwest section of the Uinta Mountains on the Duchesne River drainage. The lake lies midway between Murdock Mountain and Mirror Lake. MRN
S3,T3N,R9W,USM; 10,250' (3,124m).

FENCE CANYON (Kane) originates near the Waterpocket Fold where it drains southwest, joining the Escalante River. The canyon was fenced as a pasture at one time.
T39S,R9E,SLM. 12.

135

FERGUSON DESERT (Millard) is bound on the north by the south end of the Conger Range and US-6,50 and on the east by the Confusion Range. It was named for James (Jim) Ferguson of Ibapah*, who took up a homestead nearby, bought land, and developed a large ranch.
T20-22S,R16-18W,SLM. 153.

FERNS NIPPLE (Wayne) is a small cone-shaped butte in Capitol Reef National Park, southeast across Grand Wash from Cassidy Arch. Folklore has it that the formation was named by the notorious outlaw Butch Cassidy. Fern was supposedly a favored girlfriend of Cassidy's.
S36,T29S,R6E,SLM; 7,067' (2,154m). 360.

FERRON* (Emery) is on U-10 at the mouth of Ferron Canyon, ten miles southwest of Castle Dale*. It was named to honor A. D. Ferron, pioneer surveyor of Castle Valley, Emery, and Carbon counties.
S9,10,T20S,R7E,SLM; 5,949' (1,813m). 288, 314, 360, 542, 567.

FERRON CANYON (Emery) originates at the summit of the mountains west of Ferron*. It drains southeast past Ferron into the head of the San Rafael River. A. D. Ferron was commissioned to survey and lay out the area. There is a story that Ferron's men told him, "If you will let us duck you in the creek you can have it." He did, they did, and so it was named. The town was also named after the creek. Ferron Canyon is part of the upper drainage system of the creek. Ferron Canyon is part of the upper drainage system of the creek.
S1,T19S,R4E,SLM to S21,T19S,R9E,SLM. 360.

FIDDLER BUTTE (Garfield) is at the head of Fiddlers Cove Canyon, east of the Dirty Devil River. An old sheepherder who ran his sheep on the nearby Red Benches was a fiddle player.
6,027' (1,837m). 144.

FIDDLERS CANYON (Cache) originates two miles west of Mendon* in the north Wellsville Mountains. It drains northwest into Deep Canyon. An early settler who lived there played his fiddle for the local dances.
S12,T11N,R2W,SLM. 100(v17), 567.

FIDDLERS CANYON (Iron) originates on the Markagunt Plateau at Jones Hill, five miles northeast of Cedar City*. The canyon drains west northwest into Cedar Valley. In the early days of establishing the local settlement, a number of men engaged in building a co-op road up the canyon for a source wood fuel. During this road building, it was discovered that all the men played the fiddle. The men were Joseph Hunter, John L. Jones, Edward Parry, and Elliot Wilden.
S10,T36S,R10W,SLM to S36,T35S,R11W, SLM. 100(v17), 567.

FIDDLERS CREEK (Davis). See Holmes Creek (Davis).

FIELDING* (Box Elder) is a small agricultural town on U-81, two and one-half miles north northwest of Collinston*. The area was originally settled in 1892-93 when Jedediah Earl and Harmon D. Pierson of East Plymouth* were commissioned to establish a new town site. Fielding was an outgrowth of Plymouth*, a town that was originally named South Plymouth* in reference to its location. The town was later renamed to honor the mother of Joseph Fielding Smith, the sixth president of the Mormon Church.
S6,T12N,R2W,SLM; 4,367' (1,331m). 139, 546.

FIERY FURNACE (Grand) is in the central section of the Arches National Park. It is a concentrated area of sandstone ridges and elephant backs with deep narrow passageways between them. The brilliant red sandstone not only absorbs the heat from the sun but often

reflects the light, taking on the color of fire. During the summer months, the temperature often rises above 110°F.
S1,2,T24S,R21E,SLM; 5,000' (1,524m).

FIFTYMILE BENCH (Garfield) rests against the base of Fiftymile Mountain of the Kaiparowits Plateau with the Straight Cliffs in between. See Fiftymile Mountain.

FIFTYMILE CREEK (Garfield) originates near Fiftymile Spring at the base of the Straight Cliffs of the Kaiparowits, southeast of Cave Point. It drains northeast into the Escalante River. The creek is approximately fifty miles away from Escalante*. See Fiftymile Spring. Variant: Fiftymile Gulch.

FIFTYMILE GULCH (Garfield). See Fiftymile Creek.

FIFTYMILE MOUNTAIN (Garfield) is part of the Kaiparowits Plateau southeast of Escalante*. The name comes from the approximate fifty-mile length of the mountain, which runs from near Escalante to the end of the plateau near the Colorado River. Its escarpment is the formidable Straight Cliffs. Fiftymile Bench lies at the base of the mountain. The Hole-in-the-Rock road runs parallel to the Fiftymile Bench and the Straight Cliffs.
T38-42S,R5-8E,SLM; 7,606' (2,318m).

FIFTYMILE SPRING (Garfield) is near the Hole-in-the-Rock road and Fiftymile Bench. Seven miles southeast along the road is the Hole-in-the-Rock. The spring is approximately fifty miles out from Escalante* and was named by the members of the Hole-in-the-Rock expedition.
NE¼,T41S,R8E,SLM; 4,500' (1,372m). 12, 602.

FILLMORE* (Millard) is one hundred and forty-eight miles south of Salt Lake City on I-15 and Chalk Creek. The community was named by an act of the Utah Territorial Legislature signed by Brigham Young on October 4, 1851. President Fillmore has been honored twice by the Mormons because he was friendly and helped them. Millard County and Fillmore City* were both named for him. For a time, Fillmore was the territorial capitol.
S20,19,29,T21S,R4W,SLM; 5,135' (1,565m). 27, 275, 314, 360, 542.

FIR LAKE (Summit) is at the west end of the Uinta Mountains in the upper Bear River drainage. Hayden, Jewel, Naomi and Cutthroat lakes are in the vicinity. The lake was named for the beautiful trees so common in the area, especially the alpine fir (*Abies lasiocarpa*).
S14,T1S,R9E,SLM; 10,320' (3,146m).

FIRE LAKE (Summit) is at the west end of the Uinta Mountains in the Upper Provo River drainage, two miles west of Haystack Mountain. Duck, Weir, and Island lakes are close to Fire Lake. An old forest fire scarred the timber in the area.
S13,T2S,R8E,SLM; 10,180' (3,103m). 298.

FIRST SPRING (Beaver) is at the head of First Spring Creek on the western slope of the Tushar Mountains, northeast of Beaver*. It was the first spring encountered as one travelled north along the old mountain road, the first route developed to the Tushar Mountains.
S33,T28S,R6W,SLM; 7,580' (2,310m). 125.

FIRST SPRING (Sevier) is near the head of First Spring Hollow, five miles southwest of Sevier*. The spring was named as the first watering place on the old road up the north end of the Tushar Mountains. These springs were important watering and camping areas in horse-and-wagon days. One and one-half miles south, higher up the mountain, is Sargent Lake.
S23,T26S,R4½W,SLM; 7,700' (2,347m).

FIRST SPRING CREEK (Beaver) originates on the western slopes of the Tushar Mountains at First Spring. It drains west into Bone Hollow and received its name from the spring.
S32,33,T28S,R6W,SLM.

FIRST SPRING HOLLOW (Sevier) originates at Sargent Lake on the eastern slopes of Sargent Mountain at the north end of the Tushars. The hollow drains north into Clear Creek and was named for the spring at its head.
S26,T26S,R4½W,SLM to S34,T25S,R4½W, SLM.

FISH CREEK (Carbon) originates on Fish Creek Ridge, nine miles northwest of Scofield Reservoir. The creek drains southeast into the reservoir.
S24,T11S,R5E,SLM to S17,T12S,R7E,SLM.

FISH CREEK (Duchesne) originates in the southwest section of the Uinta Mountains at Rainbow Lake. It drains southeast into the west fork of Rock Creek. The headwaters include Governor Dern Lake and Pinto Lake.
S21,T3N,R8W,USM to S35,T3N,R8W,USM.

FISH CREEK (Piute, Sevier) originates on the western slopes of Mount Belnap of the Tushar Mountains. The creek drains north into Clear Creek.
S36,T25S,R5W,SLM (at mouth). 567.

FISH HATCHERY LAKE (Duchesne) is on the headwaters of Fish Creek in the southwest section of the Uinta Mountains, two and one-half miles southwest of Governor Dern Lake. The lake is used in fish culture.
S29,T3N,R8W,USM; 10,225' (3,117m).

FISH LAKE (Sevier) is east of Koosharem* and Burrville* as a vast depression on the Fishlake Plateau. The lake is four miles wide and seven miles long, with waters that are deep, cold, and excellent for fishing. The Mytoge Mountains are the eastern border and

the Fishlake Hightop Plateau is the western border. This lake was a major source of fish for the early Fishlake Indians.
S3-30,T26S,R2E,SLM; 8,843' (2,695m). 175, 314, 360, 546.

FISH LAKE (Summit) is a good fishing lake at the west end of the Uinta Mountains, midway between Holiday Park* and Mirror Lake.
S4,5,T1S,R9E,SLM; 10,190' (3,106m).

FISH SPRING RANGE (Juab) has a north-south orientation southwest of the Fish Springs.
T13S,R14W,SLM; 8,354' (2,546m).

FISH SPRINGS (Juab) is at the northern end of the Fish Spring Range in the Fish Springs National Wildlife Refuge. Today the springs have been developed into ponds and marshes with recreational and wildlife facilities. Prior to 1859 it was a Pony Express and Overland Stage station. At that time, many of the fish caught in the spring measured up to six inches in length.
T11S,R13,14W,SLM; 4,295' (1,309m). 100 (v17), 477, 516, 546.

FISH SPRINGS FLAT (Juab) is south of the Fish Springs.
S1,2,11,T11S,R14W,SLM; 4,200' (1,341m).

FISHER CREEK (Box Elder). See Fisher Creek Canyon (Box Elder).

FISHER CREEK (Grand) originates on the northern slopes of the La Sal Mountains, two and one-half miles north of Mount Waas. The creek drains north through Fisher Valley and Cottonwood Canyon, then flows into the Dolores River. The creek was named for Avill and Gull Fisher, early settlers and stockmen who took up land near the mouth of the creek. See also Fisher Towers.
S6,T26S,R25W,SLM to S2,T24S,R25E,SLM. 100(v17), 567.

FISHER CREEK CANYON (**Box Elder**) originates at Fisher Lake in the Raft River Mountains and drains south into the valley northwest of Park Valley*. It was named for Avill Fisher, who took up land near the mouth of the canyon.
S35,T14N,R14W,SLMtoS17-20,T13N,R13W, SLM. 100(v17), 567.

FISHER MESA (**Grand**) is east of Fisher Valley. Fisher Creek drains the south end of the mesa. The mesa is named after the creek.
T24,25S,R24E,SLM; 8,000' (2,438m).

FISHER TOWERS (**Grand**) is twenty miles northeast of Moab*. It is an area of heavily eroded clay and sandstone towers and minarets, with the tallest tower rising nine hundred feet from the desert floor. One of the towers was first climbed by man in 1962. For a short time it was believed that the name Fisher was a misspelling of Fissure. This has since been disproved.
T24S,R24E,SLM. 279, 360, 425, 542, 555.

FISHER VALLEY (**Grand**) is at the north end of the La Sal Mountains, with Fisher Creek draining through it. It was earlier named Forbidden Valley because gaining access to the area was difficult. See Fisher Creek for name source. See Fisher Towers.
T24,25S,R24E,SLM; 6,000' (1,829m). 146, 546.

FISHLAKE HIGHTOP PLATEAU (**Sevier**) is the high point of the Fish Lake Plateau, four miles northwest of Fish Lake. The plateau has a northeast-southwest orientation and receives its name from the lake.
S4,T25S,R2E,SLM to S36,T25S,R1E,SLM; 11,633' (3,546m). D.L. 7102.

FISSURE TOWERS (**Grand**). See Fisher Towers (Grand).

FIVE LAKES (**Garfield**) is a cluster of five small pond-like lakes on the southern rim of Boulder Mountain of the Aquarius Plateau. Four Lakes are located one mile northeast.
S35,T31S,R3E,SLM; 11,016' (3,358m).

FIVE MILE PASS (**Tooele, Utah**) is five miles west southwest of Fairfield*. The pass was a landmark on the old Pony Express and Overland Stage route, a lookout point, and a resting and camping area.
S4,T7S,R3W,SLM; 5,305' (1,617m).

FIVE POINT LAKE (**Duchesne**) is in the south central section of the Uinta Mountains near the head of Garfield Creek which drains into Yellowstone Creek. The lake has five main points of ingress or egress.
S29,T4N,R5W,USM; 11,009' (3,356m). 100 (v2).

FIVE POINTS (**Beaver**) is in the northwest section of Pine Valley east of the north end of the Needle Range. At this point roads branch out in five different directions.
S31,T26S,R17W,SLM; 5,659' (1,725m).

FIVE POINTS (**Weber**) is in North Ogden* where five roads, including US-30S, US-89, and US-91, branch out in five different directions. The early pioneer settlement here was Lynn(e)*. See Lynn*.
S16,17,T6N,R1W,SLM; 4,290' (1,308m). 567.

FIVEMILE WASH (**Emery**) originates twelve miles southeast of Green River*. It drains east to enter the Green River.
S36,T21S,R14E,SLM to S8,T22S,R16E,SLM.

FLAGSTAFF MOUNTAIN (**Summit, Wasatch**) is on the dividing ridge between Park City* and Midway*. In 1869 three soldiers from Fort Douglas returned to a rich ore strike they had previously marked with a red handkerchief on a stick. They named both the area and the mine the Flagstaff. The mountain is also known as Flagstaff Peak.

S33,T2S,R4E,SLM; 8,400' (2,560m). 508, 567.

FLAGSTAFF PEAK (Summit, Wasatch). See Flagstaff Mountain (Summit, Wasatch).

FLAMING GORGE (Daggett) is in the northeastern section of the Uinta Mountains in the Flaming Gorge National Recreation Area. Manila* is located eight miles northwest. Today the entire area carries the name Flaming Gorge, but the section that was specifically named Flaming Gorge is at the head of Horseshoe Canyon at the west end of the Boars Tusk. On May 26, 1869, after Major Powell and his men saw the sun reflecting off the red rocks, they coined the name Flaming Gorge. S30,T3N,R21E,SLM; 6,000' (1,829m). 160, 172, 314, 360, 422, 496.

FLAMING GORGE NATIONAL REC-REATION AREA (Daggett) is the region in northeastern Utah and south-western Wyoming centered around Major Powell's Flaming Gorge on the Green River. Dam construction was completed on the Green River in 1964 to form the reservoir. The U.S. Congress established the Recreational Area on September 16, 1968.
195.

FLAMING GORGE LAKE (Daggett). See Flaming Gorge entries above. T2,3N,R20,22E,SLM; 6,040' (1,841m).

FLAT CANYON (Carbon) originates on the West Tavaputs Plateau, eight miles north of Patmos Head. It drains east into the Green River at Desolation Canyon. This prominent canyon is wide and flat, and rests in rugged country between Steer Ridge and Cedar Ridge. S8,17,T14S,R15E (to Green River).

FLAT NOSE GEORGE CANYON (Grand) originates on the East Tavaputs Plateau and drains west southwest into Rattlesnake Canyon. Flat Nose George

(George Curry) was an outlaw of the 1890s who led the well-known Curry Gang. He was killed on April 17, 1900, by Doc King, foreman of the Webster City Cattle Company. King was a member of a posse out to capture Tom Dilly, another outlaw in the area. Curry was killed by mistake in the vicinity of the canyon that now bears his name. SW½,T18S,R18E,SLM. 25, 303, 415.

FLAT ROCK MESA (Uintah) is on the East Tavaputs Plateau between Willow and Hill creeks. T14,15S,R20E,SLM; 7,500' (2,286m).

FLAT TOPS (Emery) are fifteen miles south of the San Rafael River and ten miles east of U-24. There are three mesas in close proximity to one another. The road to the Roost area from the northwest runs between them. S15,26,T26S,R13E,SLM; 5,965'-6,089' (1,818m-1,856m). 25.

FLATIRON LAKES (Wayne) is a cluster of small lakes, two of which have the triangular shape of a flatiron. The lakes are on the northern slopes of Boulder Mountain, two miles south of Teasdale*. S29,T29S,R4E,SLM; 8,320' (2,536m). 567.

FLAXVILLE* (Box Elder). See Mantua*.

FLINT TRAIL (Garfield) drops from the Flint Flats of the Orange Cliffs onto the Black Ledge and into Big Water Canyon, East Fork. The trail leads from this point into the southern end of Elaterite Basin. The trail was used by prospectors and cattlemen who moved their cattle from summer and winter range and out to market. S35,T30½S,R16E,SLM.

FLOATING ISLAND (Tooele) is on the west side of the Great Salt Lake Desert, near the Silver Island Mountains. It receives its name from the mirage-like effect that seems to suspend the island above the horizon. The phenomenon is

common in this region of the Great Salt Lake Desert with the brilliant sun and intense radiated heat.
S14,23,T2N,R16W,SLM; 5,109' (1,557m).

FLORENCE CREEK (Grand) heads at Florence Springs of the McPherson Range on the East Tavaputs Plateau. The creek drains northwest into the Green River approximately forty miles north of Green River*. This entire region is alive with the history of early cattlemen, Indians, sheep men, outlaws, and sheriffs' posses. The Owlhoot Trail passed through the McPherson Ranch (Jim McPherson) at the mouth of the creek. Sheriff Tyler and a member of his posse, Sam Jenkins, were killed by outlaws in this area. Flat Nose George was also killed near Florence Creek. Today the ranch is part of the Uintah-Ouray Indian Reservation.
S4,T17S,R17E,SLM (at mouth). 25, 303, 415.

FLORENCE SPRING (Grand) is at the head of Florence Creek, East Tavaputs Plateau. See Florence Creek.
S32,T17S,R19E,SLM; 9,080' (2,768m).

FLORIDA* (Beaver) is an early mining boomtown site in the San Francisco Mountains northwest of Milford*.
T27S,R13W,SLM. 355.

FLOWELL* (Millard) is six miles west of Fillmore* in the Pavant Valley. There are a large number of flowing wells in the region. Flowell was known earlier as Crystal*.
S17,20,T21S,R5W,SLM; 4,702' (2,433m). 360, 542, 567.

FLOY CANYON (Grand) originates on the East Tavaputs Plateau, thirteen miles north of Crescent Junction. The canyon drains southwest into the desert as Floy Wash. The name comes from an old railroad siding nearby.
S20,T22S,R18E,SLM (at mouth). D.L. 6201.

FOOL CANYON (Millard). See Fool Creek (Millard).

FOOL CREEK (Millard) originates at Fool Peak in the Canyon Mountains east of Oak City* and drains northwest into Fool Creek Reservoir. The name comes from an incident where water in the creek was plentiful when the pioneers first arrived, but when they returned with their families, the creek was suddenly dry.
S31,T15S,R4W,SLM (at mouth). 567.

FOOL CREEK RESERVOIR (Millard). See Fool Creek (Millard).

FOOL PEAK (Millard) is in the Canyon Mountains east of Oak City* at the head of Fool Creek.

FORBIDDEN CANYON (San Juan) is west of Rainbow Bridge National Monument. Aztec Creek drains through this narrow, inaccessible, and isolated canyon.
567.

FORBIDDEN VALLEY (Grand). See Fisher Valley (Grand).

FOREST CITY* (Utah) is up American Fork Canyon, four miles northeast of Tibble Fork Reservoir at Dutchman Flat. Forest City was a mining town of the 1868-69 period. As the mine resources were depleted around 1878, the town was abandoned. The name comes from the beautiful setting in this alpine forest region. Today it is a ghost town site only.
SW¼,T3S,R3E,SLM; 7,600' (2,316m). 89, 516.

FOREST DALE* (Salt Lake) was a small community south of Sugar House*. This outgrowth of Sugar House was absorbed into Greater Salt Lake City*. Brigham Young personally laid his farm in Forest Dale.
S20,28,T1S,R1E,SLM; 4,400' (1,341m). 567.

FORGOTTEN CANYON (**San Juan**) originates east across Lake Powell from Bullfrog Marina and drains west into Lake Powell. It is between Knowles and Crystal Springs canyons.
T37S,R12E,SLM.

FORKED FLAT (**Beaver**) originates at the summit of the Tushar Mountains near the head of Straight Creek where the flat spreads out into several separate forks.
S28,33,T29S,R5W,SLM; 6,660' (2,030m). 125.

FORKED SPRING (**Beaver**) is on a small forked drainage at the north end of the Needle Range near the head of Cottonwood Wash.
S26,T26S,R19W,SLM; 7,600' (2,316m).

FORSHEA MOUNTAINS (**Piute**) is west of Otter Creek and Angle* and east of the Piute Reservoir. Malmsten Peak is the highest point. The mountains were named for James Edward Forshee. As this book goes to press, efforts are being made to correct the spelling of the name to "Forshee Mountains."
S14,T29S,R2½W,SLM to S11,T30S,R2½W, SLM; 9,794' (2,985m). 563.

FORSHEE MOUNTAINS (**Piute**). See Forshea Mountains (Piute).

FORSYTH RESERVOIR (**Sevier**) is seven miles northeast of Fremont on U M Creek. Mills Meadow Reservoir is two miles southwest.
S24,25,T26S,R3E,SLM; 7,990' (2,436m).

FORT ALMA* (**Sevier**) was where Monroe* stands today. The fort was a forerunner to the community, built during 1865-66.
368, 546.

FORT BINGHAM* (**Salt Lake**) was a small stockade built in 1864 near the head of Binghams Creek in Binghams Canyon. Today that site has been eliminated by the open-pit copper mine

in the area. See Bingham Canyon for name source.
ca. S26,T3S,R3W,SLM. 516.

FORT BINGHAM* (**Weber**) was built on Ogden City's Second Street and Washington Boulevard. Today it is known as Five Points*. In 1853 it was the forerunner of Lynn* (Lynne*), now absorbed into Ogden City*. It was named for Erastus Bingham, the 1849 settler who built the fort.
S16,17,T6N,R1W,SLM; 4,290' (1,308m). 100 (v1), 516, 567.

FORT BOTTOM (**San Juan**) was in the heart of Stillwater Canyon of the Green River, five miles south of the mouth of Horsethief Canyon. The name was applied to an ancient Indian ruin there.
4,125' (1,257m). 102, 516, 609.

FORT BUENAVENTURA (**Weber**) was in Ogden* at the west end of Twenty-eighth Street and the Weber River. Miles Goodyear built the fort in 1845, after the decline of the fur trade. The fort was well documented and considered the earliest permanent site for white men in the Great Basin area. Recent archaeological excavations have confirmed the site. In 1850, Miles moved to California after he sold all his holdings, including the fort, to Captain James Brown.
S31,T6N,R1W,SLM; 4,300' (1,311m). 274, 360, 516, 546.

FORT BUTTERMILK* (**Millard**) was built in 1855 where Holden* stands today. The fort received its name because travelers passing through could stop to obtain cold buttermilk.
S2,T20S,R4W,SLM; 5,125' (1,562m). 108, 288, 542, 567.

FORT CAMERON* (**Beaver**) was established as a military tent camp under the Grant presidency in May 1873. It was built two miles east of Beaver* on the north side of the Beaver River where units of the Eighth U.S. Infantry were

assigned. On July 1, 1874, it was named to honor Colonel James L. Cameron, who was killed during the Civil War in the battle of Bull Run. An earlier name was Post of Beaver. The camp was disbanded in April 1883.
S23,T29S,R7W,SLM; 6,000' (1,829m). 100 (v17), 355, 516, 591.

FORT CLARA* (Washington). See Fort Santa Clara* (Washington).

FORT CRITTENDEN* (Utah). See Camp Floyd*, Fairfield* (Utah).
27.

FORT DAVIS* (Box Elder). See Davis Fort* (Box Elder).

FORT DAVY CROCKETT*. Contrary to reports that list this fort in Utah, evidence points to it being located over the Colorado border. It was sometimes known as Fort Misery*.
159, 172, 271, 314, 546, 555(v9), 604.

FORT DESERET* (Millard) was nine miles southwest of Delta*. In 1866, Brigham Young ordered the construction of this fort during the Ute-Black Hawk War. The adobe walls were made from a mixture of mud and straw that had been trampled by oxen. Although portions of the fort still stand today, the adobe walls are rapidly deteriorating. It was named for the temporary State of Deseret. The word "Deseret" means "honeybee" and comes from Mormon scripture.
S8,T18S,R7W,SLM; 4,580' (1,396m). 516, 546.

FORT DOUGLAS* (Salt Lake) is on the benchland east of and near the University of Utah. It was established as Camp Douglas on October 24, 1862. The commanding officer, Colonel Patrick Edward Connor, had rejected the recommended use of the fort at Camp Floyd near Fairfield*. The troops were housed in dugouts through the first winter. At President Lincoln's request, the name of the fort was changed to Fort Douglas in 1878 honoring Stephen A. Douglas, Lincoln's opponent in the 1860 elections.
S3,T1S,R1E,SLM; 4,975' (1,516m). 100(v6), 252, 314, 360, 542, 546, 555(v33/4), 567.

FORT DUCHESNE* (Uintah) was near the Uinta River, one mile south of US-40. The site was originally a fur-trading post prior to 1841. In August 1861, the fort was established under the Lincoln presidency. On August 20, 1886, two troops of black men from the Ninth Cavalry, under Major F. W. Benteen, moved in. They served at the fort for twelve years. Because of their dark curly hair, the Indians called the troops buffalo soldiers. The fort was abandoned in 1912, then re-established as the headquarters for the Uintah Reservation. See Duchesne River for name source.
S23,T2S,R1E,USM; 4,988' (1,520m). 100 (v17), 163(6 Oct. 1934), 229, 360, 496, 555(v2,no.1), 567.

FORT EPHRAIM* (Sanpete) was the early fort built on the present site of Ephraim*.
567.

FORT ERDA* (Tooele). See Batesville* (Tooele).

FORT FARR* (Weber). See Farrs Fort* (Weber).

FORT GUNNISON* (Sanpete). See Gunnison City* (Sanpete).

FORT HAMBLIN* (Washington). See Hamblin* (Washington).

FORT HAMILTON* (Sanpete). See Mount Pleasant* (Sanpete). Do not confuse with Hamilton Fort* (Iron).

FORT HARMONY* (Washington). See New Harmony* (Washington).

FORT HERRIMAN* (Salt Lake). See Herriman*.

FORT HOBBLE CREEK* (Utah). See Springville* (Utah).

FORT HOYT* (Summit). See Hoytsville* (Summit).

FORT JOHNSON* (Iron). See Enoch*.

FORT KIT CARSON* (Uintah) was an early fort built near the confluence of the Uinta, White, and Green rivers, near the present community of Ouray*. The fort was built by Kit Carson in 1833 and was destroyed by the Ute Indians in the early 1840s.
129, 516.

FORT LOUISA* (Iron). See Parowan*.

FORT MEEK* (Kane) was built in 1869 by Jacob Hamblin and his companions. The fort was located northeast of Kanab* and named for a Mormon bishop, William Meek, the first bishop of nearby Pahreah* (Paria*).
516.

FORT MIDWAY* (Wasatch). See Midway*.

FORT MISERY*. See Fort Davy Crockett*.

FORT MONTEZUMA* (San Juan). See Montezuma Creek* (San Juan).

FORT MOUND* (Weber). See Mound Fort*.

FORT PETEETNEET* (Utah). See Payson*.

FORT PROVO* (Utah). See Provo City*.

FORT RAWLINS* (Utah) was a temporary military fort established July 30, 1870, within what is today's Provo City* boundaries. During the short period the camp was established, there was considerable friction between the local citizens and the soldiers. The camp was

shut down by June 1871. The fort was named for the late Major General John A. Rawlins.
S1,2,T7S,R2E,SLM; 4,555' (1,388m). 394, 555(v33/4, v42/1).

FORT REED* (Uintah). See Fort Uintah* (Uintah).

FORT ROBIDOUX* (Uintah). See Fort Uinta* (Uintah).

FORT ROCK* (Summit). See Rockport* (Summit).

FORT ROSE SPRINGS (Tooele). See Fort Batesville* (Bates*).

FORT SAINT LUKE* (Utah) was under construction in 1854 near the mouth of Spanish Fork Canyon. Before the fort was completed, the settlers relocated: some going back to Palmyra* and others to Spanish Fork*.
516, 567.

FORT SANFORD* (Garfield) was established one-half mile east of US-89 and seven and one-half miles north of Panguitch* near Sanford Creek. The fortification was built in early 1864 and named after Silas Sanford Smith, who was in command of the fort with its twenty-five-man detachment. After one battle with the Indians, the fort was abandoned in 1866 and was not used again. See Spry*.
S22,T33S,R5W,SLM; 6,480' (1,975m).

FORT SANTA CLARA* (Washington) was the forerunner of today's Santa Clara*, northwest of St. George*. The fort was built in 1854 by Jacob Hamblin and others and was located near and received its name from the Santa Clara River. It was also known as Fort Clara*. See Santa Clara City* for name source.
S16,T42S,R16W,SLM.

FORT SCIPIO* (Millard). See Scipio* (Millard).

FORT SHIRTS* (**San Juan**). See Shirts Fort* (San Juan).

FORT SIDON* (**Iron**). See Hamilton Fort* (Iron).

FORT SODOM* (**Utah**). See Goshen*.

FORT THORNBURG* (**Uintah**) was located where Ashley Creek emerges from the mountains. It was named for Major Thornburg(h), who was killed in the Meeker Massacre in Colorado in 1879. The fort was abandoned in 1884. S5,T4S,R21E,SLM; 5,690' (1,734m). 172, 309, 516, 555(v9,32,35).

FORT THORNBURG* (**Uintah**). An earlier Fort Thornburg is listed as having been built near Ouray* and also named for Major Thornburg(h). 516.

FORT THURSTON* (**Morgan**) was located near Milton* and was the center for subsequent Thurstonville*. It was built by Thomas Jefferson Thurston. In later years it fell into disuse. See Milton*. S28,T4N,R2E,SLM; 5,015' (1,529m). 378.

FORT UINTAH* (**Uintah**) was three-fourths of a mile east and one and one-half miles south of present-day Whiterocks*. It was on the earlier Reeds Fort site, built by Jim Reed, a fur trapper. Fort Uinta (note difference in spelling) was established in 1832 by Antoine Robidoux, a trapper and fur trader of French descent who was born in St. Louis on September 24, 1794. The fort, located on the Uinta River, was also known as Fort Uintah and Fort Wintey. It was the first year-round settlement for whites built in what is now Utah. Many well-known people stopped at the fort, including Major Powell's expedition and John C. Fremont. The fort was an important stop on the major trails used by trappers, fur traders, mountain men and Indians. In 1844 while Robidoux was away, the old fort was burned down

during the Indian uprising of 1844. S30,T1N,R1E,USM; 5,955' (1,815m). 172, 314, 516, 555(v9), 604.

FORT UTAH* (**Utah**) was an early fort built where Provo* now stands. See Provo* (Utah).

FORT WAHWEAP* (**Kane**) was near the mouth of the Paria River. The fort was established to protect travelers crossing the Colorado River from Indians. "Wahweap" is a Piute word meaning alkaline seeps or salt licks.

FORT WALKER* (**Iron**). See Hamilton* (Iron).

FORT WALL* (**Utah**). Construction of this fort began in 1852 where American Fork* now stands. It was completed in 1855, with walls built of clay.

FORT WILLDEN* (**Millard**) was built a short distance northeast of where Cove Fort* now stands. The Charles Willden family moved to the fort on September 19, 1865. 355, 567.

FORT WINTEY* (**Uintah**). See Fort Uintah*.

FORT WORDSWORTH* (**Utah**). See Alpine*.

FORTUNA* (**Beaver**) was a mining camp in Fortuna Canyon, northwest of the north end of Beaver Valley. Fortuna was the ancient Roman goddess of fortune and is Spanish for the English word "fortune" or "wealth." S19,T27S,R7W,SLM; 6,800' (2,073m). 45.

FORTUNA CANYON (**Beaver**) originates in the foothills northwest of Beaver Valley and drains southeast into Wildcat Creek. See Fortuna*. S19,T27S,R7W,SLM.

FORTYMILE (**Kane**) is approximately forty miles from Escalante*. It is the area around Dance Hall Rock and the drainage of Fortymile Gulch. The Hole-in-the-Rock group camped here while the Hole was being prepared for travel. 4,800' (1,463m).

FORTYMILE CREEK (Kane). See Fortymile Gulch, the preferred name.

FORTYMILE GULCH (Kane) originates on the Kaiparowits Plateau and drains east into Willow Creek and the Escalante River. Escalante* is approximately forty miles away from the point where the gulch crosses the old Hole-in-the-Rock road. Dance Hall Rock is in the vicinity, in addition to Fortymile Slide, Fortymile Ridge, and Fortymile Spring. All the names were given by the Hole-in-the-Rock trek pioneers. 12, 359.

FOUNTAIN GREEN* (Sanpete) is midway between Moroni* and Nephi* on U-132. The area was first named Uinta Springs* when it was an important campground and freighting stop between the early Sanpete settlements and Salt Lake City*. The springs were frequently used by the Indians. The first white people settled there in 1850, then in March 1859, George W. Johnson brought settlers from Santaquin* to start a community. He provided the present name because of the lush meadows surrounding the springs. S6,7,T14S,R3E,SLM; 5,900' (1,798m). 152, 289, 360, 567.

FOUR CORNERS is a term applied to the area where the corners of four states meet. The states are Utah, Colorado, New Mexico, and Arizona. It is the only site in the United States where this occurs.

FOUR LAKES (Garfield) are a group of lakes on the south rim of the Aquarius Plateau on Boulder Mountain. Spectacle Lake lies one-fourth mile northeast. S36,T31S,R3E,SLM; 10,850' (3,307m).

FOUR LAKES BASIN (Duchesne) is in the southwest Uinta Mountains, two miles southeast of Naturalist Basin. There are four prominent fishing lakes in the basin: Jean, Dean, Dale, and Daynes lakes. S21,11,T3N,R8W,USM; 10,800' (3,292m).

FOURMILE BENCH (Kane) is a bench-land east of Wahweap Creek and south of Fourmile Canyon from which it receives its name. Fifteen miles south is US-89 and Big Water*. T40S,R2E,SLM; 6,100' (1,859m).

FOURMILE CANYON (Beaver) originates at Fourmile Spring, seven miles southwest of Cove Fort*. The canyon is four miles long. S29,T26S,R7W,SLM (at mouth).

FOURMILE CANYON (Garfield) originates on the southern slopes of Mount Holmes of the Henry Mountains. The canyon drains southeast into the Colorado River. T35S,R13E,SLM. 567.

FOURMILE CANYON (Kane) originates between Tommy and Paradise canyons at Fourmile Water on Fourmile Bench. This four-mile-long canyon drains southwest into Tommy Smith Creek. S32,T29S,R2E,SLM.

FOURMILE CREEK (Juab) originates in the San Pitch Mountains, four miles west southwest of Fountain Green*. The creek drains west into the Juab Valley, four miles south of Nephi*. S17,T14S,R2E,SLM to S36,T13S,R1W,SLM.

FOURMILE KNOLL (Beaver) is four miles north of Minersville. S24,T29S,R10W,SLM; 5,818' (1,773m).

FOURMILE RIDGE (Beaver) is east of and near Fourmile Canyon from which it receives its name. 7,306' (2,227m).

FOURMILE SPRING (Beaver) is at the head of Fourmile Canyon where it received its name. Cove Fort* is eight miles northeast.
7,200' (2,195m).

FOURMILE WATER (Kane) is a water source at the head of Fourmile Canyon.
5,635' (1,718m).

FOURTH CHAIN LAKE (Duchesne) is in the south central section of the Uinta Mountains. This lake is the highest and smallest of the Chain Lake group. Mount Emmons is three miles west southwest. The Fourth Chain Lake drains into the headwaters of the Uinta River.
T4N,R3W,USM; 10,825' (3,299m).

FOX CREEK (Garfield). See Asay Creek (Garfield).

FOX LAKE (Duchesne) is east of the Kidney Lakes at the head of Shale Creek, which drains into the upper Uinta River. Ray C. Labrum named the lake after he scared a fox while passing through the area.
10,800' (3,292m). 165.

FRANCE CANYON (Garfield) originates seven miles southeast of Hatch* and drains northwest into the Sevier River. France Henry owned property in the canyon.
T37S,R5W,SLM. 508.

FRANCIS* (Summit) was an outgrowth of Woodland* and Kamas*, two miles south of Kamas. It was first settled in 1869 by John Williams, who was looking for a secluded spot for a homestead. The settlement was named for Francis M. Lyman, a Mormon church official. Today it is a dairy, pasture, and recreation center.
S28,29,32,33,T2S,R6E,SLM;6,560'(1,999m). 289, 360, 542.

FRANCIS CANYON (Morgan) originates northeast of the Lost Creek Reservoir and Croydon*, and drains southwest into the Lost Creek Reservoir. Samuel Francis and his sons established a ranch there in 1885 and the canyon was named for Joe Francis, Samuel's father. It had an earlier name of Red Rock Canyon.
S35,T6N,R6E,SLM to S4,T5N,R5E,SLM. 100 (v17), 567.

FRANCIS CREEK (Daggett) originates near the summit north of Flaming Gorge Reservoir where U-44 begins to descend Cart Creek. This three-mile-long creek was named by Francis Bishop, one of Major Powell's men from the second expedition. See Cart Creek.
S7,T1S,R22E,SLM to S30,T1N,R22E,SLM. 172, 496.

FRANCIS LAKE (Duchesne) is in the central Uinta Mountains on the upper reaches of Rock Creek, seven miles southwest of Explorer Peak. Four young male hikers discovered several lakes with no name signs, so they constructed makeshift signs labeled with their girlfriend's names. The hikers then placed the signs next to the lakes. Francis Lake was named for Francis Case. The other lakes were Margie, Helen, and Rosalie.
S30,T3N,R7W,USM; 9,957' (3,035m). 595.

FRANCIS PEAK (Davis, Morgan) is eight miles west of Morgan* on the headwaters of Baer and Line Creeks. The peak was named for Esther Charlotte Francis, a pioneer woman who helped early surveyors in the region.
S33,T4N,R1E,SLM; 9,547' (2,910m). 202, 360.

FREDDIES CISTERN (Garfield) is a small, isolated canyon originating near the end of Cataract Canyon. The mouth is near the Mille Crag Bend of the Colorado River and the canyon has numerous small waterpockets and rock tanks in it.
102.

FREEDOM* (Davis). See Kaysville*.

FREEDOM* (Sanpete) is a small agricultural community on U-30, four miles west northwest of Moroni* and six miles south of Fountain Green*. It was settled in 1871 during a particular post-Civil War period when several patriotic names developed. Many of the early immigrants had experienced oppression in the tyrannies of their home countries in Europe. The town was originally named Draper* for an early settler, but was changed to Freedom in 1877.
S1,T15S,R2E,SLM; 5,725' (1,745m). 152, 288, 542, 567.

FREMONT* (Wayne) is six miles north of Loa* on the upper Fremont River from which it received its name. The Fremont area was first inhabited by whites in 1875, but William Wilson Morrell and his family became the first permanent settlers; they arrived in the spring of 1876.
T27S,R3E,SLM; 7,000' (2,134m). 542, 569.

FREMONT CANYON (Garfield, Iron) originates at Fremont Pass on the west side of Dog Valley and drains into Fremont Wash. John C. Fremont passed through this area on one of his expeditions. The canyon and wash are named after him.
S30,T31S,R5W,SLM to S7,T31S,R6W,SLM.

FREMONT CANYON (Utah) originates at the Juab county line, two and one-half miles north northwest of Eureka*. It drains northeast into Chiulos Canyon.
S1,T10S,R3W,SLM to S31,T9S,R2W,SLM.

FREMONT ISLAND (Weber) is in the Great Salt Lake west of Roy*. The island was initially visited by John C. Fremont and his party on September 9, 1843. At that time, Fremont named it Disappointment Island because it had a barren, uninviting appearance. Later it was called Castle Island by a party of Mormon surveyors who visited the island and noticed a castle-like resemblance. Shortly after, Captain Stansbury decided to honor Fremont, the first white discoverer

of the island, so he named it Fremont Island. The island was referred to as Miller Island from about 1860-80 while Henry and Dan Miller ran their livestock on the island. The island is now privately owned.
4,995' (1,522m). 27, 129, 205, 360, 371, 492, 546, 567, 604.

FREMONT PASS (Iron) is the dividing line between Dog Valley and the head of Fremont Canyon at the south end of Circleville Mountain. It was named for John C. Fremont, who passed through this area.
S30,T31S,R8W,SLM; 7,522' (2,293m). 314.

FREMONT RIVER (Sevier, Wayne) originates at the Johnson Valley Reservoir north of Fishlake and drains southeast to combine with the Muddy River at Hanksville*. It then forms the Dirty Devil River. On July 27, 1869, the Powell expedition discovered an unknown river at the mouth of Narrow Canyon on the Colorado River. They named the river the Dirty Devil, but did not indicate how far up the river the name would apply, nor did they know that the river branched out. Subsequent conflicting claims forced the renaming of the upper portions of the Dirty Devil. Today the two main branches of the Dirty Devil are the Muddy and the Fremont rivers.
S30,T25S,R3E,SLM to S2,T28S,R11E,SLM. 161, 422, 494, 546.

FREMONT WASH (Iron). See Fremont Canyon (Garfield, Iron).
S6,7,T31S,R6W,SLM to S15,T33S,R9W,SLM.

FRENCH SPRING (Wayne) is at the north end of Gordon Flats at the head of North Trail Canyon. Some of the early sheepherders in the area were Frenchmen. See Gordon Flats.
NE¼,T30S,R16E,SLM; 6,200' (1,890m). 24, 102.

FRISCO* (Beaver) was at the southern end of the San Francisco Mountains and north of Squaw Peak where U-21 passes

over the summit. Silver and lead ore was discovered there in 1875 and the town was established in 1876. The adjacent mine was called the Horn Silver Mine because of the shape, texture, and color of the silver, which curled like a ram's horn when thinly cut. While the mine operated it produced a fabulous amount of valuable ore. During the 1880-85 period, over six thousand people lived in Frisco. The town had a hotel, a newspaper, a schoolhouse, and a hospital. Frisco also had a high crime rate which included murders and numerous shoot-outs. After a cave-in and other mishaps in the mine, Frisco declined into a ghost town by 1920. The name is a shortened variant of the nearby San Francisco Mountains and also honors St. Francis of Assisi, a patron saint of wildlife and nature.
S13,T27S,R13W,SLM; 6,500' (1,981m). 100 (v5,17), 314, 355, 542, 546.

FRISCO PEAK (**Beaver**) is on the west side of the San Francisco Mountains. The peak name is a contraction of the name of the nearby mountain range.
S26,T26W,R13W,SLM; 9,600' (2,926m).

FRISCO WASH (**Beaver**) originates on the south summit of the San Francisco Mountains. It drains west past the Grampian Hills, out into the Wah Wah Valley. U-21 passes through the wash, which is named for the town of Frisco*.
S24,T27S,R13W,SLM to S27,T27S,R13W, SLM.

FROGTOWN* (**Sevier**). See Austin* (Sevier).

FROGTOWN* (**Utah**). See Fairfield* (Utah).

FRUIT HEIGHTS* (**Davis**) is on Baer Creek on the upper benchland one mile east of Kaysville*. An early name for the site was East Kaysville*, a name used until August 23, 1939, when it was changed to Fruit Heights. It had long

been famous for its fruit crops and pleasant location above the valley floor. Today the area is being converted to a residential housing community.
S36,T4N,R1W,SLM; 4,800' (1,463m). 118, 360.

FRUITA* (**Wayne**) is in the heart of the Capitol Reef National Park on U-24. It was an early pioneer town first home-steaded in 1878 by Franklin D. Young. In 1880 the name was Junction*, but when the post office was established between 1900 and 1903, the name was changed to Fruita because there were too many "Junction" names in the territory. Fruita peaked as a community in the 1920-1930s when the ideal climate and soil led to development of the fruit industry. Today the fruit orchards and the one-room schoolhouse are an integral part of Capitol Reef National Park. This isolated park is known for its spectacular scenery and Indian ruins.
S14,T29S,R6E,SLM; 5,418' (1,651m). 89, 163(2 Sept. 1977), 360, 466(30 Sept. 1977), 485, 542, 546, 569.

FRUITLAND* (**Duchesne**) is a small agricultural and livestock community on US-40, twenty-four miles west of Duchesne* and three and one-half miles east of Currant Creek*. It was originally known as Rabbit Gulch* for the numer-ous jackrabbits in the area. Then in 1907, the town developers decided to change the name to Fruitland in an effort to lure land buyers, even though conditions were unsuitable for fruit growing. Today it has developed as an oil- and gas-producing and agricultural region.
T3S,R8,9W,USM; 6,611' (2,015m). 100(v17), 165, 542, 546.

FRY* (**San Juan**) is a small community centered around a service station and a grocery store on U-95 at the junction of Fry Canyon and White Canyon. Fry is ten miles west of the Natural Bridges National Monument. See Fry Canyon.
T36S,R16E,SLM; 5,315' (1,620m).

FRY CANYON (**San Juan**) originates at the Red House Cliffs two miles southwest of the Natural Bridges National Monument. It drains northwest into White Canyon near the present small community of Fry*. The canyon received its name from an early grey-bearded prospector named Charlie Fry, who camped by a spring in the canyon.
555(v32), 567.

FRY SPRING (**San Juan**) is in Fry Canyon, one and one-half miles southeast of Fry*. See Fry Canyon.

FRYING PAN, THE (**Sevier**) is a flat upland with a frying pan shape, north of Fremont*.
S12,T25S,R4E,SLM; 8,063' (2,467m).

FUNK CANYON (**Sanpete**) originates on Black Mountain southeast of Rattlesnake Peak and five miles east southeast of Sterling*. The canyon drains northwest and was named for Daniel Buckley Funk, who was the first known white man to break trail through the canyon.
S8,T19S,R3E,SLM to S35,T18S,R2E,SLM.

FUNKS LAKE (**Sanpete**). See Palisade Lake (Sanpete).

GALENA CITY* (Salt Lake) was a late 1880s temporary mining settlement up Little Cottonwood Canyon above Alta* and Union City*. The town was abandoned when the ore in the mine was depleted. Today it is a ghost town site in the heart of a year-round recreational region. Galena is a lead sulfide, the principal ore containing lead.
NW¼,T3S,R3E,SLM; 9,500' (2,896m). 454.

GANDY* (Millard) is in the Snake Valley near the Nevada border, thirty-five miles southwest of Fish Springs. This was an old ranch site owned by Isaac Gandy. It also served as a post office when the Pony Express and Overland Stage traveled this route. Partoun* is northeast.
S3,T16S,R19W,SLM; 4,925' (1,501m). 542, 567.

GARDEN CITY* (Rich) is a pleasant community at the junction of US-89 and US-30 on the western shore of Bear Lake. The site was considered a garden spot in the valley.
S21,T14N,R5E,SLM; 5,961' (1,817m). 100 (v17), 289, 542.

GARDEN CITY* (Salt Lake) is up Big Cottonwood Canyon. Garden City was a small suburb of Brighton* during the 1890s.
567.

GARFIELD* (Salt Lake) is between the Oquirrh Mountains and the Great Salt Lake. In early days the site was grassland used by ranchers and cattlemen. In 1905, the Utah Copper and American Smelting and Refining companies built a smelter in the area and established the town of Garfield to house their employees. The nearby lakeshore around Black Rock had been developed as a recreational center and there was a loading and unloading dock on the lake for boats transhipping cargo north to Corinne*. When the twentieth U.S. President, James A. Garfield, visited Salt Lake City on a campaign trip, he rode on one of the two boats, the *Kate Connor* and the *City of Corinne*, which were used for shipping. In the President's honor, the *City of Corinne* was renamed the *General Garfield*. The President's name was also given to the resort and the town. In 1904 the resort and pier were destroyed by fire and the Oquirrh Mountain forests had been cut down. Since the new recreational center to the northeast, Saltair, was rapidly developing, neither the pier nor the resort of Garfield were rebuilt. That left the smelter town of Garfield, where at one time over two thousand people lived. By 1955 transportation had improved and the mining operations were expanding, so the town of Garfield was dismantled and the houses were sold and moved to other sites. By 1956 the town had completely disappeared.
S15,22,T1S,R3W,SLM; 4,240' (1,292m). 289, 314, 542, 546, 567.

GARFIELD COUNTY. In 1882 this land was separated from Iron County and named to honor the President of the U.S., James A. Garfield, who had recently been assassinated. Panguitch* is the county seat.
6, 27, 289, 314, 602.

GARLAND* (Box Elder) is a small, thriving community on U-82, one mile north of Tremonton*. It was originally settled in 1890 and was known as Sunset* for the beautiful sunsets seen from this area. It was later named for William Garland, who led the construction of the Bothwell Canal. He was also

a leader in developing the sugar beet industry in the region.
S26,27,34,35,T12N,R3W,SLM; 4,340' (1,323m). 100(v17), 139, 542.

GARLAND* (Weber) was an early agricultural community that was recently absorbed into West Weber* and Wilson*. The community is rapidly becoming a residential area. The name signifies the feelings early settlers had about their surroundings. See West Weber*.
S22,27,T6N,R2W,SLM; 4,260' (1,298m).

GARRISON* (Millard) is on U-21 and Snake Creek near the Nevada line. Pruess Lake is four miles south. Garrison is a small ranching community settled in the 1850s by cattle rustlers and outlaws. They settled in this area because it was easy to slip back and forth between the Nevada and Utah territories. The town later became a center for mining interests. The name developed from the Garrison family who moved in and, as mining interests dwindled, developed a cattle and hay ranch. Mrs. Garrison was the schoolteacher who also managed the town mail, so it is actually her name that honors the town.
S1,T22S,R20W,SLM; 5,273' (1,607m). 314, 542, 546.

GATES OF MONROE (Sevier) is the opening gorge one mile southeast of Monroe* where Monroe Creek cuts through the rock escarpment as it emerges from the Sevier Plateau. The name was given by Captain Dutton of the U.S. Geological Survey, who did considerable research on the High Plateaus of Utah.
S23,T25S,R2½W,SLM. 175.

GATMAN LAKE (Duchesne) is at the west end of the Uinta Mountains in the Naturalist Basin. It is one of the many lakes in this area named after students of Agassiz, whose name is also honored by a nearby peak. Gatman was a naturalist and geologist.

S33,T4N,R8W,USM; 10,480' (3,194m). 298, 309, 530.

GEERTSEN CANYON (Weber) originates at the southern end of the Monte Cristo Mountains, seven miles northeast of Eden*. The canyon drains into the Pineview Reservoir and was named for Louis Geertsen, who settled in the canyon in 1863.
S16,T7N,R2E,SLM to S1,T6N,R1E,SLM. 100 (v17). D.L. 6504.

GEMINI TWINS ARCHES (Grand) are one mile north and eight miles west of Moab*. Fran Barnes named the arches.
S34,T25S,R20E,SLM. 36. D.L. 6901.

GENEVA* (Box Elder). See Mantua*.

GENEVA* (Utah) was on the northeast shore of Utah Lake near Orem*. It was settled in 1888 by Captain Dallin, who built a recreation center and named it the Geneva Bathing Resort after his daughter Geneva. The resort featured a hotel and pavilion, and offered fishing, boating, and swimming. Dallin sold Geneva in 1907 and it continued to change hands until it completely faded during the depression of 1935. In 1939 it burned to the ground. During World War II the site was used to construct the large steel plant that continues to operate today. The Geneva name was retained. An alternate claim suggests the name refers to Geneva, Switzerland.
S6,T6S,R2E,SLM; 4,490' (1,369m). 91, 314.

GENOLA* (Utah) is a fruit-growing community near US-6 between Santaquin* and Goshen*.
S32,33,T10S,R1E,SLM; 4,628' (1,411m). 249 (29 Feb. 1976).

GENTRY HOLLOW (Emery). See Gentry Mountain (Emery).

GENTRY MOUNTAIN (Emery) is between Huntington Canyon and Hiawatha*, five miles east southeast of Hiawatha. There is also a Gentry Ridge

and Gentry Hollow in the vicinity. All the Gentry names are for Bill Gentry, a stockman who ran his livestock in the area from 1876 to 1877.
S1,12,T7E,R16S,SLM; 9,700' (2,957m). 578.

GENTRY RIDGE (Emery). See Gentry Mountain (Emery).

GEORGE CREEK (Box Elder) originates in the West Raft River Mountains, seven miles east southeast of Yost*, and drains into Idaho. It was named by Charles Yost in 1865 for one of the men in his company who rode in from Nevada and homesteaded along the creek.
S26,T14N,R14W,SLM to S28,T14N,R17W, SLM (Utah border). 100(v17), 139, 542, 567.

GEORGE CREEK* (Box Elder). See Yost* (Box Elder).

GEORGE HANSEN PEAK (Juab) is the highest peak in the Fish Spring Range, seven miles north of Sand Pass and fifty miles northwest of Hinckley*. It was named for George H. Hansen, pioneer geologist of Utah and professor of geology at Brigham Young University.
S5,T13S,R14W,SLM; 8,523' (2,598m). 578. D.L. 8501.

GEORGE MOUNTAIN (Kane) is on the western slopes of the Paunsaugunt Plateau at the Sunset Cliffs. Nine miles northwest is Hatch*. George Dodds herded sheep on this mountain.
S2,T38S,R5W,SLM. 578(pers. comm.).

GEORGES DRAW (Emery) originates in the Sinbad country of the San Rafael Swell near the north end of Rods Valley. It drains east to combine with Reid Neilson Draw, then leads into Crawford Draw. The San Rafael Knob is four miles west. The area was named for George Crawford, an early cattleman of the late 1800s who ran a cattle operation there with his brother Nathaniel "Tan" Crawford. See Crawford Draw.
S10,15,T23S,R10E,SLM to S10,T23S,R11E, SLM. 193.

GEORGETOWN* (Garfield) was a small settlement on Yellow Creek, a tributary of the Paria River, three miles south of Cannonville*. In the spring of 1886 Seth Johnson and his two sons, Joseph and Eleazer, arrived and established homes. Seth named the settlement to honor George Q. Cannon, one of the general authorities of the Mormon Church. Unfortunately, the water supply was unreliable, so the settlers abandoned the town. Today the area is part of Cannonville.
S1,T38S,R3W,SLM; 5,794' (1,766m). 89, 145.

GEYSER CREEK (San Juan) originates near Geyser Pass on the northern slopes of Mount Mellenthin in the north La Sal Mountains. It drains east to join Taylor Creek. The creek was named for Al Geyser, a stockman who ran his cattle in the area.
S1,T24S,R27E,SLM to S31,T26S,R26E,SLM. 546, 567.

GEYSER PASS (San Juan) is in the La Sal Mountains, one and one-half miles north of Mount Mellenthin and eleven miles northwest of La Sal*. See Geyser Creek for name source.
S1,2,T27S,R24E,SLM; 10,700' (3,261m).

GHOST ROCK (Emery) is on the San Rafael Swell near I-70 between Secret Mesa and Head of Sinbad. Dutchmans Arch is one mile east. Early cowboys named this feature as they watched the early-morning fog shroud the base with the peak protruding above, often giving the appearance of ghost-like figures floating in the air. Ghost Rock was an important landmark in this desert region.
S33,T22S,R10E,SLM; 6,900' (2,103m). 193.

GIBSON* (Carbon). See Consumers* (Carbon).

GIFFORD CANYON (Washington) originates two miles south of the Great Arch and the east entrance of the Zion National Park tunnel. The canyon drains

into Pine Creek and is named for Oliver DeMille Gifford, an early Mormon bishop and member of a pioneer family from Springdale*.
T4S,R10W,SLM. 530.

GILBERT CREEK (Duchesne) originates in the south central section of the Uinta Mountains on the southern slopes of Gilbert Peak. It drains into the Central Fork of the Uinta River. Kings Peak, the highest point in Utah, is four miles southwest. Gilbert Creek was named after the peak.
D.L. 8404.

GILBERT LAKE (Summit) is in the north central section of the Uinta Mountains, two miles northeast of Gilbert Peak. The lake received its name from the peak.
10,905' (3,324m).

GILBERT PEAK (Duchesne, Summit) is in the central section of the Uinta Mountains at the head of the Uinta River, Center Fork, and is the second highest peak in Utah. The highest point, Kings Peak, is three and one-half miles southwest. Gilbert Peak is named for Grove Karl Gilbert, a geologist of the Wheeler survey of 1871-75 and the Powell survey of 1875-79.
13,442' (4,097m). 172, 309, 314.

GILES* (Wayne) was in Blue Valley, eleven miles northeast of Caineville* on U-24. Hanksville* is seven miles east. Hyrum Burgess was one of the first men in the Blue Valley along the Fremont River. The developing community was named to honor their religious leader and prominent citizen, Mormon Bishop Henry Giles. Alternating water shortages and floods with accumulating salts in the soil ruined the cropland and by 1919 the town was abandoned. Today the area is being reclaimed and farming is again predominant. Remnants of the former town are still evident.
S17,T28S,R10E,SLM; 4,450' (1,356m). 89, 100(v13), 303.

GILLIES HILL (Beaver) is northwest of the northern section of Beaver Valley near the head of Fourmile Canyon. The Gillies owned a ranch near the hill and Eb Gillies ran his horses in the area.
S16,17,T27S,R7W,SLM; 7,888' (2,404m).

GILLULY (Utah) was a siding on the Denver and Rio Grande Western Railroad near US-6, five and one-half miles west of Soldier Summit. It was named for James Gilluly, a government geologist who worked the San Rafael Swell and nearby areas in the early 1900s.
S19,T10S,R7E,SLM; 6,532' (1,991m). 567.

GILMER PARK (Salt Lake) was on Ninth South to Yale Avenue and Eleventh East to Fifteenth East, but is now a part of Salt Lake City*. In the early days, this beautiful section filled with springs and small brooks was the property of Jack O'Neil. O'Neil lost the property to Jack Gilmer in a card game.
S8,9,T1S,R1E,SLM; 4,600' (1,402m). 149, 508.

GILSON MOUNTAINS (Juab) are north of Leamington*. Champlin Peak is the high point.
T14S,R3W,SLM; 7,504m (2,287m).

GILSON VALLEY (Sevier) is southeast of Old Woman Plateau, two miles north of Fremont Junction. Old Spring Creek originates there.
S29,31,T23S,R5E,SLM; 6,550' (1,986m).

GILSONITE DRAW (Duchesne) originates on the East Tavaputs Plateau, twenty-six miles north northeast of Dragerton*. It drains northeast into Wells Draw. Gilsonite is a black, lustrous asphalt found only in this immediate area. This patented product is used in paints, varnishes, and inks and was named for its discoverer and developer, Samuel H. Gilson, an early Pony Express rider, prospector, and Indian scout. An early, less commonly used name, uintaite, was publicized but the name gilsonite predominated and is used today.

S24,T6S,R4W,USM to S16,T9S,R16E,SLM. 50, 89, 172, 546.

GINGERHILL* (San Juan) was a small temporary settlement near Horsehead*, southwest of Lockerby* and Eastland*. It was settled around 1917. MRN T34S,R25E,SLM; 6,800' (2,073m). 406.

GISBORN* (Tooele). See Jacob City* (Tooele).

GLADYS LAKE (Duchesne) is in the southwest section of the Uinta Mountains on the upper drainage of Rock Creek. S23,T4N,R8W,USM; 10,900' (3,322m).

GLAS EYE CANYON (Kane) originates at the Vermillion Cliffs four miles east of the mouth of Johnson Canyon. It drains north northeast into Flood Canyon. MRN S9,10,15,T43S,R4½W,SLM.

GLEN CANYON (Garfield, Kane, San Juan) is on the Colorado River, now a part of Lake Powell and the Glen Canyon National Recreation Area. It was first described and named in the late 1860s by the Powell expedition.

The area from the mouth of the Fremont (Dirty Devil) to the mouth of Trachyte Creek was first called Mound Canyon for the huge domes and rounded tops so common in this bare rimrock country. The area from Trachyte Creek to the mouth of the Paria in Arizona was called Monument Canyon, because of the baldheads and massive dome features. Monument Canyon—as described and named by Powell's group—was a serene, pastoral, smooth-flowing canyon set with large slow-moving whirlpools and walls of Navajo sandstone. Powell stated, "The next morning the second of October at eight o'clock, we continued our voyage, now entering a new canyon, then called Mound, but it was afterwards consolidated with the portion below called Monument, and together they now stand as Glen Canyon. So we have a curious ensemble of wonderful features—carved

walls, royal arches, glens, alcove gulches, mounds, and monuments. We decide to call it Glen Canyon" (422, p. 72). 159, 160, 314, 422, 496, 546, 555(v7).

GLEN CANYON CITY* (Kane) was named for the nearby canyon that is now a part of Lake Powell. See Big Water* (Kane). 455. D.L. 8002.

GLEN COVE* (Washington). See Veyo*.

GLEN COVE* (Sevier). See Glenwood*.

GLENDALE* (Kane) is on US-89 in Long Valley along the upper Virgin River. Four miles south is Orderville*. After being settled in 1862 by a party of settlers led by John and William Berry from Kanarraville*, Glendale was named Berryville* as the first settlement in the valley. At that time, Long Valley was called Berry Valley. Of those first settlers, Robert Berry and his wife Isabella were murdered by the Indians, and in 1866 Berryville was abandoned. In 1871, members of the Muddy Mission in Nevada resettled Long Valley. Led by James Leithead, the group settled on the old Berryville townsite and renamed it Glendale because of the beautiful surroundings. Another version of the naming of Glendale states that the name came from their leader and first bishop, who was reminded of his home in Scotland. Today it is a beautiful and stable community known for its scenic surroundings. S23,T40S,R7W,SLM; 5,824' (1,775m). 289, 311, 360, 455, 542, 546, 600.

GLENWOOD* (Sevier) is ten miles east of Richfield* on U-119. It was established in 1863 and named for an early pioneer, Robert Wilson Glenn. The first name was Glencoe* or Glen Cove*, but was changed in November 1864 when Orson Hyde visited the settlement and recommended Glenwood. A stone fort was constructed in April 1866.

S35,T23S,R2W,SLM; 5,300' (1,615m). 100
(v17), 289, 542, 585.

GLENWOOD SPRINGS (Sevier) is one-
half mile southeast of Glenwood*. The
springs are named after the nearby
community.
S36,T23S,R2W,SLM.

GOBLIN VALLEY (Emery) is in the
upper reaches of the Red Canyon drainage, fifteen miles north of Hanksville*. It
is a geologically unique area with unusual
highly eroded, goblin-like shapes from
which the area receives its name. It is
also whimsically known as Hoodoo Valley
or Golly Gully. The view is especially
dramatic in moonlight or when the sun is
low. At this time, the mushroom-shaped
figures appear huddled or in praying
groups.
T26S,R11E,SLM. 104.

GODIVA MOUNTAIN (Juab, Utah) is
southeast of and near Eureka* on
US-6,50. MRN
S18,19,T10S,R2W,SLM; 8,048' (2,453m).

GOLD BASIN (Grand) is on the northwest slopes of Mount Tukuhnikivatz of
the La Sal Mountains. Prospectors found
gold in this basin on Brumley Creek in
1898.
S10,15,T27S,R24E,SLM; 10,000' (3,048m).
146.

GOLD CITY* (Salt Lake) was a small
temporary mining settlement up Little
Cottonwood Canyon southeast of Salt
Lake*. The settlement developed in the
late 1800s, but only lasted a short time.
454.

GOLD CREEK (Piute) originates on the
eastern slopes of the Tushar Mountains
on Deer Trail Mountain. The creek
drains east, passing through
Thompsonville* into the Sevier River.
The name was received from the mid-
late 1800s mining activities in this region.
S10,T28S,R4W,SLM to S33,T27S,R3W,SLM.

GOLD GULCH (Piute) is eleven miles
north of Junction* where it originates on
the eastern slopes of the Tushar Mountains and drains east into the Sevier
River. Intense gold prospecting occurred
there in the 1800s.
S27,T28S,R4W,SLM to S16,T28S,R3W,SLM.
567.

GOLD HILL (Summit) is at the northwest end of the Uinta Mountains at the
head of Mill City Creek. One mile
northwest is Whitney Reservoir. The
name is a reminder of the region's
mining activity during the late 1800s.
S15,22,23,T1N,R9E,SLM; 10,563' (3,220m).

GOLD HILL* (Tooele) is on Gold Hill
Wash, three miles southeast of Woodman
Peak and five miles north of Ibapah*.
California gold seekers discovered gold
here in 1858 and a smelter was subsequently built in 1871. The town was
named after the low gold-bearing mountain to the east. The 1869 settlement
consisted of dugouts and shacks made
from willow and cedar posts. Several
mines eventually opened in this vicinity
and gold, copper, silver, lead, tungsten,
arsenic, and bismuth were mined. Ulti-
mately, the mines were thought to be
worked out and the town was abandoned. Then, in 1916 the mines were
revitalized for World War I and the
population peaked at three thousand.
In 1938 the last train pulled away and
the town died once more, only to be
reopened again for World War II, after
which it was again abandoned. Today,
eleven residents live in Gold Hill.
S1,T8S,R18W,SLM; 5,300' (1,615m). 89, 100
(v17), 153, 546.

GOLD MOUNTAIN (Piute) is one mile
south of Signal Peak in the northern
Tushar Mountains. The mountain is
named for the late 1800s mining activities
in this immediate area.
S23,T27S,R5W,SLM; 11,664' (3,555m).

GOLD QUEEN BASIN (San Juan) is
five miles southeast of Monticello* and

two and one-half miles east of Abajo Peak, on the eastern slopes of the Abajo Mountains (The Blues). The basin was named after the nearby Gold Queen Mine. See Gold Queen Gulch.
S8,T34S,R23E,SLM; 8,200' (2,499m).

GOLD QUEEN GULCH (San Juan) originates on the southern slopes of Abajo Peak, seven miles east southeast of Monticello*. It drains into the head of South Creek and receives its name from the mine at the head of the gulch.
S18,T34S,R23E,SLM (at mouth). 406.

GOLD SPRINGS* (Iron) was an early gold mining camp developed in 1897 near the Utah-Nevada border, approximately ten miles northwest of Modena*. Gold Springs was abandoned as the resources were depleted.
S25,T33S,R20W,SLM; 6,800' (2,073m). 516.

GOLD SPRINGS WASH (Iron) originates near the Utah-Nevada line, fifteen miles northwest of Modena*. It drains southeast into the Modena Draw Reservoir and was named for the ghost town of Gold Springs*.
S12,T33S,R20W,SLM to S6,T35S,R18W, SLM.

GOLDEN PASS ROAD (Salt Lake). See Parleys Canyon (Salt lake).

GOLDEN SPIKE NATIONAL HISTORIC SITE (Box Elder) is at the north end of the Promontory Mountains and the Great Salt Lake, on the old Union Pacific Railroad grade. The site was set aside to commemorate the linking of the east- and west-bound railroads. The project marked the completion of the first transcontinental railroad, and a ceremony honoring this accomplishment was held on May 10, 1869.
S8,T10N,R6W,SLM; 4,905' (1,495m).

GOOD HOPE MESA (Garfield) is on the southeast slopes of Mount Ellsworth of the Henry Mountains. To the west is

Ticaboo Mesa.
NW¼,T36S,R13E,SLM; 4,000' (1,219m).

GOODALE CREEK (Weber) originates in the Wasatch Range four miles east of Ogden* where it drains south into the Ogden River at Wildwood*. The creek was named for Isaac Newton Goodale, early pioneer and a builder of the toll road through Ogden Canyon. Goodale also harvested the timber along the creek.
S6,T6N,R1E,SLM. 100(v17), 567.

GOODRIDGE* (San Juan). See Mexican Hat*.

GOODYEARS FORT* (Weber). Miles Goodyear was the first white man to settle in the Ogden Valley. In 1844-45 he built a fort on the property, then sold it to Captain James Brown in 1850. This area then became part of present-day Ogden*. Miles named it Fort Buenaventura*.
S31,T6N,R1W,SLM.

GOOSE CREEK (Box Elder) originates in Nevada and drains across the northwest corner of Utah before entering southern Idaho. In earlier days it was a haven for wild geese.
S35,T15S,R19W,SLM. 525, 567.

GOOSE CREEK MOUNTAINS (Box Elder) range southwest and northeast in the northwest corner of the county and are named after Goose Creek, which parallels the mountains.

GOOSE EGG PEAK (Duchesne) is on the upper Uinta River in the south central section of the Uinta Mountains. Chepeta Lake is fourteen miles northeast. George Hackford named the peak after he climbed it and noticed two potholes in the meadow below. He thought the holes resembled two goose eggs.
S10,T3N,R2W,USM; 10,700' (3,261m). 309.

GOOSE LAKE (Uintah) is in the southeastern section of the Uinta

Mountains on the headwaters of Ashley Creek, South Fork. Two and one-half miles southeast is Marsh Peak. Goose Lake is one of a cluster of lakes that are a haven for wild geese.
10,252' (3,125m). 494.

GOOSEBERRY* (Sevier) is up Gooseberry Creek seventeen miles southeast of Salina*. Today there is a U.S. Forest Service ranger station on the site. In 1865 a few ranch families settled there. The name was suggested because the area has numerous wild gooseberry bushes.
S21,T23S,R2E,SLM; 7,850' (2,393m).

GOOSEBERRY CREEK (Sanpete) originates on the Wasatch Plateau seven miles east of Fairview*. It drains north through the Lower Gooseberry Reservoir into Fish Creek. Wild gooseberries are plentiful in this area.
S31,T13S,R6E,SLM to S15,T12S,R6E,SLM.

GOOSEBERRY CREEK (Sevier) originates on the eastern slopes of Indian Mountain in the Pavant Range. The creek drains southeast into the Sevier River. Gooseberries are plentiful.
S30,T24S,R4W,SLM to S11,T25S,R3W,SLM.

GOOSEBERRY CREEK (Sevier) originates at Pole Flat three miles east of Koosharem Reservoir. It drains northwest into Otter Creek. Wild gooseberries are abundant in this area.
S27,28,34,T25S,R1E,SLM.

GOOSEBERRY CREEK (Sevier) originates at Taylor Flat and Abes Reservoir, two miles southeast of the Gooseberry Ranger Station. It drains northwest through Gooseberry Valley into Salina Creek.
S23,T23S,R4E,SLM to S1,T22S,R1E,SLM.

GOOSENECKS OF THE SAN JUAN (San Juan) are a section of the canyon eroded by the San Juan River into what is now a striking example of stream erosion, or entrenched meanders. This section of the river is six miles west northwest of Mexican Hat*. The Goosenecks were previously known as The Twist.
ca. S33,T41S,R18E,SLM. 58, 314, 546.

GORDON CREEK (Morgan) originates on the eastern slopes of De Moisy Peak, south of Snow Basin, and drains southeast into the Weber River. The creek was named for Gordon Beckstead, who settled at Mountain Green* in 1860.
S8,T5N,R1E,SLM to S26,T5N,R1E,SLM. 378.

GORDON FLATS (Wayne) are a high desert region in Robbers Roost country, east of and near the Orange Cliffs. The northern boundary is the French Spring and French Spring Fork of Happy Canyon. The name is a result of the early French sheepherder's pronunciation of "garden." When the desert flats were in bloom after a wet winter they were truly beautiful, with myriads of flowers, colors, and perfumes.
6,400' (1,951m). 24.

GORGOZA* (Summit) is two and one-half miles east of Parleys Summit. The area was originally settled in 1889 and named for Rodriquez Velasquez de la Gorgozada, a Spaniard who invested almost a million dollars in a narrow-gauge railroad. This railroad was supposed to be built as an extension from Park City* to Salt Lake City*. A representative for Brigham Young traveled to France to solicit the help of the Spaniard, who was promised that a city would be built and named in his honor. The project did not fulfill its planned destiny.
S11,T15S,R3E,SLM; 6,350' (1,935m). 542, 546.

GORILLA CREEK (Beaver) is on the western slopes of the Tushar Mountains. It drains southeast into North Creek, South Fork. See Gorilla Ridge.
S17,T28S,R5W,SLM.

GORILLA RIDGE (**Beaver**) is on the western slopes of the Tushar Mountains. It has a northeast-southwest orientation from Mount Baldy. There are two versions of the name origin. First, the ridge was named after the nearby Gorilla mine. Second, the name originated when Jim Boyter and George W. Valentine of Beaver* were charged with shadowing some prospectors in the area. The prospectors saw an unshaven Valentine in the bushes at dusk and thought they had seen a gorilla.
S5,7,T28S,R5W,SLM; 10,750' (3,227m). 125.

GOSHEN* (**Utah**) is in Goshen Valley on US-6, between Santaquin* and Elberta*. The first bishop, Phineas W. Cooke, named it for Goshen, Connecticut, his birthplace. The settlement changed location several times and was successively known as Sodom*, Sandtown*, Mechanicsville*, Lower Goshen* and finally Goshen. Sandtown was an obvious name for this sandy region. "Sodum up" was a term used for the process of sodding up the roofs of the early dugout structures during the spring and fall.
S13,14,T10S,R1W,SLM; 4,530' (1,381m). 100(v17), 270, 289, 516, 542.

GOSHEN VALLEY (**Utah**) is south and southwest of Utah Lake. Goshen* and Elberta* are in the heart of the valley.
4,550' (1,387m).

GOSHUTE* (**Tooele**) is a small Indian community on the Goshute Indian Reservation. The Goshute people are of Shoshoni extraction and their name means "dust" or "desert" people in the Ute language.
S16,T11S,R19W,SLM; 6,200' (1,890m). 105, 106, 314, 546.

GOSHUTE CANYON (**Tooele**) originates in the Deep Creek Range in the western part of the county. It drains east and disappears into the Snake Valley. The canyon is named for the local Goshute Indians.

S28,T18W,SLM to S33,34,T17S,R10W,SLM.

GOSLIN MOUNTAIN (**Daggett**) is in the eastern Uinta Mountains east of and near Clay Basin. The Wyoming border is north. Charley "Goose" Goslin used the mountain as a summer range for his cattle.
S25,26,28,T3N,R23E,SLM; 8,185' (2,495m). 172.

GOULDING TRADING POST (**San Juan**) is in Monument Valley north of the Arizona line and US-163. Harry Goulding was founder and owner of the post.
S36,T43S,R15E,SLM; 5,225' (1,593m).

GOVERNMENT CREEK (**Daggett**) originates in the eastern section of the Uinta Mountains, one-half mile west of Oak Parks Reservoir. It drains south southeast to join Big Brush Creek. Government Creek is part of a complex that was the Old Carter Road running from Fort Bridger* to Fort Thornburg*. The road was built in the early 1880s to expedite the movement of government supplies and men during a period of Indian troubles.
S2,T1S,R20E,SLM to S30,T1S,R21E,SLM. 172, 494, 555(v35).

GOVERNMENT CREEK (**Tooele**) originates in the Sheeprock-Simpson Mountain area. The creek drains northwest and disappears into the desert on the Dugway Proving Grounds military reservation. MRN
S11,T10S,R7W,SLMtoSE¼,T7S,R10W,SLM.

GOVERNMENT PARK (**Daggett**) is in the eastern Uinta Mountains on Government Creek and the old Carter Road, which is now part of the Red Cloud Loop. See Government Creek (Daggett).
S13,T1S,R20E,SLM; 9,125' (2,781m). 172.

GOVERNOR DERN LAKE (**Duchesne**) is in the southwest section of the Uinta Mountains. The Naturalist Basin is three miles north. The lake was also known as

Governor Lake after former Utah governor and U.S. Secretary of War George H. Dern.
S16,T3N,R8W,USM; 9,975' (3,040). 100(v2).

GOVERNOR LAKE (Duchesne). See Governor Dern Lake.

GRABENS, THE (San Juan) are in Canyonlands National Park. These landforms have a north-south orientation and are east of and near the Colorado River. Grabens are depressed sectors of the earth's crust that are bound on each side by elevated faults. The central down-dropped block is the graben. T30½,31S,R18,19E. D.L. 6901.

GRAFTON* (Washington) is two miles west of Rockville* and one-fourth mile south of the Virgin River. Grafton was a small settlement established in 1859 by Nathan C. Tenney and others from Virgin*. The settlement was first named Wheeler*, then Grafton, another town either in Massachusetts or England—this is still a disputed matter. Grafton became a ghost town in 1921 after repeated flooding. Today vandalism is slowly destroying the abandoned buildings. Marvelous Flood Tenney's name has become folklore because his mother gave birth to her baby during the height of a flood that swept through the town.
S3,T42S,R11W,SLM; 3,700' (1,128m). 100 (v13,17), 311, 438, 542, 567, 600.

GRAFTON WASH (Washington) originates on the northern slopes of the Gooseberry Butte and drains north past Grafton* and into the Virgin River. The wash received its name from the former settlement.
S17,18,T42S,R11W,SLM to S4,T42S,R11W, SLM.

GRAFTON MESA (Washington) is near Grafton*.

GRAHAM* (Kane). See Alton*.

GRAHAM CANYON (San Juan). See Bullet Canyon.

GRAHAM LAKE (Kane). See McDonald Lake.

GRAHAM PEAK (Tooele) is the high point in the Silver Island Mountains northeast of Wendover*.
S33,T3N,R17W,SLM; 7,563' (2,305m).

GRAMPIAN* (Beaver) was on Grampian Hill at the south end of the San Francisco Mountains. This ghost town site was a "suburb" of the old mining town of Frisco*. In addition to the nearby Horn Silver Mine, there was also a Grampian Mine that opened in this area around 1874. See Grampian Hill.
S23,T27S,R13W,SLM; 6,600' (2,012m). 125, 567.

GRAMPIAN HILL (Beaver) is at the south end of the San Francisco Mountains, north of present-day U-21. The region included the fabulous Horn Silver Mine, the King David Mine, the Grampian Mine, and the notorious Frisco*—now a ghost town. The hill was reportedly named by a Scotsman and miner, Robert McGreager, who said that the surrounding hills looked like the Grampian Hills in his native land.
S23,T27S,R13W,SLM; 7,341' (2,238m). 567.

GRAND BENCH (Kane) has its southern tip at the Colorado River southwest of the Kaiparowits Plateau. It extends north as a vast bench or flatland between Rock Creek and Last Chance Bay of Lake Powell. The name suggests its size and grandeur.
T41,42S,R7E,SLM; ca. 5,000' (1,524m).

GRAND COUNTY is bordered by San Juan, Emery, and Uintah counties. The 29th Legislature of the Utah Territory established the county in 1890 and named it after the Grand River, the western boundary. In 1921 the Grand River was renamed the Colorado River.
6, 314, 542.

GRAND FLAT (San Juan) is near Grand Gulch (San Juan).

GRAND GULCH (Garfield) originates at Swap Mesa and the mouth is at Halls Crossing. The name comes from the large size of the gulch.
T34-38S,R8-10E,SLM.

GRAND GULCH (San Juan) originates at the Bears Ears and the Grand Flats and drains southwest into the San Juan River. Grand Gulch is the largest of the San Juan River tributary canyons. The gulch was named in 1879 by George B. Hobbs, Lemuel Redd, George Sevy, and George Morrill while they were scouting the region trying to find a way around this forbidding barrier for the Hole-in-the-Rock expedition. There are many Indian ruins in this area.
T37-40S,R15-18E,SLM. 359, 567, 610.

GRAND RIVER. See Colorado River.

GRAND RIVER VALLEY (Grand) lies northwest of Cisco. The name reflects the early history of this section of the Colorado River (formerly the Grand River).

GRAND VALLEY* (Grand). See Moab* (Grand).

GRAND VIEW POINT (San Juan) extends south from Island in the Sky and Grays Pasture into the region of The Confluence above the White Rim.
T28S,R19E,SLM; 6,313' (1,924m).

GRAND WASH (Wayne) is in Capitol Reef National Park where it cuts through the Capitol Reef. It drains northeast into the Fremont River, three miles east of Fruita*, and is named for its size and spectacular surroundings.
S25,T29S,R6E,SLM.

GRANDADDY LAKE (Duchesne) is at the west end of the Uinta Mountains in the Grandaddy Lake region between East and West Grandaddy mountains. Mount

Agassiz is two and one-half miles north northwest. George H. Wilcken, early pioneer and explorer, named the lake in 1897 because he thought it looked like "the Grandaddy of them all."
S4,T2N,R8W,USM; 10,318' (3,145m). 595.

GRANDDAD PEAK (Sevier) is at the southern end of the Pavant Range, thirteen miles west northwest of Sevier*. It is the most prominent peak in the Grandaddy Range.
S3,T25S,R5W,SLM; 5,854' (1,784m).

GRANGER* (Salt Lake) is west southwest of Salt Lake City* between Seventeenth and Thirty-second West and Twenty-seventh and Forty-first South. It was first settled in 1849 by emigrants from Great Britain and was known as English Fort*. English Fort was built in 1854 where today's North Jordan Cemetery is located (between Bennion* and Taylorsville*). The community was later named Granger because of the area's capacity to grow grain. The first judge of Salt Lake County, Judge Elias Smith, gave the name because the land was so productive. Granger has recently been included in a large area renamed West Valley City*.
S28,33,T1S,R1W,SLM; 4,275' (1,303m). 59, 289, 444.

GRANGER CANYON (Utah) originates on Granger Mountain east northeast of Springville* and drains southwest into Left Fork, Hobble Creek. The canyon was named for Samuel and Joseph Granger, who originally opened the canyon.
S12,16,T7S,R4E,SLM. 270.

GRANGER MOUNTAIN (Utah) is east northeast of Springville*. See Granger Canyon for the name source.
S13,23,T7S,R4E,SLM; 8,198' (2,499m).

GRANITE* (Salt Lake) is a small community at the mouth of Little Cottonwood Canyon, four miles east of Sandy City* and south of Butler*. In

1870 it was a good campsite for teamsters, quarrymen, and miners who were working in the Mormon church granite quarries and the mines in the vicinity. When transportation became more efficient during a time of reduced operations in this area, the camp was abandoned, only to be subsequently rejuvenated with modern, permanent residences. The town was named Granite because of its proximity to the granite quarries that provided the blocks for the Salt Lake Temple.
S11,T3S,R1E,SLM; 5,150' (1,570m). 252, 289, 444.

GRANITE CANYON (Beaver) originates on the southeast slopes of the Mineral Mountains. The canyon drains northeast into Cherry Creek, northwest of Adamsville*. The granite mountain range had the earlier name Granite Mountain.
S11,T29S,R9W,SLM.

GRANITE CREEK (Garfield, Wayne) originates on the northeast slopes of Mount Ellen in the Henry Mountains. It drains northeast into Granite Wash and receives its name from the Granite Ridges near the source of the creek.
S27,T31S,R10E,SLM.

GRANITE LAKE (Salt Lake). See Lake Mary.

GRANITE MOUNTAINS (Beaver) are in central Beaver County with a north-south orientation. Minersville* is on the south end of the mountains. The more popular name today is the Mineral Mountains. Commercial ores and granite have been acquired from the mountains for some time.

GRANITE PEAK (Beaver) is in the center of the Mineral Mountains and is the highest peak in the range.
S12,T28S,R9W,SLM; 9,578' (2,919m).

GRANITE PEAK (Tooele) is in the western part of the county and receives its name from the predominate type of rock in the mountain.
NW¼,T8S,R13W,SLM; 7,068' (2,154m).

GRANITE RANCH (Wayne) is a historically important ranch on the northeast side of the Henry Mountains on Granite Creek from which it receives its name.
S26,T30S,R11E,SLM; 5,160' (1,573m). 24, 25, 303.

GRANITE RIDGES (Wayne) are exposed near the head of Granite Creek on the eastern slopes of Mount Ellen of the Henry Mountains.
S26,T31S,R10E,SLM; 9,200' (2,804m).

GRANITE ROCK SPRING (Beaver) is one of a small cluster of springs on the eastern slopes of the South Twin Flat Mountains of the Mineral Mountains. There is a mass of granite boulders on the south side of the springs.
S6,T28S,R8W,SLM; 7,500' (2,286m). 578.

GRANITE WASH (Wayne) originates in the desert area where Granite Creek emerges from the northeastern slopes of the Henry Mountains. The wash drains northeast into Beaver Canyon and is named after the creek.
S26,T30S,R11E,SLM to S35,T29S,R12E, SLM.

GRANTS STATION* (Tooele). See Burmester*.

GRANTSVILLE* (Tooele) is at the south end of the Great Salt Lake on U-138, thirty-three miles southwest of Salt Lake City*. Prior to Mormon settlement, the Donner party called it Twenty Wells*. In 1850 the Mormons changed the name to Willow Creek*, which was the name of the adjoining creek where the settlers obtained their water. On February 19, 1851, Colonel George D. Grant, a military officer in the Nauvoo Legion, was sent with twenty-five men to control hostile Indians. The name of the community was then changed from

Willow Springs* to Grantsville out of gratitude to Grant.
S31,32,T2S,R4W,SLM and S36,T2S,R6W, SLM; 4,325' (1,318m). 27, 100(v17), 153, 275, 289, 498, 542, 546, 567.

GRAPEVINE PASS (Washington) is on the early trail over the Black Ridge, six miles northeast of St. George* and Washington*. The Grapevine Springs are in the vicinity. The pass was the early road leading into Utah's "Dixie." See Grapevine Springs.
S6,T42S,R15W,SLM; 3,200' (975m). 310, 423.

GRAPEVINE SPRINGS (Washington) is on the Black Ridge located above Ash Creek, six miles northeast of St. George*. Here the road down into Dixie country passes over the Black Ridge--a prohibitive barrier that is actually the edge of a lava flow. Wild grapes were common around the spring and it was a prominent resting and camping spot.
S6,T42S,R15W,SLM; 3,200' (975m). 72, 310, 438, 600.

GRASS CREEK* (Summit) is eight and one-half miles northeast of Coalville*. Coal was discovered in Grass Valley Canyon in 1860. The coal was mined, then freighted out, up, and over Parley's Summit to Salt Lake City*. The miners lived nearby with their families, calling their settlement Grass Creek. After the Grass Creek Fuel Company developed, the town began to grow. Soon afterward, the railroad line was brought into the area. Conditions then began to change and the town started to dwindle. Today Grass Creek is a ghost town site located on private property.
S18,T3N,R6E,SLM; 6,426' (1,959m). 89, 516.

GRASS CREEK (Summit) originates near the southwest corner of Wyoming. The creek drains through grass-covered hill country to the southwest, into Echo Reservoir on the Weber River.
S10,T3N,R6E,SLM to S32,T3N,R5E,SLM.

GRASS LAKE (Garfield) is nine miles north of Boulder* in a meadow on the southern slopes of Boulder Mountain.
T41S,R4E,SLM; 9,725' (2,964m).

GRASS LAKES (Garfield) are a series of small, marshy lakes in Alpine meadows on Escalante Mountain. Center Creek heads there.
S16,20,T33S,R1W,SLM; 9,600' (2,926m).

GRASS VALLEY (Sevier) is a historic, long, narrow valley walled on the west by the Sevier Plateau and on the east by the Awapa Plateau and Parker Mountain. The Otter Creek Reservoir is south. The valley houses such towns as Koosharem*, Greenwich*, Burrville*, and Angle*. The valley was named by the same group who named the community of Coyote*, which later become Antimony*. Cedar Grove, an area located on the edge of Grass Valley, was the scene of the signing of an important treaty made with the Fishlake Indians on July 1, 1873. The valley was also the site of the 1874 killing of several Indian youths by Tom and Billy McCarty. This incident led to another Indian conflict. In earlier days it was used as pastureland by herders from Sanpete County.
175, 303.

GRASS VALLEY (Washington) is a small valley to the northeast of Pine Valley* in the Pine Valley Mountains. Grass Valley Creek and New Castle Reservoir are located in the valley. The valley is good grazing territory.
S30,31,T38S,R14W,SLM; 6,950' (2,118m).

GRASS VALLEY (Summit) is an area seven to ten miles northeast of Coalville*, surrounding Grass Creek and Grass Valley Canyon.
S23,24,25,26,T3N,R5E,SLM.

GRASSY BEND (Beaver) is ten miles southwest of Milford*, a lush pastureland in the bend of the Beaver River.
S21,T29S,R11W,SLM; 5,000' (1,524m).

GRASSY CANYON (**Beaver**) originates on Black Mountain of the Tushars. The canyon drains southwest into South Canyon.
S26,T29S,R7W,SLM.

GRASSY LAKES (**Summit**) is in the northwest section of the Uinta Mountains, eight miles northwest of Christmas Meadows. The lakes are in open meadowland.
S6,T2N,R10E,SLM; 8,200' (2,499m).

GRASSY MOUNTAINS (**Tooele**) are a low range of mountains lying between Puddle Valley and Ripple Valley on the eastern border of the Great Salt Lake Desert. To the south is I-80.
T2,3N,R11W,SLM; 6,612' (2,015m).

GRAVELBED* (**Sevier**) is a small pioneer ghost town site near Sigurd* and Richfield*.
368.

GRAVELLY FORD (**Sevier**) was eight miles south of Salina* near Pelican Point where the old road crossed the Sevier River. In earlier days it was an important stop on the road to North Sevier*, south of Rocky Ford.

GRAVES VALLEY* (**Wayne**). See Hanksville* (Wayne).

GRAVEYARD HOLLOW (**Garfield**) originates five miles south of Panguitch*. It drains north past the cemetery located at the mouth of the hollow. See below.
S33,T34S,R5W,SLM.

GRAVEYARD HOLLOW (**Sevier**) is on the southwest slopes of Mount Joseph, southwest of Joseph*. It receives its name from the graveyard at its mouth. In pioneer days the graveyard was conveniently located next to a road previously built by wood haulers who cut timber in the nearby mountains.
S7,23,T25S,R4W,SLM. 567.

GRAVEYARD HOLLOW (**Wayne**) is

one mile southwest of Fremont*. It is a short hollow draining to the southwest, with the graveyard near its mouth. See above for name source.
S13,24,T27S,R2E,SLM.

GRAY CANYON (**Emery, Grand**) is that part of the Green River extending from the mouth of Florence Creek, where Desolation Canyon ends, south to where the Green River emerges into Gunnison Valley. The canyon is thirty-six miles long. Dellenbaugh wrote, "We were now actually out of the Canyon of Desolation and in the beginning of what the Major at first called Coal Canyon, then Lignite Canyon, and finally Gray Canyon, the name it bears today, because of the color of the walls" (159, p. 91).
T17-19S,R17E,SLM. 159, 160, 314, 420, 496, 609.

GRAY CLIFFS (**Washington**) are above the White Cliffs in Major Powell's Grand Staircase of geologic formations. See White Cliffs for further discussion. The Gray Cliffs are somewhat obscure because the rocks are composed of soft shale—mostly ocean deposits from the Cretaceous period—with fossils of sea life such as marine shells and sharks' teeth. Good examples are exposed northeast of the Zion National Park boundary. Here the rocks are coal-bearing sandstone and shale under the Pink Cliffs.
160, 422, 496.

GRAY HEAD PEAK (**Duchesne**) is on the West Tavaputs Plateau at the head of Lake Canyon, Right and Left Fork. The peak is gray in appearance.
S23,T6S,R8W,USM; 9,496' (2,894m).

GRAYBACK HILLS (**Tooele**) are on the eastern boundary of the Great Salt Lake Desert north of I-80 and west of Ripple Valley. The hills have a north-south orientation and receive their name from the sparse, grayish-colored vegetation growing in the area.
4,673' (1,424m).

GRAYSON* (San Juan). See Blanding*.

GREASEWOOD COUNTY was created in 1856 and named for the large amount of greasewood (*Sarcobatus*) in the region west of Great Salt Lake. The county was discontinued in January 1862.
6.

GREASEWOOD DRAW (Emery) originates on the San Rafael Swell at Arsons Garden and drains east into the San Rafael River. The desert shrub greasewood (*Sarcobatus*) is plentiful throughout the region.
S6,T23S,R13E,SLM to S3,T23S,R14E,SLM.

GREAT AMERICAN DESERT. The name refers to several dimensions in the central and western United States, some of which extend as far east as the Mississippi and Missouri rivers and west to the Sierra Nevada Mountains. Such vast dimensions for the Great American Desert were commonly accepted during the early 1800s. In 1896, when Utah became a state, it was one of sixteen states some writers included as part of the Great American Desert. Today, Utah's share of true desert could be incorporated in the Great Salt Lake Desert, consisting of western Box Elder, Tooele, and Juab counties, with isolated areas in Millard County, depending on what one's definition of a true desert is.
498, 546.

GREAT BASIN, THE, covers all or part of eight western states, with Utah and Nevada being the central points. The term was first conceptualized and identified in 1844 by Captain J. C. Fremont. The Basin extends between the Wasatch Mountains and the Sierra Nevada Mountains and is identified as having an independent inland drainage, dry climate, and scanty flora. The area is about one-sixth the size of the U.S.
159, 160, 205, 275, 314, 496, 546.

GREAT SALT LAKE was first discovered by a white man in 1824. The credit—although contested by some—is given to Jim Bridger, the well-known guide and mountain man, who acted as a scout in this area for William H. Ashley. The early explorers originally thought the lake was an arm of the Pacific Ocean because of the high salt content. Captain Bonneville (see Lake Bonneville) gave the lake his own name on subsequent maps but the name did not hold. The lake was also previously named Lake Timpanogo and still earlier, Thoago. The present name was given by Captain J. C. Fremont. The lake's mysterious background and atmosphere has been the source of legends from both Indians and whites and serious stories of giant whirlpools and water monsters have existed throughout Utah's history. The name of the lake indicates its high salt content along with other commercial minerals.
27, 129, 159, 314, 371, 372, 464, 494, 546, 555(v9).

GREAT SALT LAKE CITY* (Salt Lake). See Salt Lake City* (Salt Lake).

GREAT SALT LAKE COUNTY. See Salt Lake County.

GREAT SALT LAKE DESERT extends west and southwest of the Great Salt Lake. This salt desert is enclosed on the west by the Pilot Range north of Wendover* and by the lofty Deep Creek Range to the southwest. The desert is named after the lake. It is a remnant of ancient ice-age Lake Bonneville that once extended over most of northwestern Utah. The first recorded crossing of the Salt Desert was made in 1827 from west to east by Jedediah Strong Smith and two other fur trappers, who were returning from California. See also Great American Desert.
371, 372, 496, 498, 546.

GREAT WESTERN* (Carbon). See Coal City* (Carbon).

GREAT WHITE THRONE (Washington) is a gigantic, white, truncated sandstone monolith established on a red sandstone base. It is in upper Zion Canyon of Zion National Park near the North Fork of the Virgin River. Nearby is Angels Landing. These two formations were named in 1917 by Frederick Vining Fisher, a Methodist minister from Ogden, Utah. He wrote that the features should be spoken of reverently as the throne of God and the place where angels kneel in obeisance to God, not feeling worthy to approach closer—hence, Great White Throne and Angels Landing.
6,744' (2,056m). 438, 600.

GREATHEART MESA (Washington) is in Zion National Park, two miles northeast of the Guardian Angels. It is a white-walled mesa named for Christian's guide in *Pilgrim's Progress*. To climb this mesa requires a stout, great heart.
T40S,R10W,SLM; 7,410' (2,259m). 530, 531 (1 July 1934 to 31 June 1935).

GREEN CANYON (Beaver) originates on the western slopes of the Indian Peak Range and drains northwest into Hamlin Valley Wash. See Green Canyon Spring.
S7,T29S,R18W,SLM to S36,T28S,R20W, SLM.

GREEN CANYON (Cache) originates in the mountains six miles east of Paradise* and five miles north of Porcupine Reservoir. It drains west, combining with Hyrum Canyon, into the Little Bear River. There is a good growth of healthy green vegetation in the canyon.
S26,T10N,R1E,SLM (at mouth). 567.

GREEN CANYON (Cache) originates in the mountains east of North Logan* and Hyde Park* on the slopes of Mount Jardine. The canyon drains through North Logan into Cache Valley. The canyon is quite green, with heavy vegetation.
S24,T12N,R1E,SLM (at mouth).

GREEN CANYON SPRING (Beaver) is at the head of Green Canyon (Beaver). John Green settled in the canyon in the early 1800s.
S7,T29S,R18W,SLM. 125.

GREEN LAKE (Iron) is on the western slopes of Lone Tree Mountain, three miles south southeast of Cedar City*. The lake was sold by a Mr. Schoppman to one Mr. Green.
S36,T36S,R11W,SLM; 7,880' (2,401m). 567.

GREEN RIVER* (Emery) is on I-70 and the Green River. The town receives its name from the river and should not be confused with Green River*, Wyoming. The earlier recorded name for Green River, Utah, was Blake* for a J. P. Blake who settled on the east bank of the river. Today's town extends to both sides of the river.

This is an important, historic, river crossing. The early Indians used it for centuries and it became known as the Ute Crossing. In 1830-31 William Wolfskill and George Young crossed the river at this point and were given credit for being the first white men to do so. The Old Spanish Trail also crossed the river. Captain Gunnison and his men forded the river here, giving the crossing his name after he and some of his men were massacred by Indians a few days later. In 1883 the Denver and Rio Grande Railroad bridged the river in this area. For further history see also Green River.
S8,9,T21S,R16E,SLM; 4,079' (1,243). 27, 129, 209, 314, 494, 542, 546, 567.

GREEN RIVER is a historically important river in Utah. It originates in the Wind River Mountains of Wyoming and drains south to join the Colorado River in southwestern Utah at The Confluence. The river has had numerous names given by the early Indians, the Spanish Padres, and various mountain men, explorers, and military personnel. It has been referred to as the Seedskeedee-Agee (Prairie Hen), the Buenaventura

(Good Fortune), the Leichader, the Rio Verde (Green River), the Spanish River, and the Rio de Los Ciboles (Bison River). Despite these and other colorful names, the river ended up with the somewhat mundane name of Green River. This has posed several questions. Some say "The Green" refers to color of the water and others claim it is the vegetation along the river bank. Another report states that Ashley named the river for one of his friends living in St. Louis. Other reports say that a mysterious Mr. Green was an early trapper along the river. It has had a tumultuous history but today it is a river recognized for its electric power, recreation, and natural beauty. Backpackers, boaters, river rafters, and fishermen use the river and the surrounding area for adventure and recreation. There is still a strong sense of the unknown along stretches of The Green. See also Green River* (Utah).
27, 160, 172, 204, 240, 309, 371, 372, 496, 515(v7), 555(v28).

GREEN RIVER COUNTY was created in March 1852 and transferred to the Wyoming Territory in 1868. The county received its name from the Green River.
6.

GREEN WATER SPRING (San Juan) is near the head of Castle Creek, one mile down-canyon from the ruins that give the creek its name. The spring water has developed a beautiful green color from the green algae growing in the water. Irish Green Spring is in the vicinity.
T39S,R14E,SLM.

GREENDALE* (Daggett) was a small settlement of the 1880s where William R. Green and his sons Bill, Sanford, John, and their families lived. The settlement was centered on a fork of Skull Creek near the present-day Greens Lakes, where ranches, a school, and a post office developed. Today this alpine area is composed of campgrounds, summer homes, and a ranch or two.

SW¼,T2N,R21E,SLM. 172, 542.

GREENDALE (Daggett) is that area surrounding Greens Lakes, the early Greendale* site, and today's campgrounds and picnic sites. See Greendale*.
SE¼,T2N,R22E,SLM to SW¼,T2N,R21E, SLM.

GREENS* (Garfield) was in Main Canyon north of Escalante. Evan Green and his family lived in this small community.
602.

GREENS CANYON (Beaver) originates on the northwest slopes of Indian Peak in the Indian Peak Range. The canyon drains west into Hamlin Valley Wash. In the early 1880s John Green located on the spring at the head of the canyon.
T28,29S,R19,20W,SLM. 125.

GREENS CANYON (Sevier) originates five miles south of Ferron Mountain and drains into Muddy Creek.
S28,32,T20S,R5E,SLM.

GREENS CANYON SPRING (Beaver) is near the head of Greens Canyon (Beaver). See Greens Canyon (Beaver) for name source.

GREENS CORNER* (Cache) is a small community at the junction of US-89, US-91, and U-101 on the northeast outskirts of Wellsville*. Isaac Green settled there in 1859 and for a while it was also named Greenville*.
S35,T1E,R11N,SLM; 4,510' (1,375m).

GREENS LAKES (Daggett) are two small lakes west northwest of the junction of U-44 and U-260. One and one-half miles northeast is the Red Canyon Overlook visitor center. The lakes were originally developed in the 1880s from the surrounding marshlands by the Green families. William (Billy) Green, an old-timer and first forest ranger for the district, had the lakes named for him. Billy's son Sanford

developed the lakes as a resort. See Greendale*.
7,431' (2,265m). 100(v17), 172, 567. D.L. 6403.

GREENVILLE* (Beaver) is four and one-half miles southwest of Beaver* on U-21. In 1860 a group, including Samuel Edwards, and their families, came from Parowan* and Cedar City* to settle there. Three years before this time, they had come to cut grass for winter hay. The community is named for the lush growth of pasture and meadow grass in the region.
S25,T29S,R8W,SLM; 5,678' (1,731m). 100 (v5,17), 125, 355.

GREENVILLE* (Cache). See North Logan* (Cache).

GREENVILLE* (Cache). See Greens Corner* (Cache).

GREENWICH* (Piute) is on Otter Creek and U-62, five miles south of Koosharem*. Its early name was Box Creek* after Thomas Box and his family. The name Greenwich is recorded as an anglicized version of an earlier Indian name.
S28,29,T27S,R1W,SLM; 6,840' (2,085m). 100(v17), 360.

GREENWICH CREEK (Piute) originates at Milos Kitchen, four miles northwest of Koosharem*. The creek drains southeast into Grass Valley and is named for the community it serves.
S19,T26S,R1W,SLM to S9,T27S,R1W,SLM.

GREENWOOD* (Millard) is a ghost town site ten miles northwest of Fillmore* on the road to Delta*. The town boomed early and died quickly. It was named for Frank Greenwood, an early settler.
S31,T19S,R4W,SLM; 4,770' (1,454m). 567.

GREGORY BUTTE (Washington) is in the Kolob section of Zion National Park. Herbert E. Gregory was a well-known

U.S. Geological Survey geologist who worked extensively in Utah, especially in southern Utah.
SW¼,S2,T38S,R12W,SLM. 546, 600. D.L. 5701, 7700.

GREGORY NATURAL BRIDGE (Kane) is in Soda Gulch, a tributary of the Escalante River near its junction with the Colorado River. The name was given by Norman Nevills, a well-known river runner of Mexican Hat, Utah. The bridge is now under the waters of Lake Powell. See Gregory Butte for name source.
383(Sept. 1955), 546, 602.

GRIFFIN CREEK (Garfield) originates on top of Escalante Mountain at the western edge of the Aquarius Plateau. It drains south southwest into North Creek. See Griffin Top.

GRIFFIN TOP (Garfield) is a western section of Escalante Mountain, north of the head of Sweetwater Creek and the Escalante-Widtsoe Road. It has a north-south orientation and was the sheep range of Charles Griffin and his sons Ernest and Joseph.
S33,T34S,R1W,SLM; 10,000'-10,600' (3,048m-3,231m). 602.

GRIFFITH CREEK (Beaver) originates on the western slopes of the Tushar Mountains. It drains west into Poison Creek and was named for J. M. Griffiths, a sheep man who lived there in 1906.
S28,T28S,R5W,SLM. 125.

GRINDSTONE CANYON (Utah) originates on Grindstone Ridge and drains north into Hobble Creek. The natural stone in the canyon made excellent grindstones.
S5,9,T8S,R4E,SLM. 270.

GRIZZLY RIDGE (Beaver) is west of Puffer Lake in the Tushar Mountains between Three Creeks, North Fork, and Merchant Creek. It was here that a grizzly bear chased John C. Taylor up a tree in 1883.

S2,3,10,T29S,R5W,SLM; 9,550' (2,911m). 125.

GROSVENOR ARCH (Kane) is seventeen miles southeast of Cannonville* at the north end of the Cockscomb. The arch was named in honor of Dr. Gilbert Grosvenor, president of the National Geographic Society. The naming occurred after the society's 1947 expedition into the area.
S32,T38S,R1E,SLM. 382(v96).

GROUSE CREEK* (Box Elder) is in Grouse Creek Valley on the west banks of Grouse Creek. The area was settled in 1876 and received its name from the creek. Sage grouse were plentiful throughout this area. When the Cook family settled there, they used the name Cooksville*, a name that preceded Grouse Creek. Benjamin F. Cook dug the first well in the vicinity.
S2,T11N,R18W,SLM; 5,300' (1,615m). 139, 289, 542, 567.

GROUSE CREEK (Box Elder) originates at the junction of Cotton and Joe Dahar creeks in the extreme northwest section of Utah. It drains south through Grouse Creek Valley and disappears into the Grouse Creek Sinks in the desert west of Great Salt Lake. Early travelers found sage grouse plentiful in the region.
S13,T12N,R18W,SLM to T5N,R17W,SLM. D.L. 7804.

GROUSE CREEK MOUNTAINS (Box Elder) are in northwest Utah east of and parallel to Grouse Creek. The mountains are named for the creek.

GROUSE CREEK SINKS (Box Elder) is west of Great Salt Lake where Grouse Creek disappears into the desert soil.

GROUSE CREEK VALLEY (Box Elder) runs for twenty-one miles along middle Grouse Creek.

GROVE CREEK (Utah) originates on the west side of Mount Timpanogos and drains through Pleasant Grove* into Battle Creek. The first white settlers camped in a cottonwood grove by the creek. The area has now been absorbed into Pleasant Grove.
168.

GROVE FORT* (Utah) was built by the pioneers at the present Pleasant Grove* site on Grove Creek. See Grove Creek, Pleasant Grove*.

GROVER* (Wayne) is on the north side of the Aquarius Plateau (Boulder Mountain) on U-24. It was originally settled in 1880 and named for then U.S. President Grover Cleveland. The town had an earlier name of Carcass Creek* for the creek located adjacent to the town.
S3,T30S,R5E,SLM; 7,091' (2,161m). 100 (v17), 485, 542.

GROVER CANYON (Weber). See Grover Hollow.

GROVER HOLLOW (Weber) originates two miles west southwest of Eden* and drains into the Ogden River, North Fork. It was named for Joseph Grover, an original settler of Eden who hauled wood from the hollow.
S4,T6N,R1E,SLM to S34,T7N,R1E,SLM. 567.

GRUNDYVILLE* (Beaver). See Minersville*.

GRUVERS MESA (Emery) is thirty miles south of Green River* and west of the Trin-Alcove Bend on the Green River. Nearby to the south is Moonshine Springs where Gruver, an early moonshiner and bootlegger, made illegal liquor.
S17,18,T24S,R16E,SLM; 4,680' (1,426m). 102.

GUARDIAN ANGELS (Washington). See North and South Guardian angels.

GUILDER SLEEVE CANYON (Morgan) originates seven miles north of

Croydon*. It drains south into Lost Creek. MRN
S9,16,22,27,T5N,R4E,SLM.

GULL LAKE (**Uintah**) is on Lake Mountain on the south central slopes of the Uinta Mountains. It is one of the few places gulls are seen in this part of the country.
9,068' (2,764m).

GUN SPRING (**Beaver**) is on the eastern slope of the Wah Wah Mountains north of Revenue Basin. Elbert Cox claims this spring should be spelled with two n's and that it was developed in 1921 by T. W. Gunn.
S15,T28S,R15W,SLM; 6,000' (1,829). 125.

GUNLOCK* (**Washington**) is a small community on the Santa Clara River, twenty miles northeast of Santa Clara*. In 1857 Will Hamblin (Jacob's brother) was one of the first white settlers in the area. He was known by his friends as Gunlock or Gunshot Hamblin because he kept his guns in such good condition and was an acknowledged expert with a rifle. The settlement was named for him by a Mormon church authority, George Albert Smith, who visited the town in 1857. In 1862 the original settlement was relocated south to where the present community still stands.
T40S,R17W,SLM; 3,654' (1,114). 27, 542.

GUNNISON* (**Sanpete**) was established on US-89 and U-28 in 1859. Judge George Peacock of Manti* assigned the name to the community, honoring Captain John W. Gunnison of the U.S. railroad survey team working in that area. In August 1853 Gunnison and several of his men were murdered in western Utah by Pavant Indians. Gunnison also had an earlier name of Hog Wallow*.
S16,17,T19S,R1E,SLM; 5,100' (1,554m). 27, 289, 314, 542, 546, 569, 604. D.L. 6302.

GUNNISON BEND RESERVOIR (**Millard**) is two miles west of Delta* on the lower Sevier River. See Gunnison*

for name origin.
S10,11,15,T17S,R7W,SLM; 4,610' (1,405m).

GUNNISON BUTTE (**Emery**) is on the west side of the Green River as it emerges from the Book Cliffs. Green River City* is nearby. It was first named Cathedral Butte, then Major Powell changed it to its present name to honor Captain Gunnison. See Gunnison*.
S4,T20S,R16E,SLM; 5,230' (1,594m). 159, 160, 314, 496, 542.

GUNNISON CROSSING (**Grand**) is located at the Green River and Green River City* and was first known as the Ute Crossing. William Wolfskill and George Young have been credited with being the first white men to use the crossing, after they passed through during the winter of 1830-31. It became known as the Gunnison Crossing after Captain Gunnison and his party crossed the river here in 1853. Several days later, Gunnison and most of his men were murdered by Indians in the desert north of Sevier Lake. The crossing was a principal one on the Old Spanish Trail. The Denver and Rio Grande Railroad bridged the river here in 1883. See Green River* and Gunnison*.

GUNNISON ISLAND (**Box Elder**) is a small island one-half mile wide and one mile long (in high water), near the northwest shore of Great Salt Lake and south of Cub Island. As the water lowers, the island becomes a part of the west mainland. Gunnison Island is uninhabited, except by its famous bird population. In earlier times it was known for its guano deposits. In 1895 Alfred Lambourne lived on the island for fourteen months and wrote a book about it. The island was named for Lieutenant John W. Gunnison, second in charge to Captain Howard Stansbury, who named the island for Gunnison in his 1849 survey of the lake. Gunnison was later killed by the Indians. See Gunnison* and Gunnison Crossing.
T7N,R9W,SLM; 4,492' (1,369m). 100(v2), 133, 371, 492.

GUNNISON MASSACRE MONUMENT (**Millard**) is on the Sevier River between Crafts Lake and Alexander Lake, six and one-half miles southwest of Hinckley*. See Gunnison*.
S5,T18S,R8W,SLM; 4,555' (1,388m). 546.

GUNNISON RESERVOIR (**Sanpete**) is two miles northwest of Sterling* on the San Pitch River. It was named for Captain John W. Gunnison. See Gunnison*.
S16,21,28,T18S,R2E,SLM; 5,378' (1,639m).

GUNNISON VALLEY (**Emery, Grand**) is a large desert valley on both sides of the Green River where it emerges from the Book Cliffs. It was named for Captain John W. Gunnison. See Gunnison*.
T20,21S,R15-17E,SLM; 4,100'-4,400' (1,250m-1,341m).

GUNNISON VALLEY (**Sanpete, Sevier**) is on the upper Salina Creek drainage system, west of Island Lake and White Mountain. It was named for Captain John W. Gunnison. See Gunnison* for name source.
S13,14,23,24,25,26,T20S,R3E,SLM; 9,400' (2,865m).

GUNSIGHT BUTTE (**Kane**) is now an island in Gunsight Bay at the south end of Lake Powell. The profile of the butte has two peaks in alignment, resembling a gunsight.

GUNSIGHT FLAT (**Beaver**) is in the Tushar Mountains at the head of Three Creeks, South Fork, southwest of Puffer Lake. A break in the timberline gives one the impression of looking through a gunsight. It was named by James Puffer.
S27,T29S,R5W,SLM; 10,000' (3,048m). 567.

GUNSIGHT PEAK (**Cache**) is the highest peak on Clarkston Mountain. The peak is three miles west of Clarkston* and three miles north of Plymouth* and is well-known as a landmark for deer hunters.

S30,T14N,R2W,SLM; 8,244' (2,513m). 435.

GUSHER* (**Uintah**) was a small roadside settlement nine miles east of Roosevelt*. In derision it was originally named Sober City* because of the residents' drunkenness. The settlement was later named Moffat* for David H. Moffat, a railroad magnate who built the Moffat Tunnel in Colorado. The town was abandoned in 1901 and re-established in 1922 as Gusher when Robert Woodhave planned to develop a producing oil well—a real "gusher." The project never materialized.
T2S,R19E,SLM; 5,050' (1,539m). 100(v17), 494, 567.

GUYO CANYON (**Beaver**) originates at the southern end of the Mineral Mountains and drains southwest into the Beaver River.
S8,18,T29S,R9W,SLM.

GUYO SPRING (**Beaver**) is in Guyo Canyon.

GUYOT RANGE (**Juab, Millard**) was the name given the range of mountains by Captain Simpson to honor Professor Arnold Guyot of Princeton College. Guyot published the book *Earth and Man*, which made a deep impression on Simpson. The range extends from the south shore of the Great Salt Lake to the Sevier River. In general terms it was a combination of present-day Stansbury, Onaqui, and Sheeprock mountains.
477.

GYPSUM CANYON (**San Juan**) originates in Beef Basin northwest of the Abajo Mountains and drains northwest into the Colorado River at Cataract Canyon. While Powell's party was camped there in 1869 they experienced a dry wash flood that forced them to relocate their camp. After the flood they noticed a large quantity of gypsum deposited in the bottom of the gorge, so they named it Gypsum Canyon.
T32S,R17,18E,SLM. 159, 420, 496, 515.

- H -

HACKBERRY CANYON (Kane) originates nine miles south of Cannonville* and drains south into Cottonwood Canyon (Creek). Native hackberry (*Celtis reticulata*) is a common tree in the region.
S29,T38S,R1W,SLM to S9,T41S,R1W,SLM.

HADDEN HILLS (Emery) are a cluster of hills five miles southeast of Huntington* and three miles south southeast of Lawrence*. The hills are named after James McHadden who ran cattle in the region with Leander Lemmon in 1874.
S14,15,22,23,T18S,R9E,SLM; 5,800' (1,768m).

HADDEN HOLES (Emery) are seven miles southeast of Huntington* near the Hadden Hills and Hadden Flats. The Hadden Holes are a series of small water holes. See Hadden Hills.
S26,T18S,R9E,SLM; 5,590' (1,704m).

HADES CANYON (Duchesne) originates two miles southwest of Grandaddy Lake. Hades Creek drains through the canyon into the Duchesne River at the Hades Campground. The canyon is rugged, crooked, and steep. It was "hell" to get into, but, to avoid profanity, the word "Hades" was substituted in mixed company. The name held.
S17,T2N,R8W,USM to S26,T2N,R9W,USM. 595.

HADES CREEK (Duchesne) originates in the southwest section of the Uinta Mountains at Hades Pass. See Hades Canyon for name source.
S8,T2N,R8W,USM to S26,T2N,R9W,USM. 595.

HADES LAKE (Duchesne) is in the southwest section of the Uinta Mountains, one-fourth mile north of the head of Hades Canyon from which it receives its name. Three miles northeast is Grandaddy Lake.
S18,T2N,R8W,USM; 9,990' (3,045m).

HAILSTONE* (Wasatch) is the junction of US-40 and US-189, seven miles north of Heber City*. The junction's earliest name was Elkhorn*. The area was homesteaded in 1864 by William Paret Hailstone, Ann Davis Hailstone, and others. Mining, ranching, and lumbering were early incentives in settling in the area. It was during this time that the name was changed to Hailstone. In 1929 conditions changed when lumbering moved elsewhere. As this book goes to press, the nearby Jordanelle Dam construction is underway on the Provo River. The subsequent reservoir will cover the Hailstone site.
S32,T2S,R5E,SLM; 5,962' (1,817m). 100 (v17), 377, 546.

HALE* (Carbon) is a ghost town site near the Rio Grande Railroad on the Price River, two and one-half miles downstream from the Scofield Reservoir.
S11,T12S,R7E,SLM; 7,625' (2,324m). 89.

HALF MOON LAKE (Garfield) is midway between the headwaters of Boulder Creek, East and West forks, in the southern section of Boulder Mountain. Crescent and Circle lakes are near Half Moon Lake. The name reflects the shape of the lake.
10,800' (3,292m).

HALFWAY HOLLOW (Uintah) originates eleven miles west of Vernal* and drains southeast, crossing US-40 into Twelvemile Wash. In 1906 a saloon was established there called the Half-way Saloon.
S11,T6S,R20E,SLM (at mouth). 567.

HALL CREEK (Garfield) originates on Escalante Mountain at Griffin Top and drains south into Birch Creek of Main Canyon. It was named for the Hall family of Escalante*.
S1,T34S,R1W,SLM to S25,T34S,R1W,SLM. 12.

HALL MESA (Garfield) parallels the Grand Gulch, west of the mesa. See Halls Creek.
T37S,R10E,SLM.

HALLS CREEK (Garfield) originates at the Bitter Creek Divide on the east side of the Waterpocket Fold. It drains south southeast, paralleling the Fold, to enter Lake Powell (Colorado River) at Halls Crossing. The creek was previously known as Hoxie's Creek. See Halls Crossing*.
S13,T38S,R10E,SLM (at mouth).

HALLS CROSSING* (San Juan). In late 1879 the Mormon Hole-in-the-Rock expedition camped near the Dance Hall Rock waiting for the development of a safe crossing for the nearby Colorado River. Hall was an important part of this expedition. He stayed on at the Hole-in-the-Rock crossing hoping to make it an important one for emigrants and freighters traveling both ways across the river. The Hole-in-the-Rock crossing was used for more than a year until the travel began to decline. Hall then developed a better crossing some thirty-five miles upriver at what is today known as Halls Crossing. He settled at the mouth of Halls Creek in 1882 and ran a ferry crossing the Colorado River. Hall was well known for his projects and for his pioneering (he helped pioneer Parowan* and Escalante*). He also developed the boats used in ferrying across the Colorado River. After the dam was built and Lake Powell filled in the river and side crossings, Bull Frog Marina was developed on the west side of the lake and Halls Crossing on the east side of the lake at the end of U-263. Today a ferry makes regular crossings at this point. From 1881 to 1883 a small settlement was established at Halls Crossing, but it quickly faded into oblivion.
T38S,R11E,SLM; 3,725' (1,135m). 359, 567, 602.

HALLS DIVIDE (Garfield) is between the Water Pocket Fold and Hall Mesa.

HAMBLETON* (Sanpete). See Mount Pleasant* (Sanpete).

HAMBLIN* (Washington) was originally a fort built in 1856 by Jacob Hamblin at the north end of Mountain Meadows. As other settlers moved in, the name was reduced from Fort Hamblin* to Hamblin. The residents made a living selling butter and cheese to the emigrant trains passing through. Overgrazing and floods eventually caused the people to relocate and the site became a ghost town by 1890. The seventeen children who survived the Mountain Meadows Massacre in 1858 were brought here before they were eventually returned to their relatives in Arkansas. Today a small cemetery is all that is left of Hamblin.
S26,35,T37S,R16W,SLM; 5,800' (1,768m). 89, 100(v13), 154, 542, 546.

HAMLIN VALLEY (Iron) lies in a sixty-mile-long swath in western Millard, Beaver, and Iron counties, twelve miles north of Modena*. The valley is a good range for sheep and cattle—especially in winter.
T32,33S,R18,19W,SLM; ca. 6,200' (1,890m). 87, 567. D.L. 7402.

HAMLIN VALLEY WASH originates in the foothills north of Modena* in Iron County. It drains northwest, following

Hamlin Valley, into Nevada.
T25,32S,R18,20W,SLM.

HAMILTON* (Iron). See Hamilton
Fort* (Iron).

HAMILTON FORT* (Iron) is four miles
south of Cedar City*. The settlement was
founded in 1852 and known as Shirts
Creek* after the creek the fort was
founded on. The fort and creek were
both named for Peter Shirts, a noted
Mormon pioneer and scout. After the
Indian wars of 1853, Shirts sold the fort
and his land to his neighbor, John
Hamilton. At that time it was known as
Fort Walker*, supposedly in honor of the
noted Indian Chief Walker. It was during
the Indian wars with Chief Walker that
the settlers moved out and into nearby
Cedar City. When the settlers returned
in 1857 they renamed the settlement
Sidon* "after the Phoenician City of
Asia." In 1869 the settlers moved
one-half mile north of the old fort and
renamed the site Hamilton* in honor of
John Hamilton.
S31,T16S,R11W,SLM; 5,647' (1,721m). 27,
89, 100(v13), 289, 516, 567.

HAMMOND* (San Juan). See
Monticello* (San Juan).

HAMMOND CANYON (San Juan)
originates nine miles north northeast of
the Bears Ears and four miles north
northeast of Kigalia Ranger Station. The
canyon drains east into Cottonwood
Creek. Fletcher Hammond farmed this
area in earlier days.
NW¼,S7,T36S,R21E,SLM (at mouth). 100
(v17), 409.

HAMMOND GULCH (San Juan). See
Hammond Canyon.

HAMPTON* (Box Elder). See
Collinston* (Box Elder).

HAMPTON FORD* (Box Elder) is a
variant of Hampton* (Box Elder).

HANCOCK CANYON (Garfield) originates three miles south of Hancock Peak
and drains south southwest into Casto
Canyon. Alonzo Hancock ran his sheep
in the canyon. He also became lost in
the area and wandered around for
several days before he found his way
back.
T34S,R4W,SLM. 567.

HANCOCK CREEK (Garfield) drains in
part through Hancock Canyon (see
above).

HANCOCK FLAT (Garfield) is near
Hancock Canyon (see above).
T34S,R4W,SLM.

HANCOCK SPRING (Garfield) is near
the junction of Hancock Canyon and
Casto Canyon. See above.
T34S,R4W,SLM; 7,990' (2,435m).

HANCOCK PEAK (Iron) is at the head
of Hancock Canyon. See above.
T34S,R4W,SLM; 9,990' (3,045m).

HANGDOG CREEK (Grand) originates
on the southern slopes of the La Sal
Mountains and drains south southeast
into Twomile Creek. A dog was accidentally hung after being tied up and left
behind in a shed.
S3,T28S,R25E,SLM. 146.

HANGING ROCK (Summit) is ten
miles up Echo Canyon above Echo*. It is
a distinctive geological feature with a
small natural bridge nearby. This was the
setting for the Hanging Rock Pony
Express and Overland Stage station, also
known as Bromleys Station. Lee Daniels
was the first settler and James Bromley
ran the station for a while. See Bromleys
Canyon.
567.

HANGING ROCK STATION*
(Summit). See Hanging Rock.

HANKS STATION* (Salt Lake) was a
stop on the Overland Stage on Mountain

Dell Creek between Big and Little mountains. There is a Pony Express marker at the site. The Mountain Dell Reservoir is two miles southwest. The station was named for Ephraim K. Hanks who operated the station.
S36,T1N,R2E,SLM; 5,500' (1,676m). 89, 516.

HANKSVILLE* (Wayne) is fifty-three miles south southwest of Green River*. In its earlier days Hanksville had several other names, such as Graves Valley*, Hanks Place*, Pleasant Creek*, and Floral*. John Graves originally ran horses in the valley. In 1881, A. K. Thurber informed Ebeneazer Hanks—the man for whom the valley was named—of the possibilities the valley held. Hanks then persuaded others to join him in Parowan* before the group moved into and settled the valley. Among those who joined Hanks were the McDougalls, other Hanks, the Goalds, and Joe Sylvester. They arrived April 1, 1882. In its earlier days Hanksville, which was the closest settlement to the Robbers Roost country, was known as a hangout for Butch Cassidy and the Wild Bunch.
T28S,R11E,SLM; 4,125' (1,257m). 24, 485, 494, 542, 567.

HANNA* (Duchesne) is a small agricultural and ranching community. It is on U-35 near the Duchesne River, eleven miles northwest of Tabiona*. The community was named for William P. Hanna, the first postmaster.
T1N,T1S,R8W,USM; 6,850' (2,088m). 542.

HANS FLAT (Wayne) is a grazing area in the Robbers Roost country. It was named by the Biddlecomes for Hans Anderson, who worked for the old Biddlecome Ranch, today's Ekker Ranch.
SW¼,T29S,R16E,SLM. 25.

HANSEL MOUNTAIN (Box Elder) is north of the Great Salt Lake and east of Curlew Valley and has a northeast-southwest orientation. Monument Peak is the high point on this mountain located west of Hansel Valley from which it

is named. A Mr. Hansel was an early homesteader in the valley. Variants: Hansel Range, Summer Ranch Mountains.
T12,13,14N,R7,8,9W,SLM; 5,999' (1,828m). 100(v17), 567. D.L. 7702.

HANSEL VALLEY (Box Elder) is east of Hansel Mountain. See Hansel Mountain.
S12,T13N,R7W,SLM; 4,700' (1,433m).

HANSEN* (Box Elder). See Balfour*.

HANSEN HOLLOW (Cache) originates up Logan Canyon on the western slopes of Beaver Mountain. It drains south into the Logan River. Hans Hansen ran a dairy and logged out timber in the area. 567.

HANSEN LAKE (Box Elder) is four miles north of Mendon Peak at the north end of the Wellsville Mountains. It was named for John Hansen, an early settler of Mendon* who worked in the area between the lake and Mendon.
S34,T12N,R2W,SLM. 567.

HAPPY CANYON (Garfield, Wayne) originates at the junction of its Main and South Fork, about twelve miles southeast of the Ekker Ranch. The canyon drains west into the Dirty Devil River. One was always happy to get out of the canyon with all of its obstructions and difficulties.
T31S,R14E,SLM (at mouth). 102.

HARDESTY CREEK (Box Elder) originates in the Goose Creek Mountains northwest of the head of Grouse Creek and west of Cotton Thomas Basin. It drains northwest into Goose Creek in Nevada. It was named for an early squatter named Hardesty (Hardester), who ran his cattle along the creek.
T13,14N,R18,19W,SLM. 525, 567.

HARDSCRABBLE CANYON (Morgan) originates one mile northeast of the head of Salt Lake City's City Creek and drains north into East Canyon at Porterville*. It had an earlier name of Mill Creek. Lumber was removed from the canyon and subsequently made into thousands of railroad ties. The canyon was difficult to get into and out of. In other words, one had to "scrabble" to get back and forth. S34,T2N,R2E,SLM to S24,T3N,R2E,SLM. 378, 567.

HARDUP* (Box Elder) was a very small settlement at the mouth of Crystal Hollow at the east end of the Raft River Mountains. Six miles north northeast was Curlew Junction. MRN S31,T14N,R12W,SLM.

HARDWARE RANCH (Cache) is a large state-owned facility used for the preservation and winter feeding of elk that live wild in the surrounding region. It is on the Blacksmith Fork at the north end of Ant Valley, twenty-four miles southeast of Logan*. Alonzo Snow, a former owner of the ranch, was a hardware dealer in Brigham City*. He worked out of his store, "Box Elder Hardware." He hauled supplies from Brigham City to the loggers who lived within the vicinity of the ranch. S14,T10N,R3E,SLM; 5,587' (1,703m). 578.

HARKERS CANYON (Salt Lake) originates on the eastern slopes of the central Oquirrh Mountains. It drains northeast to enter Coon Creek near Bacchus*. Joseph Harker was an early settler in an area just west of the Jordan River. S34,T2S,R3W,SLM to S8,T2S,R2W,SLM.

HARLEY DOME (Grand) is a small community on US-6,50 (I-70) near the Colorado border. It was on the nearby sheep range that Harley Basker drilled a gas well. This was the beginning of what developed into the Harley Dome oil scandal that made national headlines during President Harding's term of office. S10,T19S,R25E,SLM; 4,740' (1,445m). 100 (v17), 146.

HARMONY* (Washington). See New Harmony*.

HARMONY FLAT (San Juan) lies at the head of Grand Gulch. In these pigmy forests of scattered cedars (*Juniperus*) and some pinyon pines (*Pinus*), an open area of grass or low shrubs was considered a "flat." The pioneers of New Harmony* in Washington County, who were part of the Hole-in-the-Rock expedition, used this flat for a period of time as they moved eastward to help settle the southeast corner of the state. T37S,R18E,SLM; 6,650' (2,027m).

HARMONY MOUNTAINS (Washington) are a comparatively small mountain range north of New Harmony* from which the mountains are named. T37S,R13W,SLM; 8,378' (2.554m).

HARMONY PARK (Beaver) is at the head of Beetle Creek and west of Big Flat. The park is one of several open, grassy flats in this spruce-fir vegetation zone. It was named by Louise Whittaker in 1922 for its peaceful and quiet atmosphere. S24,T29S,R5W,SLM; 10,000' (3,048m). 125.

HAROLD* (Utah) was a small mining community built in 1921 on Warm Spring Mountain east of Goshen*. Harold Raddatz had an interest in a mining venture there. The settlement was abandoned around 1925 when mining activities ceased. S8,T10S,R1E,SLM; 4,800' (1,463m). 516.

HARPER* (Box Elder). See Calls Fort* (Box Elder).

HARPER* (Duchesne) was a small settlement on Argyle Creek, two miles from where the creek empties into the Minnie Maude Creek in Nine Mile Canyon. Harper was on the stage road between Price* and Fort Duchesne*. S30,31,T11S,R14E,SLM. 516.

HARPOLE MESA (Grand) is in upper Castle Valley two miles south of the old Castleton* site. Joseph Harpole trapped, grazed his cattle, and homesteaded there.

S31,32,T25S,R24E,SLM; 7,150' (2,179m). 146.

HARRINGTON* (Beaver) grew up around the Harrington silver mine, four miles west of Milford* at the north end of the Star Range. Today it is a ghost town site. MRN
S9,T28S,R11W,SLM; 5,500' (1,676m). 567.

HARRIS WASH (Garfield) originates at Tenmile Spring at the mouth of Alvey Wash and drains southeast into the Escalante River. Thompson of the Powell survey called it Rocky Gulch or False Creek. Jimmy Llewellyn Harris had a homestead at the head of the wash where he ran his cattle. Today, with its wilderness canyon and numerous natural bridges and windows, it is a famous backpacking area. See Alvey Wash.
S15,T36S,R4E,SLM (head of wash). 555(v1), 602.

HARRISBURG* (Washington) is where Quail Creek crosses I-15, fourteen miles northeast of St. George*. When Moses Harris first settled on the site in 1859, it was on Cottonwood Creek where the Harrisburg Junction on I-15 is presently located. At that time the settlement was known as Cottonwood*. As the community developed, it gradually assumed Moses' name and became Harrisburg.
S23,T41S,R14W,SLM. 89, 100(v13), 289, 516, 542.

HARRISBURG JUNCTION (Washington) is four miles southwest of Harrisburg* at the junction of I-15 and U-17. See Harrisburg.
S4,T42S,R14W,SLM; 3,140' (957m).

HARRISVILLE* (Washington). See Harrisburg* (Washington).

HARRISVILLE* (Weber) is two miles north northwest of Ogden*. It was first settled in the spring of 1850 by Urban Stewart. During an altercation Stewart killed Indian Chief Terikee and was forced to abandon his farm. Then, in the

spring of 1851, Martin H. Harris, a nephew of Martin Harris—one of the three witnesses to the Book of Mormon—built the first home there.
S6,T7N,R1W,SLM; 4,290' (1,308m). 100(v5), 274, 289, 542, 567.

HARTFORD* (Duchesne) was somewhere between Myton* and Roosevelt*. This early Uinta Basin settlement did not survive. MRN
89, 165.

HARTLEYS CANYON (Juab) originates four miles northeast of Levan*. It drains west southwest into the Juab Valley and was named for Heber Wilson Hartley, an early Levan historian who settled there in 1868.
S21,22,23,T14S,R1E,SLM. 360. D.L. 8304.

HASTINGS PASS (Tooele) is in the Cedar Mountains south of Low* and Low Pass on the eastern border of the Great Salt Lake Desert. The Lansford Hastings emigrant party of 1846 used this pass.
S24,25,T1S,R10W,SLM; 5,850' (1,783m). 371, 506, 567.

HAT FLAT (San Juan) is six miles northeast of the San Juan River between Slickhorn Canyon and the Grand Gulch. The name comes from the hat-shaped rock in the center of this feature.
T39S,R16,17E,SLM; 5,517' (1,682m).

HAT ISLAND (Box Elder) is four miles north of Carrington Island in the Great Salt Lake. The island has a conical hat shape and was named by Stansbury's men, who surveyed the lake in 1849-50.
27, 133, 314, 371.

HAT ROCK (San Juan) is a small conical butte in the center of Hat Flat. See Hat Flat.

HATCH* (Garfield) is between Panguitch* and Long Valley Junction* on US-89. In 1872 the town of Aaron*, also called Asay*, was settled near the mouth

of Asay Creek. Other early settlements in this area along the Sevier River, Asay Creek, and Mammoth Creek were Proctor*, Castle*, Johnson*, and Hatchtown*. Hatchtown was settled by Meltiar Hatch, Sr., and his two wives, Parmelia Snyder Hatch and Mary Ann Ellis Hatch. Flooding and other problems forced these early communities to group together and settle one and one-half miles south of Hatchtown. This single community then took the name of Hatch, which was incorporated on January 3, 1934.
S29,T36S,R5W,SLM; 6,917' (2,108m). 145, 289.

HATCH CANYON (Garfield) originates at the junction of its North and South forks, three miles northwest of Fiddler Butte. The French Springs are fifteen miles northeast. The canyon drains west into the Dirty Devil River.
T31S,R14E,SLM.

HATCH CANYON (Piute, Wayne) originates on the west side of the Parker Plateau, overlooking Grass Valley. It drains north northeast, veering sharply to the west into Grass Valley.
S14,T27S,R1W,SLM (at mouth).

HATCH MOUNTAIN (Garfield) is six miles southeast of Panguitch Lake and four miles west of Hatch*. Ira Hatch bought land and ran livestock there.
SW¼,T36S,R6W,SLM; 8,657' (2,639m). 508.

HATCH POINT (San Juan) is a massive landform extending north between the Colorado River and Kane Springs Canyon. It was named for Alonzo Hatch. See Hatch Wash.
T27-29½S,R21-22E,SLM; 5,800'-6,000' (1,768m-1,829m).

HATCH RANCH CANYON (San Juan) originates at the south end of Hatch Point, just north of the Wind Whistle Campground and west of Hatch Rock. The canyon drains northeast into Hatch Wash. See Hatch Wash.

S25,T29S,R22E,SLM (at mouth).

HATCH ROCK (San Juan) is south of the junction of Hatch Wash and Hatch Ranch Canyon. Nearby is Wind Whistle Draw. The rock was named for Alonzo Hatch, who had a ranch in the vicinity where he ran his cattle.
S36,T29½S,R22E,SLM; 6,216' (1,895m). 514.

HATCH TOWN* (Uintah). See Vernal*.

HATCH TRADING POST* (San Juan) is at the southeast section of McCracken Mesa and eight miles west of Hovenweep National Monument of the Square Tower Group. This early trading post established by Ira Hatch still exists today.
S13,T39S,R24E,SLM; 4,680' (1,426m). 578.

HATCH WASH (San Juan) originates at the junction of East Canyon Wash, Lightning Draw, and Peters Canyon, two miles east of US-160. The wash drains northwest into Kane Springs Canyon. Alonzo Hatch ran his cattle in this area during the 1880s.
S31,T31S,R24E,SLM to S6,T28S,R22E,SLM. 475.

HATCHTOWN* (Garfield) was a forerunner of present-day Hatch* and was one and one-half miles southeast of the town. See Hatch* (Garfield).

HATTON* (Millard) is a small agricultural community three miles northwest of Kanosh*. The town was originally named Corn Creek* for the creek where the early settlers started their community. The name was later changed to Petersburg* to honor their first postmaster, Peter Robison. A new postmaster, Richard Hatton, took Robison's place and the community again changed its name, this time to Hatton. It was a main stop on the Overland Stage route to Pioche, Nevada.
S6,T23S,R5W,SLM; 4,820' (1,469m). 89, 100 (v13), 542, 567.

HAWKINS GROVE* (Weber). See Huntsville* (Weber).

HAY SPRINGS* (Beaver) is fifteen miles southwest of Minersville. The settlement was a camp stop for freighters and travelers en route to and from the eastern Nevada mines. They were also part of an early horse ranch. The Hay Springs name indicates the heavy growth of natural grasses and plentiful water found in the area during the pioneer freighting days. The springs had an earlier name of Troy.
S10,15,T29S,R11W,SLM; 4,997' (1,523m). 355.

HAY TOWN* (Box Elder). See Portage.

HAYDEN* (Duchesne) was three miles east of present-day Neola* and ten miles north of Roosevelt*. It was a temporary settlement with great plans during the Uinta Basin land rush of 1905-6. The community did not succeed as a settlement but was good cattle land with excellent pasturage and grasslands. The majority of Hayden's residents moved to nearby Neola and today it is a ghost town site. The name source for Hayden is indefinite. One cluster of references suggests it was named for its excellent hay and grasslands. Another suggests it was named for the nearby peak named for F. V. Hayden, a noted topographic engineer of early U.S. government surveys. Hayden's party did much of the surveying in this region.
S34,35,T1N,R1W,USM; 5,860' (1,786m). 89, 100(v13,17), 165, 289, 298, 567.

HAYDEN FORK (Summit) originates at the west end of the Uinta Mountains on the western slopes of Hayden Peak. It drains north, combining with the Stillwater Fork to form the headwaters of the Bear River. See Hayden Peak for name source.
S13,T9E,R1S,SLM to S32S,T2N,R10E,SLM.

HAYDEN LAKE (Summit) is at the west end of the Uinta Mountains, one and one-half miles west of Hayden Peak. See the peak for the name source.
S14,T1S,R9E,SLM; 10,420' (3,176m).

HAYDEN PASS (Duchesne, Summit) is on U-150 at the west end of the Uinta Mountains, two and one-half miles east of Mirror Lake. See Hayden Peak for name source.
S23,T4N,R9W,USM; 10,347' (3,154m).

HAYDEN PEAK (Summit) is at the west end of the Uinta Mountains, four miles northeast of Mirror Lake and one mile northwest of McPheters Lake. The peak was named for Ferdinand V. Hayden, a geologist and topographic engineer. Hayden was in charge of the U.S. Fortieth Parallel Survey when he and his team of surveyors accomplished much of the early surveying work in this region.
12,479' (3,804m). 172, 298, 309, 530, 546.

HAYMAKER BENCH (Garfield) lies southeast of The Hogsback and east of Calf Creek. It was named for Charley Haymaker who lived there with his family and farmed parts of the Escalante River bottoms.
S6,T35S,R5E,SLM; 5,980' (1,823m). 12.

HAYSTACK LAKE (Summit) is at the west end of the Uinta Mountains, one-half mile east of the south end of Haystack Mountain. Washington Lake is one and one-half miles north. The lake received its name from the mountain.
S7,T2S,R9E,SLM; 9,950' (3,033m).

HAYSTACK MOUNTAIN (Sanpete) is southeast of Ephraim* and has the general rounded shape of a haystack.
S28,T17S,R4E,SLM; 10,381' (3,164m). 152.

HAYSTACK MOUNTAIN (Summit) is at the west end of the Uinta Mountains, one and one-half miles south of Mount Watson. It has the general rounded shape of a haystack.
S1,12,13,T2S,R8E,SLM; 10,985' (3,348m).

HAYSTACK PEAK (**Juab**) is in the Deep Creek Range, one and one-half miles north northeast of Ibapah Peak. S20,T11S,R18W,SLM; 12,020' (3,664m).

HEAD OF PINE GROVE SPRING (**Beaver**) is at the head of Pine Grove, which drains west into the Pine Grove Reservoir and the Pine Valley. S35,T28S,R16W,SLM; 7,600' (2,316m).

HEAD OF WILLOW CREEK SPRING (**Beaver**) is in the Wah Wah Mountains northwest of Lamerdorf Peak, near the head of Willow Creek. S2,T29S,R16W,SLM; 8,100' (2,469m).

HEADQUARTERS VALLEY (**Kane**) is at the north end of the Cockscomb, south of Canaan Peak. The valley extends south to Headquarter Springs and Cabin, east of Butler Valley. This area served as the headquarters for the early Mormon church herds that were grazed there in pioneer days. T38S,R1E,SLM; 6,455' (1,967m). 578.

HEAPS CANYON (**Garfield**) originates on Escalante Mountain southwest of Escalante*. It drains east into lower Main Canyon and was named for the Heaps brothers who lived in the area. S20,T35S,R1E,SLM to S13,T35S,R1E,SLM.

HEART LAKE (**Duchesne**). See Scout Lake.

HEBER* (**Wasatch**) is twenty-eight miles northeast of Provo* on US-189. The area was initially settled in 1858 and known as Provo Valley* until 1861. Most of the original group of settlers to Provo Valley were Mormon converts from England, where Heber C. Kimball was instrumental in converting many people to the Mormon faith. For this reason the early community was named Heber, to honor Heber C. Kimball. S5,6,T4S,R5E,SLM; 5,595' (1,705m). 100 (v5), 289, 377, 546, 567. D.L. 6802.

HEBER MOUNTAIN (**Wasatch**) is east of Heber Valley and is named for the town. S31,T4S,R7E,SLM; 10,207' (3,111m).

HEBER VALLEY (**Wasatch**) rests in the heart of Utah's "Switzerland"—Heber*, Midway*, and Charleston* are located in this valley. The earliest name for the area was Round Prairie. The Provo Valley was a subsequent name that gradually changed after 1861 when Heber City* was named for Heber C. Kimball. See Heber*. T3S,R5E,SLM; ca. 5,600' (1,707m). 309, 477, 546.

HEBERVILLE* (**Washington**). See Price City* (Washington).

HEBRON* (**Washington**). Today Hebron is a ghost town site at the junction of the west and south forks of Shoal Creek, up-creek from Enterprise*. Hebron's first settlers were the Pulsipher brothers, John and Charles, who named the settlement Shoal Creek*. In 1866 a fort was built and in 1868 the townsite was surveyed and the name was changed to Hebron after ancient Hebron in Palestine. John Pulsipher was thinking of Abraham of old who took families, cattle, and horses, and traveled until he found a suitable place to settle—then called it Hebron. The community grew because of mining enterprises at nearby Silver Reef* and Pioche* in Nevada. After the 1902 earthquake, which extensively damaged the town, most of the residents moved down-canyon seven miles to Enterprise. The 1906 San Francisco earthquake demolished what remained of Hebron. The people who had remained were already suffering from restricted land and water problems such as a large gully washing down what was once Main Street. Finally, the rest of the people moved down-canyon to Enterprise because it remained undamaged after the San Francisco disaster.

181

S12,T37S,R18W,SLM; 5,483' (1,671m). 89, 100(v13), 154, 289, 516, 546.

HEINER* (Carbon) is a ghost town at the mouth of Panther Canyon between Castle Gate* and Helper*. The settlement was named Panther* after the adjacent coal mine when it was first settled in 1911. The name was later changed to Carbon* as a reminder of the town's ties to the coal industry. In 1914 the name was changed to Heiner for Moroni Heiner, former vice president of the U.S. Fuel Company. With improved transportation and decreasing coal use, the town faded in the 1950s.
S12,T13S,R9E,SLM; 5,984' (1,824m). 89, 516, 542, 546.

HELIOTROPE MOUNTAIN (Sanpete) is on the summit of the Wasatch Plateau between Ferron* and Mayfield*. A heliotrope is any plant that turns toward the sun. It is also a common name for flowers of the genus *Heliotropium*, several species of which are found in Utah.
S34,35,T19S,R4E,SLM; 11,130' (3,392m).

HELL CANYON (Beaver) is in the South Hills south of Beaver*. The canyon drains northeast into Nevershine Hollow where I-15 passes.
S27,T30S,R7W,SLM.

HELL CANYON (Morgan) originates at the southern end of Horse Ridge on the Morgan-Weber County line. It drains south into Lost Creek. When one hunts deer and is successful down in the canyon, it's hell to get the deer out.
S12,T6N,R4E,SLM to S18,T5N,R5E,SLM. 567.

HELL HOLE (Beaver) is on the western slopes of the Tushar Mountains between the north and east forks of Baker Canyon.
S11,T29S,R6W,SLM; 8,800' (2,682m).

HELL HOLE CANYON (Piute) originates on the Sevier Plateau, one and one-half miles south of Tibadore Canyon

and seven miles east of the north end of the Piute Reservoir. It drains west into Swift Spring Creek and is a deep, rocky canyon that is difficult to get into or out of.
S31,T28S,R2W,SLM to S5,T29S,R2½W,SLM.

HELL ROARING CANYON (Grand) originates eight miles west of Arths Pasture at the mouth of Dubinky Wash and drains southwest into the Green River. During storms, roaring torrents of muddy water rush down the rock-ribbed canyon, creating a tremendous noise.
T25,26S,R18E,SLM. 508.

HELL'N MARIA CANYON (Millard) originates in the Sawtooth Mountains of the House Range, three miles southeast of Notch Peak. It drains southwest into the White Valley (Tule) near where US-6,50 passes. This rugged canyon is very difficult to maneuver in and out of.
S36,T19S,R14W,SLM.

HELLS BACKBONE (Garfield) is on the south slope of the Aquarius Plateau with Death Hollow on one side and Sand Canyon on the other. "[It] is a knife-edged ridge with a bridge on top, spanning a streamless crevice no wider than the bridge itself" (546, p. 340). Both sides have precipitate walls that drop hundreds of feet. The bridge was built and named by the U.S. Civilian Conservation Corp in the early 1940s.
T35S,R3E,SLM; 8,854' (2,699m). 12, 145, 546, 602.

HELLS KITCHEN (Summit) is in the southwest section of the Uinta Mountains near the head of Smith and Morehouse Creek. It is a grazing area where sheepherders have found that once their sheep are in the area, they are difficult to move out.
S20,21,T1S,R8E,SLM; 10,000' (3,048m).

HELLS KITCHEN PARK (Uintah) is in the southeast section of the Uinta Mountains, three miles northeast of Paradise Park Reservoir. The area is

swampy and considered treacherous for grazing.
T4N,R1E,USM; 10,200' (3,109m).

HELPER* (Carbon) is on US-6,50 and U-244, seven miles northwest of Price*. The town was first established in 1883 with an earlier name of Pratts Landing*. In 1892, the town became known as Helper when extra engines, or "helper engines," stored there were attached to loaded trains in order to provide increased power for getting up the heavy grade to Soldier Summit*. The engines then returned to Helper under compression, using no power. This occurred during the period when steam engines controlled the rails. Today, with the heavier diesel engines and improved railroad grades, the helper engines are rarely used.
S13,24,T13S,R9E,SLM; 5,900' (1,798m). 100(v17), 289, 542, 546.

HENDERSON* (Garfield). See Osiris*.

HENDERSON CANYON (Garfield) originates on the southwest slopes of Escalante Mountain and drains southwest into the Paria River. See Osiris*.
S12,T37S,R3W,SLM (at mouth).

HENDERSON CREEK (Garfield) originates on the southwest slopes of Escalante Mountain. The creek drains southwest through Henderson Canyon into the Paria River. See Osiris*.

HENEFER* (Summit) is on I-80 between Echo* and Morgan*. It was first settled by two brothers, James and Richard (William?) Henefer. They established a blacksmith shop there in 1859 on the old Overland Stage Road. It was called Heneferville* until the late 1860s when the name was shortened.
S4,9,T3N,R4E,SLM; 5,325' (1,623m). 100 (v17), 289, 447, 542, 567.

HENEFER VALLEY (Summit) is located along the Weber River adjacent to Henefer*.

HENRIEVILLE* (Garfield) is three miles east of Cannonville* on U-12. The settlement was named for James Henrie, early Mormon settler and the first president of the Mormon Panguitch Stake. The first settlers arrived from Cannonville in 1878.
S22,27,T37S,R2W,SLM. 145, 542, 546. D.L. 6504.

HENRIEVILLE CREEK (Garfield) originates at the summit of Escalante Mountain (the west section of the Aquarius Plateau). The creek drains southwest through Henrieville* into the Paria River. See Henrieville*.
S36,T36S,R1W,SLM to S31,T37S,R2W,SLM.

HENRY MOUNTAINS (Garfield) are west of the Colorado River and south of the Fremont and Dirty Devil rivers. The mountains did not appear on any maps prior to 1869. At that time they were described as five great masses of laccolithic lava wrapped in sedimentary beds and cut through with heavy erosion. Major Powell's men first saw the mountains in their expedition down the Colorado River. At that time they made note of them as the Unknown Mountains. On Powell's second expedition the mountains were named the Henry Mountains, honoring the secretary of the Smithsonian Institution and noted physicist, Joseph Henry. Powell also named one of the peaks in the group for his sister Ellen, who was also the wife of Almon Thompson, Powell's field director.
T33S,R11E,SLM. 159, 160, 217, 422, 496, 515, 602.

HENRYS FORK (Daggett, Summit, and into Wyoming) originates at Henrys Fork Lake of the Red Castle Lakes group in the Uinta Mountains. It flows north into Wyoming, then southeast into the Flaming Gorge Reservoir at the Utah-Wyoming border. In 1823 General Ashley named this creek for his good friend and business associate in the fur-trading business, Major Andrew Henry.
172, 314, 371, 546.

HENRYS FORK LAKE (Summit) is on the northwest slopes of the Uinta Mountains at the head of Henrys Fork. Nearby are Lakes Blanchard, Grass, and Dollar. See Henrys Fork.
10,820' (3,298m). 129, 309.

HENRYS FORK PARK (Summit) is in the north central section of the Uinta Mountains as a low, marshy area along both sides of Henrys Fork.
S24,25,26,T3N,R14W,USM; 9,000' (2,743m).

HEPWORTH WASH (Washington). The mouth is at the west end of the Mount Carmel highway tunnel in Zion National Park. Thornton Hepworth was an early settler and Mormon bishop of nearby Springdale*.
T41S,R10W,SLM (at mouth).

HERB EYRE HOLLOW (Beaver) is in the southwest section of the Mineral Mountains, south of Cave Canyon. Herb Eyre was an early pioneer in Minersville*.
S13,T29S,R10W,SLM.

HERRIMAN* (Salt Lake) is in the southwest sector of the Salt Lake Valley on Butterfield Creek. Twenty-two miles northeast is Salt Lake City*. The town was first called Butterfield* for Thomas Butterfield, who settled there in 1849. Shortly after 1858 Butterfield was renamed Herriman for Henry Herriman, a prominent resident.
S35,T3S,R2W,SLM; 4,931' (1,503m). 252, 289, 360, 542, 567.

HESSVILLE* (Box Elder). See East Plymouth*.

HI LOW LAKE (Beaver) is near the mouth of the Beaver River, South Fork. The Beaver Fish and Game Club developed a small lake there that is the higher of two lakes owned by George P. Low.
S25,T29S,R6W,SLM; 7,500' (2,286m). 125.

HIAWATHA* (Carbon) is a coal mining town fifteen miles southwest of Price on U-122. Hiawatha was an important Mohawk Indian chieftain in the League of the Iroquois Indians. He also was the hero of Longfellow's famous poem of the same name. Hiawatha's name was given to a prominent Pennsylvania coal mine, then transferred to the Utah coal mine, and from the mine to the local community.
S27,34,T15S,R8E,SLM; 7,090' (2,161m). 89, 100(v17), 314, 607.

HICKERSON PARK (Daggett) is on Sheep Creek, North Fork, in the north central section of the Uinta Mountains. Jimmie Hickerson, a cowboy, built a cabin in this area in the 1890s in order to develop his holdings.
S19,T2N,R18E,SLM; 9,000' (2,743m). 172.

HICKMAN BRIDGE (Wayne) is a prominent natural bridge in Capitol Reef National Park. Early topographers called the bridge Broad Arch for its large size. The name was later changed to honor Joe Hickman, who spent twenty-five years promoting Capitol Reef as a national monument. The bridge was discovered in 1940 by Owen Hibbert, W. C. Chesnut, and Fred Fagagreen.
NE¼,S14,T29S,R6E,SLM; 5,678' (1,731m). 85, 546.

HICKMAN CANYON (Piute) originates on the southern slopes of Forshea (Forshee) Mountain of the Sevier Plateau. It drains south into Kingston Canyon. The Hickman family settled this area in the center of Kingston Canyon early in its history.
S1,12,24,T30S,R2½W,SLM. 567.

HICKMAN CANYON (Tooele) originates six miles southeast of Deseret Peak in the Stansbury Mountains. It drains east northeast into Rush Valley north of St. John*. Bill Hickman was a well-known personality in Mormon church

history. He ran his cattle in the Hickman Canyon area.
S6,T5S,R6W,SLM to S32,T4W,R5W,SLM. 100(v17).

HICKORY* (**Beaver**) is a ghost town site five miles northwest of Milford* on the old railroad bed. It was named for George Hickory, who established the nearby Old Hickory Mine in 1882. The railroad bed ran from the mine to join the Frisco branch of the Los Angeles and Salt Lake Railroad; Hickory was at the junction of these two railroads.
S27,T27S,R11W,SLM; 5,320' (1,622m). 125, 516.

HICKORY WASH (**Beaver**) originates south of the Rocky Range, five miles northwest of Milford*. It drains east into the Beaver River. See Hickory* for name source.
S26,27,T27S,R11W,SLM.

HIDDEN LAKE (**Kane**) is in Long Valley one-half mile north of the mouth of Lydias Canyon and two miles north of Glendale*. A woolen factory was built there in 1882 as part of the United Order program and it was called the Factory Farm*. The people who worked in the factory lived nearby. Baptisms were conducted in the lake. Later the name of the lake became Hidden Lake because of its solitary location as part of a recreation site.
S11,T40S,R7W,SLM; 6,013' (1,833m). 455.

HIDDEN LAKE (**Summit**) is a difficult lake to locate in the central section of the Uinta Mountains on the headwaters of Sheep Creek, Middle Fork. Spirit Lake is in the vicinity.
10,250' (3,124m).

HIDDEN LAKE (**Summit**) is in the southwest section of the Uinta Mountains near the head of the Provo River, North Fork. One and one-half miles north are Duck and Island lakes. Hidden Lake is difficult to see until you are right upon it.
S10,T2S,R1E,SLM; 9,750' (2,972m).

HIDDEN LAKE (**Summit**) is an isolated and difficult lake to locate at the west end of the Uinta Mountains between the west end of Notch Mountain and Mount Watson. It drains into the Weber River, Middle Fork.
S25,T1S,R8E,SLM; 10,260' (3,127m). 298, 530.

HIDDEN LAKE (**Summit**) is in the north central section of the Uinta Mountains, five miles northwest of North Burro Peak on the headwaters of Beaver Creek, Middle Fork. It is a lake that is difficult to reach.
10,148' (3,093m).

HIDDEN LAKE (**Summit**) is in an isolated cove in the southwest section of the Uinta Mountains, two and one-half miles southwest of the mouth of Smith and Morehouse Creek.
S6,T1S,R7E,SLM; 7,230' (2,204m).

HIDDEN VALLEY (**Duchesne**) is a small isolated valley one mile in diameter, two and one-half miles southeast of Tabiona*.
S33,34,T1S,R7W,USM; 6,600' (2,012m).

HIDEOUT CANYON (**Daggett**) is in the northeast section of the Uinta Mountains, now part of the Flaming Gorge National Recreation Area. To the north is Kingfisher Canyon, part of the earlier turbulent Green River that used to flow through the area canyons. From the 1870s into the early twentieth century, this region was a perfect hideout for cattle rustlers, bank robbers, and other outlaws. The Wild Bunch and the Powder Springs Gang, among others, frequently hid out here to camp, rest up, and hide from the law.
S11,12,13,T2N,R20E,SLM. 100(v17).

HIDEOUT CANYON (**San Juan**) originates eight miles north northeast of the Natural Bridges National Monument near Woodenshoe Buttes. It drains southwest into White Canyon. The region around the canyon was a hideout for outlaws and

their rustled horses and cattle.
S35S,R18E,SLM to S19,T36S,R17E,SLM.

HIDEOUT MESA (San Juan) is on the southeast slopes of the La Sal Mountains between Hop Creek and Trinity Canyon. The name comes from outlaws on the run who hid out on the mesa. One particular incident is cited where a bank robber from Colorado recuperated here for a period of time after being wounded.
S20,T28S,R26E,SLM; 7,375' (2,248m). 146.

HIGH CREEK (Cache) originates in the mountains north of Mount Magog and Naomi Peak. It drains northwest, then southwest into the Cub River. In the early 1800s the Hudson Bay Company trappers and traders called it the Gros Bois. During melt or flood time the creek rises dramatically.
S15,T14N,R1E,SLM (at mouth). 147(30 April 1976), 567.

HIGH PLATEAUS OF UTAH is a term that was developed and used by Captain Clarence Edward Dutton of the U.S. Geological Survey. Dutton studied and wrote a comprehensive report on prominent Utah geologic features. The Aquarius, Awapa, and Sevier plateaus are examples included in his 1880 report. Captain Dutton wrote, "The Plateau Country of the west is, I firmly believe, destined to become one of the most instructive fields of research which geologists in the future will have occasion to investigate. Thus by faults and monoclinal flexures, by deep canyons, and by lines of cliffs the surface is cut into a great number of plateaus" (175, p. ix). 175, 496.

HIGHLAND* (Utah) is a small community on U-74 two miles north of American Fork*. It was incorporated on July 13, 1977. The location on the upper benchland above the valley gives the name.
S2,T5S,R1E,SLM; 4,836' (1,474m).

HIGHLAND BOY* (Salt Lake) was a small mining community, one and one-fourth miles up-canyon from Bingham* in Carr Fork. The community received its name from the nearby mine of the same name. Highland Boy's history was closely tied to Bingham. The settlement no longer exists.
89.

HILGARD MOUNTAIN (Sevier) is ten miles northeast of Fish Lake at the head of North Last Chance Creek. It was named for J. E. Hilgard, a prominent official in the United States Coast and Geodetic Survey.
S35,T24S,R3E,SLM; 11,533 (3,515m). 497. D.L. 7103.

HILL CREEK (Grand, Uintah) originates at the Roan Cliffs on the south ridge of the East Tavaputs Plateau. It drains north through the Weaver Reservoir to join Willow Creek. The country it drains through is quite hilly.
S25,T18S,R19E,SLM to S27,T10S,R20E, SLM. 493, 567.

HILLSDALE* (Garfield) is between Panguitch* and Hatch* near the junction of US-89 and U-12. There are two sources listed for the name. (1) It was named for the hills surrounding the community. (2) It was named for Joel Hills Johnson, an early settler. The second source is preferred. The community was settled in 1871 under the leadership of George Deliverance Wilson. Wilson and Johnson established a sawmill in that same year.
S2,T36S,R5W,SLM; 6,780' (2,067m). 89, 100 (v13), 145, 289, 494, 516, 542, 567.

HILLSDALE CANYON (Garfield) originates on the western slopes of the Paunsaugunt Plateau at the Sunset Cliffs. It drains northwest into the Sevier River near Hillsdale* and receives its name from the community it serves.
S14,T36S,R4½W,SLM to S2,T36S,R5W,SLM.

HINCKLEY* (**Millard**) is five miles southwest of Delta*. It is a small agricultural community that was established as an outgrowth of nearby Deseret*. In 1877 it was named Bloomington*. Then in 1891 it was renamed Hinckley, honoring Ira N. Hinckley, who was president of the Mormon Millard Stake at that time. S19,20,T17S,R7W,SLM; 4,600' (1,402m). 494, 507, 542, 567.

HITE* (**Garfield**) is now under the waters of Lake Powell. It was located near the mouth of the Dirty Devil River across from the mouth of White Canyon. Hite was an early Colorado River outpost anciently used by the Indians as a Colorado River crossing. In the early 1870s, Cass Hite arrived in the area. He was a prospector, a former member of Quantrill's Civil War guerrillas, and was considered an outlaw. He settled at the site and became friendly with the Indians. The early whites called this Colorado River crossing the Dandy Crossing because it was relatively easy to get across. In 1881-83 a small settlement was established, centering around the ferry, and Hite's name became attached to it. The ferry was discontinued when the Glen Canyon Dam was built. Hite's name was transferred to a newly established marina, since the original Hite community is now under water. T34S,R13E,SLM; 3,480' (1,061m). 25, 303, 314, 360, 516, 546, 555(v15).

HITE CROSSING (**Garfield**). See Hite*, Dandy Crossing.

HITTLE BOTTOM (**Grand**) is in Professor Valley upriver from Moab* and ten miles southwest of Dewey*. A Mr. Hittle settled there to farm but became discouraged and moved on, even though his name remained. S35,36,T23S,R23E,SLM; 4,100' (1,250m). 146.

HOBBLE CREEK (**Utah**) See Hobble Creek Canyon.

HOBBLE CREEK* (**Utah**). See Springville*.

HOBBLE CREEK CANYON (**Utah**) originates five miles east of Springville* at the junction of the Left and Right forks. The creek drains west through Springville into Utah Lake. In February 1849 Barney Ward and Oliver B. Huntington passed through the area on a trading expedition with the Indians. They camped in the foothills east of present-day Springville and hobbled their horses for the night. The horses broke free from their hobbles and moved up toward the canyon, where Huntington caught up with and recovered them. From this incident the canyon became known as Hobble Creek Canyon. The early Spanish name for the canyon was San Nicolas. S32,T7S,R4E,SLM to S1,T8S,R3E,SLM. 275, 542, 583.

HOBBS PEAK (**Salt Lake**) is one mile east northeast of Mt. Olympus and three miles south of Mill Creek Canyon. Lee Wray Hobbs was a prominent Utah citizen and well known in Utah legal circles. He played an important role in helping to develop facets of the South Korean army. He lived near and hiked in the vicinity of his namesake peak. When he died his ashes were scattered over the peak. S8,T2S,R2E,SLM; 9,400' (2,865m). 260. D.L. 8201.

HODGES CANYON (**Rich**) originates west of Pickleville*. It drains east into Bear Lake. The name honors Nathaniel Hodges, an original settler in the canyon. S2,T13N,R4E,SLM to S33,T14N,R5E,SLM. 567.

HOG CANYON (**Garfield**) originates at Hog Spring, one and one-half miles west of U-95 and eighteen miles south of Hanksville*. It drains southeast into North Wash. Today a highway rest stop has been developed at the mouth of the canyon. See Hog Springs (Garfield) for

the name source.
360.

HOG CANYON (Kane) originates six miles northeast of Kanab* at the Hog Canyon Springs. It drains southwest into Kanab Creek. Early Kanab residents herded their hogs there to fatten them up on acorns.
S6,T43S,R5W,SLM to S17,T43S,R6W,SLM. 567.

HOG CANYON (San Juan) originates at Harts Point and drains northwest into Indian Creek, three miles south of Dugout Ranch.
S10,T32S,R22E,SLM to S6,T32S,R22E,SLM.

HOG HOLE (Cache). See Hog Hollow (Cache).

HOG HOLLOW (Cache) originates between Blacksmith Fork Canyon and its left-hand fork. It drains north. The mouth is just east of Friendship Campground and Spring Picnic Area. In pioneer days there was a splendid stand of timber in this area. Three men decided that they wanted the timber, so they cut it down. In their rush to get the timber, they greedily cut the trees haphazardly, making it impossible to move the timber efficiently. Much of it was left where it was cut. One of the men was listed as Jake Zollinger. Name variant: Hog Hole.
SW¼,T11N,R3E,SLM.

HOG MOUNTAINS (Box Elder). See Hogup Mountains.

HOG RANCH SPRING (Garfield) is on a branch of North Creek northeast of Escalante* and five miles southwest of Posy Lake. In the early days, in season, a rancher turned his pigs loose at the spring to eat the acorns.
8,775' (2,675m). 12.

HOG SPRING (Garfield) is at the head of Hog Canyon west of U-95 and eighteen miles south of Hanksville*.

Several "Hog" stories exist. One of the more reliable states that in the early 1900s, Lee Brinkerhoof was moving a load of hogs from Hite* when a wheel on his wagon broke, forcing him to unload his hogs at the spring where there was good grazing and ample water. Later the people of Hanksville brought their pigs to the spring for winter grazing. The spring was also a freighter's overnight camp stop—one day's run on the road from Hite to Hanksville.
4,500' (1,372m). 181, 360.

HOGSBACK, THE (Beaver) is a geologic formation, a sharply crested ridge, generally formed by an inclined strata that is more resistant to erosion than the surrounding area. Such an exposure is shown west of Manderfield* and northwest of Beaver*.
S17,T28S,R7W,SLM; 6,250' (1,905m).

HOGUP MOUNTAINS (Box Elder) are northwest of and near the Great Salt Lake. On some maps they are shown as the Hog Mountains. The name was given by members of the 1849 Stansbury expedition and is a contraction of the geologic term "hogback," referring to an eroded uptilted stratum. However, there is also the record of a sheep man by the name of Brown who herded sheep on that mountain range during the 1870s. He tried various means of keeping other sheep men out of the area and thus acquired the name Hogup Brown, for himself and the Hogup Mountains for the mountains. Also, prehistoric ruins and artifacts dating back approximately 7,000 years have been studied in this mountain range.
S8,T9N,R12W,SLM; 6,560' (2,007m). 100 (v17), 314, 492, 546. D.L. 5903, 6904.

HOLBROOK CANYON (Davis). See Holbrook Creek.

HOLBROOK CREEK (Davis) originates at the summit of the Wasatch Mountains east of Bountiful*. It drains west through the canyon of the same name, into the

valley. Judge Joseph Holbrook was the first probate judge in Bountiful. He joined Heber C. Kimball and Judson Tolman in building a road up the canyon, for which they charged a toll.
S19,T2N,R2E,SLM to S19,T2N,R1E,SLM. 88, 201.

HOLDEN* (Millard) is seven miles north of Fillmore* near the junction of I-15 and US-50. It was first settled in 1855 and named Cedar Springs* for the springs in the cedars that the community was built around. The town then assumed the name Buttermilk Fork* because travelers passing through were encouraged to stop for a glass of cold buttermilk while they rested. Elijah E. Holden was an early settler and an honored member of the Mormon Battalion. He froze to death in the nearby mountains and it was decided to name the community in his honor. It was incorporated in 1923.

HOLE IN THE ROCK (Iron) is four to five miles south of Parowan* and one and one-half miles west of U-143. It is a natural feature, a window or hole in a rock formation large enough to crawl through.
S3,T35S,R9W,SLM. 567.

HOLE IN THE ROCK (Millard) is a geologic feature fifteen miles west northwest of Kanosh* near the south end of Beaver Ridge.
S27,T22S,R7W,SLM; 4,920' (1,500m).

HOLE-IN-THE-ROCK (Kane) was a very steep, rugged one-fourth-mile drop-off down to the Colorado River (today's Lake Powell). It was a formidable barrier to the Mormon Hole-in-the-Rock expedition of 1879-80 that camped for four months at or near Dance Hall Rock while the Hole was widened and modified so horses, wagons, people, and livestock could be moved down to the river. Once they reached the river they were ferried across. The members of the expedition were on their

way to settle San Juan County near present-day Bluff*. For about a year this route was used for travelers going both ways until a better route was developed, after which it was abandoned. Today it is a historic landmark about sixty-five miles southwest of Escalante* in a very isolated part of Utah.
359, 360, 383(Sept. 1955), 406, 546, 555 (v26/2). D.L. 6301.

HOLE-IN-THE-ROCK ARCH (Kane) is on a high point of a sandstone cliff southwest of the Hole-in-the-Rock. The arch was named to honor the Hole expedition.
NW¼,T41S,R9E,SLM.

HOLE IN THE WALL (Iron) is a narrow cut through the hills ascending from west to east in the Bald Hills, twelve miles west northwest of Enoch*.
S29,T34S,R12W,SLM.

HOLIDAY PARK (Summit) is at the west end of the Uinta Mountains on the Weber River. This area, eighteen miles east of Oakley*, marks the convergence of Oakley, the Middle Fork, Moffit Creek, and Dry Fork. Former Salt Lake City* Mayor F. Little and some of his friends and relatives were searching for an isolated location where they could spend weekends and vacations. This was the spot they selected.
S25,26,36,T1N,R8E,SLM; 7,000' (2,134m). 298, 309.

HOLLADAY* (Salt Lake) is a southeast suburb of Salt Lake City*. It is bounded on the north by Forty-eighth South, on the south by Cottonwood Lane, and on the west by Highland Drive. In 1847 and 1848 the pioneers called it Spring Creek* because they settled along the creek which runs through the region. The settlement was then called Holladay Field*, and Holladay Settlement* or Burgh*. In 1911 it was formally named for John Holladay, an early settler. The spelling on early maps was Holiday*, but was later changed.

T2S,R1E,SLM; 4,500' (1,372m). 163(11 June 1935), 288, 314, 542, 567, 578.

HOLMES CREEK (Davis) originates at the summit east of Kaysville* and drains west into the pasturelands southwest of Kaysville. The creek was named for Samuel Oliver Holmes, an old trapper who was living by the creek when the 1849 settlers moved in. Holmes had previously purchased the property from an earlier trapper and built his own cabin there. The creek also had an early name of Fiddlers Creek because so many of the early settlers played the fiddle—Tom Bennett, Jerry Wiggill, and Lewis Whitesides. They called their group "Tom and Jerry's Music."
S28,T4N,R1E,SLM to S8,T3N,R1W,SLM. 88, 123.

HOLT* (Washington) was a pioneer village settled by the Holt family, five miles north northeast of Enterprise, near Hamblin* and the mouth of Holt Canyon.
S10,T37S,R16W,SLM; 5,420' (1,652m). 97, 516.

HOLT CANYON (Washington) originates near Hamblin Spring and the ghost town site of Hamblin*. It drains northwest into the south end of the Escalante Valley near Enterprise*. See Holt*.
S25,26,T37S,R16W,SLM to S10,T37S,R16W, SLM. D.L. 7503.

HOLT SIDING (Cache) is on the Union Pacific Railroad at the Millville station, two miles south of Trenton*. The siding was named after roadmaster Holt.
S3,T1N,R1W,SLM; 4,461' (1,360m). 567.

HOLTBYS BOTTOM (Garfield) was an area of land on Escalante Mountain between Twitchell Creek and Barker Reservoir. It was named for John Holtby, an early Escalante stockman.
9,300' (2,835m). 12.

HOLYOAK* (San Juan) was a small community of the 1880s on the San Juan River above Bluff*. The settlement was established after the Hole-in-the-Rock expedition arrived in the Bluff area. Some of the members of the expedition were Henry Holyoak and his son, Henry John Holyoak, who was only nine years old at the time. See Aneth*.
359, 406, 409.

HOMANSVILLE* (Juab) was a small mining town established in 1872 at the head of Homansville Canyon, two miles northeast of Eureka*. It was named for Sheppard Homans, a member of Captain J. W. Gunnison's party during the 1870s. The town was abandoned prior to 1900 and today is a ghost town site.
S8,T10S,R2W,SLM; 6,320' (1,926m). 89, 516, 546, 567.

HOMANSVILLE CANYON (Utah) originates near the ghost town site of Homansville*, two miles northeast of Eureka*. It is a very short canyon, draining east northeast. Pinyon Creek drains through it. See Homansville*.

HOME BASE* (Emery) is a campsite in the San Rafael Swell south of the Sinbad country. Wild horse hunters used this area as one of their main campgrounds.
S17,21,T23S,R11E,SLM; 6,800' (2,073m). 193.

HOMEBENCH (Garfield) is between Calf Creek and Dry Hollow on U-54, three miles southwest of Boulder*. At one time, plans were being made to develop this area into a subdivision, but it never materialized.
S33,T33S,R4E,SLM; 6,800' (2,073m). 578.

HOME OF TRUTH* (San Juan) is a ghost town site near the junction of US-163 and U-211, fourteen miles north of Monticello. In 1933, Marie M. Ogden came from New Jersey to establish a small religious sect, the Home of

Truth—also known as The Ogden Center. The sect was never large and Marie Ogden eventually sold her property and moved into the San Juan Nursing Home in Blanding*. She died there in 1975 at the age of ninety-one.
S26,T31S,R23E,SLM; 6,262' (1,909m). 466 (30 Sept. 1977), 516, 546.

HONAKER TRAIL (San Juan) is two miles northwest of the Goosenecks of the San Juan view point and picnic site. The trail leads from the San Juan River bluffs down to the river's edge. As a young man, Henry Honaker worked as a cowpuncher for the Carlisles. He later ran a local stage route and superintended the building of the Honaker Trail that serviced the gold claims down below, along the river's edge.
S29,T41S,R18E,SLM. 406, 409, 610.

HONDOO ARCH (Emery). See Hondu Arch.

HONDU ARCH (Emery) is on the western border of the San Rafael country, eighteen miles south of I-70. This area is known as Hondu Country. It receives its name from the arch that has the general shape of a hondu. The hondu (honda, hondo, hondoo) is the ring part of the cowboy's lariat or lasso through which the rope slides, forming the loop. It may be a metal ring, or spliced or tied rope or horse hair.
193.

HONDU COUNTRY (Emery) is around the Hondu Arch and receives its name from the arch.

HONEYVILLE* (Box Elder) is on U-69 ten miles north of Brigham City* and south of Deweyville*. It was first settled in 1861. An early name for the settlement was Hunsakerville* for the local Mormon bishop, Abraham Hunsaker, a beekeeper. The community name was changed to Honeyville, some say to honor the profession of their bishop, and others say to remind them of their location, which was like Canaan—a land flowing with milk and honey. A combination of both of these reasons is more realistic.
S4,5S,T10N,R2W,SLM; 4,265' (1,300m). 100 (v17), 289, 542, 546.

HONSLINGER CREEK (Daggett) originates in the northeast section of the Uinta Mountains, one mile east of Ute Mountain. It drains southeast into Carter Creek. The name is a corruption of Dutch John Hanselena's name. He ran his cattle along the creek. See Dutch John*.
S27,T2N,R19E,SLM to S35,T2N,R19E,SLM.

HOODLE CREEK (Garfield). See Noodle Creek (Garfield).

HOOPER* (Weber) is on U-98 and U-37 on the eastern shore of the Great Salt Lake, southwest of Ogden*. Hooper was an early herd ground for the pioneers. It was first called Muskrat Springs* and later Hooperville* for Captain William H. Hooper, an early Utah delegate to Congress. He built the first cabin in the vicinity. Today it is a dispersed, agricultural area.
S13,24,T5N,R2W,SLM; 4,237' (1,291m). 100 (v17), 274, 289, 314, 542, 567.

HOOPERVILLE* (Weber). See Hooper*.

HOOVER* (Piute) was a very small settlement on US-89 near the head of Marysvale Canyon. It was first settled in 1935 by Kenneth and Ada Hoover and family. Today it is a wayside tourist stop.
S29,T26S,R4W,SLM. 360.

HOOVER LAKE (Duchesne) is in the Murdock Basin southeast of Mirror Lake near Marshall and Shephard lakes. The lake was named for U.S. President Hoover.
S2,T3N,R9W,USM. 100(v2).

HOP CREEK (Grand) originates on the southern slopes of the La Sal Mountains

and drains southeast into La Sal Creek. Wild hops are plentiful there.
S20,T27S,R25E,SLM to S32,T28S,R26E, SLM. 146.

HOPE LAKE (Summit) is in the southwest section of the Uinta Mountains on the trail from Wall Lake to The Notch. The quiet, peaceful location of the lake suggests the name.
S29,T1S,R9E,SLM; 10,350' (3,155m). 530.

HORSE CANYON (Carbon) originates on the West Tavaputs Plateau southeast of East Carbon City* and Sunnyside*. It drains southeast into Cottonwood Creek. Horse Canyon was a small canyon where barns and pasture were located for the horses and mules used for Sunnyside Mine No. 2.
S34,T15S,R14E,SLM to S4,T16S,R14E,SLM. 567.

HORSE CANYON (Garfield) originates on top of the Circle Cliffs west of the Waterpocket Fold. It drains southwest into the Escalante River between King Bench and Big Bown Bench. The name comes from the wild horses found in the region in earlier days.
S32,T35S,R6E,SLM (at mouth); 4,840' (1,475m). 12.

HORSE CANYON (San Juan) originates seven miles southeast of the Cave Spring Line Camp and the Squaw Campground in Canyonlands National Park. It drains north into Salt Creek and is known for its natural arches, windows, and prehistoric ruins. MRN
T31S,R20E,SLM.

HORSE HOLLOW (Kane) is about forty-five miles northeast of Kanab*. George G. Mace said he named it around 1900 because he and George Greenhalgh used the canyon as a horse pasture while tending sheep there.
567.

HORSE MOUNTAIN (San Juan) is on the western border of the Abajo Mountains west of Monticello*. Horse Mountain is bounded on the east by the Seven Sister Buttes. MRN
SE¼,T33S,R19E,SLM; 9,242' (2,817m).

HORSE RIDGE (Morgan, Weber) has a north-south orientation on the county line, seven miles southeast of Monte Cristo Peak. Wild horses once thrived there. At one time between Blue Fork and Hells Canyon a herd of wild horses died during the winter when the food supply on top of the wind-swept ridge ran out and the deep ridges of snow all around the exposed ridge prevented the horses from foraging elsewhere.
S6,T7N,R4,5E,SLM; 8,000' (2,438m). 567.

HORSE SPRING (Beaver) is in the San Francisco Mountains north of the head of Sawmill Canyon and northeast of Frisco Peak, where it drains east. Wild horses watered there.
S24,T26S,R13W,SLM; 7,625' (2,324m).

HORSE SPRING (Garfield) is eighteen miles southwest of Escalante* on the eastern slopes of Mount Canaan, at the head of Horse Spring Canyon. Wild horses watered there.
S10,T37S,R1E,SLM. 12.

HORSE SPRING CANYON (Garfield) originates on the eastern slopes of Mount Canaan at Horse Spring. It drains northeast into Alvey Wash and receives its name from Horse Spring.
S10,T37S,R1E,SLM to S2,T36S,R2E,SLM. 12.

HORSE VALLEY (Wayne) is northeast of Lyman* and west of Thousand Lake Mountain. Northwest is Fremont*. Wild horses ran in this valley.
SE¼,T27S,R3E,SLM.

HORSEHEAD* (San Juan) is a small community southwest of Lockerby*. It was settled around 1917 and named for a nearby canyon.
SW¼,T34S,R26E,SLM; 6,800' (2,073m).

HORSEHEAD PEAK (**San Juan**) is in the east Abajo Mountains between Upper Spring Creek and North Canyon. An unusual arrangement of forest-growth in the general shape of a horse's head appears on the side of the peak. This strange growth inspired the name.
T33S,R22E,SLM; 11,212' (3,417m). 406, 530.

HORSESHOE BEND (**Beaver**) was two and one-half miles south of Milford* on the Beaver River. At this point the river makes a horseshoe curve. It was also a prominent ford where freighters and other travelers crossed the river.
S30,T28S,R10W,SLM; 4,995' (1,522m).

HORSESHOE CANYON (**Daggett**) is in what is today part of Flaming Gorge National Recreation Area. At this point the river makes a complete "U" turn so Powell named this stretch Horseshoe Canyon.
S31,T3N,R21E,SLM to S6,T2N,R31E,SLM. 159, 160, 420, 496, 546, 609.

HORSESHOE CANYON (**Emery**) originates eight miles east of the Ekker (old Biddlecome) Ranch and drains north northeast to the Green River. The canyon is now a part of Canyonlands National Park. It is extremely rugged and twisted and contains numerous Indian pictographs. An earlier or synonymous name was Barrier Canyon because the canyon was so difficult to cross.
T26-29S,R15-17½S,SLM. 325, 383(Jan. 1980), 546.

HORSESHOE LAKE (**Garfield**) is on the southern side of Boulder Mountain of the Aquarius Plateau. This area contains the headwaters of Boulder Creek, East Fork. The lake has the rough "U" shape of a horseshoe.
T31S,R4E,SLM; 10,800' (3,292m).

HORSESHOE MOUNTAIN (**Sanpete**) is southeast of Spring City*. The mountain includes the Big Horseshoe and the Little Horseshoe, geologic cirques resembling

the hoof of a horse. The mountain was described and named in 1852 by James Allred and family, who were the first settlers in this area.
152.

HORSETHIEF CANYON (**Wayne**) originates west of Hatch Point and Lockhart Basin. It drains northwest into the Colorado River north of Rustler Canyon. The name is related to the outlaw activities of the late 1800s.
S3,T29S,R20E,SLM. 25, 303.

HORSETHIEF CANYON (**Wayne**) originates in the Spur country west of the Green River and north of Hans Flat.

HORSETHIEF POINT (**Grand**) is east of the Green River where it extends to the west as a point of land between Mineral Canyon and Taylor Canyon. The point was a juncture of several cow-puncher and outlaw trails.
T26S,R19E,SLM; 5,500' (1,676m). 25, 146.

HOSKINNINI MESA (**San Juan**) is two miles north of Bullfrog Marina west of and near U-276. See Hoskinnini Mesa below for name source.
S32,T37S,R11E,SLM; 4,000' (1,219m).

HOSKINNINI MESA (**San Juan**) is eleven miles west of Goulding* and four miles east of Copper Creek. The name is a hybrid, with elements from Navajo and Spanish languages, and comes from "Hush-Kaaney," meaning "Angry One," in reference to the chief of that name who, during that period of strife with the whites, drove his people hard to obtain food to stay alive. Hoskinnini died in 1912 and there is a plaque honoring the chief at the junction of Swett and Trachyte creeks.
S19,29,32,T43S,R14E,SLM (in Utah); 6,400' (1,951m). 303, 314, 555(July 1953).

HOT SPRINGS (**Beaver**) are in the desert eighteen miles southwest of Minersville*. The springs are quite hot, with cold springs nearby. This was a

main stop on the old freight road to the mines of eastern Nevada.
S28,T30S,R12W,SLM; 5,037' (1,535m). 355.

HOTEL MESA (Grand) is at the junction of the Colorado and Dolores rivers.
S3,T23S,R24E,SLM.

HOURGLASS LAKE (Summit) is two miles south of Haystack Mountain and six miles southwest of Mirror Lake. It has the rough shape of an hourglass.
S24,T2S,R8E,SLM; 9,750' (2,972m).

HOUSE RANGE (Millard) is a range of mountains with a north-south orientation in the west central part of the county between White (Tule) Valley and Whirlwind Valley. In 1859 Captain J. H. Simpson named it on his road survey, "From the summit of the pass, 5,657' above the sea, could be seen, some twenty-five or thirty miles off, on the east side of the range of mountains, quite remarkable on account of its well-defined stratification and the resemblance of portions of its outline to domes, minarets, houses, and other structures. On this account I call it the House Range" (477, p. 122).
T20-23S,R13-14W,SLM. 477. D.L. 6201.

HOUSTON* (Garfield). See Widtsoe*.

HOUSTON MOUNTAIN (Garfield) is on the Markagunt Plateau between Mammoth and Tommy creeks. Eight miles northeast is Panguitch Lake. Tommy Houston ranched there.
S3,10,T37S,R8W,SLM; 10,058' (3,066m). 567.

HOVENWEEP NATIONAL MONUMENT (San Juan). The Utah section is Indian ruins in a compact group in two different areas in extreme southeastern Utah. The larger unit is eight miles east of Hatch Trading Post*. The name means deserted valley.
S20,21,T39S,R26E,SLM; 5,200' (1,585m). 163(26 Sept. 1983), 567.

HOWARDS POND (Beaver) is in the South Hills near the head of California Hollow. The Black Mountains are west.
S35,T30S,R8W,SLM; 6,780' (2,067m).

HOWELL* (Box Elder) is a small agricultural community three miles off I-84 in the central part of the Blue Creek Valley. It was first settled in 1910 after being laid out by the Promontory-Curlew Land Company. Joseph Howell was president of the company and Utah's representative to the U.S. Congress.
S5,8,T12N,R5W,SLM; 4,560' (1,390m). 100 (v17), 139, 289, 542.

HOXIE CREEK (Garfield). See Halls Creek (Garfield).

HOY MOUNTAIN (Daggett) is in northeastern Utah, with Allen Draw on the north, the Colorado line on the east, and Pot Creek on the south. J. S. and Valentine Hoy and their brothers moved into and settled this region in the early 1870s. Valentine Hoy was killed by the outlaw Harry Tracy in the spring of 1898.
S22,25,T1S,R25E,SLM; 8,716 (2,657m). 172, 303.

HOYT CANYON (Summit) originates on the southwest slopes of Hoyt Peak where it drains west into Rhodes Valley, three miles north of Kamas*. See the peak for name source.
S1,T2S,R6E,SLM to S34,T1S,R6E,SLM.

HOYT PEAK (Uintah) is in the western Uinta Mountains close to Bald Mountain. It was named for Samuel Pierce Hoyt, early pioneer of Kamas Valley and Hoytsville*. He was the valley's cattle king.
S31,T1S,R7E,SLM; 10,228' (3,117m). 309.

HOYTSVILLE* (Summit) is midway between Coalville* and Wanship*. It was first known as East Plymouth*, then Unionville*, because the people united here in time of Indian troubles. In 1875 the name was changed to Hoytsville

194

honoring Samuel P. Hoyt. See Hoyt
Peak.
S21,28,T2N,R5E,SLM; 5,700' (1,737m). 100
(v17), 289, 309, 360, 466(26 Jan. 1986),
542, 546.

HUFF CREEK (Summit) originates on
Porcupine Ridge, five miles northeast of
Upton* and drains into Chalk Creek. See
Upton for name source.
S14,T3N,R7E,SLM to S26,T3N,R6E,SLM.

HUFFVILLE* (Summit). See Upton*.

HUMBOLDT COUNTY was created in
western Utah Territory in 1856 and in
1861 it was transferred to Nevada
Territory. The county received its name
from the nearby Humboldt River, named
by Captain J. C. Fremont for Alexander
von Humboldt, an early scientist and
explorer.

HUNGRY CREEK (Garfield) originates
on the Aquarius Plateau at Posy Lake
and drains southeast into Deep Creek.
Here the pack and saddle horses began
to tire and get hungry as they worked
their way up the trail, so it was a natural
place to take a break to let the animals
graze.
12.

HUNT CREEK (Garfield) originates at
the junction of the East and West forks.
It drains northeast into Johns Valley
north of Bryce Canyon National Park.
Elk hunts were popular in this area.
S34,T34S,R3W,SLM to S19,T34S,R2W,SLM.
508.

HUNTINGTON* (Emery) is on U-10
near the mouth of Huntington Canyon
and one mile southwest of Huntington
Lake. The settlement was named for
William Huntington, an early explorer in
the area. The Huntington brothers,
Dimick, Oliver, and William, were
involved in exploration and scouting in
the region. Dimick was a well-known
Indian language interpreter. See Hobble
Creek.

S24,T17S,R8E,SLM; 5,791' (1,765m). 146,
289, 292, 322, 542.

HUNTINGTON CREEK (Emery) origi-
nates on the Wasatch Plateau northwest
of Huntington* and east of Mount
Pleasant*. The creek drains past
Huntington into the San Rafael River.
This canyon was the main line of travel
between Emery and Sanpete counties.
See Huntington*.
S5,T13S,R6E,SLM to S21,T19S,R9E,SLM.

HUNTINGTON LAKE (Emery) is one
mile northeast of Huntington*. It receives
its name from the creek.
S18,T17S,R9E,SLM; 5,839' (1,780m).

HUNTINGTON RESERVOIR (Sanpete)
is on the headwaters of the Left Fork of
Huntington Creek. It receives its name
from the creek.
S20,21,T14S,R6E,SLM; 9,014' (2,747m).

HUNTSVILLE* (Weber) is a small
community on the eastern shore of
Pineview Reservoir, east of Ogden*. It
was named for Captain Jefferson Hunt,
who arrived in the late 1860s with a
group of settlers who came to establish a
permanent settlement. It had an earlier
name of Hawkins Grove*, after James
Hawkins.
S18,T6N,R2E,SLM; 4,924' (1,501m). 100
(v17), 289, 542, 546, 567.

HURRAH PASS (San Juan) is off the
north end of Hatch Point, east of and
near Shafer Basin and the Colorado
River. It was worth a hurrah to reach the
summit of the pass.
S4,5,T27S,R21E,SLM; 4,800' (1,463m).

HURRICANE* (Washington) is at the
base of Hurricane Ridge and at the
junction of U-59 and U-9 and the Virgin
River. President Erastus Snow (the
Mormon church official in charge of the
Church's Dixie cotton mission), David H.
Cannon, Nephi Johnson, and others were
returning to St. George after a visit to
the colonies along the upper Virgin

River. As they worked their way down the lava ridge a heavy whirlwind developed, blowing the top off President Snow's buggy. He made a comment at the time that it was like a hurricane and he thought Hurricane would make a good name for the hill. After this incident the hill, fault, bench, town, and canal were named Hurricane.
S34,35,T41S,R13W,SLM; 3,250' (991m). 154, 161, 438, 542, 546.

HURRICANE FAULT (Washington) is the western edge of the Markagunt Plateau and the eastern boundary of the Great Basin in this region. The Hurricane fault' plane is over two hundred miles long—one of the most prominent in America. It extends into Arizona where the southern terminus disappears underground. See Hurricane* for name source.
175, 314.

HURRICANE WASH (Kane) originates at Fiftymile Bench and drains east northeast into Coyote Gulch near Jacob Hamblin Arch.
T39S,R8E,SLM. D.L. 7301.

HY HUNT CREEK (Beaver) originates at Big Flat in the Tushar Mountains and drains northwest into Lake Stream. Hy Hunt was an English sheepherder who herded his sheep in the area in 1876. See Iant Creek.
S13,T29S,R5W. 125.

HYATT LAKE (Duchesne) is in the southwest sector of the Uinta Mountains in the Naturalist Basin. It was named for Alpheus Hyatt, a naturalist and an Agassiz student.
S34,T4N,R8W,USM; 10,750' (3,277m).

HYDE PARK* (Cache) is five miles north of Logan* on US-91. It was settled in April 1860 by William Hyde, Robert Daines, and others. The settlement was named for William Hyde, the first presiding Mormon church elder and bishop in this area.

S2,3,10,11,T12N,R1E,SLM; 4,449' (1,356m). 100(v17), 449, 567.

HYLAND* (Duchesne) was an early temporary settlement on the benchland between Myton* and Roosevelt*.
89, 165.

HYRUM* (Cache) is eight miles south of Logan* on U-163, U-101, and U-242. The name was suggested by David Osborn when plans were made to build another city nearby that was to be named Joseph*. The towns would honor both Joseph, the Mormon prophet, and his brother Hyrum. The city of Joseph never materialized.
S4,5,T10N,R1E,SLM; 4,716' (1,437m). 289, 449, 546, 567.

HYRUM RESERVOIR (Cache) is southwest of Hyrum* from which it receives its name.
S4,5,8,9,SLM; 4,664' (1,422m).

IANT CREEK (Beaver) originates in the Tushar Mountains south of Iant Ridge and drains northwest into the Beaver River. The name comes from the local interpretation of an English sheepherder's name, Hy Hunt, as they spelled it. See Hy Hunt Creek.
T29S,R5W,SLM. 125. D.L. 7501.

IBANTIK LAKE (Summit) is in the Uinta Mountains on the north side of and near the east end of Notch Mountain. The name is of Uinta Ute Indian origin.
S20,T1S,R9E,SLM; 10,100' (3,078m).

IBAPAH* (Tooele) is at the extreme west side of the county, near the head of Deep Creek. It was an early Pony Express station that was originally founded in 1859 by Mormon missionaries, who taught the local Indians modern methods of farming. The settlement was originally known as Deep Creek* for the name of the creek where it was located. Later, Edward Ferguson suggested the present name of Ibapah, an anglicized form of the Goshute Indian word "Ai-bim-pa," which means "White Clay Water." The water is heavy with fine white clay particles. See Deep Creek.
S16,T9S,R19W,SLM; 5,288' (1,612m). 106, 153, 289, 314, 542, 567. D.L. 7403.

IBAPAH PEAK (Juab) is in the Deep Creek Range in the western part of the county. The peak received its name from the creek.
S31,T11S,R18W,SLM; 12,087' (3,684m).

IBEX* (Juab) was an old ranch and Overland Stage station on the route from Deseret* to Frisco*. It was about twenty-five miles west northwest of Black Rock and named after the nearby Ibex Mine close to the ghost town of Joy*. The ibex animal we know is not native to this country and much discussion has developed over using the word as a place name in America. Silvey comments that Indian goats often escaped captivity to run and interbreed with the wild desert sheep. Silvey (428) noted that the horns of the offspring had a more gradual curve, making them look similar to what he thought was a South American ibex. The problem with Silvey's interpretation is that the ibex is not a South American animal: it is a native to Asia, Africa, and parts of Europe. Silvey's interpretation would help explain the ibex like horned animals the early Indians chipped into rock walls in this area.
S36,T14S,R11W,SLM; 6,400' (1,951m). 89, 475, 516.

IBEX* (Millard) is a ghost town site fifty miles south of Delta* at the southern tip of the Barn Hills of the Confusion Range. It was an old mining and stockman's trading center. See Ibex* (Juab) for name source.
S20,T22S,R14W,SLM; 5,500' (1,676m).

IBEX HILLS (Millard). See Barn Hills.

IBEX POINT (Wayne) is near the Dirty Devil River, between Twin Corral Box Canyon and Sams Mesa Canyon. See Ibex* for name source.
NW¼,T30S,R14E,SLM.

ICE CAVE PEAK (Uintah) is in the eastern Uinta Mountains as the high point of Mosby Mountain.
S5,T2N,R1E,USM; 10,036' (3,059m).

ICE CAVE SPRING (Beaver) is near Jim Reed Creek on the western slopes of the Tushar Mountains, east of Johnson

Peak. The spring is near a natural rock tank that holds snow or rainwater, keeping it fresh and cold all summer.
S2,T29S,R6W,SLM. 125.

ICE SPRING (Beaver) is one-tenth mile south of the lower power station in Beaver Canyon. The water from the spring is quite cold.
S27,T29S,R6W,SLM. 125.

ICELANDER CREEK (Carbon) originates at East Carbon City* and drains south. MRN
S12,T15S,R13E,SLM (at source).

IGNACIO* (Uintah) was a stage stop on U-45 where it crosses the White River, three miles south of Bonanza*. Today it is a ghost town site. In 1905 Ignacio was built to house maintenance workers and bridge tenders, in addition to being a toll stop for the bridge and toll road built from Dragon* to Vernal*. The gilsonite operation was the primary reason for this activity. An early name for Ignacio was White River Crossing*.
S2,T10S,R24E,SLM; 5,002' (1,525m). 50, 89, 516.

IMLAY CANYON (Washington) originates at Horse Pasture and drains southeast into The Narrows of Zion Canyon. Wills Imlay ranged his sheep in the canyon.
S20,T40S,R10W,SLM (at source). 508, 530.

INDEPENDENCE* (Uintah). In 1906 the settlement was midway between Myton* and Fort Duchesne*. Independence was a monument to the folly of unhesitatingly believing land speculators. This alkaline land grew only salt grass, but was advertised and sold by speculators as prime farmland. After monies were collected, the promoters skipped town. In 1912 the site was abandoned.
S6,T3S,R1E,USM. 89, 516, 567.

INDIAN CANYON (Cache) originates on the northwest slopes of Mount Elmer and drains northwest into Summit Creek of Smithfield Canyon. Seven miles southwest is Smithfield*. While white people were settling Smithfield in the 1860s, a group of Shoshone Indians camped in this nearby canyon. A conflict ensued and several Indians and whites were killed.
567.

INDIAN CANYON (Carbon, Duchesne) originates on the west Tavaputs Plateau at the junction of the Right and Left forks. It drains northeast into the Strawberry River and Starvation Reservoir. U-33 passes through Indian Canyon and its left fork. Several Indians owned land allotments in the canyon after the Uintah Indian Reservation was opened to homesteaders. Since ancient times the canyon has been a principal Indian trail between the Uintah Basin and the Castle Valley region to the southeast.
S11,T5S,R6W,USM to S1,T4S,R5W,USM. 100(v17), 546, 567.

INDIAN CREEK (Beaver) originates in the Tushar Mountains west of Mount Belnap and northwest of Mount Baldy. Drainage is southwest through Beaver Valley. There are two versions to the name origin. The first suggests that in the fall of 1857, Captain Fancher's emigrant train was attacked by a band of Indians while passing through this area. The second states that a permanent Indian village was located there. Both versions could be correct. See Indian Creek*.
T27,28S,R6,7,8W,SLM. 125, 289, 355.

INDIAN CREEK* (Beaver) was a permanent Indian village on Beaver Creek in the late 1800s. See Indian Creek (Beaver) above.

INDIAN CREEK (San Juan) originates in the Abajo Mountains on the southern slopes of Horsehead Peak and Twin Peaks. The creek drains past Newspaper Rock and the Dugout Ranch to join Rustler Canyon. It was an area of heavy Indian activity in times past. J. S.

Newberry of the Macomb expedition wrote that they had previously named the canyon Labyrinth Canyon before changing it to Indian Creek Canyon.
28.

INDIAN CREEK (Tooele) originates in the Simpson Mountains at Indian Springs and drains west into the desert.
S2,T10S,R8W,SLM to S34,T9S,R9W,SLM.

INDIAN FARM CREEK (Juab) originates on the eastern slope of the Deep Creek Range and drains east into the Snake Valley. Mormon missionaries developed farms here to help teach the Indians to be self-sufficient.
S20,T11S,R18W,SLM to S18,T11S,R16W, SLM.

INDIAN GRAVE PEAK (Beaver) is near the south end of the San Francisco Mountains and north of the Grampian Hills. Indian graves were found on the slopes of the peak.
S14,T7S,R13W,SLM; 8,132' (2,479m). 567.

INDIAN HOLLOW (Kane) originates north of Willis Creek, southeast of Bryce Canyon National Park, and drains southeast into Sheep Creek. This was an area of early trouble between the Piute Indians and whites. See Averett Canyon.
S7,13,T38S,R3W,SLM. 100(v17), 159, 455, 515.

INDIAN PEAK (Beaver) is in the center of the Needle Mountain Range near the head of Indian Creek. Indians inhabited this region, which they called Quich-u-ant (Spirit Mountain).
S21,T29S,R18W,SLM; 9,790' (2,984m). 125, 355.

INDIAN PEAK MOUNTAINS (Beaver) are at the southern end of the Needle Mountains centered around Indian Peak. See above.

INDIAN SPRINGS PEAKS (Tooele) are at the northern end of the Simpson Mountains. Two miles south are the Indian Springs from which the peak received its name. See Indian Springs for name source.
NE¼,T9S,R8W,SLM; 8,406' (2,562m).

INDIAN SPRINGS (Tooele) are in the Simpson Mountains at the south end of Skull Valley. The springs were the site of old Indian camping grounds.
S53,T10S,R8W,SLM; 6,660' (2,030m). 100 (v17), 516, 567.

INDIAN SPRINGS* (Tooele) was located on Indian Creek, two miles north of the head of Death Canyon. It was a temporary mining camp during the 1890s at the springs of the same name.
S34,T9S,R8W,SLM; 6,560' (1,999m). 516.

INDIANOLA* (Sanpete) is east of US-89 on Thistle Creek. Twelve miles southeast is Fairview*. An early Indian village existed there. In pioneer times the site was selected for farms assigned to Indians protected by the Mormon Church. The Indians were permitted to file on land and own it if it was taken care of. This plan was discontinued when the Indian reservation in the Uintah Basin was established by the federal government.
S4,5,T12S,R4E,SLM; 5,957' (1,816m).

INGERSOLL* (Millard) was a scattered settlement on the Sevier River, approximately four miles east of Crafton*. It was settled under the Swan Lake Project by one hundred Quakers from Philadelphia. The settlement was sometimes known as Lake Town*. Earlier, Crafton settlers sold their properties to the Ingersoll Quakers, but shortly after, Ingersoll was also abandoned. See Crafton*.
89, 516, 567.

INTERPLANETARY AIRSTRIP (Carbon) is a controversial mile-long dirt airstrip on what is known as the Stone Cabin Gas Field, four miles southeast of the junction of Argyle and Nine Mile Canyons. It first appeared on U.S. Geological Survey maps with the

1968 issue of the Currant Canyon 7.5' minute quadrangle. The name origin is conjectural.
S14,T12S,R14E,SLM; 7,600' (2,316m). 466 (27 July 1979).

IOKA* (Duchesne) is a small community first established on U-87 in 1907, five miles northwest of Myton*. It was named for a Ute headman and means "bravado." S33,T2S,R2W,USM; 5,356' (1,632m). 567.

IOSEPA* (Tooele) was twenty miles south of the Great Salt Lake in the center of Skull Valley. In 1889, with the encouragement of the Mormon Church, a group of converts from Hawaii attempted to establish a colony at this location. At one time over 225 Mormon church members lived in the colony. Hansens disease (leprosy) struck the settlement in 1893. When the church built a temple in Hawaii in 1916, many of the Hawaiians returned to their homeland. By 1917 Iosepa was a ghost town centered around a cemetery. The property was later sold to the Deseret Livestock Company. "Iosepa" is Hawaiian for "Joseph."
S21,T3S,R8W,SLM; 4,500' (1,372m). 89, 314, 516, 542, 546.

IRON CITY* (Iron). See Old Irontown* (Iron).

IRON COUNTY in 1850 was called Little Salt Lake Valley County but was changed later in the year to Iron County. The name is a reminder of the early iron mines developed west of Cedar City*. 6, 542.

IRON CREEK (Beaver) is in the Tushar Mountains, where it drains northwest into Briggs Creek.
S36,T28S,R6W,SLM.

IRON MINE CREEK (Wasatch) originates on the southern slopes of Iron Mine Mountain. It drains east into the Duchesne River and receives its name from the mountain and a local mine.

S22,T2N,R9W,USM (at mouth).

IRON MINE LAKE (Wasatch) is in the southwest section of the Uinta Mountains, two miles east southeast of the Iron Mine Mountain peak. There are iron deposits in the immediate area and it receives its name from the mountain.
S17,T2N,R9W,USM; 9,580' (2,920m).

IRON MINE MOUNTAIN (Wasatch) is in the southwest section of the Uinta Mountains, two miles south of Alexander Lake. There are iron deposits in the area.
S12,T3S,R8E,SLM; 10,463' (3,189m). 314.

IRON MINE SPRING (Beaver) is in the center of the Wah Wah Mountains on the north slope of Iron Mountain. The spring received its name from a nearby mine.
S7,T30S,R14W,SLM; 6,200' (1,890m).

IRON MINE WASH (Beaver) originates in the central part of the Wah Wah Mountains and drains southwest into Blawn Wash. The wash received its name from the local mines.
S5,7,T30S,R14W,SLM.

IRON MOUNTAIN (Iron) is eighteen miles west of Cedar City*. Parley P. Pratt's expedition of 1849 discovered vast quantities of iron here. The first molten iron was run on September 2, 1852.
S25,26,35,36,T36S,R14W,SLM; 7,832' (2,387m). 100(v17), 423, 555(v1), 567.

IRON MOUNTAIN (Summit) is two miles west northwest of Park City*. This is a region of numerous mines.
S7,T2S,R4E,SLM; 9,018' (2,749m).

IRON SPRING (Uintah) is east of Bullionville* ghost town site, three-fourths of a mile west northwest of Big Lake. It has been claimed the spring was named for mineral ores found in the mountain. However, in 1941 U.S. Forest Ranger Snyder said it received its name for the underground iron pipe that was

installed to assure reliable water flow.
S28,T1S,R21E,SLM; 8,688' (2,648m). 567.

IRON SPRINGS (Iron) are nine miles
northwest of Cedar City*. The springs
were discovered and named by Parley P.
Pratt in November 1849. Early Indians
and later stockmen and prospectors
camped by the springs. Sections of the
motion picture "Union Pacific" were
filmed by the springs in 1938.
S20,T35S,R12W,SLM; 5,391' (1,643m). 567.

IRONTON* (Juab) was first established
in 1871 near the present junction of
US-6,50 and U-36 or the Tintic Junction
two miles southwest of Eureka*. Ironton
was an ore shipping and supply town for
local mines. As railroad construction
crews moved on, Ironton became a ghost
town.
S27,T10S,R3W,SLM; 5,904' (1,800m). 314,
516, 546.

IRONTON* (Utah) was a small community established two miles north of
Springville* on US-91 and US-89.
Columbia Steel operated a blast furnace
there for the manufacture of pig iron.
Since the company closed down, plans
for an industrial park have been
developing.
S20,T7S,R3E,SLM; 4,520' (1,378m). 542,
578.

IRONTOWN* (Iron). See Old Irontown*
(Iron).

ISLAND HOME ORCHARD (Grand) is
a large island in the river three miles
north of Green River*. In 1909 a plan
was filed to develop the island but
nothing ever materialized.
S22,T30S,R16E,SLM; 4,080' (1,244m).

ISLAND LAKE (Sanpete) is in the
mountains east of Mayfield, two and
one-half miles east of Woods Lake.
There is a small island in the center of
the lake.
S18,T20S,R4E,SLM; 10,322' (3,146m).

ISLAND LAKE (Summit) is in the north
central section of the Uinta Mountains.
Two miles west is South Burro Peak. An
island is located in the center of the lake.
10,777' (3,285m).

ISLAND LAKE (Summit) is at the west
end of the Uinta Mountains, two miles
west of Haystack Mountain. Included in
this group are Duck, Weir, and Fire
lakes. Island Lake has an island in the
center.
S34,T1S,R8E,SLM; 10,150' (3,094m). 298.

ISLAND PARK (Uintah) is between the
exit from Whirlpool Canyon and the
entrance to the Split Mountain Gorge in
Dinosaur National Monument. Powell
and Dellenbaugh recorded, "The valley
we were now in was not long; about four
miles in a straight line, with a width of
two. In this space the river meanders
nine miles, one detour being very long.
It spreads also amongst a number of
islands. We floated along on waters deep
and black and slow. The Major was for
a time uncertain whether to call this
'Rainbow' or 'Island' Park, the decision
finally being given to the latter" (610,
p. 183). And so Island Park was named.
The name Rainbow Park was recently
given to a nearby river area.
S31,32,T3S,R25E,SLM; 5,000' (1,524m).
160, 420, 496, 609, 610.

IVINS* (Washington) is five miles
northwest of Santa Clara* on the Santa
Clara Bench, west of Snow Canyon.
Anthony W. Ivins was a Mormon church
official and a pioneer of southern Utah.
He had accomplished a great deal to
help the Indians of the region and the
town was named for him.
S31,32,T41,42S,R16W,SLM;3,500'(1,067m).
154.

IVINS MOUNTAIN (Washington) is two
miles southeast of Greatheart Mesa and
five miles southeast of the South
Guardian Angel. See Ivins*.
T40S,R10W,SLM; 7,019' (2,139m). 530.

- J -

JACK LAKE (Wasatch) is in the southwest section of the Uinta Mountains, five and one-half miles west southwest of Mirror Lake and one mile west of Haystack Mountain. Cardie Clegg (H. Cardwell Clegg) was an early freighter and developer in the area who named the lake for his oldest son Jack.
S2,T2S,R8E,SLM; 9,990' (3,045m). 113, 379.

JACK THOMPSON SETTLEMENT* (Weber). See Riverdale*.

JACKASS BENCHES (Emery) is upland bench country on the San Rafael Swell, fifteen miles west of Green River*. For a period of time jackasses roamed in this area by escaping from domestication or from travelers on the Old Spanish Trail.
SW¼,T21S,R13E,SLM; 5,950' (1,814m).

JACKRABBIT SPRING (Beaver) is in the Mineral Mountains five miles south of the head of Cunningham Wash. Jackrabbits are plentiful in this area.
S8,T27S,R8W,SLM; 7,760' (2,365m).

JACKSON* (Washington) was about twenty-five miles up the Santa Clara Creek north of Santa Clara*. It was named for Jackson, a renegade Indian. Jackson and his men hid out where the road ran along the creek bottom through heavy underbrush, under an overhanging cliff. It was a favorite place for Indian attacks: several people traveling through this area were killed.
438.

JACKSON COUNTY (Beaver). See Jackson County Hill (Beaver).

JACKSON COUNTY HILL (Beaver) is an agricultural area one mile south of Beaver*. It was named by immigrants from Jackson County, Missouri.
S27,T29S,R7W,SLM; 6,000' (1,829m). 355, 567.

JACKSON HOLE (Grand) is a U-shaped section of the Colorado River that has been cut off by a change in the river course—a captive meander. The river section is at the southern end of the Amasa Back, six miles southwest of Moab. John Jackson was an early cattleman who ran his cattle in this area.
S19,20,29,30,T26S,R21E,SLM. 578.

JACKSON RIDGE (San Juan) is near the head of Recapture Creek. It extends from Cooley Pass to Mount Linnaeus and is named for the early prospector who founded nearby Camp Jackson*. He was killed by a double-barreled shotgun blast.
T34S,R22E,SLM. 530.

JACKSON SIDING (Box Elder) is on the Union Pacific Railroad Lucin Cutoff. In 1905 the siding was named by the railroad for a prospector of the same name who operated a mine nearby.
S22,T7N,R16W,SLM. 567.

JACOB CITY* (Tooele) was at the head of Dry Canyon two miles north of Ophir*. In 1865, the Hidden Treasure Mine was opened and the mining camp Jacob City was subsequently established. It was later absorbed into another mining camp, Gisborn* (Gisbourne*, Gibson*), which was named for Mack Gisborn, part owner of the mine. Today it is a ghost town.
S15,T5S,R4W,SLM. 89, 516.

JACOB HAMBLIN ARCH (Kane) is in Coyote Gulch west of the Escalante River. Escalante stockmen had named

the feature the Lobo Arch for a great grey wolf that roamed the region. Jacob Hamblin's name was given to the arch for his work as a guide for Almon Thompson and the men of the Powell survey as they tried to locate the mouth of the Dirty Devil River.
S16,T39S,R8E,SLM. 12.

JACOBS CHAIR (San Juan) is a geological feature resembling a gigantic straight-backed chair located twelve miles northwest of the Natural Bridges National Monument. Jacob Adams was a close friend of Al Scorup; both were well-known cattleman in the area. Adams lost his life while trying to cross nearby White Creek too soon after a storm.
T35S,R16E,SLM; 6,805' (2,074m). 471, 555 (v32).

JACOBS RESERVOIR (Garfield) is under the south rim of Boulder Mountain east of Cyclone Lake. The reservoir was named for John Jacobs.
T32S,R3E,SLM; 10,069' (3,069m). 602.

JAKE HOLLOW (Garfield). There are three hollows under Jake's name, all centered in the area west of Escalante* between Main and North canyons. They are Jake Hollow, Little Jake Hollow, and Right Fork Little Jake Hollow. They were named for Jacob Butler of Escalante.
SW¼,T34S,R1E,SLM. 12.

JAMES PEAK (Cache, Weber) is ten miles northeast of Huntsville* in the Monte Cristo Mountains. See Davenport Creek for name source.
S36,T8N,R1E,SLM; 9,422' (2,872m).

JARVIES CANYON (Daggett) originates in the northeast section of the Uinta Mountains on Dutch John Mountain. It drains south into the Flaming Gorge Reservoir in Browns Park (before 1869, Browns Hole). John Jarvie was an early settler who ran cattle in the canyon. Jarvie was the first postmaster and he also built a ferry on the nearby Green River.
S31,T3N,R22E,SLM to S6,T2N,R22E,SLM. 172, 303.

JASPER CANYON (Garfield) originates in the Land of Standing Rock, six or seven miles west of The Confluence. It drains northeast into the Stillwater section of the Green River. The jasper gemstone is found in the canyon.
S29,T30S,R18E,SLM.

JEAN LAKE (Duchesne) is in the southwest section of the Uinta Mountains as one of the lakes in the Four Lakes Basin.
S11,T3N,R8W,USM.

JEDEDIAH MOUNTAIN (Tooele) is at the north end of the Lakeside Mountains west of the Great Salt Lake. It was named to honor Jedediah Smith, one of the West's greatest explorers and mountain men.
S21,T3N,R9W,SLM; 5,838' (1,779m). 360, 371, 372.

JENNINGS WASH (Washington) is a tributary of Coalpits Wash. Henry Jennings was a pioneer who lived in this vicinity from 1862 until his death in 1874. Jennings helped settle the community of Rockville*.
S12,T41S,R11W,SLM. 567. D.L. 6402.

JENSEN* (Uintah) is a small agricultural community on US-40 and the Green River. It had earlier names of Incline* and Riverdale*. Lars Jensen settled there in 1877 and began operating a ferry on the Green River in 1885.
S21,T5S,R23E,SLM; 4,739' (1,444m). 289, 314, 542, 546, 567, 609.

JERICHO* (Juab) was an early sheep shearing corral, midway between Eureka* and Lynndyl*, on the Los Angeles and Salt Lake Railroad. Later, it was a U.S. Civilian Conservation Corps camp. The name came from the sandy, isolated, and desolate surroundings.
S29,T12S,R3W,SLM; 5,311' (1,619m). 516, 546.

JERICHO* (Sevier). See Joseph* (Sevier).

JERICHO* (Uintah). See Vernal* (Uintah).

JERRY LAKE (Summit) is in the western section of the Uinta Mountains, one mile southeast of Anchor Lake. It was named for a son of Cardie Clegg, an early pioneer and developer in the region.
S27,T1S,R8E,SLM; 10,225' (3,117m). 578.

JERUSALEM* (Sanpete) was a small agricultural settlement between Freedom* and Fountain Green*. The settlement was originally established in 1871 by Lourtz Christensen and Simion Simonson.
S25,T14S,R2E,SLM; 5,925' (1,806m). 567.

JESSE EWING CANYON (Daggett) drains from Clay Basin into the Green River at Browns Park. Jesse Ewing was an eccentric, moody prospector, outlaw, and murderer of the 1860s who lived near the head of his namesake canyon. He was killed by Frank Duncan in a dispute over a mutual lady friend.
S1,T2N,R24E,SLM to S7,T2N,R25E,SLM. 80, 172, 303.

JESSEN BUTTE (Daggett) is five miles southwest of Manila*. The butte was named for Adolph Jessen, a surveyor of the Manila region.
S32,33,T3N,R19E,SLM; 8,620' (2,627m). 172.

JEWEL LAKE (Summit) is at the west end of the Uinta Mountains near the head of the Bear River. Two and one-half miles south is Mirror Lake. The name is descriptive of the beauty of the lake and its surroundings.
S14,T1S,R9E,SLM; 10,320' (3,146m).

JIM REED CREEK (Beaver) is on the western slopes of the Tushar Mountains at the head of Baker Canyon, North Fork. Jim Reed was a sheepman in the area during the early 1890s.

S2,T29S,R6W,SLM. 125.

JIMMIE REED CREEK (Daggett). See Crouse Creek.

JIMMIE REED SPRING (Beaver) is at the head of Jimmie Reed Creek.

JIMMY KEEN FLAT (Grand) is in the western section of Wilson Mesa, fifteen miles east of Moab*. It was named for Jim Stocks, who homesteaded in this area. His nickname was Jimmy Keen.
S13,T26S,R23E,SLM; 8,000' (2,438m). 146.

JOCKEY ROAD (Beaver) is one of the early roads running east and west through the center of the county. John (Jockey) W. Myers was an early freighter on this road that was used to carry supplies and ores between the eastern Nevada mines and Milford*, Utah.
T30S,R14,15W,SLM. 578.

JOCKEYS CANYON (Beaver) is in the foothills south of Beaver* where it drains northwest. See Jockey Road for name source.
S15,T30S,R7W,SLM.

JOE AND HIS DOG (Emery) is a rock formation on the San Rafael Swell, six miles north of I-70 near the head of Saddle Horse Canyon. The feature was said to resemble Joe Swasey and his dog.
SW¼,T21S,R10E,SLM; 6,500' (1,981m). 193.

JOE LAY RESERVOIR (Garfield) is in the Escalante Mountains at the west end of the Aquarius Plateau. It is part of a cluster of small lakes and reservoirs at the head of North Creek. Joseph Lay was an early cattleman and rancher in the area.
T33S,R1E,SLM; 9,450' (2,880m). 602.

JOE WILSON CANYON (San Juan) originates one mile east of Wilson Arch. The canyon drains southwest into Hatch Wash. See Wilson Mesa for name source.
S14,T29S,R23E,SLM to S31,T29S,R23E, SLM.

JOES DUGOUT* (Utah). See Dugout Station* (Utah).

JOES VALLEY (Emery) surrounds Joes Valley Reservoir, eleven miles northwest of Orangeville* at the head of Straight Canyon. There are two versions to the name origin. One reports that early immigrants saw an Indian mistreat a fellow Indian named Joe who was then rescued by the settlers. In turn, Joe helped his rescuers in many ways. The other version reports that the valley was named for an early white settler named Joe.
S30,31,T17S,R6E,SLM to S5,6,T18S,R6E, SLM; 6,990' (2,131m). 134(4 Oct. 1981), 143, 360, 466(4 Aug. 1938).

JOES VALLEY RESERVOIR (Emery). See Joes Valley (Emery).

JOHN ALLEN BOTTOM (Garfield) is northwest of Posy Lake and named for an early Escalante* rancher.
9,100' (2,774m). 12.

JOHN HENRY CANYON (Kane) originates at Fourmile Bench and drains southeast into Warm Creek.
S35,T41S,R3E,SLM (at mouth). D.L. 8204.

JOHN R. CANYON (Kane) originates on John R. Flat ten miles northeast of Kanab* and drains southeast. John R. Young held land in this area during pioneer days.
S18,T42S,R5W,SLM to S20,T42S,R6W,SLM. 567.

JOHN R. FLAT (Kane). See John R. Canyon (Kane).

JOHNS CANYON (San Juan) originates on Cedar and Polly mesas and drains southwest into the San Juan River. An earlier name was Douglas Canyon (see Douglas Mesa). Later, John Oliver and his brother Bill ran cattle on this open range in competition with Jimmy Palmer, an alleged murderer and horse rustler. Palmer killed John then fled to Arizona.

He was later captured and died in a Texas jail.
T39,40S,R17,18E,SLM. 567, 610.

JOHNS VALLEY (Garfield) is on the upper Sevier River, East Fork, north of Bryce Canyon National Park. The valley was named for John A. Widtsoe. Nearby Widtsoe* was also named for Widtsoe, an early Mormon apostle who supervised the settling of the region.
T32-35S,R2,3W,SLM.

JOHNSON* (Garfield) was one of numerous small settlements along the upper Sevier River. Some of the others were Hatchtown*, Asay*, and Castle*. Johnson later became Hatch*. See Hatch*.
145.

JOHNSON* (Iron). See Enoch*.

JOHNSON* (Kane) was first settled up Johnson Canyon east of Kanab*. The Johnson brothers, Joel H., Joseph E., Benjamin F., and William D., along with their families, founded the community in the spring of 1871. Brigham Young wanted a settlement in this region, so he recommended the brothers leave their Virgin River Valley location to settle there.
S12,T43S,R5W,SLM; 5,240' (1,597m). 89, 289, 455, 516, 542, 500.

JOHNSON* (Tooele). See Clover* (Tooele).

JOHNSON CANYON (Garfield) originates on the Paunsaugunt Plateau six miles east of Hatch*. It drains northwest into the Sevier River. The canyon was named for Joel Hills Johnson who established a sawmill in the canyon with George Wilson. The canyon was previously named Hillsdale* for Joel's middle name, Hills. See Hillsdale text and references.
S27,T36S,R4½W,SLM to S15,T36S,R5W, SLM.

JOHNSON CANYON (**Kane**) is ten miles east of Kanab*. It had an earlier name of Spring Canyon and was the site of an early ranch owned by John D. Lee. When the Johnson brothers moved in with their families in the spring of 1871, the name was changed to Johnson Canyon. See Johnson*.
S24,T43S,R1W,SLM (at mouth).

JOHNSON CREEK (**Duchesne**) originates in the south central section of the Uinta Mountains, one and one-fourth miles west of Johnson Lake. The creek drains northwest into the upper Whiterocks River. See the lake for name source.
S32,T4N,R1W,USM (at mouth).

JOHNSON CREEK (**San Juan**) originates four miles north of Brushy Basin on the western slopes of the Abajo Mountains. It drains south southeast into the head of Recapture Creek. It was named for Zeke Johnson, an early cattleman.
S7,T36S,R23E,SLM (at mouth).

JOHNSON HOLLOW (**Beaver**) originates on the western slopes of the Tushar Mountains north of Johnson Peak. It drains southwest into Bone Hollow and was named for Samuel Johnson, a sheep man in this area in 1890.
S3,4,T29S,R6W,SLM. 125.

JOHNSON LAKE (**Uintah**) is in the south central section of the Uinta Mountains, midway between Cliff Lake and Paradise Park Reservoir. It drains into Lily Lake. Alf Johnson ran cattle in the area.
S35,T4N,R1W,USM; 10,785' (3,287m). 309.

JOHNSON PEAK (**Beaver**) is south of the head of Johnson Hollow on the western slopes of the Tushar Mountains. See Johnson Hollow for name source.
S3,T29S,R6W,SLM; 8,939' (2,725m).

JOHNSON TWIST (**Washington**) was the first trail made from the Toquerville* area, up and over the Hurricane Fault, into the upper Virgin River Valley. In 1858, on instructions from Brigham Young, Nephi Johnson pioneered this trail that led to the white man's discovery of Zion Canyon.
500.

JOHNSON VALLEY RESERVOIR (**Sevier**) is one and one-half miles north of Fish Lake. John Johnson ran a dairy there during the summer months.
S24,25,26,T25S,R2E,SLM; 8,819' (2,688m). 585.

JOHNSONS FORT* (**Iron**). See Enoch*.

JOHNSONS PASS (**Tooele**) is six miles west of Clover*. The pass separates the Stansbury Mountains and the Onaqui Mountains and was named for Luke S. Johnson, an original settler of Clover.
S36,T5S,R7W,SLM; 6,237' (1,901m). 477.

JOHNSONS SETTLEMENT* (**Iron**). See Enoch*.

JOHNSONS SETTLEMENT* (**Tooele**). See Clover* (Tooele).

JOHNSTONS PASS (**Tooele**). See Look Out Pass (Tooele).

JOHNSTOWN* (**Sanpete**) was a small temporary settlement one-half mile west of Pigeon Hollow Junction on US-89. The community was named for two Johns, Anderson and Peterson, who owned property in the area. Johnstown did not survive as a settlement.
S15,T16S,R3E,SLM; 5,480' (1,670m). 336.

JORDAN LAKE (**Duchesne**) is one of the lakes in the Naturalist Basin in the western section of the Uinta Mountains. Nearby is Mount Agassiz. The lake was named for David Starr Jordan, a noted biologist and an authority on fish. He

was a student of Agassiz.
S33,T4N,R8W,USM; 10,680' (3,255m). 298, 530.

JORDAN NARROWS (Salt Lake, Utah) is a deep, narrow defile at the Point of the Mountain where the Jordan River has cut a passageway on its course from Utah Lake to the Great Salt Lake.
S26,T4S,R1W,SLM. 494, 546.

JORDAN RIVER (Utah, Salt Lake) originates at freshwater Utah Lake in Utah County and drains north through the Jordan Narrows into the salty Great Salt Lake in Salt Lake County. The similarity of this drainage system with the Holy Land, where the Jordan River drains from the freshwater Sea of Galilee to the Dead Sea, influenced the early Mormon pioneers into naming the local river. For a while it carried other earlier names: Proveau's Fork for Etienne Proveau, and the Western Jordan River, which was soon changed to its present name, the Jordan River.
S25,T5S,R1W,SLM to S20,T2N,R1W,SLM. 27, 314, 466(3 Sept. 1987), 501, 546, 604.

JORDANELLE RESERVOIR (Wasatch) is currently under construction at Hailstone Junction eight miles north of Heber*. The reservoir is scheduled for completion in the early 1990s. The Jordanelle name originated with the grandfather of Clift Jordan who owned property there. The reservoir site had an earlier name of Bates Reservoir.
S31,30,32,T2SS,R5E,SLM. 101, 466(3 Sept. 1987).

JOSEPH* (Sevier) is on US-89 six miles southwest of Elsinore* near the Sevier River. The community was named for Joseph A. Young, first president of the Sevier Stake of the Mormon Church. It had an early name of Jericho*.
S14,14,T25S,R3W,SLM; 5,437' (1,657m). 100(v17), 289, 542, 569, 584, 585.

JOY* (Millard) was a small mining settlement in the Drum Mountains near Mount Laird, southeast of the Fish Spring Range. Today it is a ghost town site thirty miles northwest of Delta*. Harry Joy was a mining engineer from Detroit, Michigan. In 1872 he and his partner, Charles Howard, organized the Detroit Mining District with the new town of Joy as its center. Isolation and the cost of transporting ores and supplies forced the mine to shut down. The town subsequently died out.
S26,T14S,R11W,SLM; 5,940' (1,811m). 89, 516.

JUAB* (Juab) was established in 1860 and received the name Chicken Creek* from the creek the settlers built on. Shortly afterward, the town was abandoned, then resettled as John C. Widbeck's Overland Stage Station. When the Utah Southern Railroad came through in 1876, Widbecks Station became an important railroad stop and John C. renamed it Juab. In 1879, when the railroad extended its line to Milford*, Juab gradually declined in importance and population. Today it is farmland. The word "Juab" comes from the name already given to the valley by the local Indians, the Uabs, Yuabs, or Yoab Indians of the Piute Tribe and means flat or level plain. Another record also incorporates the word "thirsty" into the meaning of Juab.
S9,T15S,R1W,SLM; 5,080' (1,548m). 27, 89, 100(v13), 289, 314, 516, 542.

JUAB COUNTY. In 1852 the Utah Territorial Assembly created four new counties. Juab was one of them. See Juab* for name source.

JUAB VALLEY (Juab, Utah) has a north-south orientation between Santaquin* and Mona Reservoir. Levan* and Nephi* are in the valley. See Juab references.
T11-16S,R1E,1W,SLM.

JUDD MOUNTAIN (Box Elder) is eight miles west northwest of the junction of Dahar Creek and Cotton Creek to form

Grouse Creek. Frank Judd built a cabin there and ran a small moonshine business. He later homesteaded the site.
S2,T12N,R19W,SLM; 7,898' (2,407m). 525.

JUNCTION* (Piute) was first settled in 1880 on what is today's US-89 and U-153 at the junction of the East Fork and the Sevier River. The settlement had an earlier name of City Creek*.
S32,T29S,R3W,SLM and S5,T30S,R3W,SLM; 6,002' (1,829m). 242, 314, 546.

JUNCTION* (Wayne). See Fruita*.

JUNCTION CREEK (Box Elder) enters Utah from Idaho, then drains south into the Raft River.
567.

JUSTENSEN FLATS (Emery) are on the San Rafael Swell at the head of Devils Canyon. I-70 passes through the flats that are named (with a slight change in spelling) for Orson and Buck Justesen, sheepherders.
7,200' (2,203m). 193.

- K -

KACHINA BRIDGE (San Juan). See Natural Bridges National Monument.

KAIPAROWITS PEAK (Garfield) was the name given by the Powell survey to Canaan Mountain on the Kaiparowits Plateau.

KAIPAROWITS PLATEAU (Garfield) is approximately sixty miles long and has a northwest-southeast orientation. The plateau is located southeast of Escalante*. The southeast Navajo Point overlooks Lake Powell and the northwest rise is Canaan Mountain (Kaiparowits Peak). Stegner states that the plateau was Zane Grey's Wild Horse Mesa. Older maps refer to it as the Straight Cliffs Plateau. The Indian name for the plateau has various meanings depending upon who is interpreting. "Big Mountain's Little Brother" is one. Another is "One-Arm," in reference to Major Powell, who lost an arm in the battle of Shiloh during the Civil War. A third is "Home of Our People."
12, 46, 314, 422, 496, 602.

KAMAS* (Summit) is on U-189 and Beaver Creek, sixteen miles northeast of Heber*. Kamas was first settled in 1857 as a small farming community, but the town rapidly diversified into cattle, lumbering, dairying, and, more recently, recreation. The word "Kamas" is a modified term derived from an Indian word. Through many spelling modifications (Chamas, Camass, Kamash, Camas, etc.) it refers to an edible bulb found in the valley (*Camassia quamash*). The Indians ate it dried, roasted, or steamed; the bulb was a staple throughout this region at one time. In a broader sense the word also means "a small grassy plain among hills."

S16,17,21,T2S,R6E,SLM; 6,475' (1,974m). 289, 314, 442, 542.

KAMAS LAKE (Summit) is at the west end of the Uinta Mountains, two miles north northwest of Mirror Lake. It is a favorite recreation site for the residents of Kamas*.
S15,T1S,R9E,SLM; 10,500' (3,200m). 298.

KAMAS VALLEY (Summit). See Rhodes Valley.
D.L. 7104.

KANAB* (Kane) is on US-89 and Kanab Creek. In 1864 Jacob Hamblin played an important role in the settlement of Kanab. In 1866 the area was vacated because of Indian troubles, then resettled in 1871. The name is Piute meaning willow, referring to the numerous willows growing along the creek.
T43S,R6W,SLM; 4,973' (1,516m). 314, 455, 542, 546.

KANARRAVILLE* (Iron) is thirteen miles southwest of Cedar City* near I-15. The settlement was named for Kanarra (Quanarrah), a Piede Indian and leader of a Piute band. The band often camped where the community is located. Kanarra was killed after being thrown from a horse fourteen miles south of Cedar City.
S34,35,T37S,R12W,SLM; 5,750' (1,753m). 136, 289, 311, 314, 546, 567.

KANE CANYON (Beaver) originates in the Tushar Mountains southeast of Beaver. It drains west into South Creek and was named for the rush-like plants growing in the canyon at Kane Spring. See Kane Spring (Beaver).
T29,30S,R6,7W,SLM. 355.

KANE COUNTY was created in 1860 and redefined in 1864. The county was

211

named for a great friend of the Mormon people, Colonel Thomas L. Kane.
6, 455.

KANE SPRING (**Beaver**) is in lower Kane Canyon southeast of Beaver*. Ordinarily Kane is spelled with a "C" instead of a "K" because it refers to the rushes growing around the spring. This spring was probably named after Colonel Thomas L. Kane, a prominent non-Mormon who helped the Mormons during their times of trial.
S6,T30S,R6W,SLM; 6,600' (2,012m).

KANE SPRING (**Washington**) is west of Pine Valley adjacent to U-18 eleven miles south of Enterprise*. See Kane Spring (Beaver).
S26,T38S,R16W,SLM; 5,600' (1,707m). 100(v13).

KANE SPRING CANYON (**San Juan**) and creek originates on the western slopes of the La Sal Mountains. The canyon drains southwest into the Colorado River. See Kane Spring (Beaver).
S35,T27S,R23E,SLM to S21,T26S,R21E, SLM.

KANESVILLE* (**Davis**) is four miles south of West Weber* and four miles west of Ogden*. The first settlers were Orin Hedlock, John Atkin, and their families. On April 27, 1886, this district separated from the Hooper* Ward and organized under the name of Kanesville, honoring Colonel Thomas L. Kane, a close friend of the Mormons. Today the community has been absorbed into the surrounding communities.
S4,9,T5N,R2W,SLM; 4,260' (1,298m). 100 (v17), 274, 567.

KANOSH* (**Millard**) is on US-91 between Cove Fort* and Meadow*. The settlement was first called Corn Creek* because the first whites found Indian corn growing along the creek in 1854. Kanosh was a friendly Indian chief who camped in this area with his band. "Kan"

means "willow," as in "Kanab." "Oush" means "bowl." Chief Kanosh received his name as a baby because he enjoyed playing with his mother's willow bowl or jug.
S17,20,T23S,R5W,SLM; 5,015' (1,529m). 46, 289, 314, 542, 546.

KANOSH CANYON (**Millard**) is southeast of Kanosh*, with Corn Creek draining through it.

KAYS MEADOW (**Beaver**) is on the western slopes of the Tushar Mountains between Three Creeks, North Fork, and Twin Lakes. It was named after Charles Dent Booth (nicknamed Kay), who bred horses there in 1885.
S35,T28S,R5W,SLM; 9,745' (1,093m). 125.

KAYS WARD* (**Davis**). See Kaysville*.

KAYSVILLE* (**Davis**) is on US-91 and U-115 two miles southeast of Layton*. In 1849 Samuel Oliver Holmes, an early settler, purchased a cabin in the area from a trapper. William Kay and his family arrived one year later and he became the first Mormon bishop. Afterward, the settlement became known as Kays Settlement*. When Kay moved on, some of the people wanted to name the community Freedom*. Legend suggests that Brigham Young objected to the name by asking, "When did Kay's Ward get its freedom?" So, on Brigham Young's recommendation the name Kaysville was finally settled upon.
S34,35,T4N,R1W,SLM; 4,349' (1,326m). 27, 88, 546, 567.

KEARNS* (**Salt Lake**) is one-half mile west of Taylorsville* and two miles southwest of Granger*. It became prominent during World War II as an air base and continued as a thriving community.
S7,18,T2S,R1W,SLM; 4,550' (1,387m).

KEETLEY* (**Wasatch**) was on Silver Creek and US-40, three miles east of Park City*. The earliest name was Camp

Florence* in honor of Dan Robbins's daughter, who was the first "lady" to visit the camp. It later became a Pony Express Station and mining/lumbering center. George A. Fisher, cattleman, land developer, and mayor, named the growing community for John B. (Jack) Keetley, a Pony Express rider and then supervisor of mining construction work in the region. The community was slowly abandoned with diminished mining and lumbering. Soon the entire region will be under the waters backed up behind the Jordanelle Dam.
S35,T1S,R4E,SLM; 6,600' (2,012m). 100 (v3,17), 377, 555(v54), 567.

KELLYS GROVE (Utah) is three miles up Hobble Creek Canyon on the south side of the highway. In 1852 a sawmill was built on this site. Then, around 1875, Cyrus Sanford and Joseph Kelly located on this land and obtained title through homestead entry. The site was named for Joseph Kelly.
S32,T7S,R4E,SLM; 5,101' (1,555m). 270.

KELTON* (Box Elder) was twenty miles off the northwest corner of the Great Salt Lake. It was originally on the Central Pacific Railroad as a stage and freighting station, with hotels, saloons, post office, and homes. After the Lucin Cutoff was built across the lake, Kelton faded into a ghost town. It had an early name of Indian Creek*. The settlement was named after a Mr. Kelton, a local cattleman.
S21,T12N,R11W,SLM; 4,220' (1,286m). 89, 139, 516, 542.

KELTON PASS (Box Elder) is on US-30S eight miles west northwest of Curlew Junction. See Kelton*.
S35,T15N,R12W,SLM; 5,305' (1,617m).

KENILWORTH* (Carbon) is a coal-mining town at the end of U-157, two and one-half miles east of Helper*. The mine is no longer operating and the town is in decline. Some say the town was named for the country surrounding the Kenilworth Castle in Scotland. Others suggest the name is from the old word, "kenil" or "cannel," an old, country term for bituminous coal.
S16,21,T13S,R10E,SLM; 6,800' (2,073m). 100(v17), 542, 567, 607.

KENNECOTT COPPER CORPORATION (Salt Lake) owns the world's largest open-pit copper mine at Bingham Canyon. The corporation was named for Dr. Robert Kennecott, an early explorer and developer in Alaska. See Bingham*. 89.

KENNEDYVILLE* (Rich). See Argyle*.

KENTS LAKE (Beaver) is west of the Tushar Mountain summit on the upper Beaver River drainage between Upper and Lower Kents lakes. The lake was named for Kent Farnsworth, who first acquired land in the area by squatter's rights. He built a dam, then stocked the lake with fish and developed a resort. The property was later sold to Beaver City*.
S6,T30S,R5W,SLM; 8,790' (2,679m). 125, 355, 567.

KERR* (Iron) was a railroad stop on the Los Angeles, Salt Lake Railroad, ten miles south of Nada*. It was named for William J. Kerr, the fourth president of Utah State Agricultural College (today's Utah State University).
555(v49/1).

KESSLER PEAK (Salt Lake, Tooele) is on the crest of the Oquirrh Mountain range, four miles south of the Great Salt Lake. The Kessler family lived at the base of the mountain range for many years.
S51,R2S,R3W,SLM; 8,820' (2,688m). 508.

KETTLE CREEK (Daggett). See Carter Creek.

KILN SPRING (Beaver) is in the east central section of the Wah Wah Mountains north of Revenue Basin. Coke

ovens or kilns are located in the area.
S10,T28S,R15W,SLM; 5,825' (1,775m).

KIMBALL ISLAND (Tooele). See
Stansbury Island.

KIMBALLS* (Summit) is one and
one-half miles east of present Kimballs
Junction, north northeast of Park City*.
The area was explored by Parley P. Pratt
in 1848. George Kimball later owned a
ranch there. The community became an
Overland Stage stop and William H.
Kimball built a rock stage structure there
that still stands today.
S20,T1S,R4E,SLM; 6,388' (1,947). 89, 516,
542, 546, 567.

KIMBALLS JUNCTION (Summit) is
north northeast of Park City* at the
junction of I-80 and U-224, one and
one-half miles west of Kimballs*.
T1S,R4E,SLM; 6,366' (1,940m). 89, 516,
546.

KIMBERLY* (Piute) is a mining ghost
town site. Peter Kimberly bought the
property high in the north Tushar
Mountains. In the 1890s several gold
strikes were made and Upper and Lower
Kimberly settlements developed where
gold, silver, lead, and copper were mined.
Mining resources were being depleted by
1908 and by 1938 the towns had died.
S2,T27S,R5W,SLM; 8,250' (2,515m). 89,
233, 396, 516, 555(v35).

KING BENCH (Garfield). There are two
benches. This one is north of the
Escalante River and east of Calf Creek.
John King was a pioneer cattleman in
the area.
S34,T35S,R6E,SLM. 12, 602.

KING BENCH (Garfield). This second
bench is on the southern slopes of the
Aquarius Plateau. Hells Backbone is
seven miles northwest. See above for
name origin.
S36,T33S,R3E,SLM.

KINGFISHER CANYON (Daggett) is

now in Flaming Gorge Reservoir between
Horseshoe Canyon and Hideout Canyon.
It was named by Major Powell for the
numerous kingfishers found in the area.
S1,11,T2N,R20E,SLM. 160, 420, 496.

KINGS LAKE (Duchesne) is in the
central Uinta Mountains on the southwest slopes of Kings Peak. See the peak
for name source.
T4N,R4W,USM; 11,416' (3,480m).

KINGS PEAK (Duchesne) is in the south
central section of the Uinta Mountains
between the headwaters of the Uinta and
Yellowstone rivers. Kings Peak is the
highest point in Utah. The peak was
named for Clarence King, an early
director of the U.S. Geological Survey.
13,528' (4,123m). 314, 342, 462, 496, 546.
D.L. 6602.

KINGSTON* (Piute) is on U-62 near the
mouth of the East Fork of the Sevier
River. The community is named for
Thomas R. King and his five sons from
Fillmore. In 1876 they moved to the
mouth of Kingston Canyon in search of
a place to settle.
S15,T30S,R3W,SLM; 6,012' (1,832m). 5, 100
(v13), 289.

KINGSTON CANYON (Piute) has an
east-west orientation with the mouth near
Kingston*. The canyon received its name
from the community it serves.
S30,T30S,R2W,SLM to S15,T30S,R3W,SLM.

KINGSTON FORT* (Davis) was a
Mormon settlement built in 1853 in
South Weber* near the mouth of Weber
Canyon. It was named for the community's first bishop, Thomas Kingston
(reference 27 spells the name Kington).
The tiny fort was abandoned during the
1857 invasion by Johnston's Army. In
1859-60 Joseph Morris and his followers,
who were known as the Morrisites, took
possession of the fort and the Morrisite
"War" followed. See South Weber*.
S26,27,34,35,T5N,R1W,SLM; 4,510'
(1,375m). 27, 88, 289, 516, 542, 546, 567.

KINGSVILLE* (Emery). See Clawson*.

KIRK BASIN (San Juan) is one and one-half miles west of the Colorado line on upper John Creek. Kirk Puckett was a prospector who also raised blooded horses in the basin around 1880.
S31,32,T25S,R26E,SLM; 7,900' (2,408m). 475, 514.

KITCHEN CANYON (Kane) originates four and one-half miles west of its mouth at Nipple Lake and drains east into the Paria River. John G. Kitchen worked in the California gold mines until 1879. He was an early settler who owned a ranch near the mouth of Kitchen Canyon. He ran his cattle near Johnson*.
S29,T40S,R2W,SLM to S35,T40S,R2W,SLM. 455, 567.

KIZ* (Carbon) was fifteen miles east of Price* and ten miles northeast of Wellington* in Clark Valley. Kiz was established in the valley in 1906, but did not flourish, and was abandoned shortly after its inception. George Mead, a businessman, suggested the name in honor of the first woman who settled in the area. Her name was Kiziah and she was the wife of Ephraim Dimick.
T14S,R12E,SLM; 5,885' (1,794m). 89, 360, 510, 516, 567.

KLETTING PEAK (Summit) is at the west end of the Uinta Mountains, two and one-half miles northwest of Hayden Peak. Richard K. A. Kletting was a native of Germany and a conservationist who organized the first forest reserve in Utah on February 22, 1897. He was also the architect of the Utah State Capitol and the Saltair Resort pavilion. The peak was named for him in 1964.
S6,T1S,R10E,SLM; 12,055' (3,674m). 309, 555(Newsletter, v33), 555(v52). D.L. 6302.

KNIGHTSVILLE* (Juab) was at the north end of Godiva Mountain, one-half mile east of Eureka*. Jesse Knight was a well-known mining man, financier, and benefactor. He developed Knightsville in 1897 to house his mining employees and

their families. When the mines were closed, Knightsville was abandoned. During the town's peak it was only one of two mining camps in Utah without saloons or red-light districts. Today it is a ghost town site.
S18,T10S,R2W,SLM; 6,780' (2,067m). 89, 100(v7), 270, 289, 347, 516, 546.

KNOLL, THE (Grand) is twelve miles west of Moab. The feature is a well-known landmark used by early cattlemen and sheep men.
6,316' (1,925m). 146.

KNOLLS* (Tooele) is a siding on the Western Pacific Railroad on the eastern edge of the Great Salt Lake Desert. In the 1880s it was a camp for railroad construction and maintenance men, and later for I-80 highway construction personnel. The name refers to the numerous knolls in the area.
SE¼,T1S,R13W,SLM; 4,238' (1,292m). 498, 567.

KNOWLEN* (Tooele) was on Bates Creek one mile west of the mouth of Ophir Canyon. The community was originally settled in 1869 by Ormus E. Bates. See Batesville*.
S28,T5S,R4W,SLM; 5,700' (1,737m). 153.

KNUDSONS CORNER (Salt Lake) is at Sixty-second South and Holladay Boulevard (1715 East) on Big Cottonwood Creek. The Rasmus C. Knudson family settled in this area in 1864. Members of the Knudson family are still living on the original property today.
S23,T2S,R1E,SLM; 4,565' (1,391m). 466(19 July 1981, H11).

KODACHROME FLAT (Kane) is seventeen miles south of Cannonville*. This area was named by members of a 1947 National Geographic Society expedition. They were referring to the great variety of colored geologic formations found throughout the area.
S3,T38S,R2W,SLM; 5,900' (1,798m). 383 (Sept. 1949).

KOLMAR* (Box Elder). See Lampo*.

KOLOB ARCH (Washington) is on the northeast slope of Gregory Butte in the Kolob section of Zion National Park. Recent measurements indicate that the size of the arch is competitive with the Rainbow Natural Bridge as the world's largest single-span natural arch. See Kolob Canyons for the name source. T39S,R12W,SLM. 163(10-11 Aug. 1983). D.L. 5701.

KOLOB CANYONS (Iron, Washington) are an addition to the north end of Zion National Park. The canyons are a conglomerate of unique sandstone formations and canyons that were annexed to the park in 1955. The name Kolob is derived from Mormon Church doctrine as the star in the center of the universe—the star nearest to the throne of God.

KOLOB CREEK (Washington) originates in the Kolob section of Zion National Park and drains southeast into the North Fork of the Virgin River. See Kolob Canyons for name source. S19,T38S,R10W,SLM to S10,T40S,R10W, SLM.

KOOSHAREM* (Sevier) is in Grass Valley on U-62, five miles north of Greenwich*. The settlement was originally settled in 1877. The name is an Indian word referring to red clover or an edible tuber growing in the valley. The tuber has served as a food staple for the Indians. S35,T26S,R1W,SLM; 6,914' (2,107m). 100 (v17), 289, 314, 542.

KOOSHAREM RESERVOIR (Sevier) is in Plateau Valley north of Grass Valley. The reservoir received its name from the community it serves. S30,31,T25S,R1E,SLM; 6,995' (2,132m).

KOSMO* (Box Elder) was a temporary construction camp on the old railroad route north of the Great Salt Lake between the ghost towns Monument* and Lake*. T12N,R8W,SLM; 4,222' (1,287m). 516.

KREBS BASIN (Duchesne) is in the south central section of the Uinta Mountains at the head of Krebs Creek. Robert Krebs was an early sheep man and cattleman in the area. S4,5,6,T3N,R3W,USM; 10,600' (3,231m). 309.

KREBS LAKE (Duchesne) is in Krebs Basin. See Krebs Basin for the name source.

- L -

LA GORCE ARCH (**Kane**) is a natural arch in Davis Gulch, four miles north northwest of Hole-in-the-Rock. It was named for Dr. John Oliver La Gorce, who served the *National Geographic* magazine for fifty-four years.
T40S,R9E,SLM. 177, 369, 532(D.L. 7403), 602.

LA PLATA* (**Cache**) was near Paradise* on the East Fork of the Little Bear River in the Bear River Mountains. In 1891 silver ore was discovered there by a sheepherder named Johnson. Today it is a ghost town site located on private property. It is recorded that one of the mail riders between La Plata and Huntsville* was David O. McKay, who later became a president of the Mormon Church. "La Plata" is Spanish for silver.
516, 546, 567.

LA SAL* (**San Juan**). Old La Sal, located twelve miles east of present-day La Sal, was first settled in 1877 during the post-Civil War period by Mr. and Mrs. Tom Ray and their eight children. Because of frequent flooding, the old La Sal site was abandoned in 1930 and present-day La Sal was settled on U-46, southeast of Moab. The name means "salt" and was taken from the name of the nearby La Sal Mountains. The town of La Sal had an early name of Coyote*.
S2,T29S,R24E,SLM; 7,125' (2,172m). 89, 146, 406, 514, 542, 546.

LA SAL MOUNTAINS (**San Juan**) are near the Colorado border, north of the small community of La Sal*. The mountains are composed of subterranean igneous laccoliths forced upwards above the surrounding region. At one time they were called the Elk Mountains. It was the Domínguez-Escalante expedition that used the name La Sal for the mountain range and Hayden who made the name official. There are numerous salt deposits in this region.
T25-28S,R24-25E,SLM; 13,089' (3,990m). 100(v17), 275, 314, 475, 583.

LA VEGA* (**San Juan**) was the result of an early attempt by Bluff* residents to develop a town on Spring Creek, several miles northwest of Monticello*. "Vega" is Spanish for "fertile plain."
406.

LA VERKIN* (**Washington**) is near the junction of U-9 and U-17, two miles north northeast of Hurricane*. It is generally agreed that in this area La Verkin is a corruption of the Spanish La Virgen, referring to the Virgin River. La Verkin was first settled in 1897 by the Thomas Judd family from St. George*.
S24,T41S,R13W,SLM; 3,202' (976m). 163(26 June 1852), 289, 311, 314, 494, 496, 542, 600.

LA VERKIN HOT SPRINGS (**Washington**) is a commercial hot springs establishment near La Verkin*.
311.

LABARON CREEK (**Beaver**) originates in the Tushar Mountains and drains northwest into LaBaron Lake and the Beaver River, East Fork. The creek was named after the French LaBaron brothers—Dan, Alonzo, and William. They were early sheep men, prospectors, and trappers in the area around 1874.
S34,T29S,R5W,SLM. 100(v17), 125. D.L. 7501.

LABARON LAKE (**Beaver**) is in the Tushar Mountains near the head of LaBaron Creek. See LaBaron Creek for name source.

LABARON MEADOWS (Beaver) surrounds LaBaron Lake.

LABYRINTH CANYON (Grand) is on the Lower Green River above Stillwater Canyon. It is sixty-two and one-half miles long and was named by the Powell expedition for its tortuous, twisting meanders and overhanging cliffs.
100(v17), 159, 160, 314, 420, 422, 496, 530, 609.

LADY LAIRD PEAK (Juab) is one mile southeast of the ghost town of Joy* and Laird Peak, northwest of Delta*. Folklore suggests the peak was named for a well-known lady of dubious reputation.
S35,T14S,R11W,SLM; 6,982' (2,128m).

LADY MOUNTAIN (Washington) is in Zion National Park one mile northwest of the Zion Lodge. The mountain is named for the feature resembling the form of a woman located near the top of the mountain.
T41S,R10W,SLM; 6,940' (2,115m). 530, 602.

LAGOON RESORT (Davis) is a commercial public resort on the western outskirts of Farmington*. In earlier days it was a swampy, marshy area.
S24,T3N,R1W,SLM; 4,270' (1,301m). 567.

LAGUNA* (Utah) is a generalized area on the shore of Utah Lake. The name goes back to the 1776 Domínguez-Escalante expedition who referred to the Indians and their villages along the shores of the lake as Lagunas, or Lake People.

LAKE* (Box Elder) was a temporary railroad construction camp five miles southeast of Kosmo* on the Central Pacific Railroad route north of the Great Salt Lake. On April 28, 1869, a record was set when the crews laid ten miles of track in one twelve-hour period. The camp was named for the nearby lake.
NW¼,T11N,R7W,SLM. 516.

LAKE ATWOOD (Duchesne). See Atwood Lake.

LAKE BEARD (Duchesne). See Lake George Beard.

LAKE BLANCHE (Salt Lake) is one of a cluster of three alpine lakes in Big Cottonwood Canyon of the Wasatch Range, three miles east of Storm Mountain. The other two are Florence and Lillian at the head of Mill Fork B, South Fork. Lake Blanche was named prior to 1925 for Miss Blanche Cutler.
T2S,R2E,SLM; 8,850' (2,697m).

LAKE BONNEVILLE was a vast body of fresh water occupying the eastern part of the Great Basin during the glacial and post-glacial periods. The lake eventually drained north into the Snake River in Idaho at Red Rock Pass. In 1875, the noted geologist Grove Karl Gilbert named this extinct body of water for Captain B. L. E. Bonneville, who was publicized in Washington Irving's account of Bonneville's travels. In this publication, Irving pushed to have Bonneville's name given to the Great Salt Lake. Since Bonneville never visited the area, the recommendation was rejected. In Utah, the Sevier Lake, Great Salt Lake, and the Bonneville Salt Flats are all remnants of this prehistoric lake.
172, 218, 280, 401, 421, 496, 546.

LAKE BOREHAM (Duchesne) is between Roosevelt* and Duchesne*, two and one-half miles east northeast of Bridgeland*. The lake was previously known as Midview Reservoir and was renamed in memory of a U.S. Civilian Conservation Corps boy who lost his life at the reservoir.
S36,T3S,R3W,USM; 5,262' (1,604m). 307, 567.

LAKE BOTTOM (Grand) is on the Dolores River one mile from its junction with the Colorado River. The original

name was Waring Bottom for Jim Waring (see Waring Canyon), then the name was changed to Lake Bottom in 1910. This low area is subject to periodic flooding. The ford on the Dolores River there was often used by early outlaws.
S16,T23S,R24E,SLM; 4,175' (1,273m). 146.

LAKE CANYON (Duchesne) originates on the West Tavaputs Plateau between Sams and Indian canyons. The canyon drains northeast into the Strawberry River and receives its name from the two small lakes in its main drainage.
S31,T5S,R7W,USM to S7,T4S,R6W,USM.

LAKE CANYON (Emery) originates on the Wasatch Plateau and drains south into the headwaters of Huntington Creek. There are a number of lakes and ponds at the source.
S29,T14S,R6E,SLM to S34,T14S,R6E,SLM.

LAKE CANYON (Kane) originates on the southeast section of the Kaiparowits Plateau at a shallow marshy pond from which the canyon receives its name. It drains southwest into Dry Rock Creek.

LAKE CANYON (San Juan) originates on the Nokai Dome nineteen miles northeast of the junction of the San Juan and Colorado rivers that are now part of Lake Powell. Prior to 1915 Lake Pagahrit was located in Lake Canyon. It was formed over many years by drifting sand, which created a natural dam. The water behind this dam slowly backed up into a freshwater lake. In 1915 three days of unusual flooding caused the sand dam to break and the lake to disappear.
T39S,R11,12E,SLM. 219, 359.

LAKE CATHERINE (Salt Lake) is in Big Cottonwood Canyon near Brighton, one-half mile south of Lake Mary. The lake was named for the wife of William A. Brighton, an early settler who lived in the area during the 1870s.
T3S,R3E,SLM; 9,950' (3,033m). 100(v2), 546.

LAKE CITY* (Utah). See American Fork*.

LAKE CREEK (Millard) drains through Pruess Lake.

LAKE CREEK* (Wasatch). See Daniels*.

LAKE DESOLATION (Salt Lake) is two and one-fourth miles north of Silver Fork* and four and one-half miles northwest of Brighton*.
S10,T2S,R3E,SLM; 9,235' (2,815m).

LAKE FLAT* (Summit) was a small temporary mining settlement two miles southeast of Park City*. It was settled in 1872 by Scottish immigrants and was abandoned in 1875.
S27,T2S,R4E,SLM; 8,000' (2,438m). 89, 516.

LAKE FLORENCE (Salt Lake) is one of three small lakes in a cluster at the head of Mill Fork B, South Fork. Lakes Lillian and Blanche are the other two. Lake Florence was named before 1925 for the daughter of H. L. A. Culmer, a noted artist.
T2S,R2E,SLM; 8,795' (2,681m).

LAKE FORK* (Duchesne). See Upalco*.

LAKE FORK MOUNTAIN (Duchesne) is in the south central section of the Uinta Mountains, two miles east of Moon Lake. The mountain received its name from the river.
S9,10,15,16,T2N,R5W,USM; 10,910' (3,325m).

LAKE FORK RIVER (Duchesne) originates in the central section of the Uinta Mountains near Mount Lovenia and drains into the Duchesne River. One report states that an early trapper named Lake provided the name origin. Another suggests it was the numerous lakes the river drains.
T4N,R6W,USM to S22,T3S,R2W,USM. 163(6 Oct. 1934), 567.

LAKE GEORGE BEARD (**Duchesne**) is two and one-half miles southeast of Kings Peak. The lake was named for George Beard of Coalville*, Utah, an early settler of northern Utah. He was a noted artist and naturalist who painted and sketched in the area. Mount Lovenia is named for Beard's wife.
S9,T4N,R4W,USM; 11,410' (3,478m). 309. D.L. 6604.

LAKE GILBERT (**Summit**). See Gilbert Lake.

LAKE HARDY (**Utah**) is in the Wasatch Mountains one and one-half miles south of Bells Canyon Reservoir. MRN
T3S,R2E,SLM.

LAKE HELEN (**Duchesne**) is one of a cluster of four lakes in the southwestern section of the Uinta Mountains in the upper Rock Creek drainage. The lake was named for Helen Odekirk. See Francis Lake for details.
S13,T4N,R8W,USM; 10,869' (3,313m).

LAKE KATHERINE (**Salt Lake**). See Lake Catherine (Salt Lake).

LAKE LILLIAN (**Salt Lake**) was one of a cluster of three lakes. Lake Lillian was named for the lady who became Mrs. Andy Walker. See Lake Blanche for details.

LAKE LOVENIA (**Summit**) is one-half mile north of Wall Lake. See Mount Lovenia for name source.
S30,T1S,R9E,SLM; 10,300' (3,139m). 298.

LAKE MARTHA (**Salt Lake**) is in the Brighton area of Big Cottonwood Canyon, near Lake Mary. It was named for Mrs. Martha Lambourne, wife of William Lambourne.
T3S,R3E,SLM; 9,590' (2,923m). 100(v2), 371.

LAKE MARY (**Salt Lake**) is at the head of Big Cottonwood Canyon in the Brighton Basin. The lake had an early name of Granite Lake, but was rechristened to honor Mary Borneman, wife of Hartwig Borneman, a noted artist from New York City.
T3S,R3E,SLM; 9,550' (2,911m). 100(v2).

LAKE MOUNTAIN (**Uintah**) is in the southeast section of the Uinta Mountains. Gull Lake is near the summit and Mosby Mountain is three miles west.
SW¼,T2S,R19E,SLM; 9,068' (2,764m). 309.

LAKE NAOMI (**Summit**) is in the western section of the Uinta Mountains, two and one-half miles west of Hayden Peak. MRN
S14,T1S,R9E,SLM; 10,390' (3,167m).

LAKE OLGA (**Duchesne**) is in the southwestern section of the Uinta Mountains between Naturalist and Four Lakes basins.
S3,T3N,R8W,USM.

LAKE PAGAHRIT (**San Juan**) was also known as Hermit Lake, eight miles up Lake Canyon. "Pagahrit" is a Piute Indian word meaning "standing water." There are several variations to the spelling. See Lake Canyon.
T39S,R12E,SLM; 4,000' (1,219m). 35, 359, 406, 567.

LAKE PEAK (**Beaver**) is in the Tushar Mountains one and one-half miles north of Puffer Lake. The peak overlooks the lake.
S30,31,T28S,R4W,SLM; 11,317' (3,449m). 125.

LAKE PHILO (**Garfield**) is on the Aquarius Plateau five miles west of Roundy Reservoir. MRN
NW¼,T32S,R1E,SLM; 9,911' (3,021m).

LAKE POINT* (**Tooele**). See E.T. City*.

LAKE POINT (**Tooele**) is a prominent landpoint just west of the north end of the Oquirrh Range, one and one-half miles southwest of Lake Point Junction.
S25,T1S,R4W,SLM; 5,990' (1,826m).

LAKE POINT JUNCTION (Tooele) overlooks the south end of the Great Salt Lake where US-40, US-alt 50, U-201, U-36, and I-80 merge and diverge.
S19,T1S,R3W,SLM; 4,278' (1,304m).

LAKE POSY (Garfield) is on the Aquarius Plateau fifteen miles northwest of Escalante*. The lake was named for that well-known renegade Indian sub-chief, Posy (Posey), who was killed near Blanding* in 1923 in Utah's "last" Indian "War." See Posy Canyon.
8,676' (2,644m). 224, 409.

LAKE POWELL (San Juan) is the body of water built up behind Glen Canyon Dam. Most of the lake is on the Colorado River in Utah. It was named for Major Powell, who led the first explorations and surveys of the Colorado River. The lake now extends upriver from the dam about two hundred miles.

LAKE SHAMBIP (Tooele). See Rush Lake.

LAKE SHORE* (Utah) is a small agricultural community on the eastern shore of Utah Lake on U-228. One and one-half miles south is Benjamin*. It was first settled about 1860 by families from Spanish Fork*.
S16,17,T8S,R2E,SLM; 4,519' (1,377m). 100 (v17), 270, 289.

LAKE SOLITUDE (Salt Lake) is an isolated, quiet lake one and one-fourth miles west of Brighton* at the head of Big Cottonwood Canyon.
S34,T2S,R3E,SLM; 9,025' (2,751m).

LAKE STREAM (Beaver) originates near the southeast base of Lake Peak and drains into the Beaver River at Three Creeks.
T29S,R5W,SLM. 125.

LAKE TIMPANOGOS (Utah). See Utah Lake.

LAKE VIEW* (Utah) is a small community, an outgrowth of Provo*, on the eastern shore of Utah Lake near the mouth of the Provo River. It was first settled by whites in 1849.
S33,34,T6S,R2E,SLM; 4,544' (1,385m). 270, 289, 542.

LAKESIDE* (Box Elder) is on the western shore of the Great Salt Lake. In 1901 the settlement developed and was inhabited by people who worked for the Southern Pacific Railroad that crossed the lake. Today the area is restricted to federal government military use.
S22,T6N,R9W,SLM; 4,217' (1,285m). 100 (v17), 156, 498.

LAKESIDE MOUNTAINS (Box Elder) have a north-south orientation on the western shores of the Great Salt Lake.
S4,T5N,R9W,SLM; 6,625' (2,019m).

LAKETOWN* (Millard). See Crafton* (Millard).

LAKETOWN* (Rich) is on US-30 at the south end of Bear Lake. It was settled in 1864 and was first known as Last Chance*. The name was changed to Laketown after the establishment of a post office in 1877.
S31,T13N,R6E,SLM; 5,988' (1,825m). 100 (v17), 289, 542, 546, 567.

LAKETOWN CANYON (Rich) originates five miles south southwest of Laketown* and drains into the southern end of Bear Lake. The canyon is named for the community it serves.

LAKEVIEW* (Tooele). See Lincoln*.

LAKOTA* (Rich) is a small agricultural and recreational community at the mouth of Swan Creek on the west side of Bear Lake from which the settlement received its name.
S5,T14N,R5E,SLM; 5,950' (1,814m).

LAMBS CANYON (**Salt Lake**) originates seven miles northwest of Park City*. It drains northwest into Parleys Canyon. In the 1860s Horace and Neona Lamb built a cabin and Abel Lamb built a sawmill in the canyon.
S27,T1S,R3E,SLM. 172, 567.

LAMERDORF CANYON (**Beaver**) originates at the south end of the Wah Wah Mountains at Lamerdorf Peak and drains northeast into Willow Creek and the Wah Wah Valley. Charles Lamerdorf was an early mining man in the region. See also Lamerdorf Spring.
S18,T29S,R15W,SLM to S3,T29S,R15W, SLM. 125.

LAMERDORF PEAK (**Beaver**) is at the head of Lamerdorf Canyon. See Lamerdorf Spring for name source.
S18,T29S,R15W,SLM; 8,425' (2,568m).

LAMERDORF SPRING (**Beaver**) is at the base of Lamerdorf Peak. Charles Lamerdorf was a mining man who produced charcoal near the spring for the Frisco* smelters during the 1870s.
S18,T29S,R15W,SLM. 125.

LAMOTTE PEAK (**Summit**) is in the northwest section of the Uinta Mountains near Amethyst Basin.
S31,T1N,R11E,SLM; 12,720' (3,877m).

LAMPO* (**Box Elder**) was a construction camp on the Union Pacific Railroad northwest of the Great Salt Lake. Earlier it was known as Kolmar* (Colmer*) for a railroad official, and was also known as Junction City*. Today it is ghost town site.
S20,T11N,R5W,SLM. 516, 567.

LANDSCAPE ARCH (**Grand**) is in the Devils Garden section of Arches National Park near Moab*. It is one of the great natural arches of the known world. In 1934 Frank A. Beckwith of Delta* named the arch. He thought the area looked like a beautiful painting when you looked through the arch.

S21,T23S,R21E,SLM. 262, 325, 383(v92), 514, 546.

LAPOINT* (**Uintah**) is a small agricultural community on U-121 fourteen miles north of Roosevelt*. It was originally named Taft* to honor U.S. President William Howard Taft. The present name reflects its location on a southern spur of the Uinta Mountains.
S17,T5S,R19E,SLM; 5,562' (1,695m). 100(v17), 567.

LARK* (**Salt Lake**) was three miles south of Copperton* and three and one-half miles west northwest of Herriman* on the eastern slopes of the Oquirrh Mountains. It was settled on January 3, 1866, as a small mining community. When the nearby Kennecott Copper open-pit mining operation expanded, Lark was dismantled and by 1978 it was basically nonexistent. It is believed the community name was brought from England.
S29,T3S,R2W,SLM; 5,460' (1,664m). 360.

LAST CHANCE NAMES, some reasons for. Several specific examples are listed:
"This is it, we can go no further."
"If we can't make it here, where else can we go?"
"Men, this is the last water for the next forty-eight hours. We leave at midnight."
"This is the last water hole before we cross the desert."

LAST CHANCE (**Rich**). See Laketown* (Rich).

LAST CHANCE BAY (**Kane**) is in Lake Powell at the mouth of Last Chance Creek from which it received its name.

LAST CHANCE BENCH (**Beaver**) is on the benchland in the Beaver Valley north of Beaver*.
T28S,R7W,SLM.

LAST CHANCE CREEK (**Emery, Sevier**) originates south of I-70 and Old

Woman Plateau at the junction of North Last Chance and South Last Chance. It drains southeast through Last Chance Desert toward the Muddy River. S16,T25S,R4E,SLM (at head).

LAST CHANCE CREEK (Kane) originates on the west side of the Kaiparowits Plateau and drains south southeast into Lake Powell. It is the only source of water for cattle grazing in that area. S34,T39S,R3E,SLM (to mouth of Lake Powell). 494, 602.

LAST CHANCE DESERT (Emery, Sevier). Last Chance Creek drains through the desert. S13,14,T25S,R5E,SLM and S17,18,T25S, R6E,SLM.

LAST CHANCE HOLLOW (Beaver) is on the western slopes of the Tushar Mountains and drains into the North Fork of North Creek. It is the last draw or hollow on the way up North Fork. S3,T28S,R6W,SLM. 125.

LATUDA* (Carbon) was a mining settlement one mile up Spring Canyon. In 1914 Frank Latuda, a mine owner, developed an existing mine and settlement known earlier as Liberty*. Latuda shut down in 1954 and by 1967 all the miners and their families had vacated the town. S8,T13S,R9E,SLM; 6,865' (2,092m). 89, 516, 542, 607.

LAVENDER CANYON (San Juan) originates on the northern slopes of Salt Creek Mesa at Cathedral Butte. It drains northeast into Indian Creek. MRN S4,T31S,R21E,SLM (at mouth).

LAWRENCE* (Emery) is a small agricultural community on Roper Wash, five miles southeast of Huntington*. It was first settled in 1879 and named for the St. Lawrence River. S32,T17S,R9E,SLM; 5,645' (1,729m). 289, 567.

LAYTON* (Davis) is an outgrowth of Kaysville*. In 1885 the town was known as Little Fort*, since a larger fort had been built in Kaysville. It subsequently became Kaysville Second Ward*. In 1892 the community received its present name that honors Christopher Layton, a member of the Mormon Battalion and an early bishop who brought the first alfalfa seed into the growing community. For a short period of time it was also known as Laytona*. S16,17,20,21,T4N,R1W,SLM; 4,000' (1,219m). 88, 100(v5), 289, 542, 546, 567.

LAYTONA* (Davis) is the name of a present-day subdivision in North Layton*. See Layton*. S17,T4N,R1W,SLM; 4,525' (1,379m).

LEAMINGTON* (Millard) is on U-132 and the Sevier River, five miles east of Lynndyl*. It was established in 1871 and named after a city in England. S10,T15S,R4W,SLM; 4,738' (1,444m). 567.

LEAMINGTON HILL JUNCTION* (Millard). See Lynndyl*.

LEAN-TO CANYON (San Juan) originates seven miles east of the mouth of Dark Canyon and drains west into that canyon. A lean-to line camp was established in the area across from the mouth of Sheep Canyon. Early cattlemen and sheep men used the camp.

LEAP CREEK (Washington) originates near Anderson Valley five miles southwest of New Harmony* and drains southeast into Ash Creek. See Peters Leap. S6-36,T39S,R13W,SLM.

LEAVITT CANYON (Tooele) originates on the Oquirrh Mountain summit, one and one-half miles north of Markham Peak. The canyon drains west into Tooele Valley. In 1850 a Mr. Leavitt built a log cabin at the mouth of the canyon. S7,8,9,T3S,R3W,SLM. 153.

LEBARON CREEK (Beaver). See LaBaron Creek (Beaver).

LECONTE LAKE (Duchesne) is at the west end of the Uinta Mountains in the Naturalist Basin. This cluster of lakes at the foot of Mount Agassiz are all named for noted naturalists or scientists, most of whom were students of Agassiz. Joseph Leconte was a geologist.
S28,T4N,R8W,USM; 10,920' (3,328m). 298, 530.

LEEDS* (Washington) is southeast of the Pine Valley mountains on I-15. The community became an outgrowth of nearby Harrisburg* when settlers from Leeds*, Yorkshire, England, moved to the site in 1867. The original name was Bennington*, in honor of Benjamin Stringham, the presiding Mormon elder. He recommended the name be changed to Leeds.
S7,T41S,R13W,SLM; 3,460' (1,055m). 100 (v17), 154, 289, 311.

LEES FERRY (Arizona) crosses at the mouth of the Paria River across the Utah border on the Arizona side. This crossing was very important in Utah's history. John D. Lee settled there with his family after fleeing from the law following the Mountain Meadows Massacre. Lee's wife originally named the crossing the Lonely Dell. Lee operated a ferry across the Colorado River at this point, which was an ancient Indian crossing as well as a place where the early Spaniards, outlaws, trappers, and travelers crossed the Colorado River. Someone has said that Lees Ferry was the "Forty-second and Broadway" of this isolated region.
160, 463, 496, 546.

LEES SPRING* (Beaver) is on the southwestern slopes of the Tushar Mountains at the head of Lees Spring Wash. To the northwest is Beaver*. John P. Lee was an Indian fighter and early settler in this area.
125.

LEES SPRING WASH (Beaver) originates at Lees Spring southeast of Beaver*. See Lees Spring for name source.
S30,31,T30S,R6W,SLM.

LEESBURG* (Sanpete). See Sterling*.

LEETON* (Uintah) is five and one-half miles south of Whiterocks*. Henry Lee, an early settler and farmer, established a store there in 1910.
S18,T1S,R1E,USM; 5,500' (1,676m). 494, 542.

LEFT HAND COLLETT CANYON (Kane, Garfield) originates on the central Kaiparowits Plateau. It drains northeast to join Right Hand Collett Canyon. Together these two form Twentymile Wash. See Right Hand Collett for name source.
S27,T38S,R3E,SLM to S36,T37S,R4E,SLM.

LEHI* (Utah) is on I-15 three miles northwest of American Fork*. On February 5, 1852, David Evans presented the residents' request for the incorporation of the community of Dry Creek*. The request was granted under the name of Lehi. This name was chosen because the people of Lehi in the Book of Mormon had frequently moved, as had the pioneers. The community had an earlier name of Evansville* in honor of David Evans.
S8,9,T5S,R1E,SLM; 4,550' (1,387m). 270, 289, 384, 546.

LEIDY PEAK (Daggett) is in the east central Uinta Mountains at the head of the North Fork of Ashley Creek. Joseph Leidy was an astronomer and noted paleontologist who arrived in the West in 1871 with William Cope to study fossil remains. He developed a monograph on the fossil horse.
12,028' (3,666m). 172, 309, 494.

LELAND* (Utah) was two and one-half miles east of Benjamin*. This small settlement was absorbed into Spanish

Fork*. The town was named for Leland Creer, an early settler.
S23,26,T8S,R2E,SLM; 4,560' (1,390m). 100(v17).

LEMAY ISLAND (Box Elder) is an isolated rise in the Great Salt Lake Desert north of Wendover* and west of Great Salt Lake. These western desert islands are not islands in the general marine sense. Lemay Island is surrounded by salt beds, mud, and alkaline flats.
S1,12,13,T5N,R18W,SLM; 4,906' (1,495m).

LEMON SPRING (Washington) is near the head of Echo Canyon, which drains south southwest into Zion National Park. It was named (losing an "m") for James A. Lemmon, an early logging operator in the area.
S31,T40S,R9W,SLM. U.S.G.S. D.L. 8102.

LEMONADE SPRINGS (Sevier). See Big Rock Candy Mountain.

LEOTA* (Uinta) was an outgrowth of Randlett*. The early Leota Ranch was established in 1904 by R. S. Collett and others. The name was that of a local Indian girl given by Mrs. Annie M. Hacking, an early resident.
S22,T7S,R20E,SLM; 4,900' (1,494m). 542, 567.

LES GEORGE POINT (Kane) is a grazing area west of the Escalante River, southeast of King Mesa, and north of Coyote Gulch. It was named for Leslie George, an Escalante* cattleman.
S2,T39S,R8E,SLM (center); 4,961' (1,512m). 12.

LEVAN* (Juab) is on I-15 and U-28 eleven miles south of Nephi*. There are several French, Latin, or Piute interpretations of the name, suggesting it means East of the Sunrise, Land of the Sunrise, Rear Rank of a Moving Army, Frontier Settlement, or Little Water. The tongue-in-cheekers say the name is a reverse spelling of Navel* because it is located in

the center of the state. Several different spellings have been recorded.
S29,30,31,T14S,R1E,SLM; 5,314' (1,624m). 100(v17), 289, 347, 542, 567.

LEVAN RIDGE (Juab) is near Levan*.

LEWIS PEAK (Weber) is northeast of Ogden*. Lewis W. Shurtliff, the local postmaster, joined a group who climbed the peak in the late 1800s and placed a flag at the summit. They claimed to be the first whites to make the trek to the top.
S21,T6N,R1W,SLM; 8,031' (2,448m). 274, 494, 567.

LEWISALLEN* (Daggett). See Manila*.

LEWISTON* (Cache) is two miles south of the Idaho border on U-61. The area was originally settled in 1870, although cattle had previously been herded in this region. It was named for the first Mormon bishop in the local ward, William H. Lewis. The settlement had earlier names of Poverty Flat and in 1878, Cub Hill after the nearby Cub River. In June 1890 it was renamed Lewiston.
S4,5,8,9,T14N,R1E,SLM; 4,506' (1,373m). 289, 449, 542, 567.

LEWISTON* (Tooele). See Mercur* (Tooele).

LIBERTY* (Carbon). See Latuda*.

LIBERTY* (Uintah). See Tridell*.

LIBERTY* (Weber) is on U-162 east of North Ogden* and north of Eden*. The settlement was laid out in 1892 as an outgrowth of Eden. There are several reasons presented for the name source. One version states that shortly after the Civil War the name "liberty" was very popular throughout the country. Another source claims that after John Freeman had been having trouble with range cattle, he told his neighbors, Fisher and Morris of North Ogden, that since people

seemed to be taking a lot of liberties with property, he thought Liberty was an appropriate name for the settlement. Another reference states that the community was named after the Liberty Prison at Liberty*, Clay County, Missouri. The Prophet Joseph Smith of the Mormon Church was held in this jail at one time.
S34,35,T7N,R1E,SLM; 5,118' (1,560m). 100 (v17), 274, 289, 494, 567.

LICK SKILLET (Washington). See Tonaquint*.

LIGHTNING LAKE (Duchesne) is in the southwest section of the Uinta Mountains on the upper drainage of Rock Creek.
S23,T4N,R8W,USM; 10,819' (3,298m). D.L. 6803.

LIGHTNING PEAK (Utah) is three and one-half miles south of the head of the south fork of Provo River.
S19,T6S,R4E,SLM; 10,056' (3,065m).

LIGHTNING RIDGE (Duchesne) is between Rhoades Canyon and the North Fork of the Duchesne River, four miles northwest of Hanna. On September 6, 1919, Jess Bigler, a sheepherder from Midway*, was killed by lightning on the ridge.
309.

LIGNITE CANYON (Emery, Grand). See Gray Canyon.

LILLY LAKE (Wasatch) is at the west end of the Uinta Mountains near U-150 and Lost Lake and one-half mile east of Trial Lake. It was named for Ben Lilly, who hunted wolf and bear in this region during the early 1900s.
S4,T2S,R9E,SLM; 9,880' (3,011m). 309.

LILY LAKE (Duchesne) is in the south central section of the Uinta Mountains on the headwaters of the Uinta River. It is a shallow lake covered with yellow pond lilies (Nuphar polysepalum).
10,200' (3,109m).

LILY LAKE (Uintah) is in the southeast section of the Uinta Mountains at the head of Lily Lake Creek. It is a small shallow lake covered with water lilies.
S2,T3N,R1W,USM; 10,310' (3,142m).

LILY LAKE CREEK (Uintah, Duchesne) originates in the southeast section of the Uinta Mountains at Lily Lake and drains southwest into the Whiterocks River.
S2,11,15,T3N,R1W,USM.

LILY LAKES (Summit) are in the southwest section of the Uinta Mountains on the upper Provo River drainage. There are two Lily Lakes located among a cluster of lakes that include Washington and Trial lakes. The easternmost of the Lily Lakes is a research and study area for Brigham Young University. The yellow pond lily is plentiful in this area.
S31,T1S,R9E,SLM; 10,025' (3,056m).

LILY PAD LAKE (Duchesne) is in the southwest section of the Uinta Mountains near Pine Island Lake. Four miles north is Mount Agassiz. The yellow pond lily is abundant in this region.
S20,T3N,R8W,USM; 10,290' (3,136m).

LILY PAD LAKE (Summit) is in the north central section of the Uinta Mountains on the headwaters of Sheep Creek. This lake is located in a cluster of lakes including Spirit Lake. The yellow pond lily (Nuphar polysepalum) is plentiful there.
10,380' (3,164m).

LILY PAD LAKES (Duchesne) is a small group of lakes in the south central section of the Uinta Mountains, six and one-half miles southeast of Mount Emmons. The water lily is plentiful there.
S30,T3N,R3W,USM; 10,250' (3,124m).

LIME CREEK (San Juan) originates on the southern slopes of Cedar Mesa. The creek drains south through large lime rock formations, then into the San Juan River.
S32,T41S,R19E,SLM (at mouth).

LIME MOUNTAIN (Beaver) is the high point at the north end of the Beaver Lake Mountains and is composed primarily of limestone.
S20,T26S,R11W,SLM; 6,895' (2,102m). 125.

LIME POINT (Beaver) is near U-21 on the western slopes of the Wah Wah Mountains. The rock formation is a light-colored limestone.
S36,T26S,R16W,SLM; 6,641' (2,024m).

LIMEKILN GULCH (Salt Lake) is in the northeast section of Salt Lake City*, one-half mile east of the city cemetery. The limekilns were built during pioneer days for servicing area mines, especially those up City Creek Canyon, near the mouth of Cottonwood Gulch. As of this printing the limekilns are still there.
S33,T1N,R1E,SLM. 516.

LIMESTONE POINT (Beaver) is an area of limestone outcrops located in the foothills west of the north end of Beaver Valley, northwest of Beaver*.
S30,T27S,R7W,SLM; 7,120' (2,170m).

LIMESTONE SPRING (Beaver) is on the southeastern slopes of the Mineral Mountains northwest of Adamsville*. The spring emerges from a limestone formation.
S14,T29S,R9W,SLM; 6,600' (2,012m).

LINCOLN* (Beaver) was a former boomtown near the Lincoln Mine in Lincoln Gulch. The settlement was formerly known as the Rollins Mine for James A. Rollins, who discovered it in 1858. The town was later renamed to honor U.S. President Abraham Lincoln.
S20,T29S,R9W,SLM. 567.

LINCOLN* (Tooele) was settled in 1876 at the mouth of Pine Canyon on the west side of the Oquirrh Mountains. Although the original name was Pine Canyon*, the settlers changed it to Lake View* because the settlement had such a beautiful view of Great Salt Lake. After a post office was established, it was realized that there were numerous "Lake" names in the territory; therefore, the name was changed to Lincoln, in honor of the President of the U.S.
S11,14,T3S,R4W,SLM; 4,917' (1,499m).

LINCOLN GULCH (Beaver) originates at the south end of the Mineral Mountains northwest of Adamsville*. The name comes from the nearby Lincoln Mine.
T29S,R9W,SLM.

LINDON* (Utah) was established in 1850 as an outgrowth of Pleasant Grove*, located one mile north. The settlement had an early name of Stringtown* because the houses were built along a single road—today's US-89. An old linden tree (Tilia) growing in the town in 1901 was the inspiration for the present name. Note the difference in the spelling of the tree name. It has never been corrected.
S33,34,T5S,R2E,SLM; 4,654' (1,419m). 270, 289, 567.

LINDSAY CAVE (Beaver) is near the mouth of Cave Canyon in the Mineral Mountains that drain into the Beaver River. James Lindsay dug the cave while prospecting.
S20,T29S,R6W,SLM. 125.

LINEAR LAKE (Summit) is at the west end of the Uinta Mountains, at the southeast base of Mount Watson. The lake has a worm-like shape.
S31,T1S,R9E,SLM; 10,350' (3,155m).

LINWOOD* (Daggett) was five miles east of Manila*. The settlement consisted

of a cluster of log cabins that were built in 1900. By 1920, Linwood began to deteriorate because of developments such as improved transportation. In 1957 the government began buying up the land in this region for the development of Flaming Gorge Reservoir. What was left of Linwood went underwater in the early 1960s. The source of the name is dubious but some say it was a local name for the cottonwood trees planted along the town streets.
T3N,R20E,SLM. 89, 172, 542, 546.

LION CREEK (**Beaver**) originates on the southern slopes of Shelly Baldy Peak in the Tushar Mountains. The creek drains west into the South Fork of North Creek. Mountain lions were hunted in this region.
S20,T28S,R5W,SLM. 125.

LION FLAT (**Beaver**) is on the western slopes of the Tushar Mountains near the confluence of the East Fork of Bakers Canyon and the Beaver River. Mountain lions were once plentiful in this area.
S16,T29S,R6W,SLM; 6,700' (2,042m).

LION MOUNTAIN (**Box Elder**) is a small mountain off the northwestern slopes of the Pilot Range in northwestern Utah. Pigeon Mountain is ten miles east northeast. The name refers to the bobcat.
S4,T6N,R18W,SLM; 5,255' (1,602m).

LISBON VALLEY (**San Juan**) is eight miles southeast of La Sal*. The valley was named for Lisbon*, Portugal, by the Hayden survey party, who entered this area during the early 1870s.
S8,16,22,T30S,R25E,SLM; 6,600' (2,012m). 475.

LITTLE BEAR RIVER (**Cache**) originates south of Avon* where several creeks converge. The river drains north into the Bear River at Cutler Reservoir, northwest of Benson*. The name was derived from the river into which it drains.

S15,T9N,R1E,SLM to T12N,R1W,SLM (at Cutler Reservoir). 100(v17), 449.

LITTLE BEARSKIN MOUNTAIN (**Beaver**) is in the Mineral Range near Bearskin Mountain at the head of Wildhorse Canyon.
S18,T27S,R8W,SLM; 8,875' (2,705m).

LITTLE BOWN BENCH (**Garfield**) is north of Big Bown Bench.
T35S,R6E,SLM.

LITTLE BRIDGE (**San Juan**). See Natural Bridges National Monument.

LITTLE BROWNS HOLE (**Daggett**). See Little Hole (Daggett).

LITTLE CANYON (**Kane**). See Toms Canyon (Kane).

LITTLE CEDAR COVE (**Beaver**) is in the Mineral Mountains northwest of Bailey Mountain.
S11,T27S,R9W,SLM; 6,350' (1,935m).

LITTLE COTTONWOOD CANYON (**Salt Lake**) originates two miles southeast of Alta* in Albion Basin. The canyon drains west through Union* into the Jordan River and receives its name from the cottonwood groves near the canyon mouth.
T3S,R3E,SLM to S26,T2S,R1W,SLM.

LITTLE COTTONWOOD CREEK (**Salt Lake**) drains through Little Cottonwood Canyon.

LITTLE CREEK (**Iron**) originates on the southern slopes of Little Creek Peak. It drains northwest into Parowan Valley and is a comparatively small creek.
S10,T34S,R7W,SLM to S27,T33S,R8W,SLM.

LITTLE CREEK (**Rich**) originates at the springs three miles west of Randolph* where it drains into Big Creek.
S22,T11N,R6E,SLM to S32,T11N,R7E,SLM.

LITTLE CREEK PEAK (Iron) is at the head of Little Creek, twelve miles northeast of Paragonah*. The name was taken from the creek.
S2,T34S,R7W,SLM.

LITTLE DAVENPORT CREEK (Daggett) originates in the northeast section of the Uinta Mountains, six miles north northwest of Matt Warner Reservoir. The creek drains into the Green River. It was named for Tom Davenport, a Welsh coal miner from Rock Springs who settled and built a cabin in this area. There is a grave lying near the creek which is where Tom Crowley was put to rest. Crowley was an outlaw who was killed in a card game while hiding out in the area.
S32,28,15,22,T2N,R23E,SLM. 172, 303.

LITTLE DEER CREEK (Duchesne, Wasatch) originates in the southwest section of the Uinta Mountains and drains into the Duchesne River. Mule deer are plentiful in the region.
S29,T3N,R9W,USM to S27,T3N,R9W,USM.

LITTLE DRUM MOUNTAIN (Millard) is south of the Drum Mountains.

LITTLE DRY LAKE (Beaver) is at the north end of Beaver Valley and six miles west of the summit.
S2,T27S,R8W,SLM; 7,050' (2,149m).

LITTLE EGYPT (Garfield) is a region near U-95 and north of North Wash. The area has geologic features that reminded those who named the area of ancient Egypt.
T30,31S,R12E,SLM; 5,000' (1,524m).

LITTLE ELK LAKE (Summit) is in the southwest section of the Uinta Mountains near Big Elk Lake, four miles west of Haystack Mountain. Elk congregate in the region.
S8,T2S,R8E,SLM; 9,780' (2,981m). 298.

LITTLE HENDERSON (Garfield) drains into Tropic Canyon in Bryce Canyon National Park. It was named for William Jasper Henderson, who was born in Nauvoo, Illinois, on June 30, 1840. In 1891 and 1892, he built a log cabin and lived in the canyon with his family near Henderson Canyon Springs. Henderson died on September 22, 1919.
S10,T36S,R3W,SLM. 530.

LITTLE HOLE (Daggett) is an enclosed, rugged area on the south side of the Green River at the mouth of Little Davenport Creek. It is sometimes called Little Browns Hole after the early name of nearby Browns Park. When Powell came down the river he called it Ashley Park.
S14,15,22,23,T2N,R23E,SLM;   5,600' (1,707m). 160, 172, 496.

LITTLE HORSESHOE (Sanpete) is a small cirque west of Big Horseshoe cirque, southeast of Spring City*. The feature resembles the general shape of a horse hoof. See Horseshoe Mountain.
S35,T16S,R4E,SLM.

LITTLE LAKE (Duchesne) is in the southwest section of the Uinta Mountains. Big Lake is a larger lake located one and one-half miles northwest.
S29,T1S,R8W,USM; 9,870' (3,008m).

LITTLE LAKE (Rich). See Bear Lake (Rich).

LITTLE LYMAN LAKE (Summit). See Lyman Lake.

LITTLE MOUNTAIN (Salt Lake) is distinguished from nearby Big Mountain. Big Mountain was the most difficult mountain the pioneers had to overcome on their journey to the Great Salt Lake Valley.

LITTLE MUDDY (Iron). See Cedar City*.

LITTLE NORTH CREEK (Beaver) originates in the northern Tushar Mountains where it drains west between

Sulphur Creek and Pine Creek. See North Creek.
T26N,R6W,SLM.

LITTLE PIGEON MOUNTAINS (Box Elder) are near the Pigeon Mountains from which the mountains are named. There are numerous mourning doves in this area.
S11,14,23,T6N,R17W,SLM; 4,569' (1,393m).

LITTLE PINTO SPRING (Beaver) is one of a cluster of springs named Big, Little, and Pinto springs in a small area at the head of Pinto Creek. The name comes from the various colors in the surrounding hills.
S2,T31S,R18W,SLM; 8,000' (2,438m). 125.

LITTLE RESERVOIR (Beaver) is on the western slope of the Tushar Mountains, southwest of the powerhouse. It is the smaller of two lakes located in this region.
S25,T29S,R6W,SLM; 7,000' (2,134m).

LITTLE SALT LAKE* (Iron) was an early temporary name for Parowan*. The name was not universally accepted.

LITTLE SALT LAKE (Iron) was a seasonal, small, shallow, brackish sink lying north of Parowan* in Parowan Valley. The lake was named in contrast to the larger and better-known Great Salt Lake located near Salt Lake City*. It was also called Parowan Lake. The Piutes called it "Paragoon," which means "vile water." The adjacent town of Paragonah* takes its name from this Indian word. Parowan also evolved from Paragoons, Marsh People, the name of the Piede band living near the water in earlier days.
R9,10W,T33S,SLM; 5,675' (1,730m). 136, 314, 423, 438.

LITTLE SALT LAKE VALLEY COUNTY. See Iron County.

LITTLE SHELLY BALDY PEAK (Beaver) is in the Tushar Mountains

northwest of Mount Belnap. Elbert Cox says the present name is a corruption of Little Shaley Baldy Peak, which describes the heavy shale deposits on its slopes.
S24,T27S,R6W,SLM; 9,900' (3,018m). 125.

LITTLE SPENCER FLAT (Garfield). See Spencer Flats.

LITTLE SUPERIOR LAKE (Duchesne) is in the south central section of the Uinta Mountains and is smaller than nearby Superior Lake from which it receives its name.
S20,T4N,R5W,USM; 11,208' (3,416m).

LITTLE TWIST CREEK (Beaver) originates at Birch Creek Mountain south of Kents Lake in the Tushar Mountains. It drains southwest into South Creek and is smaller than Twist Creek. Both creeks take a twisting course.
S24,T30S,R6W,SLM. 125.

LITTLE VALLEY (Box Elder). Mantua* is located in the center of the valley. Little Valley had an early name of Box Elder Valley. Prior to 1863, some ranchers from Brigham City* used the valley as a herding ground for their livestock. A reservoir has recently been built east of Mantua.
T9N,R1W,SLM.

LITTLE VALLEY* (Box Elder). See Mantua*.

LITTLE VALLEY (Garfield) is in the upper reaches of Alvey Wash.
S25,T36S,R2E,SLM; 6,300' (1,920m).

LITTLE WARM VALLEY (Wasatch). See Wallsburg*.

LITTLE WHITE RIVER (Emery). See Price River.

LITTLE ZION* (Washington) was an early settlement in upper Zion Canyon. The settlement was established in 1861 when Joseph Black made a brief visit to the area. In 1863 Isaac Behunin also

came to the area where he built a cabin and built fences. In 1864, after two or three other cabins were built, Behunin began calling the community Zion*. When Brigham Young visited the settlement in 1870, he suggested that "this was not Zion." So for a period of time the town went by the tongue-in-cheek name of Not Zion*. Today it is a ghost town site in Zion National Park.
4,276' (1,303m). 100(v17), 600.

LITTLETON* (Morgan) was two and one-half miles west of Morgan*, near the mouth of Deep Creek. This small agricultural community was named in 1856 to honor Jesse C. Little, its founder. Flooding forced the settlers to relocate to Morgan.
S34,T4N,R2E,SLM; 5,040' (1,536m). 378, 567.

LLEWELLYN CANYON (Kane) originates in the Straight Cliffs of the Kaiparowits Plateau. It drains southeast into Mudholes Canyon. See Llewellyn Gulch and Harris Wash for name source.
S7,T40S,R7E,SLM (at head).

LLEWELLYN GULCH (Kane) originates near the southern end of the Kaiparowits Plateau and drains east into the Colorado River. Llewellyn Harris, an Indian scout who lived in Escalante*, established a homestead at the head of Harris Wash.
S16,T42S,R9E,SLM. 12, 602.

LOA* (Wayne) is in the Fremont Valley on U-24, two miles west of Lyman*. Franklin W. Young served a church mission in Hawaii. He suggested the town be named for Hawaii's Mauna Loa volcano because of the physical similarities in the Hawaiian volcano and the mountain adjacent to the settlement.
S1,T27S,R2E,SLM; 7,050' (2,149m). 289, 494, 542, 546, 569.

LOAFER MOUNTAIN (Utah) is four miles southeast of Payson*. Santaquin Peak is the high point. MRN
S32,33,T9S,R3E,SLM; 10,685' (3,257m).

LOBO ARCH (Kane) is in Coyote Gulch that drains into the Escalante River. Coyote Natural Bridge is one mile downstream. The name refers to a marauding wolf that frequented this area during pioneer days. It is also known as the Jacob Hamblin Arch.
S16,T39S,R8E,SLM. 12.

LOCKERBY* (San Juan) is two miles west of the Colorado border and two miles south of US-666. A. E. Lockerby was a prominent early resident.
S20,T34S,R26E,SLM; 6,786' (2,068m). 406, 542.

LOCKHART BASIN (San Juan) is on the west central slopes of Hatch Point. L. B. Lockhart was a prospector who settled with his family at Utah Bottoms on the Dolores River in the early 1900s.
S36,T28S,R20E,SLM; 4,300' (1,311m). 146.

LOCKHART BOTTOM (Grand). See Roberts Bottom (Grand).

LOCKHART CANYON (San Juan) originates on the southwest section of Hatch Point country southeast of Lockhart Basin. The canyon drains northwest into the Colorado River. See Lockhart Basin for the name source.
S16,T29S,R21E,SLM.

LOCKJAW HOLLOW (Beaver) originates at the east end of the South Hills, south of Beaver*. It drains into Nevershine Hollow through which I-15 passes.
S22,T30S,R7W,SLM.

LOCOMOTIVE SPRINGS (Box Elder) is composed of two main lakes just off the northwest tip of the Great Salt Lake. In 1888, J. T. Baker and Elijah Reed arrived in the area. At this time the water was gushing through the rocky precipitate and it sounded like rushing locomotives. The sound discontinued after the settlers pried and chipped away the deposits to obtain more water. Today the springs have been diked and marshland has been developed by the Locomotive Springs Wildlife Management site. T11N,R9,10W,SLM; 4,210' (1,283m). 139, 546, 567.

LODGE POLE CREEK (Daggett) originates in the northeast section of the Uinta Mountains and drains east into Sheep Creek. The lodge pole pine (*Pinus contorta*) is abundant in this area and is a source of many current timber products in addition to being commonly used by the Indians for shelters and other uses. S19,T2N,R18E,SLM to S3,T2N,R19E,SLM.

LODORE CANYON (In Colorado near Utah line). See Gates of Lodore.

LOEBER GULCH (Beaver) originates on the southwest slopes of Indian Grave Peak in the San Francisco Mountains. It drains southwest towards the Wah Wah Valley. This area is also known as Loeber Canyon. Charles G. Loeber was a well-known prospector in the region. S15,22,T27S,R13W,SLM. 100(v17), 125.

LOFGREEN* (Tooele) was settled in 1898 by Herman Lofgreen (Lofgren) along the Union Pacific Railroad track going south from Lake Point. In earlier days there was a small schoolhouse in the settlement. The residents earned their living by breaking wild horses and working as section hands for the railroad. The settlement was abandoned after creosote was discovered, since this greatly reduced the demand for section hands. (Applying creosote to railroad ties keeps them from rotting.) Variant: Lofgren Siding. T9S,R4W,SLM; 5,803' (1,769m). 367, 542, 567.

LOGAN* (Cache) is at the mouth of Logan Canyon on US-89,91. The city has several name sources. The most prominent is that Ephraim Logan, a mountain

man with Ashley's group, and a member of Jedediah Smith's party, lost his life in the 1820s along the river. The settlement was later named for the river. Peter Maughan located the site in the spring of 1859 and it was originally known as Logans Fort*. Another claim is that the settlement was named for a friendly Indian chief named Logan. There is also a letter on file (see 567) from a Mrs. Roberts stating that the town was named for her father's old ox because her father asked Apostle Hyde to do so, and he publicly consented,

> An ox called Logan tough with fame
> Came with the Reeses here
> And after it the town was named
> As items now appear.

See Logan River.
S26,27,33,34,T12N,R1E,SLM; 4,535' (1,382m). 100(v17), 172, 449, 494, 542, 546, 567.

LOGAN CANYON (Cache) originates near the summit east of Logan* at Amazon Hollow and drains west into the Bear River. It is one of the more ruggedly beautiful canyons in the West. See Logan River for name source. S36,T12N,R1E,SLM (at mouth).

LOGAN PEAK (Cache) is in the Bear River Range six miles east of Logan*. See the river for name source. T11N,R2E,SLM; 9,710' (2,960m).

LOGAN RIVER (Cache) originates in Idaho and drains south to eventually enter the Little Bear River west of Logan*. The most reliable name source is that the river was named for mountain man/trapper Ephraim Logan, whose grave rests in Logan Canyon. For further discussion on the name, see Logan. Earlier names for the river were Logans Fork, Maughans Fork, and Little Bear. 209, 249(7 Jan. 1977), 314, 476, 546.

LOGANS HOLE (Cache). See Cache Valley.

LOGGERS FORK (**Sanpete**) originates at Loggers Fork Reservoir and drains west into the North Fork of Manti Canyon. The area was named for the early logging activities.
S9,10,T18S,R4E,SLM.

LOGWAY CANYON (**Cache**) originates at South Peak in the north Wellsville Mountains and drains northeast into Gibson Canyon. The pioneers of Mendon* cut most of the timber for their homes in this canyon.
S24,T11N,R2W,SLM. 100(v17).

LONDON* (**Wasatch**) was a small settlement on a spring one mile north of Heber*. A large wickiup was set up there to house thirty men who had come from Great Britain. London was a forerunner of Heber.
S29,T3S,R5E,SLM; 5,580' (1,701m). 309, 377.

LONE MAN BUTTE (**Emery**) is near the head of Lone Man Draw in the Sinbad section of the San Rafael Swell. The imagined shape of the butte is the source for the name.
S22,T23S,R11E,SLM. 193.

LONE MAN DRAW (**Emery**) originates at Lone Man Butte where it drains to the southeast. See the butte for name source.
S22,T23S,R11E,SLM to T24S,R12E,SLM. 193.

LONE PEAK (**Salt Lake**) is a prominent peak five and one-half miles east of Draper*.
T3S,R2E,SLM; 11,253' (3,430m).

LONG CANYON (**Emery**) is near Mount Elliot on the Book Cliffs. The canyon drains southeast into the Green River. Short Canyon is nearby.
S3,T20S,R16E,SLM (at mouth).

LONG CANYON (**Garfield**) drains southeast along the east side of the Waterpocket Fold. The canyon empties into Bullfrog Bay.
T36,37S,R9,10E,SLM.

LONG CANYON (**Garfield**) originates in the southeast section of Boulder Mountain of the Aquarius Plateau and empties into the Escalante River southeast of Boulder*.
T33,34S,R5,6E,SLM.

LONG CANYON (**Grand**) drains from the west into the Colorado River, six miles southwest of Moab*.
S16,T26S,R20E,SLM to S18,T26S,R20E, SLM.

LONG CANYON (**Juab**) originates on Gilson Mountain and drains west to disappear into the desert.
S7,T14S,R3W,SLM to S10,T14S,R4W,SLM.

LONG CANYON (**Kane**) originates on the southwest corner of the Waterpocket Fold and drains south into Lake Powell. Navajo Creek flows through Long Canyon.
T38,39S,R10E,SLM.

LONG CANYON (**Kane**) originates on the Kaiparowits Plateau and drains into Right Hand Collett Canyon.
S2,T38S,R3E,SLM (at mouth).

LONG CANYON (**Kane**) originates east of the mouth of the Escalante River and drains into Lake Powell.
S32,T38S,R10E,SLM.

LONG CANYON (**Kane**) originates at Pine Point on Timber Mountain. The canyon drains southwest into Johnsons Wash and Johnsons Canyon. It is longer than the other canyons in this vicinity.
T42S,R4½,5W. 567.

LONG CANYON (**Kane**) drains east into the Paria River south of US-89.
S3,T43S,R1W,SLM (at mouth).

LONG CANYON (**San Juan**) drains into White Canyon from the northeast. The rock formation known as Jacobs Chair is located south and Short Canyon is north. T35S,R15,16E,SLM.

LONG CANYON (San Juan) drains from the northwest into Dogge and Montezuma canyons. T35S,R23,24E,SLM.

LONG LAKE (Garfield) is on the eastern slope of the Boulder Mountain section of the Aquarius Plateau. The shape of the lake suggests the name. T31S,R5E,SLM.

LONG LAKE (Summit) is one-half mile southwest of Mount Watson at the west end of the Uinta Mountains. S35,36,T1S,R8E,SLM; 10,100' (3,078m).

LONG LICK CANYON (Beaver) originates on the eastern slopes of Long Lick Mountain in the Shauntie Hills and drains southeast into the Escalante Desert. This rugged canyon is difficult to negotiate. T29S,R12W,SLM.

LONG LICK MOUNTAIN (Beaver) is the high point in the Shauntie Hills. See Long Lick Canyon. S6,S29S,R12W,SLM; 6,806' (2,074m).

LONG LICK PEAK (Beaver). See Long Lick Mountain (Beaver).

LONG VALLEY (Beaver) originates on the northeast slopes of the Wah Wah Mountains where it drains into the Wah Wah Valley. S11,15,T26S,R15W,SLM.

LONG VALLEY (Kane) stretches between Long Valley Junction and Carmel Junction. White people who originally entered the valley called it Berry Canyon after John Berry who settled Berryville* in 1864 on the site where Glendale* is presently located. Several members of the Berry family were killed by Indians while they were in the process of settling

in the valley. Dr. Priddy Meeks and his family arrived in the valley with the Berrys and settled where Mount Carmel* is today. See also Mount Carmel*, Glendale*, and Orderville*. T38-41S,R6,7W,SLM. 224, 455, 515(v7), 600.

LONG VALLEY JUNCTION* (Kane) is at the head of Long Valley where US-89 and U-14 join. This junction is at the southern edge of the Great Basin where the headwaters of the Sevier River flow north and the headwaters of the Virgin River flow south. William J. Baird built the first house there in 1927. S22,T38S,R6W,SLM; 7,454' (2,272m).

LOOKING GLASS ROCK (San Juan) is three miles south of La Sal Junction and one and one-half miles west of US-160. This natural rock window was named by John Silvey in 1889. Silvey's view through the window seemed to mirror a reflection. S17,T29S,R23E,SLM; 6,247' (1,904m). 475, 514, 546.

LOOKOUT PASS (Tooele) is on the old Pony Express and Overland Stage route that passed between the Onaqui and Sheeprock mountains west of Faust*. Captain Simpson originally named this Johnston's Pass to honor General Albert Sidney Johnston. Horace and Libby Rockwell lived there between 1866 and 1890 and it became Lookout Pass because one could see for vast distances from this area. Since this was the case, it was an ideal lookout point for the Stage or the Pony Express. There is another reason for the importance of this pass. It was there that the Rockwells' well-known dog cemetery was located. Over the years the dogs owned by the Rockwells were all carefully buried in an enclosed dog cemetery, which is still there. See Clover*. S18,T8S,R6W,SLM; 6,192' (1,887m). 153, 360, 477.

LOOP, THE (**San Juan**) is an "S" loop on the Colorado River just above The Confluence.
S34,T29½S,R19E,SLM (at tail of "S").

LOPEZ ARCH (**San Juan**) is four miles south of La Sal Junction. Fernin R. Lopez was a well-known and trusted cattle ranch foreman in La Sal*.
S34,T29S,R23E,SLM. 406, 567. D.L. 7502.

LOSEEVILLE* (**Kane**) was a small settlement two miles east of Tropic*. It was abandoned around 1900 after being named for Isaac Losee. Variants: Losee* and New Clifton*.
78, 89, 508, 516.

LOST CANYON (**San Juan**) originates in the rimrock country north of the Natural Bridges National Monument and drains northwest into Dark Canyon. The canyon was named by the local cattlemen because it was so difficult to find and easy to lose.
S5,T35S,R17E,SLM (at head). 578.

LOST CREEK (**Garfield**) originates at the Tule Lakes area of the Aquarius Plateau, one mile southwest of Posy Lake. It drains south to disappear near Skull Spring.
12.

LOST CREEK (**Morgan**) originates at the junction of Morgan, Rich, and Weber counties. The creek drains south southeast through Lost Creek Reservoir and into the Weber River. The creek had an earlier name of Plumber (Plumbar) for an early trapper of that name. It has also been claimed that the creek was named Plumber because it often disappeared and reappeared lower down. This tendency also gave the name "lost" to the creek. But here again there is controversy. It is not known if a party of scouts camping by the creek gave the name, or if it was named by Moses Tracy and Sidney Kelly, who were lost there in a snowstorm in 1855.

S17,T7N,R5E,SLM to S19,T4N,R4E,SLM.
378, 494, 542, 567.

LOST CREEK (**Sevier**) originates on the northwest slopes of Mount Terrill and drains northwest into the Sevier River. This creek is not easily located.
S14,T24S,R2E,SLM to S3,T22S,R1W,SLM.

LOST CREEK (**Summit**) originates in the north central section of the Uinta Mountains near Beaver Meadow Reservoir. It drains north one and one-half miles, then disappears into a porous limestone cavern. The waters of Lost Creek then appear again eighteen miles to the east at Big Spring on Sheep Creek.
172.

LOST CREEK RESERVOIR (**Sevier**) is in a small open valley which drains into the headwaters of Lost Creek, nine miles north of Fish Lake.
S21,T24S,R2E,SLM; 9,702' (2,957m).

LOST LAKE (**Duchesne**) is in the south-west section of the Uinta Mountains on the headwaters of Fish Creek. The lake is difficult to locate.
S21,28,T3N,R8W,USM; 10,025' (3,056m).

LOST LAKE (**Duchesne, Summit**) is in the southwest section of the Uinta Mountains on the upper Provo River drainage. The lake has a porous bed and the water level vacillates with heavy agricultural use.
S4,5,T2S,R9E,SLM; 9,900' (3,018m).

LOST LAKE (**Summit**) is in the north central section of the Uinta Mountains on the Middle Fork of Sheep Creek. The lake is difficult to locate and reach.
10,300' (3,139m).

LOST RIVER (**Beaver**). See Beaver River (Beaver).

LOTT SETTLEMENT* (**Utah**). Mrs. Pamelia Lott, a widow, settled near

Lehi* in the spring of 1854. The settlement was named for her.
567.

LOUISA* (Iron). See Parowan* (Iron).

LOUSY JIM CREEK (Beaver) originates in the Tushar Mountains east of Beaver and drains southeast into the Beaver River. The creek was named for a local sheepherder who was afflicted with a bad case of lice infestation. See Crazy Creek.
S7,T29S,R5W,SLM. 44, 100(v17).

LOW* (Tooele) was a Western Pacific Railroad siding at the northern tip of the Cedar Mountains on the eastern edge of the Great Salt Lake Desert. The settlement was established in the early 1880s as a construction and maintenance camp. Local water was unavailable and the camp was abandoned by 1955. The siding was on a low pass between two mountain ranges.
T1N,R10W,SLM; 4,614' (1,406m). 360, 498.

LOWDER SPRINGS (Garfield). See Fort Sanford* (Garfield).

LOWER BEAVER* (Beaver). See Minersville*.

LOWER BEAVER* (Beaver) is on Beaver Creek, seven miles downriver from Beaver*. In early 1859, several weeks before the men from Parowan* settled at Minersville*, a party from Cedar City* arrived in this area where they formed a settlement called Lower Beaver. Their living quarters were dugouts or cellars, which was the origin of the earlier name of Old Cellars*. The settlement was abandoned the summer of 1860.
S28,T29S,R8W,SLM; 5,604' (1,708m). 456.

LOWER CHAIN LAKE (Duchesne) is in the south central section of the Uinta Mountains. It is the lowest of four principal lakes in the Chain Lakes group.
10,580' (3,225m).

LOWER CLARA* (Washington). See Tonaquint* (Washington).

LOWER FERRON* (Emery). See Molen* (Emery).

LOWER GOOSEBERRY RESERVOIR (Sevier) is on the Wasatch Plateau on the upper reaches of Gooseberry Creek southeast of Salina.
S7,T13S,R6,SLM; 8,424' (2,568m).

LOWER GRASS VALLEY* (Sevier). See Angle* (Sevier).

LOWER INDIAN SPRING (Beaver) is below Upper Indian Spring on the Indian Peak Mountains.
S2,T29S,R18W,SLM; 6,960' (2,121m).

LOWER JOES VALLEY (Emery) is at the head of Straight Canyon, with Joes Valley Reservoir in the center. See Joes Valley.
T17,18S,R6E,SLM; 6,990' (2,131m).

LOWER KENTS LAKE (Beaver). See Kents Lake (Beaver).

LOWER PODUNK CREEK (Kane). See Podunk Creek (Kane).

LOWER RED CASTLE LAKE (Summit). See Red Castle Lake (Summit).

LOWER SHINGLE CREEK LAKE (Summit) is at the west end of the Uinta Mountains on the headwaters of Shingle Creek.
S7,T2S,R8E,SLM; 9,630' (2,935m).

LOWER TRAIL CANYON (Kane) originates near the head of Left Hand Collett on the Kaiparowits. This and Upper Trail Canyon were used by cattlemen to trail stock into the Last Chance Creek area.
S21,33,T38S,R4E,SLM. 12.

LOWER VALLEY (Millard) was an early name for Beaver Bottoms on the lower Beaver River.

LOWER YELLOW PINE LAKE (Summit) is at the west end of the Uinta Mountains and six and one-half miles east northeast of Kamas*. The name comes from the nearby creek.
S9,T2S,R7E,SLM; 9,610' (2,929m).

LUCERNE* (Daggett). See Manila* (Daggett).

LUCERNE* (Millard). See Sugarville*.

LUCERNE VALLEY (Daggett) is southeast of Manila*. Lucerne (Alfalfa) is a common name for Medicago sativa, a very important hay crop in the West. In 1893 Adolph Jessen, the developer of a canal system in Daggett County, renamed Dry Valley, to Lucerne Valley.
T3N,R19,20E,SLM; 6,200'-6,600' (1,894m-2,012m). 172.

LUCIN* (Box Elder) has been located in two places during its history. The first site was ten miles north of its present location. Lucin was a small railroad community on the west side of the Great Salt Lake. It was staffed by employees of the early Central Pacific and South Pacific railroads. Today the railroad crosses the Great Salt Lake instead of skirting the northern shore, so in 1903 the community shifted to its present location. The town died in 1936. Then from 1937 to 1972 four retired railroad workers resettled the site. The name Lucin comes from a local prolific fossil bivalve (Lucina subanta).
S3,4,10,T7N,R18W,SLM; 4,472' (1,363m). 498, 542.

LUND* (Iron) was a station on the branch line from the Union Pacific Railroad to Cedar City*, thirty-three miles southeast. It was named for Utah state legislator and local mine owner Robert C. Lund of St. George*. Lund was also a director of the railroad.
S21,T32S,R14W,SLM; 5,081' (1,549m). 314, 542.

LYDIAS CANYON (Kane) originates four and one-half miles northwest of Glendale* at the junction of the right and left forks. It drains southeast into the East Fork of the Virgin River. Lydia was an early pioneer woman who settled at the mouth of the canyon in 1899.
S5,T40S,R7W,SLM to S14,T40S,R7W,SLM. 100(v17), 567.

LYMAN* (Wayne) is two miles east of Loa* on U-24. The settlement was originally named East Loa*, then in 1893 it was changed to Wilmoth*. The following year the name was changed to honor Apostle Francis M. Lyman, a Mormon church official who had suggested they move their settlement to higher ground.
S5,T28S,R3E,SLM; 7,125' (2,172m). 100 (v17), 289, 360, 485, 542, 569.

LYMAN CANYON (San Juan) originates on the southeast slopes of the Bears Ears and drains south southwest. The canyon was named for Platt DeAlton Lyman, an early pioneer who was second in charge of the Hole-in-the-Rock expedition. The group passed through this area.
NW¼,T37S,R19E,SLM. 359.

LYN* (Millard). See Lynndyl*.

LYNN* (Box Elder) is a small agricultural settlement at the north end of the Grouse Creek Mountains on the South Fork of Junction Creek. The name is a corruption of John Lind's name. In 1882 John and his half-brother Alexander Anderson emigrated from Sweden, lived for a short time in Grantsville*, then settled in Lynn* with their families.
S1,T13N,R17W,SLM; 5,919' (1,804m). 139, 542. 567.

LYNN* (Weber) is now a part of Ogden*. Previous town names were Five Points* because five roads converged in this area, Binghams Fort for Bishop Erastus Bingham (fort construction began

in the fall of 1853), and Lynne*. One report states that the town was called Lynn after Lynn, Massachusetts, where many Mormon converts originated. Another claim suggests the settlement was named for a town in Scotland. Variant: Lynne*.
S17,T6N,R1W,SLM; 4,320' (1,317m). 27, 289, 542, 567.

LYNN SPRINGS (Box Elder) is near Lynn*.
567.

LYNNDYL* (Millard) is a small agricultural community that was an early railroad junction sixteen miles northeast of Delta*. Folklore relates one story for the name origin. Apparently, while the railroad was under construction and before the area was named, someone from Salt Lake City* asked a telegrapher where she was. While trying to think of an answer, she noticed "Lynn, Mass" printed on her shoe, so she answered, "At Lynn"—so the junction now had a name. However, when an application was filed at the post office, a Lynn* already existed in Box Elder County so "-dyl" was added.
S14,T15S,R5W,SLM; 4,784' (1,458m). 100 (v17), 314, 466(8 Nov. 1977).

MCARTHURSVILLE* (**Utah**). See American Fork* (Utah).

MCCARDY CANYON (**Piute**) originates on Table Mountain three miles south of Kingston Canyon. Billy McCarty (McCardy) owned a ranch in the immediate area and the canyon was named for him. Billy and his son Fred were both killed on September 7, 1893, while robbing the Delta, Colorado, bank. Variants: McCarty, McCarthy, McCary, etc.
S31,T31S,R2½W,SLM to S23,T30S,R2½W, SLM. 5, 25, 303, 409.

MCCARDY SPRING (**Piute**) is near the head of Steens Canyon north of Kingston Canyon. McCardy (McCarty), an outlaw, used this spring as a hideout while evading the law. See McCardy Canyon (Piute).
S35,T29S,R2½W,SLM; 8,400' (2,560m).

MCCARTY CANYON (**Emery**) originates seven miles north of the Head of Sinbad in the San Rafael Swell. It drains north northeast into Molen Seep Wash. The canyon was named after Tom McCarty, brother of Billy, both ranchers and outlaws. Tom used the canyon as a hideout in the late 1800s. See McCardy Canyon (Piute).
S17,T21S,R10E,SLM. 567.

MCCORNICK* (**Millard**) was a settlement and a siding on the Union Pacific Railroad, eleven miles northwest of Holden*. The settlement was established through a high-pressure advertising and selling scheme, but died by 1930 because of alternating floods and drought. It was named for William S. McCornick, a Salt Lake City* banker and promoter.
S27,28,T18S,R5W,SLM; 4,741' (1,445m). 89, 100(v13,17), 516.

MCCRACKEN CANYON (**San Juan**) originates on McCracken Mesa and drains south into the San Juan River.
T39,40S,R23E,SLM.

MCCRACKEN MESA (**San Juan**) is at the head of McCracken Canyon on the Navajo Indian Reservation in southeastern Utah.
T39S,R23E,SLM.

MCDONALD LAKE (**Kane**) is at the junction of U-136 and US-89 southwest of Levanger Lakes and Alton*. See Alton*.
S16,T30S,R6W,SLM.

MCELPRANG WASH (**Emery**) originates on the eastern slopes of the Wasatch Plateau, three and one-half miles southwest of Huntington*. The wash drains southeast into Huntington Creek. Sorn W. McElprang settled in this area in 1885.
S28,T17S,R8E,SLM to S8,T18S,R9E,SLM. 292.

MCGATH LAKE (**Garfield**) is on the southern slope of the Boulder Mountain section of the Aquarius Plateau. It was named for Ben McGath, an early Escalante* stockman who had a farm nearby.
32S,R3E,SLM; 9,372' (2,857m). 12.

MCGATH POINT (**Garfield**) is a large mesa-like outcropping five miles southwest of Boulder*. See McGath Lake for name source.
S22,T34S,R4E,SLM; 6,759' (2,060m). 12.

MCINTYRE CANYON (**San Juan**) originates on Three Step Hill at the south end of Lisbon Valley southeast of La Sal*. It was named for Donald

McIntyre, a cattleman and prospector who lived in the area.
S12,13,T31S,R25E,SLM (to Colorado border). 467.

MCKUNE SPRING (**Duchesne**) is on the southern slopes of the Uinta Mountains, eleven miles northwest of Altonah*. Robert and J. D. McKune operated a sawmill in this area around 1913.
S32,T2N,R4W,USM; 8,300' (2,530m). 578.

MCPHERSONS RANCH (**Grand**) is at the junction of Florence Creek and the Green River north of Green River*. Jim McPherson established his headquarters near Browns Park and the Robbers Roost, directly on the infamous Owlhoot Trail that was used by outlaws operating between Canada and Mexico. Sheriff Jesse Tyler and his deputy Sam Jenkins were murdered by outlaws in this area. The outlaw Flat Nose George was also killed in the area by Doc King, foreman of the Webster City Cattle Company. In 1942 the McPherson ranch was purchased by the federal government and included in the Uintah Ute Reservation. See McPherson Range.

MCPHERSON RANGE (**Grand**) is in the Roan Cliffs south of Moonwater Point. To the west is the Green River and to the north is Florence Creek where, at the mouth, Jim McPherson had his ranch headquarters. Jim McPherson and Preston Nutter were the first men to run a cattle operation up in the Book Cliffs country. See McPherson Ranch.
T17-18S,R8E,SLM. 25, 146, 555(v32).

MCPHERSONS FLAT (**Washington**). See Anderson Junction*.

MCPHETERS LAKE (**Summit**) is on the northern slope of the west end of the Uinta Mountains. Two miles south is Mount Agassiz. The lake was named for a deceased member of the engineering services of the U.S. Forest Service.
10,850' (3,307m). 298.

- M -

MABA LAKE (**Duchesne**) is at the west end of the Uinta Mountains in the Murdock Basin. Hoover, Shepard, and Marshall lakes are in the vicinity. The name has an Indian origin. MRN
S2,T3N,R9W,USM; 9,900' (3,018m).

MACHINE CREEK (**Washington**). See Mill Creek (Washington).

MAESER* (**Uintah**) is three miles west of Vernal*. The first sawmills in Ashley Valley were built in this area and the name of the site was Millward*. After the sawmills closed down, the settlement was temporarily renamed Buena Vista*. Karl G. Maeser, early head of the Brigham Young Academy and superintendent of the Mormon church sunday schools, made an official visit to the region. The people liked him so much they decided to name their town for him.
S8,9,16,17,T4S,R21E,SLM; 5,540' (1,689m).
289, 542, 567.

MAGNA* (**Salt Lake**) is twenty-two miles west of Salt Lake City*. The area was initially established in 1906 as a farming community, but this suddenly changed when the Utah Copper Concentrate Mill was erected. Prospectors, drifters, and miners moved in and set up tents and shanties, or lived in dugouts. At this time, the community was known as Ragtown*. When the company erected three hundred cottages, a new town name was needed and it was called Pleasant Green* for a short time. Since this name was so common in Utah, the name was changed to Magna. One report states that Magna was the name of a nearby mine. Another source reports that D. C. Jackling's use of the Latin term "magna" came from a phrase used by the Masonic Order, "Magna est veritas, et

praevalibit"–"Truth is might and will prevail."
S29,T1S,R2W,SLM; 4,300' (1,311m). 272, 360, 542, 546.

MAGOTSU CREEK (**Washington**) originates in the Mountain Meadows four miles north of Central* and drains south southwest into Moody Wash. The name is a corruption of the Piute "Ma-haut-su," which means "long slope" or "end of a long slope."
S15,T38S,R16W,SLM to S36,T39S,R17W, SLM. 314, 555(v1).

MAHOGANY CANYON (**Rich**) originates in the hill country east of the south side of Bear Lake where it drains east into Sixmile Creek. Mountain mahogany is a common name for a shrub, *Cercocarpus*, which is prominent in the area.
S14,T13N,R6E,SLM to S19,T13N,R7E,SLM.

MAHOGANY KNOLL (**Beaver**) is in the Black Mountains near Minersville Reservoir. See Mahogany Canyon for name source.
S36,T30S,R9W,SLM; 7,987' (2,434m).

MAHOGANY MOUNTAIN (**Utah**) is between Pleasant Grove* and American Fork Canyon. See Mahogany Canyon for name source.
S3,T5S,R2E,SLM; 9,001' (2,744m).

MAIN CANYON (**Garfield**) originates on the upper east slopes of the Escalante Mountains and drains east into the Escalante River. The Widtsoe*-Escalante* road crosses the summit and Birch Creek drains through the canyon. It is the most important canyon in this area.
S23,T34S,R1W,SLM to S16,T35S,R2E,SLM.

MAIN CANYON (**Summit**) originates three and one-half miles northeast of East Canyon Reservoir and drains northeast into Weber Valley. It was at Henefer* and the mouth of Main Canyon that the Mormon pioneers (and the Donner-Reed party before them) left the Weber Valley and turned southwest up Main Canyon. This change was made to avoid the formidable Devils Gate located down Weber Canyon.
S31,T4E,R3N,SLM to S8,T4E,R3N,SLM.

MAIN CANYON (**Uintah**) originates on the East Tavaputs Plateau. It drains northwest into Willow Creek and is the principal canyon in the region.
S33,T15½S,R24E,SLM to S27,T13S,R21E, SLM.

MALAD COUNTY was created in Utah Territory in 1856 and discontinued January 1862. The county was named after the Malad River. See Malad River for name source.
6.

MALAD RIVER (**Box Elder**) drains south from Idaho into Utah and the Bear River. Donald Mackenzie, a French-Canadian trapper from the Hudson Bay Company, is given credit for naming the river. He and his men became ill after eating beaver meat. "Malade" is French for "sick." Fremont called the river the Roseaux River.
S33,T15N,R3W,SLM (in Utah) to S19,T10N, R2W,SLM. 314, 464, 555(v30).

MALANS BASIN (**Weber**) is one and one-half miles east of Ogden. The Tim Bartholemew Malan family built a hotel, log cabins, and a camp there. The family moved away and the site closed down in 1905.
S1,T5N,R1W,SLM; 6,800' (1,884m). 163(30 June 1983).

MALMSTEN PEAK (**Piute**) is the high point on Forshea Mountain, six miles east of the south end of the Piute Reservoir. Harry Malmsten was a

surveyor for the U.S. Forest Service during the early 1900s.
S26,T29S,R2½W,SLM; 9,794' (2,985m).

MAMMOTH* (**Juab**) is three miles south of Eureka* in the Tintic Valley. The settlement received its name in 1870 following the discovery of rich ore in the nearby Mammoth mine. Another version suggests that someone cried "Boys, we've got a mammoth mine here."
S25,T10S,R2W,SLM; 6,026' (1,837m). 89, 100(v7,17), 289, 516, 542, 546.

MAMMOTH CANYON (**Beaver**) is in the Star Range southwest of Milford* where it drains northeast into Elephant Canyon.
S25,T28S,R12W,SLM.

MAMMOTH CREEK (**Garfield**) originates on the west ridge of the Markagunt Plateau at Mammoth Summit north of Cedar Breaks National Monument. This unusually large creek drains southeast into the Sevier River.
S12,13,T36S,R9W,SLM to S5,T37S,R5W, SLM. 567.

MAMMOTH PEAK (**Juab, Utah**) is two miles south southeast of Eureka*, near the mining community of Mammoth*, from which it received its name.
S30,T10S,R2W,SLM; 8,108' (2,471m).

MAMMOTH SPRING (**Garfield**) is five miles south of Panguitch Lake on Mammoth Creek, from which it receives its name.
S31,T36S,R7W,SLM; 8,025' (2,446m).

MANASSEH* (**Sanpete**) was a settlement that was supposed to be built across the San Pitch River from Ephraim*. Manasseh's "sister city" Ephraim succeeded and became a beautiful and prosperous town, but the plans for Manasseh did not mature. The site has been used for agricultural purposes only.
S10,15,T17S,R2E,SLM; 5,450' (1,661m). 336.

MANCOS JIM BUTTE (**San Juan**) is south of the Henry Mountains between Allen Canyon and Dry Wash. The butte was named for Mancos Jim, who was an Indian sub-chief of a local Piute clan. Jim died from wounds received in an Indian-white altercation in the Bluff*/Blanding* region in 1923.
S22,T35S,R21E,SLM; 7,180' (2,188m). 303, 409, 567, 583.

MANCOS MESA (**San Juan**) is twelve miles north of the Clay Hills. See Mancos Jim Butte for name source.
S36,T37S,R13,14E,SLM; 5,500' (1,632m).

MANDERFIELD* (**Beaver**) is five miles north of Beaver* on I-15. The settlement had an earlier name of Indian Creek*, which was the name of the creek where the community was located. Manderfield was originally settled in 1865 by the Ephraim Twitchell family. In 1910 the community was named for J. Manderfield, a railroad man.
T28S,R7W,SLM; 6,119' (1,865m). 100(v17), 125, 355.

MANHARD CREEK (**Beaver**) originates in the Tushar Mountains and drains southeast into the South Fork of North Creek. It was named for William Manhart, who prospected in this area in 1860. Variant: Manhart Creek.
S18,19,T28S,R5W,SLM. 125.

MANILA* (**Daggett**) is on U-43 and U-44 near the Flaming Gorge Reservoir. It had earlier names such as Chambers* for R. C. Chambers who helped finance the Lucerne Valley project; Lewisallen* for Lewis Allen, a prominent early settler; and the early name Lucerne* for the alfalfa grown in the valley which was sold to local stockmen for winter feed. Adolph Jessen, the surveyor for the settlement, named the settlement Manila in 1898 in commemoration of Admiral Dewey's victory over the Spanish fleet at Manila, Philippine Islands. In 1904 local sources continued to refer to the town as Lucerne or Manila.

S18,T3N,R20E,SLM; 6,375' (1,943m). 172, 289, 314, 546, 567.

MANILA* (**Utah**) was an outgrowth of Pleasant Grove* located approximately three miles northwest of that settlement. See Manila* (Daggett) for name source.
S8,T5S,R2E,SLM; 4,733' (1,443m). 567.

MANILA WARD* (**Box Elder**). See Elwood*.

MANNING* (**Tooele**) was a mining town that rapidly developed during the late 1880s in Manning Canyon southeast of Mercur*. Since nearby Mercur had a better water supply than Manning, the towns expanded into one another over the summit. Manning died out, then was rejuvenated in the 1930s. It was finally abandoned in 1937. See Manning Canyon for name source.
S15,T6S,R3W,SLM. 89, 516, 546.

MANNING CANYON (**Utah**) is over the summit east of Mercur* and drains southeast into Cedar Valley. The canyon was named for L. S. Manning, a prominent person in the mining industry in both Mercur and Manning*, adjacent mining communities of the 1890s.
S4,T6S,R3W,SLM to S25,T6S,R2W,SLM. 89, 516.

MANNING CREEK (**Piute**) originates on the northeast slopes of Marysvale Peak at Manning Meadow. The creek drains southwest into the Sevier River. The pioneer Manning family ranched in the area along the creek.
S23,T27S,R2½W,SLM to S15,T28S,R3W, SLM. 100(v17).

MANNING MEADOW (**Piute**) is on the northeast slopes of Marysvale Peak at the head of Manning Creek. See Manning Creek.
9,774' (2,979m).

MANTI* (**Sanpete**) is on US-89 between Gunnison* and Ephraim*, and was settled in 1849. Brigham Young and

Isaac Morley, one of the first settlers, named the early community for a prominent city in the Book of Mormon. It had an early name of Copenhagen*, which was a reminder of the city where many of the residents came from.
S7,T18S,R2,3E,SLM; 5,530' (1,686m). 27, 289, 314, 322, 542, 546, 555(v6).

MANTUA* (Box Elder) is eight miles east of Brigham City* on US-89. It had a series of early names, including Little Valley* for its location, Flaxville* because the early settlers concentrated on raising flax, Copenhagen* because a majority of the settlers were Danes, and Geneva* for the Swiss city. Lorenzo Snow, fifth president of the Mormon Church, named the town after his birthplace, Mantua, Ohio. There is a counterclaim by some that the name comes from the early French-Canadian trapper's loose cloak, a manteau.
S22,T9N,R1W,SLM; 5,159' (1,572m). 100 (v17), 139, 314, 449, 542, 546, 567. D.L. 6802.

MAPLE CANYON (Utah) is near Springville* and Mapleton* (at the mouth of the canyon). The town and the canyon are both named for the numerous maple trees in the canyon.
S12,T8S,R3E,SLM (at mouth).

MAPLE FLATS (Beaver) is in the foothills west of the north end of Beaver Valley. Maple trees are the dominant trees in the area.
S24,25,T27S,R8W,SLM; 7,200' (2,195m).

MAPLETON* (Utah) is southeast of Springville* near US-89. This outgrowth of Springville received its name from the groves of maple trees in the area. The settlement had an early temporary name of Union Bench* because of the united efforts the early settlers had in making the community successful.
S10,11,14,15,T8S,R3E,SLM;4,725'(1,440m). 289, 270.

MARBLE GULCH (Beaver) originates on the western slopes of the San Francisco Mountains and drains southwest toward the Wah Wah Valley. The area received its name for the large exposure of marble along the gulch.
S22,T27S,R13W,SLM. 125.

MARGIE LAKE (Duchesne) is on the southern slopes of the Uinta Mountains, one and one-half miles north of Rocky Sea Pass. Jack Fitzwater and three of his friends placed the name Margie on a slab of wood near the lake in 1936-37. The name held. See Francis Lake for further details.
S27,T4N,R8W,USM; 10,980' (3,347m). 595.

MARION* (Summit) is two miles north of Kamas* on alt. US-189. The settlement had earlier names of Morrell* after one of the pioneer settlers and Boulderville*. The present name honors Francis Marion Lyman, a Mormon church official.
S4,5,T2S,R6E,SLM; 6,425' (1,958m). 100(v17), 289, 542, 567.

MARJORIE LAKE (Wasatch) is in the southwest section of the Uinta Mountains, two and one-half miles west southwest of Trial Lake. Marjorie was the daughter of H. Cardwell (Cardie) Clegg, an early developer and freighter in the area. Jack Lake, named for Cardie's son, is also in the area.
S2,T2S,R8E,SLM; 9,990' (3,045m). 104, 578.

MARKAGUNT PLATEAU (Garfield, Iron) is the southernmost member of the western range of plateaus distinguished by Dutton in his "High Plateaus of Utah." Brian Head is the highest point at 11,315' (3,449m). The general boundaries of the plateau are U-20 on the north, US-89 on the east, U-14 on the south, and I-15 on the west. "Markagunt" is a Piute word meaning "Highland of Trees." The plateau was named by Almon Thompson, a member of the Powell surveys.

MARKHAM PEAK (Salt Lake, Tooele) is in the Oquirrh Mountains five miles northeast of Tooele*. The pioneers named the peak after one of their members.
S21,T3S,R3W,SLM; 8,702' (2,652m).

MARRIOTT* (Weber). In 1855 Lorin Farr sent John Marriott to establish a settlement three miles northwest of Ogden*. At that time, the region was overrun with wolves and bears, in addition to having an Indian encampment of two hundred lodges nearby. Marriott persevered, since he owned considerable land at the site, so the settlement was named for him.
NE¼,S24,T6N,R2W,SLM; 4,250' (1,295m). 100(v17), 274, 542, 567.

MARRS* (Grand) was a small settlement in the desert near Westwater*. The community existed during the early 1900s, but the post office closed down in 1913. George J. Marr was the postmaster.
146.

MARSELL CANYON (Duchesne) originates at Marsell and Farney lakes on the northeast slopes of West Grandaddy Mountain. The canyon drains northwest into the upper Duchesne River and was named for Dr. Ray Marsell, a noted geologist at the University of Utah.
S30,T3N,R8W,USM to S13,T3N,R9W,SLM. 298, 309.

MARSELL LAKE (Duchesne) is in the southwest section of the Uinta Mountains at the head of Marsell Canyon. See the canyon for name source.
S31,T3N,R8W,USM; 10,470' (3,191m).

MARSH LAKE (Summit) is in the north central section of the Uinta Mountains on the East Fork of Smiths Fork. Bridger and China lakes are in the vicinity. The lake was named for Yale University Professor Othniel C. Marsh, who led an 1870 expedition into this area to study fossil beds.
S30,31,T3N,R14E,SLM; 9,335' (2,845m). 309.

MARSH PEAK (Uintah) is in the southeast section of the Uinta Mountains near Chimney Rock Lake. See Marsh Lake for name source.
12,240' (3,731m).

MARSHALL LAKE (Duchesne) is in the Murdock Basin in the southwest section of the Uinta Mountains, near Hoover Lake. It was named for a former forest supervisor.
S11,T3N,R9W,USM; 9,990' (3,045m). 100 (v2).

MARTIN* (Carbon) is a small up-canyon outgrowth of Helper* that was named for a popular railroad engineer on the nearby Denver and Rio Grande Western Railroad.
S13,T13S,R9E,SLM; 5,800' (1,792m). 516.

MARTINVILLE* (Tooele). See Slagtown* (Tooele).

MARYS NIPPLE (Beaver) is on the western slopes of Indian Peak in the Indian Peak Range.
S30,T29S,R19W,SLM; 8,200' (2,499m).

MARYSVALE* (Piute) is twenty-eight miles south of Richfield* on US-89. The community was originally settled in 1863, later abandoned because of Indian troubles, and then resettled again. There are several claims for the name source. (1) It was named by a group of Catholic miners for the Virgin Mary. (2) Parley P. Pratt named it Merryville* when he passed through in 1849 because of the beautiful surroundings. The name was supposedly later changed to Marysvale. (3) Brigham Young named the settlement for his wife Mary. (4) The settlement was named Merry Valley* or Merry Vale* when Brigham Young and his party camped there when they were traveling through the area on visits to local settlements. During their visit, they

enjoyed an evening of relaxation and stag dancing. Stag dancing was common during this time because men were the predominate members of traveling groups. The name Merry Vale was gradually changed to the more euphonious Marysvale.
S19,20,T27S,R3W,SLM; 5,827' (1,776m). 27, 216, 242, 289, 314, 542, 578.

MARYSVALE PEAK (Piute) is seven miles northeast of Marysvale* on the Sevier Plateau.
S10,T27S,R2½W,SLM; 10,850' (3,307m).

MATHIAS CANYON (Box Elder) originates three miles southeast of Brigham City* and drains west into the Bear River National Wildlife Refuge. T. M. Mathias owned land near the mouth of the canyon.
S31,32,T9N,R1W,SLM. 139, 567.

MATT WARNER RESERVOIR (Uintah) is in the eastern Uinta Mountains on Pot Creek at the head of Jackson Draw. Matt Warner, an outlaw, was frequently in and out of this Browns Hole area. Warner later reformed and became sheriff of Price*, Utah. His real name was Willard Christianson. The reservoir had an earlier name of Calder Pond.
S34,35,T1N,R23E,SLM; 7,540' (2,298m). 25, 172, 303.

MATTHEW SPRING (Beaver) is on the eastern slopes of the Mineral Mountains at Cunningham Wash. The spring was named for Cunningham Matthews, a settler in this area during the 1870s.
S16,T27S,R8W,SLM; 7,200' (2,195m).

MAUGHANS FORT* (Cache). See Wellsville* (Cache).

MAVERICK NATURAL BRIDGE (Kane) spans a narrow section of a short tributary canyon that drains from the west into Phipps Canyon. A maverick is a motherless calf.
S13,T35S,R4E,SLM. 602.

MAYFIELD* (Sanpete) is twelve miles southwest of Manti* on Twelve Mile Creek. The settlement was first called Arrapene* for Chief Arrapene, a friendly Ute chief who made his camp in this area. In the early days the community was divided by the creek. The south side was called New London* because one of the settlers had recently married a young woman from London*, England. During Mayfield's early history, the name was changed several times. When the United Order was practiced, the town was known as Order*. Other names were Cobblehaven*, Skinny*, Skunk*, and Frog Hollow*. The beautiful flowers appearing along the hillsides in the early spring suggested the present name.
S32,T19S,R2E,SLM; 5,540' (1,689m). 289, 466(10 Oct. 1985, 11 March 1987), 542.

MAZE, THE (Wayne) is west of The Confluence at the head of Horse Canyon, South Fork. The tortuous twistings and turnings of the multiple waterways is how the name originated.
T30S,R18E,SLM. D.L. 6901.

MEADOW* (Millard) is eight miles south of Fillmore* on U-133. The settlement was originally called Meadow Creek* after the adjacent creek. Chief Walker and his people often used the area for a campground.
S22,T22S,R5W,SLM; 5,000' (1,524m). 289, 542.

MEADOW OF THE GATEWAY (Millard) is the area where the Beaver River, draining northward, meets the Sevier River draining southwest. The Domínguez-Escalante expedition gave the area a Spanish name, Vegas del Puerto. 129, 604.

MEADOW SPRING (Beaver) is in the Indian Peak Mountains in an alpine meadowland. The spring drains northeast into Turkey Wash.
S33,T28S,R18W,SLM; 6,625' (2,019m). 125.

MEADOWS, THE (Juab) is a railroad

siding southwest of Mills* on Chicken Creek. There is a large, prominent meadowland located in the area.
S26,35,T15S,R2W,SLM; 4,915' (1,498m).

MEADOWVILLE* (Rich) is seven miles southwest of Pickleville*. This small community was settled in 1869 and had an early name of Chimney Town*.
T13N,R5E,SLM; 6,006' (1,831m). 100(v13,17), 289, 542.

MEADOWVILLE VALLEY (Rich). Meadowville*, which is located in the valley, is the name source.

MECHAM RESERVOIR (Sevier). See Big Lake (Sevier).

MECHANICSVILLE* (Utah). See Goshen*.

MEEKS CABIN RESERVOIR (Summit) is on the Utah-Wyoming border on upper Blacks Fork. General William Henry Ashley and his trappers and mountain men were trapping in the area during the early 1820s. Joe Meeks was one of Ashley's more prominent men.
S16,T3N,R12E,SLM; 8,700' (2,652m). 237, 371, 372.

MEEKS CLIFF (Kane) is a geological feature three miles southwest of Carmel Junction*. It was named for Dr. Priddy Meeks, an early settler of nearby Mt. Carmel.

MEEKS LAKE (Garfield) is on the Boulder Mountain section of the Aquarius Plateau. The lake drains into Pleasant Creek. MRN
T31S,R5E,SLM.

MEGO* (Sanpete). See Moroni*.

MELVILLE* (Millard). See Delta* (Millard).

MELLENTHIN PEAK (San Juan) is eleven miles north of La Sal*. On August 23, 1918, Forest Ranger Rudolph E.

Mellenthin was shot to death near this peak while attempting to apprehend two draft evaders. One of the culprits, Ramon Archuletto, was wounded during the pursuit and was captured and confessed to the crime.
S11,T27S,R24E,SLM; 12,750' (3,886m). 409, 514, 530.

MENDON* (Cache) is seven miles northwest of Wellsville*. It was initially settled by Alexander and Robert Hill, and William Gardner and was known as North Settlement*. Apostle Ezra T. Benson was asked to name the new community and he renamed it Mendon for his birthplace in Massachusetts. Another reference states that Apostle H. C. Kimball named it for the town, Mendon City*, New York, where he and Brigham Young were living at the time of their conversion to the Mormon Church.
T11N,R1W,SLM; 4,500' (1,372m). 100(v17), 289, 448, 542.

MENDON PEAK (Cache) is in the Wellsville Mountains west of Mendon*.
S23,T11N,R2W,SLM; 8,766' (2,672m). 100(v17).

MERCHANT CREEK (Beaver) originates on the western slopes of Mt. Holly and Delano Peak in the Tushar Mountains. The creek drains southwest into the Beaver River. John and Charles Merchant were early settlers who ran cattle in the area in 1874. They also cut wood in this area to supply Fort Cameron, located near Beaver*.
T28,29S,R5W,SLM. 100(v17), 125, 355.

MERCHANT HOLLOW (Beaver) is northeast of North Creek* where it drains southwest into North Creek. See Merchant Creek for name source.
S20,T28S,R6W,SLM.

MERCHANT VALLEY (Beaver) is north of the head of Beaver River and Three Creeks. Merchant Creek drains through the valley. See Merchant Creek

for name source.
T29S,R5W,SLM.

MERCUR* (Tooele) is in upper Mercur Canyon, which had an earlier name of Lewiston Canyon. General Patrick E. Connor's soldiers discovered silver ore there in the 1860s. After several mines had opened, the town of Lewiston* was established. Fire then destroyed the community and, since the mines were running out, Lewiston was not rebuilt. In 1882 a Bavarian prospector, Arie Pinedo, discovered cinnabar (mercury, quicksilver). Pinedo named the strike Mercur for Mercury. By the late 1880s another town had developed, but it could not be named Lewiston because the name had been usurped by a town in Cache Valley, so Mercur was substituted. Mercur has had its ups and downs. It has been burned out and mine and ore processing have failed. But with new advancements in technology, the town has come back and continues to be active.
S7,T6S,R3W,SLM; 6,700' (2,042m). 89, 134 (29 Feb. 1976), 153, 516, 542, 546, 555 (v29).

MERCUR CANYON (Tooele) originates in the central Oquirrh Mountains where it drains west southwest into Rush Valley. See the town for the name source.
S8,T6S,R3W,SLM to S10,T6S,R4W,SLM.

MERKLEY SPRING (Uintah) is in Merkley Park three miles west of the Steinaker Reservoir. It was named for George D. Merkley.
S30,T3S,R21E,SLM. 567.

MERRILL* (Uintah). See Naples*.

MERRILL HOLLOW (Garfield) originates in the Pink Cliffs and drains southeast into Yellow Creek. It was named in 1887 for John Merrill.
S22,T37S,R3W,SLM (at mouth). 530.

MERRIMAC BUTTE (Grand) is eight miles northwest of the Moab bridge. The shape of the butte is similar to that of the famed Civil War battleship. Monitor Butte is also in this area.
S5,T25S,R20E,SLM.

MESA* (Grand) is a ghost town site nine miles east of Moab* on Wilson Mesa.
S14,15,T26S,R23E,SLM.

MEXICAN HAT* (San Juan) is on US-163 twenty miles southwest of Bluff* where a bridge crosses the San Juan River. The settlement had the early name of Goodridge* after E. L. Goodridge, a man who made an oil claim in this area in 1882. The present name comes from a sombrero-shaped rock formation that is located two and one-half miles northeast.
S71,T42S,R19E,SLM; 4,244' (1,294m). 58, 314, 542, 546, 610.

MEXICAN HAT ROCK (San Juan) is two and one-half miles north of Mexican Hat*. This feature has the general shape of a Mexican sombrero.
S32,T41S,R19E,SLM.

MIDDLE BASIN (Summit) is in the western section of the Uinta Mountains and is the middle one of three glaciated basins. To the east is Amethyst Basin.
10,000' (3,048m).

MIDDLE DESERT (Wayne) is north of Capitol Reef National Park. South Desert is further south.
T27S,R7E,SLM.

MIDDLE MOODY CANYON (Garfield) originates at Deer Point near the south end of the Circle Cliffs where it drains into Moody Creek. See Moody Creek for name source.
NE¼,T36S,R8E,SLM to T37S,R8E,SLM.

MIDDLETON* (Washington) is a community three miles east of St. George*. It was originally settled in the spring of 1863 and is midway between Washington* and St. George.
S21,T42S,R15W,SLM; 2,983' (909m). 154.

MIDDLETON* (Weber) is a settlement that was an outgrowth of Huntsville* prior to 1905. It was named in honor of Charles F. Middleton of the Mormon Church Weber Stake presidency.
289, 567.

MIDVALE* (Salt Lake) is northwest of Sandy*. The community was initially named East Jordan Ward, then Bingham Junction*, since the town was on the road west to Bingham*. The name was later changed to Midvale because it was a prosperous, centrally located, thriving community.
S25,36,T2S,R1W,SLM; 4,375' (1,333m). 289, 542.

MIDWAY* (Wasatch) is on Snake Creek four miles northwest of Heber*. In 1859 there were two settlements on the creek. The upper settlement, two miles farther up-canyon, had a temporary name of Mound City*. The two communities eventually united under the name Midway so the settlers could better protect themselves against the Indians.
S34,35,T3S,R4E,SLM; 5,550' (1,692m). 100 (v5,17), 289, 314, 542, 567.

MILBURN* (Sanpete) is an outgrowth of Fairview* on the upper San Pitch River. The community had several early names such as Milborn* and Millburn*, all of which were related to the early sawmills built at the mouth of the nearby canyons. Today it is primarily an agricultural region.
S12,T13S,R4E,SLM. 289, 542.

MILES CANYON (Cache) originates at the Bear River Reservoir where it drains west into Paradise Dry Canyon. It was named for E. D. Miles, an early laborer in the canyon.
S6,T9N,R2E,SLM (at mouth). 508.

MILFORD* (Beaver) is thirty miles northwest of Beaver* on U-21. The four-horse teams freighting ore from the Mineral Range on the east side of the river had to ford the Beaver River to get to the mill. The settlement at the ford gradually developed the name Milford.
T28S,R10W,SLM; 4,968' (1,514m). 100(v17), 314, 542, 546.

MILFORD FLAT (Beaver) is a large grazing area five miles south of Beaver*.
S31,T28S,R11W,SLM; 5,000' (1,524m).

MILFORD NEEDLE (Beaver) is a pinnacle on the north slope of Granite Peak in the Mineral Range.
S12,T28S,R9W,SLM; 9,000' (2,743m).

MILFORD VALLEY (Beaver) is the section of the old Escalante Desert that surrounds Milford*.
T28S,R10,11W,SLM.

MILK LAKE (Duchesne) is in the south central section of the Uinta Mountains, four miles northeast of Kings Peak. Suspended mineral matter in the water gives the water a milky appearance.
11,236' (3,425m).

MILK LAKE (Duchesne) is in the south central section of the Uinta Mountains on the head of Yellowstone River. See Milk Lake for name origin.
S25,T4N,R5W,USM; 10,983' (3,348m).

MILL B FORK CANYON. (Salt Lake) originates at Lake Lillian where it drains north into Big Cottonwood Canyon. Several canyons off Big Cottonwood Canyon were alphabetically named if it had a sawmill located at the mouth.
S22,T2S,R2E,SLM (at mouth).

MILL CANYON (Kane) drains south into the head of Skutumpah Creek. Bishop Levi Stewart set up a sawmill in this canyon.
S8,T40S,R4½W,SLM.

MILL CITY* (Summit) was eleven miles north of Hayden Peak and Mirror Lake. This 1880s logging camp housed the laborers and their families who were

employed in supplying timber products to the nearby transcontinental railroad.
S13,T1N,R9E,SLM; 9,400' (2,865m). 89, 516.

MILL CITY CREEK (Summit) originates in the northwestern Uinta Mountains on the north slopes of Gold Hill, one and one-half miles southeast of Whitney Reservoir. Mill City* was built near the headwaters of this creek in the 1860s.
S14,T1N,R9E,SLM to S13,T2N,R9E,SLM.

MILL CREEK (Davis) originates east of and drains through Bountiful*. The creek was named for the Heber C. Kimball mill at the mouth of Mill Creek Canyon.
S33,T2N,R1E,SLM (at mouth). 201.

MILL CREEK (Grand) originates on the western slopes of Manns Peak of the La Sal Mountains. It drains northeast through Moab* into the Colorado River. A sawmill was built on the bank of the creek.
S27,T26S,R24E,SLM to S2,T26S,R21E,SLM. 514.

MILL CREEK* (Salt Lake) is a subdivision of Salt Lake City at the mouth of Mill Creek Canyon and the east end of Thirty-third South. The community received its name from the creek. See Mill Creek (Salt Lake).
T13S,R1E,SLM; 4,975' (1,516m).

MILL CREEK (Salt Lake) originates on the southern slopes of Murdock Peak east of Salt Lake City* and drains west through Mill Creek Canyon to the Jordan River. A motion was made to name the large creek Mill Creek on August 22, 1847, at the first general conference of the Mormon Church.
S34,T1S,R3E,SLM to S36,T1S,R1E,SLM. 100 (v1), 106, 252, 542.

MILL CREEK (Washington) drains south into the Virgin River. This was Brigham Young's early "Machine Creek." It had been selected for his planned factory site, which was supposed to have originated on the south slopes of the Pine Valley Mountains. The factory plans did not transpire.
S3,T41S,R15W,SLM to S23,T42S,R15W, SLM. 154, 310.

MILL CREEK* (Weber). See Slaterville*.

MILL CREEK CANYON (Davis) originates north of Grandview Peak, east of Bountiful*, and drains west into the marshlands east of Great Salt Lake.
S33,T2N,R1E,SLM (at mouth).

MILL CREEK CANYON (Salt Lake) originates in the mountains east of Mill Creek* and Salt Lake City* and drains west. The canyon is partly precipitate, with cliffs along the side. The Indians trapped deer and elk by forcing them over the cliffs to their death in the canyon below. These activities gave the canyon the Indian name of Tin-Goup, which means "rock trap." Several mills were built in the canyon during pioneer days, thus the basis of the anglicized name.
S34,T1S,R3E,SLM to S36,T1S,R1E,SLM. 105, 252.

MILL FORK (Emery) originates east of Upper Joes Valley where it drains east into upper Huntington Creek. It was here that the pioneers set up their sawmill after the water in nearby Rilda Creek failed. Much of the lumber processed in this area was used for building homes in Huntington*.
S18,20,21,22,T16S,R7E,SLM.

MILL HOLLOW (Beaver) originates on the western slopes of Little Shelly Baldy Peak in the Tushar Mountains. It drains southwest into Indian Creek.
S27,T7S,R6W,SLM.

MILL MEADOW RESERVOIR (Sevier, Wayne) is on the county line at the junction of the Fremont River and U M

Creek. The reservoir is located in a meadow that once had a sawmill.
S24,34,T26S,R3E,SLM; 7,681' (2,341m).

MILL POND (Tooele) is a spring-fed pond one-half mile north of Tooele*.
S15,16,T2S,R4W,SLM; 4,255' (1,296m). 100(v2).

MILL WARD* (Uintah). See Maeser*.

MILLARD CANYON (Garfield) originates at French Springs southeast of Hans Flat. The canyon drains north northeast into the Green River at Queen Anne Bottom. According to Baker, "They learned later that they had misunderstood this name; instead of honoring a president, it was named for an undistinguished 'Miller' who did nothing more than leave this small, mistaken mark on the map" (24, p. 33). The name was even misspelled Millard.
T28S,R16E,SLM. 24.

MILLARD COUNTY was named for U.S. President Millard Fillmore. He signed the act creating the Territory of Utah on September 9, 1850, and then appointed Brigham Young the first governor. Fillmore* was the state capital at that time, which was also named for President Fillmore.

MILLE CRAG BEND (Garfield) is a U-shaped bend on the Colorado River between the mouths of the Dirty Devil River and Dark Canyon. The axis of the bend is more than one mile long. Major Powell named it "from the multitude of ragged pinnacles into which the cliffs broke" (159, p. 132). "In the bend on the right, vast numbers of crags, and pinnacles, and tower shaped rocks are seen. We call it Mille Crag Bend" (422, p. 67).
T33S,R15E,SLM. 159, 420, 422, 496, 515 (v7).

MILLER* (Salt Lake) was an outgrowth of Mill Creek*, settled prior to 1907. The settlement was named in honor of Bishop Reuben Miller of the Mill Creek Ward. 288.

MILLER HOLLOW (Beaver) originates on the western slopes of the Tushar Mountains and drains west. It was named for Dan Miller, a trapper and prospector who lived in the region.
S18,T28S,R6W,SLM. 125.

MILLER RIVER. See Bear River (Idaho, Utah, Wyoming).

MILLERS CREEK (Emery) originates at the coal mining town of Hiawatha*. The creek drains into the Price River and was named for Reuben Miller, a sheep man who herded his flocks in this area in 1876.
S27,T15S,R8E,SLM to T15S,R11E,SLM. 292.

MILLERS ISLAND (Weber). See Fremont Island.

MILLERS SETTLEMENT* (Davis). See Farmington*.

MILLS* (Juab). In the spring of 1880 the Union Pacific Railroad crossed the Sevier River on a grade constructed under the supervision of Henry Mills. This crossing became the construction settlement named for Superintendent Mills. It had earlier names of Suckertown* and Wellington*. The railroad also named the surrounding valley after Mills. An alternate claim is that the settlement was named for some nearby mills.
S25,T15S,R2W,SLM. 4,931' (1,503m). 100 (v17), 347, 542.

MILLS JUNCTION* (Tooele) is between Lake Point* and Tooele*. In 1855 it was a small mining town that was also the county seat. In 1856 the county seat moved south to Tooele. Mills Junction had an early name of Richville*, but after Ezra Taft Benson built a sawmill and Brigham Young had his wool processing and flour mills there, it was soon known as Milltown*, Milton*, or

Millvale*. The settlement never filled its desired potential and by 1889 the town was abandoned. Today it is Mills Junction on I-80.
S10,T2S,R4W,SLM; 4,330' (1,320m). 89, 100 (v17), 542.

MILLTOWN* (Tooele). See Mills Junction* (Tooele).

MILLVILLE* (Cache) is three miles southeast of Logan*, where the first sawmill in Cache Valley was built. The settlement was subsequently established in 1860. Prior to that, one or two individuals had taken up land in the vicinity and the area was known as the Elkhorn Ranch*.
S15,22,T11N,R1E,SLM; 4,610' (1,405m). 27, 289, 448, 449, 542, 567.

MILLVILLE PEAK (Cache) is in the Bear River Range, five miles east of Millville*, which is the source name.
T11N,R2E,SLM; 9,282' (2,829m).

MILLWARD* (Uintah). See Maeser* (Uintah).

MILTON* (Morgan) was settled in 1856 three miles northwest of Morgan* and the Weber River. It was originally called Morganville* to honor a Mormon church official, Jedediah Morgan Grant. The name was later changed to Milton to honor the late Amos Milton Musser. Another report claims the name Milton came from the gristmill built in the area.
S28,T4N,R2E,SLM; 5,015' (1,529m). 27, 289, 526(v2), 542.

MINERAL CANYON (Grand) originates east of the Green River between Hell Roaring and Taylor canyons and drains southwest into the Green River. The name reflects the prospecting and mining activities along the canyon.
T26S,R18,19E,SLM. 609.

MINERAL CANYON (Iron) originates at Mineral Springs, twelve miles northeast of Parowan*, and drains northwest. The name reflects the prospecting activities carried out in the canyon.
S7,T33S,R7W,SLM (at head). 567.

MINERAL MOUNTAINS (Beaver) run north and south between Adamsville* and Milford*. The mountains were formerly known as the Granite Mountains.
T28,29S,R8,9W,SLM; 9,578' (2,919m).

MINERS BASIN (Grand) is on the western slopes of the La Sal Mountains east of the south end of Pinhook Valley. This basin was known for having rich ores and mines. Miners settled in the basin in order to work in the nearby mines.
T26S,R24E,SLM; 9,950' (3,033m). 146, 514.

MINERS CABIN WASH (Beaver) originates on the western slopes of the Indian Peak Range and drains west into Hamlin Valley Wash.
T29S,R18,19W,SLM.

MINERS GULCH (Beaver) originates in the Indian Peak Range and drains west into Hamlin Valley. The gulch was a prospecting and mining area.
T30S,R18W,SLM. 125.

MINERS HILL RESERVOIR (Beaver) is in the Wah Wah Wash between the Wah Wah Mountains and the Shauntie Hills.
S26,T29S,R14W,SLM; 5,600' (1,707m).

MINERSVILLE* (Beaver) is eighteen miles west of Beaver* at the junction of U-21 and U-130. It was settled in the spring of 1859 and had several different names such as The Farm*, Lower Beaver*, Cottonwoods*, Grundyville*, and Punkin Center*. It was finally named Minersville to honor the miners who worked in the adjacent mines. There is an alternate claim that the settlement was named to honor a miner, Grant Prisbey, one of the early settlers who helped survey the townsite.

S12,T30S,R10W,SLM; 5,280' (1,609m). 100(v5,17), 456, 481, 542.

MINERSVILLE CANYON (Beaver) originates at Rocky Ford Dam at the south end of Minersville Reservoir. Minersville* is at the mouth of this western-draining canyon.
T30S,R9W,SLM.

MINERSVILLE LAKE STATE REC-REATION AREA (Beaver) includes Minersville Reservoir.

MINERSVILLE RESERVOIR (Beaver) is near Adamsville*. The reservoir had an earlier name of Rocky Ford Reser-voir, which is the name now used for the dam.
T30S,R9W,SLM; 5,508' (1,679m). D.L. 6802.

MINNIE MAUDE CREEK (Carbon) originates at Minnie Maude Ridge in the Roan Cliffs of the West Tavaputs Plateau, fifteen miles north northeast of Helper* and Price*. The creek drains southeast into Nine Mile Canyon. Alfred Lunt settled in this area in 1885 and named the creek for his two daughters.
S16,17,T11S,R11E,SLM to S18,T12S,R13E, SLM. 567. D.L. 5401.

MIRROR LAKE (Duchesne) is one of the more beautiful lakes located in the Uinta Mountains. It is in the southwest section at the east base of Bald Mountain. Its water surface is tranquil and reflects its alpine surroundings. Several rivers head in this vicinity: the Weber, Provo, Bear, and Duchesne.
S34,T4N,R9W,USM; 10,025 (3,056m). 247, 314, 546.

MITCHELL BUTTE WASH (San Juan) originates in Arizona southeast of Goulding* where it drains northeast into Oljeto Wash. In the early 1880s Ernest Mitchell and James Merrick (Merritt) were killed near the wash, reportedly by Ute Indians in Navajo territory. It was suspected that Mitchell and Merrick may

have discovered a hidden Indian silver mine.
T43S,R15,16E,SLM. 303, 359, 406.

MITCHELL CANYON (Garfield) is on the northeast slopes of Mount Canaan, southwest of Escalante*. It drains northeast into Coal Bed Canyon and was named for Zetland Mitchell, an early stockman.
T35S,R2E,SLM.

MITTON PEAK (Cache) is seven miles north of Brigham City*. The peak was named for John W. Mitton, a govern-ment trapper who worked in this region from 1898 to 1912.
S12,T10N,R2W,SLM; 8,657' (2,639m). D.L. 8204.

MOAB* (Grand) is on US-163 and the Colorado River near Arches National Park. It was settled in 1855 by Mormon colonists, vacated because of Indian troubles, and then resettled in 1876. Moab has had several previous names such as Plainfield*, Poverty Flats*, Bueno*, Spanish Valley*, Grand Valley*, Mormon Fort*, etc. (not in chronological order). The name Moab was first pro-posed by William Pierce who called the area "the land beyond the Jordan." Another popular claim for the name source comes from the hordes of mosquitos that breed in the swampy backwaters of the Colorado River. The Piute word for mosquito was "Moapa."
T25,26S,R21,22E,SLM; 4,042' (1,232m). 146, 314, 406, 409, 494, 514, 542, 546, 555(v1).

MOAB CANYON (Grand) is north of Moab* and the Colorado River, into which the canyon drains. US-163 passes through the canyon.
T25S,R21E,SLM.

MOAB VALLEY (Grand) was previously known as the Spanish Valley. It was in this valley that the Old Spanish Trail crossed the Colorado River. The valley is small and pear-shaped and is

approximately fifteen miles long and two to three miles wide. See Moab* for the name source.
S35,T25S,R21E,SLM and S1,T26S,R21E, SLM.

MOAP LAKE (Uintah) is in the southeast section of the Uinta Mountains on upper Dry Fork. Paradise Lake Park is eight miles south. The word "Moap" (Moapa) is Piute for mosquito. See Moab*.
10,750' (3,277m). 309.

MOCCASIN LAKE (Duchesne) is on the headwaters of the Whiterocks River in the central section of the Uinta Mountains near Chepeta Lake. See Chepeta and Papoose lakes for name source.
S28,33,T5N,R1W,USM; 10,625' (3,239m).

MODENA* (Iron) is near the Nevada border on U-56, fifty miles west of Cedar City*. The exact source for the name is unclear. The best suggestion is that a laborer of Italian origin named the railroad camp after a city in Italy. But folklore must be given its due. It is recorded that an old Chinese cook did not have a large enough cooking facility to handle the entire railroad work crew in one sitting. The cook would serve one group, then would call out, "Mo'dinna, mo'dinna" to the next group. Modena had an earlier name of Deseret Springs*.
S36,T34S,R19W,SLM; 5,462' (1,665m). 100 (v17), 314, 456, 542, 546.

MODOC CITY* (Salt Lake) was seven miles up City Creek Canyon northeast of Salt Lake City*. A mining operation was run near the mouth of nearby Cottonwood Gulch. Today it is a ghost town site. The Modocs were an Indian tribe that roamed the territory between southern California and northern Oregon.
S7,T1N,R2E,SLM. 516.

MOHRLAND* (Emery) was a coal-mining town three miles south of Hiawatha* on upper Cedar Creek. The four leading organizers of the town were Mays, Orem, Heiner, and Rice. The town name is a combination of the first initials of their names with "land" added to the end. In 1938 the mines were shut down and the town was abandoned.
S10,15,T16S,R8E,SLM; 7,100' (2,164m). 89, 494, 516, 542.

MOLEN* (Emery) became an outgrowth of Ferron* in 1877 after Mike (Mitchell) Molen brought his cattle and horses into Castle Valley and settled on Ferron Creek. An earlier name for the settlement was Lower Ferron*.
S7,T20S,R8E,SLM; 5,700' (1,737m). 100 (v17), 193, 289, 542.

MOLLIES NIPPLE (Beaver) is a small butte located four miles southwest of Milford* on the east side of the Star Range.
S15,T28S,R11W,SLM; 5,110' (1,591m).

MOLLIES NIPPLE (Kane) is two miles south of Nipple Lake and the head of Kitchen Canyon. According to early cowhands, the geologic feature was named as a compliment to John Kitchen's bride, Molly.
S6,T41S,R2W,SLM; 7,271' (2,216m). 68, 508, 555(v50).

MOLLIES NIPPLE (Utah) is two and one-half miles south southeast of Payson*.
S28,T9W,R2E,SLM; 6,277' (1,913m).

MOLLYS NIPPLE (Uintah) is south of the White River and five miles east southeast of Ouray*.
S8,T9S,R21E,SLM; 4,907' (1,496m).

MOLLYS STOCKING (Box Elder) is a two-mile-long, stocking-shaped dike located between lakes in the public shooting grounds marshland at the Bear River Migratory Bird Refuge.
S21,28,33,T10N,R4W,SLM; 4,320' (1,317m).

MONA* (Juab) is on US-91 eight miles north of Nephi*. The community was

settled in 1852 with an early name of Clover Creek* for the luxurious patches of wild clover growing in the area. The name was changed to Willow Creek*, then Starr* for an early settler. There is disagreement as to the origin of the name Mona, an Indian word meaning beautiful and a contraction of the Italian word "madonna." The name has a comical meaning. It means "Manx, by the mountains" whereby the word "Manx" refers to the people from the Isle of Mann. Dr. Matthew McCune, a former surgeon in the British Army, is reported to be the one who suggested Mona, because it was the name of his former home on the Isle of Mann.
S32,T11S,R1E,SLM; 5,000' (1,524m). 100 (v17), 289, 347, 542, 546.

MONARCH* (Duchesne) is a small community four and one-half miles west southwest of Neola*. Mrs. Lee Brown suggested the name because she said that sometime in the future the town would be the "monarch of all it surveyed." Today it is a small scattered community in a gas- and oil-producing region.
S10,T1S,R2W,USM; 5,925' (1,806m). 1, 100 (v17), 567.

MONITOR BUTTE (Grand) is eight miles northwest of the Moab bridge that crosses the Colorado River. The butte is named for the famed Civil War turreted battleship. Merrimac Butte is in the area.
S5,T25S,R20E,SLM; 5,420' (1,652m).

MONITOR BUTTE (San Juan) is in Monument Valley on Monument Mesa, twenty miles northwest of Goulding*. To some it resembles the Civil War ironclad, the *Monitor*.
S15,16,T41S,R13E,SLM; 6,117' (1,864m).

MONITOR MESA (San Juan) is in the "V" of Copper Canyon and the San Juan River. The mesa received its name from the distinctive Monitor Butte located on top of the mesa.
T41,42S,R13E,SLM.

MONKEY TOWN* (Sevier). See Monroe*.

MONROE* (Sevier) is on U-118 three and one-half miles south of Elsinore*. Monroe was originally settled in 1863 as South Bend* because the settlement was on a bend of the Sevier River. Shortly afterwards the residents were forced to move because they were having problems with the Indians. In 1870 they returned and renamed the town Alma* in honor of a prominent person in the Book of Mormon. At this time the settlers applied for a post office. The name Alma had been preempted so the name Monroe was assigned in honor of the fifth President of the United States. Monroe had one unusual variant name of Monkey Town*. An early settler, John E. Johnson, had a hobby of climbing trees and poles, so his neighbors called him Monkey John from Monkey Town.
S9,10,15,16,T25S,R3W,SLM; 5,382' (1,640m). 100(v17), 134(4 July 1920), 289, 368, 542, 567, 584, 585.

MONROE PEAK (Sevier) is on the Sevier Plateau seven miles southeast of Monroe*.
T26S,R2½W,SLM; 11,226' (3,422m).

MONTE CRISTO PEAK (Cache, Weber) is the high point in the Monte Cristo Range at the junction of Cache, Morgan, and Weber county lines. There are three different claims for the name origin. (1) It is believed that miners returning from the California gold mines thought this range resembled the Monte Cristo mountain range in California. (2) The name could have been given by early French-Canadian trappers in a hybrid form of the literal "Mountain of Christ." (3) One of the early road builders carried the book *The Count of Monte Cristo*, which he read to his coworkers around the camp fire in the evening.
S20,T8N,R4E,SLM; 9,148' (2,788m). 100(v17), 314, 567. D.L. 8401.

MONTE CRISTO RANGE is in the center of a rough triangle made by Woodruff*, Logan*, and Ogden*. Until recently it was a part of the Wasatch Mountain complex, but is now an independent mountain range. See the peak for name source.
T8N,R4E,SLM.

MONTEZUMA* (San Juan). See Montezuma Creek* (San Juan).

MONTEZUMA CANYON (San Juan). See Montezuma Creek (San Juan). D.L. 8502.

MONTEZUMA CREEK (San Juan) originates near Monticello* and drains south through Montezuma Canyon into the San Juan River. Peter Shirts is given credit for originating the creek and canyon name that is also tied into the name of nearby Recapture Creek. Shirts claimed that the Aztec ruler Montezuma was captured and killed in this area. Shirts's claim is dubious. W. H. Holmes of the Hayden survey suggests in the 1876 Hayden Report that the name was well known before Shirts's time. If so, the name origin of the two creeks is still in doubt.
T34-40S,R24E,SLM. 37, 100(v17), 314, 359, 516. D.L. 8502.

MONTEZUMA CREEK* (San Juan) was a small pioneer settlement at the mouth of Montezuma Creek. Peter Shirts initially established the community. Later, others settlers joined Shirts, especially after the Hole-in-the-Rock expedition.
S25,T40S,R23E,SLM; 4,419' (1,347m). 359, 516.

MONTEZUMA PEAK (Tooele) is the high point of the Clifton Hills, five miles south of Gold Hill*. The peak was named for a nearby mine.
SW¼,T8S,R17W,SLM; 7,370' (2,246m). 567.

MONTICELLO* (San Juan) is on US-163 twenty-five miles north of Blanding*. Since the Hayden survey found no settlers in the area in 1874, it is probable that Patrick O'Donnell, a cattleman who built a cabin there in 1879, was Monticello's first white resident. In 1887 the Mormon Church called five families from Bluff* to settle the site. Early names for the settlement were Piute Springs* and North Montezuma Creek*. In a formal meeting three names were under consideration: North Montezuma*, Hammond* for Francis A. Hammond, the local stake president, and the biblical name, Antioch*. None of the names were approved by the younger members of the community. When Hammond recommended Monticello, everyone approved and it was accepted.
S36,T33S,R23E,SLM; 7,066' (2,154m). 100 (v17), 314, 406, 409, 514, 542, 546.

MONTWELL* (Duchesne) was a small temporary community near Monarch*. The settlement had an early name of Wells* for the numerous artesian wells in the vicinity. Mormon Stake President Frederick S. Musser then suggested a permanent name of Montwell, a contraction of mountains, wells, and Monarch.
100(v17), 165.

MONUMENT BASIN (Garfield) is along the White Rim west of the Colorado River. To the north is Grand View Point. It is a region of totem-like spires and monoliths stretching up from the canyon floor.
T29S,R19E,SLM. 514.

MONUMENT CANYON (Grand). See Glen Canyon.

MONUMENT POINT (Box Elder) is north of the northernmost point of the Great Salt Lake, on the old Central Pacific Railroad grade near Pothole Springs. This was the point where the Union Pacific and Central Pacific Railroad joined on May 10, 1869. The point has been marked by a stone monument.
S3,T11N,R9W,SLM; 4,375' (1,333m). 49, 139, 546.

MONUMENT POINT (Iron) is on the top of Brian Head where the U.S. Geological Survey put survey data into a can then left it in a rock cairn.
S12,T36S,R9W,SLM; 11,307' (3,446m). 567.

MONUMENT VALLEY (San Juan) is south of the San Juan River and south and west of Mexican Hat*. The valley extends into Arizona as a desert wilderness region of pinnacles, spires, geologic "mittens" and buttes.
314, 514, 546.

MOODY CREEK (Garfield) originates on the southern slopes of the Wagon Box Mesa, west of the Circle Cliffs. It drains south into the Escalante River. John Moody, an early stockman, used the area as a cattle range. Middle Moody and East Moody canyons are also in this area.
12, 602.

MOON CANYON (Summit) originates one mile northeast of Woodland* and drains northwest into Beaver Creek at Samak*. The canyon was named for Henry and Joseph Moon, early settlers.
S26,36,T2S,R6E,SLM. 66.

MOON LAKE (Duchesne) is on the south side of the Uinta Mountains on Lake Fork. The crescent shape of the lake provides the name.
S1,12,T2N,R6W,USM. 100(v17), 314.

MOON RIDGE (Grand) is on the East Tavaputs Plateau in the fork of Meadow and Willow creeks.
T16S,R21E,SLM.

MOONLIGHT WASH (San Juan). See Oljeto Wash. "Oljeto" is Navajo for "moonlight." The anglicized form is occasionally used.

MOONSHINE CANYON (Beaver) originates in the west central part of the Wah Wah Mountains. It drains north into Pine Grove and Pine Valley Wash.
S34,T28S,R16W,SLM.

MOONSHINE SPRING (Emery) is near Gruvers Mesa and Moonshine Wash. Gruver was an early moonshiner and bootlegger who operated from this spring where he made illegal liquor.
S19,T24S,R16E,SLM. 102.

MOONSHINE WASH (Emery) originates in the "V" of the San Rafael River and the Labyrinth Canyon sector of the Green River. It drains north into the San Rafael River. See Moonshine Spring for name source.
S6,T25S,R16E,SLM.

MOONWATER POINT (Grand) has a northwest-southeast orientation on the East Tavaputs Plateau east of the Green River and north of Florence Creek.
S9,16,22,T16S,R18E,SLM; 8,644' (2,635m).

MOORE* (Emery) is on U-10 five miles northeast of Emery*. The original name for this community was Rochester*, the name of M. B. Whitney's hometown. Whitney was the promoter of the Independent Canal and Reservoir Company, which was incorporated in 1894 in order to develop the land in the vicinity. In 1940 the community name was changed to Moore to honor L. C. Moore, a landowner and manager of a local farm project.
S29,T21S,R7E,SLM; 6,269' (1,911m). 542, 546.

MOOSEHORN LAKE (Duchesne) is in the southwest section of the Uinta Mountains on the upper Duchesne River. Mirror Lake is one-half mile north. The lake has the general shape of a set of moose horns.
S34,T4N,R9W,SLM; 10,390' (3,167m). 530.

MOQUI CANYON (San Juan) originates in the northeast section of the Clay Hills and drains west into the Colorado River. The term "Moqui" is a less-favored term for the Hopi Indians. The canyon was named for the numerous Indian ruins throughout the area. Although the northern boundary of the Hopi did not extend into Utah, the state still has several Hopi place names, many of which are in the Natural Bridges National Monument area. T38S,R12E,SLM.

MORAT LAKE (**Duchesne**) is at the west end of the Uinta Mountains at the base of Mount Agassiz in the Naturalist Basin. Most of the lakes in this cluster are named for students of Agassiz, the famous naturalist. Morat was one of those students. S32,T4N,R8W,USM; 10,760' (3,280m). 298, 309.

MOREHOUSE CANYON (**Beaver**) originates at Morehouse Springs in the San Francisco Mountains and drains toward the Beaver Bottoms. The canyon was named for Charles Morehouse. He hauled water from the spring at the head of the canyon to the miners in Frisco*. S21,29,T26S,R12W,SLM. 125.

MOREHOUSE SPRING (**Beaver**) is at the head of Morehouse Canyon. See above.

MORELL* (**Summit**). See Marion* (Summit).

MORGAN* (**Morgan**) is at the mouth of upper Weber Canyon where U-66, I-80N, and US-30S intersect. An earlier name was Monday Town*. After the relocation of the community, the name was changed to honor Jedediah Morgan Grant, father of Heber J. Grant, a former president of the Mormon Church. S35,36,T4N,R2E,SLM; 5,064' (1,544m). 27, 192, 542, 546.

MORGAN COUNTY was established in 1862 and was named for Jedediah Morgan Grant. See Morgan*. 6, 27, 542.

MORGANVILLE* (**Morgan**). See Milton*.

MORMON FLAT (**Morgan**) was a prominent camping spot on the Old Mormon Trail. The route passed this area then followed through East Canyon at the mouth of Schuster Creek. S14,T1N,R3E,SLM. 378.

MORMON FLAT (**San Juan**) is five miles south southwest of the Bears Ears. It was a prominent camping spot for members of the Hole-in-the-Rock trek and subsequent travelers. T37S,R18E,SLM; 6,793' (2,071m). 359.

MORMON FORT* (**Grand**). See Moab*.

MORMON PASTURE (**San Juan**) is in the northwest sector of the Abajo Mountains, seven miles north northwest of Mount Linnaeus. In 1887 Brigham Young, Jr., and Alma and Joshua Stevens organized a cattle company, wintering their livestock between Elk Ridge and the Colorado River. They used Mormon Pasture as summer headquarters and also established a dairy there in 1889. S27,T33S,R20E,SLM to S2,T34S,R20E,SLM; 7,200' (2,195). 406, 514.

MORONI* (**Sanpete**) is six miles west of Mount Pleasant* on U-116 and U-132. The settlement had an early name of Mego* for a local friendly Indian, and Sanpitch* for a local Indian chief. In 1859 the community was organized as a ward and George Peacock of Manti* suggested Moroni as the new name. Moroni was an important figure in the Book of Mormon. A statue of Moroni is on the Salt Lake temple. S9,10,15,16,T15S,R3E,SLM. 100(v17), 542, 546, 567, 569.

MORRISSEY* (**Beaver**). See Sulphurdale* (Beaver).

MORRISON* (**Sanpete**) was two miles east of Sterling* near the mouth of Six Mile Canyon. Morrison was an English

financier who developed coal mines in this area after 1854. He also helped establish a store, homes, and other facilities. The coal veins turned out to be too thin and water continually flooded the mining operation. The community died and is a ghost town today.
T19S,R2E,SLM. 163(26 Feb. 1983), 360.

MORRISTOWN* (Washington) was a small temporary settlement established near St. George*.
311.

MORRISTOWN* (Weber). See South Weber* (Weber).

MORTENSEN CANYON (Millard) originates five and one-half miles southeast of Meadow* and drains west to Mortensen Spring. The canyon was named for the Mortensen family, who settled in the area. An earlier name was Little Cottonwood Canyon.
S10,T23S,R4½W,SLM to S12,T23S,R5W, SLM.

MOSBY MOUNTAIN (Uintah) is on the southern slopes of the Uinta Mountains, sixteen miles northwest of LaPoint*. Nearby are Mosby Creek, Sink, and Park. Dan Mosby ran his cattle on the mountain and Jim Mosby, an early settler, was accidentally killed in this area while moving a load of logs.
S20,28,32,T3N,R1E,USM; 9,941' (3,030m). 309.

MOSCOW* (Beaver) was an old mining town near the head of Moscow Wash in the Star Mountain range southwest of Milford*. It was settled in 1870 but is a ghost town site today. See Moscow Wash for name origin.
S25,T28S,R12W,SLM; 6,500' (1,981m).

MOSCOW CANYON (Beaver) originates on the north side of Picacho Peak and drains southwest into Moscow Wash. See Moscow Wash.
S25,26,T28S,R12W,SLM.

MOSCOW RESERVOIR (Beaver) is at the south end of the Star Range near the mouth of Moscow Wash.
S12,T29S,R12W,SLM; 5,100' (1,554m).

MOSCOW WASH (Beaver) originates at the junction of Moscow Canyon and Shauntie Wash in the Star Range, and drains south into the Escalante Desert. The wash received its name from the Burning Moscow Mine near the head. Matthew Cullen named the mine in 1870 for the burning red color of the ore.

MOSIDA* (Utah) was near the southwest shore of Utah Lake, eleven miles north of Elberta*. On December 5, 1908, R. F. Morrison, Joseph A. Simpson, and J. E. Davis purchased 6,880 acres of land to establish a new community. Within four to five years a hotel, schoolhouse, post office, and general store were operating. In 1915 the town was hopelessly in debt and by 1924 it was a ghost town. The community name was coined from the first two letters of the surnames of the three promoters, Morrison, Simpson, and Davis.
S9,16,T8S,R1W,SLM; 4,571' (1,393m). 89, 100(v13), 270, 516, 546.

MOSSY DELL SPRING (Garfield) is one mile west of the head of Alvey Wash at the head of Trap Canyon. Moss and Dell were the names of two early stockmen who ran their cattle in this area.
S19,T37S,R2E,SLM; 7,100' (2,164m). 12.

MOUND CANYON (Garfield). On Powell's last trip he named today's Glen Canyon by dividing the area into two sections. The first section was called Mound Canyon and the second was Monument Canyon. Powell later combined the two and changed the name to Glen Canyon. See Glen Canyon.

MOUND CITY* (Wasatch). See Midway*.

259

MOUND FORT* (Weber) was built in 1852 on a small mound at the present site of Ogden*. It was built between Tenth and Twelfth streets, west of Washington Boulevard.
ca. S10,T6N,R1W,SLM. 274, 516, 567.

MOUND SPRINGS* (Box Elder) was several miles northwest of Plymouth*, near Portage*. A large mound of gravel was once in this area. The community was originally settled by John Tims, James Spencer, and others and had an early name of Mountain Springs*. The community no longer exists.
S27,T14N,R3W,SLM; 4,406' (1,343m). 139, 567.

MOUNDS (Emery) is a Denver and Rio Grande Railroad stop southeast of Price* in an area of dome-shaped mounds. The site has springs in this area that were heavily occupied each year during sheep shearing time.
S5,8,T16S,R12E,SLM; 5,442' (1,659m). 578.

MOUNT AGASSIZ (Duchesne, Summit) is at the west end of the Uinta Mountains. In 1870 the King expedition named the mountain for Louis Agassiz, the great Swiss-American geologist and naturalist. Naturalist Basin is at the southeast base where numerous lakes are named for former students of Agassiz.
S29,T4N,R8W,SLM; 12,428' (3,788m). 298, 309.

MOUNT AIRE* (Salt Lake) is at the head of Mount Aire Canyon between Parleys Canyon and Mill Creek Canyon east of Salt Lake City*. Mount Aire is a summer home area.
S15,16,22,T1S,R2E,SLM.

MOUNT AIRE (Salt Lake) is at the head of Mount Aire Canyon east of Salt Lake City.
S23,T1S,R2E,SLM; 8,621' (2,628m).

MOUNT AIRE CANYON (Salt Lake) starts on the western slopes of Mount Aire east of Salt Lake City*. The canyon drains northwest into Parleys Canyon.
S15,16,22,T1S,R2E,SLM.

MOUNT BALDY (Beaver) is a volcanic peak at the summit of the Tushar Mountains east of Beaver*. The mountain is devoid of vegetation above the timberline.
S4,T28S,R5W,SLM; 12,082' (3,683m).

MOUNT BELNAP (Beaver) is in the Tushar Mountains east of Beaver*. It was named to honor William Worth Belnap, Secretary of War under U.S. President Grant. There are other less accurate claims that it was named for a soldier with the Eighth Infantry who was the first known white man to climb the mountain. Another claim states that the mountain was named in 1885 for a member of the U.S. Coast and Geodetic Survey. See Stegner's comments for additional information.
S34,T27S,R5W,SLM; 12,132' (3,698m). 100 (v17), 125, 314, 355, 496.

MOUNT BRIGHAM (Piute) is in the Tushar Mountains seven miles north of Puffer Lake. In 1880 a large good-natured individual named Robert Yount drifted into Marysvale*. The local miners nicknamed him Brigham, but soon shortened the name to Brig. He prospected for a time around the peak that soon adopted his name.
S8,T28S,R4W,SLM; 11,765' (3,586m). 216.

MOUNT CARMEL* (Kane) is in Long Valley, south of Glendale* on the East Fork of the Virgin River. The community was first settled in 1864 by Dr. Priddy Meeks and his family. It had an early name of Winsor* (Windsor*) for Anson P. Winsor, the Mormon church official who had jurisdiction over this area. The valley was soon vacated because of Indian problems, but was resettled in 1871 under the name of Mount Carmel, a mountain in northwest Israel.
S8,17,T41S,R7W,SLM; 5,192' (1,582m). 289, 360, 455, 501, 600.

MOUNT CARMEL JUNCTION* (Kane) is three miles south of Mount Carmel* on US-89. It is the eastern terminus of the well-known Mount Carmel highway from Zion National Park.
S9,T41S,R7W,SLM; 5,192' (1,583m). 360, 542, 546.

MOUNT DELANO (Beaver) is on the crest of the Tushar Mountains southeast of Mount Belnap. It is the tallest peak in the range and was named for the Secretary of the Interior, Columbus Delano, who served under U.S. President Grant.
S13,T28S,R5W,SLM; 12,175 (3,711m). 100 (v17), 125, 314, 355, 496.

MOUNT DUTTON (Garfield) is on the Sevier Plateau west of Bryce Canyon National Park and eight miles east of the head of Circleville Canyon. It was named for geologist Clarence Edward Dutton, who worked closely with Major Powell and who wrote the important work, *Geology of the High Plateaus*.
T32S,R3W,SLM; 11,041' (3,365m). 314, 494, 496, 497. D.L. 7403.

MOUNT ELLEN (Garfield) is the largest laccolithic dome and the highest peak in the Henry Mountains. It was named to honor Almon Thompson's wife, who was also John Wesley Powell's sister. Thompson was Powell's second in command for the government surveys that were conducted in this area.
S9,T31S,R10E,SLM; 11,506' (3,507m). 496, 567.

MOUNT ELLEN CREEK (Garfield) originates on the southern slopes of Mount Ellen Peak. It drains southeast into Bull Creek and receives its name from the nearby peak.
S14,16,T31S,R10E,SLM.

MOUNT ELMER (Cache) is in the Bear River Range eight miles northeast of Logan*. It was named for an early member of the 1878 Geodetic Survey.
9,676' (2,949m). 567.

MOUNT EMMONS* (Duchesne) is near Altonah* and Boneta* and is thirty miles south of its namesake, Mount Emmons. In 1914 E. A. Daniels laid out the townsite and named it Banner*. The name was later changed to Mount Emmons. See Mount Emmons for name source and references.
S31,T1S,R3S,USM; 6,285' (1,916m).

MOUNT EMMONS (Duchesne) is in the south central section of the Uinta Mountains. Kings Peak is six miles northwest. The mountain was named for Samuel Franklin Emmons, an American geologist who graduated from Harvard and was the U.S. Geological Survey field chief for the projects in this region.
T4N,R4W,USM; 13,440' (4,097m). 100(v17), 172, 314, 542, 567.

MOUNT ESCALANTE (Iron) is four miles southeast of Uvada*. It was in this general region that the Domínguez-Escalante expedition cast lots to decide whether to return home or to continue on to the missions in California (they returned home). The place name honors the expedition.
S4,T36S,R19W,SLM; 7,010' (2,137m). 583.

MOUNT GOG (Cache) is in the Bear River Range two miles northeast of Naomi Peak and one mile north of Mount Magog. The two place names, Gog and Magog, are referred to in the Bible (Revelations 20:7-9). See Mount Magog.
T14N,R3E,SLM; 9,714' (2,961m). 567.

MOUNT HILGARD (Sevier) is two and one-half miles west of Johns Peak and three and one-half miles south of Sheep Valley Reservoir. The mount honors Eugene W. Hilgard, a noted German-American geologist, chemist, and agriculturist.
S35,T24S,R3E,SLM; 11,533' (3,515m). 497.

MOUNT HILLERS (Garfield) is in the Henry Mountains ten miles northwest of Mount Holmes. The mountain was

named for Jack Hillers, the second photographer of Powell's Colorado River survey.
S33,T33S,R11E,SLM; 10,723' (3,268m). 485, 494, 496, 497.

MOUNT HOLLY (Beaver) is in the Tushar Mountains south of Mount Delano. The peak is named for Byron Holly, a Beaver* attorney who hunted and fished around the mountain in 1863.
S19,T28S,R4W,SLM. 125.

MOUNT HOLMES (Garfield) is one of the south central peaks of the Henry Mountains. Grove Karl Gilbert named the mountain for W. H. Holmes, the noted topographer and scientist who did early survey work in the region. Holmes was also a member of the Hayden survey that surveyed the Blue Mountains (The Abajos).
T35S,R12E,SLM. 39, 406, 497.

MOUNT JARDINE (Cache) is in the Bear River Range northeast of North Logan* at the head of Green Canyon. Jardine was a member of the U.S. Geodetic Survey of 1878.
8,848' (2,697m). 567.

MOUNT LAIRD (Juab) is north of Lady Laird Peak and the ghost town of Joy*. See Lady Laird Peak.
T14S,R10,11W,SLM; 6,433' (1,961m). 497.

MOUNT LENA (Daggett) is on the county line in the eastern section of the Uinta Mountains. The Flaming Gorge Reservoir Dam is eight miles north. The mountain was named by Francis Bishop, a botanist on Powell's second voyage. Bishop was referring to Selena, the "girl he left behind."
S27,T1N,R22E,SLM; 9,755' (2,973m). 100(v13), 172.

MOUNT LINNAEUS (San Juan) is in the Abajo Mountains, with Blue Creek heading on the north slope. The mountain was named by the Hayden survey for the famous Swedish botanist,

Carolus Linnaeus.
T34S,R22E,SLM; 10,959' (3,340m).

MOUNT LOVENIA (Duchesne) is on the crest of the Uinta Mountains near the headwaters of the East Fork of Blacks Fork. Mount Lovenia is the fifth highest peak in Utah. George Beard of Coalville*, a great lover of nature and a noted artist, named the peak for his wife, Lovenia (Lovinia) Bullock Beard.
S7,T4N,R6W,SLM; 13,227' (4,032m). 229, 298, 364.

MOUNT MAGOG (Cache) is in the Bear River Range between Tony Grove Lake and Mount Gog. Gog and Magog are the two nations Satan is supposed to lead in a final battle against the Kingdom of God at Armageddon. Mount Gog and Magog were named by Moses Thatcher while he was recuperating in his cabin in a nearby canyon.
T14N,R3E,SLM; 9,750' (2,972m). 266(Rev. 20:8), 567.

MOUNT MARVINE (Sevier) is seven miles north northwest of Fish Lake. Archibald R. Marvine was a noted geologist and a leader of one of the divisions of the 1873 Hayden survey. Marvine had also worked earlier with Lieutenant George Montague Wheeler.
S1,T25S,R2E,SLM; 11,610' (3,539m). 39, 494, 496, 497.

MOUNT MELLENTHIN (San Juan) is in the La Sal Mountains. Forest Ranger Rudolph E. Mellenthin was shot and killed on August 23, 1918, while attempting to apprehend a draft deserter.
S11,T27S,R24E,SLM; 12,646' (3,855m). 409, 514.

MOUNT NEBO (Juab) is east of Nephi* and is the southernmost point of the Wasatch Range. The Mormon pioneers named the mountain after the highest mountain east of the Jordan River in Moab where Moses died.
T11S,R1E,SLM; 11,877' (3,620m). 100(v17), 229, 314, 501, 508. D.L. 7902.

MOUNT NEBO* (Utah). See Elberta*.

MOUNT OGDEN (Weber) is three miles east of Ogden* at the head of Waterfall Canyon. On October 3, 1888, William Eimbeck of the U.S. Geodetic Survey included this peak as one of six official observation points in the Rocky Mountain and Pacific coastal regions. It was officially named Mount Henderson to honor the Ogden federal judge who had taken hikes to the top of the peak. However, use of the name Observation (Observatory) Peak continued until 1905 when Dr. A. S. Condon formally requested the peak be renamed Mount Ogden. The change was granted.
S6,T5N,R1E,SLM; 9,572' (2,918m). 274. D.L. 7001.

MOUNT OLYMPUS (Salt Lake) is east of Holladay* and south of Mill Creek* at the head of Tolcats Canyon. The ancient Mount Olympus is in northeast Greece and was the mythical abode of the gods. A view of Utah's Mount Olympus from any angle is an inspiring and beautiful sight.
T2S,R2E,SLM; 9,026' (2,751m). D.L. 7101.

MOUNT PEALE (San Juan) is in the La Sal Mountains where it was named by the Hayden survey. One report claims the mountain was so named because it reverberates and peals during thunderstorms. It is the highest peak in the La Sal range.
S24,T27S,R24E,SLM; 13,089' (3,877m). 406, 567.

MOUNT PENNELL (Garfield) is one of the five prominent peaks in the Henry Mountains. Joseph Pennell was a noted artist who created illustrations for the early government surveys.
S10,T33S,R10E,SLM; 11,371' (3,466m). 497.

MOUNT PISGAH (Box Elder, Cache) is two and one-half miles north of Mantua*. One record states that the peak was named by an early field group who got caught in a blizzard on the mountain. The name Mount Pisgah is prominent in early Mormon history and the Bible. This biblical name refers to a range of mountains near Jericho*, with Mount Nebo being its highest point.
S3,T9N,R1W,SLM; 7,140' (2,176m). 567.

MOUNT PLEASANT* (Sanpete) is on US-89 six miles south of Fairview*. The community was originally settled in 1852, vacated in 1853 because of Indian troubles, then resettled in 1859. The name is a reminder of the pleasant view of the eastern mountains and the surrounding western valley. The original name was Hambleton's Settlement*, Fort Hambleton*, and Hambleton* for Madison D. Hambledon, who came into the region in 1851-52 with Gardner Potter and others.
S23,T15S,R4E,SLM; 5,924' (1,806m). 100 (v17), 275, 289, 360, 542, 604.

MOUNT POWELL (Duchesne, Summit) is in the central region of the Uinta Mountains. Major John Wesley Powell, who lost an arm at Shiloh in the Civil War, went on to lead two expeditions down the Green and Colorado rivers. Powell was director of the U.S. Geological Survey and—among his many other achievements—he headed the Smithsonian Bureau of Ethnology. According to Stegner, Powell provided more Utah Territory place names than anyone else, excluding the Mormon Church.
S35,T5N,R5W,SLM; 13,137' (4,004m). 159, 422, 496, 497. D.L. 6804.

MOUNT STERLING* (Cache) was a small settlement one mile south of Wellsville* at the mouth of Wellsville Canyon. The community was absorbed into Wellsville.
S14,15,T10N,R1W,SLM; 4,775' (1,455m). 567.

MOUNT TERRILL (Sevier) is on the Fishlake Plateau nine miles north northeast of Fish Lake. It was named for the wife of J. H. Renshaw of the U.S.

Geological Survey.
S24,T24S,R2E,SLM; 11,547' (3,520m). 175.

MOUNT TIMPANOGOS (Utah) is in
the Wasatch Mountains northeast of
Provo* and south of American Fork
Canyon. The peak was named after the
early name of the Provo River.
"Timpanogos" is a Piute word that refers
to rock and running water. It does not
refer to a legendary sleeping Indian
princess.
S18,T5S,R3E,SLM; 11,750' (3,581m). 46,
366, 530, 546.

MOUNT TOMASAKI (San Juan) is in
the central part of the La Sal Mountains.
Tomasaki was one of the Indian guides
for the 1875 Hayden surveys.
S25,T26S,R25E,SLM; 12,230' (3,728m). 567.

MOUNT TUKUHNIKIVATS (San Juan)
is in the La Sal Mountains three miles
southeast of Mount Waas. The name is
Piute for "where the sun sets last."
S22,T27S,R28E,SLM; 12,483' (3,805m). 406,
567.

MOUNT TUSCARORA (Salt Lake) is
at the head of Big Cottonwood Canyon
just west of Lake Martha. Tuscarora was
chief of the Tuscarora Indians, who originated in North Carolina and later moved
to a region in New York.
T3S,R3E,SLM; 10,650' (3,246m).

MOUNT VAN COTT (Salt Lake) is in
the upper benchland northeast of the
University of Utah at the head of
Cephalopod Gulch. The students of
nearby University of Utah honored their
first dean of women, Lucy Van Cott, by
naming the mountain for her.
S34,T1N,R1E,SLM; 6,348' (1,935m). 578.
D.L. 6802.

MOUNT WAAS (Grand) is in the north
central section of the La Sal Mountains.
On some maps the name mistakenly
appears as Wass or Nass. See Mount
Tomasaki for name source.
S13,T26S,R24E,SLM; 12,331' (3,758m). 567.

MOUNT WATSON (Summit) is at the
west end of the Uinta Mountains, one
mile west of Wall Lake. It was named
for an early pioneer of this area.
S25,36,T1S,R8E,SLM; 11,521' (3,512m).
298.

MOUNT WOLVERINE (Salt Lake) is at
the head of Big Cottonwood Canyon,
one-half mile west of Lake Martha.
T3S,R3E,SLM; 10,795' (3,290m).

MOUNTAIN DELL* (Salt Lake) is in
Parleys Canyon where Mountain Dell
Reservoir is presently located. The road
through the canyon was built by Parley P.
Pratt and was opened for traffic on July
4, 1850, under the name of the Golden
Pass. In 1860 Leonard G. Hardy opened
a rest stop known as Hardys Place. The
name was then changed to Mountain
Dell in 1869. Ephraim K. Hanks, one of
its first settlers, contributed to the
naming of the settlement. In time
Mountain Dell became a small farming
settlement, a Pony Express stop, and
stage station. By 1910, the community of
approximately one hundred people began
to die out because of improvements in
transportation. In 1916 Salt Lake City*
bought the land for a dam, reservoir, and
recreation site.
S3,10,11,T1S,R2E,SLM. 89, 100(v13), 516,
546, 567.

MOUNTAIN DELL* (Washington) was
a small settlement about four miles up
North Creek from Virgin*. The community was first established in 1861 by Joel
Johnson when he built a sawmill in the
area, then named the community
Millville*. Although other settlers arrived,
the community was eventually abandoned
because of a lack of sufficient water.
Today the site is privately owned.
89, 100(v13), 154, 289, 311.

MOUNTAIN DELL RESERVOIR (Salt
Lake). See Mountain Dell* (Salt Lake).

MOUNTAIN GREEN* (Morgan) is in
Morgan Valley at the east end of Lower

Weber Canyon, just above Devils Gate. In 1859 George Higley built the first cabin in a lush meadowland in the valley. S25,T5N,R1E,SLM; 4,835' (1,474m). 289, 378, 567.

MOUNTAIN HOME* (Duchesne) is five miles west of Altonah* on U-134 in the upper benchland of the southwest Uinta Mountains. The settlement developed from the upper portion of the Boneta* townsite that did not develop as originally planned. Joseph D. West settled in this area in 1908. S18,T1S,R4W,USM; 7,000' (2,134m). 542, 567.

MOUNTAIN HOME RANGE (Daggett) is a small mountain west of the head of Jesse Ewing Canyon and south of Clay Basin. MRN S3,T2N,R24E,SLM and S34,35,T3N,R24E, SLM; 7,985' (2,434m).

MOUNTAIN HOME RANGE (Millard) is east of and near the Nevada border.

MOUNTAIN MEADOWS (Washington) is five miles north of St. George* near the head of Pinto Creek. John C. Fremont camped in this prime camping site on the Spanish Trail, which was previously known as Las Vegas de Santa Clara. The area had plenty of water and grazing resources for livestock. This region divides the waters of the Virgin River, which flows southwest into the Colorado River, with the water draining north into the Great Basin. In 1857 a caravan of one hundred and forty emigrants from Missouri and Arkansas were massacred in this area as they were traveling to California. The aftereffects were long lasting and quite traumatic for friends, relatives, and descendants. S10,15,T38S,R16W,SLM; 5,700' (1,737m). 74, 89, 289, 438, 516, 546, 600.

MOUNTAIN SPRING WASH (Beaver) drains from the northern mountains towards Lund* and the Escalante Desert. S4,T31S,R16W,SLM.

MOUNTAINVILLE* (Sanpete) was about six miles northeast of Mount Pleasant* when the settlement was originally established in 1882 by Allan Rowe, George Stanford, and others. Although the community was named in 1906, it no longer exists as a separate community.

MOUNTAINVILLE* (Utah). See Alpine*.

MUD CANYON (Garfield) originates on the eastern slopes of the Pink Cliffs in Bryce Canyon National Park and drains east into Sheep Creek. During the spring, after rain and melting snow, the canyon is heavy with mud that accumulates from the soft disintegrating materials of the Pink Cliffs. S26,T37S,R4W,SLM (at mouth).

MUD ISLAND (Box Elder) is in the Great Salt Lake, eight miles northeast of Fremont Island. This island is a sandbar throughout most of the year. Stansbury found "a belt of soft black mud more than knee deep between water and the hard rocky beach." It "seemed to be impregnated with all the villainous smells which nature's laboratory was capable of producing" (546, p. 486). 100(v2), 129, 546.

MUD LAKE (Beaver) is a small shallow lake in the south Tushar Mountains, east of Senseball Lake and south of Mumford Reservoir. S20,T30S,R5W,SLM; 9,440' (2,877m).

MUD LAKE (Beaver) is on the western slopes of the south side of the Tushar Mountains and north of the head of Kane Canyon. S34,T29S,R6W,SLM; 7,975' (2,431m).

MUD RIVER was an early name for the Bear River.

MUD SPRING (Beaver) is on the eastern slopes of the Mineral Mountains between Shag and Solomons hollows.

Adamsville* is north.
S30,T28S,R8W,SLM; 6,500' (1,981m).

MUD SPRING (**Beaver**) is on the eastern slopes of the Needle Range between the Needles and Sawtooth Peak. S28,T27S,R18W,SLM; 6,660' (2,030m).

MUD SPRING (**Beaver**) is at the north end of Beaver Valley on the southwest slopes of Mud Spring Ridge. S13,T27S,R7W,SLM; 6,800' (2,073m).

MUD SPRING RIDGE (**Beaver**) has an east-west orientation on the western slopes of the Tushar Mountains at the north end of Beaver Valley. S18,T27S,R6W,SLM; 7,600' (2,316m).

MUD TOWN* (**Rich**). See Round Valley* (Rich).

MUDDY CREEK (**Box Elder**) originates on the eastern slopes of the north end of the Grouse Creek Mountains. The creek drains south southeast into the Great Salt Lake Desert. The name refers to the muddy clay soil the creek passes through in its lower course.

MUDDY CREEK* (**Emery**). See Emery*.

MUDDY CREEK (**Kane**) originates at Strawberry Point nine miles northwest of Glendale* and drains southwest into the Virgin River, East Fork. The creek becomes quite muddy during high water periods. S11,T39S,R8W,SLM to S18,T41S,R7W,SLM.

MUDDY RIVER (**Cache**). See Little Bear River.

MUDDY RIVER (**Emery**) originates on the Wasatch Plateau and drains southeast to join the Fremont River in forming the Dirty Devil River. "Muddy" fits the description of the river. S2,T28S,R11E,SLM (at mouth).

MUDHOLE, THE (**Beaver**) is a spring in a muddied location in the east central part of the Wah Wah Mountains. S16,T28S,R15W,SLM; 6,310' (1,923m).

MUELLER STATE PARK (**Davis**) is east of Bountiful in the Wasatch Mountains. This beautiful camping and picnic site was named for George Mueller. S34,T2N,R1E,SLM; 5,400' (1,646m). 508.

MUKUNTUWEAP CANYON (**Washington**) is in the heart of Zion National Park. The North Fork of the Virgin River drains southwest through this canyon for about ten miles. When Major Powell named the canyon he kept the original Indian name. The meaning of the name, however, is another matter. It could mean "Straight Canyon," "The Place of the Gods," or "God's Land." It may have been named for Chief Mokun of the Virgin River Indians and would mean "Land of Mokun." The name could be a derivative of the flowering desert plant, yucca or oose, muk-unk. If anglicized, the term would mean Oose Creek or Soap Creek. One source states that the name means "Red Dirt" and another claims it is "Big Canyon." It should always be kept in mind that an Indian name is not standardized on a written map and it may apply only to a small section of a feature or area. Also, in this particular region, Piute Indian names might overlap with Navajo Indian names. In consideration of all these possible sources, it is nice to note that today the original name is not used as much as "North Fork of the Virgin (River)." T40,41S,R10W,SLM. 314, 422, 496, 546, 600.

MULE CANYON (**San Juan**) originates four miles southeast of Bears Ears and drains southeast into the Comb Wash. For a period of time mules ran wild in the canyon. T37,38S,R19,20E,SLM.

MULEY TWIST CANYON (Garfield) originates in the wild, tortuous slickrock country on the west side of the Waterpocket Fold, eight miles north northwest of the Burr Trail Pass over the Fold. This south-draining canyon was so rough, it would "twist a mule" to get through it.
T33,34S,R8E,SLM. 602.

MUMFORD RESERVOIR (Beaver) is in the south Tushar Mountains near Senseball Lake. During the 1880s George Mumford, a farmer from Beaver*, attempted to develop irrigation projects at the reservoir site.
S20,T20S,R5W,SLM. 355.

MURDOCK BASIN (Duchesne) is on the southwest slopes of the Uinta Mountains on the headwaters of the Duchesne River. Hoover, Marshall, and other lakes are in this basin. It was named in the early 1900s for Joseph R. Murdock, a developer, water specialist, and pioneer settler in the region.
379.

MURDOCK MOUNTAIN (Duchesne) is at the head of Murdock Basin in the southwest section of the Uinta Mountains. See Murdock Basin for name source.
S3,T9N,R9E,SLM; 11,212' (3,414m).

MURDOCK PEAK (Salt Lake) is in the Wasatch Mountains three miles west of Snyderville*, east of Salt Lake City*. The peak was named by the Mormon pioneers for one of their more prominent members soon after they entered the Salt Lake Valley. MRN
S34,T1S,R3E,SLM; 9,602' (2,927m).

MURRAY* (Salt Lake) is on US-89 and Big Cottonwood Creek. It was named for Eli H. Murray, the twelfth governor of Utah Territory. Murray had an early name of South Cottonwood*.
S7,18,T2S,R1E,SLM; 4,350' (1,326m). 252, 314, 542, 546, 567.

MUSKRAT* (Weber). See Hooper*.

MUSKRAT SPRINGS* (Weber). See Hooper*.

MUSSELMAN ARCH (San Juan) is one mile west of the Colorado River and two miles south of Shafer Canyon near the White Rim Jeep Trail. The National Park Service named this arch for Ross S. Musselman. Musselman was an easterner who came west in 1932. He bought land southeast of Moab* and established a guest ranch where he worked with problem children from the eastern U.S. He was a rancher, guide, youth counselor, and—with his wife—an Indian craft store operator. Musselman also enjoyed the wild, uninhabited parts of Utah.
T27S,R19E,SLM. 556. D.L. 6604.

MUSSENTUCHIT FLAT (Emery) is south of Deadman Peak. MRN
NW¼,T25S,R7E,SLM.

MUSSENTUCHIT WASH (Emery) drains from the west into Mussentuchit Flat. MRN

MUTUAL* (Carbon) is seven miles up Spring Canyon near Rains*. The Mutual Coal Company, which mined the coal and built the town, provided the name. The town opened in 1921 and died out in 1938 after the mine was shut down. The community was known earlier as Oak Springs Bench*, for the scrub oak (*Quercus*) growing in the area. Jack Dempsey, the well-known boxer (now deceased), lived there and the town adopted the name Dempseyville* for a short period of time.
S13,T13S,R8E,SLM; 7,150' (2,179m). 89, 516, 567, 607.

MUTUAL DELL* (Utah) is in the South Fork of American Fork Canyon. Mutual Dell is a beautiful picnic and camping area used for youth groups. One of the two principal hiking trails up Mount

Timpanogos starts from Mutual Dell.
S30,T4S,R3E,SLM; 6,500' (1,981m).

MYLER CREEK (Cache) originates
three miles west of Clarkston* and drains
east into Clarkston Creek. It was named
for James Myler, who settled near the
creek in the mid-1860s.
S27,28,32,T14N,R2W,SLM. 435.

MYLER GROVE (Cache) is a small
grove in the mountains three miles
northwest of Clarkston*. See Myler
Creek for name source.
S27,28,32,T14N,R2W,SLM.

MYTOGE MOUNTAINS (Sevier) is a
range of mountains with a northeast-
southwest orientation near Fish Lake.
Two small crater lakes are on the top of
the mountain, which is part of a lava
flow. The name has an Indian origin
meaning "moon."
T26S,R2E,SLM; 9,922' (3,024m). 163(30
June 1977).

MYTON* (Duchesne) is on US-40
between Roosevelt* and Duchesne*. The
community has historical significance. The
settlement was built at the only bridge
crossing the Duchesne River and for this
reason it had an early name of The
Bridge* or Bridge City*. For many years
it was a well-known trading post. The
community received its present name
when Major H. P. Myton came from
nearby Fort Duchesne* to take command
as the region was opened to settlers in
1905.
S25,26,T3S,R2W,USM; 5,084' (1,550m). 89,
494, 546, 567.

- N -

NADA* (Beaver) was a railroad siding on the Los Angeles, Salt Lake Railroad at the northern edge of the Escalante Desert, midway between Latimer* and Thermo*. It was settled in 1910 by a dry farmer. "Nada" is Spanish for "nothing." Eight miles south is where the Domínguez-Escalante expedition drew lots and decided to return home instead of trying to continue on to California. S31S,T29S,R12W,SLM; 5,054' (1,540m). 125, 314, 494, 516, 546, 555(v49).

NANCY PATTERSON CANYON (San Juan) originates fifteen miles north northwest of Hatch Trading Post between Squaw Canyon and Lake Canyon. It drains south southwest into Montezuma Creek. The canyon was named for a race horse that escaped from a nearby ranch and was captured in the canyon. S6,T37S,R26E,SLM to S5,T39S,R25E,SLM. 83.

NAPLES* (Uintah) is in the eastern section of the Ashley Valley on US-40, two miles southeast of Vernal*. The settlement was named for the prominent city in Italy. It also had earlier names (not in chronological order) such as Merrill* for Porter William Merrill, a local church official; Riverdale*, because it was located on the Green River; and Frogtown*, because of the large number of frogs in the vicinity. Bishop P. W. Merrill suggested that the name be changed from Merrill to Naples. S31,T22E,R4S,SLM; 5,220' (1,591m). 100 (v17), 289, 542, 567.

NARROW CANYON (Garfield) is about nine miles long and begins at the end of Cataract Canyon on the Colorado River between Mille Crag Bend and the mouth of the Dirty Devil River. When the Powell expedition traveled down the canyon, Powell decided to name it Narrow Canyon, which would describe the significant feature of this canyon. S32,T34S,R15E,SLM. 159, 420, 422, 496.

NASJA CREEK (San Juan) originates on Navajo Mountain and drains north into the San Juan River. The name is a corruption of the Navajo "noeshja," which means "the owls." Owls are very prominent and popular in Navajo Indian culture. T41S,R9E,SLM. 314.

NASJA MESA (San Juan) is on the northwest section of Navajo Mountain between Nasja Creek and Anasazi Creek. See Nasja Creek for name source. T41S,R9E,SLM; 4,640' (1,414m).

NATIONAL* (Carbon) was a 1920s coal mining town developed by the National Coal Company under Fred Sweet. The town name was the same as that of the mine at the end of U-139 up Consumers Wash. National was abandoned in the 1950s. There are other coal mining towns in this area, such as Consumers* and Sweet*. S17,T13S,R8E,SLM; 7,500' (2,286m). 89, 100(v17), 516, 542, 607.

NATURAL BRIDGES NATIONAL MONUMENT (San Juan) is a cluster of three natural, single-span bridges on U-95 near the junction of White and Armstrong canyons west of Blanding*. Cass Hite, a prospector who settled Hite* (now under the waters of Lake Powell) is credited as the first white man to bring the Natural Bridges to the attention of the public. This occurred in 1883. Hite named the bridges the President, Congressman, and Senator, and gave glowing reports of his find. Jim Scorup, a local cattleman, reported seeing them in 1895. In 1903 Scorup guided Horace J. Long, a mining engineer sponsored by The Commercial Club, into the region to see the bridges. By mutual agreement Long and Scorup named Cass Hite's President Bridge the Augusta for Long's wife. The Senator Bridge was named the Caroline Bridge for Jim's mother. The Congressman was named the Little Bridge because it was the smallest of the three bridges; the name was then changed to the Edwin to honor Colonel Edwin F. Holmes of Salt Lake City*, an ex-president of the Commercial Club. In 1908 President Theodore Roosevelt proclaimed the natural bridge area a national monument and this became the first site in Utah to be administered by the National Park Service. Years later a government surveyor, William Douglas, began searching for what was termed more appropriate Indian names to best identify the bridges. He learned that the local Paiute Indians called all natural bridges "Ma-Vah-Talk-Tusip" or "Under the Horse's Belly." The Caroline Bridge was the largest of the three bridges and was renamed Kachina or Sacred Dance because of the dance symbol pictographs carved into the bridge. The Augusta Bridge was renamed the Sipapu because of its unusual shape. Indian legend states the name means "the gateway through which the souls of men come from the underworld and finally return to it." The smallest bridge (the Little Bridge that became Edwin Bridge) was named the Owachomo Bridge or Flatrock Mound for a geologic formation in the vicinity. With all the effort made to obtain appropriate names for the bridges, all three names chosen were Hopi Indian names. The Hopi people were from Arizona, not Utah, but it was believed that they were descendants of the people who built the ruins at the bridges. At any rate the only recorded Hopi Indian place names in Utah today are those of the

Natural Bridges National Monument. T36,37S,R17E,SLM. 230, 314, 406, 546, 555 (v32).

NATURALIST BASIN (Duchesne) is in the southwest section of the Uinta Mountains at the base of Mount Agassiz. There are many lakes in the basin and drainage flows primarily into the East Fork of the Duchesne River. The basin received its name because many scientists and naturalists—all students of the great Swiss-American naturalist Louis Agassiz—have had their names given to various lakes in the basin. T3,4N,R8W,USM. 309, 530.

NAVAJO CANYON (Kane) originates on the west center slopes of the Kaiparowits Plateau where it drains south between Burning Hills and Croton Canyon. Almon Thompson of the Powell surveys named the canyon for the Indian ruins found there. S31,32,T39S,R5E,SLM to S12,T41S,R5E, SLM. 555(v7).

NAVAJO LAKE (Kane) is in the Duck Creek Valley on the southern margin of the Markagunt Plateau near U-14. This is the largest lake in the region and was originally named Mountain Lakelet by Grove K. Gilbert, the noted geologist, who was the first person to systematically study this region. The lake was renamed Navajo Lake after Navajo Indian raiders and stockmen from Cedar City got into a skirmish near the lake. The Piute Indian name for the lake was Pah-cu-ay, meaning Cloud Lake. S7,8,T38S,R8W,SLM; 9,035' (2,754m). 100 (v2), 399, 455.

NAVAJO MOUNTAIN (San Juan) is a solitary laccolithic dome south of the junction of the Colorado and San Juan rivers. Geologically, this sandstone surface is comparatively young, since it has not been sufficiently eroded away so the underlying lava shows. Powell first named it Mount Seneca Howland for a member of his 1869 expedition who was

killed by the Indians. Although this name didn't hold, Almon Thompson's suggestion of Navajo Mountain did and is still used today. Indian mythology credits this mountain with being the first earth home of the human race. The first couple alighted on the mountain from the tip of a rainbow. The word Navajo (navaja) is Spanish and means knife, razor, or tusk of the wild boar.
T42,43S,R9,10E,SLM; 10,220' (3,115m). 175, 314, 422, 496, 555(v7), 602, 609.

NAVAJO TWINS (**San Juan**) is a dual rock formation on the northern outskirts of Bluff* near US-191 and US-163.
S24,T40S,R21E,SLM.

NAVAJO VALLEY (**Kane**) is west of the south end of the Kaiparowits Plateau where it drains into the Colorado River. The name comes from nearby Navajo Mountain.
T42W,R8½E,SLM. 12.

NAVAJO WELLS (**Kane**) is fifteen miles east of Kanab* on present-day US-89. There are several buildings on the site now. The wells were an important stop on the old pioneer road running from Kanab to Lees Ferry.
S31,T43S,R4W,SLM; 5,290' (1,612m). 463.

NEBO CANYON (**Cache**) is southeast of Richmond*. Nebo is an extremely steep canyon that is quite treacherous to climb. Timber was harvested from this canyon for building the first homes in Richmond.
S2,T13N,R1E,SLM. 567.

NEEDLE EYE CANYON (**Kane**) originates on Smokey Mountain and drains northeast into Last Chance Creek west of the Kaiparowits. The canyon received its name from Needle Eye Point. See Needle Eye Point for name source.
S8,T41S,R4E,SLM to S34,T40S,R4E,SLM.

NEEDLE EYE POINT (**Kane**) is west of the Kaiparowits Plateau and east of Smokey Mountain near the mouth of Needle Eye Canyon. This feature is a land projection named for its peculiar shape.
S34,T40S,R4E,SLM.

NEEDLE MOUNTAINS (**Beaver**) are a north-south oriented range west of Pine Valley. They include the Mountain Home Range between The Needle and the Indian Peak Range. The Needle Mountains are a sharp, jagged row of peaks or pinnacles.
T26-31S,R17-19W,SLM; 9,784' (2,982m). 314. D.L. 7401.

NEEDLES, THE (**Grand**) is in Canyonlands National Park. This is an area of sharp pinnacles and spires in a region north of Dead Man Point and Spring Canyon Point, and south of the Blue Hills.
T31S,R19E,SLM.

NEFFS CANYON (**Salt Lake**) originates in the mountains east of Salt Lake City* and south of Mill Creek Canyon. The canyon drains west into the Salt Lake Valley. It was named for John Neff, an early settler in the area who built a flour mill in nearby Mill Creek Canyon.
T2S,R2E,SLM.

NEGRO BILL CANYON (**Grand**) originates on the western slopes of the La Sal Mountains and drains west into the Colorado River. After the Green brothers were killed by Indians in 1877, a mulatto, William Granstaff, and a French-Canadian trapper named Frenchie entered the Spanish Valley together with one trailing burro. The men were prospecting when they took possession of the abandoned fort near today's Moab*. They lived separately in the fort and each controlled a part of the valley. What we know today as Negro Bill Canyon (at that time it was called Nigger Bill's Canyon) was in Granstaff's section where he ran a few head of cattle (probably part of the Green brothers' herd). Granstaff left the area in 1881

after being charged with selling whiskey to the Indians.
T25S,R22E,SLM. 146, 409, 514.

NEGRO DAN HOLLOW (Rich) originates on the northern slopes of McKay Ridge and drains north into Saleratus Creek. MRN
S13,T7N,R7E,SLM.

NEGRO HOLLOW (Beaver) is south of Beaver* and east of I-15. It drains into Nevershine Hollow. MRN
S15,T30S,R7W,SLM.

NEGRO HOLLOW (Summit) is southwest of Park City*. MRN
S16,17,T2S,R4E,SLM.

NEGRO LIZA WASH (Iron) originates at the south end of the Needle Range and drains southeast into the desert west of Beryl*. MRN
T31,R33S,R17W,SLM.

NEGRO MAG WASH (Beaver) originates in the Mineral Mountains near Bailey Spring and drains northwest toward the Beaver Bottoms. In 1873, Mr. and Mrs. Lee, a black couple, came to Fort Cameron near Beaver*. They ran a boardinghouse on the upper floor of a large frame building one block north of the Beaver Co-op Store. Mrs. Lee was known as "Nigger Mag." After her husband's death, Mrs. Lee operated a sanitarium at the Hot Springs in the mountains northwest of Beaver.
S1,2,T27S,R9W,SLM. 355.

NELSON* (Grand) See Sego*.

NEOLA* (Duchesne) is a small community in an area of gas and oil development on U-121, ten miles north northwest of Roosevelt* and six miles south of Whiterocks*. There are several claims for the name origin: it is of Greek origin and means "new place"; it is an Indian word for "last stand"; and it means "this is the last move" or "move no more."

S31,T1N,R1W,USM. 100(v13), 165, 314, 494, 542.

NEPHI* (Juab) is on I-15 forty miles south of Provo*. It was settled in 1851 and had earlier names of Salt Creek* for the stream the pioneers settled on, and Little Chicago*. Nephi was a prophet in Mormon scriptures.
S4,5,7,8,T13S,R1E,SLM; 5,133' (1,565m). 61, 100(v17), 289, 314, 542, 546, 567, 604.

NEPHI PASTURE (Kane) is at the head of Nephi Wash, fourteen miles west of the ghost town of Paria*. The pasture and wash are named for Nephi Johnson, one of four brothers who settled nearby Johnson*.
S23,27,T41S,R4W,SLM; 6,350' (1,935m).

NEPHI WASH (Kane) originates at Nephi Pasture. See above.
S29,T41S,R3W,SLM (at mouth).

NEPONSET RESERVOIR (Rich) is ten miles south of Woodruff.
S34,35,T8N,R7E,SLM; 6,420' (1,957m).

NERVA JUNCTION (Box Elder) was a siding on the Union Pacific Railroad, three miles south of Willard*. In 1915, area farmers asked the railroad to build the siding for the local sugar beet industry. At first the railroad refused, thinking they had a lot of nerve in asking for it. Eventually the siding was built, but the railroad named it Nerva to express their feeling about the project.
S2,T7N,R2W,SLM; 4,255' (1,297m). 567.

NEVERSHINE HOLLOW (Beaver) is two miles south of Beaver* with I-15 passing through. The bottom of the canyon is shaded most of the time.
S22,27,35,T30S,R7W,SLM.

NEVERSWEAT* (Washington). See Tonaquint*.

NEVERSWEAT* (Sevier). See Vermillion*.

NEW CANYON (**Rich**) originates in the mountains west of Randolph* and drains east into Little Creek Reservoir. The first road out of the Monte Cristo Mountains toward Randolph came down Old Canyon. The road built later came down what was named New Canyon.
S20,29,T11N,R5E,SLM to S23,T11N,R6E, SLM. 567.

NEW CLIFTON* (**Garfield**). See Loseeville*.

NEW ENGLAND* (**Salt Lake**). During the early 1900s a building boom occurred on California Avenue, Concord Street, and Eleventh West Street in Salt Lake City*. This area became known as New England.
S14,T1S,R1W,SLM; 4,225' (1,288m). 508.

NEW HARMONY* (**Washington**). Fort Harmony* was built where Harmony* was established. When Harmony was flooded out, the settlers moved several miles upstream and built a new settlement, naming it New Harmony. Both were named for Harmony*, Pennsylvania, where the Mormon Prophet Joseph Smith translated the Book of Mormon. The local settlers also appreciated the name because it indicated the harmony and united action the pioneers showed during their periods of trial and hardship.
S21,22,T38S,R13W,SLM; 5,306' (1,617m). 136, 154, 289, 314, 600.

NEW HOME BENCH* (**Garfield**) is a benchland two and one-half miles west of Boulder*. Plans were made to build a subdivision on the bench, but water problems cancelled the project.
S3,T33S,R4E,SLM; 6,800' (2,073m). 567.

NEW LONDON* (**Sanpete**) was a temporary name for a settlement site on the south bank of Twelve Mile Creek. Eventually the settlers on the north and south banks united and in 1877 the entire community was established as Mayfield*.

NEW QUIGLEY CANYON (**Cache**). See Old Quigley Canyon (Cache).

NEWCASTLE* (**Iron**) is a small agricultural community on U-56, twenty-seven miles west of Cedar City* at the mouth of Pinto Canyon. In 1910 the community began moving down-canyon from Pinto* to a region offering better opportunities. The cliffs surrounding the new site were castellated. To make the name more euphonious and to signify a fresh start, the word "new" was added.
S16,17,T36S,R15W,SLM; 5,814' (1,772m). 289, 314, 542, 567.

NEWFOUNDLAND MOUNTAINS (**Box Elder**) are six miles south of Hogup Mountain, northwest of Great Salt Lake. The mountains were named by Quince Knowlton, who founded a silver mine in the area that he called the Newfoundland Mine. The mountain assumed the name of the mine.
T3-6N,R13,14W,SLM; 6,984' (2,129m). 100 (v17), 516, 567.

NEWHOUSE* (**Beaver**) was built on the western slopes of the San Francisco Range. Samuel Newhouse built the town in 1905 to house the miners who were working in his nearby Cactus mine. By Newhouse's orders, the town had no red-light district, saloons, or gambling; schools and parks were built instead. In five years the mine began to decline and the region became a center for sheep men and cattlemen, who built large sheep-shearing pens. When the last cafe burned down in 1921 it was not rebuilt. For a period of time Newhouse was a center for moving picture filming. The movie *Covered Wagon* was filmed at this site. Today it is a ghost town site.
S8,T27S,R13W,SLM; 5,180' (1,579m). 89, 355, 516, 546.

NEWHOUSE RESERVOIR (**Beaver**) is in the center of the Wah Wah Valley. It was named for the nearby ghost town.
S23,T26S,R14W,SLM; 4,760' (1,451m).

NEWTON* (Cache) was an outgrowth of Clarkston*, northwest of Logan* at the junction of U-218 and U-23. It was a farming community originally called New Town* to separate it from Clarkston. The name was soon shortened to Newton.
S17,T13N,R1W,SLM; 4,525' (1,379m). 100 (v17), 449, 567.

NEWTON CREEK (Cache) originates near Newton Reservoir and drains south into Cutler Reservoir. The creek received its name from the community.
S8,T14N,R1W,SLM.

NEWTON RESERVOIR (Cache) is southwest of Trenton* and north of Newton*. In 1871 construction began on this first storage reservoir in Utah.
S32,T14N,R1W,SLM; 4,778' (1,456m). 100 (v4).

NIBLEY* (Cache) is an outgrowth of nearby Millville*, three miles south of Logan*. It was named for Charles W. Nibley, a presiding Mormon elder in early Cache Valley.
S21,T11N,R1E,SLM; 4,942' (1,506m). 100 (v17), 289.

NIBLEY LAKE (Salt Lake). See Nibley Park.

NIBLEY PARK (Salt Lake) centers around Nibley Lake (Pond), which was once Wandermere Lake and, earlier, Calders Lake. See Nibley* and Wandermere*.
S30,T1S,R1E,SLM; 4,280' (1,305m).

NICOLLET LAKE (Millard). See Sevier Lake.

NICOLLET RIVER. See Sevier River.

NIGGER SPRING (Box Elder) is on the southern slopes of the Raft River Mountains southwest of Park Valley. The spring will undoubtedly be renamed Negro Spring or possibly Black Spring on more recent maps. MRN

S5,T12N,R13W,SLM.

NINE MILE CANYON (Carbon) is nine miles in length. See the creek.

NINE MILE CREEK (Carbon, Duchesne, Uintah) originates fourteen miles north of Sunnyside Junction on US-6,50 and U-123. The creek drains east through Nine Mile Canyon into the Green River. The canyon is nine miles long.
S35,T12S,R12E,SLM to S27,T11S,R18E, SLM. 100(v17).

NINEMILE KNOLL (Beaver) is in the Escalante Desert southwest of Minersville*. This feature was an early landmark.
S23,T30S,R11W,SLM; 5,176' (1,578m).

NINEMILE RESERVOIR (Sanpete) is nine miles south of Manti* near US-89.
S8,T19S,R2E,SLM; 5,381' (1,640m).

NINEMILE WASH (Emery) originates fourteen miles southwest of Green River*. It drains east into the Green River, nine miles south of Green River.
S12,T22S,R14E,SLM to S8,T22S,R16E,SLM.

NIOTCHE CREEK (Sevier) originates one mile north of Mount Terrill. It drains north into Salina Creek. The name is a corruption of the Ute word "no-ochi." MRN
S21,T22S,R3E,SLM.

NIPPLE BENCH (Kane). See Nipple Butte (Kane).

NIPPLE BUTTE (Kane) is at the northwest section of Nipple Bench at the head of Nipple Creek. There is also a Nipple Spring in the vicinity. The various "nipple" features all take their name from the familiar shape of many small buttes in Utah.
S1,T42S,R2E,SLM.

NIPPLE CREEK (Kane). See Nipple Butte (Kane).

NIPPLE LAKE (**Kane**) is at the head of Kitchen Canyon, which drains east into the Paria River. Ten miles southeast is the ghost town of Paria*. John Kitchen named the lake and the canyon for a nearby butte.
T30,40S,R2½W,SLM; 5,550' (1,692m).

NIX CREEK (**Summit**) originates eight miles east northeast of Oakley and drains northwest into Nobletts Creek. It was named for George Nix, who homesteaded in the area.
S16,8,T1S,R7E,SLM. 298.

NO MANS CANYON (**Wayne**) originates three miles west northwest of the Biddlecome Ranch. It is an inaccessible canyon that drains west southwest into the Dirty Devil River.
S8,T29S,R14E,SLM to S21,T29S,R13,14E, SLM.

NO MANS MESA (**San Juan**) is between Nokai Canyon and Copper Canyon on the San Juan River. The mesa is very difficult to climb.
T41,42S,R12,13E,SLM. 567.

NOAHS ARK (**Iron**) is five miles southeast of Parowan*, between Center Creek and Bowery Creek. This feature resembles an ark.
S7,T35S,R8W,SLM; 8,596' (2,620m).

NOBLETTS CREEK (**Summit**) originates at the west end of the Uinta Mountains, four and one-half miles northwest of Hoyt Peak. The creek drains west into the Weber River, South Fork. Sam Noblett was a lumberman who lived in this area during the early 1800s. He also owned several sawmills in the region. There are two Nobletts Creeks in this immediate area. See below.
S3,T1S,R7E,SLM to S8,T1S,R7E,SLM. 298.

NOBLETTS CREEK (**Wasatch**) originates at the west end of the Uinta Mountains on the northern slopes of Soapstone Mountain. It drains west into

the Provo River, South Fork. See Nobletts Creek (Summit).
S20,T3S,R8E,SLM to S24,T3S,R7E,SLM. 298.

NOKAI CANYON (**San Juan**) originates in Arizona and drains north into the San Juan River. The name is Navajo and means "Mexican waters."
S35,T43S,R12E,SLM (Utah border). 567.

NOODLE CREEK (**Garfield**) is a tributary of Pole Canyon ten miles southeast of Circleville*. Joseph Crowe hunted deer with his dog along the creek and would often urge the dog on with "Noodle 'em up, noodle 'em up." It is also listed as Hoodle Creek.
S20,T31S,R2W,SLM. 567.

NOON LAKE (**Garfield**) is on the Boulder section of the Aquarius Plateau at the head of Pleasant Creek. The lake is on a pack trail, so it was a convenient place for the cattlemen and sheep men to stop for a noon break.
T31S,R4E,SLM; 10,915' (3,327m).

NORTH BEND* (**Sanpete**). See Fairview* (Sanpete).

NORTH CANYON (**Beaver**) originates in the west central part of the Wah Wah Mountains. It drains south into Pine Grove and Pine Valley.
S26,T28S,R16W,SLM.

NORTH CANYON (**Cache**) is north of Clarkston* and drains east into Clarkston Creek.
S5,T14N,R2W,SLM (at mouth).

NORTH CANYON (**Davis**) originates three miles southeast of Bountiful* and drains west into the Jordan River. The head of the canyon is at Rudys Flat. It is the first major canyon north of Salt Lake City*.
S11,T1N,R1E,SLM (at head).

NORTH CANYON FORT* (**Davis**) was an early structure at Bountiful* (Davis).

NORTH CANYON SETTLEMENT* (**Davis**). See Bountiful* (Davis).

NORTH COTTONWOOD CREEK* (**Davis**). See Farmington*.

NORTH CREEK* (**Beaver**) is a small community northeast of Beaver on North Creek from which it receives its name. S30,31,T28S,R6W,SLM; 6,350' (1,935m).

NORTH CREEK (**Beaver**) originates on the western slopes of the Tushar Mountains and drains southwest into the Beaver River. North Creek is the first creek north of Beaver. T28,29S,R7,8W,SLM.

NORTH CREEK (**Garfield**) originates on Escalante Mountain at a series of small lakes, including Blue and Yellow lakes. It drains south southeast into the headwaters of the Escalante River. The creek is north of Main Canyon. S16,T35S,R2E,SLM (at mouth). 12.

NORTH ERICKSON LAKE (**Summit**) is in the southeast section of Erickson Basin at the west end of the Uinta Mountains. See the creek for name origin. S32,T1S,R8E,SLM; 10,030' (3,057m).

NORTH FORK TOWN* (**Weber**). See Eden* (Weber).

NORTH JORDAN* (**Salt Lake**). See West Jordan* (Salt Lake).

NORTH LAKE (**Rich**) is in North Lake Canyon three miles south of the Idaho line and one-half mile west of the Wyoming line. It is north of South Lake. S17,T14N,R8E,SLM; 6,600' (2,012m).

NORTH LAKE CANYON (**Rich**) originates five miles north of South Lake on the Idaho border. It drains south southeast through North Lake into Wyoming and receives its name from the lake. S31,T15N,R8E,SLM.

NORTH LOGAN* (**Cache**) is two miles north of Logan* at the mouth of Green Canyon. The community had an early name of Greenville*, but the name was changed when it was discovered that there was another Greenville in Utah. S23,T12N,R1E,SLM; 4,720' (1,439m). 449, 567.

NORTH MONTEZUMA CREEK* (**San Juan**) was an early name for Monticello*.

NORTH OGDEN* (**Weber**) is on U-235 three miles north of Ogden*. This outgrowth of Ogden was originally settled in 1850, vacated because of Indians, and subsequently resettled again in 1851. S28,29,T7N,R1W,SLM; 4,416' (1,346). 27, 274, 542.

NORTH OGDEN FORT* (**Weber**) was the forerunner of North Ogden* (Weber).

NORTH PEAK (**San Juan**) is in the Abajo Mountains west of Monticello*. Abajo and South peaks are south of North Peak. T33S,R22E,SLM; 10,819' (3,298m).

NORTH PEAK (**Tooele**) is five miles east of Ibapah* at the north end of the Deep Creek Range. S8,T9S,R18W,SLM; 7,708' (2,349m).

NORTH PINTO HILLS (**Wayne**) are three miles northwest of Hanksville*. The word "pinto" indicates multi-colored land formations in the area. S7,8,T28S,R11E,SLM; 4,744' (1,446m).

NORTH SALT LAKE CITY* (**Davis**) is three and one-half miles north of Salt Lake City* on Alt. US-91. During the early settlement days it was also known as Swede Town*. S1,2,T1N,R1W,SLM; 4,255' (1,297m).

NORTH SETTLEMENT* (**Cache**). See Mendon* (Cache).

NORTH SPRING (**Beaver**) is in the Tushar Mountains east of Sulphurdale*, southeast of Cove Fort*, and north of South Spring.
S9,T26S,R6W,SLM; 7,160' (2,182m).

NORTH SPRING (**Beaver**) is in the foothills south of the mouth of Cave Canyon and north of Minersville*.
S24,T29S,R10W,SLM; 5,600' (1,707m).

NORTH STAR LAKE (**Duchesne**) is in the Garfield Basin of the Uinta Mountains south of Wilson Peak.
S9,T4N,R5W,USM; 11,395' (3,473m).

NORTH SULPHUR SPRING (**Beaver**) is on the western slopes of the Needle Range in the Mountain Home Mountains. It is north of South Sulphur Springs.
S27,T27S,R19W,SLM; 7,180' (2,188m).

NORTH WARD* (**Box Elder**). See Harper*.

NORTH WASH (**Garfield**) originates at the junction of Trail Canyon and Copper Creek, eighteen miles northwest of the Hite* site, which is now under the waters of Lake Powell. The wash drains southeast into Lake Powell and was once the main trail or road between Hite and Hanksville*.

NORTH WEBER* (**Weber**). See Plain City*.

NORTH WILDCAT CREEK (**Beaver**) originates on the western slopes of the Tushar Mountains. It drains southwest into Wildcat Creek.
S17,19,T27S,R6W,SLM.

NORTH WILLOW CREEK* (**Box Elder**). See Willard* (Box Elder).

NORTH WILLOW LAKE (**Tooele**) is in the Stansbury Mountains near the head of North Willow Creek and drains toward Grantsville*.
T4S,R7W,SLM. 100(v2).

NORTHRUP* (**Washington**) was a small pioneer community at the confluence of the North and East forks of the Virgin River. Northrup was first settled in 1861 by Isaac Behunin, then was gradually absorbed into Springdale*. Variant: Northup*.
SW¼,T41S,R10W,SLM. 89, 516.

NORTONVILLE* (**Juab**) was four miles north of Nephi*. This small community was settled by John Holland, Joseph Marble, and others. After the original settlers moved on, the Norton brothers— Wesley, Isaac, and John—began homesteading much of the area. The community was named for the Nortons. By 1911 most of the families had moved into Nephi.
S8,17,T12S,R1E,SLM; 4,955' (1,510m). 100 (v13), 347.

NORWAY FLAT (**Summit**) is at the west end of the Uinta Mountains south of Big Elk Lake. The large flats in the region were timbered with Englemann spruce (*Picea englemanni*), which was harvested under the common name of Norway pine.
S8,17,20,T2S,R8E,SLM; 9,700' (2,957m). 298.

NOT ZION* (**Washington**). See Little Zion* (Washington).

NOTCH, THE (**Summit**) is the name given to the saddle in the center of Notch Mountain, one-half mile north of Wall Lake in the southwest section of the Uinta Mountains.
S30,T1S,R9E,SLM; 10,580' (3,225m).

NOTCH LAKE (**Summit**) is at the east base of Notch Mountain. See below.
S28,T1S,R9E,SLM; 10,300' (3,139m).

NOTCH MOUNTAIN (**Summit**) is in the western Uinta Mountains, one-half mile north of Wall Lake. The mountain received the name because of the unusual notch or saddle in the center of its profile. See The Notch.

S29,30,T1S,R9E,SLM; 11,263' (3,433m).
292, 532.

NOTCH MOUNTAIN (**Millard**). See
Notch Peak (Millard).

NOTCH PEAK (**Millard**) is in the
Sawtooth Mountains of the House
Range, six miles north of US-6,50 and
east of White (Tule) Valley. Its profile
from the east shows a sharp, prominent
notch.
T19S,R14W,SLM; 9,855' (3,004m).

NOTOM* (**Wayne**) is on Pleasant Creek
on the east side of Capitol Reef National
Park. The settlement was first called
Pleasant Creek*, but the postal authorities requested a change since that name
was already in use. It had also been
known as Pleasant Dale*. Notom was
finally chosen, but the name origin is not
known. The area where a small community once existed is today a large ranch
complex. See also Aldridge*. MRN
T30S,R7E,SLM; 5,250' (1,600m). 89, 485,
542.

NOWLENVILLE* (**Tooele**). See
Batesville*.

NUTTERS CANYON (**Duchesne**) flows
northeast into the Duchesne River. The
canyon was named for Preston Nutter, a
well-known cattleman of the late 1800s
and early 1900s. See Nutters Hole.
S33,T6S,R5W,USM to S12,T5S,R4W,USM.

NUTTERS HOLE (**Uintah**) is on the
Green River at the mouth of Nine Mile
Creek. Preston Nutter's cattle range
included the Hole. Preston Nutter and
Jim McPherson were the first white
cattlemen to bring their cattle up into
the Book Cliffs country.
146, 409, 555(v32).

- O -

OAK CITY* (Millard) is on U-125 ten miles east of Delta*. It was first known as Oak Creek* for the creek next to the site where the early residents settled. The area was used as an early grazing range by herders from nearby Deseret*. The town was later settled by these herders and their families.
S31,T16S,R10W,SLM and S6,T17S,R10W, SLM; 5,105' (1,556m). 289, 567.

OAK CREEK* (Millard). See Oak City* (Millard).

OAK CREEK (Millard) originates east of Oak City* and drains west into the Fool Creek Reservoir. Oak shrub is plentiful in this area.
S9,T17S,R3W,SLM to T16S,R4W,SLM.

OAK CREEK (Sanpete) originates at the foot of Haystack Mountain southeast of Spring City* and drains northwest. This area has an abundance of oak shrub (Quercus).
T15S,R3,4,5E,SLM.

OAK CREEK* (Washington). See Springdale* (Washington).

OAK SPRING (Beaver) is in the southwest section of the Mineral Mountains between Lincoln Gulch and Guyo Canyon.
S19,T29S,R9W,SLM; 6,100' (1,859m).

OAK SPRING (Garfield) is near the junction of Dave Canyon and Alvey Wash, ten miles south of Escalante*.
S13,T36S,R2E,SLM; 6,400' (1,951m). 12.

OAKLEY* (Summit) is in Kamas Valley on US-189 and U-213. It had an early name of Oak City* for the surrounding scrub oak.

S19,20,T1S,R6E,SLM; 6,475' (1,974m). 289, 542, 567.

OAKS PARK RESERVOIR (Uintah) is in the southeast section of the Uinta Mountains, twelve miles west southwest of Mount Lena. There is prolific oak growth in this vicinity.
S1,12,T1S,R20E,SLM; 9,278' (2,282m).

OAKVILLE* (Sanpete) was an outgrowth of Fairview*.

OASIS* (Millard) became an outgrowth of Deseret* in March 1891. The surroundings made the settlement seem like an oasis in the desert. See Deseret*.
S34,T17S,R7W,SLM; 4,597' (1,401m).

OBSERVATION PEAK (Weber). See Mount Ogden.

OCHRE MOUNTAIN (Tooele) is north of the Deep Creek Mountains and Pony Express Canyon, six miles northeast of Ibapah*. The mountain is a yellowish, ochre color.
S16,T8S,R18W, 7,540' (2,298m). 567.

OGDEN* (Weber) is on I-15, US-89 and the Weber and Ogden rivers, thirty-five miles north of Salt Lake City*. In 1844-45 a mountainman/trapper, Miles Goodyear, with his Indian wife, built a trading post and small fort on the site that he named Fort Buenaventura*. The 1847 arrival of the Mormons induced him to sell his land. The site was purchased by Captain James Brown, a Mormon representative. The fort and small settlement around the site then became Brownsville*. In 1850, by order of the General Assembly of Deseret, the community name was changed from Brownsville to Ogden, honoring Peter

Skene Ogden. This brigade leader for the Hudson Bay Company never entered this immediate area.
S33,T5,6N,R1W,SLM; 4,370' (1,332m). 27, 100(v5), 274, 289, 384, 464, 542.

OGDEN CANYON (Weber) is northeast of Ogden* and drains southwest. It was named for Peter Skene Ogden. See Ogden (Weber).
S15,T6N,R1E to S23,T6N,R1W,SLM.

OGDEN CENTER* (San Juan). See Home of Truth* (San Juan).

OGDEN HOLE (Weber) was for many years considered to be near North Ogden*. It is now believed to be in the valley where Huntsville* is located. In 1825 a party consisting mostly of free American trappers met Peter Skene Ogden's party of French-Canadian Hudson Bay trappers. The ensuing discussions were not friendly and Ogden retreated north to avoid any hostile actions.
T6,7N,R1E,SLM; ca. 4,900' (1,494m). 274, 371, 372, 546.

OGDEN RIVER (Weber) originates at Pineview Reservoir in Ogden Valley and drains west into the Weber River. See Ogden* for name source.
S11,14,T6N,R1E,SLM to S19,T6N,R1W,SLM.

OGDEN VALLEY (Weber) is at the head of Ogden Canyon fourteen miles east of Ogden*. Huntsville*, Pineview Reservoir, and Ogden Hole are located in the valley. See Ogden*.
T6,7N,R1,2E,SLM; 5,000' (1,524m).

OGDENVILLE* (Sevier). During the 1870s a family named Ogden took up land just south of Richfield*. For a short period of time the settlement was known as Ogdenville, but it was soon absorbed into Richfield.
S35,36,T23S,R3W,SLM; 5,265' (1,605m). 360.

OKE DOKE LAKE (Duchesne) is in the south central section of the Uinta Mountains, one and one-fourth miles northeast of Mount Emmons. George Walkup of the U.S. Forest Service named the lake because the fishing was "oke doke" there.
T2N,R4W,USM; 11,240' (3,426m). 309.

OLD CANYON (Cache) originates at Red Spur Mountains west southwest of Randolph*. See New Canyon (Cache).
S5,T10N,R5E,SLM.

OLD CELLARS* (Beaver). See Lower Beaver* (Beaver).

OLD FORT* (Box Elder) was first built where Brigham City* now stands. The name was changed to Old Fort after a new fort was built.

OLD FORT* (Grand) was in the Moab Valley area. In 1855, the Mormons built this fort, the first in that particular area.
475, 514.

OLD FORT* (Salt Lake) is where Pioneer Park is in Salt Lake City*. During the August 1, 1847, General Assembly, a vote was cast to build a stockade or fort of adobe houses at this site.
S1,T1S,R1W,SLM; 4,240' (1,292m). 100 (v17).

OLD HICKORY* (Beaver): See Hickory*.

OLD INDIAN SPRING (Beaver) is in the Mineral Mountains near the head of Cunningham Wash.
S8,T27S,R8W,SLM; 7,960' (2,426m).

OLD IRONTOWN* (Iron) was fifteen miles west of Cedar City* and two and one-half miles southwest of Iron Mountain. The settlement was established in 1850-52 specifically for the mining of iron ore. The area was abandoned shortly

after its establishment because the venture proved impractical and too costly. Later attempts also failed. Old Irontown, Iron City*, became Utah's first ghost town.
S8,T37S,R14W,SLM; 5,900' (1,798m). 27, 89, 516, 546, 567.

OLD LA SAL* (San Juan). See La Sal* (San Juan).

OLD QUIGLEY CANYON (Cache) originates in the Clarkston Mountains northwest of Clarkston* and drains east into Clarkston Creek at Hammond Flats. The canyon was first opened by Andrew Quigley, so it was named after him. There is a New Quigley Canyon just south of the Old; it has the same name origin.
S12,T14N,R3W,SLM to S4,T14N,R2W,SLM. D.L. 6504.

OLD WOMAN PLATEAU (Sevier) is on the headwaters of Convulsion Canyon, six miles northwest of Fremont*. Erosion on the plateau has formed a natural profile of an old woman. More recently, this process has disfigured the nose on the profile.
S22,T23S,R4,5E,SLM. D.L. 7103.

OLD WOMAN WASH (Emery) originates on the San Rafael Swell three miles northeast of Temple Mountain. It drains southeast into Cottonwood Wash. Nancy McCrery Harris, born in Virginia on April 29, 1836, operated a freighting station near the area where U-24 now crosses the wash.
S31,T24S,R13E,SLM; 4,800' (1,463m). 193, 508, 567.

OLJETO* (San Juan) is near the head of Oljeto Wash in Monument Valley. It received its name from the wash.
S24,T43S,R14E,SLM.

OLJETO MESA (San Juan) is west of and near Goulding*. See Oljeto Wash for name source.
T43S,R15E,SLM.

OLJETO WASH (San Juan) originates in Arizona and drains north into the San Juan River. This popular Navajo word means "moonlight." Variants: Oljato, Oljieto, etc.
S30,T40S,R15E,SLM (at mouth). 314, 542. D.L. 5903.

OLMSTEAD* (Utah) is a hydroelectric development at the mouth of Provo Canyon. It was built in 1904 as the first important hydroelectric development in Utah and was named for the designing engineer.
T6S,R3E,SLM; 4,831' (1,472m).

OLSEN RESERVOIR (Emery) is five and one-fourth miles south of Wellington* on Marsing Wash.
S4,T16S,R11E,SLM; 5,416' (1,651m).

OMAHA* (Millard). See Sugarville* (Millard).

OMNI* (Sevier). See Richfield* (Sevier).

OMNI POINT* (Sevier). See Annabella* (Sevier).

ONAQUI MOUNTAINS (Tooele) extend south from the Stansbury Mountains and separate Rush and Skull valleys. The name is Goshute Indian: "Ona" refers to salt and "qui" is a locative syllable.
T6,7S,R6W,SLM; 8,642' (2,634m). 107, 314, 567. D.L. 7304.

ONION CREEK (Grand) originates in Fisher Valley and drains northwest into the Colorado River at Professor Valley. The creek water contains arsenic and sulphur and is poisonous—hence the name.
S2,T25S,R24E,SLM to S10,T24S,R23E,SLM. 146, 546, 567.

OOWAH LAKE (Grand) is near the head of Mill Creek southeast of Moab*. The name is of Piute Indian origin.
S33,T26S,R23E,SLM; 8,800' (2,682m).

OPHIR* (Tooele) is four miles up Ophir

Canyon south southeast of Stockton*. General Connor's men discovered ore there in the 1860s in what was known at that time as East Canyon. The men named the settlement St. Louis*. A prospector named the adjacent mine Ophir because it was very rich in gold and silver. The name "Ophir," a word of biblical origin, was soon adopted by the town. The town peaked about 1880 and today is a stable community of about fifty people.
S24,T5S,R4W,SLM; 6,600' (2,012m). 153, 266(1 Kings, X:11), 314, 516, 542, 546, 549.

OPHIR CANYON (Tooele) originates at Lowe Peak on the southwest slopes of the Oquirrh Mountains and drains southwest into Rush Valley. It had an earlier name of Bates Canyon for Ormus E. Bates and family, who settled at the mouth of the canyon in the 1850s. See Ophir*.
S6,T5S,R3W,SLM to S28,T5S,R4W,SLM.

OQUIRRH CITY* (Salt Lake). See West Valley City* (Salt Lake).

OQUIRRH MOUNTAINS (Salt Lake, Tooele) have a north-south orientation at the south end of Great Salt lake. The mountains used to be heavily wooded but have been deforested by heavy logging, smelter fumes, and other problems. The communities of Magna* and Bacchus* are east. On the west is Tooele Valley. The name is Goshute Indian and has various meanings, some of which are recorded as "Wooded Mountain," "Cave Mountain," "West Mountain," and "Shining Mountain."
T1-6S,R2-4W,SLM; 10,626' (3,239m). 106, 107, 314, 466, 567.

ORANGE CLIFFS (Garfield, Wayne). The canyons of the Colorado River cut through these cliffs that were named by members of Powell's survey. The Orange Cliffs are the lower step and the Book Cliffs are the second step in this series. The Orange Cliffs are shown most predominantly along the west side of the

Colorado River at The Confluence. Here, buff sandstone rests on red shale below a five-hundred-foot vertical wall of orange-colored sandstone with no breaks. The Ute Indians called this region Toom-pin wu-near Tu-weap, a land of canyons, coves, standing rocks, buttes, and cliffs—an ensemble of strange, grand features, weird and wonderful—the Land of Standing Rocks, named for their sunset colors.
T30,31S,R16,17E,SLM. 159, 160, 314, 422, 494, 609.

ORANGEVILLE* (Emery) is a small community two and one-half miles northwest of Castle Dale*. It was named for Orange Seely, an early settler in Castle Valley. The community had an early name of Upper Castle Dale*.
S29,30,T18S,R8E,SLM; 5,772' (1,759m). 289, 314, 542, 546, 567.

ORDER* (Sanpete). See Mayfield*.

ORDER CITY* (Kane). See Orderville* (Kane).

ORDERVILLE* (Kane) is on U-89 in Long Valley, between Mount Carmel* and Glendale*. The settlement was initially established in 1875 by Mormon settlers from Glendale who had moved earlier from the settlements on the Muddy River in southern Nevada. The first families who arrived intended to discipline themselves by following a strict United Order program that was encouraged by the Mormon Church. The name comes from that United Order program.
S4,T41S,R7W,SLM; 5,480' (1,670m). 289, 311, 314, 360, 455, 542, 546, 555(v7), 567, 600.

ORDERVILLE CANYON (Kane, Washington) drains southwest into The Narrows section of Zion National Park. The canyon name comes from the community of Orderville*, located east of the canyon.
T40S,R9,10W,SLM. D.L. 6803.

OREGON SPRINGS (**Box Elder**) are at the west base of the Clarkston Mountains, three miles northeast of Portage*. The springs were on the old Oregon Trail.
S33,T15N,R3W,SLM; 4,401' (1,341m). 567.

OREJAS DEL OSO (**San Juan**) anglicized, means the Bears Ears. See Bears Ears.

OREM* (**Utah**) is on US-89 and I-15, four miles north of Provo City*. The settlement was built on the Provo Terrace of ancient Lake Bonneville. Walter C. Orem was president of the Salt Lake and Utah Electric Interurban Railroad that ran through Orem and he contributed substantially to the development of the city of Orem. His name was given to the city in 1919.
T6S,R2E,SLM; 4,756' (1,450m). 270, 314, 394, 494, 542.

OREM BENCH (**Utah**) is the section of the Provo Terrace of ancient Lake Bonneville upon which the city of Orem* is built.

ORTON* (**Garfield**). See Spry* (Garfield).

OSIRIS* (**Garfield**) is a ghost town site eight miles south of Antimony* on the east fork of the Sevier River. The settlement was established in 1910 as Henderson* after William James Henderson, an early Panguitch* sheep man who donated land for the townsite. Later W. E. Holt (Halt?) from nearby Widtsoe* built a creamery, flour mill, and home on the site, then renamed it Osiris for the king or god of the dead. The altitude and insufficient water resources prevented the growth of reliable vegetable crops, and within ten years the settlement was abandoned.
S13,T32S,R2W,SLM; 6,700' (2,042m). 89, 145, 516.

OSTLER FORK (**Summit**) originates in the northwest section of the Uinta Mountains at Ostler Lake. It drains north into the Stillwater River. See Ostler Peak for name source.
T1S,R10E,SLM to S27,T1N,R10E,SLM.

OSTLER LAKE (**Summit**) is on the headwaters of Ostler Fork of the Stillwater River in the Amethyst Basin. See Ostler Peak for name source.
T1S,R10E,SLM; 10,550' (3,216m).

OSTLER PEAK (**Summit**) is at the west end of the Uinta Mountains, six miles east northeast of Hayden Peak. It was named for J. R. Dick Ostler, a former ranger in the Grandaddy Lake region.
12,718' (3,876m). 309, 530.

OTTER CREEK (**Rich**) originates northwest of Randolph* where it drains east into the Bear River. Otter were once plentiful in this creek.
S1,2,T11N,R6E,SLM.

OTTER CREEK (**Piute, Sevier**) originates on the Fishlake Plateau eight miles north northwest of the north end of Fish Lake. It drains into the Otter Creek Reservoir. Otter were plentiful in the creek in an earlier period.
S30,T24S,R2E,SLM to S36,T29S,R2W,SLM.

OTTER CREEK RESERVOIR (**Piute**) is at the south end of Grass Valley at the junction of Otter Creek (from which it was named) and the East Fork of the Sevier River. The reservoir was completed in 1901.
T29,30S,R2W,SLM; 6,372' (1,942m). 585.

OTTER LAKE (**Beaver**) is in the Tushar Mountains at the head of Lake Stream, southwest of Puffer Lake. Otter were plentiful there in earlier days.
S12,T29S,R5W,SLM; 9,600' (2,926m). 125.

OURAY* (**Uintah**) is a small Ute Indian community near the junction of the Duchesne and Green rivers. The community was named for Chief Ouray, who was born in 1820. He was chief when the White River Utes were brought to the

Uinta Basin Reservation from Colorado. He spoke both Spanish and English and was friendly to the whites. His wife was Chepeta, an important person in her own right since she was a great help to her people. Ouray is the second oldest settlement in the Uinta Basin.
S32,T4S,R3E,SLM; 4,655' (1,419m). 100 (v17), 314, 494, 542.

OURAY LAKE (Duchesne) is in the central section of the Uinta Mountains at the head of Rock Creek. See Ouray* for name source.
S24,T4N,R8W,USM; 10,380' (3,164m).

OUTLAW SPRING (Wayne) is in the center of the Spur country at the head of Spur Canyon, west of Millard Canyon. The name reflects its early history as a water hole and hideout for early cattle rustlers and outlaws.
T29S,R16E,SLM.

OVERLAND CANYON (Tooele) is near Clifton* and Gold Hill*. The Overland Stage passed through the canyon.
S25,T8S,R18W,SLM. 89.

OWACHOMO BRIDGE (San Juan). See Natural Bridges National Monument.

OWEEP CREEK (Duchesne) originates in the central section of the Uinta Mountains, five and one-half miles east of Mount Lovenia. The creek drains southwest into the Lake Fork River. "Oweep" means "grass" and the creek flows through grassy meadows.
S12,T4N,R6W,USM to S9,T3N,R6W,USM. 530.

OWIYUKUTS MOUNTAINS (Daggett) are north of Browns Park and south of the Wyoming border, with a northeast-southwest orientation. MRN
T2,3N,R25E,SLM; 9,016' (2,748m).

OWL NATURAL BRIDGE (San Juan) is on Navajo Mountain, three miles northwest of the summit near the head of Nasja Creek. Nasja is a corruption of

"noeshja" meaning "the owls." Owls were respected birds that were well loved by the Navajo Indians. See Nasja Creek. 314.

OWLHOOT TRAIL is a general term for an outlaw trail that was traveled during the night. One of the trails in Utah entered the state from a northern route originating in Canada, followed south through Vernal*, went down the Green River past the McPherson Ranch, came out into the Robbers Roost country, then went south into Mexico. 25, 303.

OX KILLER HOLLOW (Cache) is at the summit east of Mantua Reservoir on the headwaters of the Little Bear. It is a very steep, difficult hollow to ascend.
S18,T9N,R1E,SLM and S13,24,T9N,R1W, SLM.

OX VALLEY (Washington) is between Enterprise* and the Bull Valley Mountains. See Bull Valley Mountains for name source.
S10,14,15,T38S,R17W,SLM;6,262'(1,909m).

OXKILLER HOLLOW (Cache) originates northwest of Cherry Peak and drains west, entering the Cub River between Lewiston* and Richmond*. MRN
S24,T14N,R1E,SLM (at mouth).

OYSTER SHELL REEF (Garfield) is an exposed section of the Waterpocket Fold along the headwaters of Halls Creek, south of Divide Canyon. Fossil oyster shells are exposed along the reef.
T33,34S,R8E,SLM.

- P -

PACE LAKE (Grand) is a small shallow lake near the Colorado border north of La Sal*. MRN
S9,T26S,R26E,SLM.

PACEN* (Utah). See Payson* (Utah).

PACK CREEK (Grand) had the early name of Pack Saddle Creek. The creek originates on the western slopes of the La Sal Mountains where it drains northwest into Mill Creek. It was named after two men who buried their packs along the creek in an attempt to lighten their load while fleeing from Indians.
S34,T27S,R24E,SLM to S1,T26S,R21E,SLM. 146, 514.

PACK SADDLE CREEK (Grand). See Pack Creek (Grand).

PACKARD CANYON (Utah) originates three miles west of the guard station in Diamond Fork of the Spanish Fork River; it drains north into Hobble Creek. The canyon was named after Milan Packard who opened the canyon with William Bringhurst in 1870. They built a steam sawmill in the canyon.
S32,T7S,R5E,SLM.

PACKARD LAKE (Duchesne) is in the Naturalist Basin at the base of Mount Agassiz. Alpheus S. Packard was a student of Agassiz's, along with other well-known naturalists and scientists whose names are also attached to this cluster of lakes.
S6,T3N,R8W,SLM; 9,980' (3,042m).

PACKER* (Duchesne) was a small townsite located two miles east of Neola*, into which it was eventually absorbed. See Neola* (Duchesne). MRN

89, 165.

PADRE BAY (Kane). When the waters of Lake Powell covered the mouth of Padre Canyon where the Crossing of the Fathers was located, the name of the canyon was transferred to the bay. The crossing is now several hundred feet below the surface of the water in the bay. See Crossing of the Fathers.
T43S,R5,6E,SLM.

PAHREAH* (Kane). See Paria* (Kane).

PAHVANT names. See Pavant names.

PAINTED DESERT (Kane) is a term used to describe what is today known largely as Monument Valley—colorful, with unusual geologic formations and cloud shadows.
159.

PAINTER BASIN (Duchesne) is in the south central Uinta Mountains on the headwaters of the North Fork of the Uinta River. Tom Painter was a sheep man from Evanston* who ran his sheep in the basin.
ca. 11,000' (3,353m). 309.

PAINTER LAKES (Duchesne) is a cluster of lakes southeast of Painter Basin. See the basin for the name source. 11,300' (3,444m).

PALISADE LAKE (Sanpete) is in Palisade Park, two miles east of Sterling*. There are palisade formations throughout the park. An earlier name was Funks Lake for its founder, Daniel Buckley Funk, a Sanpete County developer.
S34,35,T18S,R2E,SLM; 5,868' (1,789m). 152.

PALISADE LAKE STATE RECREA-TION AREA (Sanpete) includes an area of unusual geologic features surrounding Palisade Lake. The Mormons purchased the land from the Indians in 1873. It was also a summer camping ground of Chief Arrapene and his people.

PALMYRA* (Utah) was founded in 1852 on the banks of the Spanish Fork River. The town soon became absorbed into the city of Spanish Fork*. Present-day Palmyra is a later outgrowth of Spanish Fork. Both Palmyras were named for Palmyra, New York, a town prominent in early Mormon history. S10,T8S,R2E,SLM; 4,522' (1,378m). 27, 268, 289, 542.

PANCAKE* (Beaver). See Greenville*.

PANGUITCH* (Garfield) was settled in 1866 on Panguitch Creek near the Sevier River. The settlement was vacated because of Indian troubles, then resettled in 1871. The name comes from nearby Panguitch Lake and Panguitch Creek. Both were named by the Piute Indians and mean "water" and "fish." The settlement had an early name of Fairview*. S32,38,T34S,R5W,SLM; 6,624' (2,019m). 100(v17), 136, 314, 289, 360.

PANGUITCH CREEK (Garfield) origi-nates at Panguitch Lake and drains east into the Sevier River. See Panguitch*. S34,T35S,R7W,SLM to S21,T34S,R5W,SLM.

PANGUITCH LAKE (Garfield) is south-west of Panguitch* at the head of Panguitch Creek. The lake first became known to white men in 1852. Livestock-men and lumbermen ran their businesses around the lake in the past. Today it is a region of canyon homes, ranching, and recreation. See Panguitch*. T35,36S,R7W,SLM; 8,208' (2,502m).

PANGUITCH VALLEY (Garfield) is the area surrounding Panguitch* and the junction of Panguitch Creek and the Sevier River. The valley was originally explored by white men in June 1852, then was settled by a group of people who gathered at Parowan* before moving into the valley on March 16, 1862. 145.

PANTHER* (Carbon). See Heiner*.

PAPOOSE LAKE (Duchesne) is a small lake on the headwaters of the Whiterocks River. Nearby are Wigwam, Moccasin, and Chepeta lakes. This area was a favorite Ute Indian summer camping site. S29,T5N,R1W,USM; 10,625' (3,238m). D.L. 6901.

PARADISE* (Cache) is nine miles south of Logan* on U-165. In 1860, when the first white settlers saw the green hills and wildflowers, they named it Paradise. S27,28,33,34,T10N,R1E,SLM; 4,950' (1,509m). 27, 289, 526, 542, 567.

PARADISE CANYON (Garfield, Kane) originates on the northwest section of the Kaiparowits Plateau, south of Mount Canaan. This beautiful wilderness area drains southeast into Last Chance Creek. S36,T37S,R1E,SLM to S34,T39S,R3E,SLM.

PARADISE CREEK (Uintah) originates in the southeast section of the Uinta Mountains at Paradise Park Reservoir. It drains southwest into the Whiterocks River and receives its name from the park. S8,T3N,R1E,USM to S36,T3N,R1W,USM.

PARADISE PARK (Uintah) is in the southeast section of the Uinta Mountains on the headwaters of Paradise Creek. The area has a reservoir in it today. The name was conceived when Bill Caldwell, a sheep man of the early 1900s, was lost in the area for three days and nights. When he made his way out into what is now Paradise Park, he saw a sheep camp with food and shelter—paradise! S7,T3N,R1E,USM; 10,000' (3,048m). 309, 567.

PARADISE PARK RESERVOIR (**Uintah**). See Paradise Park.

PARADISE VALLEY LAKE (**Sevier**) is nine miles south of Fremont Junction near U-72. It is a small lake (less than a mile in length) situated in a beautiful setting surrounded by mountains and mountain meadows.
S14,T25S,R4E,SLM; 7,900' (2,408m).

PARAGONAH* (**Iron**) is four miles northeast of Parowan* and was first settled on Red Creek in the spring of 1851. The name comes from the Piede Indians, who were a clan of the Piute Indians. "Paragonah" was their name for nearby salty Little Salt Lake, which means "marshland" or "many springs," with connotations of salty, poisonous, or filthy water. Several variants are listed. Fremont called it Paragoona. Others added an "h."
S32,33,T33S,R8W,SLM; 5,897' (1,797m). 27, 72, 100(v17), 136, 289, 310, 406, 542, 567.

PARDNER CANYON (**Garfield**) is four miles northeast of Henrieville* on the southern slopes of Escalante Mountain. It drains south to empty into Dry Creek and Henrieville Creek. The Pardner sons owned a farm in this canyon.
S28,T37S,R2W,SLM. 567.

PARIA* (**Kane**) is forty-two miles northeast of Kanab* at the junction of Cottonwood Creek and the Paria River from which it receives its name. In 1865, Peter Shirts (Shurtz) became the first white man to settle there. In 1870, William Meeks and a party of Mormon missionaries arrived for the purpose of proselytizing and educating the Indians. Today it is a ghost town slowly being washed away by the Paria River. Pahreah was the early phonetic spelling of what the whites thought the Indians were saying. Major Powell was the first to spell it Paria and this is how the postal service recorded it. The post office closed in 1914 because the settlers were becoming tired of fighting floods and drought and were moving to other areas. The last moment of glory for Paria was being a western location for moving pictures. Many great movies were filmed there before the town was totally abandoned.
S18,T41S,R1W,SLM; 4,700' (1,433m). 89, 175, 289, 314, 455, 516, 542, 600.

PARIA CANYON (**Kane**). The lower Paria River runs through this canyon and empties into the Colorado River at Lees Ferry. This is a scenic wilderness region that is used by backpackers and hikers.

PARIA RIVER (**Kane**) originates on the southwestern slopes of the Aquarius Plateau and the southern slopes of Bryce Canyon National Park. It drains south to empty into the Colorado River at Lees Ferry in Arizona. Travelers used to follow the river as they moved north and south, then had to cross the river when traveling between St. George* and Kanab* or to Henrieville*-Escalante* country. In his journal, Powell used the name Ute Creek for the river. It was often spelled Pahrea(h), a Piute Indian word meaning muddy water or elk water.
175, 204, 463, 600, 602.

PARIETTE DRAW (**Uintah**) is fifteen miles south of Myton* and drains southeast into the Green River. Pariette Bench is located nearby. The Pariettes operated a gilsonite mine near the head of the draw.
T8S,R17E,SLM to S14,T9S,R19E,SLM. 567.

PARK, THE (**Beaver**) is a natural open glade in the Mineral Mountains between South Twin Flat Mountain and Granite Peak.
S1,T28S,R9W,SLM; 7,800' (2,377m).

PARK CITY* (**Summit**) is on U-248, five miles south of Kimball Junction*. In 1869, Colonel Patrick E. Connor's men from Fort Douglas discovered silver- and gold-carrying ore there. Soon after this discovery, tents and brush shelters appeared and the stampede for riches hit. The area flourished as a mining

town, peaked, then declined. In more recent times, the area has thrived as a skiing and recreational resort abounding with prosperous homes and condominiums. Park City had an early name of Upper Kimballs* for nearby Kimball's ranch, stage station, and highway junction. It was also called Upper Parleys* for nearby Parleys Park at the head of Parley P. Pratt's toll road built up Parleys Canyon. Later, it was George Gideon Snyder who came up with the present name. He was a probate judge who owned a local sawmill and held mining properties with his brother S. C. Snyder (nearby Snyderville*). George didn't like any of the previous names and on July 4, 1872, a handmade flag was hoisted and his choice of Park City (for nearby Parleys Park) was given to the town.
S16,21,T2S,R4E,SLM; 7,000' (2,134m). 89, 100(v17), 289, 542, 546, 555(v28), 567.

PARK VALLEY* (Box Elder) is on U-30 south of the Raft River Mountains. It was first settled in 1869 by William Cotton Thomas, who migrated from Brigham City* and developed a cattle ranch near Dove Creek. The heavy growth of trees along the creek and the view of the valley inspired the name. Park Valley was on the Overland Route for early immigration to California. In 1826 Jedediah Smith passed through, in 1841 the Bartelson-Bidwell party brought the first wagon through the valley, and in the 1860s the railroad was built through the valley.
S27,28,34,T13N,R13W,SLM; 5,543' (1,690m). 89, 100(v17), 139, 546, 567.

PARK VALLEY (Box Elder) has an east-west orientation and is south of the Raft River Mountains. The community, Park Valley*, is in the center.

PARKER MOUNTAIN (Piute, Wayne) is the west escarpment of the Awapa Plateau, with Angle* and Otter Creek Reservoir in the valley below. The Parker Range was probably named for Smith

Parker, who ran his cattle in Grass Valley and the adjoining region.
T27-30S,R1W,SLM; 9,481' (2,890m). D.L. 7104.

PARLEYS CANYON (Salt Lake). I-80 passes through the canyon that extends from southeast Salt Lake City* to Parleys Park at the summit. It was first named Big Canyon at the general conference of August 22, 1847. On March 18, 1849, Parley P. Pratt started building a road up the canyon that was used as a toll road called The Golden Pass. The name was eventually changed to Parleys Canyon, with Parleys Park at its head.
S9,T1S,R3E,SLM to S26,T1S,R1E,SLM. 27, 100(v17), 252, 289, 314, 423, 567, 604.

PARLEYS CREEK (Salt Lake) drains Parleys Canyon.

PARLEYS PARK (Summit) is a beautiful mountain meadow at the head of Parleys Canyon. Today it is an area of luxurious canyon homes. During the winter of 1848, Parley P. Pratt and David Lewis (a trapper and scout) went hunting in the area. It was Lewis that suggested the park be named after Pratt.
T1S,R4E,SLM; 6,472' (1,973m). 100(v17), 289, 314, 423.

PAROAN* (Iron). See Parowan*.

PAROWAN* (Iron) is near I-15, eighteen miles northeast of Cedar City*. It was founded by the Iron County Mission on January 18, 1851, as the first settlement the Mormon pioneers built south of Provo*. The name Parowan was given on May 16, 1851. The town was the center of the establishment of four neighboring settlements as far away as Bluff* in San Juan County and communities in southwestern Colorado and Arizona. The name Parowan evolved from the Piute "paragoons" and "pah-o-an," meaning "marsh people" and "bad or harmful water." Today the lake is usually a salt flat—depending on seasonal precipitation. The settlement was

originally named the City of Little Salt Lake* but this name was never used. It was also named Birch Creek* and Center Creek* after nearby creeks. Then it was named Louisa* for Louisa Beeman, one of the first Mormon women to consent to plural marriage.
T34S,R9W,SLM; 5,990' (1,826m). 46, 58, 100(v17), 136, 275, 289, 314, 423, 438.

PAROWAN CANYON (Beaver, Iron) originates near Brian Head and drains north into the valley at Parowan*.
S10,T36S,R9W,SLM to S24,T34S,R9W,SLM.

PAROWAN CANYON (Iron) originates at the summit south of Minersville* and drains north. The old road from Parowan* to Minersville and on to Beaver* came down this canyon.
S26,T31S,R10W,SLM to S10,T31S,R10W, SLM.

PAROWAN GAP (Iron) was a large cut through the Red Hills west of the Little Salt Lake. This was the old road between Cedar City*, Parowan*, and Minersville*. Today it is known for its Indian inscriptions on the gap walls.
S27,28,35,T33S,R10W,SLM.

PARRISH CREEK (Davis) originates near the summit east of Centerville*. It drains west into the valley. Samuel Parrish settled on the creek in 1848.
S2,T2N,R1E,SLM to S8,T2N,R1E,SLM. 88.

PARSON CITY* (Duchesne) is a ghost town on the eastern slopes of Dyer Mountain, twenty-four miles north of Vernal*. Dr. John Parson from nearby Browns Park prospected there.
S16,T1S,R21E,SLM; 9,700' (2,957m). 165, 172.

PARTITION ARCH (Grand) is one of the many natural rock openings in Arches National Park. The opening goes through a rock partition from one draw to another.
S21,T23S,R21E,SLM. 263.

PARTOUN* (Juab) is a small ranch settlement in the Snake Valley, midway between Trout Creek* and Gandy*.
S33,T13S,R18W,SLM; 4,818' (1,469m).

PARUNUWEAP CANYON (Washington) is drained by the East Fork of the Virgin River. It extends down to the ghost town of Shunesburg*. All of this region is now in Zion National Park. The Parunuweap joins the Mukuntuweap (the North Fork of the Virgin River) just east of Rockville*. The name is Piute and means "Roaring Water Canyon."
T42S,R9,10W,SLM. 314, 422, 496, 546, 600.

PASKETT CANYON (Box Elder) originates on the western slopes of the Grouse Creek Mountains and drains west into Grouse Creek. Philip A. Paskett and his family settled at Paskett Springs in the canyon.
S8,T11N,R17W,SLM to S11,T11N,R18W, SLM.

PASS CREEK (Garfield) originates at The Pass from which it receives its name, one mile east of Panguitch Lake.
S1,7,16,T36S,R16W,SLM.

PASS LAKE (Duchesne) is in the Mirror Lake region of the western Uinta Mountains on the divide between the Weber and Duchesne rivers' watersheds.
S27,T4N,R9W,SLM; 10,125' (3,086m). 530.

PASTRY RIDGE (Washington) is two miles west of Grafton*, a ghost town between Gooseberry Mesa and the Virgin River. Heavy erosion has given the ridge a filigreed and decorated look.
S5,8,T42S,R11W,SLM; 4,554' (1,388m).

PASTURE CANYON (Carbon) is one mile north of Sunnyside*, on the east side of the canyon. The canyon is excellent pastureland for livestock.
S31,T14S,R14E,SLM. 567.

PAT CORROLL PARK (Uintah) is in the eastern Uinta Mountains south of the summit on the Old Military Road. It was

named for Pat Correl who ran a sawmill there. Variant: Corral Park.
S6,T1S,R20E,SLM; 9,550' (2,991m). 567.

PAT WILLIS DRAW (Garfield) originates on the Paunsaugunt Plateau five miles north of Ruby's Inn. It drains southeast into the East Fork of the Sevier River and was named for William Patterson Willis. See Willis Creek.
S19,29,T35S,R3W,SLM.

PATMOS HEAD (Carbon) is an extension in the Roan Cliffs at the south end of Patmos Ridge, five miles southeast of Sunnyside*. MRN
S23,T15S,R14E,SLM; 9,641' (2,939m).

PATTERSON HOLLOW (Beaver) is on the southeast slopes of Bearskin Mountain of the Mineral Mountains. See below for name source.
S20,21,T27S,R8W,SLM; 7,300' (2,225m).

PATTERSON HOLLOW (Beaver) is in the Birch Creek Mountains near the head of the South Fork of Kane Canyon. It drains southwest into Birch Creek. Robert Patterson, a professional lumberjack, logged timber there in 1888.
S1,2,10,T30S,R6W,SLM. 125.

PAUL BUNYANS POTTY (San Juan) is in Horse Canyon several miles south of Cave Spring Line Camp in Canyonlands National Park. It is a natural opening in the cliffside with a very distinctive shape and markings.
S32,T30½S,R20E,SLM. D.L. 7503.

PAULSIN BASIN (Summit) is an the alpine area between the heads of Slate Creek and Hoyt Canyon, four miles east northeast of Samak*. Hans Paulsin homesteaded and built a sawmill there in the 1860s.
S1,T2S,R6E,SLM; 8,500' (2,591m). 151, 298.

PAUNSAUGUNT PLATEAU (Garfield, Kane) is a sedimentary rock plateau, bounded on the east by the East Fork of

the Sevier River. Red Canyon and U-12 is north. The southern boundary of the Paunsaugunt are the Pink, White, and Vermillion cliffs. The Sevier Valley and US-89 is the west boundary. Major Powell named the plateau with a Piute Indian name that means "place or home of the beavers."
175, 314, 496, 531(1 July 1934 to 31 June 1935).

PAUTCH CREEK (Washington). See Beaver Dam Wash.

PAUVAN is an early variant of Pavant.

PAVANT MOUNTAINS (Sevier). See Pavant Plateau.

PAVANT PLATEAU (Millard, Sevier) is the most northern of the three plateaus that make up Dutton's westernmost range of High Plateaus of Utah. It is bordered on the north by Scipio* and on the west by Holden* and Fillmore*. The Tushars are south and the Sevier River is east. Dutton describes the plateau as being made up of tertiary beds with a rigorously even stratification of pink, carmine, and cream, alternating with almost pure white formations. The name is Piute and means "water people." Variants: Pah Vant, Pauvan, etc. There are numerous "Pavant" place names on the maps, spelled in various ways.
175, 314, 422, 466(27 Jan. 1983), 496, 497, 567.

PAYSON* (Utah) is near I-15 and US-91, thirteen miles south of Provo*. An early name was Peteetneet* or Fort Peteetneet* for Chief Peteetneet and his people, who camped on the site at Peteetneet Creek. James Pace, John Courtland, A. J. Stewart, their families, and other Mormon pioneers settled there in 1850 and for a while after March 1851 the settlement was known as Pacen*. Pacen was changed to Payson when the town was incorporated on January 21, 1853, under Utah territorial law.

S8,9,16,17,T9S,R2E,SLM; 4,648' (1,417m).
27, 100(v5,17), 168, 270, 289, 314, 542,
546.

PAYSON CANYON (Utah) originates in
the mountains southeast of Payson* and
northeast of Mount Nebo. It empties into
the Utah Valley near Payson. Peteetneet
Creek drains through the canyon that
received its name from the town of
Payson.
S15,T10S,R2E,SLM to S21,T9S,R2E,SLM.

PAYSON LAKES (Utah) are a cluster of
small lakes midway up Payson Canyon.
SW¼,R3E,T10S,SLM; 7,900' (2,408m).

PEARL LAKE (Duchesne) is in the
Mirror Lake region in the western
section of the Uinta Mountains near
Scout Lake. It was named for its clarity
and beauty.
S22,T4N,R9W,USM; 10,390' (3,167m). 530.

PEARL LAKE (Uintah) is in the eastern
section of the Uinta Mountains on the
headwaters of the Whiterocks River, East
Fork. The lake was named after Pearl
Walkup in 1934 by U.S. Forest Service
Ranger George Walkup.
S35,T5N,R1W,USM; 10,700' (3,261m). 309.

PEERLESS* (Carbon) was in Spring
Canyon west of Helper*. It was first
settled in 1912 and was named after the
local coal mine. Peerless peaked around
the 1920s and 1930s, but the community
soon began to fade because improved
transportation allowed the miners to
commute from Helper.
S17,T13S,R9E,SLM; 6,400' (1,951m). 89,
516, 607.

PEGASUS ARCH (San Juan). See
Angel Arch (San Juan).

PELICAN LAKE (Uintah) is seven miles
north of Ouray* on U-88. Numerous
water birds, including the white pelican,
use the lake.
S20,21,T7S,R20E,SLM; 4,797' (1,462m).

PELICAN POINT (Box Elder) is a sand-
spit on the south end of Hat Island in
the Great Salt Lake. Thousands of
pelicans and other water birds congregate
on the point. See Hat Island.

PENNELL CREEK (Garfield) originates
four and one-half miles southeast of
Mount Pennell in the Henry Mountains.
It drains southwest into Bullfrog Creek.
See Mount Pennell for name source.
S29,T33S,R11E,SLM to SW¼,T34S,R10E,
SLM.

PENNELLEN PASS (Garfield) is a
mountain pass in the Henry Mountains
between Mount Ellen and Mount
Pennell.
S21,T32S,R10E,SLM; 7,857' (2,395m).

PENROSE* (Box Elder) is four miles
south of Thatcher* and southwest of
Tremonton*. It is an agricultural community named for Charles W. Penrose, a
noted editor, poet, composer, and
Mormon church official.
T11N,R4W,SLM; 4,300' (1,311m). 139, 542,
546, 567.

PEOA* (Summit) is nine miles north of
Kamas* on US-189. It was settled in
1857 by Judge William W. Phelps along
with several others. Phelps named the
town an Indian name, Pe-oh-a, "to
marry," which was found carved on a log
at the site.
S23,T1S,R5E,SLM; 6,190' (1,887m). 100
(v17), 289, 542, 546, 567.

PERRY* (Box Elder) is a small
community three miles south of Brigham
City*, which was settled by William
Plummer Tippets in 1853, then later by
Lorenzo Perry. Originally it was called
Porters Spring* for Orrin Porter
Rockwell, the original white landowner.
Later it became Three Mile Creek*
because its location is three miles south
of Brigham City. The name change to
Perry honored Lorenzo Perry, first
Mormon bishop of the town.

T8N,R2W,SLM; 4,358' (1,328m). 100(v17), 139, 289, 488, 567.

PERRY CANYON (Box Elder) originates three miles northwest of Perry Reservoir, with Three Mile Creek draining through it.
S2,T8N,R2W,SLM (at mouth).

PERRY RESERVOIR (Box Elder) is at the head of Perry Canyon east of Perry*.
S16,T8N,R1W,SLM; 7,700' (2,347m).

PESHLIKI FORK (Garfield) originates east of Mount Ellsworth in the southern Henry Mountains. It drains south into Ticaboo Creek. Cass Hite named Ticaboo Creek and the fork was named for Cass's Navajo Indian name, Peshliki, which means "silver" (Peshlaki). Cass Hite was a prospector who was constantly hunting for the big strike. See Hite*.
S32,T35S,R13E,SLM.

PET HOLLOW (Garfield) originates eight miles northeast of Canaan Peak. It drains northeast into Upper Valley Creek. A favored pet cow grazed in the hollow.
S30,T35S,R2E,SLM (at mouth). 12.

PETEETNEET* (Utah). See Payson*.

PETEETNEET CREEK (Utah) originates northeast of Mount Nebo. It drains down Payson Canyon into Utah Lake. Chief Peteetneet was a friendly Indian who camped on the creek with his people. He died near Camp Floyd in January 1862. See Payson*.
S14,T20S,R2E,SLM (at head). 100(v6), 546, 604. D.L. 6803.

PETERS CANYON (San Juan) originates eight miles north of Monticello* at Peters Spring. It drains north, emptying into Dry Valley at Church Rock. See Peters Spring.
S23,24,T32S,R23E,SLM to S23,T31S,R23E, SLM.

PETERS LEAP (Washington) is on Leap Creek, which originates near Anderson Valley, five miles southwest of New Harmony*. It drains southeast into Ash Creek. Peter Shirts (Shurtz) was paid three hundred dollars to build a road into Utah's Dixie over the formidable Black Ridge. At one point they had to dismantle their wagons to get them over the ridge. That was Peters Leap.
S6-36,T39S,R13W,SLM.

PETERS NIPPLE (San Juan) is a geologic formation five miles southeast of Aneth*. It was named after Peter Shirts, who was an early settler in the area. Shirts was a legendary figure who seemed to appear in areas destined to be settled by others. In 1852 he founded Hamilton* on Shirts Creek, south of Cedar City*. In the winter of 1865 and 1866 he holed up with a cluster of Indians on the Paria* site. On June 2, 1879, he was visited by members of the Hole-in-the-Rock expedition at the mouth of Montezuma Wash. Shirts had gone into San Juan country in 1877. See Hamilton* (Iron), Shirts Creek (Iron).
S36,T41S,R25E,SLM; 5,141' (1,567m). 131, 600.

PETERS POINT (San Juan) is at the north end of Peters Point Ridge, one and one-half miles west of Peters Canyon and seven miles north of Monticello*. See Peters Spring for name source.
S2,3,T32S,R23E,SLM; 7,233' (2,205m).

PETERS POINT RIDGE (San Juan) has a northeast-southwest orientation extending from the north end of the Abajo Mountains and ending at Peters Point. See Peters Spring for name source.
T32S,R22,23E,SLM.

PETERS SINK (Cache) is three miles west southwest of Bear Lake Summit, between Logan* and Garden City*. The area is nationally known for its extremely cold winter temperatures. MRN
T14N,R4E,SLM; 8,092' (2,466m).

PETERS SPRING (**San Juan**) is at the head of Peters Canyon, seven miles north of Monticello* near US-163. Peters (no first name has been recorded) drove two thousand head of cattle into the area in 1880. He made his headquarters at the spring and built a rock cabin nearby.
S24,T32S,R23E,SLM; 6,845' (2,086m). 406, 475, 555(v32).

PETERSBORO* (**Cache**) was a small community settled in the 1860s that concentrated on a dry-farming type of agriculture. It was named for Peter Maughan and was eventually absorbed into Mendon*.
567.

PETERSBURG* (**Millard**). See Hatton*.

PETERSON* (**Morgan**) is on Peterson Creek and I-80N, seven miles northwest of Morgan*. It was first settled in 1855 and named Weber City* because of its proximity to the Weber River. The name was changed in honor of Charles Shreeve Peterson, an early settler.
S6,T4N,R2E,SLM; 4,900' (1,494m). 289, 378, 542, 546.

PETERSON CREEK (**Morgan**) originates southwest of Peterson* and drains into the Weber River. It receives its name from the community it serves.
T4N,R1,2E,SLM.

PETERSON FLAT (**Beaver**) is in the Tushar Mountains between Gunsight Flat and Iant Ridge. It was named for J. L. Peterson, who was killed when his team of horses ran away with a load of lumber.
S26,T29S,R5W,SLM; 9,800' (2,987m).

PETES MESA (**Wayne**) is six miles northwest of The Confluence and north of The Maze. Pete Massett, an early sheep man, ran his sheep there in the early 1900s.
S32,T29S,R18S,SLM; 5,464' (1,665m). 102.

PETIT LAKE (**Summit**) is at the west end of the Uinta Mountains between Wall Lake and Cliff Lake and is east of Mount Watson. It is a small pond-like lake.
S31,T1S,R9E,SLM; ca. 10,300' (3,139m). 530.

PETTYVILLE* (**Sanpete**). See Sterling*.

PHIL PICO MOUNTAIN (**Daggett**) is in the northeast section of the Uinta Mountains near the Wyoming line. Corson Peak is the high point of the mountain. The name comes from Phil Pico, a man who ran his livestock in the area.
S20,29,T3N,R18E,SLM; 9,575' (2,918m).

PHINNEY LAKE (**Duchesne**) is in the central section of the Uinta Mountains on the headwaters of Fall Creek, which drains into Rock Creek. Dean Phinney was a forest ranger who loved to fish in the lake.
S27,T4N,R7W,SLM; 10,625' (3,238m). 595.

PHIPPS ARCH (**Garfield**) is in Phipps Wash (Canyon). See the wash for name source.
S24,T35S,R4E,SLM.

PHIPPS WASH (**Garfield**) originates ten miles east of Escalante* and drains north into the Escalante River. Washington Phipps was an Escalante* stockman who ran his cattle in the wash that was wide enough to be good pastureland. On November 30, 1878, he was killed by John F. Boynton.
S18,T35S,R35E,SLM (at mouth). 12, 315, 602.

PHOEBE LAKE (**Salt Lake**) is a small lake near Annette Lake.

PHONOLITE HILL (**Piute**) is in Kingston Canyon, east of Kingston* and north of the East Fork of the Sevier River. The name comes from the

principal rock the hill is composed of, phonolite, a gray-green lava that rings and reverberates when it is struck.
S14,23,T30S,R2½W,SLM; 7,915' (2,412m).

PICACHO PEAK (Beaver) is the high point at the south end of the Star Range, southwest of Milford*. The name is Piute Indian and means a sharp peak.
S25,T28S,R12W,SLM; 6,871' (2,094m).

PICKLEVILLE* (Rich) is a small community on US-30 at the southwest corner of Bear Lake. It was originally agricultural but is now rapidly becoming a condominium and private home complex. Charles C. Pickel was an engineer who supervised improvement of the town's water supply.
S28,33,T14N,R5E,SLM; 5,940' (1,811m). 100 (v17), 542. D.L. 7203.

PICTURE GALLERY* (Grand) is an area on Coates Creek and the Utah-Colorado border known for its picturesque ranches and open pastoral beauty. The Picture Gallery Ranch is near the center of the region.
S29,T21S,R26E,SLM; 6,249' (1,905m). 146.

PICTURESQUE LAKE (Summit) is in the Uinta Mountains southwest of Scout Lake. It is in a picturesque setting of high mountains, numerous lakes, and evergreen forests.
S23,T1S,R9E,SLM; 10,390' (3,167m).

PIGEON CREEK (Juab) originates in the San Pitch Mountains, five miles southwest of Fountain Green*. It drains into Juab Valley at Levan*. In season, the lower part of the creek swarms with mourning doves.
S28,T14S,R2E,SLM to S32,T14S,R1E,SLM.

PIGEON HOLLOW (Sanpete) has Pigeon Hollow Junction, where U-11 and US-89 join, on its west side. Mourning doves, commonly known as pigeons, were plentiful in the hollow.
S14,T16S,R3E,SLM; 5,800' (1,768m).

PIGEON MILK SPRING (Duchesne) is a trailside spring south of Naturalist Basin at the west base of Rocky Sea Pass. The spring water is not palatable and the milky color is produced by minerals suspended in the water.
S3,T3N,R8W,USM.

PIGEON MOUNTAIN (Box Elder) is in the western part of the Great Salt Lake Desert, eight miles east of Lucin*. Thousands of wild pigeons (mourning doves) congregate in this area.
S1,2,11,T7N,R17W; 5,369' (1,636m). 567.

PILAR, EL RIO DEL (Washington) was Domínguez's and Escalante's name for Ash Creek.
327, 583.

PILOT PEAK (state of Nevada). Even though Pilot Peak is in Nevada, it is close to the Utah border and is included because it was so important in Utah history. It is north of Wendover* and was a landmark to all immigrant parties moving west in this part of the country, especially the Donner-Reed party. Various explorers, mountain men, trappers, and Indians also used the peak as their guide. It could be seen from great distances as migrating parties crossed the Great Salt Lake Desert. It was named by J. C. Fremont as quoted by Creer (1947), "To the friendly mountain, I gave the name of Pilot Peak."
S8,T36N,R70E (in Nevada); 10,716' (3,266m). 100(v17), 129, 371, 506, 567.

PILOT RANGE (Utah-Nevada border) received its name from its highest peak, The Pilot, north of Wendover*. See Pilot Peak.

PILOT SPRINGS (Box Elder) is four miles southeast of Cedar Creek* in Curlew Valley. This area marks the separation of the early immigration trails moving westward.
S13,T14N,R11W,SLM; 4,655' (1,419m). 567.

PINE CANYON (**Rich**) originates in the high country east of the south end of Bear Lake where it drains west into the lake. Blue spruce and Douglas fir were harvested in the canyon for the nearby sawmills.
S15,16,20,T13N,R6E,SLM. 567.

PINE CANYON (**Tooele**) originates on the western slopes of the Oquirrh Mountains and drains west into the valley. See Lincoln*.
S11,14,T3S,R4W,SLM (at mouth).

PINE CLIFF* (**Summit**) was a sheep and cattle company fifteen miles east of Coalville*, beyond Upton*. The name is descriptive of the surroundings.
S26,T3N,R7E,SLM; 6,706' (2,044m). 567.

PINE CREEK* (**Beaver**) was an early settlement of the late 1860s and early 1870s located on the old road which later became US-91. The settlement was built on Pine Creek as it emerged from the north end of the Tushar Mountains. A stage station was built there, which was owned and operated by George Williams. He also built cabins, a small store, and operated a U.S. mail drop. The settlement took the name of the creek.
S35,T26S,R7W, 6,200' (1,890m). 125, 355.

PINE CREEK (**Beaver**) originates in the northern Tushar Mountains. It drains northwest into Cove Creek. There is a heavy growth of ponderosa pine in the region.
T26S,R6W,SLM.

PINE CREEK (**Beaver**) originates on the southwest slopes of Mount Baldy in the Tushar Mountains. It drains southwest into the south fork of North Creek.
T28S,R6W,SLM.

PINE CREEK (**Garfield**) originates on the Aquarius Plateau north of Escalante* and drains south into the Escalante River. Almon H. Thompson of Major Powell's surveys wrote, "Leaving the foot of Potato Valley, we travelled a little west of north up a creek called, from the many fine pine trees in its valley, Pine Creek" (422, p. 139).
S9,T35S,R3E,SLM (at mouth). 12, 315, 422.

PINE CREEK (**Piute**). See Bullion Canyon (Piute).

PINE CREEK* (**Sanpete**). See Ephraim* (Sanpete).

PINE GROVE CREEK* (**Beaver**) originates on the western slopes of the Wah Wah Mountains near Head of Pine Grove Springs and drains west into Pine Valley. The Dodd brothers from Pioche*, Nevada, settled the town in the early 1870s.
T28S,R16W,SLM. 355.

PINE HEN SPRINGS (**Beaver**) is on the western slopes of Pole Mountain of the Tushar Mountains. It drains into Drag Hollow. Pine hens were once plentiful around the springs.
S4,T28S,R6W,SLM; 8,300' (2,530m).

PINE ISLAND LAKE (**Duchesne**) is in the southwest section of the Uinta Mountains, four miles south southwest of Naturalist Basin. Several small islands are located within the lake boundary that are covered with dense growths of conifers.
S20,T3N,R8W,USM; 10,345' (3,253).

PINE LAKE (**Garfield**) is on the southwest slopes of Escalante Mountain at the mouth of Pine Canyon. The ghost town of Widtsoe* is located three miles north. The lake is in an area of evergreen trees.
S24,25,T35S,R2W,SLM; 8,192' (2,497m).

PINE SPRING (**Beaver**) is on the eastern slopes of The Needles in the northwest section of the Needle Range.
S21,T26S,R18W,SLM; 6,580' (2,006m).

PINE VALLEY (**Beaver, Millard**) is a vast region south of the Deseret Range Experiment Station between the Wah Wah Mountains and the Needle Range. The surrounding mountains are covered

with pinyon (pinenut) pine trees.
T25-29S,R16-18W,SLM;   5,000'-6,000'
(1,524m-1,829m).

PINE VALLEY (Washington) is in the
Pine Valley Mountains, twenty-five miles
north of St. George*. The region has a
heavy growth of ponderosa pine and
other coniferous trees. The first sawmills
were built in 1855-56 for providing
lumber to the surrounding communities.
T39S,R15W,SLM; 6,529' (1,990m). 100(v13),
154, 163(5 March 1856).

PINE VALLEY* (Washington) is a small
isolated community in Pine Valley of the
Pine Valley Mountains north of St.
George. It was settled in 1859 near the
head of the Santa Clara River. During
the early years it was primarily a lumber
town. In later years the town became a
small but stable community with many
luxurious homes. It was named by Isaac
Riddle, Jacob Hamblin, and others. See
Pine Valley for references.
S14,T39S,R15W,SLM; 4,500' (1,372m).

PINE   VALLEY   MOUNTAINS
(Washington) are a range of mountains
twenty miles north of St. George*. The
Santa Clara River heads in these
mountains where Pine Valley* is located.
See Pine Valley.

PINE VALLEY WASH (Beaver) originates at the south end of Pine Valley,
draining north into the Pine Valley
Hardpan. The wash received its name
from the valley.
T25-30S,R16,17W,SLM.

PINHOOK* (Grand) is a ghost town site
at the head of Pinhook Valley above
Castleton*. Moab* is fifteen miles west.
The people who lived there worked at
the mines in Miners Basin. The valley
was named Pinhook because it is shaped
like a giant fishhook.
NW¼,T26S,R24E,SLM. 146, 567.

PINK CLIFFS (Kane) range west of the
east fork of the Virgin River. Bryce

Canyon is part of this geologic formation.
Powell named the entire series of escarpments in this region. Starting with the
oldest they are the Vermillion, White,
Grey, and the Pink cliffs.
T38,39S,R6,7W,SLM. 314, 422, 496, 504,
530.

PINTO* (Washington) is twelve miles
east southeast of Enterprise* and is an
outgrowth of nearby Fort Harmony*. The
Spanish Trail passed through on its way
south toward Mountain Meadows. Both
the Utes and the Piutes occupied sites
along the creek in this area before 1856,
when Rufus C. Allen and others settled
there. There are different versions of
how the town received its name. First,
"pinto" is a Spanish word for "speckled"
or "spotted," which would describe the
area's multi-colored geologic formations.
In another version, Leigh writes that a
Piute Indian band, the Pintiats, lived
along the creek and the word "pinto"
comes from an Indian name rather than
from the Spanish.
S34,T37S,R15W,SLM; 6,052' (1,845m). 74,
136, 154, 289, 314, 542.

PINTO CREEK (Beaver) originates in
Iron County and drains northeast into
the Pine Valley Wash. "Pinto" is Spanish
for "mottled" or "speckled."
T30S,R16,17W,SLM.

PINTO LAKE (Duchesne) is at the west
end of the Uinta Mountains near the
head of Fish Creek and Governor Dern
Lake. Pinto Lake was a favorite fishing
lake of Governor Dern's. On one fishing
trip, his pinto horse died by the lake and
the carcass remained there for quite
some time. Gradually the lake was
referred to as Pinto Lake and the name
held.
S17,T3N,R8W,USM; 10,000' (3,048m). 100
(v2), 595.

PINTO PEAK (Washington) is two miles
east of the early Pinto* settlement from
which it received its name.
S1,T38S,R15W,SLM; 7,280' (2,219m).

PINTURA* (Washington) is on Ash Creek and I-15 between Cedar City* and St. George*. It was settled in 1858, then abandoned because of a lack of water, then resettled a second time. It was first named Ashton* because it was located on Ash Creek. In 1863 it was renamed Bellvue* (Bellview*) by Jacob Gates and James Sylvester because the landscape resembled the shape of a bell and the view was superb. In 1925, at the suggestion of Andy Gregerson, the name was changed to Pintura, a Spanish word meaning "painting," in reference to the nearby brightly colored hills.
S2,T40S,R13W,SLM; 4,000' (1,219m). 154, 311, 314, 542.

PIONEER TRAIL STATE PARK (Salt Lake) is at the mouth of Emigration Canyon where the Mormon pioneer trail entered the valley. Pioneer Village and the "This Is the Place" monument are located within the vicinity of the park.

PISHLAKI FORK (Garfield). See Peshliki Fork (Garfield).

PITT AND PAGE HILL (Summit) was a large expanse of timberland at the west end of the Uintas at the junction of the North Fork of the Provo River. Orson Page and Sett Pitt logged out this area prior to 1915.
S22,28,32,T2S,R8E,SLM. 298.

PITTSBURGH* (Utah) was a small mining community up the left fork of American Fork Canyon above Forest City*. It only existed during the 1870s.
SW¼,T3S,R3E,SLM. 89, 516.

PIUTE COUNTY was separated from Beaver County on January 16, 1865. The county was named after the Piute (Paiute) Indians who inhabited the region.
6.

PIUTE CREEK (San Juan) originates in Arizona and drains north into the San Juan River. The creek once represented a boundary between Paiute and Navajo territory.
S32,T41S,R11E,SLM (at mouth). 314.

PIUTE CREEK (San Juan) originates fourteen miles east of Monticello* near Piute Knolls. It drains southeast into Colorado. This was all Paiute country at one time.
S17,T33S,R26E,SLM (at head).

PIUTE FARMS* (San Juan) is an Indian settlement near the San Juan River at the northwest boundary of Monument Valley.
S2,T41S,R14E,SLM.

PIUTE MESA (San Juan) has a north-south orientation between Piute Creek and Nokai Canyon. The San Juan River is the northern boundary. The name "Piute" is a corruption of Paiute, which means either Pure Ute or Water Ute. The question has never been settled. There are several spellings, Pa-Ute, Pah Ute, etc.
314.

PIUTE RESERVOIR (Piute) is in the Sevier River Valley, northeast of Junction* near US-89. It received its name from the Paiute Indian Tribe that occupied this region.
T29S,R3W,SLM; 5,996' (1,828m). 285, 314.

PIUTE SPRINGS* (San Juan) is east of Monticello* near the Utah-Colorado border. The Old Spanish Trail passed by the springs, which were a favorite camping place for the Paiute Indians. Soldiers assigned to the region also camped there. In the 1880s the Carlisle Cattle Company used the springs for their headquarters. In May 1881 the Paiute Indians killed three white men, Smith, Thurman, and May, while they were camped at the springs. In 1913, after the free cattle range period, Mr. and Mrs. H. U. Butt homesteaded at the springs where they built their home.
S21,T33S,R26E,SLM; 6,800' (2,073m). 314, 330, 406.

PLAIN CITY* (Weber) is five miles northwest of Ogden*. It was initially settled in 1859 as a consolidation of Skeen*, North Weber*, and Poplar*. The settlers were former residents of Lehi*: Daniel Collet, Joseph Skeen, their families, and others, who agreed on City of the Plains* for the settlement name. This was later changed to Plain City because the town is located in a large open flat valley.
S32,33,28,T7N,R2W,SLM; 4,237' (1,291m). 100(v17), 274, 289, 542, 567.

PLAINFIELD* (Grand) was an early uranium mining settlement southwest of Moab* in upper Spanish Valley. It was also known as Bueno* and Poverty Flat*. The town was later absorbed into Moab. See Moab*.
T27,R23E,SLM. 514, 516.

PLEASANT CREEK (Sanpete) originates in the mountains east of Mount Pleasant at the junction of Straight and Blue Slide forks. It drains west into the San Pitch River. It was named for its pleasing surroundings.
S10,T15S,R5E,SLM to S32,T14S,R5E,SLM.

PLEASANT CREEK (Wayne) originates at Noon Lake and Pleasant Creek Meadow on the Boulder Mountain section of the Aquarius Plateau. The creek drains northeast into the Fremont River. A. H. Thompson named the creek because he and his group thought the groves of cottonwood trees made the area a pleasant place to be.
T30,31S,R5-8E,SLM. 159, 422.

PLEASANT CREEK* (Wayne). See Notom* (Wayne).

PLEASANT CREEK SETTLEMENT* (Sanpete). See Mount Pleasant* (Sanpete).

PLEASANT DALE* (Wayne). See Notom* (Wayne).

PLEASANT GROVE* (Utah) is on US-89 between American Fork* and Lindon*. It was established by whites in 1849 when a Mormon group, including William H. Adams, Philo T. Farnsworth, and John Mercer, settled there. They built a fort and named it Grove Fort*. After an early disagreement with local Indians under Roman Nose, the settlement became Battle Creek* and then Stringtown* because the first homes were built in a line along the creek. In March 1851 the name was changed to Pleasant Grove for the grove of cottonwood trees where the first pioneers settled.
S20,21,28,29,T5S,R2E,SLM; 4,623'(1,409m). 27, 129, 270, 384, 546.

PLEASANT SPRING* (Tooele). See Simpsons Spring* (Tooele).

PLEASANT VALLEY* (Carbon). See Winter Quarters* (Carbon).

PLEASANT VALLEY (Millard) is on the Nevada-Utah line, with Uvada* in the valley. In 1850 H. J. Faust, Howard Egan, and Al Huntington explored the valley while searching for a mail route to California.
100(v13), 347.

PLEASANT VALLEY CREEK (Carbon) originates at the junction of Long and Snyder canyons and drains north into the Scofield Reservoir. It had pleasant surroundings and an appealing view.
S4,T14S,R7E,SLM to S29,T12S,R7E,SLM.

PLEASANT VALLEY JUNCTION* (Utah). See Colton*.

PLEASANT VIEW* (Weber) is one and one-half miles northwest of North Ogden*. In 1851, it became an outgrowth of North Ogden when John and Sarah Ann Mower moved there to establish their new home, which was a one-room log cabin. From this location they had a beautiful view of the surrounding valley.

S30,T7N,R1W,SLM; 4,398' (1,341m). 100 (v5), 274, 542.

PLEASANT VIEW* (Utah) is a small subdivision in northeast Provo* near the mouth of Rock Canyon. One can get an excellent view of the valley from this location.
S30,31,T7S,R3E,SLM; 4,680' (1,426m).

PLYMOUTH* (Box Elder) is on I-15 south of the Idaho border. The town was settled in 1869 and named Squaretown* because the first four families built homes on adjoining corners of four sections of land. It was previously named Settlement over the Ridge* for a short period of time. Finally it was renamed Plymouth by Myron Abbott for the imagined resemblance of a nearby large rock to Plymouth Rock.
S12,T13N,R3W,SLM; 4,400' (1,341m). 100 (v17), 139, 488, 542, 567.

PLYMPTON RIDGE (Millard) is a large semi-circular ridge near Cowboy Pass, with Disappointment Hills to the north. It was named after Lieutenant W. L. Plympton, who was undertaking a wagon road survey with Captain Simpson. There are some springs in the vicinity that are also named for the lieutenant.
S2,T16S,R17W,SLM; 7,197' (2,194m). 477.

POCKETVILLE* (Washington). See Virgin* (Washington).

PODUNK CREEK (Kane) originates on the southwest section of Bryce Canyon National Park at the Pink Cliffs. It drains northwest into the east fork of the Sevier River. The name was created when Po Dunk, a Piute Indian, was lost for a period of time in this heavily timbered region.
S13,T38S,R4½W,SLM (at mouth). 567.

POINT LOOKOUT (Box Elder) is three miles west of Tremonton* at the south tip of Point Lookout Mountain. Sentinels were kept there to watch for Colonel Albert Sidney Johnston's army that was believed to be coming to exterminate them. They had a large pile of sagebrush ready to ignite if necessary.
S6,T11N,R3W,SLM; 4,450' (1,356m). 567.

POINT LOOKOUT MOUNTAIN (Box Elder). See Point Lookout (Box Elder).

POINT OF THE MOUNTAIN (Salt Lake, Utah). At this point, which is the boundary between Salt Lake and Utah valleys, the wave action of ancient Lake Bonneville formed a massive land barrier. When the Jordan River cut through this barrier, it created the Jordan Narrows and on the east, a gigantic spit called the Point of the Mountain.
S23,24,T4S,R1W,SLM; 5,148' (1,569m).

POISON CREEK (Beaver) originates on the western slopes of Delano Peak of the Tushar Mountains, draining southwest into Merchant Creek. The creek has plants growing along its banks that are poisonous to livestock.
S14,T28S,R5W,SLM. 125.

POISON CREEK (Garfield) originates on the western slopes of Escalante Mountain on the Aquarius Plateau. It drains northwest into Antimony Creek. The plants which grow along the creek are poisonous to sheep.
S23,T31S,R2W,SLM (at mouth). 567.

POISON SPRING (Garfield) is in the Henry Mountains, four miles east of Bull Mountain at the head of Poison Spring Canyon. The water, although tainted, can be drunk.
S1,T31S,R11E,SLM. 25, 303.

POISON SPRING BENCH (Emery) is six miles north of Huntington*. The settlers of 1877 named it once they realized that the spring water was too alkaline to drink.
T16S,R9E,SLM; 6,800' (2,073m).

POISON SPRING BENCHES (Garfield) are at the head of Poison Spring Canyon in the Henry Mountains. See Poison

Spring (Garfield) for name source.
S6,7,T31S,R12E,SLM; 5,100' (1,554m).

POISON SPRING CANYON (Garfield) originates in the Henry Mountains, four miles east of Bull Mountain where it drains east into the Dirty Devil River. See Poison Spring (Garfield) for name source.
S1,T31S,R11E,SLM to T31S,R13E,SLM.

POISON MESA (Grand) has an east-west orientation along Agate Wash, eight miles east of Arches National Park. The soil of the mesa contains arsenic, which kills sheep that graze in the area.
S31,34,T22S,R22E,SLM; 4,800' (1,463m).

POLAR MESA (Grand) is four miles south of the Dolores River between Fisher Valley and Beaver Creek. During the winter, temperatures at the top of the mesa are bitterly cold.
S25,35,T24S,R25E,SLM; 7,500' (2,286m). 146.

POLE CANYON (Beaver) originates on the western slopes of the central Tushar Mountains and drains north into Indian Creek. The quaking aspens found in the canyon produced good fence posts.
S28,33,T27S,R6W,SLM. 125.

POLE CANYON (Beaver) originates in the Mineral Mountains on the west slope of Harkley Mountain. It drains west into the Beaver River. Logs were hauled from the canyon for building cabins in nearby settlements.
S30,32,T28S,R9W,SLM.

POLE CANYON (Grand) originates on the southern slopes of the La Sal Mountains, draining south past the town of La Sal*. La Sal settlers harvested lumber from this canyon in order to build their homes.

POLE CREEK (Beaver) originates on the southwest slopes of Mount Baldy in the Tushar Mountains. It drains southwest into North Creek, North Fork.

Prior to 1870, Philo Carter hauled poles from the canyon for local use.
S12,15,T29S,R6W,SLM.

POLE CREEK (Duchesne) originates at Pole Creek Lake in the south central section of the Uinta Mountains. It drains south southeast. Lumber was harvested in the canyon.
S12,T3N,R2W,USM to S36,T2N,R2W,USM.

POLE CREEK (San Juan) flows east into Salt Creek from northeast of Abajo Peak. A great deal of the lumber used for construction in Monticello* was taken from this canyon.
530.

POLE CREEK LAKE (Duchesne) is in the south central section of the Uinta Mountains, at the head of Pole Creek from which it receives its name. It drains south into the Uinta River.
S12,T3N,R2W,USM; 10,151' (3,094m).

POLE HEAVEN (Utah) originates three miles east northeast of Springville*. It drains east into the left fork of Hobble Creek. Aaron Johnson named it because there was a large amount of pole lumber available in the vicinity.
S20,21,30,T7S,R4E,SLM. 270.

POLLY MESA (San Juan) is at the head of Slickhorn Canyon, north of the San Juan River and east of Grand Gulch.
T39S,R17E,SLM; 5,975' (1,821m).

POLLYS PASTURE (San Juan) is on Polly Mesa.

POLLYWOG LAKE (Garfield) is on the northwest slopes of the Aquarius Plateau, east southeast of Antimony*. It is a small marshy lake shaped like a pollywog.
S19,20,T31S,R1E,SLM; 9,175' (2,797m).

POND TOWN* (Utah). See Salem* (Utah).

PONDEROSA CANYON (Kane) origi-nates one mile north of Rainbow Point in Bryce Canyon National Park, draining east. The local cattlemen and sheep men named it for the preponderance of western yellow pine (*Pinus ponderosa*) in the region. Variant: Shumway Canyon for Charles Shumway, pioneer of Johnson*, who ran his livestock in the canyon. T38S,R4W,SLM. 530, 567.

PONDEROSA PARK (**Beaver**) is one and one-half miles up Beaver River Canyon in the Tushar Mountains. The name comes from the pleasant picnic area U.S. Forest Service and U.S. Civilian Conservation Corps personnel built. The picnic area is located in a large grove of ponderosa pine trees. S26,T29S,R6W,SLM; 7,200' (2,195m). 125.

PONDEROSA RIDGE (**Kane**) is between Bull Valley and Ponderosa Canyon near the southern boundary of Bryce Canyon National Park. It was named for the ponderosa pine.

PONDS, THE (**Summit**) is a small pond-like lake at the western end of the Uinta Mountains, one-half mile southwest of Wall Lake. S31,T1S,R9E,SLM; 10,350' (3,155m). 530.

PONY EXPRESS CANYON (**Tooele**) is at the north end of the Deep Creek Mountains, draining west into Deep Creek Valley. The Pony Express passed the canyon. S29,30,T8S,R18W,SLM.

POPLAR* (**Weber**). See Plain City* (Weber).

POPLAR GROVE* (**Salt Lake**) was a small community that has been absorbed into Salt Lake City*. It was on the west bank of the Jordan River in a cluster of cottonwood trees.

POPPERTON* (**Salt Lake**). See Federal Heights*.

PORCUPINE CANYON (**Beaver**) originates on the eastern slopes of Granite Peak in the Mineral Mountains. It drains southeast into Wild Cat Creek. Porcupine are plentiful in the canyon. S17,18,T28S,R8W,SLM.

PORCUPINE CREEK (**Cache**) originates at Porcupine Ridge seven miles southeast of Avon*. It drains west into Porcupine Reservoir in East Canyon. Porcupine are abundant in the area. S27-S17,T9N,R2E,SLM.

PORCUPINE MOUNTAIN (**Summit**) is the high point of Porcupine Ridge. S1,T3N,R7E,SLM; 9,195' (2,803m).

PORCUPINE RESERVOIR (**Cache**) is four miles east southeast of Avon* on the east fork of the Little Bear River. The reservoir received its name from the creek. S17,T9N,R2E,SLM; 5,381' (1,640m).

PORCUPINE RIDGE (**Summit**) has a north-south orientation east of Avon* and south of Porcupine Reservoir. The numerous porcupines in the area caused problems for the sheep and especially sheepdogs who were continually getting quills in their faces. Occasionally the situation was so serious that the sheep had to be moved from the region. T9N,R2E,SLM; 8,500' (2,591m). 100(v17), 567.

PORCUPINE RIM (**Grand**) is a twelve-mile-long escarpment along the western boundary of Castle Valley. The name came from nearby Porcupine Draw where porcupines are a problem. T24-26S,R22,23E,SLM. 146.

PORTAGE* (**Box Elder**) is west of I-15 and south of the Idaho line. It was settled in 1867 by people from Wellsville*. It had an early name of Hay Town*, which refers to the large hay fields growing there. S6,T14N,R3W,SLM.

PORTER CANYON (**Garfield**) originates on the Sunset Cliffs east of Hatch*.

It drains northwest into the Sevier River. It was named after L. L. Porter, who lived in Hatch.
S25,T36S,R6W,SLM (at mouth).

PORTERS SPRINGS* (Box Elder). See Perry*.

PORTERVILLE* (Morgan) is four miles southwest of Morgan* at the junction of Hardscrabble and East canyons. It was named for Sanford and Warriner Porter, the first settlers who came over the mountain from Centerville*. The Porters also built the first sawmill there.
S24,T3N,R2E,SLM; 5,160' (1,573m). 289, 378, 542, 567.

POST, THE (Garfield) was an old cottonwood tree that cowboys hitched their horses to on the Burr Trail, southwest of Mt. Pennell and north of Halls Crossing. Today it is a point where backpackers gauge their distance while hiking in the region.
SW¼,T34S,R8E,SLM.

POST OF BEAVER* (Beaver). See Fort Cameron* (Beaver).

POSY CANYON (San Juan) originates on the Chippean Ridge of the Abajo Mountains, draining south into Cottonwood Creek. Posy was a local Ute Indian chief who had difficulty adjusting to the encroachment of the white people. He was severely wounded during an Indian-white altercation. Posy escaped into the wilderness country west of Blanding where he was found dead near Mule Creek sometime later. This 1923 incident was often blown out of proportion as the last Indian "war" in the United States.
T35S,R20E,SLM. 406, 409, 546.

POSY LAKE (Garfield). See Lake Posey (Garfield).

POSY SPRING (Garfield) is one-half mile east of Lake Posy. See Posy Canyon for name source.

POT CREEK (Daggett, Uintah) originates northeast of Vernal* on the southwest slopes of Mount Lena, draining through Crouse Reservoir into the Green River. Three masked robbers, recorded as Matt Warner, Elza Lay, and Lew McCarty, robbed a pot peddler along the creek. They took his money and valuables, then scattered his pots and pans along the creek. The pots and pans eventually ended up in the homes of Browns Park residents.
S35,T1N,R22E,SLM to S1,T2S,R25E,SLM (in Utah). 80, 303, 567.

POT GUT (Beaver) is on the southwest slopes of the Tushar Mountains where the South Creek Road crosses South Creek and climbs up a narrow and precipitous gulch.
S7,T30S,R6W,SLM.

POT LAKE (Summit) is in the southwest section of the Uinta Mountains near Weir and Duck lakes. In the early history of the Uinta Mountains, before many lakes were named, they were designated by letters, such as "T" for Teapot Lake and "P" for Pot Lake. Both lakes are shaped like a pot.
S2,T2S,R8E,USM; 9,900' (3,018m). 379.

POTATO VALLEY* (Garfield). See Escalante* (Garfield).

POTATO VALLEY (Garfield) is at the junction of Alvey Wash and the Escalante River. The valley was originally discovered by whites in 1875 when a group from Panguitch* arrived in search of a milder climate. At the same time, Captain James Andrus arrived with his cavalrymen in pursuit of Indians. These two groups, in addition to the local Indians, subsisted on the wild potato (*Solanum jamesii*) growing in the valley. The variant name is Spud Valley.
T35S,R3E,SLM; 5,812' (1,771m). 12, 385, 496, 602.

POTHOLES, THE (Sevier) is a cluster of small ponds and lakes at the junction of the right and left forks of U M Creek, three miles west of Hilgard Mountain. S29,32,T24S,R3E,SLM; 9,450' (2,880m).

POTTAWATTAMIE* (Rich). See Round Valley*. 289.

POVERTY FLAT* (Grand) was an early name that is still used for the Bueno* or Plainfield* areas near Moab*. See Moab*.

POVERTY FLAT* (Wayne). See Torrey*.

POWELL LAKE (Duchesne) is in the southwest section of the Uinta Mountains on the upper Fish Creek drainage near Governor Dern Lake. It was named for Major John Wesley Powell, who was in charge of the Colorado and Green River explorations of 1869-72. See Mount Powell. S27,T3N,R8W,USM; 9,975' (3,040m). 100 (v2), 496.

POWELL POINT (Kane) is the southern section of the Table Cliff Plateau and Escalante Mountain. Almon Thompson named the area after Major Powell in 1872. See Powell Lake and Mount Powell. T26S,R1W,SLM; 10,188' (3,105m). 567.

PRATTS SIDING* (Carbon). See Helper* (Carbon).

PRATTVILLE* (Sevier) is at a point on the Sevier River, four miles east of Richfield*. On June 21, 1873, a group of Mormon pioneers arrived and established their community, which was named Prattville after Helaman Pratt. Unfortunately, the settlers soon moved to other locations because the soil was too alkaline and waterlogged for their purposes. S27,T23S,R2W,SLM; 5,250' (1,600m). 360.

PREACHER CANYON (Grand) originates on the East Tavaputs Plateau at the south end of Snowshoe and Cedar Camp ridges. It drains southeast into Hay Canyon. MRN S25,T16S,R22E,SLM to T17S,R23E,SLM.

PRESIDENT NATURAL BRIDGE (San Juan). See Natural Bridges National Monument (San Juan).

PRICE* (Carbon) is a focal-point city of the coal industry in Utah. It is at the junction of US-6 and U-10 between Green River* and Provo*. In 1869 William Price explored the region and named the Price River. The settlement was named after the river. S16,21,T14S,R10E,SLM; 5,550' (1,692m). 100(v17), 289, 314, 546, 567.

PRICE* (Washington) was originally settled in 1858 south of St. George and Bloomington*. It was initiated under the United Order with the name Heberville*, honoring Heber C. Kimball, a Mormon church authority. It was abandoned in 1859-60 because of floods and sickness, but was resettled in 1874 under the name Price. By the early 1900s the site was completely deserted. 89, 154, 311, 516.

PRICE CANYON (Carbon) originates on the west summit of the Roan Cliffs, draining south southeast. The mouth of the canyon is at Helper* and the Price River drains through it. See Price River for name source. T12,13S,R9W,SLM.

PRICE RIVER (Carbon) originates at Scofield Reservoir and drains southeast into the Green River at Gray Canyon. It had an early name of White River but was changed in 1865 when William Price, a Mormon bishop in Goshen*, explored the region and renamed it. T15,16S,R11,12E,SLM (at mouth). 100(v17), 159, 314, 409. D.L. 6901.

PRIEST AND NUNS (Grand) are a row of monolithic sandstone figures in Castle Valley, with Moab* on the west and the

Colorado River on the northwest.
T25S,R23E,SLM.

PRIESTHOOD CAMP* (Salt Lake) was a small mining settlement established in the early 1870s, approximately nine miles up City Creek Canyon northeast of the state capitol building. The men there worked the mines near the mouth of Cottonwood Gulch. MRN
S7,T1N,R2E,SLM. 49.

PRITCHETT ARCH (Grand) is a natural geologic window near the head of Pritchett Canyon. See Pritchett Canyon for name source.
T26S,R21E,SLM.

PRITCHETT CANYON (Grand) originates five miles south of Moab*, draining northwest into the Colorado River. Thomas Pritchett came into the Spanish Valley in 1880 and was the first justice of the peace. He lived with a group of people in a fort in Pritchett Canyon during the winter of 1880-81.
S22,23,25,T26S,R21E,SLM. 514.

PROCTOR* (Garfield) was one of the early settlements that eventually consolidated with Hatch*. It was on a side creek near the head of the Sevier River. See Asay* and Hatch*.
516.

PROCTOR CANYON (Garfield) originates on the northwest slopes of the Sunset Cliffs, five miles west of the Tropic Reservoir. It drains northwest into the Sevier River. The name comes from Bill Proctor, who homesteaded in the canyon.
S9,T37S,R4½W,SLM to S22,T36S,R5W,SLM. 508.

PROFESSOR CREEK (Grand) originates near the junction of Mary Jane and Hell Roaring canyons east of Castle Valley. It drains northwest into the Colorado River. See Richardson* for the name source.
S1,T25S,R23E,SLM.

PROFESSOR VALLEY (Grand) runs along the Colorado River midway between the Dewey Bridge and the Colorado River bridge north of Moab*. See Richardson* for name source.
S3,9,17,T24S,R23E,SLM; 4,275' (1,303m).

PROMONTORY* (Box Elder) was an early construction camp near the point where the Central Pacific Railroad from the east and the Union Pacific Railroad from the west met on May 10, 1869. It was a typical roisterous camp until it was decided that it would become the meeting place for the two railroads. The status of the town varied from complete abandonment, to cattle town, to an honored site under the National Park Service (the Golden Spike National Historical Site). The name was taken from the large promontory projecting south into the Great Salt Lake.
T10N,R6W,SLM; 4,902' (1,494m). 89, 314, 494, 516, 542, 546.

PROMONTORY MOUNTAINS (Box Elder) ranges with a north-south orientation about twenty miles out into the north end of the Great Salt Lake. See Promontory*.
T6-10N,R5-7W,SLM; 7,372' (2,247m).

PROMONTORY POINT (Box Elder) is the southern tip of the Promontory Mountains.

PROSPECT HILL (Salt Lake). See Capitol Hill.

PROVAUX CITY* (Utah). See Provo City* (Utah).

PROVIDENCE* (Cache) was an offshoot of North Ogden*, three miles south of Logan*. The settlers who moved to the site on April 20, 1859, named it Spring Creek*, a name they also used for the creek. The postal service would not accept the name, so since circumstances for settlement appeared somewhat providential in nature, the residents decided to use Providence.

S10,11,T11N,R1E,SLM; 4,600' (1,402m).
427, 449, 567.

PROVIDENCE CANYON (Cache) origi-
nates in the Bear River Range east of
Providence*, draining west into Cache
Valley.
S13,T11N,R2E,SLM (at mouth).

PROVIDENCE LAKE (Cache) is at the
head of Providence Canyon on the
southeast slopes of Providence Peak.

PROVIDENCE PEAK (Cache) is at the
head of Providence Canyon.
T11N,R2E,SLM; 9,710' (2,960m).

PROVO* (Utah) is on I-15, forty-five
miles south of Salt Lake City*. It was
founded in 1850 as Fort Utah* in honor
of the Ute Indians who inhabited the
region. The name was changed to Fort
Provo* for the well-known French-
Canadian trapper, Etienne Proveau
(Provost, Provot, Provaux, etc.), who first
arrived in 1825. Proveau and his men
had an altercation with the local Indians
under Bad Gocha and several whites and
Indians were killed. This incident led to
the area being called Proveau's Hole and
to the city eventually being named Provo.
T6,7S,R2,3E,SLM; 4,549' (1,387m). 27, 275,
289, 314, 366, 542, 546, 555(v36,42), 604.

PROVO BENCH (Utah) is on the Provo
level or terrace of ancient Lake
Bonneville, with the town of Orem*
located in the center of the bench.
S5,T6S,R2E,SLM; 4,800' (1,463m).

PROVO CANYON (Utah) originates at
Deer Creek Reservoir, with the mouth at
Olmsted*. The Provo River drains
through the canyon.
S6,T5S,R4E,SLM to S7,T6S,R3E,SLM.

PROVO RIVER (Utah, Wasatch) origi-
nates at Washington Lake in the west
Uinta Mountains. It drains southwest into
Utah Lake. The river had the early name
of Timpanogotzis (Tumpanowach) for the
Indians living along its banks. The early

white settlers decided to name the river
after Proveau and transfer the old name
to the mountain to the north, which
became Mount Timpanogos. See Provo*
(Utah).

PRUESS LAKE (Millard) is near the
Nevada line, five miles south of
Garrison*. Charles Pruess was a cartographer who joined Fremont's first and
second expeditions.
S19,29,T22S,R19W,SLM; 5,359' (1,633m).
90, 205, 314, 494, 604.

PUDDLE VALLEY (Tooele) is west of
the Great Salt Lake and the Lakeside
Mountains. The valley has a clay base
with no drainage, so when it rains,
muddy rain puddles develop.
T2,3N,R10W,SLM.

PUFFER LAKE (Beaver) is in the
Tushar Mountains east of Beaver* at the
head of Lake Stream. J. M. Puffer, an
Indian fighter and trapper, discovered the
lake in the early 1860s. When Puffer led
a party of sportsman to the lake, they
formally named it after him.
S1,T29S,R5W,SLM; 9,672' (2,948m). 100
(v17), 125, 355.

PYRAMID LAKE (Duchesne) is in the
Murdock Basin at the west end of the
Uinta Mountains. The lake is triangular
in shape.
S15,T3N,R9W,SLM; 9,725' (2,964m). 298.

- Q -

QUAIL CREEK (Washington) originates on the southern slopes of the Pine Valley Mountains and drains south into the Virgin River. The first white settlers found numerous quail along the creek. S34,T40S,R14W,SLM. 72. D.L. 8703.

QUARTER CORNER LAKE (Summit) is in the north central section of the Uinta Mountains on a quarter corner survey point. S25,T3N,R14E,SLM; 8,913' (2,717m).

QUARTZ CREEK (Beaver) originates at the south end of the Wah Wah Mountains and drains northeast into the Wah Wah Valley. The creek drains through a bed of broken and chipped quartzite. T28,29S,R14,15W,SLM.

QUEEN CITY* (Duchesne). See Altonah* (Duchesne).

QUICHAMPAU CREEK (Duchesne) originates on the west Tavaputs Plateau near the headwaters of Tabby Canyon. The creek drains east into Sowers Canyon. See below for name source. S14,T6W,R6W,USM to S18,T26,R5W,SLM. 595.

QUICHAPA CREEK (Iron) originates in the Harmony Mountains and drains northeast into Cedar Valley. The creek drains through an antelope and big horn sheep bedding ground in an alkaline area. The name is Paiute and means "dung." Other sources say it means "laxative waters." There are many spellings to the word depending on how the Indian oral language is interpreted. S12,T37S,R13W,SLM to S33,T36S,R12W, SLM. 314, 398, 399.

QUICHAPA LAKE (Iron) is three and one-half miles west of Hamilton Fort*. This brackish, stagnant, and salty lake appears and disappears with the seasons. The lake had an early name of Shirts Lake for Peter Shirts. See above for name source. S21,28,33,T36S,R12W,SLM. 508.

QUICHUPAH CREEK (Sevier) originates at the junction of Convulsion Canyon and Water Hollow on the eastern slopes of Old Woman Plateau and drains east into Ivie Creek. See Quichapa Creek for name source. S16,T23S,R6E,SLM.

QUIGLEY CANYON (Cache). There are two listed, the Old and the New Quigley canyons. Both are northwest of Clarkston* and are named for an early settler. Old Quigley Canyon originates six miles northwest of Clarkston and drains east into Clarkston Creek. S12,T14N,R3W,SLM to S6,T14N,R2W,SLM. 435.

307

- R -

RABBIT CREEK (**Rich**) originates in the hill country east of the south end of Bear Lake and drains southeast into Bear River. There are many cottontails and jackrabbits in the area.
S34,T14N,R7E,SLM.

RABBIT GULCH* (**Duchesne**). See Fruitland* (Duchesne).

RABBIT RIVER. See Sevier River.

RABBIT SPRING (**Box Elder**) is four miles south of the southern tip of the Grouse Creek Mountains. There are a cluster of springs and a small reservoir, with numerous rabbits in the vicinity.
S24,T8N,R18W,SLM; 4,500' (1,372m).

RABBIT VALLEY (**Wayne**) is west of Loa* between the Fishlake and Awapa plateaus. The Fremont River and U-24 pass through the valley. The name was suggested by General William B. Pace and his men as they passed through the region after the Indian-white Battle of Red Lake.
T28S,R2,3E,SLM; 7,000' (2,134m). 485.

RAFT RIVER (**Box Elder**) originates in northwest Utah at the junction of Junction Creek and its South Fork, five miles north of Lynn*. The river drains northeast. The early settlers often crossed the river on primitive rafts at a time when they were establishing their settlements.
100(v17), 567.

RAFT RIVER MOUNTAINS (**Box Elder**) are in northwest Utah parallel to the Idaho border. The mountains were named from the nearby Raft River.
T23-28N,R13-15W,SLM.

RAGTOWN* (**Salt Lake**). See Magna* (Salt Lake).

RAIN LAKES (**Garfield**) is a small cluster of ponds in the south section of Boulder Mountain of the Aquarius Plateau. During the frequent rain showers, the ponds quickly filled and expanded in size.
10,800' (3,292m).

RAINBOW* (**Uintah**) was a small mining community built especially for gilsonite miners, four miles south of Watson*. The town was named for the nearby Rainbow Mine, which was well developed by 1920. By 1938 the settlement was abandoned.
T11S,R24E,SLM; 5,350' (1,631m). 50, 89, 516, 542.

RAINBOW BRIDGE (**San Juan**) is on the northwest slopes of Navajo Mountain in the Rainbow Bridge National Monument at the mouth of Bridge Canyon. Lake Powell now lies at the base of the bridge. White men initially viewed this feature on August 14, 1909, when W. B. Douglass of the U.S. General Land Office, Byron Cummings of the University of Utah, and others reached the bridge. Geologically it is a part of the upper La Plata sandstone, which was deposited in Jurassic times. It was considered the largest single-span natural arch in the known world until 1983 when the Kolob Arch in Zion National Park entered the competition. Each bridge has its advocates but the Kolob seems to have an edge over the Rainbow. The name of the bridge is derived from Navajo Indian words such as "na'nanzozh" and "nannezoshie," which mean "great arch" or "stone arch." The

Piute Indian name is "Barohoine" meaning "The Rainbow."
T43S,R8½E,SLM. 163(30 Sept. 1977, 10,11 Aug. 1983), 241, 383(v21,22), 546.

RAINBOW BRIDGE CANYON (San Juan) originates on the western slopes of Navajo Mountain and drains northwest, passing under the Navajo Bridge into Forbidden Canyon and Lake Powell.
T43S,R8½E,SLM. D.L. 7203.

RAINBOW BRIDGE NATIONAL MONUMENT (San Juan). This area was set apart by President Taft in 1910 in order to surround and protect the great natural bridge. At that time the feature was several miles from the Colorado River. Today Lake Powell laps at its base. See Rainbow Bridge.
314, 546.

RAINBOW HILLS (Sevier) is a cluster of multicolored hills, two miles northeast of Glenwood*.
S19,20,T23S,R1W,SLM; 6,525' (1,989m).

RAINBOW LAKE (Duchesne) is in the southwest section of the Uinta Mountains, one-half mile southeast of Governor Dern Lake. It was one of the lakes stocked with rainbow trout and is known for excellent trout fishing. The lake was named in 1930.
S21,T3N,R8W,USM; 9,960' (3,035m). 100 (v2).

RAINBOW PARK (Uintah). See Island Park.

RAINBOW PLATEAU (San Juan) includes Navajo Mountain and the Rainbow Natural Bridge.

RAINBOW POINT (Kane) is at the south end of the Bryce Canyon National Park road where the view overlooks the Pink Cliffs and other pink, orange, and red-tinted geologic formations.
T38S,R4W,SLM; 9,115' (2,778m).

RAINS* (Carbon) was a mining community six miles up Spring Canyon, northwest of Helper*. It was named for the owner of the mine, L. F. Rains, a prominent mining engineer. The community was established 1915 and shut down in 1958.
S7,T13S,R9W,SLM; 7,042' (2,146m). 89, 494, 516, 542, 607.

RAMONA LAKE (Summit) is in the southwest section of the Uinta Mountains on the upper Provo River. Trial Lake is three miles east. Cardie Clegg named the lake for his sister.
S35,T1S,R8E,SLM; 10,350' (3,155m). 379.

RANCH* (Kane) was a group of ranches settled in the 1880s near Alton* (Upper Kanab*), at the mouth of Main and Rush canyons.
S4,39,T39S,R6W,SLM. 455, 567.

RANCH CANYON (Beaver) originates on the northern slope of South Twin Flat Mountain of the Mineral Mountains and drains west into the Beaver River. John Black established a ranch in the canyon in 1861.
S31,36,T28S,R9W,SLM. 125.

RANDLETT* (Uintah) is near the Uinta River ten miles southeast of Fort Duchesne*. The area was first settled by whites in 1892, abandoned, and resettled in 1905. Colonel James Randlett was the local Indian agent and commanding officer at nearby Fort Duchesne. Indians and whites both considered him to be a good officer who tried to help the Indians. His name was given to the settlement after it was previously called Leland* for a short period of time.
S7,18,T3S,R2E,USM; 4,820' (1,469m). 100 (v17), 457, 542, 567.

RANDOLPH* (Rich) is a ranching community in the Bear River Valley ten miles north of Woodruff*. The pioneers arrived on the site March 14, 1870.

Randolph H. Stewart initially settled the community and was the presiding Mormon elder and the first bishop.
S29,T11N,R7E,SLM; 6,289' (1,917m). 289, 542, 546.

RANGE CREEK (Carbon, Emery) originates on the East Tavaputs Plateau, south of Mount Bartles. The creek drains southeast into the Green River through Range Valley, which is known for having excellent grazing land.
S3,T14S,14E,SLM to S32,T17S,R17E,SLM. 567.

RANGE VALLEY (Carbon, Emery). See Range Creek.

RANGE VALLEY MOUNTAIN (Carbon, Emery) is east of central Range Creek from which it receives its name. It is sometimes referred to as Valley Mountain.
T15,16S,R15,16E,SLM; 9,297' (2,834m).

RANSOM* (Cache). See Cornish* (Cache).

RAT SEEP HOLLOW (Garfield, Kane) originates at the Straight Cliffs of the Kaiparowits Plateau and drains northeast into Twentyfive Mile Wash. It receives its name from a natural seep in the hollow where water was drawn for the sheep. Drowned rats would often be found in the seep.
S16,T38S,R5E,SLM. 12.

RATTLESNAKE CANYON (Grand) originates on the East Tavaputs Plateau and drains west into the Green River. There are numerous rattlesnakes in the canyon.
S35,T18S,R19E,SLM to S31,T18S,R17E, SLM. 252.

RATTLESNAKE PEAK (Beaver) is on the western slopes of the Tushar Mountains near the head of First Spring Creek. Rattlesnakes are numerous around the base of the peak.
S33,T28S,R6W,SLM; 7,900' (2,408m).

RATTLESNAKE PEAK (Sanpete) is southeast of Manti* on the Wasatch Plateau. Rattlesnakes are numerous in the lower sections of the mountain.
S6,T19S,R3E,SLM; 8,621' (2,628m).

READER LAKES (Duchesne) are in the central section of the Uinta Mountains on the headwaters of the Whiterocks River. During the early 1900s, John Reader grazed his sheep around this cluster of small lakes and high mountain meadows.
S31,T5N,R1W,USM;10,400-11,000'(3,170m-3,353m).

READS* (Beaver). See Smyths* (Beaver).

RECAPTURE CANYON (San Juan). See Recapture Creek.

RECAPTURE CREEK (San Juan) originates north of Blanding* and empties into the San Juan River. Peter Shirts (see Paria*, Shurtz Creek, etc.) settled in the San Juan country in 1877. Shirts believed that Montezuma, the last Aztec emperor in Mexico, escaped and fled to the north, and was recaptured in the canyon that he (Shirts) named. See Montezuma Creek.
T38-40S,R22,23E,SLM. 406, 546.

RED BREAKS (Garfield) is eighteen miles southeast of Escalante*. This area is several square miles in size and consists of rugged, heavily eroded rimrock and sand.
T36S,R5E,SLM; 5,800' (1,768m).

RED BUTTE (Salt Lake) is southeast of Salt Lake City*.
S35,T1N,R1E,SLM; 6,500' (1,981m).

RED BUTTE CANYON (Salt Lake). See Red Butte Creek (Salt Lake).

RED BUTTE CREEK (Salt Lake) originates in the Wasatch Mountains five miles northeast of Fort Douglas* and drains southwest into the Salt Lake Valley. In 1906 the U.S. government

restricted traffic and grazing activities after obtaining control of this region as part of the Fort Douglas Military Reservation. The creek and canyon drainage system subsequently became the water supply for Fort Douglas. The area developed a dense vegetative cover with a rich floral and faunal population, which is an excellent area for research and study. The creek was named during the first Mormon general conference on August 22, 1847, when Brigham Young moved that the small creek be named Red Butte Creek.
S20,T1N,R2E,SLM to S3,T1S,R1E,SLM. 27, 100(v17), 124, 567.

RED BUTTE HILLS (Beaver) are on the western slopes of the Tushar Mountains, between Indian and Wild Cat creeks. Prominent red ledges can be found in this area.
S19,T27S,R6W,SLM; 7,300' (2,225m). 125.

RED BUTTE SPRINGS (Sevier). See Redmond Lake (Sevier).

RED CANYON (Daggett) was a prominent section of the Green River that is now part of Flaming Gorge Reservoir. The canyon extends about twenty-five miles south from the mouth of Hideout Canyon. The rise of the reservoir waters has diminished the impact of the flaming red canyon walls that were so prominent before the dam was built. In the late 1860s, Major Powell and his men passed through the canyon and admired the beautiful surroundings.
S19,T2N,R21E,SLM (end of canyon). 160, 172, 420, 496, 609.

RED CANYON (Garfield) ends two and one-half miles east of the U-12 and US-89 junction. The head is several miles east, past the Sunset Cliffs, on the top of the Paunsaugunt Plateau. The brilliant brown, red, pink, and orange-tinted canyon walls provided the name. U-12 passes through the canyon up into Bryce Canyon National Park.

S27,T35S,R4½W,SLM to S31,T35S,R4W, SLM. 546.

RED CASTLE LAKE (Summit) is in the north central section of the Uinta Mountains near Red Castle Mountain (Peak) from which it receives its name. 11,295' (3,443m).

RED CASTLE PEAK (Summit) is in the north central section of the Uinta Mountains on the headwaters of the East Fork of Smiths Fork. The name reflects its reddish color and battlemented profile.
12,566' (3,830m).

RED COVE RESERVOIR (Beaver) is on the east central slopes of Pine Valley.
S4,T28S,R16W,SLM; 5,635' (1,718m).

RED CREEK (Daggett) originates in Wyoming and enters Utah at the west end of Clay Basin. The creek drains into the Green River at Browns Park and received its name from the color of the creek, which is loaded with suspended red sediment.
S17,T3N,R24E,SLM to S18,T2N,R24E,SLM (in Utah).

RED CREEK (Duchesne, Wasatch) originates in the southwest section of the Uinta Mountains on the southern slopes of Red Creek Mountain. The creek drains southeast into the Strawberry River and is named because the water contains suspended red sediment.
S15,T1S,R10W,USM to S13,T4S,R8W,USM.

RED CREEK* (Iron). See Paragonah* (Iron).

RED CREEK (Iron) originates in the mountains east of Parowan* and drains north through Red Creek Reservoir into the Parowan Valley. Parley P. Pratt named the creek in November 1849 for the red sediment suspended in the water.
S30,T34S,R7W,SLM to S33,T33S,R8W,SLM. 27, 136, 567.

RED CREEK RESERVOIR (**Duchesne**) is on Red Creek, four and one-half miles southwest of Tabby Mountain.
S11,13,T2S,R9W,USM; 7,224' (2,202m).

RED FLEET RESERVOIR (**Uintah**) is ten miles north of Vernal*, east of US-191. The name was suggested because the nearby row of ridges resembles a fleet of ships surrounded by waves of canyons and hills.
578(3 Jan. 1982).

RED FORK CREEK (**Summit**). See Echo Canyon Creek.

RED HILL (**Beaver**) is in the Wah Wah Mountains southeast of Iron Mountain.
S20,T30S,R14W,SLM; 6,030' (1,838m).

RED LAKE (**San Juan**) is a red-tinted lake three and one-half miles north of Boundary Butte Mesa. The surrounding red sand and rimrock reflect a reddish tone onto the lake.
4,965' (1,513m).

RED LAKE CANYON (**San Juan**) originates in the Grabens section of Canyonlands National Park, seven miles south of The Confluence. The canyon drains west into the Colorado River at the Spanish Bottoms. Evidence of a small lake caused by a flash flood or geologic movement at the mouth of the canyon was most likely the source of the name.
T30,31S,R18E,SLM.

RED MESA* (**San Juan**). See Blanding* (San Juan).

RED MOUNTAIN (**Summit**) is in the north central section of the Uinta Mountains, two and one-half miles northeast of Bridger Lake. The mountain has a reddish tint.
S22,T3N,R14E,SLM; 9,522' (2,903m).

RED MOUNTAIN (**Washington**) is a red-colored sandstone formation, eight miles north northwest of St. George*. It is especially brilliant after a rainstorm when the sun reflects off the mountain.
T40,41S,R16,17W,SLM; 5,297' (1,615m).

RED PINE CREEK (**Summit**) originates in the southwest section of the Uinta Mountains and drains north northeast into Smith and Morehouse Creek. "Red pine" is a lumbering industry term for the Douglas fir tree (*Pseudotsuga menziezii*) that is plentiful in this area.
S27,T1S,R7E,SLM to S12,T1S,R7E,SLM.

RED PINE LAKE (**Salt Lake**) is at the head of Red Pine Fork, south of Little Cottonwood Canyon and one-half mile west of White Pine Lake. See Red Pine Creek for name source.
T3S,R2E,SLM.

RED ROCK CANYON (**Morgan**). See Francis Canyon (Morgan).

REDMOND* (**Sevier**) is ten miles south of Gunnison* and west of US-89. The red-colored mounds west of the town are the source of the name.
S1,12,T21S,R1W,SLM; 5,135' (1,565m). 289, 360, 542.

REDMOND LAKE (**Sevier**) is two and one-half miles north of Salina*, near Redmond*, from which it was named. It had an earlier name of Red Butte Springs for the nearby springs.
S11,12,T21S,R1W,SLM; 5,110' (1,558m). 91, 567, 585.

REDS CANYON (**Emery**) originates at the San Rafael Knob in the Sinbad country section of the San Rafael Swell. The canyon drains southwest into Muddy River. Red-bearded "Red" Blackum lived in the area, and the canyon was named for him.
S19,T32S,R10E,SLM (at head). 193.

REDWOOD* (**Salt Lake**) is an area on the west side of Salt Lake City* between Redwood Road (1700 West) and the Jordan River. The name comes from the

principal thoroughfare in the area—Redwood Road.
S22,27,T1S,R1W,SLM; 4,230' (1,289m).

REED* (Beaver). See Smyths* (Beaver).

REED AND BENSON RIDGE (Salt Lake) has a north-south orientation two to four miles north of Alta*. In the 1870s Mr. Reed had several mining claims in the area and Mr. Benson was superintendent of the canyon railroad. They worked together on several business ventures.
S17-32,T2S,R3E,SLM; 10,561' (3,218m). 508.

REEDS FORT* (Utah). See Fort Uinta*.
516.

REESE CANYON (Kane) originates at Collett Top on the north side of the Kaiparowits Plateau and drains south into Last Chance Creek. Watkins Reese ran his cattle in the canyon.
S5,T39S,R4E,SLM to S12,T41S,R4E,SLM. 12.

REFRIGERATION CANYON (Washington) is in Zion National Park and is noted for its cool, narrow passes.

REID NEILSON DRAW (Emery) originates at the Head of Sinbad on the San Rafael Swell and drains southeast into Crawford Draw. Reid Neilson was an early sheepherder.
S23,T22S,R10E,SLM to S10,T23S,R11E, SLM. 193.

REIDS LAKE (Summit) is at the west end of the Uinta Mountains on the western slopes of Reids Peak from which it received its name.
S28,T1S,R9E,SLM; 10,350' (3,155m).

REIDS MEADOW (Summit) is at the west end of the Uinta Mountains on the northwest slopes of Reids Peak from which the area was named.
S22,T1S,R9E,SLM; 10,000' (3,048m).

REIDS PEAK (Summit) is at the west end of the Uinta Mountains, one mile west of Mirror Lake. The peak was named for an early explorer and trapper who was in the region around 1875.
S27,T1S,R9E,SLM; 11,708' (3,568m). 298.

RESERVATION RIDGE (Duchesne, Utah, Wasatch) has an east-west orientation on the West Tavaputs Plateau. The ridge is on the old Indian treaty boundary that was made with the Ute Indians in order to create their reservation.

REVENUE BASIN (Beaver) is in the central part of the Wah Wah Mountains northeast of Lamerdorf Peak. MRN
S22,T28S,R15W,SLM; 6,200' (1,890m).

REX PEAK (Rich) is the highest point in the Crawford Mountains range.
S36,T11N,R7E,SLM; 7,996' (2,437m).

RHOADES CANYON (Duchesne, Wasatch) originates at the west end of the Uinta Mountains and drains southeast into Wolf Creek. Thomas Rhoades named the canyon in honor of his older brother, Kaleb Rhoades. The Rhoades's name is associated with gold mines in the Kamas* and Rhoades Canyon areas. Rhoades supplied the gold used for decorating the Mormon temple in Salt Lake City*.
S8,T1N,R9W,USM to S7,T1N,R9W,USM. 442. D.L. 6901.

RHOADS LAKE (Summit) is in the southwest section of the Uinta Mountains, two and one-half miles northeast of the head of Smith and Morehouse Creek. See Rhoades Canyon for name source.
S15,16,T1S,R8E,SLM; 10,150' (3,094m).

RHODES VALLEY (Summit) is a beautiful valley at the western end of the Uinta Mountains. The Weber River drains the north end of the valley and the Provo River drains the south end. In the early 1860s Thomas Rhoades, George

W. Brown, and others moved into the valley, which had an early name of Kamas (Camas) Valley. See Rhoades Canyon. Variant: Rhoades Valley.
T1,2S,R5,6E,SLM; 6,500' (1,981m). 27, 289, 442, 567.

RICE CREEK (Weber) is a very short creek originating northeast of North Ogden and drains southwest. Ira and Asa Rice lived on the creek.
S22,28,T7N,R1W,SLM. 274, 360.

RICH COUNTY was created in 1863 as Richland County. Before final acceptance in 1864, the name was shortened to Rich County. The county honors Charles Coulson Rich, an early Mormon apostle and a prominent leader in the settling of the Bear Lake region.
6, 27, 555(v2).

RICHARDSON* (Grand) was twenty-seven miles south of Cisco* and seventeen miles northeast of Moab*. The settlement was developed in 1879 on Professor Creek, two miles from the Colorado River. In 1898 the town was a uranium shipping point named for Dr. Sylvester Richardson, who was also known as Professor. Richardson was the postmaster and a teacher in a small school in Professor Valley. Today Richardson is a ghost town site. See Professor Creek.
S22,T24S,R23E,SLM; 4,250' (1,295m). 89, 146, 409, 514, 516, 555(v31).

RICHARDSON AMPHITHEATER (Grand) is a partially enclosed area between the Colorado River and the hill country to the southeast. See Richardson* and Professor Creek for name source.
S12,14,22,T24S,R23E,SLM; 4,200' (1,280m).

RICHFIELD* (Sevier) is ten miles south of Salina* on US-89 and I-70. The area was first used by whites in 1863. In January 1864 Albert Lewis led a party of ten men to settle the site. Their families arrived in March. Richfield was originally

known as Warm Springs*, but was later changed to Omni* in honor of a prophet mentioned in the Book of Mormon. After a good crop of wheat was produced in 1865, the community name was changed to Richfield.
S25,26,T23S,R2½W,SLM; 5,308' (1,618m). 100(v17), 163(22 Sept. 1934), 285, 289, 542, 567, 585.

RICHLAND COUNTY was an early name for Rich County.

RICHMOND* (Cache) is at the junction of US-191 and U-142 north of Logan*. It was settled in 1859 by a group led by John Bair and Nels Empey. Several claims are made for the name origin. (1) It was named for Mormon church apostle and regional elder, Charles C. Rich. (2) It was named for the extremely rich soil in the region. (3) It was named for Richmond, Missouri, where Mormon church official Orson Hyde had lived.
S26,27,34,35,T14N,R1E,SLM; 4,607' (1,404m). 100(v17), 289, 449, 542.

RICHVILLE* (Morgan) is on U-66 south of Morgan*. It is a small farming community founded in 1860 and named for Thomas Rich, an early settler and presiding Mormon elder.
S11,T3N,R2E,SLM; 5,118' (1,560m). 378, 567.

RICHVILLE* (Tooele) was located between Lake Point* and Tooele* near the former site of E. T. City*. Saw, woolen, and flour mills were built nearby and subsequent names were developed: Mills*, Milton*, Millvale*, and Milltown*. For a short period of time Richville was the county seat. After the county seat was moved to Tooele and the mills shut down, the community was abandoned. Today it is Mills Junction, on I-80. See Mills Junction*.
89, 100(v17).

RICKS CANYON (Cache) originates fifteen miles east of Logan* and drains north into the Right Fork of Logan

Canyon. The canyon was named for Thomas E. Ricks, an early pioneer and a prominent Cache Valley citizen. Ricks worked the canyon for lumber.

RICKS CREEK (Davis) originates on the southern slopes of Bountiful Peak and drains southwest through Ford Canyon into the west valley. It was named for Joel Ricks, who settled on the creek in the spring of 1849.
S27,T3N,R1E,SLM to S1,T2N,R1W,SLM. 88.

RIGGS SPRING (Kane) is near the head of Podunk Creek just inside the southern border of Bryce Canyon National Park. It had an earlier name of The Bunk because an old sheep wagon was kept there for the stockmen in the Riggs family. In 1934 the name was changed to Riggs Spring to honor one of the Riggs boys who was killed in World War I.
S4,T39S,R4W,SLM; 7,443' (2,269). 530.

RIGHT HAND COLLETT CANYON (Garfield) originates on the Kaiparowits Plateau one mile west of Death Ridge Reservoir and drains east into Left Hand Collett Canyon. The canyon was named for Reuben Collett, an early Escalante settler and cattleman who ran his cattle on the Kaiparowits Plateau.
S24,T37S,R1E,SLM to S36,T37S,R4E,SLM. 12.

RILDA CREEK (Emery) originates on the Wasatch Plateau east of Upper Joes Valley where it drains east into Huntington Canyon. An early settler, Elam McBride, and his wife, Rilda, named the creek when they established a sawmill in the area. After the water failed, they moved to the next creek to the north, which was Millfork Canyon.
S24,T16S,R6E,SLM to S22,T16S,R7E,SLM. 292, 508.

RILEYS CANYON (Summit) originates three miles northeast of Woodland* and drains southwest into the Provo River. It was named for an early prospector who

had several claims in the canyon.
S7,T3S,R7E,SLM (at mouth). 298.

RIM LAKE (Garfield) is a small lake on Boulder Mountain of the Aquarius Plateau. The lake is located at the head of Boulder Creek near the rim of a dropoff.
10,900' (3,322m).

RINCON* (San Juan) was a small trading post and settlement ten miles southwest of Bluff*. In 1887 Amasa M. Barton was killed by Navajo Indians at Rincon.
409, 567.

RINCON, THE (San Juan) is on the southern side of the Colorado River (Lake Powell), northeast of the mouth of the Escalante River. A rincon is an old waterway or meander that has been cut off or bypassed, leaving a high and dry area or a horseshoe-shaped lake.
T40S,R10E,SLM; 4,600' (1,402m).

RIO BLANCO (Uintah). See White River (Uintah).

RIO COLORADO DEL OCCIDENTE is the Colorado River of the West or the present Colorado River.

RIO DE AQUAS CALIENTES (Utah) is the Spanish Fork River (Utah).

RIO DE LA VIRGEN (Washington) is the Virgin River (Washington).

RIO DOLORES (Grand) is also listed as the Rio Dolores Chiquito. See Dolores River (Grand).

RIO DOLORES CHIQUITO (Grand). See Dolores River (Grand).

RIO GRANDE DEL NORTE is the Grand River of the North. The Grand River was an early name for a section of the Colorado River.

RIO DE SAN COSME (Uintah) was Domínguez's and Escalante's name for the Uinta River.

RIO SAN BUENAVENTURA (Uintah) is the Buenaventura River.

RIO SAN JUAN is the San Juan River.

RIO SAN RAFAEL is the San Rafael River.

RIO SANTA CLARA (Washington) is the Santa Clara River.

RIO SEVERO is the Sevier River.

RIO VIRGIN COUNTY was created in 1869 from the western part of Washington County. The county was named for the nearby Virgin River. However, the action was cancelled in 1872, so the section was returned to Washington County.

RIPGUT CREEK (Beaver) originates on the eastern slopes of the White Rock Mountains where it drains east into Hamlin Valley Wash. MRN
S36,T29S,R20W,SLM.

RIPGUT SPRING (Beaver) is at the head of Ripgut Creek.

RIVER HEIGHTS* (Cache) is across the Logan River south of Logan*. It was settled in 1882 as an outgrowth of Logan and Providence*. The community had an early name of Dry Town*, but it was later changed to the present name.
S3,T11N,R1E,SLM; 4,560' (1,390m). 289, 449.

RIVERBED STATION (Tooele) was a stop on the Pony Express route from Simpson Springs to Dugway Station. The station was nine miles southwest of Simpson Springs in the ancient Sevier River riverbed. This riverbed was believed to have existed when the Sevier River drained directly into the Great Salt Lake.

S18,T10S,R9W,SLM; 4,410' (1,344m).

RIVERDALE* (Uintah). See Jensen* (Uintah).

RIVERDALE* (Uintah). See Naples* (Uintah).

RIVERDALE* (Weber) is near I-15 north of Sunset*. The settlement was an outgrowth of Ogden* that was named for its proximity to the Weber River. It had earlier names of Jack Thompson Settlement* for John C. Thompson, an early settler. Before this it was called Stringtown* because the homes were built along the single road leading to and from Ogden.
S7,T5N,R1W,SLM; 4,355' (1,327m). 100 (v17), 274, 289, 516, 567.

RIVERSIDE* (Box Elder) is a small agricultural community on I-15, eight miles north of Tremonton*. The settlement was originally established in 1893 as an outgrowth of nearby Fielding*. It was named because of its proximity to the Bear River.
S11,T12N,R3W,SLM; 4,360' (1,329m). 139, 289, 542, 546.

RIVERTON* (Salt Lake) is on U-68 and U-71 three miles south of South Jordan*. In 1870, the settlement was established as an outgrowth of South Jordan. The name reflects its proximity to the Jordan River.
S27,34,T3S,R1W,SLM; 4,435' (1,352m). 100 (v17), 252, 289, 542.

ROAD CANYON (San Juan) originates on Cedar Mesa, seven miles north of the Valley of the Gods where it drains southeast into Comb Wash. George Hobbs, George Morrell, Lemuel Redd, and George Sevy named the canyon while they were working on a path through it, in search of an eastern route for the Hole-in-the-Rock expedition.
S13,T39S,R18E,SLM to S1,T40S,R20E,SLM. 359.

ROAN CLIFFS (**Grand**) are the blue, grey, and buff cliffs Powell named that are north of and above the Book Cliffs on the East and West Tavaputs Plateaus. Further south are the Orange Cliffs that are also a part of this series. The Roan Cliffs, which Powell originally named the Brown Cliffs, extend roughly parallel to the Book Cliffs.
T16-19S,R18-26E,SLM (in Utah). 160, 175, 422, 496.

ROBBERS ROOST (**Beaver**) is a small meadowland in the Tushar Mountains at the junction of the Beaver River and its East Fork. The name suggests a quiet, isolated enclosed area.
S20,T29S,R5W,SLM; 9,200' (2,804m). 125.

ROBBERS ROOST (**Garfield, Wayne**) is a large isolated region between the Dirty Devil and Green rivers, and The Confluence of the Green and Colorado rivers. This high desert country was surrounded by deep canyons, high cliffs, and difficult rivers. The area was treacherous to maneuver into and out of. As such, it became a hideout for bank and train robbers, bandits, horse and cattle rustlers, and various types of outlaws on the run, all of whom hit the Owlhoot Trail. The law never penetrated the Robbers Roost.
24, 25, 54, 303.

ROBBERS ROOST (**Millard**) is near the Juab-Millard County line at the head of Robbers Roost Canyon near Robbers Roost Spring, four miles north of Swasey Peak. Outlaws robbed the store at Deep Creek*, stole horses, and then robbed a Central Pacific Railroad train. They fled into a cave at the Roost and built a rock fort. Eventually they were captured and sentenced in a Nevada court in 1882.
S2,T16S,R13W,SLM; 7,150' (2,179m). 567.

ROBBERS ROOST* (**Washington**) was a campsite near Hurricane* where a group of laborers who were working on the Hurricane Canal set up camp. The

shelter was a wagon cover and all the cooking was done in the open. One of the men, as told by Morris Wilson, facetiously gave the name Robbers Roost to the camp. The name held. Nearby was Chinatown*, another camp for workers. 311.

ROBBERS ROOST CANYON (**Garfield**) originates at the junction of the North Fork of Robbers Roost Canyon and White Roost Canyon. It drains west southwest into the Dirty Devil River and receives its name from the surrounding Robbers Roost.
T29S,R13E,SLM (at mouth).

ROBBERS ROOST SPRING (**Wayne**) is five miles north of the old Biddlecome (today's Ekker) Ranch in the heart of the Robbers Roost country.

ROBERTS BOTTOM (**Grand**) is on the Dolores River, one mile from its junction with the Colorado River. It had an early name of Lockhart Bottom for L. B. Lockhart, a prospector. Lafe Roberts, a farmer, moved onto the bottomland and built a cabin. In the spring of 1896 Roberts was found dead in his cabin and the bottoms assumed his name.
S9,16,T23S,R24E,SLM; 4,150' (1,265m). 146.

ROBERTS LAKE (**Duchesne**) is in the south central section of the Uinta Mountains, south southwest of Lake Atwood. The lake was named for George Roberts, who grazed his sheep in the vicinity.
11,550' (3,520m). 309.

ROBERTS MESA (**Grand**) is near Roberts Bottom, with the same name source.

ROBERTS PASS (**Duchesne**) is in the south central section of the Uinta Mountains one mile north of Upper Chain Lake. Three and one-half miles west northwest is Roberts Lake from

which the pass received its name. George Roberts developed the trail over the pass.
11,160' (3,402m). 165.

ROBINSON* (Juab) was an old mining settlement west of Mammoth* and north of Silver City*. It was developed by George H. Robinson, a mining engineer employed by the McIntyres of Mammoth. Even though Robinson was fired by the McIntyres, he continued to develop the community that he named for himself.
S25,T10S,R3W,SLM. 89, 516.

ROCHESTER* (Emery). See Moore* (Emery).

ROCK CANYON (Utah) originates in the mountains east of Provo* near the head of Pole Canyon. It drains west into Utah Lake and is a rugged, rocky canyon with steep walls.
S27,T6S,R3E,SLM (at head).

ROCK CORRAL (Beaver) is a natural enclosure surrounded by granite cliffs at the head of Corral Canyon on the northwest slopes of the Mineral Mountains.
S14,T28S,R9W,SLM; 7,500' (2,286m).

ROCK CORRAL SPRING (Beaver) is at the head of Corral Canyon from which it receives its name.
S14,T28S,R9W,SLM; 7,500' (2,286m).

ROCK CREEK (Duchesne) originates in the west central section of the Uinta Mountains near Lightning and Helen Lakes. It drains southeast into the Duchesne River through a very rocky creekbed.
T4N,R7,8W,USM to S19,T2S,R5W,USM.

ROCK CREEK (Kane) originates on the Kaiparowits near the head of Blackburn and Steer canyons. It drains south through rocky terrain into the Glen Canyon section of the Colorado River.
S29,T40S,R7E,SLM. 12.

ROCK CREEK (Summit) originates at the west end of the Uinta Mountains on Pitt and Page Hill where it drains south through rocky terrain into the Provo River.
S28,T2S,R8E,SLM to S5,T3S,R8E,SLM. 298, 567.

ROCK FORT* (Summit). See Rockport* (Summit). Variant: Rockfort*.

ROCK LAKE (Beaver) is in the south Tushar Mountains northeast of Senseball Lake. The lake is in rocky terrain.
S17,T30S,R5W,SLM; 9,760' (2,975m).

ROCK LAKE (Summit) is at the west end of the Uinta Mountains, one and one-half miles southwest of Washington Lake. Rock Lake is surrounded by loose rock detritus.
S12,T2S,R8E,SLM; 10,150' (3,094m). 530.

ROCKHOUSE* (Kane) was established in 1865, five miles south of the ghost town Paria* (Pahreah*) on the Paria River. Water was unreliable and after several years the settlers moved elsewhere, making the area a ghost town. The settlement received its name after Peter Shirts, an early settler, built a large sandstone blockhouse at the site.
S9,T42S,R1W,SLM. 89.

ROCKPORT* (Summit) is today under the waters of the Rockport Lake State Recreation Area (Summit), two miles south of Wanship*. It was originally known as Three Mile Creek* for the creek where the people settled. The name was subsequently changed to Crandall* after a nearby canyon. In 1861, the name was again changed to Enoch City*, a biblical name. In 1866 and 1867 a rock fort was built to protect the settlers from Indians, so the town was renamed Rockport in remembrance of the fort. In 1950 the government purchased the land and relocated the residents.
T1,2S,R5E,SLM; 6,037' (1,840m). 89, 100 (v17), 516, 546, 567.

ROCKPORT LAKE STATE RECREA-
TION AREA (**Summit**). See Rockport*
(Summit).

ROCKS, THE (**Emery**) is four miles
southeast of Cleveland*. This is an area
of unusual rock formations that protrude
in a concentrated area anywhere from
two to six feet out of the ground.
S33,T17S,R10E,SLM.

ROCKVILLE* (**Washington**) is a canyon
community on U-9, four miles southwest
of Springdale*. It was originally settled in
late 1860 and early 1861 under the
direction of Mormon Apostle Orson
Pratt. The original name was Adventure*
but it was subsequently changed to
Rockville because of the rocky soil and
surroundings along the Virgin River.
S1,T42S,R11W,SLM; 3,746' (1,142m). 154,
289, 311, 542, 546, 600.

ROCKWELLS STATION* (**Salt Lake**)
was a stop on the Overland Stage at the
Point of the Mountain, just before the
road crossed the Jordan River to head
southwest. The station was manned by
Porter Rockwell, famous Mormon scout
and one-time bodyguard for Brigham
Young.

ROCKY CANYON (**Beaver**) is in the
south Tushar Mountains where it originates at Rocky Reservoir. It drains
northwest into Wide Mouth Wash and
receives its name from the large amount
of lava rock in the canyon.
S27,33,35,T30S,R6W,SLM. 125.

ROCKY FORD (**Beaver**) was on the
Beaver River where the Rocky Ford
Dam is presently located. Early travelers
crossed the Beaver River at this point.

ROCKY FORD CREEK (**Piute**) originates at the Rocky Ford Reservoir on
Table Mountain, six miles southeast of
Kingston*. The creek drains north into
the Sevier River, East Fork. The early
settlers were able to cross the river at
the mouth of the creek. A bridge was

built later.
S8,T31S,R2½W,SLM to S13,T30S,R3W,SLM.
567.

ROCKY FORD HOLLOW (**Beaver**)
originates in the Black Mountains at
the Blue Ribbon Summit, south of
Minersville*. It drains northeast into the
Minersville Reservoir at the Rocky Ford
Dam.
S27,11,T30S,R9W,SLM.

ROCKY FORD RESERVOIR (**Beaver**)
was a synonym for today's Minersville
Reservoir (Beaver).

ROCKY FORD RESERVOIR (**Piute**).
There are two listed on this particular
creek. One is two miles south of the
mouth of Rocky Ford Creek. The other
is six miles south of the mouth of the
creek up on Table Mountain. Both
reservoirs were named for the creek.
S26,T30S,R3W,SLM; 6,650' (2,027m) and
S8,T31S,R2½W,SLM; 9,300' (2,835m). 567.

ROCKY FORD RESERVOIR (**Sevier**)
is near Vermillion* and Sigurd* on U-24,
eight miles south southwest of Salina*.
The reservoir received its name from the
old rocky ford where the early settlers
crossed the Sevier River.
S30,31,T22S,R1W,SLM; 5,210' (1,588m).
584.

ROCKY PASS PEAK (**Box Elder**) is
near Rocky Pass over the crest of the
Grouse Creek Mountains.
S2,T9N,R17W,SLM; 6,900' (2,103m).

ROCKY RANGE (**Beaver**) is northwest
of Milford and southeast of the Beaver
Lake Mountains. It was named for
J. F. M. Rockyfeller, a prospector of the
1870s.
S15,T27S,R11W,SLM; 6,035' (1,839m). 100
(v17).

ROCKY RESERVOIR (**Beaver**) is in the
south Tushar Mountains near the head of
Rocky Canyon. This region was once
subject to heavy volcanic activity, which

320

explains the abundance of lava boulders.
S35,T30S,R6W,SLM; 7,650' (2,332m).

ROCKY SEA PASS (Duchesne) is at the
west end of the Uinta Mountains, one
and one-half miles southeast of Naturalist
Basin. The pass winds its way over rocky
ridges of detritus, which reminds one of
waves in heavy seas.
S3,T3N,R8W,USM; 11,500' (3,505m).

RODS VALLEY (Emery) is on the San
Rafael Swell, ten miles northwest of
Temple Mountain, and south of the
Head of Sinbad on the San Rafael Swell.
Rod Swasey, a member of the Swasey
family who helped to settle this region,
thought this was a beautiful valley so he
named it in the late 1800s.
S21,28,T23S,R10E,SLM; 6,800' (2,073m).
193.

ROGER PEAK (Garfield) is on the
Aquarius Plateau southwest of McGath
Lake and two miles northwest of Hells
Backbone. See Rogers Canyon.
10,115' (3,083m). 12.

ROGERS CANYON (Garfield) origi-
nates on the Kaiparowits Plateau, at the
Straight Cliffs and Left Hand Collett
Wash and drains southeast to join
Sunday Canyon. The canyon was named
for the Rogers brothers (John, Noah,
Washington, and Henry) who were early
Escalante cattlemen.
S1,T41S,R5E,SLM (at mouth). 12.

ROLAPP* (Carbon). See Royal*
(Carbon).

ROOSEVELT* (Duchesne) is at the
junction of US-40 and U-121. The
settlement was called Dry Gulch before
the area was platted in 1905-6. At this
time it was renamed for U.S. President
Theodore Roosevelt.
T2S,R1W,USM; 5,100' (1,554m). 289, 457,
542.

ROOST FLATS (Wayne) is a large flat
upland at the head of Robbers Roost

Canyon, South Fork, with Deadman Hill
to the west. The flats are part of the
Robbers Roost region.
SW¼,T28S,R15E,SLM; 5,800' (1,168m).

ROSALIE LAKE (Duchesne) is on the
upper Rock Creek drainage. See Francis
Lake for name source.
S26,T4N,R8W,USM; 10,900' (3,322m).

ROSE SPRING FORT* (Tooele). See
Fort Erda* and Batesville*.

ROSEBUD CREEK (Box Elder) originates on the east central slopes of
the Grouse Creek Mountains and
drains southeast to join Muddy Creek.
There are abundant wild roses along the
creek.
S20,T11N,R16W,SLM (at head).

ROSEDALE* (Davis) is on U-106 and
Ricks Creek between Centerville* and
Farmington*. Wild roses are abundant in
the area.
S6,T2N,R1E,SLM; 4,309' (1,313m).

ROSESPRING CANYON (Beaver) originates on the western slopes of Lamerdorf
Peak in the south Wah Wah Mountains
where it drains southwest into Pine
Valley. Wild roses are plentiful in the
area.
S13,23,T29S,R16W,SLM.

ROSETTE* (Box Elder) is a small
ranching community five miles west of
Park Valley*. Jonathan Campbell, the
first postmaster, named it in 1871 for the
wild roses in the area.
S26,T13N,R14W,SLM; 5,679' (1,731m). 139,
542, 567.

ROUND LAKE (Millard) is eight miles
southwest of Delta. This dry lake bed is
a captured meander on the old channel
of the Sevier River.
S3,T18S,R8W,SLM.

ROUND LAKE (Millard) is a small
body of water in the center of Round
Valley, south of Scipio*.

ROUND LAKE (**Summit**) is a circular lake at the west end of the Uinta Mountains, four miles south of Whitney Reservoir.
S5,T1S,R9E,SLM; 9,950' (3,033m).

ROUND LAKE (**Summit**) is a circular lake in the north central section of the Uinta Mountains, one-half mile east of Island Lake.
10,622' (3,238m).

ROUND VALLEY* (**Millard**). See Scipio* (Millard).
542.

ROUND VALLEY (**Millard**) is an oval-shaped valley nine miles south of Scipio*.
T19,20S,R1,2W,SLM; ca. 6,000' (1,829m).

ROUND VALLEY* (**Rich**) was a small community settled in 1864 in Round Valley, southeast of Bear Lake. This was one of several nearby communities that were eventually absorbed into Laketown*. Some of the early settlements were Chimney Town*, Sly Go*, Pottawattamie*, and Mud Town*.

ROUND VALLEY (**Rich**) is an oval-shaped valley three miles southwest of Bear Lake and two miles southwest of Laketown*. On May 12, 1863, Luther Reed settled there with his family. See Round Valley* (Rich).
S2,3,10,T12N,R5E,SLM; 5,971' (1,820m). 89, 100(v13,17), 289, 567.

ROUND VALLEY* (**Wasatch**). See Wallsburg* (Wasatch).

ROUND VALLEY (**Wasatch**) is four miles southeast of Deer Creek Reservoir, with Wallsburg* in the center. The valley is oval in shape.
T5S,R4,5E,SLM; ca. 5,600' (1,707m).

ROUND VALLEY CREEK (**Millard**) drains through Round Valley into Scipio Valley.
T19S,R2W,SLM.

ROUNDY CANYON (**Kane**) originates three miles northeast of Alton* where it drains south into Kanab Creek. It was named for Lorenzo Wesley Roundy who settled Alton with his family in 1865.
S30,31,T38S,R5W,SLM.

ROUNDY RESERVOIR (**Garfield**) is west of Barney Lake and southeast of Antimony* on the south edge of the Aquarius Plateau. Napoleon (Pole) Roundy built a dam at this site in order improve his irrigation supply and to provide water for his sheep.
NW¼,T32S,R2E,SLM; 9,958' (3,035m). 12, 602.

ROUNDY STATION* (**Kane**) was an early name for Alton* (Kane).

ROW LAKES (**Garfield**) is a series of lakes on the Aquarius Plateau. The lakes are situated in a row, one mile north of Jacobs Reservoir.
S28,32,33,T31S,R3E,SLM; ca. 10,225' (3,117m).

ROWLEY JUNCTION* (**Tooele**) is forty-four miles west of Salt Lake City* on I-80. The settlement had an earlier name of Timpie Junction, "timpie" being Goshute Indian for "rock." The name was changed to Rowley Junction around 1970 when a chemical processing plant was built on the shore of nearby Great Salt Lake.
S8,T1S,R7W,SLM; 4,215' (1,285m). 542.

ROWVILLE* (**Box Elder**). See Bothwell* (Box Elder).

ROY* (**Weber**) is at the junction of U-26 and U-126 between Clearfield* and Ogden*. The area was used as a grazing range before 1876 when it became an outgrowth of Kanesville* and Hooper*. William E. Baker, Justin Grover, and others were early settlers. It was first called The Sandridge then Central City for its location. In 1894 an application was made for a post office under the

name of Roy. David P. Peebles was a prominent citizen whose young son Roy had recently died.
S11,14,T5N,R2W,SLM; 4,436' (1,352m). 289, 542, 546, 567.

ROYAL* (Carbon) was on US-6,50 south of and near Castle Gate*. The area was gradually consumed by coal-mining activities. Throughout the history of this community, the name has changed several times. It was originally Bear Canyon* for the canyon where the early miners settled. In 1913 Frank Cameron developed a mine in the vicinity and the community became Cameron*. In 1917, Cameron sold the mine to Henry Rolapp whose name then was used for the town (Rolapp*). In the 1920s the Royal Coal Company purchased the mine and the town had its newest and last name, Royal. Today the community is completely gone, except for a few stone walls and lilac bushes.
S35,T12S,R9E,SLM; 6,273' (1,912m). 100 (v17), 494, 542.

ROZEL* (Box Elder) was an early construction camp on the old Central Pacific Railroad near the Golden Spike National Historic Site. MRN
S16,T10N,R7W,SLM; 4,593' (1,400m). D.L. 6701.

RUBYS INN* (Garfield) is on U-12 two and one-half miles north of the Bryce Canyon National Park visitors center. In 1916 Reuben (Ruby) C. Syrett built a small lodge and some cabins near Sunset Point. Today it is a prominent junction with several motels and a small community.
S18,T36S,R3W,SLM; 7,661' (2,335m). 546.

RUDE HOLLOW (Duchesne) originates at the west end of the Uinta Mountains and drains south into the Duchesne River, West Fork. It was named for Rudolph (Rude) Wilcken, who homesteaded the mouth of the hollow.
S9,16,21,28,29,T1N,R8W,USM. 595.

RUDOLPH LAKE (Duchesne) is at the southwest end of the Uinta Mountains near the head of Rock Creek drainage. Diamond Lake is in the vicinity. The lake was named for Rudolph Wilcken, who built trails in this area for the U.S. Forest Service. Rudolph and Dean Phinney named this lake and nearby Phinney Lake. See Rude Hollow (Duchesne).
S35,T3N,R7W,USM; 10,470' (3,191m). 595.

RUIN CANYON (San Juan) originates on the western slopes of the Abajo Mountains where it drains north north-west into Beef Basin Wash. The canyon is known for its prehistoric ruins.
S36,T32S,R18E,SLM (at mouth).

RUSH CANYON (Kane) originates four miles east northeast of Alton*. It drains west into Kanab Creek. Rush and reed plants are plentiful along the canyon bottom.
S32,T38S,R5W,SLM (at mouth).

RUSH LAKE (Tooele) is one mile south-west of Stockton*. The lake is shallow and marshy, with abundant reeds and rushes growing in it. In pioneer times, when Colonel Steptoe camped there with his men, the lake was known by its Indian name, Lake Shambip. For a period of time it was also known as Stockton Lake. In the 1870s Godbe's Chicago Smelter, known as Slagtown*, was located on the eastern shore of the lake.
S26,T4S,R5W,SLM; 4,960' (1,512m). 530, 546.

RUSH VALLEY (Tooele) is a desolate valley of public lands and several ranches west of the south Oquirrh Mountains. The Pony Express and Overland Stage passed this area. The valley is named after Rush Lake.
T4-8S,R4,5W,SLM; 5,100' (1,554m). 314, 367, 546.

RUSH VALLEY CITY* (Tooele) is the new name for the recent merging of

Clover* and Saint John*.
367.

RUSSELL GULCH (**Washington**) is in
the northwest corner of Zion National
Park as a tributary of the Left Fork of
North Creek. It was named for Alonzo
Havington Russell, who lived in the gulch
from 1861 until his death in 1914.
S36,T40S,R11W,SLM (at head).

RUSSIAN KNOLL (**Box Elder**) is ten
miles south of Park Valley* near the
ghost town site of the former Russian
Settlement*.
T12N,R13W,SLM; 4,941' (1,506m). 516.

RUSSIAN SETTLEMENT* (**Box Elder**)
is a ghost town site ten miles south of
Park Valley*. It was established in 1914
by a small group of Russian migrants.
After about six years the settlement
failed and there is nothing left of the site
except a small cemetery, one-half mile
east of Russian Knoll.
T12N,R13W,SLM; 4,850' (1,478m). 516, 546.

RYDER LAKE (**Summit**) is at the west
end of the Uinta Mountains between
Hayden Peak and Mount Agassiz on the
headwaters of Stillwater Fork. It was
named for a member of the engineering
department of the U.S. Forest Service.
10,625' (3,238m). 530.

- S -

SADDLE HORSE CANYON (Emery) originates on the San Rafael Swell west of Sinbad country near Joe and His Dog. It drains north northwest into Molen Seep Wash. Saddle horses were kept separated from the rest of the stock in this canyon.
T21S,R10E,SLM. 193.

SADIES NIPPLE (Garfield) is a geologic formation one-half mile north of Boulder Town*.
S24,T33S,R4E,SLM.

SAGE CANYON (Rich) originates near the south end of Bear Lake where it drains east. The creek running through the canyon empties into the Bear River after passing through sagebrush country.
S9,T12N,R6E,SLM (at head). 567.

SAGE CREEK* (Rich) was located north of present-day Sage Creek Junction and Randolph*. Before 1870 residents of nearby Randolph moved into and settled the region. Today the area has reverted to grazing lands and one or two scattered ranches. See Sage Canyon for the Sage Creek location.
T12N,R7E,SLM. 100(v13,17).

SAGEBRUSH BENCH (Emery) is on the San Rafael Swell two miles south of the San Rafael Knob and I-70. There is an abundance of sagebrush in the region.
S16,T23S,R9E,SLM; 7,150' (2,179m). 193.

SAHARA* (Iron). See Zane* (Iron).

SAHARA VILLAGE* (Davis) is southeast of Syracuse* near Clearfield*.
S8,9,T4N,R1W,SLM; 4,720' (1,301m).

SAINT ELMO* (Emery). See Elmo* (Emery).

ST. GEORGE* (Washington) is on I-15, fifty-two miles southwest of Cedar City*. The settlement was named prior to its establishment in 1861. The name honored the presiding Mormon elder, counselor to Brigham Young, and "Father of the South," George Albert Smith. It was half-humorously suggested that if other churches could have saints, Mormons could too.
S29,30,T42S,R15W,SLM; 2,761' (842m). 27, 155, 275, 289, 438, 542, 546.

SAINT JAMES* (Washington). See Bloomington* (Washington).

SAINT JOHN* (Tooele) is eight miles southwest of Stockton*. The area was settled in 1867 by a group from Clover* who named the settlement in honor of John Rowberry, the presiding Mormon elder. Recently, Saint John and Clover have merged to form Rush Valley City*.
S30,T5S,R6W,SLM; 5,050' (1,539m). 289, 367, 542, 546, 567.

SAINT JOHN STATION* (Tooele) is a siding on the Union Pacific Railroad line in Rush Valley. The station was named for Saint John*, which is three miles west.

SAINT MARYS COUNTY was created in Utah Territory in 1857 then transferred to Nevada Territory in 1861. The early name for the Humboldt River was Marys River, honoring the Indian wife of Peter Skene Ogden, the noted Hudson Bay trapper. The county received its name from the river.
6.

SALDURO SIDING* (Tooele) was established on the railroad eight miles east of Wendover*. It was most prominent during the 1930s and 1940s when salt and potash were mined in the area. The settlement was finally abandoned in 1944 when the potash plant closed and, shortly afterwards, a fire swept through the small community. The name is a combination of Spanish and Latin and means rock or hard salt. T1S,R18E,SLM; 4,219' (1,286m). 314, 498.

SALEM* (**Utah**) is on old US-91 east of Payson*. It was first settled in 1851 near a large pond. Lyman Curtis, the oldest man in the early community, was asked to suggest a name. He chose his birthplace of Salem*, Massachusetts. There is a counterclaim that the community was named for Salem* (Jerusalem*) of biblical note. It has also been suggested that it had an earlier name of Pond Town* for the small body of water close to the settlement. S1,2,11,12,T9S,R2E,SLM; 4,600' (1,402m). 270, 289, 542, 546.

SALEM HILLS* (**Utah**) is a recently incorporated community three miles southeast of Payson*. The community receives its name from nearby Salem*. S23,T9S,R2E,SLM; 5,200' (1,585m). 163(2 Nov. 1977).

SALEM POND (**Utah**) is the small body of water surrounded by Salem*, from which it receives its name.

SALERATUS CANYON (**Grand**) originates on the McPherson Range where it drains west to the Green River. The name reflects the alkaline condition of the canyon. S1,2,T18S,R17E,SLM.

SALERATUS CREEK (**Rich**) originates in the Monte Cristo Mountains where it drains north northeast into the Bear River. The early settlers collected saleratus along the creek bank. They used the substance for soda. S28,T6N,R6E,SLM to S14,T9N,R7E,SLM. 360.

SALERATUS RESERVOIR (**Emery**) is north of Big Hole Wash and west of Fry Mesa. See Saleratus Canyon for name source. S8,T19S,R13E,SLM.

SALERATUS WASH (**Emery**) drains from west to east to enter the Green River at Green River*. The waters are alkaline. S15,T21S,R16E,SLM (at mouth).

SALERATUS WASH (**Grand**) drains from north to south, crossing US-6,50 into Pinto Wash, ten miles southwest of Cisco* (Grand). The waters are alkaline. S4,T22S,R22E,SLM (at mouth).

SALINA* (**Sevier**) is ten miles north of Richfield* at the junction of US-89 and I-70. It was settled in 1863, vacated in 1866 because of white-Indian problems, then resettled in 1871. When Captain Dutton was investigating the high plateaus in Utah he commented that "Salina was a little Mormon village, a wretched hamlet, that made its living by lixiviating salt from the nearby salt deposits" (175, p. 170). The word "salina" is Spanish and refers to salt seeps or deposits. S24,25,T21S,R2W,SLM; 5,160' (1,573m). 175, 289, 314, 546.

SALINA CANYON (**Sevier**) is drained by Salina Creek.

SALINA CREEK (**Sevier**) originates near the head of Gunnison Valley between Woods and Island lakes. It drains south into Salina Canyon and into the Sevier River. The creek is on the Old Spanish Trail and was named by the Spanish for salt marsh, salt seep, or pond. Commercial sources of salt are near the creek. S11,13,14,T20S,R3E,SLM to S23,T21S,R1W, SLM.

SALINE* (**Box Elder**) was a Southern Pacific Railroad siding on Promontory Point. The name reflects the nearby salt works.

S25,T6N,R6W,SLM; 4,225' (1,288m). 542.

SALLYS HOLLOW (Grand) originates in the northeast section of the La Sal Mountains and drains southeast into Taylor Creek. There are two versions of the name source. One claims Sally was a cook at the Pace Cattle Ranch in Castle Valley who was supposedly known for her ability to vocally get the men in for dinner. The other records Sally being Sally Culberson, a man who settled in the hollow in 1886.
S19,30,T26S,R26E,SLM. 146, 475.

SALT CABIN SPRING (Beaver) is on the southwest slopes of Indian Peak in the Indian Peak Range at the head of Salt Cabin Spring Wash. An old log cabin there was used to store rock salt for the livestock.
S5,T30S,R18W,SLM; 7,600' (2,316m). 125.

SALT CABIN SPRING WASH (Beaver) originates on the southwest slopes of Indian Peak where it drains west into Hamlin Valley Wash. See the spring for name source.
S7,T27S,R6W,SLM.

SALT CREEK* (Juab) was an early name for Nephi*. The early non-Mormons did not appreciate using a Mormon name for the town and were reluctant to change after Nephi was approved. For some time non-Mormons continued to use the name Salt Creek. See Nephi* (Juab).

SALT CREEK (Juab) originates on the eastern slopes of Mount Nebo. The creek drains west through Salt Creek Canyon and southwest into the Sevier River. There are commercial salt deposits along the creek.
S5,R2E,T12S,SLM to S5,T13S,R1E,SLM.

SALT CREEK* (Weber). See Warren*.

SALT CREEK CANYON (Iron) originates three miles northeast of Cedar City* where it drains south into Coal Creek of Cedar Canyon.
S7,18,T36S,R10W,SLM.

SALT CREEK CANYON (Juab). See Salt Creek (Juab).

SALT HOLLOW (San Juan) originates at Salt Creek Mesa and drains north into Horse Creek in Canyonlands National Park, north of The Confluence. The water draining the hollow is alkaline.
T30-31S,R19,20E,SLM.

SALT LAKE. See Great Salt Lake.

SALT LAKE CITY* (Salt Lake) is located at the interchange of I-80 and I-15, midway between Ogden* and Provo*. It was settled on July 24, 1847. At a general gathering of colonists on August 22, 1847, it was moved and seconded to call the city the City of the Great Salt Lake or Great Salt Lake City, thus acknowledging the great body of salt water to the west. The word "Great" was deleted for practical purposes on January 29, 1868.
T1S,R1E,SLM; 4,331' (1,320m). 27, 100 (v17), 314, 417, 542, 546, 604.

SALT LAKE COUNTY was established in 1850 and named for the adjoining Great Salt Lake. The county was originally named Great Salt Lake County as one of the first six counties organized in the territory, but in 1868 it was formally shortened.
6, 542.

SALT LAKE VALLEY (Salt Lake) extends from the Point of the Mountain to Salt Lake City* and from the Wasatch Mountains to the Oquirrh Mountains. The Jordan River drains down the center of the valley.
371, 604. D.L. 8301.

SALTAIR (Salt Lake) was a large recreational facility on the south end of Great Salt Lake, twelve miles west of Salt Lake City near I-80. A large Moorish pavilion was built in 1893.

Picnicking, swimming in the lake, and dancing on the "largest ballroom floor in the world" were principal attractions. A 1925 fire at the resort, followed later by another fire and heavy vandalism, contributed to the decline of the resort. In recent years attempts to rejuvenate the old resort have been hampered by an unexpected rise of the lake level.
S34,T1N,R3W,SLM; 4,213' (1,284m). 360, 371.

SALVATION KNOLL (San Juan) is located northeast of Grand Flats and southwest of the Bears Ears. After being lost in midwinter while scouting for the Hole-in-the-Rock expedition, George Hobbs and his three companions were able to reorient and save themselves.
NE¼,T37S,R18E,SLM. 359.

SAMAK* (Wasatch) is a small community southeast of Kamas* on U-150. The spelling of the name was reversed to distinguish this community from nearby Kamas.
S22,23,T2S,R6E,SLM; 6,900' (2,103m).

SAMS CANYON (Duchesne) originates on the West Tavaputs Plateau and drains northeast into the Strawberry River.
S35,T5S,R8W,USM to S15,T4S,R7W,USM.

SAMUELS LAKE (Duchesne) is on the southern slopes of the Uinta Mountains between Fox and Kidney lakes. Ed Samuels ran sheep in this area in 1903.
309.

SAN ARROYO CANYON (Grand) originates on the East Tavaputs Plateau above the Book Cliffs, near the San Arroyo Ridge. The canyon drains south through the Book Cliffs into Bitter Creek. This creek should not be confused with the Bitter Creek on the north side of the plateau, which drains north. The name is Spanish and means "holy stream or creek."
S9,T16S,R25E,SLM to S30,T18S,R26E,SLM.

SAN ARROYO RIDGE (Grand). See San Arroyo Canyon (Grand).

SAN CLEMENTE RIVER (Uintah) was the name Domínguez and Escalante used for the White River (Uintah).
159, 583.

SAN DOMINGO CITY* (Salt Lake) is a 1870s ghost town site seven miles up City Creek Canyon, northeast of the state capitol building. The men who lived in the camp worked in the mines near the mouth of Cottonwood Gulch.
S7,T1N,R2E,SLM. 516.

SAN FRANCISCO MOUNTAINS (Beaver) are south of Sevier Lake and northwest of Milford*. The mountain name is a reminder of the Domínguez-Escalante expedition of 1776. The group passed this area and that resulted in the development of the Old Spanish Trail. The name refers to Saint Francis of Assisi, patron saint of wildlife and founder of the Franciscan Order of the Catholic Church.
T26,27S,R12,13W,SLM; 9,660' (2,944m). 125.

SAN JUAN COUNTY. In 1880 the Territorial Legislature carved San Juan County from Iron, Kane, Sevier, and Piute counties. The name comes from the San Juan River.
6, 314, 406, 542, 546.

SAN JUAN HILL (San Juan) was the most difficult obstacle for the Hole-in-the-Rock group as they came down Comb Ridge Wash trying to overcome the forbidding Comb Ridge. Between the ridge and the San Juan River they turned east and went up and over what came to be known as San Juan Hill, which was on the way to Bluff*.
S15,T41S,R20E,SLM; 4,757' (1,450m). 359.

SAN JUAN RIVER (San Juan) drains from Colorado and New Mexico into

Utah near Four Corners, and into the Colorado River (Lake Powell). The history of the origin of the river name is extensive and dates back to the early Spanish and Mexican explorers who came from Mexico and New Mexico into the Great Basin to trade. Both Don Juan de Oñate's and Don Juan Maria de Rivera's names are mentioned. 314, 530, 555(v3), 610.

SAN LINO, EL RIO DE (Utah). See Diamond Fork (Utah).

SAN NICOLAS, EL RIO DE (Utah). See Hobble Creek (Utah).

SAN PETE COUNTY. See Sanpete County.

SAN PITCH MOUNTAINS (Sanpete) are between Levan* and Freedom*. See San Pitch River for name source. T15,16S,R1,2E,SLM.

SAN PITCH RIVER (Sanpete) originates in the mountains northeast of Milburn* and drains south southwest into the Sevier River. The river was named for a chief of the San Pitch (Sanpitch, Sampitch) tribe or clan of Piute Indians who lived along the river. S13,T12S,R4E,SLM to S14,T19S,R1W,SLM. 100(v17), 314.

SAN RAFAEL DESERT (Emery) is between the San Rafael River and the San Rafael Reef, with the Flat Tops to the southwest. The desert received its name from the river.

SAN RAFAEL KNOB (Emery) is the highest point on the San Rafael Swell. Reds, Sulphur, and Devils canyons head near The Knob. See San Rafael River for name source. NE¼,T23S,R9E,SLM; 7,921' (2,414m). 193.

SAN RAFAEL REEF (Emery) is the cliff-like eastern border of the San Rafael Swell. See San Rafael River for the name source.

SAN RAFAEL RIVER (Emery) originates at the junction of Huntington, Cottonwood, and Ferron creeks. The river drains southeast near the Old Spanish Trail into the Green River. It was named by early Spanish Franciscan friars who used the trail. The friars were referring to Archangel Saint Rafael, the angel of the spirits of men, the Healer, one of the four angels who stood around the throne of God. S21,T19S,R9E,SLM to S8,16,T24S,R15E, SLM. 100(v17), 193, 314, 422.

SAN RAFAEL SWELL (Emery) is approximately thirty by fifty miles in size, located between Green River* and Castle Valley. The San Rafael River is on the north. The Swell received its name from the river. It is a geologic anticlinal uplift, a massive swell, and inverted bowl that has been heavily eroded into towers, buttes, crags, rocklands, and canyons.

SAN RAFAEL VALLEY (Emery) is north of the San Rafael River and west of its junction with the Green River. See San Rafael River for name source. S7,8,T24S,R15E,SLM.

SAND CREEK (Garfield) originates on Burr Top of the Aquarius Plateau, two miles south of Jacobs Reservoir. It drains south into the Escalante River. The creek bottom is sandy in many areas. S10,T35S,R4E,SLM (at mouth). 12.

SAND FLATS (Box Elder) are between Elwood* and Garland*. The flats were named in 1878 for the deep sand in the area. 567.

SAND HILLS, THE (Kane) is an area of sand and rimrock sandstone, surrounding the site where US-89 crosses the summit ten miles north of Kanab*. Before the highway was built, Kanab was quite isolated because of this sand region. T42S,R7W,SLM.

SAND HOLLOW (**Beaver**) is in the South Hills south of Beaver*, where it drains north into South Creek. S20,28,33,T30S,R7W,SLM.

SAND MOUNTAIN (**Juab**) is seven miles north of Lynndyl* in the sand dune area west of Jericho*. It is a huge rock outcropping with accumulated sand dunes surrounding the mountain. Today it is a popular recreation area. S10,T14S,R5W,SLM; 5,702' (1,738m).

SAND POND (**Beaver**) is a small shallow body of water near Ninemile Knoll in the Escalante Desert. S23,T30S,R11W,SLM; 5,050' (1,539m).

SAND RIDGE* (**Davis**). See Clearfield* (Davis).

SAND RIDGE (**Davis**) is north of Layton* and extends into Weber County. The ridge was formed through the wave and backwash action of ancient Lake Bonneville. 88.

SAND SPRING (**Beaver**) is in the Mountain Home Range south of Mountain Home Pass. The spring rises to the surface through sand. S9,T26S,R19W,SLM; 7,775' (2,370m).

SAND SPRING (**Iron**) is in Sand Spring Canyon on the northwest slopes of the Antelope Range east of Enterprise*. During the early days when the Old Spanish Trail was being utilized, the spring was a favorite camping spot. The ghost town site of Chloride* is in this vicinity. S24,T35S,R15W,SLM; 5,533' (1,686m). 360.

SAND SPRING CANYON (**Iron**) is near Chloride Canyon and includes the Sand Spring (Iron).

SANDTOWN* (**Utah**). See Goshen* (Utah).

SANDY CITY* (**Salt Lake**) is twelve miles south of Salt Lake City* on the sand bench from which the name is derived. It was settled as an agricultural community when the first post office was established in 1871. The community rapidly changed to a mining, smeltering, and teamster center for the mines in the adjacent Wasatch Mountains. It was also known for the depot where blocks of granite from Little Cottonwood Canyon were reloaded onto rail cars. The blocks were used for the construction of the Salt Lake City Mormon temple. There is one alternate claim to the origin of the city name. When the first locomotive came to the expanding city the engineer was a very popular red-headed, sandy-bearded man named Alexander Kinghorn. Some claim the town was named Sandy after Kinghorn. S6,T3S,R1E,SLM; 4,450' (1,356m). 252, 444, 542, 546.

SANDY CREEK (**Wayne**) originates twelve miles west of Mount Pennell in the Henry Mountains. It drains north through very sandy terrain and empties into the Fremont River. T33S,R8E,SLM to S15,T29S,R8E,SLM.

SANFORD CREEK (**Garfield**) originates on the western slopes of the Sevier Plateau and drains west into the Sevier River. See Fort Sanford* for name source. S16,T33S,R5W,SLM (at mouth); 6,440' (1,963m).

SANPETE COUNTY was created when a congressional act founded the Utah Territory in 1850. The county is one of the original eight counties of the territory. Sanpete is a corruption of San Pitch, the name of the Ute Indian chieftain whose people lived in the region.

SANPETE VALLEY (**Sanpete**) is a large beautiful valley with the San Pitch River draining through it. To the north is Fairview* and at the south end is Manti*. It was originally called San Pitch Valley for the local Ute Indian chieftain.

SANTA CLARA* (Washington) is on Santa Clara Creek four miles northwest of St. George*. Jacob Hamblin, an early Mormon scout and church authority, helped establish an Indian mission on the site in 1854. In 1856 a fort was built. The settlement was destroyed by floodwaters in 1862, then rebuilt on higher ground. The river was named by early travelers on the Old Spanish Trail that followed the river. It refers to the exceptionally good weather in this region.
S16,T42S,R16W,SLM. 22, 289, 310, 311.

SANTA CLARA BENCH* (Washington). See Ivins*.
100(v17).

SANTA CLARA RIVER (Washington) originates in the Pine Valley Mountains near Pine Valley* and drains into the Virgin River south of St. George*. The river was named by the early travelers of the Old Spanish Trail that followed the river. For a short time it was known as the Tonaquint River, named for the small tribe of Tonaquint Indians living further downriver, near the mouth.
S15,T39S,R15W,SLM to S6,T43S,R6W,SLM. 240, 311, 546, 600.

SANTA ISABEL, EL RIO DE. See Sevier River.

SANTAQUIN* (Utah) is four miles southwest of Payson* on Summit Creek. It was settled by Benjamin Johnson and others in 1851. The community was originally named Summit City* because it was situated on a summit between Utah and Juab valleys. In 1856 the community name was changed to honor a San Pitch Indian chief of the Ute Indian nation who lived with his clan in the area.
S1,2,T9S,R1E,SLM; 4,880' (1,487m). 270, 289, 468, 546.

SANTAQUIN DRAW (Duchesne) originates in the southwest area of the Uinta Mountains at Santaquin Springs and drains east into Rabbit Gulch. The draw was named for the spring.
S17,T2S,R8W,USM. 595.

SANTAQUIN PEAK (Utah) is a high point on Loafer Mountain east of Santaquin*.
S32,T9S,R3E,SLM; 10,685' (3,257m).

SANTAQUIN SPRING (Duchesne) is at the head of Santaquin Draw in the southeast Uinta Mountains. See Santaquin* for name source.
S17,T2S,R8W,USM; 7,920' (2,414m). 595.

SAPPHIRE MOUNTAINS (Tooele) are included in the U.S. Military Dugway Proving Grounds, five miles south of Granite Peak. MRN
NE¼,T9S,R13W,SLM.

SARATOGA SPRINGS (Utah) are on the northwest shore of Utah Lake. John C. Nagle, an early settler, owned the springs. When John Beck purchased the ranch and springs, he developed the area as a public resort for swimming and picnicking and named it Saratoga* for the famous resort in New York.
S26,T5S,R1W,SLM; 4,510' (1,375m). 100 (v2).

SARA ANN CANYON (Garfield) originates at the north end of the Kaiparowits Plateau and drains southeast into Right Hand Collett Canyon. MRN
S20-35,T37S,R3E,SLM.

SARDINE CANYON (Cache) originates near Sardine Summit in the Wellsville Mountains and drains northeast into Cache Valley. The small sardine-size fish found in the river is one reason for the name. However, the best recorded alternate claim reports that on September 15, 1858, the Wellsville pioneers traveling through this canyon stopped to lunch on their last can of sardines.

S34-S18,T10N,R1W,SLM. 100(v17), 249(21 Nov. 1977), 546, 567.

SARDINE PEAK (Weber) is one and one-half miles north of Snow Basin at the head of Wheeler Creek. See Sardine Canyon.
S20,T6N,R1E,SLM; 7,486' (2,282m).

SARGENT LAKE (Summit) is in the north central section of the Uinta Mountains on the East Fork of Smiths Fork. In 1883 Nephi and Amos Sargent converted the lake into a reservoir.
9,690' (2,954m). 508.

SAUCER LAKE (Uintah) is in the eastern section of the Uinta Mountains on the headwaters of the Whiterocks River, East Fork. The lake has a circular shape.

SAWMILL CANYON (Beaver) originates on the northeast slopes of Frisco Peak in the San Francisco Mountains and drains east into Morehouse Canyon. A sawmill was built in the canyon in the 1870s.
S23,24,25,T26S,R13W,SLM. 125.

SAWMILL CANYON (Beaver) originates on the southwest slopes of Blawn Mountain of the Wah Wah Mountains. The canyon drains southwest into Pine Valley.
T29,30S,R15,16W,SLM.

SAWMILL CREEK (Beaver) originates on the eastern slopes of White Rock Peak in Nevada and drains northeast into Utah at Hamblin Valley Wash.
S13,23,24,T29S,R20W,SLM.

SAWMILL FORK (Beaver) originates on the southwest slopes of Delano Peak in the Tushar Mountains and drains southwest into Merchant Creek. Sawmills were built at the head of the fork.
S23,27,34,T28S,R5W,SLM.

SAWTOOTH PEAK (Beaver) is on the northeast slopes of the Needle Range.

The peak has a jagged profile.
S15,T28S,R18W,SLM; 7,273' (2,217m).

SCARECROW PEAK (Washington) is in the Beaver Dam Mountains west of Beaver Dam Wash. MRN
S18,T41S,R19W,SLM; 4,492' (1,369m).

SCHARF MESA (Grand) is north of the Dolores River and seven miles west of the Colorado border. John and Samuel R. Scharf developed a ranch there in the 1890s.
S5,6,7,8,T23S,R25E,SLM; 5,222' (1,522m). 25, 146.

SCIPIO* (Millard) is near I-15, thirty-seven miles south southwest of Nephi*. It was originally settled in 1859 with an early name of Round Valley* for the oval-shaped valley where the community is located. For a while it was also called Craball*. In 1861 the name Scipio was finally agreed upon for Scipio Kenner, an early settler. An early Fort Scipio* also existed in this area.
S17,T18S,R2W,SLM; 5,296' (1,614m). 100 (v5,17), 289, 314, 516, 542, 567.

SCIPIO LAKE (Millard) is in Round Valley, nine miles south of Scipio*.
S2,11,T20S,R2W,SLM; 5,961' (1,817m).

SCOFIELD* (Carbon) is on U-96 south of Scofield Reservoir at the junction of Pleasant Valley Creek and Winter Quarters Canyon. It was settled in 1879 as a ranching community that utilized the wild meadow grasses in the area. Coal was discovered shortly after and by 1882 the railroad was brought into the valley. The rapidly developing community was named for General Charles W. Scofield, a timber contractor and a local mine official. The town had an early name of Pleasant Valley*.
S5,T13S,R7E,SLM; 7,702' (2,348m). 89, 100 (v17), 360, 542, 546.

SCORPIO PEAK (Box Elder) is high point of the Hogup Mountains west of the Great Salt Lake. MRN

SCORPION FLAT (Garfield) is south of the Escalante River and Twentyfive Mile Wash. Scorpions are numerous in this region.
T37,38S,R7E,SLM; 5,100' (1,554m). 12.

SCORPION GULCH (Kane) originates on Scorpion Flat and drains east into the Escalante River. See Scorpion Flat (Garfield) for name source.
T38S,R7,8E,SLM. 12.

SCORUP CANYON (San Juan) is between White and Blue Notch canyons and drains west into Lake Powell. Al and Jim Scorup, early cattlemen, ran their cattle in this region from the 1890s onward.
T35S,R14E,SLM. 555(v32).

SCOUT LAKE (Duchesne) is at the west end of the Uinta Mountains, one and one-half miles north of Mirror Lake. The Boy Scout Camp Steiner is located on the banks of the lake. It had an early name of Hearts Lake.
S22,23,T4N,R9W,USM; 10,375' (3,162m). 309.

SCRABBLE CANYON (Beaver) originates on the southwest slopes of the Tushar Mountains and drains west into Kane Canyon. One has to "scrabble" to get through the canyon.
S5,6,T30S,R6W,SLM.

SCRANTON* (Tooele) was a small mining ghost town site in the East Tintic Mountains southeast of Vernon*. It was settled in 1908 and was abandoned in 1910 after the ore was depleted. What was left of the site was burned out in a 1971 range fire. MRN
S8,T9S,R3W,SLM. 89.

SEAMON CANYON (Kane) originates five miles east of Johnson* and drains south into Arizona. It was named for Captain John Seamon, who settled in the canyon in 1874.
S34,T42S,R4W,SLM (at head). 567.

SCUDDER LAKE (Duchesne) is at the west end of the Uinta Mountains, midway between Mirror Lake and Naturalist Basin. It was named for one of Agassiz's students, Samuel Hubbard Scudder, an entomologist. See Naturalist Basin.
S36,T4N,R9W,USM; 10,050' (3,063m). 298, 530.

SEARS CREEK (Daggett) originates on the northern slopes of the Uinta Mountains, six miles south of the west end of Browns Park. The creek drains north into the Green River. Charles B. Sears and his wife, Elizabeth, moved into the area to develop a ranch in 1875.
S35,T1N,R24E,SLM. 172.

SECOND SPRING CREEK (Beaver) originates on the western slopes of the Tushar Mountains and drains north into the South Fork of North Creek. This is the second spring creek adjacent to the old road that works its way up the west face of the Tushars.
S27,T28S,R6W,SLM. 125.

SECRET LAKE (Salt Lake). See Cecret Lake (Salt Lake).

SECRET MESA (Emery) is on the San Rafael Swell between the heads of Eagle Canyon and Coal Wash, South Fork. Since the mesa was isolated, it was often used as a holding area for rustled livestock.
S30,31,T22S,R10E,SLM; 6,900' (2,103m). 193.

SEEDSKEDEE RIVER is an Indian name for the Green River. Variants: Seedskeedee-Agie, Seedskeeder, and others.
159, 237, 372, 609.

SEELEY CREEK (Emery) originates near the head of Cottonwood Canyon east of Ephraim* and drains east into Joes Valley Reservoir. Wellington Seeley was a pioneer stockman out of Castle Dale* who ran his cattle along the creek.

S26,T17S,R4E,SLM to S6,T18S,R6E,SLM. 100(v17), 360, 567.

SEEP FLAT **(Garfield)** is fifteen miles out from Escalante* on the Hole-in-the-Rock road. The flat is a water seep at the base of the Kaiparowits Plateau. S1,2,11,12,T37S,R4E,SLM; 5,426' (1,654m). 12.

SEGO* **(Grand)** was a small coal mining community established in 1910 up Sego Canyon north of Thompson Springs. Sego was first known as Ballard* for Harry Ballard, who discovered hard anthracite coal in the area. After Ballard sold the mine, the community became Neslin* for Richard Neslin, the general manager of the American Fuel Company that purchased the property. Neslin was fired in 1915 and the name was changed to the Utah state flower, the sego lily, which was plentiful on the slopes around the community. By 1955, the railroad was using diesel engines, replacing the steam engines, thus decreasing the need for coal. The town was then closed down and the houses were moved to Moab* to be sold. S10,T20S,R20E,SLM; 6,000' (1,829m). 542, 567.

SEGO CANYON **(Grand)** originates in the Book Cliffs. It drains south past Sego* into Thompson Canyon. S10,15,T19S,R20E,SLM.

SELDOM STOP* **(Washington)**. See Tonaquint* (Washington).

SENATOR NATURAL BRIDGE **(San Juan)**. See Natural Bridges National Monument.

SENSEBALL CANYON **(Beaver)**. See Senseball Creek (Beaver).

SENSEBALL CREEK **(Beaver)** originates in the southwest Tushar Mountains and drains southwest through Senseball Canyon into the South Creek, South

Fork. See Senseball Lake for name source. S19,30,T30S,R5W,SLM.

SENSEBALL LAKE **(Beaver)** is at the head of Senseball Creek in the southwest Tushar Mountains. Senseball was an expert one-armed logger who worked in the area in 1873. S19,30,T30S,R5W,SLM; 9,200' (2,804m). 125.

SESSIONS SETTLEMENT* **(Davis)**. See Bountiful* (Davis).

SESSIONS MOUNTAIN **(Davis)** is east of Bountiful* and named for Perrigrine Sessions, the first settler of Bountiful. S29,T2N,R2E,SLM; 9,248' (2,819m).

SETTLEMENT CANYON **(Tooele)** originates in the Oquirrh Mountains on the northwest slopes of Lowe Peak and drains northwest into Tooele Valley. The 1849 pioneers of Tooele Valley initially settled near the mouth of Settlement Canyon. S32,T4S,R3W,SLM to S33,T3S,R4W,SLM. 153, 275, 367.

SETTLEMENT OVER THE RIDGE* **(Box Elder)**. See Plymouth* (Box Elder).

SEVEN SISTERS **(San Juan)** is a north-south-oriented, three-mile-long ridge, west of the Abajo Mountains. There are seven prominent rises on the ridge. S21,28,33,T33S,R20E,SLM; 8,560' (2,609').

SEVENMILE CANYON **(Grand)** originates at Bartlett Flats, fifteen miles northwest of Moab*. The canyon drains northeast into Courthouse Wash, crossing US-160 seven miles northwest of Moab. S31,T24S,R21E,SLM (at mouth).

SEVENMILE CREEK **(Sevier)** originates on the western slopes of Mount Terrill, east of Lost Creek Reservoir. This seven-mile-long creek drains south into Johnson Valley Reservoir at the north end of Fish Lake.

S14,T24S,R2E,SLM to S24,T25S,R2E,SLM.
175.

SEVIER* (**Sevier**) is on US-89 seventeen miles south of Richfield*. The settlement was named for the river it is situated on. It had an earlier name of Cove* because the community is in a secluded area. S29,T25S,R4W,SLM; 5,536' (1,687m). 100 (v17), 542.

SEVIER BRIDGE RESERVOIR (**Juab**) is on the Sevier River east of Scipio*. T16-18S,R1,2W,SLM; 5,014' (1,528m). 285.

SEVIER CANYON (**Piute, Sevier**) is a rugged Sevier River canyon between Marysvale* and Sevier*. S32,T26S,R4W,SLM to S7,T27S,R3W,SLM.

SEVIER COUNTY. On January 16, 1865, Sevier County was formed from the south section of Sanpete County. The name came from the Sevier River, which was included in the county boundary. 6, 242.

SEVIER LAKE (**Millard**) is a remnant of ancient Lake Bonneville located at the mouth of the Sevier River, west of Richfield* and the Cricket Mountains. The lake was once much larger, but it is slowly disappearing. It has had several earlier names. Miera, who was a cartographer with Domínguez and Escalante in 1776, named it Laguna de Miera for himself. General Ashley trapped this far south in 1825 and the lake was known as Ashley Lake for a short period of time. Joseph N. Nicollet, noted French explorer and geologist on U.S. government assignment, explored the region in the mid-1800s. Some maps use his name for the lake. In general the naming of the lake follows that of the Sevier River. See the river for name source. T20-24S,R11,12W,SLM; 4,519' (1,377m). 81, 129, 175, 285, 368, 496, 604.

SEVIER PLATEAU is approximately eighty miles long and twelve to twenty miles wide. The plateau is cut by the East Fork, Sevier River. See the Sevier River for name source. 175, 314.

SEVIER RIVER originates in Kane County near the summit of Long Valley at Long Valley Junction*. The river drains north through the Sevier River Bridge Reservoir, making a dramatic "U" turn south near Delta*, then flows into the seasonal Sevier Lake. The river is prominent in western and Utah history and it is the longest river located entirely within the state of Utah. The present name is a corruption of Rio Severo, the name used by the Spanish. It means severe and violent, which is an appropriate way to describe the river as it drains through difficult terrain. Domínguez and Escalante called it El Rio de Santa Isabel. The river, as did the lake, carried the name Nicollet for a short period of time. Jedediah Smith named it the Ashley River, in honor of his former employer. Several references give Brigadier General John Sevier of Kentucky credit for the name of the Sevier River, but this is incorrect. See also Sevier Lake. 175, 237, 240, 285, 289, 314, 583, 584, 585, 604.

SEWING MACHINE PASS (**Beaver**) is on the west central slopes of the Wah Wah Mountains. The rock structure resembles an old-fashioned sewing machine. S1,T27S,R16W,SLM; 6,100' (1,859m).

SEYMOUR CANYON (**Summit**) originates in the mountains four miles east southeast of Oakley* and drains west northwest into the Weber River. John Seymour homesteaded the mouth of the canyon. S22,26,T1S,R6E,SLM. 298.

SHADOW LAKE (**Summit**) is at the west end of the Uinta Mountains on the upper Provo River, close to the east base of Haystack Mountain. The lake is

shaded for the better part of the day.
S12,T2S,R8E,SLM; 10,050' (3,063m). 530.

SHAFER BASIN (San Juan) is west of
the Colorado River, north of The
Confluence, and east of Dead Horse
Point. The basin was named for Frank
and John H. Shafer, cattlemen in the
region during the 1870s. John Shafer
homesteaded in the Moab* area in the
early 1880s.
S1,T27S,R20E,SLM. 409, 475, 555(v36).

SHAFER CANYON (San Juan) is a
short canyon originating one mile
southwest of Dead Horse Point. It drains
southeast into the Colorado River. See
Shafer Basin for name source.
S7,T27S,R20E,SLM.

SHAFER TRAIL (Grand) is north of
The Confluence between the Green and
Colorado rivers. It leads from Red Sea
Flat and Grays Pasture down into Shafer
Canyon. As the cattle rustling and other
outlaw gangs began to die out, the trail
was developed by Frank and J. H. Shafer
who used it to move their cattle to
market and into winter and summer
range. Later, the trail was used by
people working in the uranium industry.
T27S,R19E,SLM. 146, 409, 514.

SHAG HOLLOW (Beaver) originates on
the eastern slopes of the Mineral
Mountains and drains east into
Cunningham Wash. It was named for
James (Shagg) McEwan of Beaver.
S32,33,T27S,R8W,SLM. 125.

SHAG HOLLOW (Beaver) originates on
the eastern slopes of the Mineral
Mountains and drains southwest into
Wildcat Creek. See Shag Hollow for
name source.
S30,32,T28S,R8W,SLM.

SHAKESPEARE ARCH (Garfield) is in
the Kodachrome Basin State Reserve,
nine miles south of Cannonville*. Tom
Shakespeare, park superintendent,

discovered the arch and named it after
early family members who settled the
area.
NE¼,T38S,R2W,SLM. 466(20 March 1983).

SHALE CREEK (Duchesne) is a short
precipitous creek in the central section of
the Uinta Mountains. The creek originates in a cluster of lakes including Dime
and Divide lakes and drains northwest
into the Uinta River. The creek is named
for the steep shale slopes it drains.

SHALE LAKE (Duchesne) is at the base
of steep shale slopes at the west end of
the Uinta Mountains, one mile west of
Mount Agassiz.
S30,T4N,R8W,USM; 10,580' (3,225m). 530.

SHALER LAKE (Duchesne) is in the
Naturalist Basin as one of a cluster of
lakes at the west end of the Uinta
Mountains, at the foot of Mount Agassiz.
These lakes were named in honor of
students of Agassiz. Nathanial Southgate
Shaler was a geologist.
S27,28,T4N,R8W,USM; 10,910' (3,325m).
298, 309, 530.

SHALLOW LAKE (Summit) is at the
west end of the Uinta Mountains
between Washington Lake and the Provo
River Falls. The lake depth is only two
feet.
S7,8,T2S,R9E,SLM; 9,825' (2,995m). 298,
530.

SHAMBIP* (Tooele). See Stockton*.

SHAMBIP COUNTY was established on
January 12, 1856. In 1862 the county was
absorbed back into Tooele County. The
name is Goshute Indian and means water
rushes and reeds.
6, 542.

SHANGHAI CANYON (Weber) is opposite Pineview Reservoir Dam east of
Ogden*. The bridge that once crossed
the Ogden River at this point was often
called the Shanghai Bridge, so the

canyon was given that name. The site where this bridge was located is now under water.
S9,16,T6N,R1E,SLM. 567.

SHANNON HOLLOW (**Beaver**) originates ten miles south of Beaver* and drains northwest into California Hollow and the Greenville Bench. Dave Shannon owned a ranch nearby and the hollow was named for him.
S25,36,T30S,R8W,SLM. 567.

SHARP PEAK (**Cache**) is in the Monte Cristo Mountains ten miles north of Monte Cristo Peak. It is a sharp, steep-sided peak.
S9,T8N,R2E,SLM; 9,082' (2,768m). 567.

SHAUNTIE* (**Beaver**) is a ghost town site at the head of Shauntie Wash in the southeast section of the Star Range, fourteen miles southwest of Milford*. In 1870 it was a miner's tent town. After 1876 the settlement declined as the nearby mines were worked out. It was eventually abandoned. The name is of Piute Indian origin and means "much" or "a whole lot."
S26,T28S,R12W,SLM; 6,100' (1,859m). 89, 355, 516, 567.

SHAUNTIE WASH (**Beaver**) originates in the Star Range southwest of Milford* and drains south into the Escalante Desert. See Shauntie* for the name source.
S25,T28S,R12W,SLM to S12,T29S,R12W, SLM.

SHAY MOUNTAIN (**San Juan**). See Abajo Peak (San Juan). MRN

SHEARING CORRAL (**Rich**) is on Shearing Corral Creek at the Reservoir. This was the center for shearing and shipping out sheep.
S28,T6N,R7E,SLM; 6,800' (2,073m).

SHEARING CORRAL CREEK (**Summit**) originates near the Morgan-

Rich County border, six miles west of Wahsatch*. It drains northeast through the Shearing Corral Reservoir into Wyoming. Shearing corrals were established near the reservoir site and vast herds of sheep were brought in at shearing and shipping time.
S1,T5N,R6E,SLM (into Wyoming).

SHEARING CORRAL RESERVOIR (**Rich**) is on upper Shearing Corral Creek.
S28,T6N,R7E,SLM.

SHEARING CORRAL SPRING (**Beaver**) is in the foothills of the Mineral Mountains between Minersville* and the mouth of Cave Canyon.
S13,T29S,R10W,SLM; 6,000' (1,029m).

SHEEP CREEK (**Beaver**) originates in the Indian Peak area of the Needle Range and drains northeast into Pine Valley.
T30S,R17W,SLM.

SHEEP CREEK (**Cache**) originates four miles northeast of Monte Cristo Peak and drains northwest into Blacksmith Fork.
S28,T9N,R4E,SLM to S25,T10N,R3E,SLM.

SHEEP CREEK (**Daggett**) originates five miles south of Corson Peak of the Phil Pico Mountains and drains east into Flaming Gorge Reservoir. It was named for the mountain sheep that once existed in this area. Powell originally called it Kingfisher Creek, but the name was soon changed.
S21,T2N,R18E,SLM to S8,T2N,R20E,SLM. 172.

SHEEP CREEK LAKE (**Daggett**) is in the northeast section of the Uinta Mountains on the headwaters of Sheep Creek from which it receives its name.
8,600' (2,621m).

SHEEP CREEK RESERVOIR (**Beaver**) is at the junction of Cottonwood and

Sheep creeks on the east slope of the Needle Range.
S35,T29S,R17W,SLM.

SHEEP VALLEY (Sevier) is a good sheep-grazing valley three miles north of Hilgard Mountain.
S14,22,23,T24S,R3E,SLM; 9,400' (2,865m).

SHEEPPEN CREEK (Rich) originates in the mountains east of the central section of Bear Lake and drains north into North Eden Canyon. The name is tied to the early overgrazing of sheep that occurred in this area.
S28-S4,T14N,R7E,SLM.

SHEEPROCK CANYON (Beaver) originates on the western slopes of the Tushar Mountains at Pole Mountain, and drains southwest into Big Hollow, northeast of Manderfield*.
S7,8,T28S,R6W,SLM.

SHEEPROCK MOUNTAINS (Tooele) are at the south end of the Onaqui Mountains with Rush Valley on the east. Big horn sheep were plentiful in these mountains when the settlers arrived.
T8,9,10S,R5,6,7W,SLM; 8,010' (2,441m).

SHEFFIELD ROAD, BEND, AND ALCOVE (Garfield). The road originates twelve miles out from Escalante* on U-12, which is the highway to Boulder. It ends at a large bend and alcove of the Escalante River where Sam Sheffield ranched during the early days of Escalante.
S36,T35S,R5E,SLM (the bend). 12.

SHELLY BALDY CREEK (Beaver) originates in the Tushar Mountains between Delano and Shelly Baldy peaks, and drains south into Merchant Creek, West Fork. The creek received its name from the peak.
S15,22,T28S,R5W,SLM.

SHELLY BALDY PEAK (Beaver) is at the head of Shelly Baldy Creek. The peak is bare and covered with shale.

"Shelly" is claimed to be a corruption of "Shaley."
S16,T28S,R5W,SLM; 11,326' (3,452m). 125.

SHENANDOAH CITY* (Beaver) is a ghost town site in the central section of the Star Range, twelve miles southwest of Milford*. This early 1870s mining camp was named by Confederate war veterans of the Civil War.
S25,T28S,R12W,SLM; 5,900' (1,798m). 89, 355, 516.

SHEPHARD LAKE (Duchesne) is at the west end of the Uinta Mountains in the Murdock Basin. Hoover and Marshall lakes are in the vicinity. The lake was named for a former forest supervisor.
S2,T3N,R9W,USM; 9,975' (3,040m). 100(v2).

SHINGLE CREEK (Piute, Sevier) originates in the northwest Tushar Mountains, three miles northwest of Little Shelly Baldy Peak, and drains north into Clear Creek. The lumber harvested in this region made good shingles.
S3,T27S,R4W,SLM to S34,T26S,R5W,SLM.

SHINGLE CREEK (Summit) originates at the southwest section of the Uinta Mountains at East Shingle Creek Lake. It drains south into the Provo River. Jed Lambert operated a shingle mill in the canyon during the 1880s.
S6,T2S,R8E,SLM to S2,T3S,R8E,SLM. 298.

SHINGLE MILL CANYON (Kane) originates at the base of the Pink Cliffs, eight miles north northwest of Glendale*, and drains southeast into Stout Canyon. An early shingle-producing sawmill was located in the canyon.
S16,T39S,R7W,SLM.

SHINGLE MILL CREEK (Summit) originates at the west end of the Uinta Mountains at Shingle Mill Lake and drains north northwest into Smith and Morehouse Creek. This region is important timber country.
S11,T1S,R7E,SLM to S33,T1N,R7E,SLM.

SHINGLE MILL LAKE (**Summit**) is at the head of Shingle Mill Creek, six miles northeast of Hoyt Peak. The lake received its name from the creek.
S11,T1S,R7E,SLM; 9,550' (2,911m).

SHINOB-KIAB MOUNTAIN (**Washington**) is southeast of Washington* and is named for an important god of the local Indians. "Kiab" means mountain.
S24,T42S,R10W,SLM. 310.

SHIP MOUNTAIN POINT (**Kane**) is fifteen miles northeast of Big Water* (Kane). The mountain is shaped like a ship.
S26,27,T40S,R3E,SLM; 6,519' (1,987m).

SHIRTS CREEK (**Iron**) originates in the Cedar Mountains at the head of Shurtz Canyon, five miles southeast of Hamilton Fort. It drains northwest into Quichapa Lake. The creek was named for Peter Shirts (Shurtz), a pioneer from Europe. The early Utah Territory places that were named after Shirts were spelled with a European spelling. Shirts later anglicized his name, so both spellings are used on more recent maps. Sidon Creek was an early name for the creek.
S24,T37S,R11W,SLM to S27,T36S,R12W, SLM. 72, 359, 409, 567, 600.

SHIRTS FORT (**Kane**) was four miles south of Paria* on the Paria (Pahreah) River. Peter Shirts (Shurtz) and others built this small fort in 1865. For safety reasons the group soon moved upstream to the site of Paria.
131, 516.

SHITAMARING CREEK (**Garfield**) originates in the Henry Mountains on the south slopes of Mount Hillers, and drains south into Hansen Creek. The water of the creek is poisonous and very diarrheic. The creek name on the U.S. Geological Survey 15' 1952 Mount Hillers map is now controversial and does not fit the standards set by the U.S. Board on Domestic Geographic Names. The name of the creek has been changed on more recent maps, although the new maps have not yet been made available.
T34S,R11E,SLM to S16,T35S,R11E,SLM.

SHIVWITS* (**Washington**) is a small Indian village on the Shivwit Indian Reservation, eight miles northwest of Santa Clara*.
S33,T41S,R17W,SLM.

SHOAL CREEK (**Washington**) originates at the summit eleven miles west of Enterprise*, and drains northeast into the desert near Beryl*. John and Charles Pulsipher named the creek when they were exploring this area in search of a place to develop a settlement (Hebron*). The creek name refers to the shallow, sandy bottom.
S31,T36S,R18W,SLM to S6,T36S,R18W, SLM. 89, 100(v13).

SHOESTRING LAKE (**Summit**) is on the Provo River drainage at the west end of the Uinta Mountains. Trial Lake is one mile north. The lake is long, narrow, and slightly curved.
S5,8,T2S,R9E,SLM; 9,825' (2,995m).

SHORT CANYON (**Emery**) originates on the Beckwith Plateau eleven miles north of Green River and drains east into the Green River. This canyon is shorter than Long Canyon, which is also in this area.
S24,T19S,R15E,SLM.

SHOT CANYON (**Wayne**). Lou Chaffin and his son Ned joined the Ekkerses in building a trail from Jasper Canyon into their newly named Shot Canyon. The trail was built by blasting or "shooting" out the path with explosives.
T30S,R18E,SLM. 102.

SHOWALTER BENCH (**Garfield**) is ten miles north of Bryce Canyon National

Park and west of Johns Valley. It was named for Clarence Showalter, who ran sheep there in the 1890s. See also Clarence Creek.
S2,3,T35S,R4W,SLM; 8,200' (2,499m).

SHOWALTER CREEK (Garfield) originates twelve miles northwest of Bryce Canyon National Park and drains southeast into the Sevier River, East Fork at Johns Valley. See Showalter Bench for name source.
S28,T35S,R3W,SLM (at mouth).

SHUMWAY CANYON (Kane). See Ponderosa Canyon (Kane).

SHUNES CREEK (Kane, Washington) originates four miles southeast of the ghost town of Shunesburg* and drains northwest into the East Fork of the Virgin River. See Shunesburg for name source.
T42S,R10W,SLM. D.L. 7902.

SHUNESBURG* (Washington) is a ghost town three miles up the East Fork of the Virgin River, at the base of the old Wiggle Trail. Oliver DeMille and others settled there on January 20, 1862. Recurring Indian-white conflicts, drought, and flooding problems forced the abandonment of the settlement in 1903. The name refers to a local Indian (Shunes) who was the headman of a clan living in this area. Today the locale is private and unavailable to public access.
S10,T42S,R10W,SLM; 3,979' (1,213m). 100 (v13), 154, 289, 311, 600.

SID AND CHARLEY (Emery) is a rock formation in North Salt Wash, two miles south of its junction with Eagle Canyon. The feature was named for its imaginary likeness to Sid and Charley Swasey, who ran their cattle in this region.
S26,T21S,R8E,SLM; 6,000' (1,829m). 193.

SIDON* (Iron). See Hamilton Fort* (Iron).

SIDON CREEK (Iron). See Shirts Creek.

SIDS DRAW (Emery) originates on the San Rafael Swell, two miles southeast of The Wickiup and one mile northwest of I-70. It drains north into Cottonwood Draw and was named for Sid Swazy (Swasey), a San Rafael Swell cattleman.
S23,T22S,R11E,SLM. 193.

SIDS MOUNTAIN (Emery) is east of Castle Valley on the San Rafael Swell. Sid Swasey wintered his livestock on the mountain. See Sids Draw for name source.
T20S,R10E,SLM. 193.

SIGURD* (Sevier) is near the junction of I-70 and U-24. The community was settled in 1874 as an outgrowth of nearby Vermillion*. The U.S. Post Office named the settlement Sigurd because many Danish people lived there and the name had a Danish origin.
S36,T22S,R2W,SLM and S1,T23S,R2S,SLM; 5,270' (1,505m). 100(v17), 289, 542, 585.

SILVER CANYON (Iron) originates one mile north of Silver Peak in the Crows Nest section of the Antelope Range, twenty-three miles west of Cedar City*. The canyon drains west into the desert. Several silver mines were discovered in the area during the 1890s and numerous mining camps were built to house the miners.
S25,T36S,R15W,SLM (at mouth).

SILVER CITY* (Juab) is an old mining ghost town site, five miles south of Eureka* and east of US-6,50. Silver City was originally settled in 1870, peaked in 1908, and was deserted by the early 1930s. Vast amounts of silver were extracted from the mines in this area.
S36,T10S,R3W,SLM; 6,100' (1,859m). 289, 542.

SILVER CREEK (Summit) originates in the mountainous country near Park City* and drains north northeast into the Weber River. The creek was named for its crystal clear, sparkling water.
S22,T2S,R4E,SLM to S20,T1N,R5E,SLM.

SILVER FALLS CREEK (Garfield) originates near the south end of the Wagon Box Mesa and drains southwest into the Escalante River. The creek received its name from the falls area where streaks of desert varnish draped the wet canyon walls, glistening in the sunlight.
T36S,R6E,SLM. 12.

SILVER FORK* (Salt Lake). See Silver Fork (Salt Lake).

SILVER FORK (Salt Lake). The mouth of Silver Fork Canyon is two miles down-canyon from Brighton*. This area has an interesting history. It began in 1854 when sawmills were built to produce timber and timber products such as shingles. Lumber from this area was used in the construction of the famous Mormon Tabernacle. The lumbermen and their families lived at the mouth of what became Silver Fork Canyon. The emphasis on lumbering operations began to change in the 1870s when ore products were discovered in the vicinity. Several mines were then developed and the local emphasis began to shift towards mining. It was at this time that the lumbering community received the named Silver Fork*. As the timber resources were depleted and the mines were worked out, the area reverted to grazing lands. Then, in the early 1900s, transportation to and from the canyon improved and building lots were sold for cabins and summer homes. Today Silver Fork thrives as a year-round community.
S21,T2S,R3E,SLM. 89, 546.

SILVER ISLAND MOUNTAINS (Box Elder) is northeast of and near Wendover*. The mountains are in the heart of the Salt Flats of the Great Salt Lake Desert. The strong shimmering sunlight and rising heated air imparts a silvery reflection and often produces a mirage effect in the region. Silver outcrops have been found there.
T1-5N,R17-19W,SLM; 7,300' (2,225m). 498, 567. D.L. 6001.

SILVER LAKE (Salt Lake) is one-fourth mile west of Brighton* and named for its crystal clearness and silver-like reflection. Variant: Brighton Lake for William A. Brighton, a pioneer settler in the basin.
S35,T2S,R3E,SLM; 8,725' (2,659m). 100(2), 289, 494.

SILVER LAKE* (Salt Lake). See Brighton* (Salt Lake).

SILVER LAKE (Wasatch) is a beautiful reflecting lake in the Cloud Rim area over the summit, three miles east from the head of Big Cottonwood Canyon.
S31,T2S,R4E,SLM; 9,300' (2,835m).

SILVER PEAK (Iron) is on the Antelope Range (including Silver Canyon), five miles east of Newcastle*. Silver ore was discovered in the region in the 1890s.
T36S,R14W,SLM; 7,273' (2,217m). 567.

SILVER REEF* (Washington) was established in 1866 one mile west of Leeds* at the southwest edge of the Pine Valley Mountains. The original name was Bonanza Flats*, which was taken from the name placed on Hyrum Jacobs's store. Prior to 1866 silver had never been found in sandstone, so it created quite a sensation when silver lode was discovered in a protruding sandstone ledge. By the 1880s the reef was mined out and the settlement was abandoned.
S1,T41S,R14W,SLM; 8,730' (2,661m). 27, 89, 154, 403, 438, 516, 542, 546, 600.

SILVERTIP SPRING (Wayne) is in the Robbers Roost Flats near the head of the south fork of Robbers Roost Canyon. The spring was named for Silver Tip (Jim Wall), who was born sometime

around 1850. He became an outlaw and was active in and around the Roost area during the 1890s. Wall received the nickname because his hair was turning grey.
SW½,T28S,R14E,SLM. 25, 303.

SIMPSONS MOUNTAINS (Tooele) have a north-south orientation west of Eureka* and southwest of the Onaqui Mountains. Captain J. H. Simpson originally named this mountain range for Captain Stephen Champlin of the U.S. Navy. The mountains were later renamed to honor Captain Simpson himself. See Simpson Springs for further information.
T9,10S,R7,8W,SLM; 8,406' (2,562m). 371, 477, 546.

SIMPSON SPRINGS (Tooele) are twenty-five miles west of Vernon*. Captain J. H. Simpson was a U.S. military officer sent by the government to explore a western railroad route. Simpson's route was later used for the Pony Express and Overland Stage. He camped at the springs on October 23, 1853, and first named them Pleasant Springs because the water was excellent. The springs were later named to honor Captain J. H. Simpson. See references under Simpson Mountains.
S18,T9S,R8W,SLM; 5,097' (1,554m). 134(29 Feb. 1976), 466(8 July 1978), 477, 545.

SINBAD COUNTRY (Emery) is in the center of the San Rafael Swell at the head of Straight Wash, Cottonwood Draw, and Ernie Canyon. It is an area of "arabesque monoliths of multiple shapes and colors" representing "scenes or castles described in the Arabian Knights" (546, p. 167).
T22S,R12E,SLM. 193, 497, 546.

SINK, THE (Beaver) is a low water-collecting area in the Escalante Desert, west of Minersville* and southwest of Milford*.
S29,T30S,R11W,SLM; 5,025' (1,532m).

SINK HOLES, THE (Garfield) is an area of bogs on Escalante Mountain. The Sink Holes are located east of Griffin Top and north of Barkers Reservoir.
T33S,R1E,SLM; 10,000' (3,048m). 12.

SINK VALLEY (Kane) is at the head of Sink Valley Wash; Alton* is northwest. The valley is a partially enclosed area that is two miles in diameter.
S20,29,T39S,R5W,SLM; 6,950' (2,118m). 455.

SIPAPU BRIDGE (San Juan). See Natural Bridges National Monument.

SISTERS LAKES (Salt Lake) is a cluster of lakes in Hidden Valley between the headwaters of Little and Big Cottonwood canyons. Lake Lillian was named for Mrs. Andy Walker, Lake Florence for the daughter of H. L. A. Culmer, and Lake Blanche for Miss Blanche Cutler.
100(v2).

SIT DOWN BENCH (Kane) is at the confluence of the two arms of Last Chance Creek in the drainage of Roger, Monday, and Sunday canyons. The name of the bench seems to have been acquired over a period of time, depending on who you ask. One version suggests that most people would want to sit down and rest after climbing to the top. Another suggests that the sheepherders had more time to sit and rest there because the grazing was so good the sheep didn't wander.
T42S,R5E,SLM; 4,200' (1,280m). 12, 578. D.L. 8602.

SIXMILE CREEK (Sanpete) originates in the mountains east of Sterling* and drains west into the San Pitch River. One crosses the creek six miles south of Manti* on the old pioneer road.
S35,T18S,R3E,SLM to S32,T18S,R2E,SLM. 514.

SIXMILE PONDS (**Sanpete**) are near the skyline drive on the headwaters of Sixmile Creek.
S2,T19S,R3E,SLM; 8,970' (2,734m).

SIXMILE RESERVOIR (**Rich**) is north northeast of Randolph* near the mouth of Sixmile Creek from which it receives its name.
S25,T13N,R7E,SLM; 6,300' (1,920m).

SIXSHOOTER PEAK, NORTH (**San Juan**) is near Indian Creek and the east entrance to Canyonlands National Park. South Sixshooter Peak is also in the vicinity. The peak has the general shape of a handgun or pistol pointing straight up.
T30S,R20E,SLM.

SIXSHOOTER PEAK, SOUTH (**San Juan**) has the same general shape as North Sixshooter Peak, which is in the same area.
T30½S,R21E,SLM.

SKEEN* (**Weber**). See Plain City*.

SKINNY* (**Sanpete**). See Mayfield*.

SKOOTS CREEK (**Garfield**) drains from the north into Clear Creek near Lake Panguitch. Skoots was a Piute Indian who lived by the creek.
S30,31,T35S,R7W,SLM.

SKOOTSPAH* (**Kane**). See Clarkdale* (Kane).

SKULL FLAT (**Beaver**) is on the western slopes of the Tushar Mountains, between the Beaver River and the East Fork of Baker Canyon. A skull was found on the flat.
S23,T29S,R6W,SLM; 9,000' (2,743m). 125.

SKULL SPRING (**Garfield**) is on the Aquarius Plateau near the mouth of Lost Creek, nine miles northwest of Escalante*. Cattle skulls were found alongside the spring: apparently the animals had been marooned and died

there during the wintertime.
6,600' (2,012m).

SKULL VALLEY (**Tooele**) is a broad valley between the Stansbury and Onaqui mountains, and the Cedar Mountains. Dugway* and Timpie* (Rowley Junction*) are two settlements in this valley that had an earlier name of Spring Valley. The families of Harrison Severe and James McBride were early white settlers. When prehistoric buffalo skulls were found in the valley in 1853-54, people began using the name Skull Valley. Another claim for the name source is that native Indian skulls were reportedly found in area springs.
T3-5S,R8,9W,SLM; 4,500' (1,372m). 314, 506, 546.

SKUMPAH CANYON (**Sevier**) originates at Skumpah Reservoir and drains southwest into Salina Creek. See Skumpah Creek for name source.
S32,T21S,R4E,SLM.

SKUMPAH CREEK (**Sevier**) originates five miles north of Acord Lakes and drains southwest through Skumpah Reservoir and Canyon, then flows into Salina Creek. "Skumpah" is a Piute word referring to the rabbitbrush that grows along the creek.
S22,T21S,R4E,SLM to S12,T22S,R3E,SLM.

SKUTUMPAH* (**Kane**). See Clarkdale* (Kane).

SKUTUMPAH CANYON (**Kane**). Skutumpah Creek drains through the canyon.

SKUTUMPAH CREEK (**Kane**) originates at the junction of Mill and Mineral creeks near the south side of Bryce Canyon National Park. The creek drains south into Johnson Wash. This region is one where the Navajo, Piute, and Ute Indian tribes overlapped. Since no written Indian language existed, the whites wrote down their interpretation of the Indian spoken word. These interpretations created many variations such as Skootumpa and Skutempah. "Skoots-pa" meant "the creek where the squirrels live" and "skoom-pa" meant "the creek where the rabbitbrush grows." Therefore, Skutumpah, and other words, are a combination of words that the white people had interpreted. T40S,R4½W,SLM. 100(v17), 422, 455.

SKYLINE ARCH (Garfield). See Stevens Arch (Garfield).

SLAGTOWN* (Tooele) is a ghost town site on the eastern shore of Rush Lake (Lake Shambip), southwest of Stockton*. Slagtown was known earlier as Martinville* because of its resemblance to the nests of the well-known birds, the martins. The settlement was established near the Old Chicago Smelter that was built in 1871. Slagtown lasted until 1880 when it was abandoned because the smelter closed down. S26,T4S,R5W,SLM; 5,000' (1,524m). 97(v8), 100(v17), 516.

SLATE CANYON (Summit) originates in the west end of the Uinta Mountains, five and one-half miles northeast of Kamas*, and drains south into Beaver Creek. The predominant bedrock in the canyon is slate, a sedimentary rock. S5,8,17,20,T2S,R7E,SLM.

SLATERVILLE* (Weber) was settled in the fall of 1850 between Plain City* and Roy* and was initially known as Mill Creek*. The three original families drew lots for the honor of having the settlement named after them. Richard Slater won the draw. S11,T6N,R2W,SLM; 4,240' (1,292m). 27, 274, 289, 542, 567.

SLICKHORN CANYON (San Juan) originates on Polly Mesa, east of Grand Gulch, and drains south into the San Juan River. It was named for a distinctive herd of longhorn cattle. S9,T40S,R16E,SLM (at mouth). 610.

SLICKROCK BENCH (Kane) is at the head of Hackberry Canyon, fifteen miles north of the ghost town of Paria*. This area is an open benchland composed of sandstone slickrock with no vegetation. T38S,R1W,SLM.

SLIDE CANYON (Utah) originates three miles north of Springdell* and drains southeast into Provo Canyon. A two-mile-long timber slide was constructed from the top to the bottom of the canyon in order to move logs down to the sawmill. S21,27,T5S,R3E,SLM. 100(v17), 567.

SLY GO* (Rich) was a temporary 1864 settlement in Round Valley. See Round Valley* (Rich). MRN

SMITH* (Beaver). See Smyths* (Beaver).

SMITH AND MOREHOUSE CREEK (Summit) originates at the west end of the Uinta Mountains in Hells Kitchen and Erickson Basin. The creek drains west northwest into the Weber River. Smith and Morehouse was an early logging company that operated in the area. S28,T1S,R8E,SLM to S28,T1N,R7E,SLM. 298.

SMITH AND MOREHOUSE RESERVOIR (Summit) is at the west end of the Uinta Mountains on Smith and Morehouse Creek. S1,12,T1S,R7E,SLM; 7,650' (2,332m).

SMITH CANYON (Garfield) originates on the western slopes of Mount Dutton and drains southwest into the Sevier River. George Smith was a black man who hauled logs out of the canyon. S35,T32S,R5W,SLM (at mouth). 567.

SMITH CREEK (Morgan) originates at the Smith Creek Lakes on the Davis County line, and drains east northeast into the Weber River. Smith Creek had an earlier name of Swan Creek for

Ephraim Swan. After Swan moved out of the area, William Smith moved in.
S28,T4N,R1E,SLM to S17,T4N,R2E,SLM. 378.

SMITH CREEK LAKES (**Morgan**) is a cluster of small lakes at the head of Smith Creek, north of Francis Peak. The lakes received their name from the creek.
S28,T4N,R1E,SLM; 8,800' (2,682m).

SMITHFIELD* (**Cache**) is six miles north of Logan*. This small town was originally settled in 1859 as Summit Creek*. The name was soon changed to its present name to honor John Glover Smith, a Mormon who served as the first bishop.
S27,28,33,34,T13N,R1E,SLM; 4,595' (1,401m). 100(v17), 448, 449, 542.

SMITHFIELD CANYON (**Cache**) originates in the Bear River Range and drains west into the Bear River. The canyon is named for the town it serves.
S23,24,T13N,R1E,SLM.

SMITHS FORK (**Summit**) originates near Mount Wilson and Red Castle Lake, and drains north into Wyoming. It was named for Jedediah S. Smith, a noted trapper, mountain man, and explorer.
309, 372, 496.

SMITHSONIAN BUTTE (**Washington**) is south of Rockville*. The butte was named by Captain Clarence Edward Dutton, a noted geologist who worked closely with Major Powell in the surveying of this region. Dutton also wrote *Geology of the High Plateaus*.
T42S,R11W,SLM; 6,773' (2,064m). 286, 496, 530.

SMOKEY MOUNTAIN (**Kane**) is northeast of Big Water* (Glen Canyon City*), west of lower Last Chance Creek, and south of Henrieville*. Stockmen tell of smoke columns rising from cracks in the ground and of burning underground coal deposits. In 1967 and 1968 the U.S.

Bureau of Mines attempted to extinguish underground fires by plugging up the ground fissures.
T40,42S,R4,5E,SLM; 5,840' (1,780m). 12, 455, 546, 602.

SMYTHS* (**Beaver**) is presently a railroad siding twelve miles north of Milford* where John Smyth developed a ranch. The ranch then evolved into a small settlement. The community was also known as Read* (Reed*) for a short period of time.
T26S,R10W,SLM; 4,925' (1,501m). 355, 516.

SNAKE CANYON (**San Juan**) is west of Bluff* and drains east, crossing US-163. The canyon is known for its crooked course.
S27-25,T40S,SLM. 546, 567.

SNAKE CREEK (**Kane**) originates seven miles northeast of Nipple Lake and drains southwest into the Paria River. Rattlesnakes are common in the region.
T39-40S,R2W,SLM.

SNAKE CREEK (**Wasatch**) originates on the southeast slopes of Sunset Peak, three miles south of Brighton*. The creek drains southeast into Pine Creek. Numerous snakes—usually rattlesnakes—live in the rocky areas along the creek.
T3S,R3E,SLM to S22,T3S,R4E,SLM. 100 (v17), 567.

SNAKE VALLEY (**Juab, Millard**) is an extensive valley with a north-south orientation west of the Conger and Confusion ranges. The valley is known for its rattlesnakes.
T21S,R18,19W,SLM. 477, 567.

SNOW BASIN (**Weber**) is northeast of Mount Ogden and south of the Ogden River. It was originally known as Wheeler Basin for Levi and Simon Wheeler who operated a sawmill in this area. In 1939 the name was changed to Snow Basin when it became a popular ski area.
S28,32,T6N,R1E,SLM. 567.

SNOW CANYON (Washington) is a state park north of Santa Clara*. The canyon was named in 1861 for Mormon Apostle Erastus Snow, a prominent figure in helping develop Utah's Dixie.
S4,5,T41S,R16W,SLM to S33,34,T41S,R16W, SLM. 546, 567.

SNOWBIRD* (Salt Lake) is a renowned ski and recreation resort at the head of Little Cottonwood Canyon, southeast of Salt Lake City*.

SNOWVILLE* (Box Elder) is on US-84 near Deep Creek and the Idaho border. It was settled in 1871 by Idahoans who named their community after Mormon Apostle Lorenzo Snow, who was assigned to supervise the development of this section of the Utah Territory.
S2,11,T14N,R8W,SLM; 4,544' (1,385m). 289, 542, 546, 567.

SNYDERS STATION* (Summit). See Snyderville* (Summit).

SNYDERVILLE* (Summit) is four miles northwest of Park City*. It was settled in 1865 by J. M. Grant, H. C. Kimball, and Samuel C. Snyder, who developed mine holdings and a sawmill in the area. After the Overland Stage went through this area, it became known as Snyders Station* and later Snyderville, for G. G. Snyder, the younger brother of Sam. G. G. was a probate judge who named Park City.
T1S,R4E,SLM; 6,554' (1,998m). 542, 555(v28), 567.

SOAPSTONE BASIN (Wasatch) is in the Soapstone Creek drainage, two miles south of its junction with the Provo River. See the creek for name source.
S17,21,22,T3S,R8E,SLM.

SOAPSTONE CREEK (Wasatch) originates one mile southwest of Iron Mine Mountain and drains northwest into the Provo River. Soapstone, a variety of talc that has a soapy or greasy feel, is prevalent along the creek bed.

S9,T3S,R8E,SLM. 298.

SOAPSTONE MOUNTAINS (Wasatch) are at the west end of the Uinta Mountains, one mile southwest of Soapstone Basin. See Soapstone Creek for name source.
S29,T3S,R8E,SLM; 9,473' (2,887).

SOB RAPIDS (Uintah) are on the Green River within Split Mountain Canyon in the Dinosaur National Monument. Originally these were the S.O.B. rapids, but the name was modified by the National Board on Geographic Names to conform to present-day regulations.

SOBER CITY* (Uintah). See Gusher*.

SODOM* (Utah). See Goshen* (Utah).

SOLDIER BENCH* (Salt Lake) is in the upper reaches of Coon Canyon on the eastern slopes of the Oquirrh Mountains. Colonel Steptoe's troops bivouacked there during the winter of 1854.
S15,T2S,R3W,SLM; 6,200' (1,890m). 360.

SOLDIER CANYON (Morgan) originates four miles southwest of Lost Creek Reservoir and drains south into Lost Creek. In the 1880s an Indian by the name of Old Soldier camped in the canyon.
S23,26,T5N,R4E,SLM. 567.

SOLDIER CREEK (Carbon) originates at Whitmore Park sixteen miles northeast of Wellington* on the West Tavaputs Plateau. It drains southwest into the Provo River. This was the trail used by soldiers moving between Fort Duchesne* and the Price* area.
S33,T12S,R12E,SLM to S9,T15S,R11E,SLM. 165.

SOLDIER CREEK (Utah) originates at Soldier Summit between Thistle* and Helper* and drains west down Spanish Fork Canyon, into the Spanish Fork

River at Thistle. Federal troops used this route when they moved through the area. S25,T10S,R7E,SLM. to S33,T9S,R4E,SLM. 567.

SOLDIER CROSSING (San Juan) is in White Canyon near U-95, fourteen miles northwest of the Natural Bridges National Monument. Soldier Crossing is the site where Captain Perrine and his cavalry overtook a group of Indians on July 15, 1884. The Indians, including Mancos Jim, were fleeing the cavalry when a skirmish ensued. Rowdy Higgins and a Mr. Worthington, a government scout, were killed in the skirmish. A small soldier cemetery is nearby. NW¼,T36S,R16E,SLM. 409.

SOLDIER PASS (Beaver) is in the Mineral Mountains at the summit of the Pass Road southwest of Adamsville*. In 1880 the soldiers from Fort Cameron built a road through the pass so they could quickly reach the Milford* region. S3,T29S,R9W,SLM; 7,408' (2,258m). 567.

SOLDIERS SPRING* (San Juan) is south of Monticello*. Soldiers camped in this area during the summer of the mid-1880s while they were protecting settlers during the Indian-white skirmishes. 409, 567.

SOLDIER SUMMIT* (Utah, Wasatch) is at the summit midway between Thistle* and Helper*. It is a fact that several soldiers are buried at the summit, but the exact details of how they got there vary. One of the more reliable versions is that shortly after the beginning of the Civil War, when Camp Floyd* (near Fairfield*) was disbanded, the soldiers were reassigned to other posts. Several soldiers either became ill and died at the summit or were caught there in a blizzard. The small community of Soldier Summit developed in 1862. In recent years, as transportation has improved, the community has diminished in size and importance. 89, 292, 377, 516, 546.

SOLDIERS CANYON (Sevier) originates at Gooseberry Valley and drains northwest into Salina Creek. The government used this canyon to pass from one area to another. S22,T25S,R1E,SLM. to S5,T22S,R1E,SLM. 100(v17), 567.

SOLOMONS TEMPLE (Sevier) is a sharply rising rock formation at the south end of the Last Chance Desert, north of Temple Wash. It has a fancied resemblance to ancient Solomon's temple. S12,T26S,R5E,SLM; 6,476' (1,974m).

SOONER BENCH (Garfield) is east of the Kaiparowits Plateau and south of Fortymile Gulch. Nearby are Sooner Flat, Rocks, and Gulch. A young, homesick, tenderfoot sheepherder gave the name because he'd "sooner be home than out in this forsaken region." S16,T40S,R8E,SLM; 4,300' (1,311m). 12, 602.

SOUTH BENCH (Beaver). See Jackson County Hill (Beaver).

SOUTH BEND* (Sevier). See Monroe*.

SOUTH CAMP* (Beaver) is a ghost town site at the south end of the Star Range. This settlement had the southernmost location of several mining camps that were active in this area during the 1870s. S36,T29S,R12W,SLM; 5,700' (1,737m). 355.

SOUTH CANYON (Cache) is a short canyon one mile southwest of Clarkston*. It originates in the Clarkston Mountains and drains east into City Creek. S27,T14N,R2W,SLM (at mouth).

SOUTH CANYON (Garfield) originates eight miles southwest of Panguitch* and drains northeast into the Sevier River. S16,T35S,R6W,SLM to S33,T34S,R5W,SLM.

SOUTH COTTONWOOD* (Salt Lake) is located between Big and Little Cottonwood Canyon creeks, ten miles

southeast of the Great Salt Lake Fort. The approximate location today is Twentieth East and Seventieth South, where Cottonwood Heights* is now located. Amasa M. Lyman and his company of pioneers settled in this area in October 1848 after they arrived in Salt Lake City*. The settlement was named for the two creeks.
SE¼,T2S,R1E,SLM; 4,800' (1,463m). 163(7 Jan. 1935).

SOUTH CREEK (Beaver) originates in the south Tushar Mountains and drains northwest into the Beaver River. It is the first principal creek south of Beaver*.
T29,30S,R6,7W,SLM.

SOUTH ERICKSON LAKE (Summit) is in the southwest section of the Uinta Mountains in the Erickson Basin. See Erickson Creek for name source.
S5,T2S,R8E,SLM; 10,100' (3,078m).

SOUTH HILLS (Beaver) are a large group of hills south of Beaver* and Greenville*.
T30S,R7,8W,SLM.

SOUTH HOOPER* (Davis). See West Point* (Davis).

SOUTH JORDAN* (Salt Lake) is midway between Riverton* and West Jordan*. In 1859 this early farming settlement was established as an outgrowth of West Jordan.
S15,T3S,R1W,SLM; 4,300' (1,311m). 289, 542.

SOUTH LAKE (Rich) is one mile west of the Wyoming border and five miles south of the Idaho border. It is south of North Lake (Rich).
S30,T14N,R8E,SLM; 6,500' (1,981m).

SOUTH MESA (Grand) is east of Moab* and south of Wilson Mesa. The mesa was well known because it was a point where the settlers lowered as much as twelve hundred pounds of produce two thousand feet to the valley below. A

similar procedure was developed at the Wiggle Trail near Shunesburg* and at Cable Mountain in Zion Canyon.
T26S,R23E,SLM.

SOUTH MILFORD* (Beaver) was also known as Milford Flat*.

SOUTH MONTEZUMA* (San Juan). See Verdure*.

SOUTH OGDEN* (Weber) was settled in 1848 south of and as an outgrowth of Ogden*. The settlement was known earlier as Burch Creek*.
S4,5,T5N,R1W,SLM; 4,400' (1,341m). 567.

SOUTH PEAK (San Juan) was also known as South Mountain as one of the peaks in the Abajo Mountains, south of Abajo Peak.
T34S,R22E,SLM.

SOUTH PEAK (Tooele) is at the north end of the Deep Creek Range south of North Peak.
S17,T9S,R18W,SLM; 8,136' (2,480m).

SOUTH PINTO HILLS (Wayne) are three miles west of Hanksville* and south of the North Pinto Hills.
S25,26,T28S,R10E,SLM and S30,31,T28S, R11E,SLM; 4,848' (1,478m).

SOUTH PLYMOUTH* (Box Elder). See Fielding* (Box Elder).
289.

SOUTH SALT LAKE* (Salt Lake) was developed between Murray* and Salt Lake City*. This area was briefly known as Central Park*.
T1S,R1E,1W,SLM; 4,253' (1,296m). 542.

SOUTH SPRING (Beaver) is in the northwest Tushar Mountains at the head of Sulphur Creek. It is south of North Spring.
S17,T26S,R6W,SLM; 7,600' (2,316m).

SOUTH SULPHUR SPRING (Beaver) is on the west central slopes of the Needle

Range, south of North Sulphur Spring. See Sulphur Spring (Beaver) for name source.
S10,T28S,R19W,SLM; 6,760' (2,060m).

SOUTH TENT MOUNTAIN (Sanpete) is twelve miles southeast of Spring City*, near the skyline drive. The mountain is shaped like an old-fashioned tent.
S33,T16S,R5E,SLM; 11,285' (3,440m). 152.

SOUTH TWIN FLAT MOUNTAIN (Beaver) is in the Mineral Mountains between Granite Peak and North Twin Flat Mountain, and south of North Twin Flat Mountain.
S1,T28S,R9W,SLM; 7,957' (2,425m).

SOUTH WASH (Washington) originates on the north slopes of Smithsonian Butte and drains north into the Virgin River. It is directly south of the ghost town of Grafton*.
S21,22,T42S,R11W,SLM to S3,T42S,R11W, SLM.

SOUTH WEBER* (Davis) was settled in 1851 on the south side of the Weber River, southeast of Ogden*.
S26,27,34,35,T5N,R1W,SLM; 4,510' (1,265m). 27, 88, 289, 516, 542, 567.

SOUTH WEBER* (Weber). See Riverdale*.

SOUTH WILLOW CREEK* (Salt Lake). See Draper*.

SOUTH WILLOW LAKE (Tooele) is in the Stansbury Mountains at the head of Mining Fork of South Willow Creek. It is south of North Willow Lake (Tooele).
T4S,R7W,SLM. 100(v2).

SOWERS CANYON (Duchesne) originates on the West Tavaputs Plateau north of the Badlands Cliffs. The canyon drains northeast into Antelope Creek south of Bridgeland*.
S36,T6S,R7W,USM to S6,T5W,R3W,USM.

SPANISH BOTTOMS (Garfield) is a wild, seldom-used crossing of the Colorado River at the head of Cataract Canyon. Cattle rustlers and outlaws were the most frequent users of the crossing.
T30S,R18E,SLM.

SPANISH FORK* (Utah) is eight miles south of Provo* on I-15 and the Spanish Fork River. Spanish Fork was an outgrowth of Palmyra*, located to the northwest. As the community developed, Palmyra diminished and eventually became a suburb of Spanish Fork. In the early days, both settlements existed with one fort, Fort St. Luke*. Spanish Fork received its name from the adjacent river, which was named by the 1776 Domínguez-Escalante expedition.
S13,24,T8S,R2E,SLM and S18,19,T8S,R3E, SLM; 4,549' (1,387m). 270, 289, 542, 546.

SPANISH FORK CANYON (Utah) originates at Soldier Summit, drains northwest through Thistle Junction*, then ends in Utah Lake. The canyon carries Soldier Creek from the summit to Thistle Junction and from there it carries the Spanish Fork River. See the river for name source.
T8-10S,R3-6E,SLM.

SPANISH FORK PEAK (Utah) is six miles east of Spanish Fork* and receives its name from the river.
S30,T8S,R4E,SLM; 10,192' (3,107m).

SPANISH FORK RIVER (Utah) originates at Thistle*, the junction of Soldier and Thistle creeks, and drains through Spanish Fork Canyon into Utah Lake. The early Spaniards named the river El Rio de Aquas Calientes, "the Fiery River," most likely for the nearby hot springs. The river name was later changed to the Spanish Fork River as a reflection of the region's early Spanish history.
S33,T9S,R4E,SLM to S32,T7S,R2E,SLM. 27, 129, 168, 360, 583.

SPANISH TRAIL was pioneered in 1829 by Antonio Armijo and a party of thirty-one men. The trail runs between the Santa Fe* and Los Angeles*. Note, however, that in 1776 the Domínguez and Escalante expedition initiated a section of the Old Spanish Trail beginning at Utah Lake, crossing the Green River at today's Jensen*. The trail had to circumvent the southern deserts and the Grand Canyon country; therefore, the men had to find a practical crossing of the Colorado and Green rivers. So, from Santa Fe the trail swings northwest to cross the Colorado River at Moab* and the Green River at Green River*, Utah Territory. The route then veered southwest toward Los Angeles. Minor variations occurred along the route. The "Old Spanish Trail" is used in some references.
240, 372, 514, 546.

SPECTABLE LAKE (**Garfield**) is on Boulder Mountain of the Aquarius Plateau, five miles northwest of Jacobs Reservoir. The lake is divided into two sections that are joined by a narrow neck.
T31S,R4E,SLM; 10,859' (3,310m). 508.

SPECTACLE LAKES (**Wasatch**) are in the southwest section of the Uinta Mountains, three miles south of Washington Lake and seven miles southwest of Mirror Lake. These two small lakes are situated in such a way that they look like spectacles.
S24,T2S,R8E,SLM; 9,690' (2,953m).

SPENCER CAMP (**San Juan**) was established in the 1890s on the south side of the San Juan River, six miles southeast of the mouth of Alcove Canyon. Today it is under the waters of Lake Powell. Charles H. Spencer was a prominent prospector, promoter, and adventurer in that wild region.
S12,T41S,R1E,SLM. 463, 516.

SPENCER FLAT (**Garfield**) is near the head of Phipps Wash. Note also the related Spencer Flats. William Spencer was an early cattleman in the region.
S29,32,T35S,R5E,SLM; 5,900' (1,798m). 12, 602.

SPIDER LAKE (**Duchesne**) is in the south central section of the Uinta Mountains, at the head of Yellowstone Creek. The lake has a very irregular shoreline with extensive narrow inlets.
S32,T4N,R5W,USM; 10,876' (3,315m).

SPIRIT LAKE (**Daggett**) is in the north central section of the Uinta Mountains on the headwaters of Sheep Creek, Middle Fork. Daggett Lake is two and one-half miles southeast. A feathery mist often hangs over this lake. The lake name is derived from an Indian legend claiming that a group of Shoshone braves were camped by the lake while on an elk hunting excursion. As the moon rose over the lake, one brave woke up and saw a group of snow-white elk through the mist and the broken clouds. The animals were plunging through the water, throwing a spray that mingled with the mist and the clouds. He awakened his companions and told them of his vision and they named the lake Spirit Lake.
10,166' (3,099m). 100(v2,17), 172.

SPITZENBERG SPRING (**Daggett**) is between Tolivers Canyon and the mouth of Sears Canyon. Spitzenberg was an early trapper who camped by the spring.
S35,T2N,R24E,SLM. 309.

SPLASH DAM LAKE (**Duchesne**) is at the head of Hades Canyon, three and one-half miles southwest of Grandaddy Lake. In 1916 a dam was built on the lake to control the water for floating logs down Hades Canyon. Although the plan was unsuccessful, the impoundment remains.
S18,19,T2N,R8W,USM; 9,150' (2,789m). 595.

SPLIT MOUNTAIN (**Uintah**) is bisected by the Split Mountain Canyon through which the Green River drains. See Split Mountain Canyon.

SPLIT MOUNTAIN CANYON (**Uintah**) has its mouth at the north end of Wonsits Valley. The Green River has cut a course through the Split Mountain section of the eastern Uinta Mountains in the Dinosaur National Monument. Major Powell's group first named it Craggy Canyon because it is a very ragged, craggy canyon, but later changed the name to Split Mountain Canyon. T4S,R24E,SLM. 159, 160, 422, 496.

SPOTTED WOLF CANYON (**Emery**) originates in the eastern section of the San Rafael Swell and drains east through the San Rafael Reef into the San Rafael River. A rock formation in this canyon resembles an imaginary spotted wolf. S5,T22S,R14E,SLM (at mouth). 193.

SPREAD EAGLE PEAK (**Duchesne, Summit**) is in Naturalist Basin at the western end of the Uinta Mountains. S22,T4N,R8E,SLM; 12,540' (3,822m).

SPRING BAY (**Box Elder**) is a large bay at the north end of the Great Salt Lake, south of Monument Point. The 1934 earthquake caused the development of a large number of saltwater springs in this area. T11N,R9W,SLM; 4,193' (1,278m). 133.

SPRING CANYON* (**Carbon**) is one mile northeast of Standardville* at the junction of Sowbelly Gulch and Spring Canyon. In 1912, Jesse Knight established this community for the miners working in his local coal mines. Knight named the community Storrs* for his mine superintendent, George A. Storrs. In 1924 the name was changed to Spring Canyon. By 1954 the demand for coal began to dwindle so the miners began moving their families out of the settlement. Shortly after, Spring Canyon became a ghost town. S9,T13S,R9E,SLM; 6,600' (2,012m). 542, 567, 607.

SPRING CANYON (**Carbon**) originates at the junction of the Left Fork, Spring Canyon and Cliochetto Canyon, and drains southeast into the Price River at Helper*. S7-24,T13S,R9E,SLM.

SPRING CITY* (**Sanpete**) is seven miles south of Mount Pleasant* on Oak and Canal creeks. The Indians used the freshwater springs at this site for centuries. The area was first settled by whites in 1852. Since the original group included many Danish families, the first community name was Little Denmark*. S29,T15S,R4E,SLM. 89, 152, 289, 322.

SPRING CREEK* (**Sevier**). See Angle*.

SPRING GLEN* (**Carbon**) is near US-6,50 and the Price River, one mile south of Helper*. This small mining community was first settled in 1880 in a beautiful cove or glen, by a freshwater spring. S30,31,T13S,R10E,SLM; 5,750' (1,753m). 100(v17), 542, 567.

SPRING HOLLOW* (**Summit**). See Cluff* (Summit).

SPRING LAKE* (**Utah**) is a small community settled in 1850 near a large spring, three miles south of Payson*. In 1852 Joseph E. Johnson bought the property and moved his family of five wives and their children into a large adobe house and built an adobe wall around it for protection. They named it Spring Lake Villa*, which was later shortened to Spring Lake. Black Hawk, the instigator of the Black Hawk War between the whites and Indians, is buried at Spring Lake. T9S,R2E,SLM; 4,730' (1,442m). 270, 289, 542.

SPRING LAKE VILLA* (**Utah**). See Spring Lake* (Utah).

SPRING VALLEY* (**Tooele**). See Skull Valley* (Tooele).

SPRINGDALE* (**Washington**) is at the west entrance to Zion National Park. In 1862 Albert Petty, George Petty, J. H. Whitlock, and others arrived here after spending the summer at Shunesburg*. Albert Petty's wife suggested the name because the settlement was adjacent to some freshwater springs.
T41S,R10W,SLM; 3,913' (1,193m). 289, 311, 438, 600.

SPRINGDELL* (**Utah**) is a small enclosed community three miles up Provo Canyon. The community has its own freshwater spring.
S5,T6S,R3E,SLM; 5,000' (1,524m). 578.

SPRINGVILLE* (**Utah**) was settled in October 1850 between Provo* and Spanish Fork*. The settlement was originally called Hobble Creek* for the creek the people settled on. A large freshwater spring was located in the vicinity.
S33,T7S,R3E,SLM; 4,515' (1,376m). 270, 289, 542, 567.

SPRY* (**Garfield**) is eight miles north of Panguitch*. The settlement was established in 1872 and had several early name changes as clusters of families were absorbed into the settlement. Fort Sanford* was named for Silas Sanford Smith, who was in command of the fort; Lowder Spring* for John Lowder; Tebbs Springs* (later Tebbsdale*) for Daniel F. Tebbs; Orton*, after William F. Orton, was used for a short time; Bear Creek* was derived from the nearby creek; and Cleveland* was used for a while in honor of President Grover Cleveland. When Jesse LeFevre became postmaster in 1908, he renamed the established community of Spry in honor of Utah Governor William Spry.
T34S,R5W,SLM. 100(v17), 143, 289, 360, 466(3 Feb. 1985), 516, 542.

SPUD VALLEY* (**Garfield**). See Escalante* (Garfield).

SPUD VALLEY (**Garfield**). Escalante* is in the center of the valley and the head of the Escalante River is nearby. The early settlers found a wild edible potato growing in this area. Variant: Potato Valley.

SPUR, THE (**Emery**) is a twenty-two-mile-long and six-mile-wide feature located near Low Spur, Head Spur, and Spur Canyon. The Orange Cliffs and the Green River are east and Horseshoe Canyon is west. This massive landform has a northeast-southwest orientation and is shaped like a hook.
T26-29S,R16-17E,SLM; ca. 5,000' (1,524m). 25.

SQUARETOWN* (**Box Elder**). See Plymouth*.
542.

SQUAW PEAK (**Utah**) is northeast of the Provo* Mormon temple, near the mouth of Rock Canyon. In February 1850 a white-Indian conflict developed near the mouth of the Provo River. Big Elk, a chief of the local Piute Indians, was killed and his squaw fled with others toward the foothills to the east. She died from a fall from the peak that was then named in her honor. There are other versions to the peak's name origin.
S28,T6S,R3E,SLM; 7,876' (2,401m). 597.

SQUAW PEAK (**Duchesne**) is in the central Uinta Mountains between Explorer and Cleveland peaks. This is a summer camping site of the Uinta Basin Ute Indians.
S35,T4N,R7W,USM; 12,855' (3,918m).

STAG SPRING (**Beaver**) is in the Tushar Mountains northwest of Kents Lake, near Willow Lake. Assistant Forest Supervisor C. J. Olsen killed an elk or mule deer by the spring.
S31,T29S,R6W,SLM; 8,120' (2,475m). 125.

STANDARDVILLE* (**Carbon**) was up Spring Canyon, four and one-half miles

northwest of Helper*. In 1911 the settlement was built for miners working for the Standard Coal Company, which operated several mines in the area. Standardville had the reputation of being an ideal mining town, a standard for others to achieve. After the mines closed down in 1950 the people moved out and/or down to Helper. Standardville is now a ghost town.
S17,T13S,R9E,SLM; 6,630' (2,021m). 89, 516, 542, 607.

STANSBURY GULCH (Tooele) is at the southwest corner of Stansbury Island. The gulch was named by G. K. Gilbert for Captain Stansbury, who conducted geological work in the region.
S28,T1N,R6W,SLM.

STANSBURY ISLAND (Tooele) is usually a peninsula extending from the southwest shore of Great Salt Lake, but it becomes an island during high water. Captain Howard Stansbury's officers named the feature in his honor when they were surveying the lake in 1850. For a short period of time, it was previously known as Kimballs Island for H. C. Kimball, a member of the 1847 pioneers. Kimball ran his livestock on the island. Albert Carrington, an assistant to Captain Stansbury, recorded an early name of "Dome" for the island.
T1N,R6W,SLM. 100(v2), 133, 371, 492, 546.

STANSBURY MOUNTAINS (Tooele) are between Tooele and Skull valleys. See Stansbury Island (Tooele) for name source.
T1-5S,R6,7W,SLM. 314.

STAR CITY* (Beaver) is a ghost town site in the Star Range mining district, twelve miles southwest of Milford*. There are other famous ghost towns in this vicinity, such as Shauntie*, Shenandoah City* and Moscow*. Star City was settled in the 1870s. The name was derived from the Star mining district.
T28S,R11,12W,SLM. 89, 516.

STAR LAKE (Summit) is in the southwest section of the Uinta Mountains on the upper Provo River. Nearby are Wall and Trial lakes. The lake has an irregular shoreline with deep, narrow inlets.
S32,T1S,R9E,SLM; 9,995' (3,046m).

STAR RANGE (Beaver) is several miles southwest of Milford*. It has a north-south orientation and was named for the Star mining district which was formed in this area.
T28S,R11W,SLM; 6,871' (2,094m).

STARR* (Juab) is a small, scattered agricultural settlement three miles north of Mona*. In 1858 the soldiers of Johnston's Army established a ranch for holding government livestock. When it became available to the public in 1880, Albert W. Starr and his son William A. Starr purchased the property. Starr's name was used for the settlement that has been absorbed into nearby Mona.
S8,T11S,R1E,SLM; 4,906' (1,495m). 100 (v13), 347, 516.

STATE LINE* (Iron) is a ghost town at the south end of Hamblin Valley near the Nevada border. Nelson Millet and a Mr. Popliss discovered silver ore in this area in 1894. In the early 1900s, the settlement peaked as a supply town for nearby farmers, lumbermen, and stock-men. It was also a well-known outlaw and cattle rustler hangout. As commercial activities diminished, the people moved out and the town was abandoned by the 1940s.
S19,T32S,R19W,SLM; 7,000' (2,134m). 89, 516, 567.

STATELINE DRAW (Grand) originates on the eastern slopes of the La Sal Mountains and drains south along the state line into Lion Canyon.
S4-S8,T28S,R26E,SLM.

STEAMBOAT MESA (Grand) is near the Dolores River and the Colorado state

line. The shape of the mesa resembles an old-time steamboat.
S30,32,T23S,R26E,SLM; 6,306' (1,922m).

STEENS CANYON (Piute) originates on the southern slopes of Forshea (Forshee) Mountain near McCardy Spring. It drains south into Kingston Canyon. See Steens Meadow for name origin.
S2,11,22,T30S,R2½W,SLM.

STEENS MEADOW (Piute) is at the head of Kingston Canyon near the south end of Otter Creek Reservoir. John Steen, a bachelor, homesteaded a ranch in the meadow.
S29,30,T30S,R2W,SLM; 6,325' (1,928m). 5.

STEER GULCH (San Juan) originates at Red House Cliffs and drains south southwest into the San Juan River, near the south end of Grand Flat. Culled steers were pulled from the herd and gathered here prior to being trailed out to market.
T38S,R16E,SLM to S18,T40S,R15E,SLM.

STEER PASTURE CANYON (San Juan) originates north of the Clay Hills and drains southwest into Castle Creek. See Steer Gulch for name source.
T39S,R15E,SLM.

STEINAKER RESERVOIR (Uintah) is three and one-half miles north of Vernal*. In 1877 John Steinaker settled in the area that is now taken up by the reservoir.
S26,34,35,T3S,R21E,SLM; 5,520' (1,682m). 567.

STERLING* (Sanpete) is on US-89 midway between Manti* and Gunnison*. The community was settled in 1873 and had several early names. The first was Pettyville* for the William G. Petty family. Other names were Pettytown*, and Leesburg*, then Buncetown* for the Bunce family. The community finally chose the name Sterling for the progressive, sterling qualities of its people.

S4,T19,R2E,SLM; 5,414' (1,650m). 152, 289, 542.

STEVENS ARCH (Kane) is considered the grandaddy of the Escalante Arches. The arch is formed near the junction of Stevens Canyon and the Escalante River and is sometimes called Skyline Arch. Al Stevens ran his cattle along the Stevens Canyon drainage system.
T39S,R8,8½S,SLM. 12, 383(Sept. 1955), 602.

STEVENS CANYON (Kane) originates in the Pink Cliffs and drains into the Escalante River. See Stevens Arch for name source.

STEVENSVILLE* (Iron) is a ghost town site four miles northwest of Enoch*.
S33,T34S,R11W,SLM; 5,452' (1,662m).

STEVES MOUNTAIN (Sevier) is on the Sevier Plateau six miles east of Salina* at the head of Steves Wash.
T21S,R2E,SLM; 8,761' (2,670m).

STILLWATER CANYON (San Juan, Wayne) is one of the several canyons through which the Green River drains. It starts at the end of Labyrinth Canyon and ends at the junction of the Green and Colorado rivers, a distance of about forty-two miles. It is a quiet section of the river where the water slowly winds through a strange region of high walls, rock terraces, crags, and pinnacles. This section of the river is devoid of any vegetation.
T26-30,R17,18E,SLM. 314, 420, 422, 496. D.L. 7301.

STILLWATER FORK (Summit) originates in the northwest section of the Uinta Mountains where it drains north from McPheters and Amethyst lakes. The name comes from the way the river slowly meanders through Christmas Meadows on its course to the Bear River.
T1S,R10E,SLM to S32,T2N,R10E,SLM.

STOCKMORE* (Duchesne) was at the junction of the Duchesne River and its West Fork. This community was allegedly planned for development during the land rush of 1905. A Mr. Stockman and Mr. Moore "founded" the town and advertised lots for sale by displaying gold nuggets that came from "Stockmore." Stockman and Moore fled when federal marshals entered the scene. Today the U.S. Forest Service Stockmore Ranger Station is on the site.
T1N,R8W,SLM. 89, 309, 567, 595.

STOCKTON* (Tooele) is one-half mile east of Rush Lake at the north end of Rush Valley. The settlement was originally called Camp Relief* by soldiers of the California Volunteers under General Connor. They later changed the name to Stockton for the California town many of the soldiers were from.
S24,T4S,R5W,SLM; 5,100' (1,554m). 100 (v17), 153, 314, 542, 546, 567.

STOCKTON BAR (Tooele) is the boundary between Tooele and Rush valleys. This geological phenomenon is a massive ridge of gravel deposits formed by the water movements of ancient Lake Bonneville when the lake level was at its highest point. The feature was named by G. K. Gilbert in 1890.
S13,14,23,24,T4S,R5W,SLM. 314. D.L. 8702.

STODDARD* (Morgan) is in the Morgan Valley three miles northwest of Morgan* near I-80. This small agricultural community was settled in 1860 by the Judson L. Stoddard family.
S22,T4N,R2E,SLM; 5,000' (1,524m). 378, 542.

STODDARD FORT* (Davis). In 1854 Judson Stoddard made a start on his own fort at the mouth of Bernard Creek near Centerville*.
S6,T2N,R1E,SLM. 567.

STOKER* (Davis). See Bountiful* (Davis).

STONE CANYON (Davis) originates in the Wasatch Range east of Bountiful* and drains west into the valley. Large rocks and stones have been deposited along the canyon course.
S13-20,T2N,R1E,SLM. 88.

STORM MOUNTAIN (Salt Lake) is four miles up Big Cottonwood Canyon near Stairs Gulch. Although this is a popular hiking and rock climbing area, it is very rugged and quite dangerous. Unexpected storms make the rocks slippery and unstable.
S20,T2S,R2E,SLM; 9,524' (2,903m).

STORRS* (Carbon). See Spring Canyon*.

STRAIGHT CANYON (Washington). See Mukuntuweap Canyon (Washington).

STRAIGHT CANYON (Garfield) is a six-mile-long canyon on the Colorado River, east of the mouth of the Dirty Devil River. It was named by Powell's expedition for the narrow, straight course of the canyon.
T33S,R14,15E,SLM. 160, 420, 422, 496.

STRAIGHT CLIFFS (Kane) are the straight perpendicular cliffs making up the edge of the Kaiparowits Plateau on the northeast front. The southeast point is Navajo Point, which faces Lake Powell. The name was given by Herbert E. Gregory, a noted geologist.
T37-42S,R3-8E,SLM. 12, 602. D.L. 6504.

STRAWBERRY* (Duchesne) was the name applied by early settlers who lived along the Strawberry River. The community, per se, no longer exists.
567.

STRAWBERRY CREEK (Kane) originates on Strawberry Point at the southwest edge of the Markagunt Plateau. It drains northeast into Asay Creek and received its name from the wild strawberries growing along the creek's course.
S2,T39S,R8W,SLM to S5,T38S,R6W,SLM.

STRAWBERRY FLAT (Beaver) is on the western slopes of the Tushar Mountains near the junction of Merchant Creek and Beaver River. Wild strawberries are plentiful along the flat.
S16,T29S,R5W,SLM; 8,900' (2,713m). 125.

STRAWBERRY PEAK (Wasatch) is six miles east southeast of the Strawberry Reservoir and the early Strawberry Valley from which the peak received its name.
S14,T5S,R10W,USM; 10,335' (3,150m).

STRAWBERRY PINNACLES (Duchesne) are striking geologic formations near the Strawberry River junction with Red Creek and Avintaquin Canyon.
S14,T4S,R8W,USM; 6,100' (1,859m).

STRAWBERRY RESERVOIR (Duchesne) is a man-made lake in the Strawberry Valley. The impounded water is tunneled southwest so the Colorado River drainage is diverted into the Great Basin, especially for use along the Wasatch Front.
T3,4S,R11W,USM; 7,558' (2,304m). 289, 314, 546.

STRAWBERRY RIVER (Duchesne, Wasatch) originates three miles southeast of Heber* and drains into Strawberry Reservoir and east into the Duchesne River. The members of the Domínguez and Escalante expedition named it the El Rio de Santa Catarina de Sena, then Fremont called it the Uintah River before the name was changed to the Strawberry River.
S15,T5S,R12W,USM to S6,T4S,R4W,USM. 100(v17), 314.

STRAWBERRY VALLEY (Cache) is a small isolated valley southwest of the south side of Bear Lake. Wild strawberries are plentiful there.
S11,14,15,T11N,R4E,SLM; 6,900' (2,103m).

STRINGTOWN* (Cache). See Clarkston* (Cache).

STRINGTOWN* (Utah). See Lindon* (Utah).

STRINGTOWN* (Weber). See Riverdale* (Weber).

STRIP, THE (Uintah) was located between Fort Duchesne* and Gusher*. It was a small seven-hundred-acre section of land that, through legal maneuvering, was neither federal nor territorial land. The settlement had no laws restricting gambling, prostitution, or liquor control. The result was a wild, lawless town that attracted outlaw gangs. The town existed until 1905 when the federal government opened up the vast Uintah-Ouray Indian Reservation, which included the strip. 89.

STRONGS KNOB (Box Elder) is one and one-half miles northwest of Lakeside*, on the western shore of the Great Salt Lake. It was named for William Strong, a member of Stansbury's survey party.
S9,T6N,R9W,SLM. 100(v2), 567.

STUDHORSE PEAKS (San Juan) are west of the Waterpocket Fold and five miles northwest of Wagon Box Mesa. It was from these high points that wild stallions stood guard over the mares and colts grazing nearby.

SUCKERTOWN* (Juab). See Mills* (Juab).

SUGAR HOUSE* (Salt Lake) was settled just west of the mouth of Parleys Canyon, southeast of Salt Lake City*. The settlement was established to manufacture sugar but the project was unsuccessful. An earlier attempt was made to produce paper in this area. Today it is a thriving section of Greater Salt Lake City.
S20,T1S,R1E,SLM; 4,366' (1,331m). 100 (v17), 289.

SUGARVILLE* (Millard) is a small community northwest of Delta*. The

early settlers named it Omaha* for Omaha, Nebraska. It later became Alfalfa* because the grazing plant grew so well in the region. As the sugar industry developed and the sugarbeet crop became successful, the name was changed to Sugarville.
S5,T16S,R7W,SLM; 4,585' (1,398m). 89, 542.

SUICIDE PARK (Summit) is on the Wyoming state boundary and Smiths Fork, west of Gilbert Creek. Charley Matson, Jack Rose, and Olaf Olson died here of alleged suicide. They are buried nearby.
S16,T3N,R13E,SLM; 9,000' (2,743m). 309.

SULPHUR CANYON (Emery) originates two miles southwest of the San Rafael Knob on the San Rafael Swell, and drains southwest into Reds Canyon. Sulphur was discovered in the canyon.
T23S,R9E,SLM.

SULPHUR CREEK (Beaver) originates at South Spring on the northwest slopes of the Tushar Mountains and drains northwest through Sulphurdale* into Cove Creek. There is a sulphur mine close to the creek.
S17,18,T26S,R6W,SLM.

SULPHUR CREEK (Wayne) originates on the eastern slopes of Boulder Mountain and drains southeast into Pleasant Creek. The creek water has a strong sulphur odor.
S26,T30S,R5E,SLM to S36,T30S,R6E,SLM.

SULPHUR CREEK (Wayne) originates on the southeast slopes of Thousand Lake Mountain, north of Teasdale*, and drains southeast into the Fremont River. The creek water has a strong sulphur odor.
S3,T29S,R5E,SLM to S14,T29S,R6E,SLM.

SULPHUR SPRING (Beaver) is on the west central slopes of the Needle Range. Nearby are the North and South Sulphur springs. All the springs have a strong sulphur odor.
S3,T28S,R19W,SLM; 6,775' (2,065m).

SULPHUR SPRINGS (Iron) are two miles northwest of Lund* on the west side of the Escalante Desert. Although the springs were sulphur-tainted, they were the only water available to the freighters passing through. Peter Guio scratched out an existence while living near the springs by helping to make the water available and ready when the freighters travelled through the area.
S18,T32S,R14W,SLM; 5,084' (1,550m).

SULPHURDALE* (Beaver) was three miles south of Cove Fort, near I-15. Sulphur was discovered at the site in the mid-1850s. A mine was established in 1870 by Charles Dickart, who was then the U.S. Deputy Surveyor. The site was not completely developed until 1883 when it received a temporary name of Morrissey* for the man who developed the area. The small settlement grew but the sulphur was of unreliable quality. The community was abandoned after the owner died and is now a ghost town located on private property. For a short period of time it was Utah's only sulphur-producing mine.
S7,T26S,R6W,SLM; 6,190' (1,887m). 89, 100 (v17), 516, 546.

SUMMIT* (Davis). See Clinton*.

SUMMIT* (Iron) was a small hamlet settled in 1858 on the divide midway between Parowan* and Cedar City*.
S36,T34S,R10W,SLM; 6,130' (1,868m). 136, 289, 314, 542.

SUMMIT BASIN* (Utah). See Birdseye* (Utah).

SUMMIT COUNTY was created on January 13, 1854, from the west end of Green River County. The balance of Green River County was transferred to Wyoming Territory. Summit County embraces the high country separating the drainage of the Green River (and Colorado River) from the Great Basin. 6, 542.

SUMMIT CREEK* (Cache). See Smithfield* (Cache).

SUMMIT CREEK (Utah) originates in the mountains northeast of Mount Nebo and drains north northwest into Santaquin Canyon. See Santaquin* for name source.
S9,T11S,R2E,SLM to S11,12,T10S,R1E,SLM.

SUMMIT CREEK* (Utah). See Santaquin* (Utah).

SUMMIT PARK (Daggett) is in the eastern Uinta Mountains, four and one-half miles east northeast of Leidy Peak. The park is at the summit of the mountain range where the Old Carter Road passes through.
T1N,R19E,SLM; 9,800' (2,987m).

SUMMIT POINT* (San Juan) is sixteen miles north of Eastland*. It divides the San Juan drainage from the Colorado River drainage. A Mr. Lorenzo settled here in 1915 and a small ranching settlement developed.
S30,T31N,R26E,SLM; 7,113' (2,168m). 406.

SUNDANCE* (Utah) is a rapidly developing, year-round recreational and educational center, one and one-half miles southeast of Aspen Grove*. It was named in 1968 by owner and developer Robert Redford, who wanted a name with a local Indian connotation.
S11,T5S,R3E,SLM; 6,100' (1,859m).

SUNFLOWER* (Millard) was settled in 1912 when irrigation water became available in the area. The settlement was three and one-half miles west of Sugarville* and named for the unlimited fields of sunflowers. The community was abandoned in 1920.
S35,T15S,R8W,SLM; 4,575' (1,394m). 89, 567.

SUNKEN RIVER was an early name Major Powell's party used for the Green River. The name refers to the deep canyons surrounding the river.
159.

SUNNYSIDE* (Carbon) is located on U-123 at the base of the Book Cliffs. This coal mining town developed in 1912 on the sunny side of the canyon. It had an earlier name of Verdi* after a nearby railroad camp.
S6,T15S,R14E,SLM; 6,523' (1,988m). 100 (v17), 607.

SUNNYSIDE HOLLOW (Beaver) originates on the eastern slopes of South Twin Flat Mountain in the Mineral Mountains. It drains east into Burnt Hollow and Cunningham Wash.
S7,8,T28S,R8W,SLM.

SUNSET* (Box Elder). See Garland* (Box Elder).

SUNSET* (Davis) was on U-84 and US-91 as an outgrowth of nearby Clinton*. The name Sunset was used because the community was set up on an elevated location on a sand ridge, giving the residents a clear view of the magnificent sunsets over the Great Salt Lake.
S23,26,35,T2W,R5N,SLM; 4,567' (1,392m). 289, 542.

SUNSET CANYON (Millard) originates at Sunset Peak in the Pavant Mountains, nine miles east northeast of Kanosh*. The canyon drains west into the Pavant Valley and received its name from the peak.
S6,T23S,R4W,SLM to S1,T23S,R5W,SLM.

SUNSET CLIFFS (Garfield) is part of the western border of the Paunsaugunt Plateau east of the Sevier River Valley. The cliffs face west and are most visible when the afternoon sun reflects off them.
T35,36S,R4½W,SLM.

SUNSET FLAT (**Kane**) is on the Hole-in-the-Rock road, twenty miles from Escalante*. It is an open, exposed flat that was named by the local stockmen.
T38S,R5E,SLM; 5,200' (1,585m). 12.

SUNSET PEAK (**Millard**) is at the head of Sunset Canyon in the Pavant Range, nine miles east northeast of Kanosh*. At the end of the day the peak receives the sun longer than the surrounding region.
S5,T23S,R4W,SLM; 10,088' (3,075m).

SUNSHINE* (**Tooele**) was a small mining town one mile up Sunshine Canyon at the southwest tip of the Oquirrh Mountains. Although the town was established in the 1890s, it was abandoned by 1918 and is now a ghost town.
S28,T6S,R3W,SLM; 6,200' (1,890m). 89, 92, 516.

SUNSHINE CANYON (**Tooele**) originates on the southeast slopes of Eagle Hill on the western slopes of the Oquirrh Mountains, and drains southwest into Rush Valley. The canyon was named for the mine and resultant community that developed partway up the canyon. See Sunshine*.
S17,T6S,R3W,SLM to S29,T6S,R3W,SLM. 89, 516.

SUPERIOR LAKE (**Duchesne**) is in the south central Uinta Mountains on the headwaters of Garfield Creek, which drains into Yellowstone Creek. The name suggests its relative superior or higher position compared to the larger Five Point Lake below.
S20,T4N,R5W,USM; 11,163' (3,402m).

SURPRISE VALLEY (**Garfield**) is between the Kaiparowits Plateau and Reese Canyon near Smokey Mountain. Seth Johnson and Sam Spencer were surprised when they found such a good sheep range in this isolated region, which is surrounded by impossibly chopped up country. The sheep stayed in good condition throughout the winter.

S17,18,20,T40S,R5E,SLM; 5,000' (1,524m). 12.

SUTHERLAND* (**Millard**) is a small farming community on U-99, four miles northwest of Delta*. It was settled in the early 1900s and named for George Sutherland, a U.S. Senator from Utah and an associate justice of the U.S. Supreme Court.
S27,28,T16S,R7W,SLM; 4,629' (1,411m). 289.

SWAINS CREEK (**Garfield**) originates in the Pink Cliffs ten miles north of Orderville*, and drains northeast into the head of Asay Creek.
T39S,R7W,SLM to S32,T37S,R6W,SLM. 508, 600.

SWAINS HOLLOW (**Garfield**) is a tributary of Dry Wash, two miles northeast of Glendale*. In pioneer days, Sven (Swain) Anderson ran a dairy in the hollow.
S18,19,T40S,R6W,SLM. 567.

SWALLOW CANYON (**Daggett**) is on the Green River in Browns Park and extends east almost to the Colorado line. Major Powell named the canyon for the thousands of swallows swarming throughout the canyon.
S7-9,T1N,R25E,SLM. 159, 420, 422, 496.

SWAN CREEK (**Rich**) originates on the northern slopes of Swan Peak, three miles west of Lakota*, and drains east into Bear Lake. Several pairs of swans lived along the creek.
S5,T14N,R5E,SLM (at mouth). 567.

SWAN CREEK MOUNTAIN (**Rich**) is at the head of Swan Creek.

SWAN LAKE (**Millard**) is near Black Rock as a shallow, marshy area that picks up seepage and drain water from the nearby Sevier River and what is left of the Beaver River. The lake is inhabited by local and migratory birds.
T18S,R8,9W,SLM; 4,555' (1,388m).

SWAN PEAK (Rich) is at the head of Swan Creek, three miles west of Lakota*. See Swan Creek (Rich) for name source. T14N,R4E,SLM.

SWAPP CANYON (Kane) originates three miles northeast of Sink Valley and five miles southeast of Alton*. It drains east to combine with Robinson Canyon to form the headwater of the East Fork of the Sevier River. James Swapp, a rancher in nearby Sink Valley, ran his cattle in Swapp Canyon. S15,T39S,R5W,SLM to S10,T39S,R4½W, SLM. 567.

SWASEY MOUNTAINS (Juab, Millard) have a north-south orientation east of Tule (White) Valley and south of the Fish Spring Mountains. See the peak for name source. T16S,R13W,SLM; 9,669' (2,947m).

SWASEY PEAK (Millard) is the high point of the Swasey Mountains (variant: Swazey). Rodney Swasey was a pioneer in this region. T16S,R13W,SLM; 9,669' (2,947m). 100(v17).

SWASEYS LEAP (Emery). See Swazys Leap (Emery).

SWAYBACK KNOLL (Iron) is on the eastern slopes of Parowan Valley, one mile east of I-15. This feature is an isolated rise with the profile of a sway-backed horse. S7,8,T32S,R7W,SLM; 6,171' (1,881m).

SWAZYS LEAP (Emery). Swaseys is the more commonly used spelling, but it is listed as Swazys on maps listing this feature. The leap site is in the Black Box section on the San Rafael River, three miles north of I-70 and sixteen miles west of Green River*. All agree that Sid Swazy (Swasey) took a leap on his horse across the San Rafael River at this point but the distance jumped and the distance to the river water below, varies. One report states the distance was eleven feet across, with the river one hundred feet straight down. There are other versions and estimates but the leap was made and the achievement was no small feat—and Swazy lived to tell about it. T21S,R13E,SLM. 193.

SWEDE TOWN* (Salt Lake). See North Salt Lake City*.

SWEDISH KNOLL (Sanpete) is one and one-half miles south of John August Lake, on the summit southeast of Ephraim*. The name indicates the strong influence of the early Scandinavian settlers who came to the region during pioneer times. Niels Anderson, a Swedish pioneer, herded his sheep in this locality. Danish Knoll is nearby. S11,T18S,R4E,SLM; 10,488' (3,197m). 100 (v17).

SWEET ALICE CANYON (San Juan) originates at Sweet Alice Hills and drains north into Beef Basin Wash. See Sweet Alice Springs for name source. S2,T18S,R33E,SLM.

SWEET ALICE HILLS (San Juan) are near Sweet Alice Springs (San Juan). See the springs for name source. T33S,R18E,SLM; 8,486' (2,587m).

SWEET ALICE SPRINGS (San Juan) are between the heads of Dark Canyon and Fable Valley. During the early cattlemen heyday in this region, the springs were the home of an Indian maiden of various talents who entertained cowboys, prospectors, and other male passerbys. T33S,R18E,SLM.

SWEETS* (Carbon) is at the head of the North Fork of Gordon Creek at the end of U-139. The town took the name of the nearby coal mine developed by Charles and Will Sweet. The town peaked in the 1920s, then closed down with the mines during the depression. S17,T13S,R8E,SLM; 7,700' (2,347m). 89, 516.

SWEETWATER CANYON (Garfield) originates at the summit of Escalante Mountain, east of the ghost town of Widtsoe*. It drains west into Johns Valley and the East Fork of the Sevier River. The water has a mildly sweet, alkaline flavor.
S22,T34S,R1W,SLM to S5,T34S,R2W,SLM. 567.

SWEETWATER CREEK (Beaver) originates on the northern slopes of Shelly Baldy Peak in the Tushar Mountains and drains west into North Creek, South Fork. The water is sweet and fresh tasting.
S16,17,T28S,R5W,SLM.

SWEETWATER CREEK (Garfield) originates east of McGath Lake on the south slopes of Boulder Mountain of the Aquarius Plateau, and drains south into Sand Creek. The water is less bitter than that of other creeks in this area.
S8,T34S,R4E,SLM (at mouth). 12. D.L. 6504.

SWEETWATER CREEK (Garfield, Wayne) originates west of Mount Ellen in the Henry Mountains and drains north into the Fremont River. The water is potable.
S24,T31S,R8E,SLM to S25,T28S,R9E,SLM.

SWEETWATER CREEK (Uintah) originates at the south end of the Tom Patterson Ridge, eight miles west of the Colorado line and drains north to join Bitter Creek. Sweetwater Creek, unlike Bitter Creek, is mildly alkaline but potable.
S4,T16S,R25E,SLM to S3,T13S,R23E,SLM. 567.

SWIFTS CANYON (Summit) originates on the northwest slopes of Hoyt Peak, six miles east of Oakley*, and drains northwest into the Weber River. The Swift family homesteaded in the canyon during the late 1800s.
S12,24,36,T1S,R6E,SLM. 298.

SYRACUSE* (Davis) was settled in 1878, two and one-half miles west southwest of Clearfield* as an outgrowth of South Hooper* and Kaysville*. In 1887 a bathing resort was built on the shores of Great Salt Lake and named for Syracuse, New York. The name was also accepted by the nearby community.
S9,10,15,16,T4N,R2W,SLM; 4,260' (1,305m). 289, 567.

SYRETT HOLLOW (Garfield) drains from the southwest to the northeast past Rubys Inn into the East Fork of the Sevier River. Reuben (Ruby) C. Syrett built Rubys Inn.
T36S,R3W,SLM.

- T -

TABBY CANYON (**Duchesne**) originates on the West Tavaputs Plateau and drains northeast into Sowers Canyon, seven miles south of Duchesne*. The canyon was named for Chief Tabby of the local Ute Indians.
S20,T6S,R6W,USM to S13,T5S,R5W,USM.

TABBY CREEK (**Duchesne**) originates on the western slopes of Tabby Mountain and drains southwest into Red Creek.
S30,T1S,R8W,SLM to T11S,R9W,SLM. 100 (v17).

TABBY MOUNTAIN (**Duchesne**) is in the southwest section of the Uinta Mountains between Timber Canyon and Trail and Mill hollows. Tabiona* is located to the southeast. Before the arrival of the pioneers, Chief Tava (Tabby) and his Ute Indians spent much of their time in this region. The mountain was named for the chief.
S29,33,T1S,R8W,USM; 10,001' (3,048m). 314, 595.

TABBYS CANYON (**Tooele**) originates on Stansbury Island at the south end of the Great Salt Lake. The canyon drains to the west.
S2,27,T1N,R6W,SLM.

TABBYS PEAK (**Tooele**) is in the south central section of the Cedar Mountains, west of Skull Valley.
S16,T4S,R10W,SLM; 6,921' (2,110m).

TABBYUNE CREEK (**Utah, Wasatch**) originates six miles east of Soldier Summit* and drains southwest into the White River.
S25,T10S,R8E,SLM; to S5,T11S,R8E,SLM.

TABIONA* (**Duchesne**) is a small agricultural community southwest of Tabby Mountain on the Duchesne River. In 1860 a military fort was built on this site. The fort was named Tabiona, but was also known as Tabbyville* and, until 1915, it was often called Tabby*. The name refers to two Ute Chiefs, Tava (Tabby) and Tayneena. They lived in the area with their people. In 1915 Tabiona became the formal name.
S31,T1S,R7W,SLM; 6,517' (1,986m). 165, 198, 314, 457, 546, 567, 595.

TABLE CLIFF PLATEAU (**Garfield**) was Almon Thompson's name for what is today part of Barney Top, southwest of Escalante*. Thompson was Powell's chief of surveys for this region.

TABLE MOUNTAIN (**Garfield**) is on the south Sevier Plateau near Kingston Canyon. It has a comparatively flat top.
T31S,R2½W,SLM; 9,372' (2,857m).

TABLE MOUNTAIN (**Tooele**) is an isolated, unusually flat-topped mountain rising above the surrounding desert at the north end of the Slow Elk Hills and Dugway Valley.
S20,T10S,R9W,SLM; 5,766' (1,757m).

TABLE TOP MOUNTAIN (**Garfield**) is another name for Barney Top on Escalante Mountain, southwest of Escalante*.

TADPOLE SPRINGS (**Beaver**) are near the Union Pacific Railroad, two and one-half miles southwest of Milford*. The springs create a swampy area that is populated with numerous frogs.
S24,25,T28S,R11W,SLM; 4,970' (1,515m).

TAIL LAKE (**Summit**) is at the west end of the Uinta Mountains. A small rivulet attaches this lake to Washington Lake.
S6,T2S,R9E,SLM; 9,990' (3,045m). 530.

TALMAGE* (**Duchesne**) is a small ranching community eight miles west of Altamont* and fourteen miles north of Duchesne*. White settlers originally established this community in 1907 and in 1912 it was named Winn* when the settlement was platted. In 1914 the name was changed to Talmage to honor James E. Talmage, a Mormon church official.
S2,T2S,R5W,USM; 6,830' (2,082m). 100 (v17), 542, 567.

TAMARACK LAKE (**Summit**) is in the north central section of the Uinta Mountains near Spirit Lake. Tamarack is a lumberman's term for the Englemann spruce (*Picea engelmanni*), a tree that is quite common in this region.
10,429' (3,179m).

TAN SEEP (**Emery**) is a small water source on the San Rafael Swell at the south end of Rods Valley. The San Rafael Knob is five miles northwest. Tan Seep was named for Nathaniel (Tan) Crawford, who ran sheep in this area with George Crawford.
6,750' (2,057m). 193.

TANGENT PEAK (**Box Elder**) is the high point of the Hogup Mountains west of the north end of the Great Salt Lake. The name was given during Clarence King's 1877 expedition. See Hogup Mountains.
D.L. 6402.

TANK MESA (**San Juan**) is a benchland two by ten miles in size, extending north from the San Juan River between Butler and Cottonwood washes. Cattlemen hollowed out depressed areas (water-pockets) in the slickrock for storing additional water so the cattle could graze for a longer period of time in this desolate area.
T39,40S,R21E,SLM; 4,969' (1,515m). 12, 567.

TANNER CANYON (**Beaver**). See Tanner Hollow (Beaver).

TANNER FLAT (**Salt Lake**) is four and one-half miles down-canyon from Alta* in Little Cottonwood Canyon, southeast of Salt Lake City*. See Tannersville* for name source.
NE¼,T3S,R2E,SLM; 7,200' (2,195m).

TANNER HOLLOW (**Beaver**) is on the western slopes of the Tushar Mountains. The hollow originates at Tanner Peak and drains south. Shepherd Tanner ran his cattle in this area.
S9,15,T28S,R6W,SLM. 100(v17), 125.

TANNER MOUNTAIN (**Beaver**) is nine miles northeast of Beaver* on the west central slopes of the Tushar Mountains. See Tanner Hollow for name source.
S9,T28S,R6W,SLM; 8,484' (2,586m).

TANNERSVILLE* (**Salt Lake**) was four and one-half miles down-canyon from Alta* at Tanner Flat. In 1851 John Tanner and his sons built a sawmill and a boardinghouse for mining and timber workers. This soon developed into a settlement called Tannersville. In 1872 the hotel burned down and was not rebuilt and the town was subsequently abandoned. Today nothing remains.
NE¼,T3S,R2E,SLM; 7,200' (2,195m). 89, 454, 508, 567.

TANTALUS CREEK (**Garfield**) originates east of Bowns Reservoir at the eastern end of the Aquarius Plateau and drains northeast into Pleasant Creek. In Greek mythology Tantalus was a wealthy king who was punished for his sins by being placed in a lake whose waters receded whenever he stooped to drink.
T31S,R6E,SLM. 314, 602.

TARANTULA MESA (**Garfield**) is east of the Waterpocket Fold and seventeen miles south of Notom*. The mesa is noted for its tarantulas.
T32S,R8,9E,SLM.

TATOW KNOB (**Millard**) is at the north end of the House Range, north of Swasey Peak. The name refers to a pair

of buttes that represent the big toes (Ta-too, ta-taugh = big toe) of an Indian giant.
NW¼,T16S,R13W,SLM; 8,416' (2,565m). 46.

TAVAPUTS PLATEAU is north of Green River*. The Green River divides the plateau into the West Tavaputs and East Tavaputs Plateaus. The Roan or Brown Cliffs are the southern scarp of this feature. Tavaputs was a Uinta Ute Indian chief.
314, 555(v39).

TAYLOR* (Davis) was a small community located three and one-half miles west of Ogden*. Taylor was absorbed into the surrounding communities. MRN
S28,29,T6N,R2W,SLM; 4,230' (1,289m).

TAYLOR CANYON (San Juan) originates at Grays Pasture in the Canyonlands National Park and drains west into Upheaval Canyon. The canyon was named for Arth Taylor, an early cattleman in the region. Nearby Arths Pasture was also named for Arth Taylor. See Taylor Creek.
T27S,R17½-19E,SLM. 514, 530, 555(v64).

TAYLOR CANYON (Weber) originates on the northwest slopes of Mount Ogden and drains west into the Weber River. It was named for John Taylor, a man who built a limekiln at the mouth of the canyon.
S35,36,T6N,R1W,SLM. 274.

TAYLOR CREEK (San Juan) originates at Taylor Flat on the northeast slopes of the La Sal Mountains east of Mount Waas. The creek drains southeast into Rock Creek. Lester, Buddy, Arthur, and Crispin Taylor entered this part of the country in the 1870s. The Taylor family ran their cattle along the creek on Arths Pasture, as well as other places.
S9,17,T26S,R25E,SLM to S31,T26S,R26E, SLM. 514, 530, 555(v64).

TAYLOR FLAT (San Juan) is at the head of Taylor Creek (San Juan) with the same name source.

TAYLOR FORK (Summit) originates five miles northeast of Woodland* and drains north into Beaver Creek at Beaver Creek Campground. It was named for John Taylor, who ran a sawmill in the canyon.
S27,34,T2S,R7E,SLM. 298.

TAYLOR LAKE (Duchesne) is in the central Uinta Mountains on the headwaters of the Whiterocks River, four miles west of Chepeta Lake. Rex Taylor was the first person to stock the lake with fish.
11,225' (3,421m). 309.

TAYLOR MOUNTAIN (Uintah) is twenty-four miles north northwest of Vernal* near the Red Cloud Loop Road. In 1878 Teancum and Alma Taylor ran their cattle on the mountain.
S23,T1S,R20E,SLM; 10,190' (3,106m). 567.

TAYLORSVILLE* (Salt Lake) is between Kearns* and Murray* on U-68. Taylorsville was originally known as North Jordan* and was part of West Jordan*. The settlement was renamed Taylorsville to honor John Taylor, an early president of the Mormon Church and a member of the Taylor family, early settlers in this area.
S10,T2S,R1W,SLM; 4,299' (1,310m). 144, 289, 542, 567.

TAYLORSVILLE* (Weber) is two miles south of West Weber* and was named for Samuel Walker, a tailor by trade. Taylorsville was separated from West Weber on March 14, 1909, but is again part of West Weber today.
S29,T6N,R2W,SLM; 4,245' (1,294m). 476, 567.

TEAL LAKE (Summit) is at the west end of the Uinta Mountains three miles north of Mirror Lake. A large number of teal, a small freshwater duck, inhabit the lake.
S10,T1S,R9E,SLM; 10,280' (3,133m).

TEAPOT LAKE (Summit) is one of a cluster of lakes in the southwest section of the Uinta Mountains between Trial Lake and Lost Lake. The outline of the lake represents the rough shape of a teapot. Also, before many lakes were named in this region, this lake was designated "T" Lake and a nearby lake was designated "P" Lake. Both resembled pots, hence the names Pot Lake and Teapot Lake.
S5,T2S,R9E,SLM; 9,900' (3,018m). 379.

TEASDALE* (Wayne) is at the junction of Bullberry Creek and the Fremont River. The settlement was originally established in 1879 and was named for George Teasdale, a Mormon church apostle and pioneer.
S16,T29S,R4E,SLM; 7,125' (2,172m). 289, 485, 542, 602.

TEAT MOUNTAIN (Utah) is ten miles east of the junction of Diamond Fork Creek and Spanish Fork River. The name reflects the general shape of the mountain.
S16,T9S,R5E,SLM; 8,537' (2,602m).

TEBBSDALE* (Garfield). See Spry*. 100(v17), 143.

TEBBSVILLE* (Garfield). See Spry*.

TEMPLE FORK (Cache) originates south of Temple Peak up Logan Canyon. An earlier name was Maughns Fork for Peter Maughn, who ran a sawmill in the canyon. The name was changed after a decision was made to harvest the timber in this canyon for building the Logan* Mormon temple. Private lumbering interests agreed to go elsewhere to obtain lumber supplies while the temple was under construction. All the temple names in this immediate area are derived from this name source.
567.

TEMPLE FORK (Sanpete). The Mormon church built a lumbermill on the left-hand fork of Canal Creek, southeast of Spring City*. This lumber mill was used to produce lumber for the Manti Temple.
S29,30,T16S,R5E,SLM. 152.

TEMPLE MOUNTAIN (Emery) is seven miles west of U-24 and twenty-three miles north of Hanksville*, at the south end of the San Rafael Swell. The mountain resembles a cathedral or chapel with its spires pushing up into the sky.
T24S,R11E,SLM; 6,773' (2,064m). 193.

TEMPLE PEAK (Cache) is at the head of Temple Fork up Logan Canyon. See Temple Fork (Cache) for name source. 9,026' (2,751m).

TEMPLE WASH (Emery, Sevier) originates near Solomons Reservoir and drains east northeast into Last Chance Wash. The name was derived from Solomons Temple.
T26S,R5E,SLM to S26,T25S,R6E,SLM.

TENMILE CANYON (Grand) originates on the East Tavaputs Plateau near the head of Westwater Creek and drains northwest into Willow Creek. The canyon is approximately ten miles long.
S25,T17R,R21E,SLM to S8,T16S,R21E,SLM.

TENMILE CREEK (Piute) originates on the eastern slopes of the Tushar Mountains and drains east into the Sevier River. The creek is ten miles south of Marysvale* and was a popular camping spot for freighters.
S22,T28S,R3W,SLM (at mouth).

TENMILE FLAT (Garfield) is ten miles out from Escalante* on the Hole-in-the-Rock road.
S21,22,T36S,R4E,SLM; 5,423' (1,653m).

TENMILE WASH (Garfield). See Alvey Wash (Garfield).

TENT TOWN* (Beaver). See Newhouse* (Beaver).

TERRACE* (Box Elder) was an early construction town on the Central Pacific Railroad right-of-way, twenty-eight miles southwest of Park Valley*. The name reflects the nearby terraces of ancient Lake Bonneville. In 1900 the railroad shops were moved into Nevada and a subsequent fire damaged the remainder of the settlement. No one lives there today.
S13,T7N,R15W,SLM.

TERRACE MOUNTAINS (Box Elder) are west of the north end of the Great Salt Lake. When Captain Howard Stansbury made his survey of the Great Salt Lake region on October 29, 1849, he observed the prominent shorelines or terraces of extinct Lake Bonneville. The terraces are found along the slopes of the mountain.
T9N,R14W,SLM; 7,028' (2,142m). 314, 371, 492.

TERRITORY OF UTAH. See Utah Territory.

TETONS, THE (Beaver) are a series of sharply rising peaks in the south central section of the Wah Wah Mountains. "Tetons" is the French term for breasts.
S7,8,T30S,R15W,SLM; 7,953' (2,424m).

TETSLAFF PEAK (Tooele) is the high point of the Silver Island Mountains, nine miles northeast of Wendover*. MRN
S16,T1N,R18W,SLM; 6,267' (1,910m).

TEXAS CANYON (San Juan) originates one mile northeast of the Bears Ears and drains southeast into Arch Canyon. Kigalia Rest Area is four miles north. The name comes from the early Texans who moved their herds of longhorn cattle into southeastern Utah Territory in the 1870s.
T36S,R19E,SLM. 409, 514, 555(v32).

TEXAS FLAT (San Juan) is near Texas Canyon. See the canyon for name source.

THATCHER* (Box Elder) is a small farming community three miles southwest of Bothwell*. It was named for Moses Thatcher, an apostle of the Mormon Church.
S15,T11N,R4W,SLM; 4,300' (1,311m). 139, 289, 542.

THATCHER MOUNTAIN (Box Elder) is two miles west of Thatcher* from which it received its name.
S15,16,21,22,T11N,R4W,SLM; 4,360' (1,329m).

THAYNES CANYON (Summit) originates at Shadow Lake in the Wasatch Mountains, two and one-half miles east northeast of Brighton*. The canyon drains north northeast into the upper section of Parleys Park.
S30-8,T2S,R4E,SLM.

THERMO* (Beaver) is a siding on the Union Pacific Railroad southeast of the Shauntie Hills. The name comes from the hot spring thermal activity of this area. See Thermo Springs.
S11,T30S,R12W,SLM; 5,037' (1,535m).

THERMO SPRINGS (Iron) are in the western Escalante Desert near Thermo siding. The U.S. Geological Survey named the springs for their high temperature.
S28,T30S,R12W,SLM; 5,037' (1,535m). 314.

THIRD SPRING HOLLOW (Beaver) originates on the western slopes of the Tushar Mountains and drains north into North Creek, South Fork. It is the third hollow with a spring located along the old road going up the west face of the mountain.
S35,T28S,R6W,SLM. 125.

THISTLE* (Utah) was a small community on US-6, 89 at the junction of Thistle Creek and Soldier Creek, twenty-three miles southeast of Provo*. The settlement was established in 1883

when the Denver and Rio Grande Railroad pushed its line through from Denver*. The name comes from the numerous thistles growing in the area. On April 14, 1983, the people of Thistle were evacuated when a mountain slide blocked the two creeks. The subsequent flooding transformed Thistle into a ghost town lying beneath an artificial lake.
S32,33,T9S,R4E,SLM; 5,033' (1,534m). 89, 163(19 Aug. 1983, U1), 289, 542, 546.

THISTLE CREEK (Utah) originates three and one-half miles east of Indianola* and drains northwest. Thistle Creek joins Soldier Creek to form the Spanish Fork River. See Thistle*.
S1,T12S,R4E,SLM to S28,T9S,R4E,SLM.

THOMAS RANGE (Tooele) is near Fish Springs north of Topaz Mountain. Captain Simpson named it for Lieutenant Colonel Lorenzo Thomas, the Assistant Adjutant General of the U.S. Army in Utah in 1859.
T11,12S,R12,13W,SLM. 477.

THOMPSON* (Grand) is east of Crescent Junction and near I-70 at Sego* junction. E. W. Thompson lived near the springs and operated a sawmill to the north near the Book Cliffs. It was also a prominent shipping point for cattle that were run in the Book Cliffs area. Stockmen from both San Juan and Grand counties used Thompson. The original name for this settlement was Thompson Springs*, a name that has recently been revived and reinstated.
T21S,R20E,SLM; 5,134' (1,565m). 100(v17), 146, 514. D.L. 8603.

THOMPSON CANYON (Grand) originates on the East Tavaputs Plateau in the Book Cliffs and drains south through Thompson* (now Thompson Springs*). See Thompson* for name source.
S16,T21S,R2E,SLM.

THOMPSON HOLLOW (Beaver) originates in the southwest part of the Tushar Mountains and drains north into South Creek, South Fork. In 1860, E. W. Thompson operated a sawmill in the hollow.
S25,T30S,R6W,SLM. 100(v17), 125.

THOMPSON MESA (Wayne) is ten miles northwest of Mount Ellen in the Henry Mountains. Three miles west is Sandy Creek. The mesa was named for Almon Thompson of the Powell surveys who worked extensively in this area.
T30S,R8E,SLM.

THOMPSON RIDGE (Beaver) is in the Tushar Mountains near Thompson Hollow. See the hollow for name source.
S25,36,T3S,R6W,SLM; 8,200' (2,499m).

THOMPSON WASH (Grand) originates at the mouth of Thompson Canyon near Thompson Springs* (Thompson*) and drains southwest into Tenmile Canyon.
S21,T21S,R20E,SLM to S13,T23S,R18E, SLM.

THOMPSONVILLE* (Piute) is three miles southeast of Marysvale* near US-89 at the mouth of Gold Creek. It is a small farming community named for the Thompson family, who live in the community.
S32,33,T27S,R3W,SLM; 6,000' (1,829m). 242.

THOUSAND LAKE MOUNTAIN (Wayne) is north of Torrey*, Bicknell*, and the Fremont River. Capitol Reef National Park is east. The mountain was named by the Mormons who pastured their flocks in the valley below. However, it is widely thought that cartographers erred by giving these mountains the Thousand Lake Mountains name. Apparently, the name should have been given to the Aquarius Plateau across the Fremont River to the south where the lakes are almost too numerous to count. There are no lakes found in today's Thousand Lake Mountains.
T27S,R4E,SLM; 11,306' (3,446m). 100(v2), 175, 314, 546.

THREE CANYON (Emery) drains from the southwest to the northeast into the Green River at Trin-Alcove Bend. The name reflects what is seen from the mouth of the canyon—the image of three canyons. See Trin-Alcove Bend.
S4,T25S,R16E,SLM to S23,T24S,R16E,SLM. 160, 422, 496.

THREE CREEKS (Beaver) is in the western Tushar Mountains at the confluence of the North Fork of Three Creeks, Lake Stream, and the South Fork of Three Creeks. The name extends downstream to the junction of Merchant Creek.
S9,16,T29S,R5W,SLM. 125.

THREE DIVIDE LAKES (Summit) are in the southwest section of the Uinta Mountains. The three lakes are in a line on the divide between the upper Provo River and the upper Middle Fork of the Weber River. Wall Lake is also in the vicinity.
S30,T1S,R9E,SLM; 10,460' (3,188m).

THREE FORKS (Wasatch) are four miles down Daniels Canyon southeast of Heber*. Three forks on both sides of Daniels Canyon meet at this point.
S33,T15S,R6E,SLM.

THREE KILN SPRING (Beaver) is northwest of Lime Mountain in the Beaver Lake Mountains and south of Little Frisco Mountain. Charcoal kilns are located by the spring.
S10,T26S,R12W,SLM; 5,950' (1,814m).

THREE LAKES (Kane) are a series of small lakes or large ponds in Three Lakes Canyon north of Kanab*. The water draining down the canyon accumulates into large waterpockets that are located in the sub-surface sandstone.
S19,30,31,T42S,R6W,SLM; 5,475' (1,669m).

THREE LAKES (Sanpete, Sevier) are a series of small lakes in the mountains southeast of Mayfield* on White Mountain. The lakes straddle the county line.

S30,31,T20S,R3E,SLM.

THREE LAKES CANYON (Kane) originates on top of the sand hills, nine miles north of Kanab. The canyon drains south into Kanab Creek, four miles north of Kanab*. US-89 passes through the canyon. See Three Lakes (Kane) for name source.
S18,19,30,31,32,T42S,R6W,SLM.

THREE MILE CREEK (Box Elder) originates east of Perry* and drains west through Perry Canyon into Willard Bay. The point where the creek crosses US-89 is approximately three miles south of Brigham City*.
S1,2,10,T8N,R2W,SLM. 567.

THREE MILE CREEK* (Box Elder). See Perry*.
139, 542.

THREE PATRIARCHS (Washington) are three prominent sandstone monoliths in Zion National Park. The landforms are close together across the river from Zion Lodge. Claude Hirschi, a Mormon stake president, named the monoliths because they reminded him of the character strength of the three biblical patriarchs: Abraham, Isaac, and Jacob.
T41S,R10W,SLM. 438.

THREE PEAKS (Iron) are a cluster of low peaks, one and one-half miles northeast of the Iron Springs. These landmarks were named by the stockmen who ran their herds in the area. The peaks should not be confused with the Three Peaks located ten miles west.
S16,T35S,R12W,SLM. 567.

THREE PEAKS (Iron) are a cluster of peaks in the south central section of the Escalante Desert, twenty-five miles northeast of Enterprise* and twenty miles south of Lund*. These peaks should not be confused with Three Peaks located ten miles east.
S1,2,T35S,R14W,SLM.

THREE STEP HILL (**San Juan**) is near the head of Dry Wash southwest of Lower Lisbon Valley. In the early wagon freighting days, there were three switchbacks or jump-offs that had to be overcome on the hill between La Sal* and Mancos*.
S1,2,12,T31S,R25E,SLM. 475, 514.

THREEMILE CREEK (**Garfield**) originates six miles northwest of Panguitch* and drains east. The creek crosses US-89, three miles north of Panguitch.
S7,T34S,R6W,SLM to S8,T34S,R5W,SLM.

THURBER* (**Wayne**). See Bicknell* (Wayne).

THURBER FORK (**Piute**) originates five miles northwest of Koosharem* and drains southeast into Greenwich Creek. Albert K. Thurber was an early Mormon explorer and prominent negotiator with the Indians. Thurber and others signed a peace treaty with the Fishlake Indians in Cedar Grove, which is also in this vicinity.
S14,T26S,R2W,SLM to S32,T26S,R1W,SLM. 585.

THURSTONVILLE* (**Morgan**). See Fort Thurston* (Morgan).

TIBADORE CANYON (**Piute**) originates in the mountains eight miles east of the north end of the Piute Reservoir and drains west into the Sevier River. The canyon was named for James Thibadeau (Tibadeau), an early settler in the canyon and in nearby Marysvale*.
S20,T28S,R2W,SLM to S27,T28S,R3W,SLM. 100(v17), 462, 567.

TICABOO CANYON (**Garfield**) originates in the Henry Mountains east of Mount Ellsworth and north of Ticaboo Mesa, and drains into Lake Powell. "Ticaboo" is an Indian word for "friendly."
T39S,R9E,SLM.

TICABOO CREEK (**Garfield**) originates three miles east of Ticaboo Mesa on the east side of the Henry Mountains, and drains southeast into Lake Powell. "Ticaboo" is the Piute Indian word for friendly. Cass Hite named the creek in the 1880s.
S32,T35½S,R13E,SLM. 181, 303, 466(27 Jan. 1978).

TICABOO MESA (**Garfield**) is between Cane Spring Desert and the Henry Mountains. The mouth of Ticaboo Creek is located three miles east, from which the mesa received its name.
S2,T36S,R12E,SLM; 5,166' (1,575m).

TICKVILLE GULCH (**Utah**) originates on the Camp Williams Military Reservation at Tickville Spring and drains southeast into Utah Lake. The Rocky Mountain spotted tick is quite common in this area.
S26,T4S,R2W,SLM to S26,T5S,R1W,SLM.

TIDWELL BOTTOM (**Emery**) is on the Green River between Fort Bottom and Bowknot Bend. Clyde Tidwell and his two brothers ran their cattle in this area in the early 1900s. See Tidwell Bottoms.
T26S,R17½E,SLM. 102, 193.

TIDWELL BOTTOMS (**Emery**) is on the San Rafael River at the mouth of Tidwell Draw and I-70. Clyde Tidwell ran cattle on the bottoms until he was killed there in a fire.
S28,32,T21S,R14E,SLM. 127, 193.

TIDWELL CANYONS (**Sevier**) originate six miles north of Forsyth Reservoir and drain south into Short Creek.
T25,26S,R3,4E,SLM.

TIE FORK (**Utah**) is a branch of Soldier Creek. The mouth of the fork is eight miles west of Soldier Summit. Railroad ties for the Denver and Rio Grande Railroad were obtained from this area.
S14,T10S,R6E,SLM (at mouth).

TIMPANOGOS CAVE NATIONAL MONUMENT (**Utah**) is centered around a beautiful natural cave located several miles up American Fork Canyon, east of Alpine*.

TIMPANOGOS RIVER (Utah). See Provo River.

TIMPIE* (Tooele). See Rowley Junction*.

TIMPIE LAKE (Tooele) is a widening in an impounded stream at the north end of the Stansbury Range. Variant: Big Spring.
S8,9,T1S,R7W,SLM; 4,223' (1,287m). 100 (v2).

TINTIC* (Juab) was a small community settled in 1903. It is now a highway junction for U-36 and US-6 west of Mona*. Tintic (Tintick) was a renegade Indian chief who, with his small local band of Goshute Indians, claimed the country on the west side of Utah Lake in Cedar, Tintic, and Skull valleys.
T10S,R3W,SLM; 5,859' (1,786m). 100(v3), 314, 516, 542.

TINTIC VALLEY (Juab) is between the East and West Tintic mountains west of Eureka*. See Tintic* for name source.
T10,11S,R3W,SLM. 163(5 March 1856), 224, 526(v3).

TOAD, THE (Beaver) is an odd-shaped rock formation in The Needles, at the north end of the Needles Range.
S28,T26S,R18W,SLM; 7,542' (2,299m).

TOKAWANA PEAK (Uintah) is in the north central section of the Uinta Mountains between the East and West forks of Blacks Fork. According to Uinta Ute Indian legend, there were once two Indian chiefs: one was good and one was bad. Tokawana was the good Indian's name, meaning peace.
13,173' (4,015m). 309, 567.

TOLIVERS CREEK (Daggett, Uinta) originates in the northeast section of the Uinta Mountains and drains north into the Green River. J. Frank Tolliver and

his family were well-known settlers in Browns Park history. They arrived in 1885 and ran cattle in the area. Joe Tolliver, a son of J. Frank, committed suicide in a Vernal saloon while trying to prove his loaded pistol was really empty.
S17,T1N,R24E,SLM to S25,T2N,R24E,SLM. 172, 303, 567.

TOM PATTERSON CANYON (Uintah) originates on the East Tavaputs Plateau, six miles west of the Colorado line at Tom Patterson Point. It drains northwest into Sweet Water Canyon.
S19,T15S,R25E,SLM to S21,T14S,R24E, SLM.

TOMMY CREEK (Garfield). See Houston Mountain.

TOMMY SMITH CREEK (Kane) originates on the southern slopes of the Kaiparowits Plateau and drains south into Wahweap Creek.
T39-40S,R1,2E,SLM.

TOMS CABIN CREEK (Box Elder) originates in northeastern Nevada and drains east into Grouse Creek. Uncle Tom Warburton was an unmarried man who built a cabin on the creek. During roundups, cowboys gathered at his cabin.
S32,33,T10N,R18W,SLM (at mouth).

TOMS CABIN SPRING (Box Elder) is located on the creek. See above.

TOMS CANYON (Kane) originates three and one-half miles northeast of Kanab* and drains southwest into Kanab Creek. Thomas E. Robinson purchased the canyon from James A. Little, who was using the canyon as a cow pasture. Soon afterward, Little Canyon was being called Toms Canyon.
S14,22,28,T43S,R6W,SLM. 100(v17), 567.

TOMSICK BUTTE (Emery) is up the Muddy River on the San Rafael Swell. Tomsick, accompanied by his dog, was prospecting near the butte when both he and the dog drank poison creek water.

The dog died, but Tomsick survived. T24S,R9E,SLM. 508.

TONAQUINT* (Washington) was a small 1855 pioneer settlement at the junction of Santa Clara Creek and the Virgin River. The settlement had several names, including Lower Clara* because it was further down the creek from Santa Clara*, Seldom Stop* because it was away from the main line of travel, Never Sweat* because it was a hot, sweltering place to live in, and Lick Skillet* because the people were so poor that this is what one had to do to survive. It was first named for the small clan of Tonaquint Indians living there when Mormon missionaries arrived to help the Indians farm, build dams, and improve their lot. Tonaquint should not be confused with Tonaquint Station* (Santa Clara*). S6,T43S,R15W,SLM; 2,500' (762m). 89, 100 (v17), 154, 311, 516, 600.

TONAQUINT STATION* (Washington). See Santa Clara* (Washington).

TONY GROVE* (Cache) is eighteen miles up Logan Canyon at Tony Grove Creek. The name developed as loggers and stockmen observed well-to-do people—the "tony" people of the 1880s— come to the site to enjoy the recreation it provided. The term was gradually transferred from the people to the site. Utah State University presently maintains a forestry training station in this area. 249(22 April 1977).

TONY GROVE CREEK (Cache) originates at Tony Grove Lake and drains into the Logan River near Tony Grove*.

TONY GROVE LAKE (Cache) is at the head of Tony Grove Creek.

TOOELE* (Tooele) was settled in 1851 on the west base of the Oquirrh Mountains and received its name from the Tooele Valley where the community is located. The valley lies between the Oquirrh Mountains and the Stansbury

Mountains. The definition of the word "Tooele" is in dispute. Some say it refers to the name of a Goshute Indian chief, Tuilla. Others claim a reference to the rushes and reeds that are so common in the tules, the swampy areas in the valley. S21,22,27,28,T3S,R4W,SLM; 5,050' (1,539m). 27, 58, 153, 275, 314, 367, 542, 546, 567.

TOOELE COUNTY was originally known as Tuilla County and was one of the first six counties created by the General Assembly of the State of Deseret on January 31, 1850. The spelling was changed to Tooele in March 1852 when the boundaries were extended to the California border. See Tooele* for further discussion.

TOOELE VALLEY (Tooele) is at the south end of the Great Salt Lake and is bordered by the Oquirrh and Stansbury mountains. See Tooele* for name source. T2,3S,R4,5W,SLM.

TOPACHE PEAK (Beaver) is a high point of the Star Range, southwest of Milford*. MRN S36,T8S,R12W,SLM.

TOPAZ* (Juab) is three miles northwest of Abraham*. Topaz was a resettlement camp for Japanese internees after Pearl Harbor and during World War II. The name was derived from the nearby mountain where topaz crystals are often found. The camp was established in September 1942 and was shut down in 1945. Today it is a ghost town site. S20,T16S,R8W,SLM; 4,570' (1,393m). 89, 314, 501, 516.

TOPAZ MOUNTAIN (Juab) is part of the south end of the Thomas Range. The gem topaz is found on this mountain. S8,17,18,T13S,R11W,SLM; 7,046' (2,148m).

TOPLIFF* (Tooele) was an 1870 quarrying settlement ten miles southwest of Fairfield*. The sole product was limestone, which was in demand at

nearby smelters. The smelters all closed by 1937 and Topliff soon became a ghost town. MRN
T8S,R3W,SLM; 4,986' (1,520m). 89, 516, 542.

TOQUERVILLE* (Washington) is on U-17 north of La Verkin*. The area was settled in 1858 as the second town located on the lower Virgin River. The community name is that of Chief Toquer of the local Piute Indians. The Toquer name evolved through Tokar*, Toker*, Tokerville* and finally Toquerville, which means black. The name refers to the surrounding black lava rock that is so abundant in this area. The name does not refer to grapes.
S2,T41S,R13W,SLM; 3,200' (975m). 154, 163(1 Oct. 1862), 289, 311, 314, 438, 542, 600.

TORREY* (Wayne) is a small agricultural community on U-24 between Bicknell* and Capitol Reef National Park. It was named in honor of Colonel Torrey, who fought in the Spanish American War. Torrey has had several earlier names such as Poverty Flat*, Youngstown*, Central*, Popular*, and Bonita*.
S12,T29S,R4E,SLM; 6,843' (2,086m). 100 (v17), 289, 542.

TRACHYTE CANYON (Garfield) originates on the northern slopes of Mount Hillers in the Henry Mountains and drains southeast into Lake Powell. The canyon was named on June 20, 1872, by Almon H. Thompson of the Powell surveys. Trachyte is a light-colored volcanic rock that is quite common in the canyon.
T33S,R12,13E,SLM. 159, 422, 496.

TRAIL CANYON (Kane) originates three miles northwest of Kanab* at the top of the Vermillion Cliffs. The canyon drains east into Kanab Creek. It was an early 1872 mail route that was used instead of the old Shunesburg* route.
S17,18,24,T43S,R6W,SLM. 567.

TRAIL CANYON (San Juan) originates in Canyonlands National Park near Aztec Butte at the north end of Grand View Point. It drains northwest into Taylor Canyon and was developed by early stockmen.
T27S,R18E,SLM.

TRAIL CREEK CANYON (Morgan) originates at the Rich County line and drains west southwest into Francis Canyon at Lost Creek Reservoir. Stockmen used the canyon to move sheep to and from a grazing area and the Shearing Corral area.
S34,T6N,R6E,SLM to S10,T5N,R5E,SLM. 567.

TRAIL MOUNTAIN (Sevier) is at the south end of the Pavant Mountains. Three early military trails cross this range then go in three different directions.
S15,T25S,R5W,SLM; 7,850' (2,393m). 567.

TRAIL POINT (Garfield) is a southern extension of Boulder Mountain, an eastern part of the Aquarius Plateau. A stock trail from the low country works its way up onto the plateau near Crescent, Circle, and Half Moon lakes.
10,834' (3,302m). 12.

TRAIN ROCK (San Juan) is an extended butte one and one-half miles long, east of Oljeto Wash.
S33,T42S,R15E,SLM; 5,834' (1,778m).

TRAIN ROCK WASH (San Juan) originates seven miles northeast of Goulding*, passes Train Rock, and drains northwest into Oljeto Wash.
S11,12,T43S,R16E,SLM to S19,T42S,R15E, SLM.

TRAP CANYON WASH (Garfield) originates at Death Ridge Reservoir on the Kaiparowits and drains northeast into Little Valley Wash. The canyon was used by early stockmen for capturing wild horses.
S19,T37S,R2E,SLM to S35,T36S,R2E,SLM. 12.

TRAVELERS REST STATION (**Salt Lake**) was an Overland Stage stop where State Street now passes through Murray City*. Here the passengers took a brief rest stop while the horses were watered. S6,T2S,R1E,SLM; 4,285' (1,306m). 516.

TRAVERSE MOUNTAINS (**Salt Lake**). The name reflects the east-west orientation instead of the usual north-south orientation. The Jordan River cuts through the Traverse Mountains at the Point of the Mountain, from Utah Lake into the Great Salt Lake. T4S,R1W,SLM; 6,331' (1,930m).

TREASURE HILL (**Juab**) is three and one-half miles south of Eureka* near Ruby Hollow. This is one of the most heavily prospected areas in the state. S6,T11S,R2W,SLM; 6,860' (2,091m). 100 (v17).

TREMONT* (**Box Elder**). See Tremonton*.

TREMONTON* (**Box Elder**) is on I-15 and the Malad River. White people first settled in this area in 1888, although French-Canadian trappers had entered the area much earlier. There are two versions to the name origin. One suggests the town was named for Tremont*, Illinois. The other states that the name was given by the early French-Canadian trappers, "tres" means three and "monton" means hill, thus Tremonton. S2,3,10,11,T11N,R3W,SLM; 4,322' (1,317m). 100(v17), 139, 314, 542.

TRENTON* (**Cache**) is a small agricultural community on U-142 and U-23 south of Lewiston*. The community was settled in 1870. The early Mormon bishop, William B. Preston, suggested the name of his former hometown, Trenton*, New Jersey. S28,34,T14N,R1W,SLM; 4,455' (1,358m). 100(v17), 289, 449, 542, 567.

TRIAL LAKE (**Summit**) is at the west end of the Uinta Mountains near Wall Lake. In 1893 it was the first lake in this vicinity to be used as a reservoir. In other words it was a trial lake. An error on some maps show it as Tryol or Tyrol Lake. Washington Lake is another reservoir that is located in this vicinity. S32,T1S,R9E,SLM; 9,825' (2,995m). 100(v2), 530.

TRIANGLE CANYON (**Grand**) originates near the Colorado line north of the Dolores River. The canyon drains southwest then west to enter Coates Creek. With the Colorado River, the three form a Big Triangle, as the enclosed area is named. S7-11,T22S,R25E,SLM.

TRIDELL* (**Uintah**) is a small agricultural community twenty miles north of Roosevelt* on U-246 and the junction of three canyons. S26,T1N,R1E,USM; 5,650' (1,722m). 542.

TRIDENT LAKE (**Summit**) is at the west end of the Uinta Mountains, two miles south of Washington Lake. The lake has a triangular shape. S18,T2S,R9W,SLM; 9,754' (2,973m). 530.

TRIN-ALCOVE BEND (**Emery, Grand**) is on the Green River at the mouth of Three Canyon in Labyrinth Canyon. Powell wrote, "These canyons are very tortuous, almost closed in from view, and, seen from the opposite side of the river, they appear like three alcoves; and we name this Trin-Alcove Bend" (420, p. 200). S23,T24S,R16E,SLM; 3,990' (1,216m). 160, 420, 496.

TRINITY CANYON (**Grand**) originates on the southeast slopes of the La Sal Mountains and drains south to the junction of Dry Canyon and Stateline draws. MRN S8,17,20,T28S,R26E,SLM. 146.

TROPIC* (**Garfield**) is on U-12, east of Bryce Canyon National Park. The original settlers came from Panguitch*

and named their new community Tropic because the region had a milder climate in comparison to Panguitch.
S35,T36S,R3W,SLM; 6,298' (1,920m). 145, 289, 542.

TROPIC RESERVOIR (Garfield) is on the Sevier River, East Fork, seven miles southwest of Bryce Canyon National Park. The reservoir received its name from the town it services.
S8,T37S,R4W,SLM.

TROUT CREEK* (Juab) is between Callao* and Gandy* on the fishing creek from which it was named.
S13,T13S,R18W,SLM; 6,675' (2,035m). 100 (v17), 347.

TROUT CREEK PEAK (Uintah) is seven miles north of Marsh Peak and east of the head of Trout Creek. The peak was named after the creek.
S9,T1N,R20E,SLM; 10,519' (3,206m).

TROY* (Beaver) was a small settlement near the Troy smelter, five miles south of Milford*, along the Beaver River. After five years of operation, the smelter burned down, was not rebuilt, and the community was abandoned. Troy was an early name for Hay Springs*. MRN
S31,T28S,R10W,SLM; 5,000' (1,524m).

TUB SPRING (Beaver) is in the San Francisco Mountains between Sawmill and Barrel Spring canyons.
S25,T26S,R13W,SLM; 7,100' (2,164m).

TUB SPRING (Beaver) is in the Mountain Home Range north of the head of Cottonwood Wash.
S16,T26S,R19W,SLM; 7,750' (2,362m).

TUCKER* (Utah) was an early railroad stop between Thistle* and Soldier Summit*. Today it is a highway rest stop. An earlier name was Clear Creek*, from the name of the nearby creek. The name was later changed to Tucker for James Tucker, an 1883 settler. The use of this area as a freight and engine-helper stop

diminished in 1915 when the railroad was realigned and engines were improved.
S24,T10S,R7E,SLM; 5,236' (1,901m). 89, 270, 516.

TUERTO CANYON (San Juan) originates on the northwest slopes of Mount Linnaeus in the Abajo Mountains, and drains northwest into Cottonwood Creek. "Tuerto" is Spanish for crooked.
T33,34S,R21E,SLM.

TUILLA COUNTY. See Tooele County.

TULE LAKES (Garfield) are several small lakes one-half mile southwest of Posy Lake on the Aquarius Plateau. The lakes are named for the reeds and rushes that grow around the water.
9,108' (2,776m).

TULE VALLEY (Millard). See White Valley (Millard).

TUNNEL SPRING (Millard) is on the western slopes of Tunnel Spring Mountains. MRN
S8,T24S,R17W,SLM.

TUNNEL SPRING MOUNTAINS (Millard) are named for the Tunnel Spring that flows on the western slopes of the mountain.
S9,17,20,T24S,R17W,SLM.

TUNGSTEN HOLLOW (Beaver) originates on Baldwin Ridge of the Tushar Mountains and drains south into North Creek, South Fork. MRN
S24,25,T28S,R6W,SLM.

TURKEY WASH (Beaver) is on the eastern slopes of the Needle Range and drains northeast into Pine Valley Wash.
T28S,R17W,SLM.

TUSHAR CANYON (Grand) originates twelve miles northwest of Moab* and drains north northeast into Bartlett Wash.
S36,T24S,R19E,SLM to S8,T24S,R20E,SLM.

TUSHAR MOUNTAINS (**Beaver**) is a mountain range between Beaver* on the west and Junction* and Marysvale* on the east. There are two versions of the name origin. Dutton described two pre-eminent cones (Belnap and Baldy) that ended in sharp cusps. The words "cusp" and "tush" are similar in meaning and tushar becomes a descriptive name–the Tushar Mountains. Beckwith writes that the local Indian word for the mountain was "t'shar," meaning the white mountain, because it was always covered with snow. Anglicized, T'shar becomes Tushar–the Tushar Mountains. Cox also points out that legend records an ancient tribe of Indians called the Tushari lived on the mountains.
T27-29S,R4,5W,SLM; 12,160' (3,706m). 12, 46, 175, 314.

TUSHAR RIDGE (**Beaver**) is in the Tushar Mountains near Puffer Lake. See the mountain for name source.
S1,2,10,11,T29S,R5W,SLM.

TUSHER CANYON (**Grand**) originates on the East Tavaputs Plateau and drains west into the Green River. Dave Tushar ran a few cattle and horses in the canyon that was named after him.
S16,T20S,R16E,SLM (at mouth).

TUXEDO BOTTOM (**Wayne**) is on the Green River between the mouths of Dead Horse and Millard canyons. An early claim for this land was written on a piece of paper and placed in an empty Tuxedo tobacco can found on an exposed rock at the site.
S32,T28½S,R18E,SLM; 4,000' (1,219m). 102.

TWELVE HUNDRED DOLLAR RIDGE (**Wasatch**) is six miles south of Currant Creek, with Strawberry Peak at its southwest point. MRN
S29,T4S,R9W,USM to S15,T5S,R10W,USM; 10,335' (3,150m).

TWELVEMILE CREEK (**Duchesne**) originates on the West Tavaputs Plateau and drains northeast into the Right Fork of Indian Canyon.
S36,T6S,R8W,USM to S30,T6S,R7W,USM.

TWELVEMILE CREEK (**Sanpete**) originates at Twelvemile Flat east of Mayfield* and drains west into the San Pitch River. The road crosses the creek twelve miles south of Manti*.
S29,T10S,R4E,SLM to S13,T19S,R1E,SLM. 494.

TWELVEMILE KNOLL (**Beaver**) was an early freighter's landmark on the Old Jockey Road, twelve miles out from Milford*.
S13,T29S,R12W,SLM.

TWENTY WELLS* (**Tooele**). See Grantsville* (Tooele).

TWENTYFIVE MILE WASH (**Garfield**). The Hole-in-the-Rock road crosses the wash twenty-five miles out from Escalante*.

TWENTYMILE WASH (**Garfield**). The Hole-in-the-Rock road crosses the wash twenty miles out from Escalante*.
S¼,T37S,R8E,SLM.

TWIN LAKES (**Beaver**) are two small lakes located close together in the Tusher Mountains, northwest of Puffer Lake.
S26,T28S,R5W,SLM.

TWIN LAKES (**Duchesne**) are in the Brown Duck Basin of the central Uinta Mountains between the Brown Duck Mountains and Clements Lake. The lakes are similar and close together.
S30,T3N,R7W,USM; 10,594' (3,229m).

TWIN LAKES (**Salt Lake**) are up Big Cottonwood Canyon one mile southwest of Brighton*. These similarly shaped small lakes were named during a July 24th celebration in the 1880s. The lakes were developed as a reservoir with the building of a dam.
S34,T2S,R3E,SLM; 9,450' (2,880m). 100(v2).

TWIN LAKES (**Summit**) are two adjoining lakes of similar shape in the southwest section of the Uinta Mountains, between Wall Lake and Notch Mountain. S30,T1S,R9E,SLM; 10,420' (3,176m).

TWIN LAKES (**Uintah**) are two lakes close together in the southeast section of the Uinta Mountains, four miles west of Marsh Peak. 10,300' (3,139m).

TWIN PEAKS (**Beaver**) is in the Indian Peak Range at the head of Sheep Creek. S27,T30S,R18W,SLM; 9,546' (2,910m).

TWIN PEAKS (**Salt Lake**) is two miles southwest of Lake Blanche and one mile west of Dromedary Peak. T2S,R2E,SLM.

TWIN PEAKS (**Salt Lake**) is two miles north of the University of Utah campus. S28,T1N,R1E,SLM; 6,291' (1,917m).

TWIN PEAKS (**Salt Lake**) is on the Utah County line, four miles south southwest of Alta*. T3S,R3E,SLM; 11,433' (3,485m). 252.

TWIN PEAKS (**Utah, Wasatch**) is a pair of peaks on the county line, three miles southwest of Daniels Pass. S29,T6S,R6E,SLM.

TWIN POTS RESERVOIR (**Duchesne**) is a lake with two separate prominent underwater holes in the south central section of the Uinta Mountains. S3,T1N,R5W,USM; 7,611' (2,320m).

TWIST CREEK (**Beaver**). See Big or Little Twist Creek (Beaver).

TWITCHELL CANYON (**Beaver**) originates on the northwest slopes of the Tushar Mountains and drains southwest into Indian Creek. The canyon was named for James Twitchell of Beaver* who kept a garden in the canyon in the 1860s. S22,28,T27S,R6W,SLM. 100(v17), 125.

TWITCHELL CREEK (**Garfield**) originates on Escalante Mountain west of Escalante* at the Long and Round Willow Bottom reservoirs. It drains east into North Creek. The Edwin Twitchell family were early Escalante pioneers who used the creek. SW¼,T3S,R1E,SLM. 12.

TWO TOM HILL (**Utah**) is one and one-half miles east of the headwaters of Diamond Fork. MRN S30,T7S,R6E,SLM; 8,325' (2,357m).

TWOMILE CANYON (**Garfield**) originates in the Henry Mountains and drains east into the Colorado River. Before Lake Powell was dammed, Twomile Canyon was located two miles downriver from Hite*. Today both Hite and the mouth of the canyon are under the waters of Lake Powell. S2,T35S,R12E,SLM (to the Colorado River). 567.

- U -

U M CREEK (Sevier, Wayne) originates at the junction of the Left and Right forks of U M Creek, south of the Pot Holes and the U M Plateau. It drains south into Mill Meadow Reservoir. The creek was named for the United Moroni Order, a group of Mormon stockmen who worked in the area as a united group during pioneer days. U M was the brand used on their cattle and Moroni was a noted Mormon prophet.
S5,T25S,R3E,SLM to S35,T26S,R3E,SLM. D.L. 7103.

U M PASS (Sevier) is on the saddle between Mount Marvine and Mount Terrill, just south of the headwaters of the U M Creek, Left Fork. See the creek for name source.
S31,T24S,R3E,SLM.

U M PLATEAU (Sevier) is on the headwaters of U M Creek, Right Fork. See the creek for name source.
S8,17,21,T24S,R3E,SLM; ca. 11,100' (3,383m).

UCOLO* (San Juan) is a small ranching community west of the Colorado border and north of US-666. Ucolo encloses Piute Spring country and was headquarters for the Carlisle Cattle Company in the 1880s. In 1912, as the open range became more restricted with fencing, the families of John T. Cardwell and Frank Ellington became the first settlers. Ucolo is an anagram for Utah-Colorado.
T33S,R26E,SLM; 6,875' (2,095m). 406, 409.

UINTA BASIN (Uintah) is drained by the Uinta and White rivers complex with the Uinta Mountains on the north. The entire basin drains into the Green River. It is a favored region in the West, with numerous streams of clear cold water, springs, much arable land, and unlimited resources. The name comes from the Uinta Utes who live in the basin.
160, 314, 422, 496, 546.

UINTA MOUNTAINS are a wide upheaval in northeast Utah with an east-west axis—an unusual orientation in the United States. Early maps generally attached an "H" to the end of the word, until it was left off in Major Powell's publications as being unnecessary to the pronunciation. Inasmuch as the county name was already assigned, the name remains unchanged along with one or two other special cases. The name Uinta originated from the Ute Indians who lived in the basin.
172, 275, 420, 422, 530, 546.

UINTA RIVER (Duchesne, Uintah) originates on the eastern slopes of Kings Peak (Utah's highest peak), and drains south southeast into the Duchesne River. In the early mountain men/trapper period of Utah Territory, the relationship of the Uinta and Duchesne rivers was occasionally confused; even the nearby Whiterocks River was called the Uinta River prior to the 1870s. See Uinta Mountains for name source.
S17,T3S,R2E,USM (at mouth). 309, 555(v9). D.L. 8404.

UINTA SPRINGS (Sanpete). See Fountain Green*.

UINTAH* (Weber) was settled as East Weber in 1850 at the mouth of the Weber River Canyon. On March 4, 1867, the Union Pacific Railroad named the nearby stop Deseret*. This was changed to Uintah out of respect for the local Ute Indians and soon the entire community carried the same name.

S25,T5N,R1W,SLM; 4,497' (1,371m). 27, 289, 314, 516, 542.

UINTAITE (**Uintah**). See Gilsonite Draw.

UINTAH COUNTY is one of the original eight counties organized in 1850. The name is taken from the early Ute Indian tribe, who continue to live in the adjacent Uinta Basin. See Uinta Basin for further name source.
6, 27, 163(6 Oct. 1941), 309, 542, 567.

UINTAH LAKE (**Duchesne**) is at the west end of the Uinta Mountains and drains southeast into Rock Creek. The name is taken from the local Ute (Uinta Ute) Indians.
S26,T4N,R8W,USM; 10,960' (3,341m).

UNDER THE LEDGE (**Garfield**) is a term applied by the local stockmen to the massive shelf country between the inner canyons of the Colorado and Green rivers complex. Most of this area is now located in Canyonlands National Park and the high country above The Ledge. The Robbers Roost is part of the country above The Ledge.
24.

UNDINE SPRINGS (**Emery**) boil up as a branch of, and flows into the mouth of, the San Rafael River. The springs effervesce and throw a column of water into the air. "Undine" means nymph.
159, 555(v7).

UNION* (**Box Elder**) was a small temporary settlement during early 1900, two and one-half miles southwest of Tremonton*. MRN
T11N,R3W,SLM. 11.

UNION* (**Salt Lake**) is in the southeast part of the Salt Lake Valley at Seventh East and Seventy-fifth South. The community was settled in 1849 by brothers John and Elmer Cox. It was first known as Little Cottonwood* until 1854

when the name was changed to South Cottonwood*. When South Cottonwood was divided, the southern half became Union (the name of the fort), a name suggestive of the unity, energy, good feeling, and cooperation displayed in order to accomplish their united goals.
S29,T2S,R1E,SLM; 4,500' (1,372m). 252, 289, 567.

UNION* (**Weber**). See Riverdale* (Weber).

UNION BENCH (**Utah**) is a term for the benchland southeast of Springville* where Mapleton* is now located. The early settlers of Springville united in grazing their livestock on the bench.
S2,3,10,11,T8S,3E,SLM. 134(29 Feb. 1976).

UNION CITY* (**Salt Lake**) was a small mining community in the late 1800s up Little Cottonwood Canyon between Galena City* and Alta*. It was abandoned when the mines were shut down.
T35S,R3E,SLM. 454.

UNION FORT* (**Salt Lake**). See Union* (Salt Lake).

UNION SPRINGS* (**Juab**). See Fountain Green*.

UNIONVILLE* (**Summit**). See Hoytsville* (Summit).

UNKNOWN MOUNTAINS (**Garfield**). See the Henry Mountains.

UPALCO* (**Duchesne**) is seven and one-half miles southeast of Altamont* near the Lake Fork River. Upalco's first name was Lake Fork* for the river. The name is drawn from the initial letters of the Utah Power and Light Company that furnished power for the project.
S28,T2S,R3W,USM; 5,765' (1,757m). 89, 100(v17), 542.

UPHEAVAL CANYON (**San Juan**) originates at the Upheaval Dome and

380

drains northwest into the Green River. See Upheaval Dome. T27S,R18E,SLM.

UPHEAVAL DOME (San Juan) is in Canyonlands National Park at the head of Upheaval Canyon. The dome is believed to have formed when a three-thousand-foot-layer of salt pushed up through an area of overlying weakness. The dome then bulged onto the surface as a mountain that eventually cracked open into a series of concentric stone strata or ridges. As the salt dissolved it left monuments of towers and odd rock formations. The overall formation has been heavily eroded. T18E,R27S,SLM. 383(v140), 514.

UPPER BINGHAM* (Salt Lake). See Copperfield* (Salt Lake).

UPPER CASTLEDALE* (Emery). See Orangeville* (Emery).

UPPER CHAIN LAKE (Duchesne) is three miles east of Mount Emmons in the south central section of the Uinta Mountains. This lake is the third from the lowest and also the largest of the Chain Lakes group. 10,623' (3,238m).

UPPER INDIAN SPRING (Beaver) is in the Indian Peak Range near the head of Antelope Wash. This spring is higher in altitude than Lower Indian Spring. S11,T29S,R18W,SLM.

UPPER JOES VALLEY (Emery) is on Indian Creek, eight miles north of Lower Joes Valley. See Joes Valley for name source.

UPPER KANAB* (Kane). See Alton* (Kane).

UPPER KENTS LAKE (Beaver) is in the south Tushar Mountains east of and above Kents Lake. S5,T30S,R5W,SLM; 8,989' (2,740m).

UPPER PINE SPRING (Beaver) is at the north end of the Needles Mountain Range and west of and higher than Pine Spring. S21,T26S,R18W,SLM; 6,850' (2,088m).

UPPER RED CASTLE LAKE (Summit) is in the north central section of the Uinta Mountains on the headwaters of the East Fork of Smiths Fork. It drains into Red Castle Lake. 11,542' (3,518m).

UPPER TRAIL CANYON (Kane) originates near the head of Left Hand Collett on the Kaiparowits Plateau into which it drains. Cattle were trailed through this and Lower Trail Canyon into the Last Chance Creek area. S31,T38S,R4E,SLM. 12.

UPPER VALLEY (Garfield) is ten miles southwest of Escalante* with U 54 passing through. The valley is higher than Lower Escalante Valley to the northeast. S19,T36S,R1E,SLM to S16,T35S,R2E,SLM. 12.

UPPER VALLEY CREEK (Garfield) originates at the summit between Henrieville* and Escalante* on U-54, and drains northeast through Upper Valley into the Escalante River. S30,T36S,R1E,SLM to S16,T35S,R2E,SLM. 12.

UPPER YELLOW PINE LAKE (Summit) is at the west end of the Uinta Mountains, one and one-half miles east southeast of Castle Peak and above Lower Yellow Pine Lake. S9,T2S,R7E,SLM; 9,700' (2,957m).

UPTON* (Summit) was a small settlement up Chalk Creek, above Coalville*. An early name was Huffville* for the Joseph Huff family who originally settled on the creek. That name now clings to a fork of Chalk Creek. As more people moved in, Huffville became Up Town* then Upton as being "up the creek" from

Coalville.
T3N,R6E,SLM; 6,182' (1,884m). 100(v17),
289, 542, 567.

URADO* (San Juan) was a small 1918
settlement on the Colorado border east
of Monticello*. Urado is an anagram for
Utah and Colorado.
406.

UTAH COUNTY was established on
January 31, 1850, as one of the first six
counties created by the General
Assembly of the State of Deseret. The
name is drawn from the local Ute
Indians.
6, 27, 501, 546, 604.

UTAH LAKE (Utah) is about thirty
miles long and seven to eleven miles
wide, located in the Utah Valley. It has
had earlier names of Ashley Lake, Little
Uta Lake, Utaw Lake, and Laguna de
Nuestra Senora de la Merced de
Timpanogotziz. See Utah State for
further name source.
T5-9S,R1W,1E,SLM; 4,488' (1,368m). 27,
205, 270, 371, 546, 583.

UTAH STATE. The Mormon pioneers
first settled in their promised land
between July 21 and 24, 1847, although
trappers and mountain men had thoroughly covered the region during the
previous twenty-five years. The
Domínguez and Escalante party had also
penetrated the region in 1776. Before
this exploration and settlement, the area
was home to the native Indians. The
Mormons established their State of
Deseret on March 12, 1849. The term
"Deseret" comes from their scriptures
and means "honey bee." Deseret was
later changed to the Territory of Utah
on September 9, 1850. The word "Utah"
was taken from the native Ute Indians.
The State of Utah was formalized on
January 4, 1896.
27, 209, 314, 371, 546, 604.

UTAH TERRITORY. See Utah State.

UTAH VALLEY (Utah) is south of the
Jordan Narrows and the Point of the
Mountain, between Utah Lake and the
Wasatch Mountains. Utah Lake is the
predominant feature. It was named for
the Ute Indians who inhabited the valley.

UTAHN* (Duchesne) was a product of
the 1905 land rush into the Uintah Basin.
The settlement was nine miles north of
Duchesne on U-35 and the Duchesne
River. After peaking in 1920 with two
hundred citizens, it finally stabilized as a
small agricultural community.
S27,34,T2S,R5W,SLM; 5,865' (1,788m). 89,
457.

UTE CROSSING (Emery). See
Gunnison Crossing (Emery).

UTE FORD (Kane, San Juan) is now
under the waters of Padre Bay of Lake
Powell. See Crossing of the Fathers.

UTELAND BUTTE (Uintah) is a prominent landmark in the heart of the Uinta
Basin and the Uinta Indian Reservation,
near Fort Duchesne.
S4,5,8,9,T5S,R2E,USM; 5,192' (1,583m).

UVADA* (Iron) is in Pleasant Valley,
which lies in both Nevada and Utah,
southwest of Modena*. Uvada is an
anagram of Utah-Nevada.
S35,T35S,R20W,SLM. 100(v17).

- V -

V, THE (Garfield) is an open V-shaped range at the junction of Harris Wash and the Escalante River.
T36S,R6E,SLM; 5,250' (1,600m). 12.

VACA* (Sevier) is across the Sevier River from Cove* (between Joseph* and Sevier*) where the old Vaca Road drops over the ridge into Long Valley. "Vaca," meaning "cow" in Spanish, was an old livestock shipping point.
S34,T25S,R3W,SLM; 5,658' (1,725m). 368, 584.

VADO DE LOS PADRES, EL (Kane, San Juan). See The Crossing of the Fathers.

VAL VERDA* (Davis) is in the foothills southeast of Bountiful*. The name was also attached to a nearby spring where John McNeil, a shoemaker, settled in 1875. Val Verda is an anglicized version of the Spanish term for green valley.
S6,T2N,R1E,SLM; 4,500' (1,372m).

VALLEY CITY* (Grand) is a ghost town site on US-160, five and one-half miles south of Crescent Junction*. A nearby reservoir, Valley City Reservoir, carries on the name. In 1908 an earthen dam washed out and flooded the homesteads below. By 1930, flash floods finally forced the last settlers to move out of the area.
S27,T22S,R19E,SLM; 4,622' (1,409m). 89, 409.

VALLEY MOUNTAIN (Carbon, Emery). See Range Valley Mountain.

VALLEY OF THE GODS (San Juan) is west of Lime Creek and north of US-163. This is a desert region with unusual, eroded formations.
T40,41S,R19E,SLM.

VANCE SPRING (Beaver) is on the eastern slopes of the Indian Peak Range, northwest of Buckhorn Spring. A Mr. Vance built his cabin at the spring in 1880.
S16,T28S,R18W,SLM; 6,670' (2,033m).

VEGA CREEK (San Juan) originates on the northeast slopes of the Abajo Mountains and drains northeast across the rolling flatlands north of Monticello* into Montezuma Creek. "Vega" is a Spanish term for "fertile plain."
S30,T33S,R23E,SLM to S4,T34S,R24E,SLM. 406.

VENICE* (Sevier) is an outgrowth of Glenwood*, located east of Richfield*. In 1875, Francis G. Wall built a cabin on the banks of the Sevier River; the early settlement was named Wallsville*. When the post office was established around 1894 the name was changed to honor Venice*, Italy.
S15,T23S,R2W,SLM; 5,235' (1,596m). 100 (v17), 542, 567.

VERDI* (Carbon). See Sunnyside*.

VERDURE* (San Juan) is several miles south of Monticello*. In 1887 Verdure was established as the first settlement in The Blues (Abajo Mountains). The community was inhabited by people from Bluff* who settled on South Montezuma Creek, which was later known as Verdure Creek. Although Monticello was settled one year after Verdure, Monticello proved to be a more productive agricultural area. Therefore, as Monticello grew, Verdure declined. Today it is private ranch property.
S25,T34S,R23E,SLM; 6,760' (2,060m). 100 (v13), 406, 409, 462, 546, 567.

VERDURE CREEK (San Juan) originates in the Abajo Mountains and drains east to join Vega Creek. See Verdure* for name source.
S34,T34S,R24E,SLM (at mouth).

VERMILLION* (Sevier) is ten miles northeast of Richfield*. In 1874, white settlers established this small agricultural community on the west bank of the Sevier River. The community had an earlier name of Neversweat* because of the midsummer humidity and heat. It was renamed Vermillion because the settlement was adjacent to Vermillion Mountain. The brilliant red coloring of the mountain inspired Brigham Young to name it on October 8, 1876.
S25,T22S,R2W,SLM; 5,240' (1,597m). 289, 542, 585.

VERMILLION CLIFFS (Kane, Washington) extend more than a hundred miles in length and hundreds of feet high across southern Utah. The cliffs are the lowest of the series of cliffs called the The Grand Staircase that extend north out of the Grand Canyon. The staircase includes the White Cliffs, which are higher and located to the north, the Gray Cliffs, then the beautiful shining Pink Cliffs. Beyond these are the Paunsaugunt Plateau and the towering Table Cliffs. Members of Major Powell's 1869-72 expedition used the name to describe the dramatic coloring of the cliffs.
159, 160, 175, 232, 314, 420, 422, 496.

VERNAL* (Uintah) is on US-40 and US-191 in the heart of Ashley Valley. It was settled in 1876, although trappers and mountain men previously explored the region and the Ute Indians had inhabited the area even earlier. Vernal has had various names, such as Ashley* for the valley where the settlement is located (General William H. Ashley led the early trappers into the valley). Jericho* was another early name used to compare the walls of the early local fort and the walls of ancient Jericho. Vernal was also known as The Bench* for its location, and Hatchtown* for the several Hatch families who settled in the area. In the late 1800s the town name was finally formalized as Vernal, which refers to a beautiful spring-like green oasis covered with grasses and numerous trees.
S22,23,T4S,R21E,SLM; 5,315' (1,620m). 100 (v7,17), 172, 289, 309, 314, 372, 375, 494, 496, 542.

VERNON* (Tooele) is a small agricultural, cattle, and hay settlement on U-36, thirty-six miles south of Tooele*. The area was settled by whites in April 1862. One of the settlers was Joseph Vernon, who was killed by a local Indian, Tabby Weeput, during the early settlement days.
S29,T8S,R5W,SLM; 5,511' (1,680m). 100 (v17), 289, 314, 542.

VERNON CREEK (Tooele) originates at J Hill in the Sheeprock Mountains and drains north northeast into Rush Valley. The town of Vernon* utilizes the creek water.
S25,T10S,R5W,SLM (at head).

VERRILL LAKE (Duchesne) is in the Naturalist Basin at the west end of the Uinta Mountains. This is another lake that was named for one of Agassiz's students, Addison Emory Verrill, a zoologist.
S32,T4N,R8W,USM; 10,500' (3,200m). 530.

VEYO* (Washington) is a hamlet on U-18 and the upper Santa Clara River, eighteen miles north of St. George*. When the area was originally settled in 1911, it was called Glen Cove*. When the townspeople later decided to have a permanent name, they asked the local Mormon "Beehive" girls to provide a name. The girls came up with an acronym of virtue, enterprise, youth, and order. Another version records the girls creating the name from parts of the words "verdure" and "youth."
S6,T40S,R16W,SLM; 4,025' (1,227m). 100 (v17).

VICTOR* (**Emery**) was ten miles south of Wellington*. This small community was initially established in 1885 near a small lake formed from seepage waters. The original name was Desert Lake*, which was derived from the small lake. By 1920, the settlers were worn out by the unending struggle to survive with insufficient water, so they moved away and Victor became a ghost town.
S29,T16S,R11E,SLM; 5,500' (1,676m). 89, 100(v13), 516.

VICTOR SPRING (**Beaver**) is in the Mountain Home Range near the head of Cottonwood Wash.
S26,T26S,R19W,SLM; 7,560' (2,304m).

VINEYARD* (**Utah**) is an outgrowth of Lake View* and Provo* on the east shore of Utah Lake. John Gillies planted the first grapevines in the area and is credited with naming the community.
S16,T6S,R2E,SLM; 4,555' (1,388m). 270, 289, 542.

VIRGIN* (**Washington**) was first settled by whites in 1857 on U-9, six miles east of La Verkin*. The site is enclosed by red sandstone cliffs and had an early name of Pocketville* because the local Indian name meant a pocket or hole. The settlement soon took the name of the nearby Virgin River.
T41S,R12W,SLM; 3,400' (1,036m). 27, 289, 311, 372, 542, 600.

VIRGIN RIVER (**Washington**) originates east of Rockville* at the junction of the North and East forks and drains southwest into Lake Mead. The early Spaniards named it El Rio de Sulfureo for the nearby hot sulphur springs. Jedediah Smith named it the Adams River for John Adams, who was president of the United States at that time (this name never held). Some records claim Smith named the river after Thomas Virgin, a member of his 1827 party. Virgin was severely wounded by Indians in this area and was later killed in the fight on the Umpqua River.

The name Virgin is of Spanish origin in honor of the Virgin Mary. Major Powell named the two forks of the Virgin River the Parunuweap and the Mukuntuweap.
160, 311, 314, 372, 438, 496, 546, 600, 601, 604.

VIVIAN PARK* (**Utah**) is a small community at the mouth of the South Fork of Provo River between Wildwood* and Bridal Veil Falls.
S26,T5S,R3E,SLM; 5,196' (1,584m). 270.

- W -

WAGON BOX MESA (Garfield) is within the Circle Cliffs on the headwaters of Silver Falls Creek. The mesa was named for an old abandoned wagon box the San Juan pioneers left beside the early Escalante*-Halls Crossing road. T34S,R7,8E,SLM; 7,270' (2,216m). 12, 530.

WAGON ROAD RIDGE (Sanpete) is near the skyline drive along the summit, three miles west southwest of Joes Valley Reservoir and east of Manti*. The first wagon road between Sanpete and Emery counties ran along the ridge. Dan Overlade named the ridge. S9,15,T8S,R5E,SLM; 10,157' (3,108m). 567.

WAH WAH MOUNTAINS (Beaver) are a north-south oriented range located between the Wah Wah Valley and Pine Valley. The mountains extend into neighboring counties. See Wah Wah Springs for name source. T24-29S,R15,16W,SLM. 100(v17), 125.

WAH WAH SPRINGS (Beaver) are on the eastern slopes of the Wah Wah Mountains, seven miles west of the ghost town of Newhouse*. These historically well-known springs were first owned by Edwin and Lydia Squire, who sold them to Samuel Newhouse, who then piped the water to his mining town, Newhouse. "Wah Wah" means good clear water. S12,T27S,R15W,SLM; 5,500' (1,676m). 89, 125.

WAH WAH VALLEY (Beaver, Millard) is between the Wah Wah Mountains and the San Francisco Mountains. See Wah Wah Springs for name source. T25,26S,R13,14W,SLM; 4,700' (1,433m).

WAH WAH VALLEY HARDPAN (Beaver) is at the north end of the Wah

Wah Valley where water accumulates and then dries, creating a rock-hard flat. T25S,R13W,SLM; 4,600' (1,402m).

WAH WAH WASH (Beaver) originates at Miners Hill at the south end of the Wah Wah Valley and drains north into the Wah Wah Valley Hardpan. T26-29S,R13,14W,SLM.

WAHSATCH* (Summit) was built eleven miles west of Evanston*, Wyoming, as a principal camp on the Union Pacific transcontinental railroad that was under construction at the time. The site was located at the Echo Canyon summit between the Weber and Bear rivers drainage systems and was a livestock shipping center as well as an engine-cutting or drop-off point. The camp was named for Chief Wahsatch, the local Shoshone Indian chief who was on friendly terms with the whites. The chief and most of his clan converted to the Mormon faith as they sought to learn farming and agriculture in the Mormon manner. Today the site is railroad property and evidence of the former town has disappeared. Variant: Wasatch. S1,2,T5N,R7E,SLM; 6,742' (2,055m). 314, 542, 567, 546.

WAHWEAP BAY (Kane) is a part of Lake Powell at the mouth of Wahweap Creek.

WAHWEAP CREEK (Garfield, Kane) originates on the southern slopes of Canaan Peak on the Kaiparowits Plateau and drains south southeast into Lake Powell. It had an early name of Sentinel Rock Creek because a sandstone tower stood at the mouth of the creek. Wahweap is an Piute Indian reference to alkaline seeps containing stagnant or

brackish seeps.
S9,10,T37S,R1E,SLM to T43S,R3E,SLM.
136, 555(v7), 567. D.L. 6504.

WALCOTT LAKE (**Duchesne**) is in the
Naturalist Basin at the west end of the
Uinta Mountains. The lake was named
for an Agassiz student, Charles Doolittle
Walcott, a geologist and paleontologist.
S32,T4N,R8W,USM; 10,980' (3,347m). 530,
595.

WALES* (**Beaver**). See Adamsville*
(Beaver).

WALES* (**Sanpete**) is four miles west of
Chester* on U-177. The community was
settled by Mormon immigrants from
Wales who named their community in
memory of their mother country. The
settlers were coal miners who came to
mine the newly discovered coal beds. The
first name for the community was
Coalbed*, later Coalville*. The name
Wales was formally adopted on
September 6, 1869.
S30,T15S,R3E,SLM; 5,600' (1,707m). 152,
289, 314, 542, 567.

WALKER FLAT (**Sevier**) is four miles
northeast of Fremont Junction between
U-10 and I-70. The flat was a camping
area for Chief Walker and his people.
T23S,R5,6E,SLM; ca. 6,130' (1,868m).

WALKER FLAT (**Utah**) is south of and
adjacent to Payson* along the west side
of Peteetneet Creek. The flat was
another favorite camping site for Chief
Walker and his people.
S16,T9S,R2E,SLM; 4,795' (1,462m). 168.

WALKERS CANYON (**Millard**) originates on the northwest slopes of Sunset
Peak, nine miles southeast of Meadow*.
The canyon drains west northwest into
the Pavant Valley. Walker was a noted
Piute Indian chief who was important in
early Mormon history in the territory. He
died at Meadow Creek and was buried
there in the canyon in January 1855.
S34,T22S,R4W,SLM (at head). 136, 442,

555(v30), 567.

WALKUP LAKE (**Duchesne**) is on the
headwaters of the Whiterocks River,
northwest of Chepeta Lake. The lake
was named for U.S. Forest Ranger
George Walkup, and also for the long
walk or hike up to the lake.
S19,T5N,R1W,USM; 11,114' (3,388m). 309.

WALL LAKE (**Duchesne**) is in the south
central section of the Uinta Mountains,
east of the Uinta River and between
Rock Canyon and Bluebell Creek. The
lake is in a cove up against a cliff.
10,859' (3,310m).

WALL LAKE (**Summit**) is at the west
end of the Uinta Mountains, one-half
mile east of Mount Watson and four
miles west of Mirror Lake. One name
origin suggests the lake was named for
the nearby cliffs. Another claim states
that the lake was named for Lawrence
Wall, who was the first to stock the lake
with fish.
S30,31,T1S,R9E,SLM; 10,155' (3,095m).
298.

WALLACE PEAK (**Beaver**) is nine miles
west of the ghost town of Newhouse*
and one-half mile south of U-21. Wallace
Wintch lived in the area in the 1890s and
the peak was named for him.
S11,T27S,R15W,SLM; 6,539' (1,993m). 578.

WALLSBURG* (**Wasatch**) is a small
agricultural community on U-282, four
miles southeast of Deer Creek Reservoir.
The early Indian name for the settlement
was Little Warm Valley or Round Valley.
It was finally named for William Madison
Wall, a native of North Carolina, who
helped build the road through Provo
Canyon. He was an explorer, colonizer,
military officer, and church leader.
S18,T5S,R5E,SLM; 5,625' (1,715m). 100
(v17), 289, 377, 542, 567.

WALLSVILLE* (**Sevier**). See Venice*
(Sevier).

WANDERMERE* (**Salt Lake**) was an early settlement adjacent to Lake Wandermere, which later became Lake Nibley in Nibley Park. Wandermere was later absorbed into Salt Lake City*. In 1895, E. McClelland purchased the property around Seventh East and Twenty-seventh South and offered a prize for the most appropriate name. The name chosen was a combination of "Wando," a Piute word for "a pleasant place," and the Anglo-Saxon word "mere," meaning "a small lake or pond." S20,29,T1S,R1E,SLM; 4,280' (1,305m). 508.

WANSHIP* (**Summit**) is a small agricultural community at the junction of Silver Creek and the Weber River near I-80, eight miles southwest of Coalville*. The community was named for a friendly Shoshone Indian chief, Wanship (meaning good man). S20,T1N,R5E,SLM; 5,842' (1,781m). 27, 371, 384, 542, 546, 567.

WARD CANYON (**Davis**) originates in the mountains east of Bountiful* and drains west into the valley. The canyon had an early name of Stone Creek. The timber and water in the canyon were valuable to the surrounding settlers, so the local Mormon North Canyon Ward assumed responsibility for proper utilization of these resources. T2N,R1E,SLM. 88, 201.

WARDS CACHE LAKE (**Beaver**) is a small lake in the south Tushar Mountains, between Anderson Meadow Reservoir and LaBaron Lake. MRN S9,T30S,R5W,SLM; 9,500' (2,896m).

WARDSWORTH CANYON (**Utah**) originates on the southern slopes of Strawberry Peak, northeast of Wardsworth Peak, and drains southwest into Hobble Creek, Right Fork. Wardsworth Canyon is a fork of Hobble Creek Canyon. William Wardsworth opened the canyon, then built a sawmill there with Solomon Chase. S19,T2S,R6E,SLM to SW¼,T7S,R5E,SLM.

270.

WARDSWORTH PEAK (**Utah**) is in the southwest section of the Uinta Mountains, five miles southwest of Daniels Pass. See Wardsworth Canyon for name source. S35,T6S,R5E,SLM; 8,839' (2,694m).

WARING BOTTOM (**Grand**). See Lake Bottom (Grand).

WARING CANYON (**Grand**) originates at the Fisher Towers upriver from Moab* where it drains north, entering the Dolores River at its junction with the Colorado River. Jim Waring was one of the earliest settlers in this region. He arrived prior to 1880 and had a livestock ranch in Fisher Valley. 146.

WARM CREEK* (**Sanpete**). See Fayette.

WARM SPRING HILLS (**Box Elder**) are on the south central section of the Raft River Mountains. Warm Springs is nearby and is the name source. S21,22,27,28,SLM; 6,023' (1,836m).

WARM SPRINGS (**Beaver**) is east of Minersville* near the Beaver River. S7,T30S,R9W,SLM; 5,300' (1,615m).

WARM SPRINGS (**Box Elder**) is on the southern slopes of the Raft River Mountains between Dennis Hill and Warm Spring Hills. The springs drain east toward Dove Creek. S19,T12N,R15W,SLM; 5,720' (1,743m).

WARM SPRINGS (**Salt Lake**) was in north Salt Lake City* near the location of today's Salt Lake City Childrens Museum (See Becks Hot Springs). The journal of Erastus Snow quoted Young saying: "We came to a small lake also fed by warm springs. The largest and warmest spring bursts from the base of a perpendicular ledge of rock about forty feet high and emits a volume of water

sufficient for a mill. We had no instrument to determine the degree of temperature, but suffice it to say that it was about right for scalding hogs" (604, p. 542).
S14,T1N,R1W,SLM; 4,221' (1,287m). 604.

WARNER LAKE (Grand) is in the La Sal Mountains north of Mill Creek. Orlando Warner settled there and his name was given to the lake.
S28,T26S,R24E,SLM. 146, 514.

WARNER VALLEY (Washington) is a hockey-stick-shaped valley south of the Virgin River and twelve miles southwest of Hurricane*. The ruins of Fort Pierce* lie at the extreme south end of the valley. MRN
ca. 3,000' (914m).

WARREN* (Weber) was settled in 1870 as an outgrowth of Plain City*, five miles northwest of Ogden* on Salt Creek (Salt Creek* was also the original settlement name). High winds would wash salt water from the Great Salt Lake up the creek, where it would crystallize and be harvested. On June 7, 1896, the settlement was officially named Warren to honor Mormon Stake President Lewis Warren Shurtliff.
S6,T6N,R2W,SLM; 4,219' (1,286m). 274, 289, 542, 567.

WARREN DRAW (Uintah) is in the eastern Uinta Mountains, with Tolivers Creek draining through the draw. Jim Warren, a part-time outlaw, settled near the creek in 1876.
S9,T1N,R24E,SLM. 80, 172, 567.

WASATCH* (Summit). See Wahsatch* (Summit).

WASATCH* (Salt Lake) is one and one-half miles up Little Cottonwood Canyon, southeast of Salt Lake City*. It was an early summer resort for those able to get away from the summer heat of the valley. In 1859 it became a residential area for quarrymen who worked the nearby quarries where granite for the Salt Lake Mormon temple was prepared for shipment. The settlement also became a transfer and railroad point for ore, lumber, and trimmed stone that was harvested from the canyon. In 1893, after the completion of the temple, the community evolved back into a recreational area. See Wasatch County for name source.
T3S,R2E,SLM; 5,600' (1,707'). 252, 289, 444, 454, 567.

WASATCH COUNTY was established in January 1862 and received the name of the Wasatch Mountains. "Wasatch" is an Ute Indian word meaning "mountain pass" or "low place in a high mountain" and is generally assumed to refer to the site where the Weber River cuts through the Wasatch Range.
6.

WASATCH MOUNTAIN STATE PARK (Wasatch) is on the western slopes of Heber Valley, two miles west of Midway*. The Wasatch is the largest of Utah's state parks and was named for the Wasatch Mountains.

WASATCH MOUNTAINS extend in a north-south orientation from the point where the Bear River cuts through the mountain range near Collinston*, south to Mount Nebo. The range forms part of the eastern boundary of the Great Basin and the western slopes, known as the Wasatch Front. This is the most heavily populated region in the state. The original name was Wahsatch, but the "h" was dropped because it was unnecessary. See Wasatch County for name source.
175, 314, 496, 530. D.L. 8002.

WASHAKIE* (Box Elder) is the center of a small Shoshone Indian reservation on the Malad River, south of Portage*. The settlement was named for Shoshone Chief Washakie, who was on friendly terms with the Mormons. The Indians requested help from the Mormons, who sent missionaries to educate them in

farming and stock raising techniques.
S17,20,T14N,R3E,SLM; 4,370' (1,332m).
289, 314, 449, 542.

WASHBOARD WASH (Carbon, Emery)
originates south of Hiawatha* and drains
east into the Price River. The wash was
named in 1877 when the settlers
discovered that the numerous small
washes were difficult to travel through.
S35,T15S,R8E,SLM to S24,T16S,R11E,SLM.
292.

WASHBOARDS, THE (Cache) are in
the foothills three miles north of
Clarkston*. This series of numerous small
draws look like an old-fashioned
washboard.
S3,4,9,10,T14N,R2W,SLM.

WASHINGTON* (Washington) is on
I-15, six miles east of St. George*. The
community was founded in 1857, several
years before St. George was settled. It
was noted for the local factory that made
cotton cloth from home-grown cotton.
The settlement was named to honor
George Washington, the first President of
the United States.
S14,15,T42S,R15W,SLM; 2,800' (853m).
154, 289, 310, 542, 546, 600.

WASHINGTON COUNTY was established in March 1852 and named to
honor George Washington, the first
President of the United States.

WASHINGTON DOME (Washington) is
a geologic feature three miles southeast
of Washington*, from which it receives
its name.
S30,36,T42S,R14,15W,SLM.

WASHINGTON LAKE (Summit) is at
the west end of the Uinta Mountains,
one mile south of Wall Lake. The lake
was one of the earlier lakes in the region
to be developed as a reservoir. It honors
the first President of the United States,
George Washington.
S6,T2S,R9E,SLM; 9,980' (3,042m). 100(v2),
298, 530.

WASHINGTON TERRACE* (Weber) is
a subdivision of southeast Ogden* built
on one of the ancient Lake Bonneville
terraces.
S17,T5N,R1W,SLM.

WATER CANYON (Beaver) originates
at Carlyle Spring in the northeast section
of the Mineral Mountains and drains
north into Antelope Valley.
S4,T27S,R8W,SLM.

WATER CANYON (Garfield) originates
on the northeast boundary of Bryce
Canyon National Park and drains east.
The water resources are used by the
settlement of Tropic*.
567.

WATERCRESS JUNCTION* (Box
Elder) was a railroad construction camp
built in 1868, seventeen miles east of
Lucin*. The camp's water was obtained
from a nearby spring where watercress
grew profusely.
T9N,R15W,SLM. 516, 567.

WATERFALL CREEK (Beaver) origi-
nates in the west central Tushar
Mountains and drains west into Bosman
Creek.
S29,T28S,R5W,SLM.

WATERPOCKET FOLD. This vast area
has a northwest-southeast orientation as
a doubling up of the earth's crust that
created the upheaval, a cliff or an
escarpment, extending from Capitol Reef
National Park to the Colorado River and
beyond. This region was named by
Almon Thompson of the Powell surveys
for the numerous waterpockets created
by erosion in this naked Navajo
Sandstone formation.
12, 160, 315, 496, 546, 555(v7).

WATSON* (Uintah) is a ghost town site
on U-45 and Evacuation Wash, eight
miles south of the White River Crossing.
Wallace G. Watson was the engineer in
charge of the survey work for the Uintah
Railroad that was built through this

region in 1911.
S7,T11S,R25E,SLM; 5,347' (1,630m). 50, 89,
100(v17), 516, 542, 567.

WATSON LAKE (Summit) is in the
western section of the Uinta Mountains,
between Wall Lake and Mount Watson
from which it is named.
S31,T1S,R9E,SLM; 10,425' (3,178m). 298,
530.

WATTIS* (Carbon) is a coal mining
town up Serviceberry Canyon, eleven
miles southwest of Price*. W. H. Wattis
and his brother established the community in 1912 in order to operate the
nearby mines.
S10,T15S,R8E,SLM; 7,600' (2,316m). 89,
100(v17), 494, 516, 607.

WATTS SPRING (Millard) is six miles
southeast of Kanosh*. Baldy Watts was
an early settler who worked the area
around the spring, improving it and
making the springwater more available
to livestock.
S2,T24S,R4½W,SLM. 567.

WAYNE COUNTY was established in
1892. Willis E. Robinson, a member of
the state legislature, named the county in
honor of his son Wayne. A counterclaim
suggests it was named for General
Anthony Wayne.
6, 485, 494, 542.

WEBB HOLLOW CREEK (Grand)
originates twenty miles east southeast of
Moab* on Bald Mesa and drains into the
North Fork of Mill Creek. J. H. Webb
homesteaded the site and prospected in
the area.
S19,20,T26S,R24E,SLM.

WEBER CANYON (Morgan) is east of
Ogden*, with the Weber River draining
through it. The obstructions in the Lower
Weber Canyon where the cliffs extend to
the waterline, caused the pioneers a
great deal of trouble, forcing them to
seek another route. Weber Canyon is the
"low pass" (an Indian term for Wasatch)
to the Wasatch Mountains. See Wasatch
County for additional information.
372, 546.

WEBER CITY* (Morgan). See
Peterson* (Morgan).

WEBER COUNTY was one of the first
six counties created by the General
Assembly of the State of Deseret on
January 31, 1850. The name comes from
the Weber River.

WEBER RIVER originates at the west
end of the Uinta Mountains on the north
slopes of Reids Peak and Bald Mountain,
and drains northwest into the Great Salt
Lake. The consensus of opinion suggests
the river was named for a Dutch sea
captain, John H. Weber, who travelled
west as a trapper with General Ashley in
1823. He was killed near the river shortly
after his arrival. Counterclaims state that
the river was named for Pauline Weaver,
an Arizona frontiersman who was also in
the region.
129, 274, 314, 378, 464, 546, 555(Jan.
1941), 567.

WEBER STATION* (Summit) was an
important Overland Stage station at the
mouth of Echo Canyon, two miles southeast of Echo City*. The station was
eventually absorbed into Echo City. The
name came from the nearby river.
S32,T3N,R5E,SLM; 5,480' (1,670m). 516.

WEBSTER CITY* (Piute) was a small
mining community built up around the
Daniel Webster Mine, one and one-half
miles west of Bullion City*. Daniel
Webster had taken a lease on the
property on April 20, 1869, but the
operation was unprofitable and the
community was abandoned after 1914.
S6,T28S,R4W,SLM. 89, 413.

WEBSTER CITY* (Grand) was near the
head of Willow Creek in the Book Cliffs,
north of Sego*, which is now a ghost
town. Webster City was established in the
1880s by British interests. Today the area

is included in the Ute Indian Reservation.
516.

WEIR LAKE (**Summit**) is at the west end of the Uinta Mountains near Duck, Island, and Ramona lakes. Water from nearby lakes drain into Weir Lake, which is used as a control lake.
S2,T2S,R8E,SLM; 9,950' (3,033m). 379.

WELCH CANYON (**Summit**) originates in the west Uinta Mountains seven miles northeast of Kamas and drains north northeast into the Weber River, South Fork. The canyon was named for James Welsh, an early settler in nearby Peoa*. The difference in spellings is a typographical error on the map.
S20,21,29,T1S,R7E,SLM. 588.

WELCOME SPRING (**Washington**) is on the western slopes of the Beaver Dam Mountains north of US-91 where it drains into Beaver Dam Wash.
T42S,R18W,SLM.

WELLINGTON* (**Carbon**) is six miles southwest of Price* on US-6,191. The community was settled in 1878 by a band of thirteen Mormons led by Jefferson Tidwell. The town was named for Justus Wellington Seeley, Jr., of the Emery County Court.
S6,7,T15S,R11E,SLM; 5,415' (1,650m). 163(14 April 1973), 289, 360.

WELLINGTON* (**Juab**). See Mills*.

WELLSVILLE* (**Cache**) is eight miles southwest of Logan*. The settlement was established in 1856 and was originally known as Maughans Fort* for Peter Maughan, an early settler. At a public meeting in the fall of 1859 the permanent name of Wellsville was decided upon, honoring Daniel H. Wells, pioneer settler, second counselor to Brigham Young, and a former commander of the Nauvoo Legion.
S2,3,11,T10N,R1W,SLM; 4,495' (1,370m). 27, 289, 449, 567.

WELLSVILLE MOUNTAINS (**Cache**) were known earlier as Mount Logan. The mountains have a north-south orientation, with Wellsville* and Mendon* on the east and Deweyville* on the west. The mountains received their name from the town of Wellsville.
T9,11N,R1,2W,SLM. 249(30 April 1976).

WENDOVER* (**Tooele**) was first settled on I-80 and the Nevada line in 1906. Even though there are several versions to the name origin, all the versions refer to "wending over the desert." Wendover is completely surrounded by desert.
S17,18,19,20,T1S,R19W,SLM; 4,256' (1,297m). 100(v17), 153, 314, 367, 498, 542, 546.

WENDOVER PEAK (**Tooele**) is one and one-half miles north northeast of Wendover* and is now part of the Danger Cave State Park.
S8,T1S,R19W,SLM; 5,087' (1,551m).

WEST BASIN (**Summit**) is a glacially gouged-out basin on the northwest slopes of the Uinta Mountains, bordered on the south by Hayden Peak and on the east by Middle Basin.

WEST CLARK BENCH (**Kane**) is south of US-89, between the Cockscomb and the Paria River. It was named for Owen Washington Clark, who ran cattle on the bench.
T43S,R1W,SLM.

WEST DIP* (**Tooele**) was an outgrowth of Mercur*, sometimes referred to as West Mercur*.
89.

WEST GRANDADDY MOUNTAIN (**Duchesne**) is in the southwest section of the Uinta Mountains at the head of Hades Canyon, one mile west of Grandaddy Lake, from which it receives its name.
S2,T3N,R8,9W,USM; 11,494' (3,503m).

WEST HARRISVILLE* (Weber). See Farr West*.
542.

WEST HILLS (Summit) are five miles west of Kamas* and Oakley*.
S1,T2S,R5E,SLM; 7,961' (2,427m).

WEST JORDAN* (Salt Lake) was first settled in 1848 and, at that time, included the area west of the Jordan River, then south to Herriman*.
S27,34,T2S,R1W,SLM; 4,360' (1,329m). 252, 289, 542.

WEST LAYTON* (Davis) is an outgrowth of Layton*.
S19,T4N,R1W,SLM.

WEST MERCUR* (Tooele). See West Dip*.

WEST MOUNTAIN PEAK (Washington) is the high point in the Beaver Dam Mountains west of St. George*.
T42S,R18W,SLM; 7,746' (2,361m).

WEST OGDEN* (Weber) is an outgrowth of Ogden*.
S30,T5N,R1W,SLM; 4,350' (1,326m).

WEST POINT* (Davis) is a scattered agricultural community, three miles west of Clearfield* on U-107. The community was an outgrowth of Syracuse*, with an early name of South Hooper*. The origin of the name is the result of locating the settlement on a point or small peninsula extending out into the Great Salt Lake. Another record suggests it was named for the famous military school in the state of New York.
S32,33,T5N,R2W,SLM; 4,311' (1,314m). 555 (v1), 567.

WEST SHINGLE CREEK LAKE (Summit) is at the west end of the Uinta Mountains, on the headwaters of Shingle Creek.
S1,T2S,R7E,SLM; 9,950' (3,033m).

WEST TAVAPUTS PLATEAU (Carbon, Duchesne) is west of Desolation Canyon on the Green River, with the Brown Cliffs as its southern scarp. John W. Powell named the Tavaputs Plateau to honor a local Ute Indian headman. See East Tavaputs Plateau.
175, 314, 422, 555(v39).

WEST TINTIC* (Juab) is a ghost town site at the south end of the West Tintic Mountains. The settlement was originally established in 1920 by Moses and Octavius Gudmundson and others. Various problems caused the failure of the community.

WEST VALLEY CITY* (Salt Lake) is a rapidly growing area in west Salt Lake Valley. It includes Granger*, Hunter*, and Chesterfield*, which were all incorporated into West Valley City on July 1, 1980.
360, 466(8 and 27 March 1980).

WEST WARREN* (Weber) separated from Warren* and became a separate community on March 25, 1917, seven miles west northwest of West Weber*. See Warren* for name source.
S14,T6N,R3W,SLM; 4,221' (1,287m). 274.

WEST WEBER* (Weber) was settled in 1850 along the Weber River, west of East and South Weber*. This rapidly expanding, populated area soon branched into towns such as Taylor*, Hooper*, Kanesville*, and Weston*. The settlement was known earlier as Alma*, a prominent person in the Book of Mormon.
S16,T6N,R2W,SLM; 4,240' (1,292m). 100 (v5), 274, 289, 542, 567.

WESTERN JORDAN RIVER. See Jordan River.

WESTON* (Weber). See West Weber*.

WESTWATER* (Grand) is a ghost town site near the west end of Ruby Canyon on the Colorado River. The Colorado border is eight miles east. After mining and railroad construction in the region declined, the town was abandoned and the area was used for grazing. The name indicates where the railroad exits into the valley at the west end of Ruby Canyon. 516.

WESTWATER CREEK (Grand) originates on the East Tavaputs Plateau and drains southeast into the Colorado River.
T17S,R22E,SLM to T20S,R25E,SLM.

WETHERILL CANYON (San Juan) originates on the Rainbow Plateau south of the San Juan River and west of the Rainbow Natural Bridge National Monument. The canyon drains south into Arizona and was named for John Wetherill, a rancher at Kayenta, Arizona, and early explorer of the region.
T43S,R7E,SLM (at head). 241, 546. D.L. 7902.

WHEAT GRASS CANYON (Weber) drains southwest into the Causey Reservoir. The canyon has been replanted with a good range grass.
S26,T7N,R3E,SLM (at mouth).

WHEELER CREEK (Weber) drains from Snow Basin into Ogden Canyon at the Pineview Reservoir Dam. Levi and Simon Wheeler operated a sawmill there on the Ogden River. They later moved their mill into Wheeler Basin, which is now known as Snow Basin.
S32,T6N,R1E,SLM to S16,T6N,R1E,SLM. 274, 567.

WHIRLPOOL CANYON (Uintah) is that part of the Green River below Lodore Canyon at the mouth of the Yampa River. The canyon continues to the beginning of the Island Park area and was named by members of Powell's expedition, who thought the canyon was quite rugged and gloomy.
T3S,R25E,SLM (in Utah). 160, 422, 496, 546.

WHIRLWIND CANYON (San Juan) originates at the Red House Cliffs east of the Clay Hills and drains south into the San Juan River. The canyon was known for its unexpected gusty dust devils that the cowboys watched, as rising heat pushed them slowly dancing and streaming up the canyon.
S23,T40S,R14E,SLM (at mouth). 610.

WHIRLWIND VALLEY (Millard) is on the east side of Confusion Valley between the House Range and the Drum Mountains. When the desert heats up and the thermal winds and updrafts develop, the dust devils begin to dance up and down the valley.
S15,T16S,R11,12W,SLM; ca. 5,200' (1,585m).

WHISKY ISLAND LAKE (Summit) is at the west end of the Uinta Mountains, four miles north northwest of Mirror Lake. MRN
S3,T1S,R9E,SLM; 10,350' (3,155m).

WHISKY SPRINGS (Wasatch) is presently a rest stop up Daniels Canyon, southeast of Heber*. During the fall, Heber cowboys brought their cattle down from the mountains and stopped at the springs to cool their whisky in the cold springwater.
S6,T5S,R6E,SLM; 6,400' (1,951m). 590.

WHITE CANYON (San Juan) originates on the southwest slopes of the Bears Ears and drains west into the Colorado River near its junction with the Dirty Devil River. The canyon drains through a white sandstone area.
T36S,R19E,SLM to T34S,R14E,SLM.

WHITE CITY* (Salt Lake) was an early subdivision or outgrowth of Sandy* covering that area from Seventh East to Twentieth East and from Ninety-fourth South to One Hundred and Sixth south. It was named for Kenneth White, the developer.
S89,T3S,R1E,SLM; 4,600' (1,402m). 444.

WHITE CLIFFS (Kane) are one of a series of cliffs identified and named by Major Powell. The White Cliffs are famous for the spectacular white sandstone called the Navajo Sandstone formation. Below and to the south of the White Cliffs are the Vermillion Cliffs. The succeeding steps of Powell's Grand Staircase are north, starting with the Gray Cliffs then the Pink Cliffs. The formations are clearly visible in Bryce Canyon National Park.
160, 325, 422, 496, 504.

WHITE CREEK (Garfield) originates on Escalante Mountain three miles south of Barker Reservoir and drains east into North Creek. Henry J. White had a sawmill at the mouth of the creek.
12.

WHITE HOUSE* (Kane) is a ghost town site three miles south of Adairville*. The 1890s droughts caused the settlers to abandon the settlement and resettle elsewhere. The majority of the residents moved north to Paria*.
S15,T43S,R5E,SLM. 516.

WHITE MARL BLUFF (Tooele) is seven and one-half miles southwest of Simpson Springs. The bluff is an exposed ten-foot-thick layer of Lake Bonneville white marl sediments.
S6,7,8,9,T10S,R9W,SLM.

WHITE MESA (San Juan) is composed of white sandstone. The mesa is ten miles east northeast of the Boundary Butte Mesa.
T42S,R24E,SLM; 5,896' (1,797m).

WHITE MESA* (San Juan). See Blanding*.

WHITE MESA VILLAGE* (San Juan) is a Navajo Indian community nine miles south of the San Juan River on White Mesa.
T42S,R24E,SLM; 5,500' (1,676m).

WHITE MOUNTAIN (Beaver) is a small, geologic, white-colored feature south of the San Francisco Mountains.
S9,10,T29S,R13E,SLM; 6,781' (2,067m).

WHITE MOUNTAIN (Millard) is ten miles southwest of Fillmore* and made up of volcanic rock, impregnated with white gypsum sand.
S11,T22S,R6W,SLM. 567.

WHITE PINE CREEK (Cache) originates in the Bear River Range at White Pine Lake and drains east into the Logan River. White pine is the lumbering industry name for blue spruce and Englemann spruce, which is common in this area.
T14N,R3,4E,SLM.

WHITE PINE LAKE (Cache) is in the Bear River Range at the head of White Pine Creek.

WHITE PINE LAKE (Salt Lake) is at the head of White Pine Fork of Little Cottonwood Canyon. See White Pine Creek for name source.
T3S,R2E,SLM; 9,985' (3,043m).

WHITE RIM (Garfield) is a white sandstone formation between the Green River level and Grand View Point above. This area can be traversed by horse, four-wheel drive, or afoot, and is well known for its White Rim Trail.

WHITE RIM TRAIL. See White Rim.

WHITE RIVER* (Uintah). See Ignacio*.

WHITE RIVER (Uintah) enters from Colorado and drains into the Green River at the south end of the Wonsits Valley south of Ouray*. The 1776 Domínguez-Escalante expedition called it the El Rio de San Clemente. Later the Spaniards named it the Rio Blanco, which was eventually anglicized to White River.

S4,T9S,R20E,SLM (at mouth). 27, 157, 314, 567, 583.

WHITE RIVER (**Carbon**) originates six miles northeast of Soldier Summit* and drains south into the Price River at Colton*.
S4,T9S,R8E,SLM to S26,T11S,R8E,SLM.

WHITE ROCK CURVE VILLAGE* (**San Juan**) is a Navajo Indian community nine miles south of the San Juan River, on the northern slopes of White Mesa.
T41S,R24E,SLM; 4,600' (1,402m).

WHITE ROCK MOUNTAINS (**Beaver**) are on the Nevada line at the head of Willow Creek.
T30S,R20W,SLM.

WHITE VALLEY (**Millard**) has a north-south orientation between the Confusion Range and the House Range. The whiteness of the rocks was the basis for Captain J. H. Simpson's choice in naming the valley in 1859 during his road survey. The valley is also known as Tule Valley on some maps.
T15-18S,R14,15W,SLM. 477.

WHITEROCKS* (**Uintah**) was established in 1868 as the first white settlement in eastern Utah. The settlement is near the Whiterocks River and the mouth of Whiterocks Canyon. It received the name of the river that the Ute Indians named for the prominent white outcropping near the mouth of the canyon. Today it is a predominantly Ute Indian community.
S19,T1N,R18,19E,SLM; 6,025' (1,836m). 309, 314, 457, 542, 567.

WHITEROCKS CANYON (**Uintah**). See Whiterocks River (Uintah).

WHITEROCKS LAKE (**Uintah**) is at the head of the Whiterocks River from which it received its name.
S1,T4N,R1W,USM; 10,555' (3,217m).

WHITEROCKS RIVER (**Duchesne, Uintah**) originates in the central section of the Uinta Mountains at Chepeta Lake. The river drains south through Whiterocks Canyon into the Uinta River and receives its name from the prominent white rocks at the mouth of the canyon. Prior to the 1870s the Whiterocks River was called the Uinta River. See references for the other Whiterocks place names.
S29,32,T5N,R1W,USM to S32,T1N,R1E, USM. 555(v9).

WHITES COVE (**Garfield**) is near Whites Flat. See White Creek for name source.

WHITES FLAT (**Garfield**) is on Escalante Mountain, three miles south of Barker Reservoir, between Whites Cove and East Fork, North Creek. See White Creek for name source.
7,900' (2,408m).

WHITMORE CANYON (**Carbon**) originates at the junction of the Left and Right forks, four miles north of Sunnyside* where it drains south. This region was public domain until J. M. Whitmore claimed it as personal grazing territory. He held it until it was granted to the Denver and Rio Grande Railroad. Later Sunnyside was built on former Whitmore Ranch property.
S7,T14S,R14E,SLM to S6,T15S,R14E,SLM. 100(v17), 303, 567.

WHITMORE PARK (**Carbon**) is at the head of Coal Creek and Whitmore Canyon. See the canyon for name source.
T12S,R11,12E,SLM; 7,500' (2,286m).

WHITNEY RESERVOIR (**Summit**) is at the west end of the Uinta Mountains, four miles northeast of Holiday Park.
S9,T1N,R9E,SLM; 9,260' (2,822m).

WHITTMORE CANYON (**Utah**) originates northeast of Provo Peak and drains southeast into Hobble Creek, Left Fork.

The canyon was first opened for use by Aaron Whittmore.
S32,T6S,R4E,SLM to S10,T7S,R5E,SLM.

WICKIUP, THE (Emery) is a large pointed rock formation in the general shape of an Indian lodge, formed of cream-colored sandstone at the bottom and reddish sandstone in the upper half. This feature is on the San Rafael Swell at the north end of the Sinbad country. Sids Draw originates in this area.
S16,T22S,R11E,SLM; 6,984' (2,129m). 578.

WIDE HOLLOW (Garfield) is an open valley west of Escalante* surrounding the head of the Escalante River and the Wide Hollow Reservoir.
S2,3,10,12,T35S,R2E,SLM; 5,880' (1,792m).

WIDE MOUTH WASH (Beaver) originates in the southwest Tushar Mountains and drains west into Lees Spring Wash.
S31-33,T30S,R6W,SLM.

WIDTSOE* (Garfield) is a ghost town at the junction of the East Fork of the Sevier River and Sweetwater Creek. In 1872 it was open range and James Houston, a Mormon stake president of Panguitch*, ran his cattle in this area. On April 15, 1902, the Adair family homesteaded the site and it became Adairville* on ground donated by Julia Ann Adair. Then three families, including the Winder family, moved close by and in 1910 their settlement was named Winder*. The postal service objected to Winder because there were already several Winders in Utah Territory, so after a short period of time, the name was followed by Houston* for James Houston. In 1915 Adairville and Winder (Houston) joined and named their community Widtsoe in honor of John A. Widtsoe, a Mormon church official, president of the University of Utah, and a dry-farm expert. But this was an area too high and cold for good vegetable crops to grow. The soil was poor and unexpected floods and drought occurred, so by 1920 the settlers gave up and moved out. In 1936 the Federal Resettlement Administration stepped in and bought out the entire project and returned it to the public domain.
S21,T34S,R2E,SLM; 7,623' (2,323m). 89, 100(v13), 145, 508, 516, 542.

WIG MOUNTAIN (Tooele) is not available to the general public because the mountain is within the confines of the Dugway Proving Grounds, a U.S. military testing site. MRN
T6S,R11W,SLM; 5,194' (1,583m).

WIGGLE TRAIL (Washington). During the 1870s, the mail between St. George* and Kanab* was routed through Shunesburg* where it was lifted up over a 1500-foot cliff on a cable, winch, and wheels. This circumvented the tedious and often dangerous trail down the cliff side at the head of Shunesburg Canyon that came to be known as the Wiggle Trail. David Flanigan developed and improved on the same procedure for lowering timber from the top of what came to be known as Cable Mountain in Zion Canyon.
T42S,R7½W,SLM.

WIGGLER WASH (Garfield, Kane) originates on the southwest slopes of Canaan Peak of the Kaiparowits and drains southwest into Dry Valley Creek. The wash is known for its crooked course.
S18,T37S,R1E,SLM to S18,T38S,R1W,SLM.

WIGWAM LAKE (Duchesne) is in the central Uinta Mountains on the headwaters of the Whiterocks River. The Uinta Ute Indians often camped around the lake.
S28,T5N,R1W,USM; 10,850' (3,307m).

WILD COW POINT (San Juan) is north of Dark Canyon. This area was known for the cattle that gathered here after they had broken away from established herds then became wild.
S16,T33S,R18E,SLM. 555(v32).

WILD GOOSE LAKE (**Duchesne**) is in south central section of the Uinta Mountains near the headwaters of the Uinta River. Albert Crumbo, Lee Kay, Fred Reynolds, and George Walkup were involved in a wild goose chase while trying to locate the lake.
10,650' (3,246m).

WILDCAT CREEK (**Beaver**) originates on the northwest slopes of Little Shelly Baldy Peak in the Tushar Mountains and drains southwest into Indian Creek. The wildcat (bobcat) was common in this region in early days.
T27-29S,R7,8W,SLM. 100(v17).

WILDCAT CREEK (**Box Elder**) originates in the west Raft River Mountains and drains north into the Raft River, west of Yost*. Bobcat and cougar were common along the creek.
S2,T13N,R16W,SLM to S35,T15N,R16W, SLM.

WILDCAT FIELDS (**Beaver**) is along the upper reaches of Wildcat Creek.

WILDCAT HOLLOW (**Beaver**) originates on the northern slopes of Bearskin Mountain and drains southeast into Cunningham Wash, then into Wildcat Creek.
S15-17,T27S,R8W,SLM.

WILDCAT MESA (**Garfield**) is eight miles west of Mount Ellen in the Henry Mountains. The wildcat (bobcat) and cougar were prevalent in this area.
S11,14,T31S,R8E,SLM; 5,600' (1,707m).

WILDER LAKE (**Duchesne**) is near Agassiz Peak at the west end of the Uinta Mountains in the Naturalist Basin. This clutch of lakes are all named after students of Agassiz, the noted glaciologist and naturalist. This particular lake was named for Dr. Burt G. Wilder, a biologist from Cornell University.
S6,T3N,R8W,USM; 9,900' (3,018m). 530.

WILDWOOD* (**Utah**) is a small residential community in Provo Canyon at the junction of the Provo River and its North Fork. The name comes from the wild profusion of native vines and shrubs.
S24,T5S,R3E,SLM; 5,218' (1,590m). 268.

WILLARD* (**Box Elder**) is midway between Brigham City* and Ogden* on US-89. It was settled in 1851 and called North Willow Creek* for the name of the creek the people settled on, and to separate it from South Willow Creek* (Draper*). In 1857 a mass meeting was called to select a new name. Solomon Warner moved that the name be changed to Willard to honor Willard Richards, a counselor to Brigham Young.
S23,26,T8N,R2W,SLM; 4,350' (1,326m). 27, 100(v17), 139, 542, 567.

WILLARD BAY (**Box Elder**) is a freshwater recreational site developed on the eastern shore of the Great Salt Lake, west of Willard*.

WILLARD CANYON (**Box Elder**) originates on the northern slopes of Willard Peak and drains west into Willard Bay.

WILLARD CANYON (**Kane**) originates on the Kaiparowits Plateau at Big Sage Flat and drains northeast into Left Hand Collett Canyon. It was named for Willard Heaps, an early stockman in the area.
S23,T38S,R3E,SLM to S21,T38S,R4E,SLM. 12.

WILLARD MOUNTAIN (**Box Elder**) is at the head of Willard Creek east of Willard*.
S32,T8N,R1W,SLM; 9,422' (2,872). 567.

WILLIES HOLLOW (**Cache**) originates in the north Wellsville Mountains and drains northeast into the Little Bear River. James G. Willie was an early settler of nearby Mendon*.
S36,T12N,R2W,SLM.

WILLIS CREEK (**Garfield, Kane**) originates in the Pink Cliffs at the south end of Bryce Canyon National Park and drains southeast into Sheep Creek. The creek was named in 1874 for William P. Willis, a member of the Kanarra Co-op Livestock Company.
S33,T37S,R4W,SLM to S25,T38S,R3W,SLM. 530.

WILLIS CREEK (**Kane**) originates at the Pink Cliffs, four miles southeast of Navajo Lake, and drains east into Strawberry Creek. It was named for Willis Webb, an early pioneer.
S22,T38S,R8W,SLM to S21,T38S,R7W,SLM.

WILLOW BEND* (**Sevier**). See Aurora* (Sevier).

WILLOW CREEK (**Garfield**) originates on the northern slopes of Canaan peak of the Kaiparowits Plateau and drains northeast into Coal Bed Canyon.
S4,T37S,R1E,SLM to S4,T36S,R2E,SLM. 12.

WILLOW CREEK* (**Juab**). See Mona* (Juab).

WILLOW CREEK* (**Tooele**). See Grantsville* (Tooele).

WILLOW GULCH (**Kane**) originates at the Straight Cliffs of the Kaiparowits Plateau, south of Fortymile Gulch, and drains northeast into the Escalante River. The gulch is well known by backpackers and nature lovers.
12.

WILLOW GULCH (**Kane**) originates at Collett Top on the Kaiparowits Plateau and drains southeast into Rogers Canyon.
S14,T39S,R4E,SLM to S27,T39S,R5E,SLM. 12.

WILLOW SPRINGS* (**Juab**). See Callao* (Juab).
289.

WILLOW SPRINGS* (**Tooele**). See Grantsville* (Tooele).

WILLOW SPRINGS* (**Tooele**) is a small community west of Clover* and Johnson Pass on U-199.
S35,T5S,R7W,SLM.

WILLOW VALLEY (**Cache**). See Cache Valley.

WILMOTH* (**Wayne**). See Lyman* (Wayne).

WILSON* (**Uintah**) was named for Barlow B. Wilson, an early settler. See Ballard* (Uintah).
S25,T6N,R2W,SLM; 4,277' (1,303m). 100 (v17), 567.

WILSON ARCH (**San Juan**) is near the head of Joe Wilson Canyon and US-160, four miles south of La Sal Junction*. The formation was originally named Window Arch, then Wilson Arch to honor Joe Wilson, a local pioneer. See Wilson Mesa for further information.
S15,T29S,R23E,SLM. 514. D.L. 6803.

WILSON CANYON (**Garfield**) originates on the southwest slopes of Wilson Peak and drains west into Hillsdale Canyon. The canyon was named for George Deliverance Wilson, who, with Joel Hills Johnson, established a sawmill near Hillsdale* in 1871.
S9,10,T36S,R4½W,SLM.

WILSON CREEK (**San Juan**) originates on Wilson Mesa near the junction of the Colorado and San Juan rivers and drains south into the San Juan River. See Wilson Mesa (San Juan).
T41S,R10E,SLM.

WILSON MESA (**San Juan**) is in the "Y" of the Colorado and San Juan rivers. The Wilson family were prominent settlers and stockmen in this region.
T40,41S,R10,11E,SLM; 4,400' (1,341m). 409.

WILSON MESA (**Grand**) is seven miles east of Moab* near the head of Negro Bill Canyon. The mesa was named for A. G. Wilson and his sons. In June 1880

A. G.'s sons, Joe and Ervin, were attacked by Indians while working stock up nearby Pack Creek. One was badly wounded but survived. Such incidents perpetuated the Wilson name in the region. The Wilsons wintered their livestock on the desert and sandflats and summered the animals on the mesa.
S10,15,T26S,R23E,SLM. 100(v17), 146, 303, 409, 494.

WILSON PEAK (**Garfield**) is on the Paunsaugunt Plateau eight miles northeast of Hatch*, near the head of Wilson Canyon. George Wilson and Joel Hills Johnson helped settle the nearby community of Hillsdale*. See also Wilson Canyon.
S11,T36S,R4½W,SLM; 9,034' (2,754m).

WILSON PEAK (**Summit**) is in the Uinta Mountains at the head of the Yellowstone River, six miles east of Mount Lovenia. The peak was named for a topographer who was a member of the King survey.
S4,T4N,R5W,USM; 13,095' (3,991m). 172, 309, 494, 496.

WILSONVILLE* (**Emery**) is two and one-half miles southeast of Castle Dale*. The families of Sylvester Wilson and his brothers George, Nick, Chris, Davis, and Silas were first to settle in this area.
S21,T19S,R9E,SLM; 5,250' (1,600m). 100 (v13,17), 193, 542, 567.

WIND WHISTLE CANYON (**San Juan**) originates at Wind Whistle Rock and drains north into Hatch Wash. See Wind Whistle Rock for name source.
S31,T29S,R23E,SLM (at mouth).

WIND WHISTLE ROCK (**San Juan**) is at the head of Wind Whistle Canyon between Bobbys Hole Canyon and Hatch Ranch Canyon. The region's frequently blowing wind creates unusual sounds as it whistles through the cracks and crevices of eroded rock formations.
T30S,R22E,SLM; 6,350' (1,935m).

WINDER* (**Garfield**). See Widtsoe* (Garfield).

WINDER* (**Salt Lake**) was an outgrowth of Mill Creek. In 1904 it became a separate community and was named to honor Mormon Stake President John R. Winder.

WINDOW ARCH (**San Juan**). See Wilson Arch (San Juan).

WINDOW BLIND PEAK (**Emery**) is on the San Rafael Swell three miles west of the San Rafael River and twenty-eight miles east southeast of Ferron*. The natural rock formations on the peak resemble windows with the blinds drawn. An earlier name was Window Blind Castle.
7,030' (2,143m). 193.

WINDOWS, THE (**Grand**) is an area of gigantic, naturally eroded openings in the sandstone buttes or walls in Arches National Park, eight miles north of Moab*. The name has naturally developed from common usage.
S19,30,T24S,R22E,SLM.

WINDOWSASH BENCH (**Kane**) is near the head of Reese Canyon on the western slopes of the Kaiparowits Plateau. The Rogers brothers ran their cattle on the bench and branded their cattle with a window sash brand.
12.

WINDSOR* (**Kane**). See Mount Carmel* (Kane).

WINN* (**Duchesne**). See Talmage* (Duchesne).

WINSOR* (**Kane**) is an alternate spelling for Windsor*. See Mount Carmel* (Kane). The name refers to Anson Perry Winsor, an early settler and Mormon bishop of Grafton*.

WINTER QUARTERS* (**Carbon**) is near the mouth of Winter Quarters

Canyon west of Scofield*. The name was a result of a situation that occurred during the winter of 1879. Peter Morgan was leading a party of thirteen male coal miners and one woman over the mountains from Fairview to settlements in Sanpete County. After they arrived in Sanpete County, they were trapped for several months by the deep snow of a very severe winter. This was the first of Utah's community coal mines. Winter Quarters, with an earlier name of Pleasant Valley*, was a forerunner of nearby Scofield. See Scofield*.
S6,T13S,R7E,SLM; 8,100' (2,469m). 89, 100 (v17), 494, 516, 542, 607.

WINTER QUARTERS CANYON (Carbon) originates in the mountains four miles west of Scofield*, and drains into Pleasant Valley Creek. See Winter Quarters* (Carbon) for name source.
S5,T13S,R7E,SLM (at mouth).

WIRE FENCE CANYON (Duchesne) originates on the north slopes of the West Tavaputs Plateau and drains north into Sowers Canyon. The canyon has been fenced off.
S5,T7S,R5W,SLM to S34,T5S,R5W,USM.

WISTERIA* (San Juan). See Lockerby* (San Juan).

WITTS LAKE (Wasatch) is three and one-half miles east of the east side of Heber Valley, between Lake and Center creeks.
S10,T4S,R6E,SLM; 7,330' (2,234m).

WOLF CREEK (Duchesne, Wasatch) originates in the southwest section of the Uinta Mountains near Wolf Creek Summit and U-35. The creek drains southeast into the West Fork of the Duchesne River. When U-35 was being built the construction crew found it necessary to hire trappers to keep the wolves under control. This situation served as the basis for the creek name.
S16,T1N,R10W,USM to S26,T1N,R9W,USM. 595.

WOLF CREEK SUMMIT (Wasatch) is at the head of Wolf Creek from which it receives its name. At this point, U-35 passes between the Provo and Duchesne rivers drainage systems.
S16,T1N,R8E,SLM; 9,476' (2,888m).

WOLVERINE BENCH (Garfield) is between Wolverine Creek and Horse Canyon.
S16,T35S,R6E,SLM (south end); 5,800' (1,768m).

WOLVERINE CREEK (Garfield) originates southwest of Studhorse Peaks and drains southwest into Horse Canyon.
S16,T35S,R6E,SLM (at mouth).

WONSITS VALLEY (Uintah) is the open flat plain where the Duchesne, White, and Green Rivers converge. Members of Powell's survey named the valley with the Indian words, "wonsits yu-av," meaning "antelope valley." The valley also had the early name Uinta Valley. Domínguez and Escalante forded the Green River near the upper end of the valley. Berthoud's wagon track crossed the center near the mouth of the Uinta River. Manly, a member of the Forty-niners, left the river here in 1849.
T8S,R21E,SLM; ca. 4,700' (1,433m). 314, 372, 496.

WOODENSHOE* (Garfield) was an early settlement near Georgetown*, south of Cannonville*, into which it was absorbed. The name comes from the first white settlers who were from Holland and wore wooden shoes. See Georgetown*, Clifton*, and Cannonville*.
508.

WOODENSHOE BUTTES (San Juan) is near Woodenshoe Canyon between Hideout and Deer canyons. It is composed of two sandstone features, the heel and the toe. The buttes and the canyon were named by Al and Jim Scorup, who ran cattle in this region.
S4,5,T36S,R18E,SLM; 8,894' (2,711m). 555 (v32).

WOODENSHOE CANYON (San Juan) originates four miles north of the head of Grand Gulch and two miles southeast of Woodenshoe Buttes. It drains northeast into Dark Canyon.

WOODLAND* (Summit) is a small rural community on the Provo River and U-35, four miles southeast of Francis*. The area was first settled in 1867 by Hans Larson. The site is in a beautiful woodland country where mine timbers and railroad ties were harvested from the surrounding forests then floated down to Provo* via the Provo River.
S2,11,T3S,R6E,SLM; 6,822' (2,079m). 100 (v17), 542, 567.

WOODMAN PEAK (Tooele) is on Dutch Mountain, four miles southeast of Twin Peak and three miles northwest of the ghost town of Gold Hill. The peak was named for a prominent local prospector.
T7S,R18W,SLM; 7,262' (2,213m). 530.

WOODROW* (Millard) was seven and one-half miles northwest of Delta*. Gerome Tracy and Judge Rock settled this area in 1909. The settlement had an early name of Rock District*, but this was changed in 1913 to honor the President of the United States, Woodrow Wilson. Today the area is agricultural.
89, 567.

WOODRUFF* (Rich) is a farming and ranching community on Woodruff Creek, U-16, and U-39, ten miles south of Randolph*. It was first settled in 1865 and named for Wilford Woodruff, the fourth president of the Mormon Church. President Woodruff passed through this settlement quite often while travelling north to visit his family in nearby Randolph.
S16,T9N,R7E,SLM; 6,340' (1,932m). 100 (v17), 289.

WOODRUFF CREEK (Rich) originates on the eastern slopes of the Monte Cristo Mountains and drains northeast through Woodruff* into Saleratus Creek. See Woodruff*.
S21,T8N,R5E,SLM to S23,T9N,R7E,SLM.

WOODS CROSS* (Davis) is west of Bountiful* and named for Joseph R. or Daniel C. Wood, who settled here in 1865. The name was shortened from Wood's Crossing*. Several roads and a railroad intersect at this point.
S25,36,T2N,R1W,SLM; 4,320' (1,317m). 542, 567.

WOOD'S CROSSING* (Davis). See Woods Cross* (Davis).

WOODSIDE* (Emery) is at the crossing of the Price River and US-6,50. It was settled by whites in 1881 and soon became a thriving farming community and a busy livestock loading station. The Price River occasionally flooded, the open range disappeared, and railroad facilities improved to the point where nearby Helper* became a more important town. After the cafe and store burned down in 1970, Woodside became a ghost town.
S9,T18S,R14E,SLM; 4,633' (1,412m). 89, 466(15 July 1973), 542.

WOOLEY LAKE (Uintah) is in the eastern section of the Uinta Mountains on the headwaters of the East Fork of the Whiterocks River. About 1902 an individual named Wooley was a permittee on this allotment, which allowed him to graze his livestock in the vicinity of the lake.
S11,T4N,R1W,USM; 10,700' (3,261m). 309.

WORKMAN LAKE (Uintah) is in the eastern section of the Uinta Mountains on the headwaters of the Whiterocks River, East Fork. Bill Workman was a sheepherder in the area and this was his favorite fishing lake.
S10,T4N,R1W,USM; 10,450' (3,185m). 309.

WYCROFT CANYON (Beaver) originates in the west Mineral Mountains on the northwest slopes of Granite Peak and

drains northwest into Ranch Canyon.
S3,11,T28S,R9W,SLM.

WYCROFT SPRING (**Beaver**) is in the
Mineral Mountains at the head of
Wycroft Canyon. MRN
S11,T28S,R8W,SLM; 7,000' (2,134m).

WYMAN LAKE (**Duchesne**) is at the
west end of the Uinta Mountains in the
Naturalist Basin. This is one of the many
lakes named after an Agassiz student.
Jeffries Wyman was a scientist.
S6,T3N,R8W,SLM; 9,980' (3,042m). 530.

WYNO* (**Millard**) was a small
temporary smelter-related camp that
moved several times to carry on its
water-dependent work. One of these sites
was Smelter Knolls, four miles west of
the Japanese internment camp of
Topaz*. MRN
516.

WYNOPITS MOUNTAIN (**Washington**)
is in Zion National Park on the North
Fork of the Virgin River. Wynopits was
the Indian deity of evil.
T40S,R10W,SLM.

- X -

XMAS CANYON (**Emery**) originates twelve miles east of Woodside*, eighteen miles north of Green River*, and drains northeast into Turtle Canyon. MRN S6,T18S,R16E,SLM to S33,T17S,R16E,SLM.

XMAS MOUNTAIN (**Emery**) is two miles west of the Green River and nineteen miles north of Green River*. S35,T17S,R16E,SLM; 6,007' (1,831m).

- Y -

Y MOUNTAIN (**Utah**) is in the Wasatch Mountains range, east of Brigham Young University. The mountain is named for the giant "Y" the university students placed on the west slope to advertise and honor the university.
S33,T6S,R3E,SLM; 8,568' (2,612m).

YAMPAH PLATEAU (**Uintah**) is northeast of Jensen* and southwest of Pats Hole in Colorado. The plateau was named from the river and the river was named for the yampah plant (*Anethum graveolens*), a staple food of the local Yam Pah Ute Indians.
T4S,R24E,SLM. 314, 494.

YANKEE MEADOWS (**Iron**) is six miles southeast of Parowan* near the head of Bowery Creek Canyon.
S20,T35S,R8W,SLM.

YELLOW BANKS (**Beaver**) is on the east bank of the Beaver River at the junction of Ranch and Corral canyons. The soil of the riverbank is predominantly yellow.
S33,T27S,R10W,SLM; 5,000' (1,524m).

YELLOW CREEK (**Garfield**) originates at Yellow Spring at the base of the Pink Cliffs and on the eastern side of Bryce Canyon National Park. The creek drains east southeast into the Paria River and receives its name from the yellowish cast of the sediment-laden water.
S6,T38S,R2W,SLM (at mouth).

YELLOW JACKET CANYON (**Grand**) originates on the Dome Plateau, six miles west of the Dewey Bridge above Moab*, and drains east into Bull Canyon. The yellowjacket wasp is quite common in the canyon.
S19,T23S,R23E,SLM.

YELLOW JACKET CANYON (**Kane**) originates in the mountains west of the Coral Sand Dunes and drains northwest into the Clay Flats where it disappears into the ground. See above for name source.
S15,T43S,R8W,SLM to S18,T42S,R7W,SLM.

YELLOW LAKE (**Garfield**) is at the head of North Creek on Escalante Mountain. At various times of the year, the lake is covered with a heavy algae growth that soon turns yellow.
9,640' (2,938m). 12.

YELLOW MOUNTAIN (**Beaver**) is part of the southwest section of the Mineral Mountains. The soil has a yellowish tint.
S5,T20S,R9W,SLM; 6,307' (1,922m).

YELLOW PINE CREEK (**Summit**) originates at the west end of the Uinta Mountains on the southwest slopes of Castle Peak, and drains southwest into Beaver Creek. This region was an important lumbering center in the late 1800s. Yellow pine (*Pinus ponderosa*) was the predominant tree harvested.
S3,10,16,20,T2S,R7E,SLM.

YELLOW PINE MOUNTAIN (**Summit**) is between Kamas* and Bald Mountain near Beaver Creek. See Yellow Pine Creek for name source.

YELLOWSTONE RIVER (**Duchesne**) originates on Mount Powell in the central section of the Uinta Mountains and drains south into the Lake Fork River. There are yellowish bluffs along the upper course of the river.
S2,T4N,R5W,USM to S2,T1N,R4W,USM. 100 (v17). D.L. 6603

YOGO CREEK (Sevier) originates on the Sevier Plateau, two miles north northeast of Mount Terrill, and drains northeast into Meadow Creek.
S6,T24S,R3E,SLM to S2,T23S,R3E,SLM.

YORK* (Utah) was a prominent terminal and railroad center on the old Utah Southern Railroad, approximately fifteen miles north of Nephi* and four miles south of Santaquin*. York lasted for several years until the next terminal was established to the south (Juab*). York was then promptly abandoned.
S27,T10S,R1E,SLM; 4,920' (1,500m). 89, 355, 516.

YOSEMITE GULCH (Salt Lake) originates in the south Oquirrh Mountains and drains northeast into Butterfield Canyon. The gulch was named for Yosemite, California.
S31,T3S,R2W,SLM. 360.

YOST* (Box Elder) is on the north central slopes of the Raft River Mountains. The first name was George Creek* for George, an early range rider who came into this area with Charles Yost. Yost remained in the area, built the first cabin on George Creek, then became the first postmaster in 1887. Yost and George arrived as cowboys from the Nevada Territory and worked for William Emery. After Yost built his cabin, he lived in it alone for six years until he married Maria Larsen from Terrace*, on the south side of the mountains. For four years she was the only woman living in Yost.
S2,3,T14N,R15W,SLM; 5,980' (1,823m). 139, 289, 391, 391, 542, 567.

YOUNG PEAK (Tooele) is in the Deep Creek Mountains. The peak was named for one of the early settlers of the now abandoned town of Clifton*.
S27,T9S,R18W,SLM; 8,028' (2,447m). 242.

YOVIMPA PASS and YOVIMPA POINT (Kane) are close together at the south end of Bryce Canyon National Park. The name Yovimpa comes from the Piute "Uimpabitz," meaning Pine Tree Ridge. For a short time it carried the name Podunk, which now is the name of a nearby creek honoring the Indian Po Dunk, who was once lost in this region.
T38S,R4W,SLM. 530, 531(1 July 1934 to 31 June 1935).

- Z -

ZAHNS CAMP* (San Juan) was a temporary mining camp the five Zahn brothers built on the San Juan River in 1892. They settled on the south side of the river, two and one-half miles west of the mouth of Nokai Canyon. The Honaker Trail was built to service these river mining camps that were so difficult to reach.
S21,T41S,R12E,SLM. 516.

ZANE* (Iron) was a siding on the Union Pacific Railroad, five miles northeast of Beryl*. The settlement was named for Zane Grey, the noted western author. Southern Utah was the setting for many of Grey's novels as he traveled extensively throughout these isolated regions.
S19,T33S,R15W,SLM; 5,202' (1,586m). 542.

ZION* (Washington). See Little Zion*.

ZION CANYON (Washington) is one of the principle scenic and historical areas in Zion National Park. It was first discovered by whites in 1858 when Nephi Johnson, a Mormon pioneer, entered the canyon. The original white settlement in the park was known as Little Zion, a name used by Isaac Behunin from his little cabin built deep within the canyon. In 1909 President Taft set part of the area aside and named it the Mukuntuweap National Monument. Nine years later President Wilson enlarged the area and changed the name to Zion. The national monument was enlarged and established as a national park in 1929.
154, 438, 546, 600, 604.

ZION NATIONAL PARK (Washington) encompasses Zion Canyon.

ZION NARROWS (Washington) are in the upper part of Zion Canyon. The North Fork of the Virgin River emerges from the narrows into Zion Canyon proper. It is a popular backpacking area unavailable to the ordinary tourist. Some of the hiking is done along the river bottom that hides submerged potholes. If you reach out in opposite directions, your hands can often touch both sides of the canyon. Flash floods are a frequent possibility.
T40S,R10W,SLM.

Bibliography

1. Abbey, Edward. *Slickrock: The Canyon Country of Southeast Utah.* San Francisco: Sierra Club, 1971.
2. Alder, Douglas D. "The Ghost of Mercur." *Utah Historical Quarterly* 29 (January 1961): 33-42.
3. Alexander, Thomas G. and Leonard J. Arrington. "The Utah Military Frontier, 1872-1912, Forts Cameron, Thornburg and Duchesne." *Utah Historical Quarterly* 32 (Fall 1964): 330-354.
4. _____. "Camp in the Sage Brush: Camp Floyd, Utah, 1858-1861." *Utah Historical Quarterly* 34 (Winter 1966): 3-21.
5. Allen, A. D. "History of Kingston." Written from memory by A. D. Allen. Typescript. Piute County Courthouse, Junction, Utah.
6. Allen, James B. "The Evolution of County Boundaries in Utah." *Utah Historical Quarterly* 23 (1955): 261-278.
7. _____ and Ted J. Warner. "The Gosiute Indians in Pioneer Utah." *Utah Historical Quarterly* 39 (Spring 1971): 162-177.
8. Allred, R. Clay, et al. Davis County Master Plan, A Guide for Growth, 1970 to 1990. For the County and its Sixteen Incorporated Cities and Towns. Davis County Community Correlation Council, 1970.
9. Alter, J. C. "Fort Bridger." *Utah Educational Review* 21 (1927): 140.
10. _____. *Jim Bridger.* Columbus, OH: Longs College Book Company, 1951.
11. _____. "W. A. Ferris in Utah, 1830-1835." *Utah Historical Quarterly* 9 (January, April 1941): 81-108.
12. Alvey, Edson. "Place Names in the Escalante Area." Typescript. Utah Historical Society, Salt Lake City, Utah, 1982.
13. *Amalga in Retrospect, The Story of Amalga, Utah.* Amalga, UT: Town Board, 1951.
14. Anderson, Bernice Gibbs. "The Gentile City of Corinne." *Utah Historical Quarterly* 9 (January, April 1941): 141-154.
15. _____. "Stansbury's Survey of the Inland Sea." *Utah Historical Quarterly* 26 (January 1958): 64-81.
16. *Arizona Highways Magazine,* Utah Issue. Phoenix: Arizona Highway Department, 23 (April 1947).
17. Arrington, Leonard J. *Great Basin Kingdom.* Lincoln, NB: University of Nebraska Press, 1966.
18. Athearn, Robert G. "Opening the Gates of Zion: Utah and the Coming of the Union Pacific Railroad." *Utah Historical Quarterly* 36 (1968): 291.
19. Auerbach, Herbert S. "Old Trails, Old Forts, Old Trappers and Traders." *Utah Historical Quarterly* 9 (January, April 1941): 13-63.
20. Averett, Walter R. *Directory of Southern Nevada Place Names.* rev. ed. [Las Vegas, Nevada], 1963.
21. Bailey, Alfred M. "Desert River Through Navaho Land." *National Geographic* 5 (August 1947): 149-172.
22. Bailey, Paul. *Walkara.* Los Angeles: Westerlore Press, 1954.
23. Baker, Daran J. *Early History of Providence.* Logan, UT: Utah State University Press, 1973.

24. Baker, Pearl. *Robbers Roost Recollections*. Logan, UT: Utah State University Press, 1976.

25. _____. *The Wild Bunch at Robbers Roost*. New York: Abelard-Schuman, 1971.

26. Baldwin, Thomas and J. Thomas. *Gazetteer of the United States*. Philadelphia: Lippincott, Grambo & Co., 1854.

27. Bancroft, Hubert Howe. *History of Utah, 1540-1886*. Salt Lake City: Bookcraft, 1964. (1st ed. 1889).

28. Barnes, F. A. Canyon Country: Arches and La Sal Areas, Off-Road Vehicle Trail Maps, No. 7. Salt Lake City: Wasatch Publishers, [1979].

29. _____. Canyon Country: Exploring, No. 12. Salt Lake City: Wasatch Publishers, 1978.

30. _____. Canyon Country: Geology, No. 11. Salt Lake City: Wasatch Publishers, 1978.

31. _____. Canyon Country: Hiking and Natural History. Salt Lake City: Wasatch Publishers, c1977.

32. _____. Canyon Country: Off Road Vehicles Trails, Island Area, No. 4. Salt Lake City: Wasatch Publishers, 1978.

33. _____. Canyon Country: Off Road Vehicles Trails, Rims and Needles Area, No. 8. Salt Lake City: Wasatch Publishers, 1978.

34. _____. Canyon Country: Prehistoric Rock Art, No. 14. Salt Lake City: Wasatch Publishers, 1982.

35. Barnes, F. A. and Michaelene Pendleton. Canyon Country, Prehistoric Indians, Their Cultures, Ruins, Artifacts and Rock Art, No. 13. Salt Lake City: Wasatch Publishers, 1979.

36. Barnes, Fran. "Utah's Gemini Twins." *Western Gateways* 9 (March 1969): 18-20, 107-110.

37. Barnes, Will C. *Arizona Place Names*. Revised and Enlarged by Byrd H. Granger. Tucson, AZ: University of Arizona Press, 1960.

38. Barney, Lewis. "Life of Lewis Barney, 1808-1894." Manuscript. Provo, UT: Brigham Young University, 1963.

39. Bartlett, Richard A. *Great Surveys of the American West*. Norman, OK: University of Oklahoma Press, 1962.

40. Bean, George Washington. "The Journal of George Washington Bean, Las Vegas Springs, New Mexico Territory, 1856-1857." Edited by Harry C. Dees. *Nevada Historical Quarterly* 15, no. 3 (Fall 1972): 3-29.

41. _____. *Autobiography of George Washington Bean*. Comp. by Flora Diana Bean Horne. [Salt Lake City: Utah Printing Company, 1945.]

42. _____. "First Settlements in Sevier Valley, 1863." *Utah Genealogical and Historical Magazine* 6 (1915): 83, 141.

43. *Beautiful Logan, Cache Valley*. Logan, UT: n.p., n.d.

44. Beaver County Publicity Folder.

45. *Beaver Press*, Beaver, Utah, August 7, 1914.

46. Beckwith, Frank A. *Indian Joe, 1915-1940*. Delta, UT: DuWil Publishing Co., 1975.

47. _____. *Trips to Points of Interest in Millard County and Nearby*. Springville, UT: Art City Publishing Co., 1947.

48. Belknap, William. "Bryce Canyon." *National Geographic* 114 (October 1958): 490-511.

49. _____. "Shooting Rapids in Reverse." *National Geographic* 121 (April 1962): 562-565.

50. Bender, Henry E. Jr. *Uintah Railway, The Gilsonite Route*. Berkeley: Howell-North Books, 1970.

51. Bernheimer, Charles Leopold. *Rainbow Bridge: Circling Navajo Mountain and Explorations in the "Bad Lands" of Southern Utah*. Garden City, NY: Doubleday, 1924.

52. Bero, John A. "Utah Place Names." *Utah Humanities Review* 2 (January 1947): 79-80n.

53. Best, Gerald M. *Iron Horses to Promontory*. San Marino, CA: Golden West Books, 1969.

54. Betenson, Lula Parker. *Butch Cassidy, My Brother*. As told to Dora Flack. Provo, UT: Brigham Young University Press, 1975.

55. Billington, Ray Allen. *The Far Western Frontier, 1830-1860*. San Francisco: Harper & Row, 1956.

56. *Bingham Canyon*. Bingham Canyon, UT: The Bingham Commercial Club, 1909.

57. Biographical Memoirs of the National Academy of Science, vol. 21. Washington, DC: Government Printing Office, 1924.

58. Birney, Hoffman. *Zealots of Zion*. Philadelphia: Pennsylvania Publishing Co., 1931.

59. Black, Rose Vida. *Under Granger Skies, 1879-1963*. Granger Stake Relief Society, Church of Jesus Christ of Latter-day Saints, [1963].

60. Bolton, Herbert E. *Pageant in the Wilderness: The Story of the Escalante Expedition*. Salt Lake City: Utah State Historical Society, 1951.

61. *The Book of Mormon*. Salt Lake City: Church of Jesus Christ of Latter-day Saints, 1981.

62. Borah, Leo A. "Utah Carved by Winds and Waters." *National Geographic* 69 (May 1936): 577-623.

63. Borovatz, Steve Nick. "The Settlement of Carbon County and the Development of Schools." Thesis, University of Utah, Salt Lake City, Utah, 1953.

64. *Bountiful Area Historic Sites*. A Tour Guide Booklet. Bountiful Area Historic Sites Committee. 1976 ed.

65. Bowman, Anthony Will. *From Silver to Skis, A History of Alta, Utah and the Little Cottonwood Canyon, 1847-1966*. Logan, UT: Utah State University Press, 1967.

66. Boyce, Ronald R. "An Historical Geography of Greater Salt Lake City, Utah." Thesis, University of Utah, Salt Lake City, Utah, 1957.

67. Bradshaw, Hazel, ed. *Under Dixie Sun: A History of Washington County*. St. George, UT: Washington County Daughters of Utah Pioneers, [c1950].

68. Breed, Jack. "First Motor Sortie into Escalante Land." *National Geographic* 96 (September 1949): 369-404.

69. _____. "Roaming the West: Fantastic Four Corners." *National Geographic* 101 (June 1952): 705-742.

70. _____. "Shooting the Rapids in Dinosaur Country." *National Geographic* 105 (March 1954): 363-390.

71. _____. "Utah's Arches of Stone." *National Geographic* 92 (August 1947): 175-192.

72. Brooks, Juanita, ed. *Journal of the Southern Indian Mission, Diary of Thomas D. Brown*. Logan, UT: Utah State University Press, 1972.

73. _____. "The Land That God Forgot." *Utah Historical Quarterly* 26 (July 1958): 206-219.

74. _____. *The Mountain Meadows Massacre*. Palo Alto, CA: Stanford University Press, 1950, and Norman, OK: University of Oklahoma Press, 1962.

75. _____. "Silver Reef." *Utah Historical Quarterly* 29 (July 1961): 281-287.

76. _____. "The Mountain Meadows: Historic Stopping Place on the Spanish Trail." *Utah Historical Quarterly* 35 (Spring 1967): 137-143.

77. _____. *Silver Reef: Fact and Folklore*. Charles Redd Monographs in Western History, vol. 3. Provo, UT: Charles Redd Center for Western Studies at Brigham Young University, 1972.

78. Bruhn, Arthur F. *Your Guide to Southern Utah's Land of Color*. Salt Lake City: Author, 1952.

79. Bureau of Land Management, Moab District, Utah. Leaflet, September 1977.

80. Burroughs, John Rolfe. *Where the Old West Stayed Young*. New York: Bonanza Books, 1962.

81. Burton, Sir Richard. *The Look of the West*. Lincoln, NB: University of Nebraska Press, 1962.

82. *Butlerville, 1847-1967*. Comp. by Arnold C. Pope for the Butler Stake 5th Anniversary, Church of Jesus Christ of Latter-day Saints, November 18, 1967.

83. *BYU Today*. Provo, UT: Brigham Young University Alumni Association, December 1984.

84. Campbell, Roald Fay. *Utah Materials: A Collection of Pertinent and Factual Information About the State*, 1943.

85. Capitol Reef Natural History Association. Leaflet.

86. Carbon School District. Brief History of Price, Utah, 1930.

87. Carlson, Helen S. *Nevada Place Names*. Reno, NV: University of Nevada Press, 1974.

88. Carr, Annie Call, comp. *East of Antelope Island*, rev. ed. n.l.: Daughters of Utah Pioneers, North Davis County Company, 1961.

89. Carr, Stephen L. *The Historical Guide to Utah Ghost Towns*. Salt Lake City: Western Epics, 1972.

90. Carson, Christopher. *Kit Carson's Autobiography*. Edited by Milo M. Quaife. Lincoln, NB: University of Nebraska Press, 1935.

91. Carson, L. F. "Geneva—Then and Now." *Mountainwest Magazine* 2 (November 1976): 6-7.

92. _____. "Sunshine—A Ghost Town." *Mountainwest Magazine* 2 (September 1976): 42-43.

93. Carter, Kate B. "Among the First in Utah." *Heart Throbs of the West*, vol. 9. Daughters of the Utah Pioneers, 1948, pp. 217-268.

94. _____, comp. *Bibliography of Utah Writings and History*. Salt Lake City: n.p., 1947.

95. _____, comp. *Ghost Towns of the West*. Salt Lake City: Daughters of the Utah Pioneers, 1947.

96. _____, comp. "Origin of Mormon Names of Cities, Mountains, Streams, Counties, etc., in the United States." In *Heart Throbs of the West*, vol. 5. Daughters of the Utah Pioneers, 1944.

97. _____, comp. *Heart Throbs of the West*, vol. 8. Daughters of the Utah Pioneers, 1947.

98. _____, comp. "Utah Rivers, Part 2." In *An Enduring Legacy*, vol. 10. Daughters of Utah Pioneers, 1987, pp. 49-100.

99. _____, comp. "Origins of Mormon Place Names." In *Our Pioneer Heritage*, vol. 8. Daughters of Utah Pioneers, March 1975, pp. 305-368.

100. _____, comp. *Our Pioneer Heritage*, 17 vols. Daughters of the Utah Pioneers.

101. Central Utah Water Conservancy District Pamphlet. Jordanelle Dam, Orem, Utah.

102. Chaffin, Ned. Personal Communication.

103. Challis, Arthur T. "Handbook of Utah First Facts, 1540-1896." Thesis, University of Utah, Salt Lake City, Utah, 1959.
104. Chamberlin, Blair. "The Goblins'll Getcha in Goblin Gully." *Western Gateways* 9 (March 1969): 65-68, 98-99.
105. Chamberlin, Ralph V. "Animal Names and Anatomical Terms of the Gosiute Indians." Contributions from the Zoological Laboratory of Brigham Young University No. 1, and Proceedings of the Academy of Natural Sciences of Philadelphia, April 1908. Issued July 22, 1908.
106. _____. "The Ethno-Botany of the Gosiute Indians of Utah." Reprinted from the Academy of Natural Sciences of Philadelphia, 1911.
107. _____. "Place and Personal Names of the Gosiute Indians of Utah." American Philosophical Society, Proceedings 52 (January 1913): 1-13.
108. Christensen, Earl M. and Hyrum B. Johnson. "Presettlement Vegetation and Vegetational Change in Three Valleys in Central Utah." Brigham Young Science Bulletin. Biological Series 4 (August 1964): 1-13.
109. Christensen, James Boyd. "Function and Fun in Utah Danish Nicknames." *Utah Historical Quarterly* 39 (Winter 1971): 23-29.
110. Christy, Howard A. "Open Hand and Mailed Fist: Mormon-Indian Relations in Utah, 1847-52." *Utah Historical Quarterly* 46 (Summer 1978): 216-235.
111. Churchill, Stephanie D. *Utah: A Guide to Eleven Tours of Historic Sites*. Salt Lake City: Utah Heritage Foundation, 1972.
112. Clark, Thomas L. "A Semantic Class in the Great Basin." *Names* 26 (March 1978): 48-57.
113. Clegg, John C. Personal Communication.
114. Cleland, Robert Glass. *This Reckless Breed of Men*. New York: Alfred A. Knopf, 1950.
115. Cline, Gloria G. *Exploring the Great Basin*. Norman, OK: University of Oklahoma Press, 1963.
116. _____. *Peter Skene Ogden and the Hudson Bay Company*. Norman, OK: University of Oklahoma Press, 1974.
117. Cole, Gordon. "Peter Maughan, Cache Valley Pioneer." Thesis, University of Utah, Salt Lake City, Utah, 1950.
118. Collett, Carol Ivins. *Kaysville—Our Town*. Kaysville, UT: Kaysville City, 1976.
119. Combs, Barry B. *Westward to Promontory*. New York: American West Publishing Co., 1969.
120. Cooley, Everett L. "Clarion, Utah: Jewish Colony in Zion." *Utah Historical Quarterly* 36 (Spring 1968): 113-131.
121. _____. *Utah: A Student's Guide to Localized History*. New York: Teachers College Press, 1968.
122. Cornwall, Rebecca and Leonard J. Arrington. *Rescue of the 1856 Handcart Companies*. Charles Redd Monographs in Western History, vol. 2. Provo, UT: Charles Redd Center for Western Studies at Brigham Young University, 1982.
123. Correll, J. Lee. "Navajo Frontiers in Utah and Troublous Times in Monument Valley." *Utah Historical Quarterly* 39 (Spring 1971): 145-177.
124. Cottam, Walter P. and Frederick R. Evans. "A Comparative Study of the Vegetation of Grazed and Ungrazed Canyons of the Wasatch Range." *Ecology* 26 (1945): 171-181.
125. Cox, Elbert L. "Beaver County Gazetteer." *Beaver Press*, March 7, 14 and April 4, 11, 1930. Beaver, Utah.
126. Cox, Frank. "Canyonland Safari." *Western Gateways* 9/2 (March 1969): 38-40, 102-107.

127. Cracroft, Richard H. "Heraldry of the Range, Utah Cattle Brands." *Utah Historical Quarterly* 32 (Summer 1964): 217-231.

128. Crampton, C. Gregory. "Humboldt's Utah." *Utah Historical Quarterly* 26 (July 1958): 268-281.

129. Creer, Leland Hargrave. *The Founding of an Empire: The Exploration and Colonization of Utah, 1776-1856.* Salt Lake City: Bookcraft, 1947.

130. Culmer, Henry L. A. *Utah Directory and Gazetteer for 1879-89.*

131. Culmsee, Carlton. *Utah's Black Hawk War.* Logan, UT: Utah State University Press, 1973.

132. Cummings, Byron. "The Great Natural Bridge of Utah." *National Geographic* 21 (February 1910): 157-167.

133. Czerny, Peter G. *The Great Great Salt Lake.* Provo, UT: Brigham Young University Press, 1976.

134. *Daily Herald,* Provo, Utah.

135. Dale, Harrison C., ed. *The Ashley-Smith Exploration and the Discovery of a Central Route to the Pacific, 1822-1829.* Glendale, CA: The Arthur H. Clark Co., 1941.

136. Dalton, Luella Adams. *History of Iron County Mission.* Parowan, UT: n.p., n.d.

137. Darrah, William C. *Powell of the Colorado.* Princeton, NJ: Princeton University Press, 1951.

138. Daughters of American Revolution. "Utah Historic Spots Marked." *Daughters of the American Revolution Magazine,* (September 1937): 782-856.

139. Daughters of Utah Pioneers, Box Elder Chapter. *History of Box Elder County.* n.l.: n.p., 1942.

140. Daughters of Utah Pioneers. *Builders of Uintah, A Centennial History of Uintah County, 1871 to 1947.* Springville, UT: Art City Publishing Co., 1947.

141. _____, Carbon County. *Centennial Echoes from Carbon County,* 1948.

142. _____, Davis County Company. *East of Antelope Island.* 2nd ed. Bountiful, UT, 1961.

143. _____, Emery County. *"Castle Valley," A History of Emery County,* 1939.

144. _____, English Fort Camp. *History of Taylorsville and Bennion.* n.l.: n.p., 1949.

145. _____, Garfield County. *Golden Nuggets of Pioneer Days: History of Garfield County.* [Panguitch, UT]: Garfield County News, 1949.

146. _____. *Grand Memories, Grand County, Utah.* n.l.: n.p., 1972.

147. _____, Kane County. *History of Kane County.* Salt Lake City: n.p. 1960.

148. _____, Millard County. *One Hundred Years of History of Millard County.* n.l.: n.p., 1951.

149. _____, Salt Lake County. *Tales of a Triumphant People, A History of Salt Lake County, Utah, 1847-1900.* n.l.: n.p., 1947.

150. _____, San Juan County. *Saga of San Juan.* Monticello, UT: n.p., 1957.

151. _____, Summit County. *Echoes of Yesterday.* Summit County Centennial History, 1947.

152. _____. *These Our Fathers: A Centennial History of Sanpete County, 1849 to 1947.* Springville, UT: Art City Publishing Co., 1947.

153. _____, Tooele County Camp. *History of Tooele County.* Salt Lake City: Daughters of Utah Pioneers, 1961.

154. _____. *Under Dixie Sun: A History of Washington County.* St. George, UT, 1950.

155. _____. *Under Wasatch Skies, A History of Wasatch County, 1885-1900.* [Salt Lake City]: Deseret News Press, 1954.

156. Davis, Oscar King. "The Lucin Cut-off." *Century Illustrated Monthly Magazine* 71 (1905-06): 459-468.

157. Dawson, J. Frank. *Place Names in Colorado*. Lakewood, CO: Jefferson Record, 1954.

158. Day, Stella H. and Sebrina C. Ekins, comps. *One Hundred Years of History of Millard County*. Springville, UT: Art City Publishing Company, 1951.

159. Dellenbaugh, Frederick S. *A Canyon Voyage*. New York: G. P. Putnam's Sons, 1908.

160. _____. *The Romance of the Colorado River*. New York: Knickerbocker Press, 1906.

161. DeMille, Janice F. *Portraits of the Hurricane Pioneers*. St. George, UT: Dixie College Press, 1976.

162. _____. "Shonesburg: The Town Nobody Knows." *Utah Historical Quarterly* 45 (Winter 1977): 47-60.

163. *Deseret News*. Salt Lake City: Deseret News Publishing Company.

164. "Diary of Almon Harris Thompson." Edited by Herbert E. Gregory. *Utah Historical Quarterly* 7 (1939): 11-140.

165. Dillman, Mildred Miles, comp. *Early History of Duchesne County*. Daughters of Utah Pioneers. Springville, UT: Art City Publishing Co., 1948.

166. Dingman, Lester F. "Geographic Names—Colorful or Offensive." Typescript. Domestic Geographic Names, United States Board on Geographic Names, Washington, D.C., n.d.

167. Dinosaur National Monument. Leaflet, December 1965.

168. Dixon, Madoline Cloward. *Peteetneet Town: A History of Payson, Utah*. Provo, UT: Press Publishing Co., 1974.

169. Dodge, Natt. "Sandstone Rainbow." *Utah Magazine* (May 1947): 28.

170. Dressman, Michael R. "'Names are Magic': Walt Whitman's Laws of Geographic Nomenclature." *Names* 26 (March 1978): 68-79.

171. Dunham, Dick. *Our Strip of Land: A History of Daggett County, Utah*. Manila, UT: Daggett County Lions Club, 1947.

172. Dunham, Dick and Vivian Dunham. *Flaming Gorge Country, The Story of Daggett County, Utah*. Denver: Eastwood Printing and Publishing Co., 1977.

173. Dunlop, Richard. *Wheels West, 1590-1900*. San Francisco: Rand McNally & Co., 1977.

174. Durrington, William Robb. "History of South Davis County, 1847-1920." Thesis, University of Utah, Salt Lake City, Utah, 1959.

175. Dutton, C. E. *Geology of the High Plateaus*. United States Geographical Survey of the Rocky Mountain Region. Washington, DC: Government Printing Office, 1880.

176. Dwyer, Joseph. *The Gentile Comes to Utah*. Salt Lake City: Western Epics, 1971.

177. Edwards, Walter Meayers. "Lake Powell: Waterway to Desert Wonders." *National Geographic* 132 (July 1967): 44-75.

178. Egbert, Marie. "A Brief History of Marysvale." *Snake River Echoes* 4 (1975): 9.

179. Eichler, George R. *Colorado Place Names*. Boulder, CO: Johnson Publishing Co., 1977.

180. Ekker, Barbara. Personal Communication.

181. _____. Typescript. Utah State Historical Society Archives, Salt Lake City, Utah.

182. Ellis, Charles. *Utah, 1847-1870*. Salt Lake City: Author, 1891.

183. Ellsworth, Samuel George. "Utah History: Retrospect and Prospect." *Utah Historical Quarterly* 40 (Fall 1972): 342-367.

184. _____. *Utah's Heritage*. Santa Barbara, CA: Peregrine Smith, 1972.

185.   Emery County Historical Society. *Emery County, 1880-1980.* n.l.: Craftsman, n.d.

186.   Ephraim City Corporation. *A Golden Quarter of Ephraim History.* Provo, UT: Community Press, 1981.

187.   Evans, John Henry. *The Story of Utah, the Beehive State.* New York: Macmillan, 1933.

188.   Fabian, Josephine. "Dead Horse Point." *Utah Historical Quarterly* 26 (July 1958): 240-245.

189.   *Fanning's Illustrated Gazetteer of the United States.* New York: Ensign, Bridgman and Fanning, 1855.

190.   Fiack, Henry. "Fort Duchesne's Beginnings." *Utah Historical Quarterly* 2 (1929): 31-32.

191.   Findley, Rowe. "Canyonlands." *National Geographic* 140 (July 1971): 71-91.

192.   Fine Arts Study Group, Morgan, Utah. *Mountains Conquered: The Story of Morgan with Biographies.* Morgan, UT: Morgan County News Publisher, 1959.

193.   Finken, Dee Anne. *A History of the San Rafael Swell.* Price, UT: Resources Development Internship Program, Bureau of Land Management, Moab District Office, 1977.

194.   Flake, Chad J., ed. *A Mormon Bibliography, 1830-1930: Books, Pamphlets, Periodicals and Broadsides Relating to the First Century of Mormonism.* Salt Lake City: University of Utah Press, 1978.

195.   Flaming Gorge National Recreation Area. Leaflet 69-1093.

196.   Florin, Lambert. *Colorado-Utah Ghost Towns.* Seattle, WA: Superior Publishing Company, 1971.

197.   Fohlin, Ernest Victor. *Salt Lake City, Past and Present.* Salt Lake City: n.p., 1908.

198.   *Footprints in a Beautiful Valley.* Compiled and published by Tabiona and Hanna Communities, [1980].

199.   Forsgren, Lydia Walker, comp. *History of Box Elder County.* Salt Lake City: Daughters of Utah Pioneers, 1937.

200.   Fowler, Catherine S. and Don D. Fowler. "Notes on the History of the Southern Paiutes and Western Shoshones." *Utah Historical Quarterly* 39 (Spring 1971): 95-113.

201.   Foy, Leslie T. *Bountiful: The City.* Bountiful, UT: Horizon Publishing Co., 1975.

202.   Francis, J. H., Morgan, Utah. Letter to Mr. Van Hixon, Adjutant General, Utah National Guard, May 14, 1982.

203.   Freeman, Dick. "Land of the Arches." *Ford Times,* June 1948.

204.   Freeman, Lewis R. *The Colorado River: Yesterday, Today, and Tomorrow.* New York: Dodd, Mead and Co., 1923.

205.   Fremont, John Charles. *The Exploring Expedition to the Rocky Mountains in the Year 1842.* Washington, DC: Gales and Seaton, Printers, 1845.

206.   Friedman, Ralph. "Big Rock Candy Mountain." *Westways* 57 (November 1965): 41.

207.   Gadd, John D. C. "Saltair, Great Salt Lake's Most Famous Resort." *Utah Historical Quarterly* 36 (Summer 1968): 195-221.

208.   Gallagher, John S. *The Post Offices of Utah.* Burtonsville, MD: The Depot, 1977.

209.   Gannett, Henry. *A Gazetteer of Utah.* United States Geological Survey, Bulletin No. 166. Washington, DC: Government Printing Office, 1900.

210. _____. *Origins of Certain Place Names in the United States*. United States Geological Survey Bulletin 197. Detroit: Gale Research Company, Book Tower, 1971.

211. Gardner, Hamilton. *Lehi, Centennial History: 1850-1950*. Published by Lehi Pioneer Committee. Salt Lake City: Deseret News, 1973.

212. Gaul, R. Wharton. "The Poisonous Beaver of Sick River." *Utah Historical Quarterly* 30 (Summer 1962): 263-271.

213. *Gazetteer of Utah Localities and Altitudes*. Zoology Department, University of Utah, Utah State Institute of Fine Arts, United States Work Projects Administration. Salt Lake City: Division of Biology, University of Utah, June 30, 1952.

214. Gibbons, Helen Bay. *Letters to Mary, 1879-1929*. Salt Lake City: Helen Bay Gibbons, 1972.

215. Gibbs, Josiah F. "'Pah-Yaqua'–Death Lake, an Indian Legend." *Native American* 27 (December 1927).

216. _____. *The Railroad Red Book*. n.l.: n.p., January 1917.

217. Gilbert, Karl Grove. *Report on the Geology of the Henry Mountains*. United States Geographical and Geological Survey of the Rocky Mountain Region, Department of the Interior. Washington, DC: Government Printing Office, 1877.

218. _____. "The Ancient Outlet of Great Salt Lake." *American Journal of Science and Art*, Third Series, 15/88 (1878): 256-259.

219. Golay, A. "Lake Powell Idyl." *Western Gateways* 2 (March 1969): 48-53, 91-97.

220. *Golden Quarter of Ephraim History, 1954-1979*. Provo, UT: Community Press, 1981.

221. Goodman, Jack. "The Shining Mountains." *Utah Historical Quarterly* 27 (July 1959): 285-296.

222. _____. "The Shining Mountains: The Oquirrh Range." *Utah Historical Quarterly* 27 (July 1959): 284-295.

223. _____. "Wandering the Wasatch." *Utah Historical Quarterly* 27 (July 1959): 312-327.

224. Gottfredson, Peter. *History of Indian Depredations in Utah*. Salt Lake City: Skelton Publishing Co., 1919.

225. Gowans, Fred R. *Rocky Mountain Rendezvous*. Provo, UT: Brigham Young University Publications, 1976.

226. Grater, Russell K. *The Rainbow Canyon Country, on National Park, Utah*. n.l.: n.p., 1946.

227. Grauman, Melody Webb. "Kennecott: Alaskan Origins of a Copper Empire, 1900-1938." *Western Historical Quarterly* (April 1978): 197-211.

228. Gray, Ralph. "Three Roads to Rainbow." *National Geographic* 111 (April 1957): 547-561.

229. Greer, Deon C., et al. *Atlas of Utah*. Provo, UT: Brigham Young University Press, 1981.

230. Gregory, Herbert E. *The San Juan County: A Geographic and Geologic Reconnaissance of Southeastern Utah*. U.S. Geological Survey Professional Paper 188. Washington, DC: U.S. Government Printing Office, 1938.

231. _____. *Bryce Canyon National Park, Utah*. Washington, DC: U.S. Geological Survey, 1939.

232. _____. *The Geology and Geography of the Paunsaugunt Region, Utah*. U.S. Geological Survey Professional Paper 226. Washington, DC: U.S. Government Printing Office, 1951.

233. Gulbransen, Myrna C. *A History of the Mines and Town of Kimberly, Utah.* n.l.: n.p., 1964.

234. *Gunnison Valley's Centennial Memory Book.* Gunnison Valley Centennial Committee, 1959.

235. Hafen, LeRoy R. "Etienne Provost, Mountain Man and Utah Pioneer." *Utah Historical Quarterly* 36 (Spring 1967): 99-112.

236. ____. "Fort Davy Crockett, Its Fur Men and Visitors." *Colorado Magazine* 29 (January 1952): 17-33.

237. ____, ed. *The Mountain Men and the Fur Trade.* 10 vols. Glendale, CA: The Arthur H. Clark Co., 1965-1972.

238. ____. "Mountain Men Before the Mormons." *Utah Historical Quarterly* 26 (October 1958): 307-326.

239. ____ and Ann W. Hafen. *Handcarts to Zion, 1856-1860.* Glendale, CA: Arthur H. Clark Co., 1960.

240. ____ and Ann W. Hafen. *Old Spanish Trail, Santa Fe to Los Angeles.* Glendale, CA: Arthur H. Clark Co., 1954.

241. Hall, Ansel Franklin. *General Report, Rainbow Bridge: Monument Valley Expedition of 1933.* Berkeley, CA: University of California Press.

242. Halladay, Wilford Meeks. "A Brief History of Piute County and Its Educational Development." Thesis, Brigham Young University, Provo, Utah, 1951.

243. Harris, Beth Kay. *Towns of Tintic.* Denver: Sage Books, 1961.

244. Harris, William Richard. *History of the Catholic Church in Utah.* Salt Lake City: Intermountain Catholic Press, 1909.

245. Hartley, William. "Mormons, Crickets, and Gulls: A New Look at an Old Story." *Utah Historical Quarterly* 38 (Summer 1970): 224-239.

246. Hatch, Boyd O. "Utah Trails Before the Mormons." *Instructor* 92 (June 1957): 169.

247. Hayward, C. Lynn. *The High Uintas, Utah's Land of Lake and Forest.* Provo, UT: Monte L. Bean Life Science Museum, June 1983.

248. Henderson, Russell. "We Camped on Kaiparowits." *Desert Magazine* (September 1951).

249. *Herald Journal.* Logan, UT.

250. Herring, Elmo. *History of the Kimberly Mine.* n.l.: n.p., n.d.

251. Hess, Margaret Steed. *My Farmington.* Helen Mar Miller Camp, Daughters of Utah Pioneers, 1976.

252. Historical Record. Church of Jesus Christ of Latter-day Saints. Salt Lake City, Utah.

253. *History of Clover, Centennial Year, 1856-1956.* Tooele, UT: Genealogical Committee, 1956.

254. "History of Education in Piute County." *County Officer* 9 (July, 1945): 54.

255. *History of Emery and Sanpete Counties.* Ogden, UT: W. H. Lever, 1898.

256. *History of Fort Douglas, 22 October 1861 to 30 September 1954.* Salt Lake City: 1954.

257. History of Piute County. Pamphlet published by Piute County, 1960.

258. History of Smithfield. Published by Smithfield City, 1927.

259. History of Weber County. Taken from the original *Tullidge's Quarterly Magazine,* 11/4 (July 1883).

260. Hobbs, Lee Wray. Correspondence to Utah Historical Society.

261. Hodson, Dean. *The Origin of Non-Mormon Settlements in Utah, 1847-1896.* East Lansing, MI: Author, 1971.

262.   Hoffman, John F. *Arches National Park*. National Parks and Monuments Series. San Diego, CA: Western Recreational Publications, 1981.

263.   _____. *Arches National Park, An Illustrated Guide*. San Diego, CA: Western Recreational Publications, 1985.

264.   Holmes, E. F. "The Great Natural Bridge of Utah." *National Geographic* 18 (March 1907): 199-204.

265.   Holt, Alfred H. *American Place Names*. New York: Thomas Crowell Co., 1938.

266.   Holy Bible. Containing the Old and the New Testament. Authorized King James Version, by His Majesty's Special Command. Salt Lake City: Deseret News Press.

267.   *Home in the Hills of Bridgerland*. Hyrum City, UT: Deseret News Press, 1969.

268.   Horton, George A., Jr. "An Early History of Milford up to Its Incorporation as a Town." Thesis, Brigham Young University, Provo, Utah, 1957.

269.   Hovey, M. R., comp. *An Early History of Cache County*. Logan, UT: Logan Chamber of Commerce, 1923.

270.   Huff, Emma N., comp. *Memories That Live: Utah County Centennial History*. Salt Lake City: Daughters of Utah Pioneers, 1947.

271.   Hughel, Avvon Chew. *The Chew Bunch in Browns Park*. Centerville, MA: Scrimshaw Press, 1970.

272.   Hulse, Irene. *From Rags to Riches. A Resume of Area History from the Middle Eighteen Hundreds, Beginning in Salt Lake Valley, to the Present Time*. Tooele, UT: Tooele Transcript Press, 1964.

273.   Hunt, Charles S. Geology and Geography of the Henry Mountains Region, Utah. United States Geological Survey, Professional Paper, No. 228, Derivation of Place Names, pp. 21-24. Washington, DC: Government Printing Office, 1953.

274.   Hunter, Milton R. *Beneath Ben Lomond's Peak: A History of Weber County, 1824-1900*. Daughters of the Utah Pioneers, Salt Lake City: Deseret News Press, 1944.

275.   _____. *Brigham Young, the Colonizer*. Salt Lake City: Deseret News Press, 1940.

276.   _____. *Utah Story*. Salt Lake City: Author, 1960.

277.   _____. *Utah, The Story of Her People, 1540-1947: A Centennial History of Utah*. Salt Lake City: Deseret News Press, 1946.

278.   Idaho Department of Highways, Highway Planning Survey. *Gazetteer of Cities, Villages in the State of Idaho*. 3rd ed., January 1966.

279.   Ingalls, Huntley. "We Climbed Utah's Skyscraper Rock." *National Geographic* 122 (November 1962): 704-721.

280.   Irving, Washington. *The Adventures of Captain Bonneville, U.S.A. in the Rocky Mountains and the Far West*. Edited by Edgeley W. Todd. Norman, OK: University of Oklahoma Press, 1961.

281.   Jackson, Donald. *The Expeditions of John Charles Fremont, Commentary on Map Portfolio*. Urbana, IL: University of Illinois Press, 1970.

282.   Jackson, Richard H. and R. W. Cransby. Delimitation of the Pony Express Trail Through Utah. Typescript. Utah Historical Society, Salt Lake City, June 14, 1971.

283.   Jacobs, Jim. Personal Communication.

284.   Jacobson, Gwendolyn, et al., comp. and ed. *Memories of "Little Denmark": History of Elsinore and Brooklyn, Utah*. Elsinore Literary Club and Daughters of Utah Pioneers. Richfield, UT: Richfield Reaper, [1962].

285.   Jacobsen, Pearl F., comp. *Golden Sheaves from Richfield, Utah*. Richfield, UT: Richfield Centennial Committee, 1964.

286. James, George Wharton. *Utah, Land of Blossoming Valleys*. Boston: The Page Co., 1922.

287. James, Harry C. "Ghost Towns of the Parunuweap." *National Parks Magazine* 25 (July-September 1951): 82-88.

288. Jameson, Jesse Harold. "Corinne: A Study of a Freight Transfer Point in the Montana Trade, 1869 to 1878." Thesis, University of Utah, Salt Lake City, Utah, 1951.

289. Jenson, Andrew. *Encyclopedic History of the Church of Jesus Christ of Latter-day Saints*. Salt Lake City: Deseret News Publishing Co., 1941.

290. _____. "Origin of Western Geographic Names." *Utah Genealogical and Historical Magazine*, vols. 10-13 incl. (1919-1922).

291. Jenson, Willard Conrad. *History of Logan*. Salt Lake City: n.p. 1927.

292. Jones, J. Albert. *A Story of the Settling of Huntington, Utah*. n.l.: J. A. Jones, n.d.

293. Jordan School District. Communities of Jordan School District. 2 vols. [Salt Lake City]: n.p., 1945-46.

294. Jorgenson, John L. *A History of Castle Valley to 1890*. Salt Lake City: n.p., 1955.

295. Journal History of the Church. Salt Lake City. Archives Division. Historical Department. The Church of Jesus Christ of Latter-day Saints.

296. Judd, Neil M. "Beyond the Clay Hills." *National Geographic* 45 (March 1924): 275-302.

297. Judge, Joseph. "Retracing John Wesley Powell's Historic Voyage Down the Grand Canyon." *National Geographic* 135 (May 1969): 668-713.

298. Kamas Ranger District, Kamas, Utah. "Place Names of this United States Forest Service District." Typescript. Kamas, UT: Kamas Ranger District, [1976].

299. Keck, W. G. and W. R. Hassibe. *The Great Salt Lake*. Washington DC: Government Printing Office, 1979.

300. Kelly, Charles. "Capitol Reef National Monument." *Utah* 9 (May 1947): 22.

301. _____. "Chief Hoskaninni." *Utah Historical Quarterly* 21 (July 1953): 219-226.

302. _____. "On Denis Julien." *Utah Historical Quarterly* 59 (July 1933): 84.

303. _____. *The Outlaw Trail*. New York: Bonanza Books, 1938.

304. King, Clarence E. *The Three Lakes and How They Were Named*. San Francisco: Sierra Club (privately published, 3 copies), 1870.

305. Knowlton, George Quincey. *A History of Farmington, Utah*. Comp. and ed. by Jannetta K. Robinson. [Kaysville, UT: Inland Printing Co.], 1965.

306. Koch, Walter H. "Boat Trip on the San Juan." *Desert Magazine* 15 (March 1952): 14-16.

307. Lake Boreham, Duchesne County. Information plaque at site.

308. Lambert, Neal. "Al Scorup, Cattleman of the Canyons." *Utah Historical Quarterly* 32 (Summer 1964): 301-320.

309. Lambert, Roy. *High Uintahs, Hi!* Kamas, UT: Author, 1964.

310. Larson, Andrew Karl. *Red Hills of November*. Salt Lake City: Deseret News Press, 1957.

311. _____. *I Was Called to Dixie*. Salt Lake City: Deseret News Press, 1961.

312. Larson, Gustive O. "Journal of the Iron County Mission, John D. Lee, Clerk." *Utah Historical Quarterly* 20 (April, July, October 1952): 109-134, 253-282, 353-383.

313. _____. *Outline History of Utah and the Mormons*. 3rd ed. Salt Lake City: Deseret Book Co., 1965.

314. Layton, Stanford J. "Fort Rawlins, Utah: A Question of Mission and Means." *Utah Historical Quarterly* 42 (Winter 1974): 68-83.

315. LeFevre, Lenore Hall, comp. *Boulder Country and Its People, 1872-1973.* Springville, UT: Art City Publishing Co., [1973].

316. Leigh, Rufus Wood. *Five Hundred Utah Place Names: Their Origin and Significance.* Salt Lake City: Deseret News Press, 1961.

317. _____. "Lake Bonneville, Its Name and History." *Utah Historical Quarterly* 26 (April 1958): 150-159.

318. _____. "Naming of the Green, Sevier, and Virgin Rivers." *Utah Historical Quarterly* 29 (April 1961): 137-147.

319. _____. *Nevada Place Names.* Salt Lake City: Deseret News Press, 1964.

320. Leighly, John. "Biblical Place-Names in the United States." *Names* 27 (March 1979): 46-59.

321. Leonard, Glen Milton. "A History of Farmington, Utah to 1890." Thesis, University of Utah, Salt Lake City, Utah, 1966.

322. Lever, W. H. *History of Emery and Sanpete Counties.* Ogden, UT: W. H. Lever, 1898.

323. Logan, Ida-Marie Clark. "A Bibliography of Theses and Dissertations Concerning Utah Written Outside the State of Utah." Thesis, Utah State University, Logan, Utah, 1966.

324. _____. "Utah, the Mormons and the West: A Bibliography." *Utah Historical Quarterly,* (July 1954, January 1955, July 1955, July 1956, April 1957, January 1959, and April 1959).

325. Lohman, S. W. *The Geologic Story of Arches National Park.* U.S. Geologic Survey Bulletin 1393. Washington, DC: Government Printing Office, 1975.

326. _____. *The Geologic Story of Canyonlands.* Geologic Survey Bulletin 1327, United States Department of the Interior. Washington, DC: Government Printing Office, 1974.

327. Longsdorf, Hilda Madsen, comp. *Mount Pleasant, 1859-1939.* Salt Lake City: Stevens & Wallis, 1939.

328. Luce, Willard. *Utah.* Salt Lake City: Peregrine Smith, 1975.

329. _____. *Utah, Past and Present.* Provo, UT: Utah Color, 1955.

330. Lyman, Albert R. *Indians and Outlaws: Settling of the San Juan Frontier.* Salt Lake City: Bookcraft, 1961.

331. Lyon, T. Edgar. "This Is the Place." *Utah Historical Quarterly* 27 (July 1959): 203-208.

332. Lythgoe, Dennis L. "Negro Slavery in Utah." *Utah Historical Quarterly* 39 (Winter 1971): 40-54.

333. Macomb, John N. *Report of the Exploring Expedition from Santa Fe, New Mexico, to the Junction of the Grand and Green Rivers of the Great Colorado of the West, 1859.* Washington, DC: Government Printing Office, 1876.

334. Madsen, Brigham D. and Betty M. "Corinne, the Fair." *Utah Historical Quarterly* 37 (Winter 1969): 102-123.

335. Madsen, C. H. *Carbon County: A History.* Price, UT: n.p., 1947.

336. Madsen, Eleanor P. *A Time to Plant, A Biography of Leslie Lorenzo Madsen.* Salina, UT: Valley Printing Company, 1984.

337. Madsen, Reed. "Looks Like Rock Candy." *Deseret News,* December 27, 1971.

338. Mahan, Russel L. "Arches National Monument." *Utah Magazine* (May 1947): 34.

339. Malouf, Carling I. "A Study of the Gosiute Indians of Utah." Thesis, University of Utah, Salt Lake City, Utah, 1940.

340. Mann, David H. "Castle Valley's History." *Utah Farmer* (November 19, 1964).

341. Mariger, Marietta M. *Saga of Three Towns: Harrisburg, Leeds, Silver Reef.* 2nd ed. St. George, UT: Washington County News, n.d.

342. Marsell, Ray E. "Landscapes of the North Slopes of the Uinta Mountains." A Geological Guidebook of the Uinta Mountains, 1969.

343. Mauerman, Lawrence Albert. *Early Exploration and the Initial Settlement of Emery County, Utah.* Salt Lake City: n.p., 1967.

344. McCarry, Charles. "Utah's Shining Oasis." *National Geographic* 147 (April 1975): 440-473.

345. McConkie, Bruce R. *Mormon Doctrine.* 2nd ed. Salt Lake City: Bookcraft, 1966.

346. McCullough, C. W. "Giles, the Town the Dirty Devil Took." *Improvement Era* 54 (January 1957): 26.

347. McCune, Alice Paxman, comp. *History of Juab County, Centennial History 1847-1947.* Daughters of Utah Pioneers, Juab County Chapter. Springville, UT: Art City Publishing Company, 1947.

348. McDonald, Russell. "Explorer Peak." *Improvement Era* 58 (April, May 1948): 514.

349. McElprang, Stella, comp. *Castle Valley, A History of Emery County.* Daughters of Utah Pioneers. Castledale, UT: n.p., 1947.

350. McKay, Donald D. *The Founding of Huntsville.* Huntsville, UT: D. D. McKay, n.d.

351. _____, comp. *Memories of Huntsville and Its People.* Huntsville, UT, 1960.

352. McPhee, William M. "Vignettes of Park City." *Utah Historical Quarterly* 28 (April 1960): 137-153.

353. McVaugh, Rogers and F. R. Fosberg. *Index to the Geographical Names of Nevada. A Flora of Nevada, No. 29.* Works Project Administration of Nevada. Washington, DC: U. S. Department of Agriculture, June 1, 1941.

354. Mecham, Everett H. "The History of the Sheep Industry in Utah." Thesis, University of Utah, Salt Lake City, Utah, 1925.

355. Merkley, Aird G. *Monuments to Courage, A History of Beaver County.* Daughters of Utah Pioneers, Beaver County Chapter, 1948.

356. *The Millennial Star.* Vol. 33: 511, 1871.

357. Miller, David E. "The First Wagon Train to Cross Utah, 1841." *Utah Historical Quarterly* 30 (Winter 1962): 41-52.

358. _____, ed. "A Great Adventure on Great Salt Lake, A True Story by Kate Y. Noble." *Utah Historical Quarterly* 33 (Summer 1965): 218-236.

359. _____. *Hole-in-the-Rock.* Salt Lake City: University of Utah Press. 1966.

360. _____. Personal place name manuscript records.

361. _____, ed. "Peter Skene Ogden's Journal of His Expedition to Utah in 1825." *Utah Historical Quarterly* 20 (April 1952): 159-186.

362. _____. *Peter Skene Ogden Discovered Indians.* Charles Redd Monographs in Western History, vol. 3. Provo, UT: Charles Redd Center for Western Studies at Brigham Young University, 1972-73.

363. _____. "The San Juan Mission Call." *Utah Historical Quarterly* 26 (April 1958): 161-168.

364. _____. *Utah History Atlas.* 2nd rev. ed. Salt Lake City: Smiths Printing Service, 1968.

365. Miller, Donald C. *Ghost Towns of Wyoming.* Boulder, CO: Pruett Publishing Co., 1982.

366. Miller, Marilyn McMeen and J. C. Moffitt. *Provo, A Story of People in Motion.* Provo, UT: Brigham Young University Press, 1974.

367. Miller, Orrin. "Place Names in Tooele County." Typescript, 1984.

368. Monroe Centennial Committee and Monroe City. *Monroe, Its First One Hundred Years, 1864-1964.*

369. Moore, W. Robert. "Escalante: Utah's River of Arches." *National Geographic* 108 (September 1955): 399-425.

370. Morgan, Dale L. "The Changing Face of Salt Lake City." *Utah Historical Quarterly* 27 (July 1959): 209-246.

371. _____. *The Great Salt Lake.* Albuquerque, NM: University of New Mexico, 1947.

372. _____. *Jedediah Smith.* Lincoln, NB: University of Nebraska Press, 1953.

373. _____. "Miles Goodyear and the Founding of Ogden." *Utah Historical Quarterly* 21 (July, October 1953): 195-218, 307-329.

374. _____, comp. "The State of Deseret." *Utah Historical Quarterly* 8 (April, July, October 1940): 65-239.

375. _____, ed. *The West of William H. Ashley.* Denver: The Old West Publishing Co., 1964.

376. Morrill, A. Reed. "The Site of Fort Robidoux." *Utah Historical Quarterly* 9 (January, April 1941): 1-11.

377. Mortimer, William James. *How Beautiful Upon the Mountains: A Centennial History of Wasatch County.* Salt Lake City: Wasatch County Chapter of the Daughters of Utah Pioneers, 1963.

378. *Mountains Conquered: The Story of Morgan with Biographies.* Fine Arts Study Group. Morgan: Morgan County News Publishers, 1959.

379. Murdock, Joseph R. (Dick). Personal Communication.

380. _____ and Stanley L. Welsh. "Land Use in Wah Wah and Pine Valleys, Western Utah." Biological Series, vol. X11, no. 4, Brigham Young University Science Series. January 1971.

381. Murdock, Wilford and Mildred Murdock. *Monroe, Utah, Its First One Hundred Years, 1864-1964.* Monroe Centennial Committee and Monroe City, 1964.

382. National Committee on Geographic Names. Washington, DC. Personal Correspondence.

383. *National Geographic.* Washington, DC: National Geographic Society.

384. Neff, Andrew Love. *History of Utah, 1847-1869.* Edited by Leland Hargrave Creer. Salt Lake City: Deseret News Press, 1940.

385. Nelson, Lowry. *The Mormon Village.* Salt Lake City: University of Utah Press, 1952.

386. Newton, Charles H. *Place Names in Arizona.* Phoenix: Charles H. Newton Publishing Co., 1954.

387. Nielsen, Mabel Woodward. *Johns Valley: The Way We Saw it.* Springville, UT: Art City Publishing Co., 1971.

388. Nielsen, Vaughn J., comp. *History of Box Elder Stake.* Brigham City, UT: Pats Print Shop, 1977.

389. Nilsen, Don L. "American Proper Noun Reference: The Humorous Naming of Persons, Places, and Things." *Names* 30 (September 1982): 171-182.

390. Notarianni, Philip F. "Utah's Ellis Island: The Difficult Americanization of Carbon County." *Utah Historical Quarterly* 47 (Spring 1979): 178-193.

391. *Ogden Standard Examiner,* December 30, 1977.

392. Olsen, Robert W. "Winsor Castle: Mormon Frontier Fort at Pipe Springs." *Utah Historical Quarterly* 34 (Summer 1966): 218-226.

393. O'Neil, Floyd. "The Reluctant Suzerainty: The Uintah and Ouray Reservations." *Utah Historical Quarterly* 39 (Spring 1971): 129-144.

394. Orem Bicentennial History Committee. *It Happened in Orem*. Orem City, UT, 1978.

395. *Origins of Utah Place Names*. 3rd ed. Utah Writers Project, United States Work Projects Administration. Salt Lake City: Utah Department of Education, 1940.

396. Pace, Josephine. "Kimberly as I Remember Her." *Utah Historical Quarterly* 35 (Winter 1967): 112-120.

397. Palmer, William Rees. "Early Day Trading with Nevada Mining Camps." *Utah Historical Quarterly* 26 (October 1958): 352-368.

398. _____. "Home Lands of the Pahute." *Utah Historical Quarterly* 1, 6 (January 1928, July 1933): 19-36, 88.

399. _____. "Indian Names in Utah Geography." *Utah Historical Quarterly*. 1 (January 1928): 5-26.

400. _____. "Pahute Indian Government and Laws." *Utah Historical Quarterly* 2 (April, 1929): 35, 37, 43.

401. Peale, A. C. "The Ancient Outlet of Great Salt Lake." *American Journal of Science and Art*, Third Series, vol. 15, no. 90 (1878): 439-44.

402. Pearce T. M., ed. *New Mexico Place Names*. Albuquerque, NM: University of New Mexico Press, 1965.

403. Pendleton, Mark A. "Naming Silver Reef." *Utah Historical Quarterly* 5 (January 1932): 29-30.

404. _____. "Memories of Silver Reef." *Utah Historical Quarterly* 3 (1930): 99-118.

405. _____. "The Orderville United Order of Zion." *Utah Historical Quarterly* 7 (October 1939): 141-159.

406. Perkins, Cornelia A., et al., comp. *Saga of San Juan*. Monticello, UT: Daughters of Utah Pioneers, San Juan County Chapter, 1957.

407. Perry, J. F. "Cache County, the Eden of Utah." Logan, UT: Logan Republican, n.d.

408. Peterson, Charles S. *San Juan in Controversy: American Livestock Frontier vs. Mormon Cattle Pool*. Charles Redd Monographs in Western History, vol. 3. Provo, UT: Charles Redd Center for Western Studies at Brigham Young University, 1972-73.

409. Peterson, Charles Sharon. *Look to the Mountains: Southeastern Utah and the La Sal National Forest*. Provo, UT: Brigham Young University Press, 1975.

410. Peterson, Marie Ross and Mary M. Pearson. *Echoes of Yesterday: Summit County Centennial History*. Daughters of Utah Pioneers, Summit County, 1947.

411. Phillips, Maxine Brown. "The Strange New Language of a Magic Land." *Denver Post, Empire Magazine*, March 14, 1965, pp. 6-9.

412. "Piute County." *Utah Fish and Game Magazine* 19 (November 1963): 22.

413. Piute County Records, Book 2, p. 64.

414. Pogue, Joseph E. "The Great Rainbow Natural Bridge of Southern Utah." *National Geographic* 22 (November 1911): 1048-1056.

415. Pointer, Larry. *In Search of Butch Cassidy*. Norman, OK: University of Oklahoma Press, 1977.

416. Polk and Company. *Utah State Gazetteer and Business Directory*. 1st ed. Salt Lake City: 1900.

417. Poll, Richard D., et al., eds. *Utah's History*. Provo, UT: Brigham Young University Press, 1978.

418. Porath, Joseph H. *History of Big and Little Cottonwood Canyons*. Typescript. Utah State Historical Society, Logan, Utah.

419. Powell, Allan Kent. *Emery County*. Utah Historical Society, 1979.

420. Powell, J. W. *The Exploration of the Colorado River and Its Canyons*. New York: Dover Publications, Inc., 1961.

421. _____. "Geographical and Geological Survey of the Rocky Mountain Region. . . ." *American Journal of Science and Art*, Third Series, vol. 15, no. 89 (1878): 342-58.

422. _____. *Explorations of the Colorado River of the West and Its Tributaries, 1869, 1870, 1871, 1872*. Under the Direction of the Smithsonian Institute. Washington, DC: Government Printing Office, 1875.

423. Pratt, Parley P. *Autobiography of Parley P. Pratt*. Edited by his son, Parley P. Pratt. Salt Lake City: Deseret Book Co., 1970.

424. Price, Raye Carlson. *Diggings and Doings in Park City*. Salt Lake City: University of Utah Press, 1970.

425. _____. *Guidebook to Canyonlands Country*. n.l.: Ward Ritchie Press, 1974.

426. Price, Virginia N. and John T. Darby. "Preston Nutter: Utah Cattleman, 1886-1936." *Utah Historical Quarterly* 32 (1964): 232-251.

427. *Providence and Her People*. Comp. and ed. by Historical Society of Providence. Logan, UT: Herald-Journal Printing Co., 1949.

428. Purdy, William M. *An Outline of the History of the Flaming Gorge Area*. Salt Lake City: University of Utah Press, 1962.

429. _____. "Green River, Main Stem of the Colorado." *Utah Historical Quarterly* 28 (July 1960): 252-261.

430. Purrington, William Robb. "History of South Davis County 1847-1870." Thesis, University of Utah, Salt Lake City, Utah, 1959.

431. Putman, John J. "India Struggles to Save Her Wildlife." *National Geographic* 150 (September 1976): 341.

432. Rabbitt, Mary C. *Minerals, Lands, and Geology for the Common Defence and General Welfare, vol. 2, 1879-1904*. United States Geological Survey: Government Printing Office, 1980.

433. Raty, Leslie S. "A History of Wasatch County 1859-1899." Thesis, Brigham Young University, Provo, Utah, 1954.

434. _____. *Under Wasatch Skies: A History of Wasatch County, 1858-1900*. Wasatch County Chapter, Daughters of Utah Pioneers. Salt Lake City: Deseret News Press, 1954.

435. Ravsten, Ben J. and Eunice P. Ravsten, comps. *History of Clarkston*. n.l.: n.p., 1966.

436. Reagan, Albert B. *Some Notes on the History of the Uintah Basin in Northeastern Utah to 1850*. Reprint ed. from Proceedings of the Utah Academy of Sciences, Arts and Letters, Vol. XI, 1934.

437. Redford, Robert. *The Outlaw Trail*. New York: Grosset & Dunlap, 1976.

438. Reid, Hyrum Lorenzo. *Brigham Young's Dixie of the Desert: Exploration and Settlement*. Zion National Park, UT: Zion Natural History Association, 1964.

439. _____. "Early History of Utah's Dixie." Thesis, Brigham Young University, Provo, Utah 1931.

440. Rennick, R. M. "The Alleged 'Hogg Sisters,' or Simple Ground Rules for Collectors of 'Odd' Names." *Names* 30 (September 1982): 193-197.

441. Reynolds, Thursey Jensen. *Centennial Echoes from Carbon County*. Daughters of Utah Pioneers, Carbon County Chapter, 1948.

442. Rhoades, Gale R. and Kerry Ross Boren. *A History of the Lost Rhoades Mines*. Salt Lake City: Dream Garden Press, 1980.

443. Rice, Cindy. "Spring City: A Look at a Nineteenth Century Mormon Village." *Utah Historical Quarterly* 43 (Summer 1975): 260-277.

444. Rich, Roxie N. *The History and People of Early Sandy*. n.l.: n.p., [1976].

445. Rich, Russell Rogers. "History of the Latter-day Saints Settlements of Bear Lake Valley 1863-1900." Thesis, Brigham Young University, Provo, Utah, 1948.

446. Richans, Frederick Partridge. "The Geography of Pavant Valley, Utah." Thesis, University of Utah, Salt Lake City, Utah, 1957.

447. Richins, Fannie J. and Wright Richins. *Henefer, Our Valley Home*. [Salt Lake City]: Utah Printing Co., 1958.

448. Ricks, Joel Edward. *The Beginnings of Settlement in Cache Valley*. Logan, UT: Faculty Association, Utah State Agricultural College, 1953.

449. _____. and E. L. Cooley, eds. *The History of a Valley*. Cache Valley Centennial Commission, Logan, UT: Deseret News Publishing Co., 1956.

450. Rider, Rowland W. *Sixshooters and Sagebrush*. As told to Deirdre Paulson. Provo, UT: Brigham Young University Press, c1979.

451. Riggs, Effel Harmon, comp. *History of Hatch, Utah*. Hatch Company, Daughters of Utah Pioneers. Beaver, UT: Beaver Printing Co., 1978.

452. Roberts, B. H. *Comprehensive History of the Church of Jesus Christ of Latter-day Saints*. 6 vols. Salt Lake City: Deseret News Press, 1930.

453. Robertson, Frank C. and Beth K. Harris. *Boom Towns of the Great Basin*. Denver: Sage Books, 1962.

454. Robertson, Ruth Winder. *This Is Alta*. n.l.: Ruth W. Robertson, 1972.

455. Robinson, Adonis Findlay. *History of Kane County*. Salt Lake City: Kane County Daughters of Utah Pioneers, 1970.

456. Robinson, Alvaretta, ed. *They Answered the Call, A History of Minersville, Utah*. Minersville Centennial Committee, 1962.

457. *Roosevelt Standard*, December 8, 1938.

458. Rose, Marie, comp. and Mary H. Pearson. *Echoes of Yesterday: Summit County Centennial History*. Salt Lake City: Daughters of Utah Pioneers of Summit County, 1947.

459. Rosenvall, Lynn A. "Defunct Mormon Settlements: 1830-1930." In *The Mormon Role in the Settlement of the West*, edited by Richard H. Jackson. Charles Redd Monographs in Western History, no. 9. Provo, UT: Brigham Young University Press, 1978.

460. Roylance, Ward Jay. *Derivation of County Names*. In Materials for the Study of Utah's Counties. Salt Lake City, 1962, pp. 17-18.

461. _____. *Utah, the Incredible Land: A Guide to the Beehive State*. Salt Lake City: Utah Trails Co., 1965.

462. _____. *Utah's Geography and Counties*. Salt Lake City: Author, 1967.

463. Rusho, W. L. and C. Gregory Crampton. *Desert River Crossing, Historic Lee's Ferry on the Colorado River*. Salt Lake City: Peregrine Smith, Inc., 1981.

464. Russell, Osborne. *Journal of a Trapper, 1834-1843*. Edited by Aubrey L. Haines. 5th Bison Book Printing. Lincoln, NB: University of Nebraska Press, October 1970.

465. Salt Lake City, Chamber of Commerce. *Utah the Unique*. 1947.

466. *Salt Lake Tribune*. Salt Lake City: Kearns Tribune Corporation.

467. Salter, Richard Gene. *Tooele Valley, Utah: A Regional Interpretation of the Changing Economics*. Salt Lake City: n.p., 1953.

468. *Santaquin Through the Years*. Santaquin Centennial History, 1956.

469. Savage, Charles Roscoe. *Views of Utah and Tourist's Guide, Containing a Description of the Views and General Information for the Traveler, Resident, and Public Generally*. Salt Lake City: n.p. 1887.

470. Schindler, Harold. *Orrin Porter Rockwell, Man of God, Son of Thunder*. Salt Lake City: University of Utah Press, 1966.
471. Scorup, Stena. *J. A. Scorup; A Utah Cattleman*. [n.p., n.d.].
472. "Selected Readings on Utah's Historic and Scenic Wonders." *Utah Historical Quarterly* 26 (July 1958): 299-304.
473. Shelley, George F. *Early History of American Fork*. American Fork City, UT, 1942, 1945.
474. Silversberg, Robert. *Ghost Towns of the American West*. New York: Thomas Y. Crowell Co., 1968.
475. Silvey, Frank. *History of Northern San Juan County*. Published privately, n.d.
476. Simmonds, A. J. *On the Big Range: A Centennial History of Cornish and Trenton, Cache County, Utah*. Logan, UT: Utah State University Press, 1970.
477. Simpson, James H. *Explorations Across the Great Basin of the Territory of Utah*. Washington, DC: Government Printing Office, 1876.
478. Sloan, Edward L. *Gazetteer of Utah and Salt Lake City*. Salt Lake City: Herald Publishing Co., 1874.
479. Smith, David F. *My Native Village, Centerville*. n.l.: n.p., 1943.
480. Smith, Gary and Michael E. Long. "Utah's Rock Art Wilderness Louvre." *National Geographic* 156 (January 1980): 94-117.
481. Smith, Jesse Nathanial. His Journal, 1834-1906. Salt Lake City: Jesse Nathanial Smith Family Association, 1970.
482. Smith, Melvin T. "Forces that Shaped Utah's Dixie: Another Look." *Utah Historical Quarterly* 47 (Spring 1979): 110-129.
483. Smith, Thomas W. A Brief History of Early Pahreah Settlements. Typescript. Utah State Historical Society, Salt Lake City, n.d.
484. Smoot, Mary Ellen and Marilyn Sheriff. *The City In-Between. History of Centerville, Utah*. Bountiful, UT: n.p., 1975.
485. Snow, Anne, comp. *Rainbow Views: A History of Wayne County*. Daughters of Utah Pioneers. Springville, UT: Art City Publishing Co., 1953.
486. _____, comp. *Tales of a Triumphant People: A History of Salt Lake County, 1847-1900*. Utah County Daughters of Utah Pioneers. Springville, UT: Art City Publishing Company, 1953.
487. Sonne, Conway B. "Royal Blood of the Utes." *Utah Historical Quarterly* 22 (July 1954): 271-276.
488. Sons of the Utah Pioneers. "Box Elder Lore of the Nineteenth Century." Brigham City, UT: Box Elder Chapter, Sons of the Utah Pioneers, September 1951.
489. Sorenson, Phillip E. "The Utah-Idaho Central Railroad." *Utah Historical Quarterly* 27 (April 1959): 145-155.
490. Standing, A. R. "Through the Uintas: History of the Carter Road." *Utah Historical Quarterly* 35 (Summer 1967): 256-267.
491. Stanford, Joseph. *Brief Historical Sketch of the Settlements in Weber County*. n.l.: n.p., n.d.
492. Stansbury, Howard. *Exploration and Survey of the Valley of the Great Salt Lake of Utah*. Senate Executive Document No. 3, Special Session, March 1852. Philadelphia: Lippincott, Grambo and Co., 1852.
493. Steel, Raymond D. *Goshen Valley History*, 1960.
494. Steel, William Gladstone. "A Story of Names." Typescript. Washington, DC: United States Board on Geographic Names Library, 1956.
495. Steen, Charlie R. "The Natural Bridges of White Canyon: A Diary of H. L. A. Culmer." *Utah Historical Quarterly* 40 (Winter 1972): 55-87.

496. Stegner, Wallace. *Beyond the Hundredth Meridian*. Boston: Houghton Mifflin, 1954.

497. _____. "Powell and the Names on the Plateau." *Western Humanities Review* 7, no. 2 (Spring 1953): 105-10.

498. Stevens, Dale J., ed. *The Great Salt Lake Desert, A Geographic Survey*. Provo, UT: Brigham Young University, 1975.

499. Stewart, George. *American Place Names*. New York: Oxford University Press, 1970.

500. _____. "The Day the Bridge Went Dry." *Salt Lake Tribune*, June 20, 1971.

501. _____. *Names on the Land. A Historical Account of Place Naming in the United States*. New York: Random House, 1945.

502. Stewart, Omer C. "Ute Indians: Before and After White Contact." *Utah Historical Quarterly* 34 (Winter, 1966): 38-61.

503. Still, Bayrd, ed. *The West, Contemporary Records of America's Expansion Across the Continent: 1607-1890*. New York: Capricorn Books, 2nd Impression, 1961.

504. Stokes, William Lee. *Scenes of the Plateau Lands and How They Came to Be*. Salt Lake City: William Lee Stokes, 1961.

505. Stone, Elizabeth Arnold. *Uinta County: Its Place in History*. Laramie, WY: Larami Print Co., 1924.

506. Stookey, Walter M. *Fatal Decision, The Tragic Story of the Donner Party*. Salt Lake City: Deseret Book Co., 1950.

507. Stout, Wayne. *A History of Hinckley, Utah. 1858-1973*. Salt Lake City: n.p., 1973.

508. Streadbeck, Arval. *Personal Geographic Names File*, unpublished.

509. Sumsion, Aneita B. *Springville, Utah*. [Springville, UT]: Art City Publishing Co., 1983.

510. *Sun Advocate*, Price, Utah, December 7, 1984.

511. *Sunset Travel Guide to Utah*. Menlo Park, CA: Jane Books, 1971.

512. Sutton, Ann and Myron Sutton. *The Secret Places, Arches, Utah*. San Francisco: Rand McNally & Co., 1970, pp. 87-116.

513. Sutton, Wain. *Utah, A Centennial History*. New York: Lewis Historical Publishing Company, 1949.

514. Tanner, Faun McConkie. *The Far Country*. Salt Lake City: Olympus Publishing Co., 1976.

515. Thompson, Almon Harris. "Diary of Almon Harris Thompson." Edited by Herbert E. Gregory. *Utah Historical Quarterly* 7 (1939): 11-140.

516. Thompson, George A. *Some Dreams Die, Utah's Ghost Towns and Lost Treasures*. Salt Lake City: Dream Garden Press, 1982.

517. Thompson, Grant and Don Dunn. "Udy Hot Springs: A Bogey." *Western Folklore* 18 (April 1959): 166.

518. Thompson, S. *Utah Landmarks*. Salt Lake City: First Federal Savings, 1976.

519. Thomson, Mildred Hatch. *Rich Memories: Some Happenings in Rich County from 1863-1960*. Springville, UT: Art City Publishing Co., c1962.

520. Tilden, Freeman. *The National Parks, What They Mean to You and Me*. New York: Alfred A. Knopf, 1963.

521. Tippetts, Della Ludlow. *A Town Is Born*. Spanish Fork, UT, 1969.

522. Tolton, John Franklin. "From the Halls of Memory." Typescript. Utah Historical Society, Salt Lake City, Utah, 1861.

523. *Tooele Stake History, 1847 to 1900*. Published for Stake Centennial Observance, Centennial Edition, June 1977.

524. "Trains of Yesterday, Marysvale Branch, Denver and Rio Grande Western Railroad." *Deseret News*, Magazine Section, October 16, 1949.

525.   Toyn, Rhea E. Personal Correspondence.
526.   Tullidge, Edward Wheelock. *Histories*. Containing the History of all the Northern, Eastern and Western Counties of Utah; also the Counties of Southern Idaho. Salt Lake City: Juvenile Instructor, 1889.
527.   _____. *History of Salt Lake City*. Salt Lake City: Star Printing Co., 1886.
528.   _____, ed. *Tullidge's Quarterly Magazine of Utah*. Salt Lake City: Star Printing Company, 1881-1885.
529.   Union Pacific Railroad Company. *Utah, Sights and Scenes for the Tourist*. Omaha, NB: n.p., 1888.
530.   United States, Board on Geographic Names, Archives, Unpublished. Washington DC.
531.   _____, Board on Geographic Names, Decisions List.
532.   _____, Board on Geographic Names, Decisions. No. 38, rendered April 4, 1934. Zion National Park, Utah. Washington, DC: Government Printing Office, 1934.
533.   _____, Bureau of the Census. 1970 Census of the Population. 1. Characteristics of the Population. Part 46, Utah. Washington, DC, 1973.
534.   _____, Bureau Land Management, Central Utah. *Recreation and Wildlife on BLM Lands*. Richfield, UT: Bureau of Land Management, 1969.
535.   _____, Department of Agriculture. *Irrigation Water Management: Sevier River Basin, Utah*. U.S. Department of Agriculture, 1976.
536.   _____, 88th Congress, 1st session. House. Joint resolution to designate the lake to be formed by the waters impounded by the Flaming Gorge Dam, Utah, as "Ashley Lake." J.H. Res. 604. July 31, 1963. Washington, DC, 1963.
537.   _____, 88th Congress, 1st session, House. Joint resolution to designate the lake to be formed by the waters impounded by the Flaming Gorge Dam, Utah, and the recreation area contiguous to such lake in the states of Wyoming and Utah as "O'Mahoney Lake and Recreation Area." H.J. Res. 293. Feb. 28, 1963. Washington, DC, 1963.
538.   _____, 88th Congress, 1st session. Senate. Designating the lake to be formed by the waters impounded by the Flaming Gorge Dam, Utah, in the states of Wyoming and Utah, as "Lake O'Mahoney." Report no. 279, to accompany S.J. Res. 17. June 19, 1963, Calendar No. 160. Washington, DC, 1963.
539.   _____, 88th Congress, 1st session. Senate. Joint resolution to designate the lake to be formed by the waters impounded by the Flaming Gorge Dam, Utah, and the recreation area contiguous to such lake in the states of Wyoming and Utah, as "O'Mahoney Lake and Recreation Area." S.J. Res. 17. Jan. 15, 1963. Washington, DC, 1963. 2p.
540.   _____, Geological Survey. Kamas Quadrangle, Utah. Topographic Map. Denver: U.S.G.S., 1967.
541.   _____, Writers' Program. *Gazetteer of Utah Localities and Altitudes*. Zoology Department, University of Utah, Utah State Institute of Fine Arts, United States Work Projects Administration. Salt Lake City: Division of Biology, University of Utah, 1952.
542.   _____, Writers' Program. *Origins of Utah Place Names*. 3d ed. Comp. and written by Utah Writers Project, Work Projects Administration. Sponsored and published by Utah State Department of Public Instruction. Salt Lake City, 1940.
543.   Untermann, G. E. and B. R. "Dinosaur Country." *Utah Historical Quarterly* 26 (July 1958): 246-256.
544.   Urbanek, Mae. *Wyoming Place Names*. Boulder, CO: Johnson Publishing Co., 1967.

545. U.S. Bureau of Land Management. "Simpson Springs Campground." Information Leaflet.

546. *Utah, A Guide to the State.* Work Projects Administration. Comp. by Utah State Institute of Fine Arts, Salt Lake County Commission. New York: Hastings House, 1941.

547. Utah Centennial Commission. *This Is the Place: Utah Centennial, 1847-1947.* Salt Lake City: 1947.

548. Utah Chamber of Commerce. *Utah and the Intermountain Empire.* Salt Lake City, 1946.

549. *Utah County Journal,* October 18, 1986.

550. Utah Department of Public Instruction. Utah's Community Beginnings. Salt Lake City, 1949.

551. *Utah Gazetteer, 1892-93.* Salt Lake City: T. B. H. Stenhouse, 1892.

552. *Utah Gazetteer and Directory of Salt Lake, Ogden, Provo, Logan Cities for 1888.* Salt Lake City, 1888.

553. *Utah, Her Cities, Towns and Resources.* Chicago: Manly and Litteral Publishers, 1891-92.

554. "Utah Historic Spots Marked." *Daughters American Revolution Magazine* (September 1937): 782-856.

555. *Utah Historical Quarterly.* Salt Lake City: Utah State Historical Society.

556. Utah Historical Society. *Beehive History,* vol. 6.

557. Utah Industrial Promotion Division. Piute County 4. Salt Lake City, 1974.

558. Utah Place Name Society. Newsletter. Salt Lake City, Utah.

559. Utah Planning Board. Piute County: Basic Data of Economic Activities and Resources. Salt Lake City, 1940.

560. Utah Road Commission. *Utah, Land of Endless Scenic Discovery.* Salt Lake City: 1939.

561. Utah Sketches, 1880. Copies of Histories of 38 Communities, Compiled mainly by the Bishops between June and November 1880.

562. Utah State Committee on Geographic Names. *Utah Geographic Names Handbook.* 1976 edition.

563. Utah State Committee on Geographic Names. Agenda, August 16, 1984.

564. Utah State Department of Publicity and Industrial Development. *Utah, Land of Color.* Salt Lake City, 1948.

565. _____. *Utah, Land of Endless Scenic Discovery.* Salt Lake City: 1942.

566. _____. *Utah, the Friendly State.* Salt Lake City: 1948. Includes leaflets on the Uintah Basin, and Carbon and Emery counties.

567. Utah State Historical Society. Unpublished Archives on Geographic Names.

568. _____. *The Valley of the Great Salt Lake.* 3d ed. Salt Lake City: Utah State Historical Society, 1967.

569. Utah Tourist and Publicity Council. *Facts About Utah.* 2nd Printing revised. Salt Lake City: Utah Tourist and Publicity Council, 1959.

570. _____. *Tour the Different World of Utah's Panorama Land.* Salt Lake City: Utah Tourist and Publicity Council, 1961.

571. Utah Travel Council. A Guide to Utah's Panoramaland, Salt Lake City: Utah Travel Council, 1967.

572. "Utah's Parks and Scenic Wonders." *Utah Historical Quarterly* 26 (1958): 207-304.

573. Ute Bottle Hollow Resort. Information Brochure.

574. Utley, Robert M. "The Dash to Promontory." *Utah Historical Quarterly* 29 (1961): 98-117.

575. *Valley Tan,* November 19, 1858.

576. Van Alfen, Nicholas. "Porter Rockwell and the Mormon Frontier." Thesis, Brigham Young University, Provo, Utah, 1938.

577. Van Cott, John W. "Geographic Names of Utah, A Compilation: Beaver County." Typescript. Utah Historical Society Library, Salt Lake City, Utah, 1978.

578. Van Cott, John W. Personal records.

579. Wahlquist, Wayne L. "A Review of Mormon Literature." *Utah Historical Quarterly* 45 (Winter 1977): 4-21.

580. Walker, Don D. "The Carlisles: Cattle Barons of the Upper Basin." *Utah Historical Quarterly* 32 (Summer 1964): 268-284.

581. _____. "The Cattle Industry of Utah, An Historical Profile, 1850-1900." *Utah Historical Quarterly* 32 (Summer 1964): 182-197.

582. _____. "Cowboys, Indians and Cavalry, A Cattleman's Account of the Fights of 1884." *Utah Historical Quarterly* 34 (Summer 1966): 255-262.

583. Warner, Ted J., ed. *Dominguez-Escalante Journal.* Translated by Fray Angelico Chavez. Provo, UT: Brigham Young University Press, 1976.

584. Warnock, Irvin J. *Our Own Sevier: A Comprehensive, Centennial Volume, Sevier County, Utah, 1865-1965.* [Richfield, UT]: Sevier County Commissioners, 1966.

585. _____. *Through the Years: Sevier Centennial History.* Springville, UT: Sevier County Centennial Committee, 1947.

586. Warrum, Noble. *Utah Since Statehood, Historical and Biographical.* Chicago: S. J. Clarke Publishing Co., 1919.

587. Weber, David J. *The Taos Trapper: The Fur Trade in the Far Southwest. 1540-1846.* Norman, OK: University of Oklahoma Press, 1971.

588. Welsh, Stanley L. Personal Communication.

589. Whipple, Maurine. *This Is the Place: Utah.* New York: Alfred A. Knopf, 1945.

590. Whiskey Springs, Wasatch County. U.S. Forest Service sign at site.

591. Whitney, Orson Ferguson. *History of Utah.* Salt Lake City: G. Q. Cannon, 1892-1904.

592. _____. *The Making of a State: A School History of Utah.* Salt Lake City: The Deseret News, 1908.

593. _____. *Popular History of Utah.* Salt Lake City: The Deseret News, 1916.

594. Wilcken, Elden R. *Lakes of the Uinta Mountains.* Ashley National Forest, United States National Forest Service, 1978.

595. _____. Personal Correspondence.

596. Willis, Ann Bassett. "Queen Ann of Brown's Park." *Colorado Magazine* 29 (April, July, October): 81-98, 218-235, 284-298, and 30 (January 1953): 58-76.

597. Wilson, William M. *Pictorial Provo.* 1910.

598. Wolle, Muriel Sibell. *The Bonanza Trail.* New York: Bonanza Books, 1953.

599. Wolsey, Sarah. *Early Days in Cedar Valley.* American Fork, UT: Alpine School District, 1964.

600. Woodbury, Angus Munn. *A History of Southern Utah and Its National Parks.* Salt Lake City: State Historical Society, 1950.

601. _____. "The Route of Jedediah Smith in 1826 from the Great Salt Lake to the Colorado River." *Utah Historical Quarterly* 4 (April 1931): 3.

602. Woolsey, Nethella Griffin, comp. *Escalante Story.* Springville, UT: Art City Publishing, Co., 1964.

603. Wright, Marguerite. "Echoes from the Past: The Story of the Echo Flour Mill." *Utah Historical Quarterly* 34 (1966): 161.

604. Young, Levi Edgar. *The Founding of Utah.* San Francisco: Charles Scribners Sons, 1923.

605.   _____. *The Story of Utah*. Dansville, NY: F. A. Owen Publishing Co., 1913.

606.   Young, Merrill Yvonne. *Cache Valley: In and Out and Round About*. Logan, UT: Herald Press, 1970.

607.   Zehnder, Chuck. *Coal Camps and Ghost Towns*. n.l.: C. Zehnder, 1984.

608.   Zion-Bryce Natural History Association. National Parks and National Monuments of Utah, 1947, 1953, 1958.

609.   Zwinger, Ann. *Run, River, Run*. Tucson, AZ: University of Arizona Press, 1975.

610.   _____. *Wind in the Rock*. San Francisco: Harper & Row, 1978.

INDEX

Cullen, Matthew (Mat), 98, 259
Culmer, H. L. A., 219, 342
Cummings, Byron H., 98, 309
Curry, Flat Nose George, xviii, 99;
    death of, 140, 141, 240
Curry Gang, 140
Curtis, Lehi, 99
Curtis, Lyman, 326
Cutler, Blanche, 218, 342

Daggett, Ellsworth, 101
Daines, Robert, 196
Dallin, Captain, 152
Dallin, Geneva, 152
Dalton, Harry, 9
Dalton, Isabella, 9
Dalton, John, 101
Dalton, Ted, 101
Danger Cave State Historical
    Monument, 102
Danger Cave State Park, 393
Daniels, Aaron, 102
Daniels, E. A., 261
Daniels, Lee, 175
Daniel Webster Mine, 392
Davenport, James, 103
Davenport, Tom, 229
Davidson, Mr. (rancher), 127
Davis, Bill, 103–4
Davis, Bob, 104
Davis, Cyrus, 99
Davis, Daniel C., 103
Davis, George, 103
Davis, J. E., 259
Davis, Johnny, 103
Davis, William, 48, 103
Day, Abraham, 104
Day, Thomas, 104
Delano, Columbus, 261
Dell (stockman), 259
Dellenbaugh, Frederick, 11, 81, 107,
    164, 201
De Mille, Oliver, 104, 340
Dempsey, Jack, 85, 267
Denver and Rio Grande Railroad, 33,
    166, 170, 173, 245, 368, 370, 397;
    sidings on, 29, 126, 154, 260
Dern, George H., 160, 296
Deseret Livestock Company, 200
Deseret News, 59
DeSmet, Father, 118

Detroit Mining District, 208
Deuel, Osmyn M., 74
Dewey, George, 110, 127, 243
Dewey, John C., 110
Diamond, Jim, 111
Dickart, Charles, 357
Dilly, Tom, 111, 140
Dimick, Ephraim, 215
Dimick, Kiziah, 215
Dinosaur National Monument, 201, 346,
    351
Dodd brothers, 295
Dodds, George, 153
Dodds, Pardon, 46, 113
Domínguez-Escalante expedition, 7, 52,
    96, 131, 261, 269, 350, 382, 402;
    names by, xiii, xviii, 27, 113, 130,
    217, 218, 246, 294, 317, 328, 335,
    349, 356, 396
Donner-Reed party, xviii, 38, 114, 124,
    162, 242, 294
Dorton, Joe "Shropshire," 118
Douglas, Jim (James), suicide of, 114
Douglas, Stephen A., 143
Douglas, William, 270
Douglass, Earl, 111
Douglass, W. B., 309
Dowd, Cleophas J., death of, 115
Dragon Mines, 115
Draper, William, 115
Du Chasne (trapper), 118
Duchesne, Andre, 118
Du Chesne, Rose, 118
Duckett, John, 118
Dugway Proving Grounds, 63, 159, 331,
    398
Duncan, Chapman, 119
Duncan, Frank, 205
Durkee, Mr. (rancher), 119
Dutch John. *See* Hanselena, "Dutch"
    John
Dutch Pete (prospector), suicide of, 119
Dutton, Clarence Edward, 11, 152, 186,
    261, 326, 345, 376
Dyer, Lewis, B., 120

Earl, Jedediah, 136
Earth and Man (Guyot), 171
Edson, Alvey, 51
Edwards, Samuel, 168
Egan, Howard, 124, 298